GENOCIDE

◆ ◆ ◆

A Reader

GENOCIDE

A Reader

◆ ◆ ◆

EDITED BY

JENS MEIERHENRICH

OXFORD

UNIVERSITY PRESS

OXFORD
UNIVERSITY PRESS

Oxford University Press is a department of the University of Oxford. It furthers the University's
objective of excellence in research, scholarship, and education by publishing worldwide.

Oxford   New York
Auckland   Cape Town   Dar es Salaam   Hong Kong   Karachi
Kuala Lumpur   Madrid   Melbourne   Mexico City   Nairobi
New Delhi   Shanghai   Taipei   Toronto

With offices in
Argentina   Austria   Brazil   Chile   Czech Republic   France   Greece
Guatemala   Hungary   Italy   Japan   Poland   Portugal   Singapore
South Korea   Switzerland   Thailand   Turkey   Ukraine   Vietnam

Oxford is a registered trademark of Oxford University Press in the UK and certain other countries.

Published in the United States of America by
Oxford University Press
198 Madison Avenue, New York, NY 10016

Library of Congress Cataloging-in-Publication Data
Genocide : a reader / [edited by] Jens Meierhenrich.
pages   cm
Includes bibliographical references and index.
1. Genocide. I. Meierhenrich, Jens.
HV6322.7.G447 2013
364.15'1—dc23   2013024970

Printed in the United States of America
on acid-free paper

CONTENTS

CHAPTER THREE
Courses   171

CHAPTER SIX
Courts   316

CHAPTER SEVEN
Coping   361

CHAPTER EIGHT
Compensation   398

CHAPTER NINE

Cures   422

PREFACE AND ACKNOWLEDGMENTS

This collection has been in the making for a long time. I conceived the project while I was an assistant professor in the Department of Government at Harvard University. It was there that I designed and taught various courses on genocide and other types of collective violence. In the midst of my decade-long stint in Cambridge, the conflict in Darfur made headlines the world over, drawing attention to the meaning of genocide in an unprecedented manner. Perhaps inevitably, many questionable assertions about the nature, logic, and dynamics of violence in times of genocide found adherents in scholarship and practice. The moral imperative to respond, or so it seemed, caused many observers to make assumptions about the nature of the problem— and advocate rapid solutions, including military intervention—on the basis of incomplete or imperfect knowledge.

This was unfortunate because anthropologists, historians, political scientists, and sociologists had a fairly good understanding of what genocidal violence looks like, what triggers it, and the effects that it has on the peoples and regions in which it occurs. Little of this sophisticated scholarship, however, found its way into the emotionally charged discourses about Darfur at the time. This collection is an effort to make available some of that vast foundation of knowledge. By acquainting interested readers with the most important scholarly (as well as several nonacademic) accounts currently available, I am hoping to encourage more critical thinking about what I have come to call the darkest of human phenomena.

The all-encompassing nature of the project accounts for its long duration. Searching for the most illuminating or otherwise noteworthy texts from numerous disciplines to include in the *Reader* required a great deal of reading and culling, as did the careful editing of the 150 selections that made the final cut. I personally selected, typed, and introduced every single extract appearing in this collection. Many important examples of scholarship that I had preselected for inclusion, unfortunately, fell by the wayside in the end, especially texts from the burgeoning literature on civil war in political science, which, though conceptually, theoretically, and methodologically relevant for re-imagining (and making more sophisticated) the study of genocide, did not always have an immediate bearing on genocide, narrowly conceived. I therefore omitted them for this edition.

One of the most time-consuming tasks was the securing of copyright permissions to reproduce material that appears in these pages. It was a major logistical challenge that took several years to meet. I was very lucky that Victoria Phan was willing to oversee this part of the endeavor with her characteristic grace, professionalism, tenacity, and good humor. I could not have imagined a better research assistant. Evidence of the project's long gestation is the fact that Victoria was an undergraduate at Harvard when I commenced it and is a PhD candidate at the University of Cambridge, almost ready to submit her doctoral dissertation, now that I have completed it. Victoria and I received tremendous help from numerous publishers and rights holders who not infrequently were willing to waive or reduce their fees. I am enormously grateful for this generosity, as the project would not—on this scale—have been feasible otherwise. I also appreciate the support of Yuna Han, Eunice Kim, and Martha Lagace, who all contributed to the making of the volume in key ways.

I have had the unique opportunity to test the appeal and utility of the *Reader* as a teaching tool on a number of audiences while it was still in manuscript form. I am particularly grateful to Debórah Dwork, the inimitable director of the Strassler Family Center for Holocaust and Genocide Studies at Clark University. She has been a wonderful supporter and, in 2008, invited me to present the first draft of the book manuscript to the PhD students at the Strassler Center. The intellectually stimulating encounter aided me in tweaking the selections at a critical stage. Raz Segal and Jody Russell Manning deserve particular mention. Dwork and her colleagues, Thomas Kühne and Taner Akçam, also kindly invited me to spend the spring semester 2010 as the Cathy Cohen Lasry Visiting Professor of Holocaust and Genocide Studies at the Strassler Center. It was a marvelous experience that I look back on fondly. On that occasion I used the penultimate version of this *Reader* as the foundational text for a course on the advanced study of genocide. I am grateful to the terrific students who enrolled, notably Cristina Andriani, for their deep engagement with the material and their valuable feedback on the readings and organization of the volume. My stay at Clark was facilitated greatly by Mary Jane Rein, executive director of the Strassler Center, and by Tatyana Macauley, its program director. I am also grateful to the U.S. Holocaust Memorial Museum, where I had occasion to discuss my perspectives on the study of genocide, and the museum's role within it, at an extraordinary staff meeting. Bridget Conley-Zilkic and Mike Abramowitz made this visit possible, and I thank Sara Bloomfield, the director of the USHMM, and her colleagues for engaging with my presentation, and the Committee on Conscience for hosting me.

Finally, there is the London School of Economics and Political Science, where I tested out the manuscript of the volume that you are holding in your hands. It was a final opportunity to explore the book's suitability at both the undergraduate and graduate levels, and I incorporated a last round of comments and suggestions. My thanks go to my teaching assistant Mark Kersten and the many students who were willing to leave behind their preconceived notions about genocide and to approach the phenomenon from a number of different perspectives, and on the basis of sometimes challenging readings. I was heartened by this intellectual curiosity and the willingness to prioritize rational over moral sentiments in thinking about what used to be called the unthinkable.

Trusted fellow travelers on the scholarly road to a more critical genocide studies include Alexander Laban Hinton, Dirk Moses, Dan Stone, and Andrew Woolford. These accomplished scholars plow different corners of the field of genocide studies, but each took time out of his busy schedule to comment on a considerably longer draft of the introductory chapter than is included here. I appreciate greatly their incisive comments and intellectual support as well as friendship over the years. Other scholars who offered comments and suggestions early on include Christopher Browning, Jane Caplan, James Waller, and Eric Weitz. At Oxford University Press, Nancy Toff was a hands-on editor who championed this project and its companion volume, *Genocide: A Very Short Introduction*, from their inception. I have benefited from her insights, editorial and otherwise. Sonia Tycko calmly and expertly shepherded the book into production, where it was copyedited by Judith Hoover and Joellyn Ausanka oversaw its publication.

I was in the fortunate position of being able to put final touches to the *Reader* while in residence as the Louise and John Steffens Founders' Circle Member at the Institute for Advanced Study, Princeton. I am grateful to the School of Social Science, especially to Didier Fassin, for the financial but above all the intellectual support that I was afforded during my sabbatical year there.

GENOCIDE

◆ ◆ ◆

A Reader

Introduction: The Study and History of Genocide

Genocide is a phenomenon that has confounded scholars, policymakers, and ordinary bystanders for decades. In the late 1970s a field of inquiry emerged that began to concern itself exclusively with the study and history of genocide. Since that time a considerable amount of literature—academic and otherwise—has emerged to shed light on this darkest of human phenomena. And yet our understanding of genocide remains partial, not least because vocational and methodological differences have inhibited intellectual progress in the field of genocide studies. This is unfortunate, because the policy imperative to respond to the specter of genocide in the twenty-first century is greater than ever before. Governmental and international initiatives the world over have begun to take concrete steps aimed at forecasting—and coordinating responses to—large-scale social violence. The creation in 2012 of the Atrocities Prevention Board in the United States is emblematic of this trend. It goes hand in hand with advocacy on behalf of the responsibility to protect (R2P), a nascent idea according to which states have a moral responsibility to protect its citizens from genocide and other forms of mass violence on the international stage.

Given the unprecedented demand for knowledge about genocide, this anthology provides an overview of the state of the art in this field. By presenting key texts that are essential to explaining and understanding the complexity of genocide, it relates theory to practice. The volume is designed as an introduction to the myriad dimensions of genocide and to various ways of making sense of it, from autobiography to game theory to international law. Such stocktaking is opportune because the specter of genocide in recent years has given rise to new and improved lines of inquiry. This collection represents our extant knowledge about the violent phenomenon. The assembled writings offer a series of alternative answers to fundamental questions: What is genocide (as we now use the term)? What causes genocidal behavior? How do cases of genocide compare, and contrast? How does genocide relate to *other* types of collective violence, such as civil war and interstate war? What happens in genocide's aftermath? Can genocide be foreseen and prevented?

Although the field of genocide studies is now firmly established, it continues to face intellectual as well as practical challenges. A first step toward meeting these challenges is to recognize what the English art critic John Berger called different "ways of seeing."[1] The goal here is to highlight these contending perspectives on genocide and to acknowledge the limits of our knowledge. The anthology points to cases of immediate relevance for the study of genocide. In addition to focusing attention on the modern world, it also incorporates examples of collective violence from both the ancient and the medieval worlds. The objective is *not* to create

1. John Berger, *Ways of Seeing* (London: Penguin, 1972).

a new canon of acceptable cases but rather to *resist* the formulation of such a canon. In fact the analysis of nongenocidal cases is as important to the study of genocide as is the consideration of unambiguously genocidal ones.

The brief historical examination aims to make clear that *any* determination of temporal parameters, whether restrictive or expansive, embodies a particular way of seeing genocide. Alexander Laban Hinton, the president of the International Association of Genocide Scholars (IAGS), put it thus in his call for a "critical genocide studies": "As disciplinary structures of knowledge become ensconced, habit and tradition, as well as the interests that sustain them, also become factors in directing our attention to certain cases."[2] The field of genocide studies has—very problematically—foregrounded cases of twentieth-century violence, especially the Holocaust. As Hinton writes, "There has been a strong bias toward a genocide studies canon."[3] This canonization of collective violence is counterproductive for both scholarship and policy. One objective of this anthology is to *decenter* genocide studies, to acquaint readers with nonconventional approaches as well as to introduce them to nonconventional cases. By so doing, this book revisits the past of genocide studies and imagines its future.

The Study of Genocide

The adjectives *vocational* and *methodological* capture some of the major differences in ways of seeing genocide. What I term *vocational cleavages* refer to the different values and objectives that various professional groups have brought to their engagement with the subject matter of genocide. Three principal vocational groups have cornered the field: activists, scholars, and policymakers. Although the boundaries demarcating these groups are not always sharply drawn, they nevertheless have given rise to professional agendas that are regularly at odds with one another. What makes matters worse is the fact that these groups do not interact as frequently or regularly as would be desirable given the multidimensional nature of the subject matter.

Methodological cleavages refer to disagreements about the collection and interpretation of evidence, what in the social sciences is known as research design.[4] At present, vastly divergent standards of evidence exist among those working on questions of genocides. Far-ranging conclusions are often drawn on the basis of merely anecdotal evidence. Moreover vastly different skill levels are brought to bear when it comes to the identification of significant research questions and the formulation of viable research projects. Sometimes methodological differences have disciplinary roots. Inasmuch as the field is situated at the intersection of numerous disciplines, ranging from anthropology to sociology, cross-fertilization across boundaries is not yet the professional norm. At present, many of the existing literatures do not speak to one another, or do so only perfunctorily. Few are the scholars of genocide who have a firm grasp

---

2. Alexander Laban Hinton, "Critical Genocide Studies," *Genocide Studies and Prevention* 7, no. 1 (2012): 11.
3. Hinton, "Critical Genocide Studies," 12.
4. For an overview, see, for example, John Gerring, *Social Science Methodology: A Unified Framework*, 2nd edition (Cambridge: Cambridge University Press, 2011). See also Janet Box-Steffensmeier, Henry E. Brady, and David Collier, eds., *The Oxford Handbook of Political Methodology* (Oxford: Oxford University Press, 2010).

not only of the history of genocide but *also* of, say, the sociology of genocide, not to mention the law of genocide or the philosophy of genocide. Because different scholars attach varying levels of significance to methodological rigor, a gulf has opened up between different generations of genocide scholars. Scott Straus has usefully distinguished between "first-generation" and "second-generation" comparative research on genocide to describe this gulf, which has had significant consequences for the production of knowledge.[5]

Vocational Cleavages

The question of how to relate theory to practice has been a challenge for scholars, activists, and policymakers ever since the late 1970s, when genocide studies had its beginnings. More so than other fields, it has been Janus-faced since its inception. Just like the god of beginnings in ancient Roman mythology, genocide studies has been characterized by two contrasting vocational desires: advocacy and scholarship. The term *vocation* is useful in this context because it draws attention to the calling behind a person's professional occupation. The conflicting imperatives of advocacy and scholarship represent the first—and deepest—division in genocide studies.

In the 1950s and 1960s interest in genocide was virtually nonexistent. Despite, or rather because of the recent experience of the Holocaust, there was little appetite worldwide for a closer inspection of genocide, whether in the recent or the distant past. As the sociologist Jeffrey Alexander writes, with the United States in mind, "News about the mass murder [of the Jews of Europe], and any ruminations about it, disappeared from newspapers and magazines rather quickly after the initial reports about the camps' liberation, and the Nazis' Jewish victims became represented as displaced persons, potential immigrants, and potential settlers in Palestine, where a majority of Americans wanted to see a new, and redemptive, Jewish state."[6] It was precisely this quest for a redemptive narrative that precluded scholarly inquiry on a broad basis. Emblematic of the postwar disinterest in the systematic study of genocide (*even* of the Holocaust) is the fate of Raul Hilberg, the founding father of Holocaust studies.

His monumental three-volume study, *The Destruction of the European Jews,* which today is hailed as a classic, for numerous years languished unpublished because no American publishing house saw a market for a scholarly book on the Nazi genocide.[7] Interestingly, even Hilberg's doctoral adviser at Columbia University, Franz Neumann, a refugee from Nazi Germany, had warned that Hilberg's choice of subject might be his academic "funeral."[8] Although it is difficult to imagine today, before Hilberg's magisterial treatment of the Holocaust "there was not a

5. Scott Straus, "Second-Generation Comparative Research on Genocide," *World Politics* 59, no. 3 (2007): 476–501.

6. Jeffrey C. Alexander, "On the Social Construction of Moral Universals: The 'Holocaust' from War Crime to Trauma Drama," in Jeffrey C. Alexander, Ron Eyerman, Bernard Giesen, Neil J. Smelser, Piotr Sztompka, eds., *Cultural Trauma and Collective Identity* (Berkeley: University of California Press, 2004), 219.

7. The trilogy was eventually published in 1961 by Quadrangle Books. Holmes and Meier brought out a revised edition in 1985, and Yale University Press a third edition in 2003. For a moving and angry account of his professional struggles to establish the scholarly study of the Holocaust, see Raul Hilberg, *The Politics of Memory: The Journey of a Holocaust Historian* (Chicago: Ivan R. Dee, 2002).

8. Douglas Martin, "Raul Hilberg, 81, Historian Who Wrote of the Holocaust as a Bureaucracy, Dies," *New York Times*, August 7, 2007.

subject," as the historian Michael Marrus once put it.[9] The publication of and popular interest in Hannah Arendt's important but analytically problematic book *Eichmann in Jerusalem*, which relied heavily—although without proper acknowledgment—on Hilberg's magnum opus, was not representative of the intellectual mood in the 1950s and 1960s. Despite the adoption of the Genocide Convention in 1948, interest in genocide was scant in this postwar world. As the late Peter Novick showed, focusing on the United States, between the end of World War II and the 1960s "the Holocaust made scarcely any appearance in American public discourse, and hardly more in Jewish public discourse."[10] If not even this most far-ranging of genocides managed to capture the public imagination barely more than a decade after its perpetration, it is easy to imagine how little interest there was in making sense of genocide elsewhere.

On the few occasions when genocide became topical, it served mainly ideological purposes. A case in point is Jean-Paul Sartre's deliberate use of the label in 1968, in an attempt to stoke moral outrage about the Vietnam War.[11] At long last, in the 1970s, a small band of scholars emerged whose biographies led them, albeit in different ways and to different degrees, to discover genocide as an object worthy of study. This group included Israel Charny, Vahakn Dadrian, Helen Fein, Irving Louis Horowitz, Richard Hovannisian, Leo Kuper, Robert Melson, and Jack Nusan Porter.[12] In the 1980s other scholars joined their ranks. Of particular significance were Frank Chalk, Barbara Harff, Herbert Hirsch, Henry Hutttenbach, Rudolph Rummel, and Ervin Staub.[13] An intellectual community of scholars began to take shape. The combination of individuals and interests led to the emergence of institutions. The Cambodian Genocide Project (formed in 1981 at Yale University), the Institute for the Study of Genocide

9. As quoted in Nathaniel Popper, "A Conscious Pariah," *Nation*, March 31, 2010.

10. Peter Novick, *The Holocaust in American Life* (Boston: Houghton Mifflin, 1999), 103.

11. Jean-Paul Sartre, "Genocide," *New Left Review*, no. 48 (March–April 1968): 13–25.

12. Representative publications include Israel Charny, ed., *Toward the Understanding and Prevention of Genocide* (Boulder, Colo.: Westview, 1984); Vahakn N. Dadrian, *The History of the Armenian Genocide: Ethnic Conflict from the Balkans to Anatolia to the Caucasus* (New York: Berghahn, 2003); Helen Fein, *Genocide: A Sociological Perspective* (London: Sage, 1993); Irving Louis Horowitz, *Genocide: State Power and Mass Murder* (New Brunswick, N.J.: Transaction, 1976); Richard G. Hovannisian, *The Armenian Genocide in Perspective* (New Brunswick, N.J.: Transaction, 1986); Leo Kuper, *Genocide: Its Political Use in the Twentieth Century* (New Haven, Conn.: Yale University Press, 1981); Robert Melson, *Revolution and Genocide: On the Origins of the Armenian Genocide and the Holocaust* (Chicago: University of Chicago Press, 1996); Jack Nusan Porter, *Genocide and Human Rights: A Global Anthology* (Washington, D.C.: University Press of America, 1982).

13. Representative publications include Frank Chalk and Kurt Jonassohn, eds., *The History and Sociology of Genocide: Analyses and Case Studies* (New Haven, Conn.: Yale University Press, 1990); Barbara Harff, "No Lessons Learned from the Holocaust? Assessing Risks of Genocide and Political Mass Murder Since 1955," *American Political Science Review* 97, no. 1 (2003): 57–73; Herbert Hirsch, *Genocide and the Political Memory: Studying Death to Preserve Life* (Chapel Hill: University of North Carolina Press, 1995); Henry R. Huttenbach, "Locating the Holocaust on the Genocide Spectrum: Towards a Methodology of Definition and Categorization," *Holocaust and Genocide Studies* 3, no. 3 (1988): 289–303; R. J. Rummel, *Death by Government* (New Brunswick, N.J.: Transaction, 1994); Ervin Staub, *The Roots of Evil: The Origins of Genocide and Other Group Violence* (Cambridge: Cambridge University Press, 1989). For an introduction to the work and biographies of this first generation of genocide scholars, see Samuel Totten and Steven Leonard Jacobs, eds., *Pioneers of Genocide Studies* (Piscataway, N.J.: Transaction, 2002). See also some of the entries in Paul R. Bartrop and Steven Leonard Jacobs, eds., *Fifty Key Thinkers on the Holocaust and Genocide* (London: Routledge, 2011).

(created in 1982 at the John Jay College of Justice in New York City), and the Montreal Institute for Genocide Studies (established in 1986 at Concordia University) in particular laid the groundwork for what became the field of genocide studies.[14]

Although most genocide scholars in the 1970s and 1980s proved adept at separating their advocacy from their scholarship, a considerable number of individuals active in early genocide studies saw their calling as the prevention of genocide. Representative among them were Gregory Stanton, a lawyer who contributed to the creation of Yale's Genocide Studies Program and also played an important role in helping get under way the investigation and prosecution of Khmer Rouge crimes in Cambodia, and Ervin Staub, a psychologist and Holocaust survivor who has dedicated his life to fostering healing, forgiveness, and reconciliation.[15] However, the missionary zeal with which some members of the genocide studies community embraced the slogan "Never Again" has caused discomfort on the part of other members who are far less confident about the lessons that can be learned from studying genocide, including the Holocaust. As the communications director of the International Crisis Group put it in 2009, shortly after attending an educational seminar at Auschwitz, "I suspect too many people in the wider international community still only recognize genocide in this one most specific sense. They are always looking for Birkenau—expecting industrialized killing rather than seeing genocide the way it unfolds today."[16]

Although both vocational imperatives—advocacy and scholarship—should in principle be compatible, in practice the tensions between them opened up a deep rift in genocide studies that has still not healed. This rift received organizational expression with the founding in 2005 of the International Network of Genocide Scholars (INOGS).[17] The leading architect behind the initiative was Jürgen Zimmerer, a German historian whose work has focused on the destruction of the Herero in South West Africa. Donald Bloxham, Mark Levene, Dirk Moses, Martin Shaw, and Dan Stone quickly became major intellectual voices of INOGS.[18] INOGS was created in direct opposition to the U.S.-based, more established IAGS.[19] Its mission was to emphasize the primacy of scholarship over advocacy—a mission that, in the eyes of these mostly Europe-based scholars, had been largely abandoned by IAGS. A critical junc-

---

14. Although all three institutions are still in existence, the Yale initiative has eclipsed the other two in importance. In 1994 the U.S. government awarded it an $800,000 contract for research in postgenocide Cambodia. In 1998, on the heels of a grant from the Andrew W. Mellon Foundation, the initiative was renamed the Genocide Studies Program. The program has done more to draw scholarly attention to the phenomenon of genocide than any of the other contending institutional platforms.

15. Nowadays Stanton is best known for his argument that genocide can be broken down into "eight stages." See also Ervin Staub, *The Psychology of Good and Evil: Why Children, Adults, and Groups Help and Harm Others* (Cambridge: Cambridge University Press, 2003).

16. Andrew Stroehlein, "Never Again? What the Holocaust Can't Teach Us about Modern-day Genocide," *Foreign Policy*, December 2, 2009, available at http://www.foreignpolicy.com/articles/2009/11/25/never_again?page=0,0&hidecomments=yes.

17. The association's original name was the European Network of Genocide Scholars.

18. Representative publications include Donald Bloxham, *The Great Game of Genocide: Imperialism, Nationalism, and the Destruction of the Ottoman Armenians* (Oxford: Oxford University Press, 2007); Mark Levene, *Genocide in the Age of the Nation State*, vol. 1: *The Meaning of Genocide* (London: I. B. Tauris, 2005); Mark Levene, *Genocide in the Age of the Nation State*, vol. 2: *The Rise of the West and the Coming of Genocide* (London: I. B. Tauris, 2008); Martin Shaw, *What Is Genocide?* (Cambridge, U.K.: Polity, 2007); Dan Stone, *Histories of the Holocaust* (Oxford: Oxford University Press, 2010).

19. The IAGS was founded in 1994, originally as the Association of Genocide Scholars.

ture on the road to dissociation was the increasing use of resolutions to condemn collective violence the world over. The most controversial resolution was issued on February 1, 2006, when the IAGS formally condemned Iranian president Mahmoud Ahmadinejad's call for the destruction of Israel because the professional association's leadership felt the statement was tantamount to incitement to genocide.[20] Other members disapproved. Many, foremost among them Shaw, did not believe that it was IAGS's place to become embroiled in matters of international politics, least of all when Israel's actual treatment of Palestinians and Arab citizens was not receiving the same attention as the threats by Israel's enemies.[21]

The activist impulse remains strong in the field of genocide studies even in the twenty-first century. This was very apparent in the context of the armed conflict in Darfur, Sudan. For more than any other case, the controversy in the period 2004–10 over the classification of the conflict reminded the field that the vocational cleavage between advocacy and scholarship may have become less important, but certainly not unimportant. What the anthropologist Mahmood Mamdani called "the politics of naming" for years distracted from the reality of the intersecting and long-standing conflicts that lay at the heart of the destruction of villages and communities in the province of Darfur. In June 2005 the IAGS adopted a resolution calling for a military intervention "in order to stop the ongoing war crimes, crimes against humanity, ethnic cleansing, and genocide being perpetrated by Sudanese government troops and Janjaweed Arab militias against black African ethnic groups in Darfur."[22] By most accounts the IAGS's diplomatic intervention was misguided because it fell prey to a highly simplistic interpretation of the conflict—and rallied around a misguided solution. As the advocacy officer of a major international relief agency with a presence in Darfur explained a few years later, "Many activists were hugely detrimental in terms of looking for solutions. They created mass hysteria which limited the ability of decision-makers to pursue legitimate options. They have no concept of the fact that Sudan is a country and Darfur is just one part of it. These groups sucked up the space available for seeking solutions to the immediate needs of the people on the ground in Darfur because they focused all the attention of decision-makers on the far-fetched, long-term and debatable notion of a 'military' solution to the conflict, and of a UN-led intervention being the panacea to all Darfur's problems."[23]

The journalist Rob Crilly shone a bright light on the unintended consequences produced by another professional association that had become seized by the cause of Darfur. Reporting on the advocacy of the Save Darfur movement, he encountered "a more black and white,

20. International Association of Genocide Scholars, "Resolution Condemning Iranian President Ahmadinejad's Statements Calling for the Destruction of Israel and Denying the Historical Reality of the Holocaust; and Calling for Prevention of Iranian Development of Nuclear Weapons," February 1, 2006, available at http://www.genocidewatch.org/images/Iran-IAGS_Resolution.pdf

21. The controversy reached new heights in 2010, when Shaw, in an exchange with the Holocaust historian Omer Bartov, argued that the Zionist project of state formation in the late 1940s embodied "an incipiently genocidal mentality." Martin Shaw and Omer Bartov, "The Question of Genocide in Palestine, 1948: An Exchange between Martin Shaw and Omer Bartov," *Journal of Genocide Research* 12, nos. 3–4 (2010): 243–59.

22. International Association of Genocide Scholars, "Resolution on Intervention in Darfur," June 7, 2005, available at http://www.genocidescholars.org/sites/default/files/document%09%5Bcurrent-page%3A1%5D/documents/IAGS%20Resolution%20on%20Darfur-passed%207%20June%202005.pdf.

23. As quoted in Julie Flint and Alex de Waal, *Darfur: A New History of a Long War*, revised and updated edition (London: Zed Books, 2008), 185.

rights-based analysis often developed thousands of miles from Sudan. That analysis is not just misguided. It is not just inaccurate. It is leading us to the wrong solutions. Sometimes these are almost comical. . . . But they are also dangerous. By focusing on criminalising a government and making military intervention the top priority, Save Darfur has made peace more elusive and increased the suffering of ordinary Darfuris. Prescriptions based on the wrong diagnosis rarely work."[24] The last sentence encapsulates a general sentiment shared by the latest crop of leading genocide scholars: that prescriptions for saving strangers must be based on incontrovertible evidence. Unlike Charny, Stanton, and many of the individuals who founded the field of genocide studies, the generation of scholars who inherited it are far more ambivalent about the ethos of "Never Again." They point to the considerable knowledge gaps that vitiate the development of ready-made solutions in times of collective violence. Generally speaking, this circumspection is felt more strongly outside the United States, but even in the United States, critics have pushed back against the continued prevalence of moralism in the study of genocide studies. Very vocal among them has been Alan Kuperman, whose warnings against the moral hazard of humanitarian intervention have caused a stir in genocide studies.[25]

In 2006 the IAGS, in collaboration with the International Institute for Genocide and Human Rights Studies (a division of the Zoryan Institute for Contemporary Research and Documentation), launched the journal *Genocide Studies and Prevention* (GSP) to accommodate the policy concerns of many of its oldest members. The new journal was intended as a deliberate counterpoint to the scholarly *Journal of Genocide Research*, where evidence-driven rather than policy-oriented research was becoming the order of the day. Despite publishing a number of useful symposia on current affairs (e.g., on the 2008 report of the U.S. Genocide Prevention Task Force), GSP has been faltering, as the demand for analytical rigor in the field of genocide studies has increased. The maturation of genocide studies, and the more sophisticated methodological techniques brought to the field by the many disciplines that now regularly supply it with scholars and insights, has created a situation in which policy considerations have finally—and rightly so—taken a backseat to explanation and understanding. A new generation of scholars had a large hand in this deepening and broadening of genocide studies that commenced in the late 1990s. In addition to the INOGS community, it was the scholarship of Taner Akçam, John Hagan, Alexander Hinton, Ben Kiernan, Mahmood Mamdani, Michael Mann, Manus Midlarsky, Jacques Semelin, Scott Straus, Benjamin Valentino, and Eric Weitz, among others, that put on a more solid theoretical and empirical footing the study of collective violence in times of genocide.[26] Leading scholars of genocide now believe that "the fixa-

---

24. Rob Crilly, *Saving Darfur: Everyone's Favorite African War* (London: Reportage Press, 2010), 186–87.

25. See, for example, Alan J. Kuperman, "The Moral Hazard of Humanitarian Intervention: Lessons from the Balkans," *International Studies Quarterly* 52, no. 1 (2008): 49–80; Alan J. Kuperman, "Mitigating the Moral Hazard of Humanitarian Intervention: Lessons from Economics," *Global Governance* 14, no. 2 (2008): 219–40.

26. Representative publications include Taner Akçam, *The Young Turks' Crime against Humanity: The Armenian Genocide and Ethnic Cleansing in the Ottoman Empire* (Princeton, N.J.: Princeton University Press, 2012); Daniel Chirot and Clark McCauley, *Why Not Kill Them All? The Logic and Prevention of Mass Political Murder* (Princeton, N.J.: Princeton University Press, 2006); John Hagan and Wenona Rymond-Richmond, *Darfur and the Crime of Genocide* (Cambridge: Cambridge University Press, 2008); Alexander Laban Hinton, *Why Did They Kill? Cambodia in the Shadow of Genocide* (Berkeley: University of California Press, 2005); Ben Kiernan, *Blood and Soil: A World History of Genocide and Extermination from Sparta to Darfur* (New

tion on prevention" has diverted attention from more important issues in the study of geno-cide.[27] This emerging consensus notwithstanding, the scholarly community itself remains divided.

Methodological Cleavages

It is not surprising that scholars with very different and often contending ideas about what makes the world hang together have devoted their careers to studying genocide. On the upside, the deeper disciplinary grounding of genocide studies in the twenty-first century has been reflected in more compelling and more empirically grounded research projects. More than ever before scholars are embarking on carefully conceived archival, ethnographic, juris-prudential, laboratory, statistical, and other forms of qualitative and quantitative research in a number of disciplines. Whereas descriptive accounts based on secondary sources were the norm in the first generation of genocide scholars, the current field, with adherents in disci-plines ranging from anthropology to economics, from history to law, from literature to po-litical science, and from psychology to sociology, has a more reflexive understanding of its chosen vocation. And its leading members are methodologically more aware than those who went before. As a result "the limitation of the self-proclaimed pioneers of genocide studies are being surmounted by scholars who have made themselves experts in a particular field before embarking on comparative research."[28] In analytical terms, this has made the study of geno-cide more methodologically rigorous, more theoretically sophisticated, and more empirically discerning than it had been.

Yet disciplinary specialization has produced not just positive results; any such grounding invariably also has an immediate effect on the identification of research questions, the formu-lation of research designs, and the selection of methodological tools. For example, disciplin-ary socialization plays an important role in inculcating ideas about the determinants of social action. One perennial division relates to the so-called agent-structure problem. This problem concerns the relationship between agents and structures in the production of social out-comes, that is, the question of what is a *cause* in the social world and what is an *effect*. Do indi-viduals have the capacity to act independently (with agents constituting structures) in their

---

Haven, Conn.: Yale University Press, 2007); Mahmood Mamdani, *When Victims Become Killers: Colonial-ism, Nativism, and the Genocide in Rwanda* (Princeton, N.J.: Princeton University Press, 2001); Michael Mann, *The Dark Side of Democracy: Explaining Ethnic Cleansing* (Cambridge: Cambridge University Press, 2005); Manus Midlarsky, *The Killing Trap: Genocide in the Twentieth Century* (Cambridge: Cambridge Uni-versity Press, 2005); Jacques Semelin, *Purify and Destroy: The Political Uses of Massacre and Genocide* (New York: Columbia University Press, 2007); Scott Straus, *The Order of Genocide: Race, Power, and War in Rwanda* (Ithaca, N.Y.: Cornell University Press, 2006); Benjamin A. Valentino, *Final Solutions: Mass Killing and Genocide in the 20th Century* (Ithaca, N.Y.: Cornell University Press, 2004); James Waller, *Becoming Evil: How Ordinary People Commit Genocide and Mass Murder*, 2nd edition (Oxford: Oxford University Press, 2007); Eric D. Weitz, *A Century of Genocide: Utopias of Race and Nation* (Princeton, N.J.: Princeton University Press, 2003). In the interest of space, I have omitted relevant articles and chapters published by the aforementioned authors.

27. The formulation is Hinton's. See his "Critical Genocide Studies," 8.
28. A. Dirk Moses, "Toward a Theory of Critical Genocide Studies," *Online Encyclopedia of Mass Violence*, April 18, 2008, 11, available at http://www.massviolence.org/IMG/article_PDF/Toward-a-Theory-of-Critical -Genocide-Studies.pdf.

pursuit of collective violence, or is their ability to exercise a free will to kill governed by recurrent patterns of social organization (with structures constituting agents)?[29] Or are agents and structures mutually constitutive?

These questions from the philosophy of science are neither trivial nor abstruse. To the contrary, they help us to disaggregate what we might call, following the sociologist Emile Durkheim, the elementary forms of genocide. Only with this knowledge in hand does it become conceivable to distinguish possible and impossible responses to the specter of genocide. However, the questions have been answered differently across the universe of disciplines involved in the study of genocide. Scholars who emphasize primarily the role of agents are generally concerned with the *microdynamics* of genocide (e.g., the role of individuals, preferences, and choices in the actual pursuit of destruction). Scholars who turn first and foremost to the role of structures are more likely to be concerned with the *macrodynamics* of genocide (e.g., the role of ideology, modernity, revolution, and war in creating the conditions for destruction).

An example of the kinds of intellectual fault lines that appear when scholars disagree about the relationship between agents and structures is the well-worn (although now largely settled) debate between so-called intentionalists and functionalists in the study of the Holocaust. The former believed that the origins of the "Final Solution" go back as far as 1924 and are intimately bound up with the person and preferences of Adolf Hitler. The latter, by contrast, emphasized the cumulative radicalization of Nazi Jewish policy, noting in particular the enabling and constraining significance of bureaucratic structures. The substance of the debate need not concerns us here. But the underlying difference between intentionalists and functionalists is methodological in the sense that each perspective owes to a particular view of how the world hangs together. Intentionalists and functionalists have different understandings of the basic categories of being and their relations— what philosophers of science call ontology. At the risk of oversimplification, intentionalists believe that agents (such as Hitler) are more important that structures in bringing about social outcomes, whereas functionalists are convinced that structures (such as bureaucracies) govern the actions and omissions of individuals. In the study of genocide more generally, it is essential to appreciate the interaction effects between agents and structures in the real world. Doing so persuasively requires a fair amount of methodological training and sophistication. It necessitates careful reflection on the demands of conceptualization and measurement.

It is important to take methodological questions seriously because they directly affect the way we view the world—and genocide within it. Although genocide scholars in the humanities—in disciplines such as history, philosophy, and literature—are not concerned with measurement per se, an appreciation of the methodology of the social sciences does go a long way toward fostering the kind of interdisciplinary ethos that the subject matter demands and the study of genocide requires. Likewise social scientists less interested in interpretation and more focused on generalization would do well to become more open-minded about the use of humanistic approaches in the study of genocide. Such approaches are of particular significance when it comes to making sense of genocide's aftermath, an ever more important topic in the field. To give but one example, the study of memory and with it research on memorial-

29. As in all spheres of social life, structures can be material in nature (e.g., classes) or cultural (e.g., customs).

ization has seen a steady rise in interest. Because the consequences of genocide include the necessity of coping on the part of those who survive, memory deserves more careful scrutiny than it sometimes receives. Inasmuch as the origins of genocide deservedly generate a great deal of attention in the literature, original research on the effects of genocide is equally relevant. But given the sensitive nature of such research and the methodological awareness that this sensitivity requires from scholars, interpretive reasoning rather than positivist reasoning will often be most suitable.

Even though methodological divisions are gradually becoming less pronounced in genocide studies, they have shaped the field during the past few decades and thus provide an important key to unlocking some of the mysteries of the vast literature. Some of the most important advances in the study of genocide have come from within the discipline of sociology. Interestingly most of the better known of these contributions prioritized structures over agents in accounting for genocidal outcomes. Two key works illustrate the point. The first is Zygmunt Bauman's *Modernity and the Holocaust* (1989). This pathbreaking account made the controversial claim that the modernization of life in spheres from art to industry was a necessary condition for the death and destruction that the Holocaust brought. The catastrophe in the heart of Europe was not an aberration from the achievements of civilization, observed Bauman, but the logical outgrowth of a hyperrationalized way of life. Next is Michael Mann's *The Dark Side of Democracy* (2005). Mann's focus is also on modernity, but more so on democracy, notably the organic kind that presumes a congruence of *demos* (the people) and *ethnos* (an ethnic group). What he calls "murderous ethnic cleansing" is the result of democracy gone wrong. It is, says Mann, "the dark side of democracy." This dark side has come to the fore because "the ideal of rule by the people began to entwine the *demos* with the dominant *ethnos*, generating organic conceptions of the nation and the state that encouraged the cleaning of minorities."[30] Mann does not deny that agents matter, perceptively distinguishing among nine different types of perpetrators, all with different motives, that can be found in contexts of mass killing. However, the fact that he cares rather more about structures than agents is exemplified in this observation: "To understand ethnic cleansing, we need a sociology of power more than a special psychology of perpetrators."[31]

Among other things, the statement is a rebuke to the handful of psychologists of genocide. Although psychologists were the first social scientists to take seriously the Holocaust as an object of study, their contributions have, by and large, been marginal and not stood the test of time. The "mad Nazi thesis," which held that the perpetrators of the Holocaust were psychologically deranged, for example, barely survived after World War II. Subsequent interventions, notably by the psychologists Ervin Staub and James Waller, drew attention to more relevant factors such as difficult life conditions, prejudice, and discrimination, but psychological explanations have struggled to account for genocidal outcomes in anything but the most general terms. As Straus notes, "Deep divisions, prejudice, and discrimination are fairly constant; genocide is not."[32] This is why Mann believes that methodological individualism—the prioritizing of agents over structures that is germane to psychological reasoning as well as to

30. Mann, *The Dark Side of Democracy*, 3.
31. Mann, *The Dark Side of Democracy*, 9.
32. Straus, "Second-Generation Comparative Research on Genocide," 481.

economic reasoning and to some political science reasoning—is of limited explanatory value in the study of genocide. Mann has a point, and yet things are more complicated than he allows.

The insights generated by sociologists have taught us a great deal about the long-term dynamics of genocide. However, alternative solutions to the agent-structure problem have called into question the explanatory power of the works listed above or others like them. For the study of long-term causes of genocide usually sheds little light on faster moving developments at ground level, where individuals undoubtedly matter. Because large processes such as modernization, state building, and democratization are typically slow-moving, understanding their logic does not always contribute to knowledge about individual and collective decision making in times of genocide or the spread of violence at particular moments in time. To put it differently, knowing that the incentives for genocidal violence are sometimes greater in times of large-scale social change does not explain why different kinds of individuals (e.g., farmers, workers, mothers, bureaucrats, soldiers) choose to participate in genocidal campaigns when they do. As a result, structural perspectives offer little purchase to address questions about the timing of genocide or about the peculiar forms of violence that we see in these extreme situations.

In the mid-1990s the field of genocide studies began to change—not rapidly, but noticeably. The impetus came mostly from Europe. Young historians were responsible for a large proportion of the pathbreaking contributions at that time. Around the turn of the millennium, a growing recognition of the importance of studying the case-specific interaction effects among local, national, and international (especially regional) levels of analysis began to pervade the field of genocide studies. Bloxham, Gerlach, Kiernan, Levene, Moses, George Steinmetz, and Weitz have made most of this avenue of research. Inspired by the "global turn" in historiography more generally, these scholars of genocide started to look for "micro-macro links."[33] Much of this research was located one step below the macro level of analysis that sociologists favored, at the so-called meso level.

By scaling down to an intermediate perspective on genocide, scholars gained greater purchase on the many moving parts that must combine for genocidal violence to transpire. The authors in question understood that what the historian and sociologist Charles Tilly once referred to as "big structures" and "large processes" had to be related to specific goings-on within countries, especially at the level of states, organizations, and communities.[34] Kiernan's successive and extremely detailed accounts of the Cambodian genocide, including their convoluted international politics, led the way. Bloxham's highly influential and controversial book *The Great Game of Genocide* (2005) followed suit by presenting a revisionist history of the Armenian genocide based on a wide-ranging reappraisal of primary and secondary sources. Bloxham succeeded with his skillful interweaving of local, regional, and international dimensions of the much-disputed genocide.

33. On the problem of the micro-macro link in the social sciences, especially in sociological theory, see Jeffrey C. Alexander, Bernhard Giesen, Richard Münch, and Neil J. Smelser, *The Micro-Macro Link* (Berkeley: University of California Press, 1987).
34. Charles Tilly, *Big Structures, Large Processes, and Huge Comparisons* (New York: Russell Sage Foundation, 1984).

Hand in hand with this disciplinary reorientation of the field came a focus on the microdynamics of genocide, which just a few years prior had taken hold in political science, where a new generation of scholars—Stathis Kalyvas, Roger Petersen, Nicholas Sambanis, Jeremy Weinstein, Steven Wilkinson, and Elisabeth Wood, to name but a few—had begun to overhaul the study of civil war.[35] Inspired by this burgeoning literature, a number of political scientists working on genocide have incorporated this newfound perspective into their work. The majority of work on the so-called micropolitics of genocide has been developed in the context of the Rwandan case. The work of Straus, Lee Ann Fujii, and Omar McDoom best illustrates the quality of genocide scholarship that can result when the individuals undertaking this research are not only theoretically sophisticated but are *also* methodologically aware *and* empirically immersed in the field. This, perhaps, is the greatest paradigm shift in the methodology of genocide studies: the substitution of primary research for secondary research. An empirical imperative has begun to supplant the moral imperative that drove the first generation of genocide scholars. Historians and political scientists alike subjected local dynamics as well as national and international dynamics to scrutiny in a manner they had rarely done. Whereas genuine and extensive primary research had been missing from most first-generation accounts of genocide, it has become a sine qua non of the latest literature. This scholarship has sought to deepen theoretical insights with knowledge gained in the archives and in the field.

A final and, until very recently, very divisive methodological issue has to do with the use of comparative historical analysis in the study of genocide. In addition to the emerging focus in the early 2000s on local and regional dynamics of genocide, which had its beginnings in Holocaust studies, the second generation of genocide scholars was adamant not to view the Holocaust as the archetypal genocide. The result was a reorientation of existing scholarship. But even more important, many of the upcoming historians also discovered nonconventional cases and issues in the study of genocide. They insisted that there were comparable cases of genocide before the Holocaust and after it. This was a far cry from the 1980s, when attempts to place the Holocaust in comparative perspective were often accompanied by accusations that the scholars in question were intent on minimizing Jewish suffering at the hands of Nazi Germany.

To fully appreciate the significance of this methodological broadening of genocide studies it is useful to briefly consider the motivation behind the founding of the *Journal of Genocide Research*, the field's flagship publication, which was initially published as a newsletter, the *Genocide Forum*. Henry Huttenbach, the founder of both GF and JGR, was keen to establish a learned journal for research on genocides *other* than the Holocaust. Huttenbach, a professor of history at City College of the City University of New York, articulated his intellectual vision in no uncertain terms: "Whenever comparisons were made by those engaged in Holocaust

---

35. The literature is immense, but in book form, see, most important, Stathis N. Kalyvas, *The Logic of Violence in Civil War* (Cambridge: Cambridge University Press, 2006); Roger Petersen, *Understanding Ethnic Violence: Fear, Hatred, and Resentment in Twentieth-Century Eastern Europe* (Cambridge: Cambridge University Press, 2002); Jeremy M. Weinstein, *Inside Rebellion: The Politics of Insurgent Violence* (Cambridge: Cambridge University Press, 2006); Steven I. Wilkinson, *Votes and Violence: Electoral Competition and Ethnic Riots in India* (Cambridge: Cambridge University Press, 2004); Elisabeth Jean Wood, *Insurgent Collective Action and Civil War in El Salvador* (Cambridge: Cambridge University Press, 2003).

studies, they were done largely to set the Holocaust *apart* rather than integrating it into the larger 20th century phenomenon of genocide in general and ethno-genocide in particular. On the whole, the strategy of comparison taken by Holocaust scholars was largely one-directional, namely, to keep the Holocaust *separate*, an event standing distinctly alone. The obverse, underlying muted assumption implied that the study of non-Holocaust genocides would contribute little of substance towards understanding the depths of the genocide experienced by European Jewry."[36]

GF and *JGR* were meant as alternative outlets to Oxford University Press's journal *Holocaust and Genocide Studies*, or *HGS*. Huttenbach, with good reason, at the time bemoaned the fact that *HGS* was not fulfilling its mandate. He found that the number of articles published on non-European genocides was unacceptably small. Other scholars too chided *HGS* for this omission and suspected that the journal's association with the U.S. Holocaust Memorial Museum was partially responsible for the centrality of the Nazi genocide in its pages. Some observers were also uncomfortable with the journal's title, which was also popular when it came to the naming of research centers: "Dozens of centers, off and on campuses, named 'Holocaust and Genocide' center or institute have proliferated throughout the United States, thereby perpetuating the tendency to keep the Holocaust distinct and, by inference, . . . an event that supposedly is, by its nature, trans-genocide. The purpose is not to emphasize the Holocaust but to diminish the 'others.'"[37]

The issue is anything but trivial, and it has to be grasped by anyone interested in the study of genocide, and the politics thereof. For the question of "the uniqueness of the Holocaust" accounted for one of the most contentious debates in genocide studies, which continues to flare up occasionally.[38] Although the debate has been won, on most accounts, by those who argued that the Holocaust is neither unique nor unprecedented in the annals of genocide, much of the published work is still preoccupied with the Holocaust, as exemplified by the writings in this *Reader*. (My hope is that future editions of this *Reader* will feature a greater share of scholarship from other settings and historical periods.)

In light of this intellectual history, we can distinguish between a *disciplinary center* and the *disciplinary periphery* of the field of genocide studies. The former revolves around scholarship on the most destructive of the twentieth-century genocides. I have in mind the cases most frequently featured on syllabi and in the media, notably, in chronological order, the Armenian genocide, the Holocaust, the Cambodian genocide, the case of the former Yugoslavia, and the Rwandan genocide. By contrast, the disciplinary periphery revolves around an entirely different universe of cases, of which more in the historical section of this introduction. Usefully for the field of genocide studies, the second generation of scholars has brought the

36. Henry R. Huttenbach, "The Convergence of Holocaust and Genocide Studies," *Genocide Forum* 1, no. 1 (1994), available at http://www.chgs.umn.edu/educational/genocideForum/year1/no1.html. Huttenbach edited *Genocide Forum*, an influential newsletter whose success was a major impetus behind the launch of the *JGR*, between 1994 and 2000. All fifty issues of *Genocide Forum* are available at http://www.chgs.umn.edu/educational/genocideForum/.

37. Henry R. Huttenbach, "Vita Felix, Via Dolorosa: An Academic Journey Towards Genocide," in Totten and Jacobs, *Pioneers of Genocide Studies*, 56.

38. For an overview, see, for example, Alan S. Rosenbaum, ed., *Is the Holocaust Unique? Perspectives on Comparative Genocide*, 3rd edition (Boulder, Colo.: Westview, 2009).

periphery to the center. What used to be a minor concern has become a major current in the field, namely the study of "forgotten genocides" (René Lemarchand) and "hidden genocides" (Alexander Hinton).[39] Although no consensus exists regarding its composition, this subset of cases ranges from instances of ancient destruction (e.g., Carthage) to examples of colonial destruction (e.g., Australia) to episodes of ideological destruction (e.g., the Soviet Union). A veritable cottage industry has sprung up in recent years dedicated to understanding the microdynamics of collective violence in these unconventional settings.

Although the comparative historical analysis of genocide is now well established in general terms, methodologically speaking much remains to be done. Most important, genocide studies must pay more attention to instances of collective violence *other than* genocide. For this reason, the French political scientist Jacques Semelin decided to make the phenomenon of the massacre, not genocide, his preferred unit of analysis.[40] But the broadening of genocide studies' ambit must also include the study of so-called negative cases, that is, cases in which genocidal violence was in the offing but did not, for whatever reasons, materialize. Explicating these reasons in great empirical detail is of utmost relevance for explaining and understanding the dynamics of genocide. Compared to scholars of genocide, scholars of civil war, especially in political science, have proved more adept at figuring out why collective violence occurs in some settings of contentious politics but not in others. Straus is right: "Genocide studies would do well to take a methodological page from that literature's playbook, by focusing less on no-variance, country-case comparisons and more on comparisons with increased variance on the outcome of interest."[41] Because genocide represents but one of many forms of collective violence that are theoretically conceivable and empirically verifiable, we must understand the entire universe of collective violence before reaching conclusions about the logic and determinants of specifically genocidal outcomes. For it is an undeniable empirical fact that genocidal violence is perpetrated in the context of other mass atrocities, most commonly (though certainly not exclusively) interstate war. It is essential to make better sense of the interaction effects among these varieties of collective violence. Benjamin Valentino was among the first to draw attention to this methodological issue, in his *Final Solutions*, but he addressed it only briefly. In *Extremely Violent Societies* Christian Gerlach has gone some way toward accomplishing this goal. By considering the Holocaust alongside other central (e.g., the case of the Ottoman Empire) and peripheral (e.g., the case of East Pakistan) cases in genocide studies, he raised important questions about the boundaries of the genocide phenomenon.

Next and related, longitudinal analyses of mass violence in a given setting are extremely valuable. Instead of studying extremely violent episodes in temporal isolation, as genocide scholars have tended to do, a great deal of important knowledge can be gained from taking a longer-term view. For example, Alex de Waal, a leading interpreter of Sudan, has bemoaned the fact that those writing about the Darfur conflict in the early twenty-first century took it out of its context. De Waal showed that comparisons with other violent episodes in Sudan

---

39. See, for example, René Lemarchand, ed., *Forgotten Genocides: Oblivion, Denial, and Memory* (Philadelphia: University of Pennsylvania Press, 2011); Alex Hinton, Thomas LaPointe, and Douglas Irvin, eds., *Hidden Genocides: Power, Knowledge, Memory* (Newark, N.J.: Rutgers University Press, 2013).
40. Semelin, *Purify and Destroy*.
41. Straus, "Second-Generation Comparative Research on Genocide," 479.

renders a more complete picture of the logic of atrocities committed by Janjaweed militias at the behest of and with the support of the government of Sudan starting in 2003. It is essential to appreciate the social meaning of large-scale violence in Sudan in general and in Darfur in particular. Absent that, warns de Waal, we may misinterpret what we see: "In Darfur, cutting down fruit trees or destroying irrigation ditches is a way of eradicating farmers' claims to the land and ruining livelihoods. But this is not the genocidal campaign of a government at the height of its ideological hubris, as the 1992 jihad against the Nuba was, or coldly determined to secure natural resources, as when it sought to clear the oilfields of southern Sudan of their troublesome inhabitants. This is the routine cruelty of a security cabal, its humanity withered by years in power: it is genocide by force of habit."[42] Regardless of whether we agree with de Waal's interpretation of large-scale violence in Darfur, the analytical act of placing contemporary atrocities in the context of prior atrocities promises to surface remote or even proximate causes that otherwise might remain hidden.

Finally, inasmuch as the intellectual decentering of genocide studies has generated exciting new insights into the mechanisms and processes of what policymakers are wont to refer to as "mass atrocities," it is essential that we not lose sight of the fact that our stock of knowledge regarding the twentieth century's genocides is not as solid as it seems at first sight. In fact the professionalization of genocide studies demands that we revisit what we thought we knew about the conventional cases as well.

More sustained engagements across the vocational and methodological divides are necessary if we are truly serious about uprooting genocide in the international system. The field of genocide studies is in dire need of more and improved translational research. Scholarly discoveries must be translated more effectively into practical applications without being "dumbed down" in the process. Progress on this front has been tardy because policy oriented observers in advocacy organizations, governments, think tanks, international organizations, and NGOs have regularly demonstrated a perfunctory grasp of the complexity of genocide and related types of collective violence. Although highly relevant knowledge is available, it is not being used to the extent that it could—and should.

Progress has also been retarded because much of the available bench research in associated disciplines is theoretically underdeveloped or empirically inadequate. In the natural sciences, bench research attracts a great deal of attention and funding and is concerned with the microfoundations of life, its molecules and cells. In genocide studies the equivalent of bench research is in its infancy (except in Holocaust studies, which preceded by several decades the emergence of genocide studies and ever since the mid-1990s in particular has contributed a vast amount of knowledge to our understanding of the Nazi genocide, though this knowledge is rarely noticed let alone taken on board by the vast majority of genocide scholars).

We do not yet have a good enough understanding of the microfoundations of genocide, its mechanisms and processes. What genocide studies needs, in other words, is more and improved basic or pure research, that is, research undertaken with the sole objective of increasing understanding of fundamental aspects of genocidal dynamics. Pure research, thus defined, is not moved by questions of genocide prevention or related policy questions that all

42. Alex de Waal, "Counter-insurgency on the Cheap," *Review of African Political Economy* 31, no. 102 (2004): 723–24.

too often muddy intellectual endeavors. Pure research will rarely help policymakers directly with the challenges involved in responding to the specter of genocide. Although fundamental research of this kind does not yield immediate policy benefits, it is high time that genocide studies emulated the natural sciences in their quest for identifying the basic building blocks of life.

It is an unfortunate legacy of a field founded in the 1980s on the borderline between moral indignation and academic inquiry that many of its protagonists have been willing to advocate for solutions to the problem on the back of partial or incomplete understanding of the phenomenon. In few other walks of life would we be content to stake so much on so little. The intention of this *Reader* is to help "unsimplify" genocide, to borrow a phrase from René Lemarchand, a long-standing scholar of Africa. For rarely are perpetrators of genocide "mad" or otherwise abnormal. Nor, in most cases, are they motivated primarily by hatred or have in store a well-constructed genocidal plan. Nor are national, ethnic, racial, or religious cleavages as central to their motivation as is often thought. Typically the idea of destroying a targeted group, regardless of its nature, emerges when all else fails, for example, when homogenization has proved ineffective, repression insufficient, or resettlement impossible. Another simplistic notion to be dislodged has to do with genocide prevention. As several of the selected writings make clear, military intervention is not a panacea. It may not always be an effective, let alone a humanitarian response to suffering in a genocidal campaign. The list of simplistic notions goes on. In order to provide enough empirical background for readers to be able to appreciate the many contributions assembled here, the next section offers up a brief history of genocide.

A new era in genocide studies has begun. Although the Holocaust is the subject of many of the writings included here, this overrepresentation is chiefly a function of the dearth of scholarship on other genocides rather than the result of an inherent belief in the uniqueness of the event and its consequences. This *Reader* aims to inspire scholarship that will redress this imbalance and ensure that future editions of this collection represent an even greater diversity of knowledge.

The History of Genocide

Sketching the history of genocide is far trickier—and more controversial—than a casual observer might think. Unfortunately it is not at all obvious which cases of genocide constitute the field's ambit. Usually the inclusion and exclusion of cases reflect the bias of the person doing the selecting. Hinton therefore recently challenged us "to consider why we focus on certain cases and topics and what sorts of inclusions and exclusions ensue. What is left invisible to us and what can we do to cast light on what has formerly been opaque."[43] Hinton rightly implored scholars of genocide "to consider how such biases have shaped our own research and teaching and, through decentering, to re-envision our field of study."[44]

43. Hinton, "Critical Genocide Studies," 13.
44. Hinton, "Critical Genocide Studies," 12.

Although a considerable number of voices in the field of genocide studies continue to be wary of broadening the meaning of the phenomenon, this *Reader* treats the Holocaust as one genocide among many. This decentering of genocide studies does not relativize the massive suffering inflicted by Germans and their collaborators on millions of Jews and other victims in the context of World War II. What it does do is draw our attention to the inescapable fact that the study of genocide is far more recent than the phenomenon itself. The term *genocide* is a neologism of relatively recent pedigree; the practice of collective violence for the purpose of absolute destruction is anything but. Classifications that declare the twentieth century to be "the century of genocide" are therefore suspect.[45] Although the genocidal violence perpetrated in the Ottoman Empire, the Soviet Union, the Nazi empire, Cambodia, parts of Bosnia, and Rwanda during that century account for the vast majority of scholarship on the topic of genocide, not to mention a staggering number of victims, the violent destruction of lands and people has a very long history. Accordingly this anthology takes the ancient period as the starting point for this brief history of genocidal acts, campaigns, and regimes.[46]

This conception of the temporal parameters of the history of genocide is entirely in keeping with some of the earliest political thought on the Holocaust. Enter Raphaël Lemkin, who coined the term *genocide* by conjoining the Greek root *genos* (meaning "family," "tribe," or "race") and the Latin suffix *-cide* (from the verb *occidere*, meaning "to kill," "to slay," "to slaughter"). Unbeknown to many observers, Lemkin was convinced that we had to take a perspective from the longue durée to understand what the Nazis had euphemistically come to call "the final solution" in the 1940s. Unlike many scholars who came in his wake, Lemkin did *not* think that the Holocaust was unique in the sense that it is often said to be today. Here is a representative statement, taken from an article that he published in the *Christian Science Monitor* in 1948: "The destruction of Carthage, the destruction of the Albigenses and Waldenses, the Crusades, the march of the Teutonic Knights, the destruction of the Christians under the Ottoman Empire, the massacres of the Herero in Africa, the extermination of the Armenians, the slaughter of the Christian Assyrians in Iraq in 1933, the destruction of the Maronites, the pogroms of Jews in Tsarist Russia and Romania—all these are classical genocide cases."[47] In fact we now know that Lemkin, while advocating for the adoption of the Genocide Convention, was also busily at work on a massive scholarly history of genocide. Although the completion of the book was cut short by Lemkin's death in 1959, the historian Ann Curthoys has found several typescripts of chapters as well as outlines for the envisaged book. These documents show that Lemkin was planning on writing separate chapters on forty-one different

45. See, for example, Samuel Totten and William S. Parsons, eds., *Century of Genocide: Critical Essays and Eyewitness Accounts*, 3rd edition (London: Routledge, 2008). Note that the latest edition of this collection has been renamed, resulting in a qualitatively different classification of the twentieth century. It is now published as Samuel Totten and William S. Parsons, eds., *Centuries of Genocide: Essays and Eyewitness Accounts*, 4th edition (London: Routledge, 2012). The issue is not just one of semantics; it is deeply intertwined with the vocational and methodological cleavages in genocide studies that I discussed earlier.

46. I have elaborated this distinction elsewhere. See, for example, Jens Meierhenrich, *The Rationality of Genocide* (Princeton: Princeton University Press, forthcoming).

47. Raphael Lemkin, "War against Genocide," *Christian Science Monitor*, January 31, 1948, quoted in A. Dirk Moses, "Raphael Lemkin, Culture, and the Concept of Genocide," in Donald Bloxham and Dirk Moses, eds., *The Oxford Handbook of Genocide Studies* (Oxford: Oxford University Press, 2010), 26.

genocides. According to Curthoys's research in the archives, Lemkin's study was "to include case studies from antiquity, with chapters on the early Christians, the Pagans, Carthage, Gaul, the Celts, Egypt and Ancient Greece. Then there would be a section on the Middle Ages, with chapters on genocides committed by groups such as the Goths, Huns, Mongols, Vikings, French and Spanish against peoples and groups like the Albigensians, Jews, Valdenses, Moors and Moriscos. In the section on 'Modern Times,' chapters on a large number of cases were envisaged, including the forced deportation of the Cherokee, the Herero in South-west Africa, the Gypsies, the Armenian genocide and genocides against Polish Jews, Russian Jews, Romanian Jews and others."[48]

Lemkin's reluctance to consider unique the Nazi genocide gives us both an intellectual and a moral license to locate the Holocaust on the spectrum of genocide. Interestingly even the 1948 Genocide Convention in its preamble affirms that "at all periods of history genocide has inflicted great losses on humanity." At the same time it is important not to rush to judgment about the nature of collective violence perpetrated in the distant past. Not even all of the empirical illustrations that follow constitute fully fledged instances of genocide. The point is rather that the destruction wrought in each of the many cases to be discussed in passing is so serious and heinous that it must be taken seriously and studied closely in order to illuminate as precisely as possible its relationship—causal, geographical, temporal—to the phenomenon with which this *Reader* is primarily concerned: genocide. At the same time it is imperative that in each instance we identify better than we have thus far modes of transitions *to* and *from* genocidal violence. For history—ancient, medieval, and modern—teaches us that most conquerors "do not begin with an overtly genocidal intent, in the sense of planning to physically exterminate the pre-existing people."[49] The sociologist Michael Mann arrived at a similar conclusion in his extended study of ethnic cleansing:

> It is rare to find evil geniuses plotting mass murder from the very beginning. Not even Hitler did so. Murderous cleansing typically emerges as a kind of Plan C, developed only after the first two responses to a perceived ethnic threat fail. Plan A typically envisages a carefully planned solution in terms of either compromise or straightforward repression. Plan B is a more radically repressive adaptation to the failure of Plan A, more hastily conceived amid rising violence and some political destabilization. When these both fail, some of the planners radicalize further. To understand the outcome, we must analyze the unintended consequences of a series of interactions yielding escalation. These successive Plans may contain both logical and more contingent escalations. The perpetrators may be ideologically determined from quite early on to rid themselves of the ethnic out-group, and when milder methods fail, they almost logically seems to escalate with resolute determination to overcome all obstacles by more and more radical means.[50]

48. Ann Curthoys, "Raphaël Lemkin's 'Tasmania': An Introduction," *Patterns of Prejudice* 39, no. 2 (2005): 166.
49. David Day, *Conquest: How Societies Overwhelm Others* (Oxford: Oxford University Press, 2008), 182.
50. Mann, *The Dark Side of Democracy*, 7–8.

The argument holds true not only for the twentieth century but for much of the rest of human history as well. When conceived literally as a "final solution," the absolute destruction of real or imagined enemies becomes more comprehensible than when it is portrayed as a problem from hell. Political scientists were among the first scholars to emphasize and explicitly theorize the logic of strategic choice that has underpinned much of modern genocide.[51] A close study of premodern societies reveals that genocidal violence often served a similarly instrumental function then. What follows, then, is a set of empirical vignettes *selectively* culled from a much longer and fuller history of collective violence than can be recounted here.[52] There are the major set pieces of genocide—the Armenian genocide, the Holocaust, the Cambodian genocide, the genocide in Srebrenica and northern Bosnia, the Rwandan genocide, the conflict in Darfur—but they are interspersed with sketches of collective violence not always deemed archetypal in scholarship: the destruction of Carthaginians, the persecution of Huguenots, the extermination of Herero, the removal of Aborigines, the starvation of Ukrainians, and the suppression of Guatemalans, to name but a few of many relevant cases.

Genocide in the Ancient World

Leo Kuper, the most influential twentieth century scholar of genocide, observed that "the word is new, the crime ancient."[53] With the opening sentence of his classic account, Kuper introduced a new way of seeing genocide. More than any other previous scholar, he emphasized the importance of the comparative method for coming to terms with what the 1948 Genocide Convention described as an "odious scourge." Among other lasting contributions that he made, Kuper, following in Lemkin's footsteps, was among the first scholars to reach deep into the distant past for his comparative analysis: "One recalls the . . . horrifying genocidal massacres, such as the terror of Assyrian warfare in the eighth and seventh centuries BC, when many cities were razed to the ground and whole populations carried off or brutally exterminated, until the Assyrian empire itself became the victim of its own wars of annihilation; or the destruction of Troy and its defenders, and the carrying off into slavery of the women (as described in the legendary accounts and the Greek tragedies which have come down to us); or the Roman obliteration of Carthage, men, women and children, the site of the devastated city sown with salt, symbolic of desolation."[54]

At the same time it is very difficult to reconstruct with any degree of certainty the nature and role of collective violence in the ancient world. As Michael Freeman notes, "We know very little about unrecorded wars of extermination, the unwritten archaeological record being very recalcitrant to interpretation."[55] It follows that we must be careful before pronouncing

---

51. Valentino, *Final Solutions*.
52. The empirical vignettes included here are neither comprehensive nor conclusive. Their principal purpose is to frame the writings that make up this *Reader*. For the first attempt at a global history of genocide, see Kiernan, *Blood and Soil*.
53. Kuper, *Genocide*, 11.
54. Kuper, *Genocide*, 11.
55. Michael Freeman, "Genocide, Civilization and Modernity," *British Journal of Sociology* 46, no. 2 (1995): 218.

on the existence and nature of genocidal violence in the distant past. The ability to do so requires an "archaeology of genocide," as Frank Chalk and Kurt Jonassohn pointed out several decades ago.[56] Although no such archaeology has developed in any true sense of the word, a comparative historical approach to the study of destruction—even if undergirded with imperfect evidence—promises to bring into sharper relief the changing character of genocide across time and space.

Some of the earliest episodes of large-scale destruction that *may* be deserving, in some instances at least, of the adjective *genocidal* include the so-called rape of Troy (ca. 1194–1184 BCE), the razing of Babylon (ca. 689 BCE), the wiping out of Melos (416 BCE), and the destruction of Carthage (ca. 149–146 BCE).[57] The point of introducing these ancient cases is not to reach definitive conclusions as to the nature of the collective violence that they experienced. Quite the contrary, they are relevant to the study of genocide because they allow us to highlight varieties of violence.[58]

In Homer's *Iliad*, for example, the Greek conquerors of Troy have no qualms about the absolute destruction of the city and its inhabitants. If we believe the ancient legend, Agamemnon, King of Mycenae and the leader of the Achaeans (Greeks), laid siege to Troy, a city located near the strait of the Hellespont (now the Dardanelles) on the Aegean coast, in support of his brother, Menelaus, the husband of Helen, whose abduction by Paris, a prince of Troy, was the root cause of the Trojan War. Nine years of force did not bring about the city's destruction, despite the famed Achilles and Ajax successfully conquering cities and islands for the Achaean cause. Then came the invention of the Trojan Horse, at least according to Virgil's *Aeneid*. In fact in this much later account, the Roman poet has his main protagonist, Aeneas, speak of an "orgy of killing" in Troy as a result of which "the bodies of the dead lay through all its streets and houses and sacred shrines of its gods."[59] Odysseus's deceptive tactic, in the ancient telling of the tale, facilitated indiscriminate bloodletting. Once the Greek forces hidden in the hollow vehicle had penetrated Troy's defenses, they let loose on their enemies. Another ancient poet memorialized the destruction in equally disturbing terms:

> Blood ran in torrents, drenched was all the earth,
> As Trojans and their alien helpers died.
> Here were men lying quelled by bitter death
> All up and down the city in their blood.[60]

---

56. Frank Chalk and Kurt Jonassohn, "On Cases from Antiquity," in *The History and Sociology of Genocide*, 64.
57. Note that I am using the abbreviation BCE (Before the Common Era) rather than the traditional designation BC (Before Christ) to refer to ancient dates. This is intended as a religiously neutral alternative to the Christian convention. Likewise the abbreviation CE (Common Era) replaces the conventional AD (Anno Domini). This usage is in line with modern practice. It has been championed by former UN Secretary-General Kofi Annan and has become preferred practice at the BBC, where, in the fall of 2011, certain journalists chose to forgo the birth of Christ as a principal reference point in order not to offend non-Christians.
58. On varieties of violence more generally, see Charles Tilly, *The Politics of Collective Violence* (Cambridge: Cambridge University Press, 2003), especially chapter 1.
59. Virgil, *The Aeneid: A New Prose Translation*, translated by David West (London: Penguin, 1991), 41, 45.
60. Quintus Smyrnaeus, *The Fall of Troy*, translated by A. S. Way (Cambridge: Harvard University Press, 1913), 100–104. "Quintus of Smyrna" was a Greek epic poet whose *Posthomerica* continued Homer's account of the Trojan War. *Posthomerica*, often translated as *The Fall of Troy*, is believed to have been written in the middle of the fourth century BCE.

Homer's writings have been mined for centuries for clues about ancient Greece. The poet's oeuvre is both an indispensable and a problematic source for our undertaking, for it remains unclear whether his poems are reliable guides to the politics and society of that all-important civilization. Two other Greek authors, Herodotus and Thucydides, for example, were doubtful about the veracity of some of Homer's facts. And yet Jonathan Gottschall recently argued that "the Homeric epics can be used as primary sources for reconstructing an anthropologically coherent picture of Greek social life."[61] At a minimum the Homeric epics raise questions about the reliability of the information conveyed in them. If true, the destruction of Troy in the tenth year of the city's siege warrants close inspection for traces of genocidal and other forms of violence. If merely imagined it stands to reason that Homer's poetry of genocide—begun in the *Iliad* and continued masterfully in the *Odyssey*, which traces the aftermath of the Trojan War—captures general ancient attitudes toward the function and ethics of destruction of populations deemed unworthy of life or co-existence.

Aside from poetry, another controversial source for information about the salience of genocide in the ancient world is the Old Testament (which corresponds closely to the Hebrew Bible). This colorful source comes into play in a second case from the ancient world, the razing of Babylon, a city-state in Mesopotamia, whose remains lie in contemporary Iraq, just south of Baghdad. Since Babylon features centrally in the Old Testament, where both its rise and decline are narrated, it is worthwhile to quickly explore the portrayal of collective violence in the Bible more generally.

Like Homer's *Iliad* and *Odyssey*, the Bible too raises questions about empirical validity. The archaeological evidence supporting Old Testament accounts of widespread destruction is thin. At the same time it could be said that the biblical depictions of large-scale violence at a minimum are suggestive of everyday life in Mesopotamia. Bible references that can be used to support the argument that genocide was an ancient phenomenon are plentiful. They can be found in the Book of Joshua, which describes the conquest of Canaan.[62] Another oft-invoked example is a prophecy in Deuteronomy that calls for the Israelites to "annihilate" the Hittites and the Amorites, the Canaanites and the Perizzites, the Hivites and the Jebusites and to "not let anything that breathes remain alive."[63] As a student of genocide, it is not easy to know what to make of these sources. If we believe the psychologist Steven Pinker, "though the historical accounts in the Old Testament are fictitious (or at best artistic reconstructions, like Shakespeare's historical dramas), they offer a window into the lives and values of Near Eastern civilizations in the mid-1st millennium BCE. Whether or not the Israelites actually engaged in genocide, they certainly thought it was a good idea."[64] On this argument, it is from the language—more so than from the mythological events depicted—that we can draw tentative inferences about the meaning of large-scale collective violence in ancient Mesopotamia.

What, then, are we to make of the destruction of Babylon in 689 BCE and the attendant examples of large-scale collective violence perpetrated by the Assyrians up until the Iron Age?

61. Jonathan Gottschall, *The Rape of Troy: Evolution, Violence, and the World of Homer* (Cambridge: Cambridge University Press, 2008), 11.

62. Joshua 8:18–28, *The New Oxford Annotated Bible*, 3rd edition (Oxford: Oxford University Press, 2001), 327.

63. Deuteronomy, 20:16–18, *The New Oxford Annotated Bible*, 277.

64. Steven Pinker, *The Better Angels of Our Nature: The Decline of Violence in History and Its Causes* (London: Allen Lane, 2011), 11.

One way of looking at these relevant (though not necessarily genocidal) cases is to reserve judgment on the authenticity of all of the historical evidence but to take seriously the fact that the ancient reporting of absolute destruction was relatively casual. One could read this non-chalance as tentative evidence of the fact that the peoples of Mesopotamia were *generally speaking* not completely unfamiliar with what we call genocidal violence. In fact the barbaric use of collective violence where destruction rather than defeat is the aim was hardly exceptional at the time. The wall reliefs in the Assyrian palaces at Nimrud, Khorsabad, and Nineveh are replete with brutal battle scenes where no quarter is given to enemies.[65] The Royal Annals too bespeak violent excess.

While we may be unable to verify the *acts* portrayed in them, these and other sources provide circumstantial evidence for the *attitudes* that existed in the ancient world toward the value of human life in times of war. Mark Freeman puts it well: "Assyrian warfare was probably extremely cruel and destructive, but whether it was genocidal is uncertain.... Imperialism cannot be at the same time exterminatory and exploitative. It can, however, be destructive and exploitative. The Assyrians may have perpetrated subjugatory massacres but not extermination. Destruction of cities was common. The records are not always clear whether this was accompanied by genocide. It does appear to have been a form of cultural genocide. It is therefore not certain whether the Assyrians committed genocide in the stricter Lemkinian sense (i.e. extermination of peoples) but they did commit acts that were genocidal in the looser sense that Lemkin also employed (i.e. destruction of alien ways of life), and these they recorded and justified."[66]

Another contested case from the ancient world concerns the Athenian assault on Melos in the context of the Peloponnesian War. As Thucydides tells it in his history of the great war, Athens violently subjugated the ostensibly neutral island in the Aegean Sea. Given the centrality of Thucydides to the Western canon of political thought, the depiction of absolute destruction in what is known as his "Melian Dialogue" has greatly influenced the interpretation of collective violence in 416 BCE.[67] Was it genocide? Observers who are reluctant to include the destruction of Melos in the annals of genocide point to the fact that Athens offered the encircled Melians the terms of an unconditional surrender. Others argue that what reportedly transpired in Melos was simply the ancient way of war. The scant historical evidence makes it very difficult to adjudicate among the contending positions. This notwithstanding, the siege of Melos is relevant for any discussion of genocidal violence in the ancient world, at a minimum for understanding the relationship between war and the treatment of civilians in war.

A final case from the ancient world is the destruction of Carthage. The razing of the ancient city in 146 BCE was the culmination of the Third Punic War in which the Carthaginian city-state suffered defeat at the hands of the Roman Republic. After defeating Hannibal in the Battle of Zama, on the outskirts of Carthage, the commander of the Roman forces, Scipio, imposed a punitive peace. When the leaders of Carthage eventually violated the terms of the peace treaty in 150 BCE, Rome dispatched a military contingent. On this occasion the destruc-

65. Charles Freeman, *Egypt, Greece, and Rome: Civilizations of the Ancient Mediterranean* (Oxford: Oxford University Press, 1996), 67.
66. Freeman, "Genocide, Civilization and Modernity," 220.
67. Thucydides, *History of the Peloponnesian War*, translated by Rex Warner (London: Penguin, 1972), 407.

tion of Carthage became the principal war aim. Scipio's son, Scipio Aemilianus, eventually broke the two-year-long resistance to the Roman siege, taking the ancient city house by house. In 146 BCE Carthage was no more. Out of an estimated 250,000 inhabitants, only 50,000 are believed to have survived. And yet Brian Warmington remains unconvinced that Scipio and the Romans harbored any genocidal motivations when they did away with the city-state: "The Romans, like most people in antiquity, attached little importance to the idea of race, and the destruction of the Carthaginian civilization did not mean there was any attempt to root out Carthaginian civilization."[68]

Although the fact of the destruction of Carthage is borne out by archaeological and historical evidence, various details of the Roman onslaught remain unsubstantiated. For example, the frequently invoked anecdote that the victors poured salt into the plowed soil of Carthage so as to render it permanently uninhabitable finds no support: "The 'sowing of salt' at Carthage is a contamination from the widely known rituals of city destruction in the ancient Near East."[69] Regardless of various holes in the historical record, the cumulative radicalization of Roman warfare against the Punic Empire warrants closer inspection when it comes to tracing the ancient salience of genocide. If we believe the historian Ben Kiernan, the relevance of the Carthaginian case cannot be overstated: "The destruction of Carthage set a precedent for genocide. Rome ruled the Mediterranean, and its legions marched into northern Europe, occasionally employing genocidal massacres against enemies."[70] Though plausible, more fine-grained scholarship by experts of the ancient world is required to understand the salience and logic of genocide through the millennia.

Genocide in the Medieval World

Is it appropriate to speak of genocide when interpreting particular episodes of destruction in the medieval world? Three incidents are illustrative: the destruction of European Jewry in the course of the First Crusade (1096), the Mongol invasions (1206–1321), and the violent treatment of the Huguenots in the 1572 Massacre of St. Bartholomew's Day. Just as in the preceding subsection, the purpose of the selected illustrations is to provide initial information to make possible, and ultimately advance, the comparative historical analysis of genocide. Unlike Steven Katz and Ben Kiernan, the only two scholars who, albeit with very different motivations, have attempted to write global histories of genocide, the point of the exercise is neither to defend the uniqueness of the Holocaust (as Katz does) nor to advance an argument according to which genocide has been with us from time immemorial (as Kiernan does). Rather the focus in these individualizing comparisons is on the singularities of each case in an effort to bring the complexity of genocide into sharper relief.[71]

Beginning in the late eleventh century the Christians of western Europe, encouraged by a newfound confidence due to creative and ecclesiastical advances, resolved to mount violent

68. B. H. Warmington, Carthage, 2nd edition (New York: Robert Hale, 1969), 237–38.
69. R. T. Ridley, "To Be Taken with a Pinch of Salt: The Destruction of Carthage," Classical Philology 81, no. 2 (1986): 145–46.
70. Kiernan, Blood and Soil, 58.
71. Tilly, Big Structures, Large Processes, Huge Comparisons.

campaigns to thwart the threat of Muslim expansionism, to halt the spread of Islam, to conquer pagan lands, and to seize lost territory from the nonbelievers. At the Council of Clermont in 1095, Pope Urban II called upon those assembled to aid the Eastern Christians and to fight the infidels in the Holy Land. Unbeknown to many, some of the earliest victims of the Crusades were not Muslims, but Jews. These were killed en route to Jerusalem in 1096.[72] The targeting of Jews, who had lived more or less amicably and prosperously alongside their Christian neighbors, came despite formal (and half-hearted) calls by the Catholic Church for toleration of Jewish life within Christendom.[73] And it appears that only one of the military expeditions, the one led by Peter the Hermit, focused its attention on the Jews. The baronial armies administered no such anti-Jewish violence on their way to the Holy Land: "The bulk of the crusaders departed for the East without inferring from the call to the crusade an imperative to destroy the Jews."[74]

What exactly happened in 1096? As far as we know, while making their way through the Rhineland the crusading forces of Peter the Hermit largely destroyed the Jewish communities in five urban centers of what today is Germany: Speyer, Worms, Mainz, Cologne, and Trier. The crusading army is said to have numbered fifteen thousand men. Although the Crusades continued—in the Holy Land, but also in Spain and the Baltic—up until the sixteenth century, when the Protestant Reformation challenged the authority of the papacy, the largely incidental destruction of the Jews of the Rhineland in 1096 ranks as one of the most notorious examples of collective violence directed against a presumed internal enemy in the medieval world. Having said that, many medieval historians are reluctant to read too much into the violent episode. Christopher Tyerman, for example, insists that "the Rhineland pogroms did not mark 'the first holocaust,'" as another historian has claimed.[75] Although Robert Chazan, another influential historian, shares Tyerman's general proclivity for circumspection—insisting, as he does, that no straight line leads from medieval to modern anti-Semitism—he is nevertheless convinced that the historical evidence supports a classification of genocide, although he does not use the term. He writes, "During the eleventh century, a new aggressiveness developed in western Christendom and expressed itself in a new potential for persecution of the Jews. This new-style persecution . . . involves the notion of the total destruction of Jewishness and the Jews. Conversion of individual Jews is not the desideratum nor is expulsion of allegedly offending Jews from a given area; the goal is rather a removal of Judaism from the world, preferably by mass conversion or, failing that, by slaughter."[76] At the same time Chazan is careful to emphasize that the genocidal impulse that he identified in the medieval sources was "restricted to small and marginal groups of popular crusaders."[77] This emphasis on the microfoundations of genocidal violence is of utmost importance for second-generation scholars of

72. Robert Chazan, *European Jewry and the First Crusade* (Berkeley: University of California Press, 1987).

73. For a helpful overview, see Robert Chazan, *Reassessing Jewish Life in Medieval Europe* (Cambridge: Cambridge University Press, 2010).

74. Chazan, *European Jewry and the First Crusade*, 66.

75. Christopher Tyerman, *God's War: A New History of the Crusades* (Oxford: Oxford University Press, 2006), 105. See also Jonathan Riley-Smith, *The First Crusade and the Idea of Crusading*, 2nd edition (New York: Continuum, 2009).

76. Chazan, *European Jewry and the First Crusade*, 219.

77. Chazan, *European Jewry and the First Crusade*, 219.

comparative genocide. By disaggregating a larger phenomenon—the destruction of German Jewry during the First Crusade—into discrete agents (e.g., Peter the Hermit, Count Emich of Flonheim), preferences (e.g., acquisition of wealth, purity of the Rhineland), strategies (e.g., plunder, burning of synagogues, mass slaughter), and outcomes (e.g., Jewish suicides, destruction of Jewish communities), we are in a much better position to make sense of the dynamics of contention at that time, including transitions to and from genocidal violence.

The targeting of internal enemies as a byproduct of the First Crusade stands in stark contrast to the destruction wrought by our next set of perpetrators, the Mongols, who directed their violence primarily at external enemies. Some observers have likened aspects of the destruction brought about by the conquering forces of the Mongol Empire to genocide. Under the regimes of Genghis Khan (1206–27) and his successors, the Mongols violently built and consolidated history's largest contiguous empire. In the process of these Mongol invasions, civilian populations were often annihilated as par for the course. Yet unlike the roving perpetrators Peter the Hermit and Count Emich, the Mongol forces waged large-scale violence largely indiscriminately. "Their genius," according to Chalk and Jonassohn, "was confined to doing what others did but doing it much better. This applies even to their genocides. Massacres, wanton cruelty, the destruction of cities, and the devastation of whole regions were commonplace in Central Asia and Persia as well as in many other areas that they conquered. The Mongols simply killed on a greater scale and as a deliberate part of their policy."[78] As plausible as this claim is, it behooves us to take a closer look at what transpired in the application of large-scale violence during the Mongol campaigns.

A people of the steppe, the vast greenbelt that stretches from Hungary to Manchuria via Central Asia, the Mongols were a Turkish tribe that stealthily incorporated into their growing empire lands that belonged to China (during several invasions between 1205 and 1234), Persia (1218–20, 1251–59), Russia (1237–40), Mesopotamia (1251–59), and India (1222–1327), to name but the most significant territorial conquests. Genghis Khan is credited with uniting the Mongol Empire, which he forged in 1206, and with inventing the order of terror that sustained it.[79] The reason that the case of the Mongols is occasionally discussed in the context of genocide scholarship has to do with the empire's pattern of absolute destruction.

Two aspects of Mongol destruction are particularly noteworthy: their recognition of the value of absolute destruction for the purpose of propaganda and the centrality of mobility to the order of terror. As for the former, Saunders has highlighted the role played by psychological warfare in the making of the Mongol Empire. In his account, the Mongol invaders, initially under Genghis Khan's leadership, "deliberately set out to create a reputation for ferocious terror, in the expectation (often realized) of frightening whole nations into surrendering without resistance."[80] If these accounts are correct, the Mongols perfected destruction as a mode of governance. In other words, some historical evidence suggests that the use of barbarism was neither wanton nor senseless. It was a carefully honed and effectively administered strategy of conflict. Regardless of this policy of calculated destruction, the first Mongol Empire declined in the late fourteenth century. Military defeats and territorial losses, especially the

78. Frank Chalk and Kurt Jonassohn, "The Empire of the Mongols," in *The History and Sociology of Genocide*, 95.
79. J. J. Saunders, *The History of the Mongol Conquests* (London: Routledge, 1971), 70.
80. Saunders, *The History of the Mongol Conquests*, 59.

loss of China to the Ming Dynasty in 1368, together with imperial infighting ensured a temporary end of the order of terror. Not all too long after the defeat of the Mongol Empire, Tamerlane, also known as Timur the Great (1411–49), fought to reestablish Mongol supremacy.[81]
This gave rise to new annihilation campaigns against enemies and their brethren. Under Tamerlane the centralization of control increased even further when it came to the deployment
of Mongol forces, which, unlike Genghis Khan, he personally led. It is often said that Tamerlane the Great, as he became known on account of his exploits, surpassed his predecessor in
brutality and ruthlessness.[82] Whether the large-scale violence inflicted by Genghis Khan,
Tamerlane, or any of the other Mongol rulers was indeed genocidal, and how and when, remains open to debate. But the question certainly is worthy of further inquiry. At a minimum
it forces us to home in on the similarities and differences of varieties of collective violence,
then and now.

This linkage also plays a role in a final episode of destruction from the medieval world,
that of the Huguenots in the wake of the Protestant Reformation that Martin Luther had
unleashed in Germany in 1517. France's Protestants suffered severe prosecution in the sixteenth and seventeenth century, causing many of them to seek refuge elsewhere, including
John Calvin, who left France for Switzerland in 1534. The religious conflict between Roman
Catholics and Huguenots turned violent in the late sixteenth century, not least because the rise
of Protestantism posed a challenge to the French state. A policy of arrests and assassinations,
together with anti-Protestant legislation and the occasional public execution of heretics,
paved the way for an increasingly confrontational situation. Especially under King Henry II,
talk of destruction of what was viewed as the Huguenot menace took on new extremes. In
1557 the monarch reportedly called for putting an end to the "notorious Lutheran rabble."
What can be seen as an incitement to large-scale collective violence had predictable consequences: an angry mob stormed a meeting of Huguenots in the rue Saint-Jacques, Paris.
Deadly events soon followed, set off by the massacre in 1562 of a Huguenot congregation at
Vassy by partisans of one of France's powerful Roman Catholic families, the house of Guise.[83]
It also provoked an uprising in the provinces. Thus began a series of civil wars, collectively
known as the Wars of Religion (1562–1629), that caused havoc throughout the country.[84]

Despite numerous attempts at constructing sustainable peace agreements, hostilities continued, culminating on August 24–25, 1572, in the Massacre of St. Bartholomew's Day. The
principal objective of the orchestrated killing spree was the murder of all Huguenot leaders in
the French capital. The extermination plan was a cover-up for an earlier, failed assassination
of Admiral Gaspard II de Coligny, an influential Huguenot leader whose increasing influence
on the policy of the Crown had angered Catherine de Médici.[85] The campaign of destruction
also swept the provinces, where Protestants were murdered en masse in Rouen, Lyon, Bourges,

81. See, for example, Beatrice Forbes Manz, *The Rise and Rule of Tamerlane*, new edition (Cambridge: Cambridge University Press, 1999).
82. See, for example, Arnold Toynbee, *A Study of History* (Oxford: Oxford University Press, 1947), 347.
83. Donald R. Kelley, "Martyrs, Myths, and the Massacre: The Background of St. Bartholomew," *American Historical Review* 77, no. 5 (1972): especially 1335.
84. For an overview, see Mack P. Holt, *The French Wars of Religion, 1562–1629* (Cambridge: Cambridge Uni-
versity Press, 2005).
85. Barbara Diefendorf, "Prologue to a Massacre: Popular Unrest in Paris, 1557–1572," *American Historical Review* 90, no. 5 (1985): 1089. For a comprehensive treatment, see Barbara Diefendorf, *Beneath the Cross: Catholics and Huguenots in Sixteenth-Century Paris* (Oxford: Oxford University Press, 1993).

Orléans, and Bordeaux.[86] Was this an instance of genocidal violence being applied to a real or imagined enemy? In contemplating this question, it is important to appreciate that "the massacre immediately took its place as the pivotal event in the martyrological tradition and became a central force in the flood of propaganda that poured from Protestant presses at a greater than average rate in succeeding years."[87] As with many other cases of interest to the study of genocide, the St. Bartholomew Massacre quickly became a legend that continued to grow.[88]

Steven Katz, well known for his effort to establish the uniqueness of the Holocaust by way of comparative historical analysis, is unconvinced that the partial destruction of the Huguenots in 1572 has anything to do with genocide. According to Katz, the assassination of Coligny in the context of the Massacre of St. Bartholomew's Day was nothing out of the ordinary: "Other leading Huguenots were likewise dispatched in the late 1560s and 1570s."[89] From this it follows, says Katz, that we are nowhere near the province of genocide when talking about the destruction of Huguenots: "These destabilizing acts represent a reciprocal policy of *leadership elimination* rather than one of *mass annihilation*. Only the Saint Bartholomew's Day massacre was more than this, though even it was not a total assault, taking place within very circumscribed limits."[90]

What Katz overlooks is the fact that very few scholars *ever* believed that mass annihilation on the scale of the Holocaust was a necessary requirement for a determination of genocidal violence. In recent decades this sentiment has grown even stronger, notably on account of the influential jurisprudence that has come out of the International Criminal Tribunals for the former Yugoslavia (ICTY) and Rwanda (ICTR). In a series of judgments the judicial chambers of the ICTY and ICTR have stated clearly that no numerical threshold of fatalities had to be crossed for atrocities to count as genocide (as long as the mental and physical elements of the crime of genocide are met) and that the killing of a targeted group's leaders (what Katz terms "leadership extermination") could under certain circumstances constitute genocide (again, as long as the mental and physical elements of the crime of genocide are met *and* provided that the targeted group's survival is placed in jeopardy as a consequence of the destruction of its leaders).[91]

It stands to reason that just as the meaning of war has changed over the millennia, the meaning of categorical destruction may have as well. What, then, are we to conclude about genocide in the medieval world more generally? Len Scales puts it best: "Medieval people thought genocidally. This was partly a consequence of their disposition radically to simplify their world, its past and imagined future, into a story of peoples. Because it was a dynamic story, in which some people rose and prospered, others necessarily fell, and even disappeared."[92] Although some medieval people apparently *did* think genocidally, as Scales points out, not all

86. On the diffusion of collective violence in the provinces, see Philip Benedict, "The Saint Bartholomew's Massacres in the Provinces," *Historical Journal* 21, no. 2 (1978): 205–25.
87. Kelley, "Martyrs, Myths, and the Massacre," 1340.
88. Kelley, "Martyrs, Myths, and the Massacre," 1342.
89. Steven T. Katz, *The Holocaust in Historical Context*, vol. 1: *The Holocaust and Mass Death before the Modern Age* (New York: Oxford University Press, 1994), 549.
90. Katz, *The Holocaust in Historical Context*, 549–50.
91. For an overview of the relevant jurisprudence, see Guénaël Mettraux, *International Crimes and the Ad Hoc Tribunals* (Oxford: Oxford University Press, 2005), especially 217–23.
92. Len Scales, "Central and Late Medieval Europe," in Bloxham and Moses, *The Oxford Handbook of Genocide Studies*, 284.

of them did. This being so, it is important to explore the conditions under which genocidal violence materialized in the medieval world *and* the conditions under which it did not. This requires us to situate the phenomenon of genocide alongside other varieties of medieval violence because transitions from one type of destruction to another are not always obvious at first glance, then and now. What began as warfare or another form of collective violence in medieval times may have turned into a campaign of absolute destruction and vice versa. Identifying such transition points is critical, especially for considering instances in which genocidal violence was in the offing but did not materialize. This brings us to the modern world, where the pursuit of destruction as a strategy of conflict has been as pervasive as in the medieval world—arguably more so.

Genocide in the Modern World

The modern history of genocide can be said to have began in 1492, with the first transatlantic voyage of Christopher Columbus. A vital part of early modernization, the colonial expansion of the Western world was an important expression of the power of the modern state. Not surprisingly the projection of this power to overseas territories inhabited by indigenous populations caused death and destruction on an extremely large scale. It remains an empirically contested question as to whether and, if so, when and how these colonial encounters amounted to genocide.

In the late twentieth century Kuper was adamant that the history of colonization had to be parsed for evidence of genocidal violence. But he was also careful not to automatically equate colonial violence with genocidal destruction: "It is overstated to equate colonization with physical genocide. The issue of decolonization could not arise in countries where there had been extensive genocide, and much of colonization has proceeded without genocidal conflict. But certainly the course of colonization has been marked all too often by genocide. In the colonization of North and South America, the West Indies, Australia and Tasmania, many native peoples were wiped out, sometimes as a result of wars and massacres, or of disease and ecological change, at other times by deliberate policies of extermination."[93] For far too long scholarship has been obsessed with the dichotomous classification of violent histories as either "genocide" or "not genocide." More fruitful, and in keeping with Kuper's caution, is an in-depth consideration of relevant histories of colonial destruction, including genocidal and nongenocidal cases. For it is theoretically plausible and empirically verifiable that in many instances of colonial subjugation, genocidal acts were committed on a limited scale and during particular moments of the colonial experience, even though no all-encompassing genocidal campaign was planned in and waged from the European capital in question. It is only when we are trying to find "colonial holocausts" directly comparable in either scale or logic to the Nazi genocide that the inclusion of colonial settings into the province of genocide studies seems odd. Given this, more attention should be paid to the many different logics of violence, colonial and otherwise.

The history of colonial destruction, deliberate and otherwise, began in the Caribbean, on Hispaniola, the island that Christopher Columbus named "little Spain." In this first European

93. Kuper, *Genocide*, 15.

settlement in the New World, the native *taíno* population was virtually wiped out by the early sixteenth century. Yet contrary to some claims that the mass death on Hispaniola constituted a "Caribbean holocaust," recent scholarship has shown that it was largely sickness and starvation in combination with forced mining and wanton massacres rather than a conscious attempt at extermination.[94] In other words, the violent repression and rapid vanishing of local populations, on Hispaniola and elsewhere, was amplified by structural factors, notably ecology. However, it is without a doubt that the European conquerors exploited, primarily as forced labor, the Native Americans they encountered, whom they also ruthlessly killed when it was expedient to do so.[95]

At the same time it is not particularly helpful to ask whether this episode of destruction, or any other, constituted genocide, as we use the term today. More helpful would be an in-depth consideration of the long-run evolution of relations between newcomers and natives on the Caribbean island and the role that violence played therein. For Spain's empire project was far less single-minded and coherent and the colonial impact on indigenous populations (who themselves were hardly identical) far less uniform than is sometimes suggested. It is remarkable, for example, that the colonial experience in the Greater Antilles was significantly different from that in the Lower Antilles, where the destruction of natives was far more muted. As the Spanish forces moved from the Caribbean islands to the mainland, they faced considerably more resistance, notably from the Aztec Empire in the valley of Mexico. The amount of state power at the disposal of this advanced civilization was considerable, and the Spanish conducted numerous violent campaigns to make an example of supposedly disloyal communities. Often the purpose of collective violence meted out by the conquistadors was categorical defeat rather than categorical destruction, however. This is not to say that the colonial conquest in Central and South America proceeded without genocidal violence. Far from it, as the brutal displacement and regular destruction of *indios* in Mexico, Guatemala, and Peru attest.[96] Generally speaking, however, the colonial impulse in Spanish America was to use rather than to destroy outright the native population. The situation was, on the whole, rather different in North America. There the period between the late sixteenth century and the late eighteenth was the era of French, Dutch, and above all English colonialism. The interactions among settlers and natives did not follow one coherent pattern; the dynamics of contention, violent and otherwise, varied significantly across space and time. The term "American Holocaust" is therefore not very helpful for describing the subjugation and destruction of indigenous populations.[97] It reduces several centuries of vastly different colonial encounters on the American continent to a uniformity of experience and causation that never existed.

94. Noble David Cook, "Sickness, Starvation, and Death in Early Hispaniola," *Journal of Interdisciplinary History* 32, no. 3 (2002): 349–86. See also Noble David Cook, *Born to Die: Disease and New World Conquest, 1492–1650* (Cambridge: Cambridge University Press, 1998). For the specious claim that the decimation of the native population was akin to the Holocaust, see David E. Stannard, "Genocide in the Americas," *Nation*, October 19 1992, 430.

95. Neil L. Whitehead, "The Crisis and Transformations of Invaded Societies: The Caribbean (1492–1580)," in Frank Salomon and Stuart B. Schwartz, eds., *The Cambridge History of the Native Peoples of the Americas*, vol. 3: *South America*, part 1 (Cambridge: Cambridge University Press, 1999), 871.

96. Mann, *The Dark Side of Democracy*, 78.

97. David E. Stannard, *American Holocaust: The Conquest of the New World* (Oxford: Oxford University Press, 1993).

Considerably more is known about the micropolitics of collective violence in the colonization of Australia. The case is interesting and important for a number of reasons. First, it was the principal vehicle for broadening the scope of genocide studies in the twenty-first century. The colonization of Australia commenced on January 28, 1788, when Britain's First Fleet arrived on the continent's shores. Two different modes and stages of destruction are usually at issue in discussions about genocide in colonial Australia: physical destruction, primarily in the mid- to late nineteenth century, and cultural destruction, chiefly in the early to mid-twentieth century.[98]

In the former, Australia's settlers coveted not so much the labor of the country's indigenous population (although they did exploit it in parts of northern and western Australia) as their land.[99] Consequently the first stage of colonization saw a great deal of roving and bottom-up extermination on a relatively small scale: "Across the country, squatters, and the Native Police in Queensland, destroyed Aboriginal communities by shooting small groups in countless incidents."[100] It is here that we see the limits of the conventional focus in genocide studies on a state machinery of death à la Nazi Germany. Historically speaking, the dynamics of large-scale destruction were considerably more complex. Newcomers and natives exhibited diverse patterns of interaction. Far from trivial differences existed in the colonization of Queensland, Western Australia, and South Australia. In these different parts of the country, the onset, duration, and severity of colonial violence differed, not to mention the fact that differences within each of these areas were pronounced as well.

However, most of the debate about the existence or not of genocidal violence in colonial Australia has centered on the practice of child removal. This refers to the de facto theft of Aboriginal children by white settlers for the purpose of exploitation or purification or both. This ostensible form of cultural destruction commenced in around 1840 but hit its full stride in the early twentieth century. In the first decade of the twentieth century, according to estimates at the time, the Aboriginal population was largest in Western Australia, Queensland, and the Northern Territory. In each of these territories, settlers estimated the population to number between twenty thousand and twenty-five thousand.[101] It was against this demographic backdrop that child removal took shape. Notably the practice emerged from below, from within civil society, but it was condoned and eventually facilitated by the colonial state.

Although not widely accepted as an instance of genocide, the Irish Potato Famine, which led to the mass starvation of an estimated one million Irish and the emigration of another million, is sometimes placed alongside other examples of colonial genocide. In this interpretation the responsibility for the death toll rests with the United Kingdom, which is said to have created and condoned conditions of life calculated to bring about mass death in Ireland. In

98. I am sidestepping the case of Tasmania, or Van Diemen's Land, as it used to be known in colonial times, which is often said to have been the site of genocidal violence.
99. A. Dirk Moses, "Moving the Genocide Debate beyond the 'History Wars,'" *Australian Journal of Politics and History* 54, no. 2 (2008): 263.
100. Moses, "Moving the Genocide Debate beyond the 'History Wars,'" 263. See also Tony Barta, "'They Appear Actually to Vanish from the Face of the Earth': Aborigines and the European Project in Australia Felix," *Journal of Genocide Research* 10, no. 4 (2008): 519–39; Tony Barta, "After the Holocaust: Consciousness of Genocide in Australia," *Australian Journal of Politics and History* 31, no. 1 (1985): 154–61.
101. Andrew Markus, *Governing Savages: Commonwealth and Aborigines, 1911–39* (Sydney: Allen and Unwin, 2000), chapter 1.

what is arguably the most authoritative statement on the matter, the economist Cormac Ó Gráda, after having considered a wealth of macroeconomic and other data, comes to the conclusion that "doctrinaire neglect" it was, but genocide it was not.[102] Why, then, talk about the Irish case at all? Because famines, especially in modern times, are political as well as environmental phenomena, and the case offers ample opportunities to explicate the interaction effects among political and environmental causes of mass death. Interestingly, despite the preeminent place that the Potato Famine occupies in modern Irish history—not to mention folklore—the existing literature is minuscule despite an abundance of data and records. What the people of Ireland refer to as *An Gorta Mór* (the Great Hunger) took place in the years 1845–49. During this period an estimated one million Irish from all walks of life perished, predominantly in the far western counties, as a result of a succession of major crop failures.[103] This unexpected devastation, and its repetition in the years that followed, caused a severe shortage in Ireland's most important food supply. Apart from a high incidence of starvation-induced deaths, the country was set back in another way: one million Irish are believed to have emigrated, many to the United States. The Great Irish famine caused a 25 percent population decline in a mere six years.[104]

Though it is generally accepted as fact among scholars that the British government did not set out to systematically destroy the Irish, it is undeniable that beginning in the fall of 1847 any humanitarian impulse that might previously have existed on the part of government representatives was snuffed out.[105] Could genocide have transpired inadvertently? Had large-scale violence been perpetrated by omission rather than by commission? Can negligence or recklessness cause genocide? Lacking the financial wherewithal to adequately respond to the food crisis, the Irish Executive and the Poor Law Commission, which had been created in 1834 to alleviate poverty in Ireland, looked to London for major relief during the famine. There, one argument goes, "the relief of famine was regarded essentially as a local responsibility rather than a national one, let alone an imperial obligation."[106] It is this reckless endangerment of an entire population in the name of neoliberal orthodoxy—with mass death and emigration by most accounts as natural and foreseeable consequences—that has persuaded some to counter revisionist historians of Ireland for whom the Great Irish Famine was nothing more than an unavoidable natural disaster.[107] The issue is far from settled.

102. Cormac Ó Gráda, *Black '47 and Beyond: The Great Irish Famine in History, Economy, and Memory* (Princeton, N.J.: Princeton University Press, 1999), 10.
103. On the accuracy of mortality figures, see, for example, Joel Mokyr and Cormac Ó Gráda, "What Do People Die of During Famines: The Great Irish Famine in Comparative Perspective," *European Review of Economic History* 6, no. 3 (2002): 339–63. See also Joel Mokyr, *Why Ireland Starved: A Quantitative and Analytical History of the Irish Economy* (London: Allen and Unwin, 1983). For a spatiotemporal analysis of population change (including mass death) in nineteenth-century Ireland, see Paul S. Ell and Ian N. Gregory, "Demography, Depopulation, and Devastation: Exploring the Geography of the Irish Potato Famine," *Historical Geography* 33 (2005): 54–77.
104. Christine Kinealy, "Beyond Revisionism: Reassessing the Great Irish Famine," *History Ireland* 3, no. 4 (1995): 28.
105. George L. Bernstein, "Liberals, the Irish Famine, and the Role of the State," *Irish Historical Studies* 29, no. 116 (1995): 536.
106. Christine Kinealy, *This Great Calamity: The Irish Famine, 1845–52* (Dublin: Gill and Macmillan, 1994), 343.
107. For a brief overview of the major historiographical currents, see James S. Donnelly Jr., "The Great Famine: Its Interpreters, Old and New," *History Ireland* 1, no. 3 (1993): 27–33.

Also relevant to consider in the colonial context is the case of Southwest Africa, where German settlers destroyed large parts of three indigenous ethnic groups—the Herero, Witbooi (after their chief, Hendrik Witbooi, but also known as Hama), and the Damara—in the years 1904–7. The absolute destruction was initially targeted at the seventy-five thousand Herero cattle herders, the largest of the three African societies. Settled in the center of the colonial territory, between Windhoek and the Waterberg Mountains to the north, the Herero came to be seen as inferior and a thorn in the side of the German settlers. It is contested whether the so-called Herero revolt was at all premeditated. What is undisputed are the ensuing battles between the colonizers and the colonized and the subsequent, gradual radicalization of the colonial administration's policy toward the Herero. Their destruction unfolded in waves, following different modes. In the six weeks between August 11 and September 29, 1904, two thousand German troops were dispatched to the Waterberg Mountains, where sixty thousand Herero had gathered. The increasingly indiscriminate pursuit left many of them dead, often due to starvation. Shortly thereafter Germany's military objectives shifted from defeat to absolute destruction.

On October 2, 1904, despite some reservations on the part of the colony's first governor, Colonel Theodor Leutwein, the commander of the German forces in Southwest Africa, Lieutenant General Lothar von Trotha, issued an "extermination order." This order called for "every male Herero, armed or unarmed," to be shot dead. Two days later von Trotha further clarified his instructions: "I believe the [Herero] nation must be destroyed as such."[108] Many of the victims died on death marches during the punishing dry season because von Trotha had ordered his men "to seal off the western edge of the Sandveld along a cordon stretching about 250 kilometers and to occupy the water holes."[109] Mass death was the predictable result. Unlike the Herero, the Witbooi were seen, in the eyes of the German administration, as "noble savages." In fact in the period 1894–1904, prior to the destruction campaign, the German colonial administration extended to the Witbooi a number of concessions under a "protection and friendship treaty."[110] And yet the Witbooi too were eventually destroyed.

Unlike their African adversaries, the German army did not spare women and children. Theirs was a policy of what the historian Isabel Hull described as "absolute destruction." On this argument Wilhelmine Germany's peculiar military culture dictated that victory in war meant the utter annihilation of the enemy; where once defeat was sufficient, destruction henceforth was the order of the day. General Julius von Hartmann, a retired German naval officer, described "the great, final purpose of war" in the following terms in 1877: "the defeat of the enemy's power, the overcoming of the enemy's energy, the overwhelming of the enemy's will."[111]

According to Hull, traces of this cultural practice of war resurfaced in another genocidal setting: the disintegrating Ottoman Empire. Although the destruction of the Armenians in 1915–16 has taken center stage for many years in discussion of genocide in this part of the

---

108. As quoted in Kiernan, *Blood and Soil*, 383.
109. George Steinmetz, *The Devil's Handwriting: Precoloniality and the German Colonial State in Qingdao, Samoa, and Southwest Africa* (Chicago: University of Chicago Press, 2007), 194.
110. Steinmetz, *The Devil's Handwriting*, 147.
111. As quoted in Isabel V. Hull, *Absolute Destruction: Military Culture and the Practices of War in Imperial Germany* (Ithaca, N.Y.: Cornell University Press, 2006), 123.

world, a new generation of scholars has demonstrated that the Young Turks sought to cleanse the Ottoman Empire not only of Armenians but of numerous others minorities as well.[112]

The dynamics of destruction are highly complex, involving complicated interactions of domestic, regional, and international variables. In this sense the extermination and expulsions of Armenians from eastern Anatolia were truly transnational phenomena. Taking seriously the transnational dimension is imperative for making sense of the evolution of the destruction policy of the Committee of Union and Progress (CUP), the Young Turks' underground movement–turned–political party. Three transnational processes are of particular significance: the diffusion of nationalist norms, regional disintegration, and interstate war. The concatenation of these processes illuminates the frequently obscured dynamics of contention within the beleaguered empire.

Take nationalism: the reception of this quintessentially Occidental norm in the Ottoman Empire, and the successes of nationalist movements in Italy and Germany, spurred on the exclusionary variant of nationalism ("Turkification") pursued by the CUP.[113] Young Turk intellectuals began to redefine the nation in Turkish terms. Whereas the Ottoman nation tolerated ethnic heterogeneity, the new concept of the Turkish nation revolved around ethnic homogeneity. Exclusion rather than inclusion was the sign of the times. Yet this exclusionary ideology was not enough to create incentives for genocide. Moreover the appeal of nationalism affected not just the CUP but the Armenian community (and other subject peoples of the empire) as well. In some respects two dueling nationalisms, and the excesses committed by extremists within each movement, created the background conditions for the orchestration of a violent, eventually genocidal campaign. The genocide was not provoked by its victims, but the mobilization of nationalist ideas in Anatolia undoubtedly shaped its dynamics.

The spillover of military norms of institutional extremism from Imperial Germany too left a mark, notably on the genocidal practices of the so-called Special Organization, a mixed-military CUP institution. Several German military officers (although for the most part wary of the cumulative radicalization of CUP policy) advised the Turkish Third Army to deport Armenian civilians in an attempt to advance the Ottoman war effort in World War I. Such final solutions were increasingly appealing in the context of regional disintegration, the second transnational process that was intractably associated with the atrocities committed by Ottomans against Armenians.

The CUP's commitment to rationalization and centralization—and eventually the ethnic homogenization of the "Turkish" nation—promised to stave off the disintegration of the Ottoman Empire, to ensure the territorial integrity of the state. Borrowed from the West, it was the Young Turks' (members of the CUP) solution to the problem of institutional design. The farther the declining empire was pushed out of Europe in the late nineteenth century, the more visible within it—and targeted—were the Armenians as a community of "others." It would be inaccurate, however, to conclude that extermination rather than centralization was on the Young Turk agenda from the outset. Inasmuch as elements within the CUP (particu-

112. Akçam, *The Young Turks' Crime against Humanity*, 449.
113. For a comprehensive analysis, see, for example, Kemal H. Karpat, *The Politicization of Islam: Reconstructing Identity, State, Faith, and Community in the Late Ottoman State* (Oxford: Oxford University Press, 2001).

larly those aligned with the Central Committee) coordinated and perpetrated mass atrocities, indeed genocide, no a priori blueprint for a genocidal campaign appears to have existed.

If we believe recent scholarship, it was above all the internationalization of the "Armenian question" that provided the necessary impetus for the cumulative radicalization of CUP ideology and the consideration within the CUP Central Committee of eliminationist practices. Donald Bloxham, for example, highlighted the crucial role of the Great Powers on the road to the Armenian genocide. He and other scholars have shown that a proximate cause of the Armenian genocide was World War I. It transformed latent contention into manifest, violent contention. Significant was the Ottoman fear that Armenian leaders and their brethren were colluding with the Entente powers: Russia, Britain, and France. The spread of an imperialist norm among these Great Powers had spawned a brand of interventionism that did its share to radicalize the Young Turk leadership, contributing to a security dilemma in the context of which a genocidal campaign became increasingly desirable.

In key respects the 1915–16 Armenian genocide was the result of structured contingency. It was mediated and affected decisively by the interplay of several processes. These processes, the most important of which are outlined here, gave rise to incentives that shaped CUP choices and thus the causes and courses of collective violence in the final days of the Ottoman Empire. The destruction of the Armenians, however, was but one of numerous genocidal campaigns that materialized in the context of several fractured empires. Aside from the disintegration of the Ottoman Empire, the decline of the Romanov and Habsburg empires also spawned large-scale violence against unwanted populations. As Gerlach writes, "The Armenians were just the worst affected of several victim groups in the late Ottoman Empire. Hundreds of thousands of Greeks, Kurds, Turks, Assyrians, and Chaldeans perished in massacres, deportations, expulsions, and starvation, as well as tens of thousands of Arabs."[114]

The dynamics of genocidal violence in the Soviet Union were also diverse and varied. An increasing number of scholars have—somewhat controversially—located a number of extremely violent episodes in Soviet history squarely within the genocide spectrum. Most recently Norman Naimark unequivocally argued that "Stalin's mass killings of the 1930s should be classified as 'genocide.'"[115] In fact Naimark found evidence to suggest that we are dealing with several genocidal campaigns in the Soviet Union. He singles out four episodes: dekulakization in 1929–31, the Ukrainian famine of 1932–33, the so-called Great Terror of 1937–38, and the violent destruction of non-Russians in the 1930s and 1940s. What sets Naimark's comparative historical analysis apart from other attempts to classify episodes of collective violence in the Soviet Union as genocidal is that he goes one step further. Rather than merely documenting the existence of genocidal campaigns, he insists that we must appreciate "the genocidal character of the Soviet *regime* in the 1930s, which killed systematically rather than episodically."[116]

How do we explain Stalin's various genocidal campaigns? For Naimark, "there is no single key to understanding Stalin's violence in the 1930s, but rather—as is so often the case in

---

114. Christian Gerlach, *Extremely Violent Societies: Mass Violence in the Twentieth-Century World* (Cambridge: Cambridge University Press, 2010), 93.
115. Norman M. Naimark, *Stalin's Genocides* (Princeton, N.J.: Princeton University Press, 2010), 1.
116. Naimark, *Stalin's Genocides*, 3.

the history of genocide—a perfect storm of factors intersected that brought Stalin to engage in the mass murder of millions."[117] We must take leave of the Holocaust as archetypal example of genocide in order to appreciate the many varieties of genocidal violence that history has offered up during the past two thousand years. Just because the dynamics of destruction do not exactly look alike, we should not conclude that the collective violence that drives them is not part of the same class of events. It is for this reason that we should set aside tired arguments about whether Stalin's victims were members of a protected group, as spelled out in the 1948 Genocide Convention. The crimes predated the international treaty, so the exercise is academic. More is to be gained from comprehending the nature and logic of collective violence in the Soviet Union than from primarily reading it in terms of a legal construct.

This brings us to the Holocaust, the genocide that occasioned the codification of genocide as an international crime in the 1948 Genocide Convention. Even though the Holocaust has loomed large for several decades in the public discourse about genocide, not to mention school curricula, the conventional view of its origins and development is largely out of step with Holocaust scholarship. It will come as no surprise to anyone that the Holocaust is the most deeply researched of all genocides. The scholarship is so vast, published in dozens of languages, that any single researcher would be hard-pressed to digest it all. From among this overwhelming material a few general, widely accepted findings have emerged, however. Most important, the Nazi genocide was the sum of many violent parts, often with little direct connection to one another.[118]

Thinking about the Nazi genocide in terms of multiple genocidal campaigns, some interlinked, others not, runs counter to conventional wisdom. Yet contrary to popular belief, no straight causal path ran from anti-Semitism to Hitler to the destruction of some six million European Jews. While essential to explaining the transition from authoritarianism to totalitarianism in Nazi Germany, racial ideology was of considerably less significance to the development of genocidal violence than is commonly thought. Although it was certainly the background against which a whole host of actors calculated their interests, anti-Semitism is not particularly helpful as an explanatory variable in accounting for the timing of the various genocidal campaigns in the 1940s. Anti-Semitism was a necessary condition of the Holocaust, but not a sufficient one. It was a constant throughout the duration of the "Third Reich", and it was Nazi Germany's overriding reason of state. But although anti-Semitism became more virulent at certain junctures, other factors had a far greater causal influence on the cumulative radicalization of Nazi strategies toward resolving the "Jewish question." At least as important as race in the ideology of Nazism was space.

Lebensraum, or living space for the Aryan race, especially in the vast non-German lands in the east, was a key intellectual tenet of Nazi ideology. In the quest for Lebensraum, not only Jews but also other, ostensibly inferior races were marked for expulsion, removal, and eventually destruction. Yet territorial conquest was a long-term objective. The vision became strategy, rather prematurely, in the early phase of Operation Barbarossa, Nazi Germany's invasion of the Soviet Union, which commenced in the summer of 1940. Emboldened by the euphoria of the initial military advances there and the rapid conquest of Poland in 1939 that had

117. Naimark, *Stalin's Genocides,* 35.
118. Stone, *Histories of the Holocaust,* 15.

preceded it, the genocidal imagination of Nazi leaders as well as the technocrats concerned with population policy took a leap of faith. Suddenly anything seemed possible.[119]

The Holocaust occurred in four different yet overlapping phases of destruction; this fact is a necessary corrective to the erroneous yet still widespread assumption that the Nazi genocide of the Jews was primarily accomplished by way of industrial killing in Auschwitz and other death camps. The first killing phase of the Holocaust targeted Soviet Jews. The Reich Security Main Office or *Reichssicherheitshauptamt* (RSHA), headed by Heinrich Himmler, ordered several *Einsatzgruppen,* or mobile death squads, to deploy in the Soviet Union on the heels of the Germany military. By late August 1941 some twenty thousand mobile militia were on the hunt for Jews there. At around the same time a number of mobile gas vans came to be used in order to speed up the killing process in the east. Yet the SS eventually concluded that stationary gas vans would be more efficient tools of destruction, which is why Polish Jews from the city of Lodz and environs began to be deported to the newly created Chelmno extermination camp. As a result of these and other operations like it, an estimated 20 to 25 percent of all Holocaust victims had perished by March 1942. This is noteworthy because the notorious Wannsee Conference, at which high-ranking Nazi bureaucrats coordinated the implementation of the previously decided "Final Solution," took place only on January 20, 1942.

In the wake of the planning meeting in Berlin's Wannsee suburb, the remaining three overlapping phases of destruction got under way. The next phase involved a stepped-up campaign of genocidal cleansing operations in the Soviet Union. "East of the old Nazi-Soviet demarcation line, numerous mobile killings squads—usually organized by the Higher SS and Police Leaders or Security Police successors to the Einsatzgruppen but comprising a bewildering array of available manpower, including local militias—conducted regional sweeps and liquidated the Jewish communities in one city, town, and village after another."[120] The third phase saw the beginning of industrialized killing on a massive scale. In addition to Chelmno, Belzec, Sobibor, and Treblinka became the regime's principal killing centers. The latter three are collectively known as the "Operation Reinhard camps," after the code name for the genocidal campaign to exterminate all of the two million Jews in the part of German-occupied Poland, known as the "Government General," which had not been incorporated into the Reich proper.[121] An estimated 1.7 million Jews are believed to have been destroyed in these extermination camps in the three years after they became operational in the fall of 1941. The same year also saw the beginning of the major deportation programs from western Europe. At the same time deportations from eastern Europe began to slow down as a result of a resurgent Soviet Union. One major exception was Hungary, from which an estimated 440,000 Jews were sent to their industrial deaths, mainly to Auschwitz, in May 1944.

The fourth and final phase of the Holocaust consisted of death marches. In view of advancing Soviet forces, Himmler ordered SS concentration camp authorities to retreat toward the interior of the Nazi empire with all surviving inmates in tow. Because many of these forced evacuations took place in the winter of 1944–45, thousands of concentration camp

---

119. Christopher R. Browning, "The Nazi Empire," in Bloxham and Moses, *The Oxford Handbook of Genocide Studies,* especially 420.

120. Browning, "The Nazi Empire," 423.

121. The most comprehensive analysis of Operation Reinhard remains Yitzhak Arad, *Belzec, Sobibor, Treblinka: The Operation Reinhard Death Camps* (Bloomington: Indiana University Press, 1999).

inmates died as a result of exposure, exhaustion, and starvation. Many others were tortured or shot to death.[122]

The Holocaust was a multifaceted phenomenon that, first, is neither reducible to a particular ideology (e.g., anti-Semitism) or a specific individual (Hitler) nor to particular interests (population policy) or institutions (RSHA). Second, the Holocaust was not solely a German enterprise. As it evolved, the extent of local initiative and collaboration in eastern Europe was considerable, indeed essential to the progression and diffusion of genocidal violence against Jews. Third, neither the Holocaust nor the other genocidal projects with which it became intertwined was planned very far in advance. Rather the architects of the "Final Solution" to the "Jewish question" proceeded in fits and starts, only gradually building one overarching project of destruction.

The all-out extermination of Jews was decided only when other violent strategies had failed and a window of opportunity—in the form of the initially successful invasion of the Soviet Union—opened up. Until 1941 forced migration and violent deportation were the Hitler regime's preferred responses to the "Jewish problem." Palestine and Madagascar were high on the list of possible destinations for forcible resettlement. Notwithstanding the propaganda of *Mein Kampf* and other Nazi rhetoric so frequently invoked in popular discussion, the Holocaust, as we know it, was *not* the solution to the "Jewish Question" that Nazi elites had contemplated for most of the duration of the "Third Reich." In Mann's parlance, "the Final Solution" really *was* a final solution, resembling a "Plan D" more than a "Plan A." It was fashioned, though not always coordinated, by a diverse set of Nazi elites and collaborators in all corners of the Nazi empire. Put more abstractly, it was an amalgam of individuals and institutions as well as of ideas and interests that caused the final solution to the "Jewish question" to end up becoming the most destructive solution imaginable.

Turning eastward, the case of twentieth-century China, more specifically the Cultural Revolution in 1966–76, has always lingered on the margins of genocide studies. Like the destruction of political and other enemies in the Soviet Union, the mass killing of real and imagined adversaries in the course of the Cultural Revolution was viewed by many for decades as tragic but probably not genocidal.[123] However, in order to be able to locate genocidal violence within the coordinates of collective violence more generally and to appreciate connection points and interaction effects among varieties of such violence, the Chinese case must be probed. As before, the point of the exercise is not to classify the case or aspects thereof but merely to draw some attention to the complicated causes and meanings of large-scale violence there. The objective is to broaden the canon of genocide studies, to travel along the border of all types of mass violence so as to shed light on similarities and differences.

In June 1966 Mao Zedong, chairman of the Chinese Communist Party (CCP), incited the country's youth in schools and colleges to "sweep away" traditional class enemies such as the "seven black categories" (landlords, rich peasants, counterrevolutionaries, evildoers,

---

122. For a seminal treatment, see Daniel Blatman, *The Death Marches: The Final Phase of Nazi Genocide*, translated by Chaya Galai (Cambridge, Mass.: Belknap Press of Harvard University Press, 2010).

123. On the historiography of the Cultural Revolution, see, most important, the contributions in Joseph W. Esherick, Paul G. Pickowicz, and Andrew G. Walder, eds., *The Chinese Cultural Revolution as History* (Stanford: Stanford University Press, 2006). For a comprehensive, one-volume history, see Roderick MacFarquhar and Martin Schoenhals, *Mao's Last Revolution* (Cambridge, Mass.: Harvard University Press, 2008).

rightists, capitalists, and reactionary intellectuals) as well as otherwise suspect elements who exhibited insufficient revolutionary zeal, such as teachers and intellectuals.[124] Heeding the call, millions of students formed paramilitary groups, the Red Guards, and set about re-revolutionizing their land. As many as one hundred thousand Chinese are estimated to have been killed in the course of these campaigns in 1966. Others victims were intimidated, were expelled from their homes, or saw their "reactionary" property, notably books, confiscated and burned. As significant, key Politburo members and rivals of Mao's were removed in pursuit of a more streamlined and more dependent CCP.

A new phase of violence began in 1967, when Mao ordered the military to resolve an ideological conflict between rival factions in the country's Red Guards.[125] This "all-round civil war," as Mao once called it, led to frequently indiscriminate killing campaigns because the armed forces and so-called revolutionary committees were under orders to violently suppress all "counterrevolutionaries" they encountered.[126] Since it is inherently difficult to distinguish at the mass level revolutionaries from counterrevolutionaries, many of the involved army units erred on the side of risk, not caution. According to recent tallies, nearly five hundred thousand Chinese were killed during this second phase of the Cultural Revolution. Importantly, however, what for several decades was considered the most destructive period of the Cultural Revolution was just the beginning. Based on unprecedented access to more than two thousand local archives in the Chinese countryside where communities kept "county annals" (*xianzhi*) that frequently contained narratives of life during the 1960s and 1970s, Andrew Walder and Yang Su have demonstrated in detail how the violent consequences of the Cultural Revolution grew over time.[127] It appears that the destruction at the hands of the Red Guards was considerably less well planned than the collective violence that followed, which drew to a much larger extent on the despotic power of the Chinese state. Walder and Su write, "We suspect that the massive toll of the years after 1968 could only have been sustained by large-scale military and bureaucratic organization that spanned entire counties and rural prefectures. It is unlikely that such casualty rates were generated simultaneously and independently in hundreds of thousands of villages throughout China. It is unlikely that this occurred without active participation by politically active villagers in townships and villages."[128]

In an even more comprehensive study that is focused on two provinces, Guangxi and Guangdong, Su contrasts this state-centered account with what he calls a "community model" of explanation. Among other things, he shows that local agents sometimes perpetrated kill-

---

124. Lü Xiuyuan, "A Step Toward Understanding Popular Violence in China's Cultural Revolution," *Pacific Affairs* 67, no. 4 (1994–95): 533–63.

125. On the rise and almost immediate fall of the Red Guards as vanguards of the Cultural Revolution, see Andrew G. Walder, *Fractured Rebellion: The Beijing Red Guard Movement* (Cambridge, Mass.: Harvard University Press, 2009). For a mostly sympathetic critique, see Jonathan Unger, "The Cultural Revolution Warfare at Beijing's Universities," *China Journal*, no. 64 (July 2010): 199–211.

126. On Mao's role in and responsibility for stoking factionalism within the Red Guards and his strategic supply of arms and ammunition to workers and students in 1967, see Michael Schoenhals, "'Why Don't We Arm the Left?' Mao's Culpability for the Cultural Revolution's 'Great Chaos' of 1967," *China Quarterly*, no. 182 (June 2005): 277–300.

127. Andrew G. Walder and Yang Su, "The Cultural Revolution in the Countryside: Scope, Timing and Human Impact," *China Quarterly*, no. 173 (March 2003): 87.

128. Walder and Su, "The Cultural Revolution in the Countryside," 99.

ings at higher rates in the shadow of the state rather than under its direction. Moreover he adduces evidence according to which these village- and commune-level cadres pursued targets *not* identified by central authorities as worthy of destruction, especially landlords and wealthy peasants.[129] What is the upshot of this for the study of genocide? Like some of the other cases, the Cultural Revolution drives home the importance of studying center-periphery dynamics in times of destruction. Even in totalitarian regimes like Hitler's Germany and Mao's China the application of collective violence is rarely linear. Understanding nonlinearity and the relationship between top-down and bottom-up dynamics in the causation of destruction is a central analytical challenge.

A relatively recent addition to debates in genocide studies is the case of East Pakistan, what became the independent state of Bangladesh in 1971. What is often described as a genocidal campaign began on March 25, 1971, when the Pakistani army launched Operation Searchlight in an attempt to uproot Bengali nationalism. In the course of 267 days, Pakistani army units killed a large number of Muslim Bengalis, mostly in the countryside. Estimates range from twenty-six thousand (in the Pakistani version) to three million (in the Bangladeshi version) victims. Most scholarly observers work with figures in the range of two hundred thousand to five hundred thousand deaths. India's intervention in Pakistan on December 3, 1971, was the beginning of the end of the genocidal campaign. Two weeks later Pakistan's armed forces surrendered. The swift termination of the genocidal violence—known in Bengali as the *muktijuddho*, or the Bangladesh Liberation War—paved the way for the independence of East Pakistan, which became the sovereign state of Bangladesh.

The origins of the conflict in East Pakistan go back to the partition of India in 1947. In the process of state formation in Pakistan, competing elites in the eastern and western parts of the newly created country vied for power, wealth, and security. In the 1960s in particular, Pakistan was deeply divided along class lines, with a landed gentry and industrial elites in the western part of the state, and urban elites and the middle class in the eastern territory. Despite the fact that most of Pakistan's population resided in the east, West Pakistan reaped most of the country's economic benefits. Per capita income, to reference but one economic indicator, was twice as high in the east than in the west. This caused a great deal of Bengali discontent and led to the Awami League, the leading political party in East Bengal, demanding redistributive policies. The party also demanded participation and representation in central decision making. This push for economic and political parity left Pakistan's military dictatorship unsettled.[130] The situation became dire when the Awami League won the November 1970 general elections, the first such elections held in the country.[131] The fear of a violent uprising and a push for independence from Pakistan led to the formulation of the previously mentioned Operation Searchlight in March 1971.

129. Yang Su, *Collective Killings in Rural China during the Cultural Revolution* (Cambridge: Cambridge University Press, 2011).

130. Gerlach, *Extremely Violent Societies*, 126–27.

131. Although the Awami League did not win a single seat in West Pakistan (where 26 million voters were registered), it secured 167 out of the 169 seats in East Pakistan (31 million registered voters) in addition to 288 of the 300 provincial seats that were contested there. The party's overall performance gave it a comfortable majority (160 seats out of 300) in the Pakistan National Assembly.

Although the military order did not mandate killings but rather arrests and disarmament of Bengali soldiers (the East Pakistan Rifles company and the East Bengal Regiment), police, and intellectuals, the atmosphere of incitement that had accompanied the order's issuance caused Pakistani troops to employ lethal tactics from the get-go.[132] A series of armed militias—Razakar, Al-Bardr, and Al-Sham—was formed to incorporate volunteers into what to many looked like a genocidal campaign. However, Sarmila Bose has cautioned that we should be skeptical of accounts that automatically and categorically classify all of the violence of 1971 as genocidal. The reality of destruction was far more complex.[133]

Interestingly this finding is not entirely new. Already in 1972 the International Commission of Jurists had found that the complexity of the violence in East Pakistan was such that genocidal acts may well have been committed but that these were perpetrated in the context of a much more complicated conflict involving a broader set of international crimes.[134] This finding by the International Commission is not all dissimilar from the finding in 2005 by the UN International Commission of Inquiry on Darfur, where visiting jurists were similarly reluctant to use the genocide designation to make sense of the collective violence before them.

The country of Burundi in Central Africa, which borders on Rwanda, the Democratic Republic of Congo (formerly Zaire), and Tanzania, has seen its share of large-scale violence in the twentieth century. The deadliest conflict reached its peak in 1972, when a large number of mostly Hutu victims—estimates range between 150,000 and 300,000 persons—were killed primarily by Tutsi elements in the country's ethnically mixed armed forces. The genocidal violence was preceded by a failed coup attempt. On April 29 a Hutu-led insurrection against many perceived injustices of Tutsi-minority rule led within a few days to the death of somewhere around one thousand Tutsi troops and civilians. The insurgents, who briefly proclaimed the creation of the Martyazo Republic, began their killing spree in the town of Rumonge, located on Lake Tanganyika, about forty-five miles south of the capital, Bujumbura, from which it spread inland and southward. It was a failed coup attempt, however. The government of Burundi responded almost immediately with repressive as well as retaliatory violence. The Burundian army took the lead in the extermination of presumed enemies and sympathizers in the Hutu population. Much of the escalation, however, was orchestrated by Artémon Simbabaniye, the country's foreign minister. On his orders roving soldiers and militia went particularly after educated Hutu, so as to destroy that ethnic group's intellectual leadership.

Nevertheless the Tutsi-led genocidal campaign, while strategically waged, was not the result of a well-laid master plan. Genocidal violence was the result—as in so many other cases—of a cumulative radicalization rather than the outcome of years of predetermination. As René Lemarchand, the foremost scholar of the tiny landlocked country, cautioned, "Far from representing the culmination of a long-standing, carefully elaborated master plan . . . , the systematic massacre of Hutu elites came almost as an afterthought, long after 'peace and order' had been reestablished in the south, in an atmosphere saturated by persistent rumors of external

132. Gerlach, *Extremely Violent Societies*, 130.
133. Sarmila Bose, "The Question of Genocide and the Quest for Justice in the 1971 War," *Journal of Genocide Research* 13, no. 4 (2011): 394. For a more comprehensive treatment, see Sarmila Bose, *Dead Reckoning: Memories of the 1971 Bangladesh War* (London: Hurst, 2011).
134. Secretariat of the International Commission of Jurists, *The Events in East Pakistan, 1971: A Legal Study* (Geneva: International Commission of Jurists, 1972).

intervention—some hinting at the impending arrival of European mercenaries in the pay of the ex-king Ntare and others raising the specter of a Mulelist invasion from Zaire; hence the perceived urgency to strike a decisive blow."[135]

This contentious episode points to a dynamic rather than a static relationship between adversaries. This elasticity of ethnic relations must be taken into account, in Burundi and elsewhere, before pronouncing on the significance of ethnic cleavages in the causation of large-scale social violence. Of particular importance is the issue of intraethnic divisions that often gets lost in accounts of genocide that pit entire collectivities—whether racial, ethnic, or national in character—against one another. The imputations of intentions and behavior to large groups can be self-defeating in the study of genocide. The case of Burundi exemplifies the need for nuance in historical explanation.

Burundi was also the site of another episode of large-scale social violence, in 1993. (In addition to being noteworthy on its own, the mass violence that wrecked the country at century's end was an important catalyst for the 1994 genocide in Rwanda.) The country's first democratically elected president, who also was its first-ever Hutu leader, was assassinated in October 1993, setting the country once again on the path to large-scale ethnic violence. In the course of the popular unrest that ensued, thousands of Tutsi were killed, especially in the northern and central parts of the country. The Burundian army and gendarmerie as well as Tutsi civilians retaliated by indiscriminately killing Hutus. Some scholars estimate that between fifty thousand and one hundred thousand persons were murdered in the months following the assassination. Another one million Burundians fled the volatile country, and hundreds of thousands ended up internally displaced.[136] It remains unclear to what extent the insurgent violence of Hutu perpetrators in 1993 was spontaneous or orchestrated. It is plausible that ordinary Hutus took up arms to avenge the assassination of what they might have considered the country's first legitimate president. Equally plausible is the argument that the Hutu political party Frodebu (the Front for Democracy in Burundi) instigated the peasant uprising in order to redress Burundi's ethnic imbalance. Be that as it may, in 2002 the International Commission of Inquiry on Burundi declared that acts of genocide had been committed against the country's Tutsi minority in October 1993.

More firmly established in the annals than Burundi's two genocides is the case of Cambodia under the Khmer Rouge. Formally known as the Communist Party of Kampuchea (CPK), the Khmer Rouge captured the country in the final throes of the Vietnam War, sometimes referred to as the Second Indochina War, which lasted from 1954 until 1975. After several years of civil war the insurgent movement overthrew the military dictatorship of Lon Nol, a client regime of the United States. Upon liberating Phnom Penh, Cambodia's capital, in April 1975, the Khmer Rouge renamed the country Democratic Kampuchea (DK). In the course of the communist dictatorship that ensued, which lasted until Vietnam invaded its neighbor in 1979 and overthrew the genocidal regime of Pol Pot, the leader of the CPK, Cambodia was subjected to a radical overhaul of the cultural and political foundations of its society.

135. René Lemarchand, *Burundi: Ethnic Conflict and Genocide* (Cambridge: Woodrow Wilson Center Press and Cambridge University Press, 1994), 102.
136. Peter Uvin, "Ethnicity and Power in Burundi and Rwanda: Different Paths to Mass Violence," *Comparative Politics* 31, no. 3 (1999): 262.

At the end of this extreme experiment in social engineering, a significant portion of Cambodia's population lay dead, much of the country devastated.

Estimates of mortality under the Khmer Rouge regime vary widely and are the subject of an intense debate, one that is sometimes more ideological than scholarly. This is not surprising, given that the government overthrown by the Khmer Rouge, led by Lon Nol from 1970 until 1975, was pro-American, that the Khmer Rouge under Pol Pot advocated a radical form of Marxism, and that the regime that wrested control from the Khmer Rouge in 1979 was backed by the government of Vietnam. This draws attention to one of the thorniest yet most fundamental methodological challenges in the study of genocide: how to count the dead. Most of Cambodia's victims died as a result of starvation, illness, and exhaustion rather than as a result of mass killings and executions, although scholars disagree about exact percentages of each of these methods of destruction. Equally interesting is the question of why so many Cambodians had to die in the first place.

In his account of the Cambodian genocide, the historian Eric Weitz argues that the regime embodied an ideology of "racial communism" that played a major role.[137] The term captures neatly the twin utopian elements that drove the destruction of a large segment of the country's population. The Khmer Rouge directed its violent energies toward the invention of a racialized order that sought to improve on what were seen as the insufficiently rigorous communist regimes in the Soviet Union and China. According to the DK recipe for egalitarianism, the developmental state that was required for leapfrogging from agrarianism over capitalism to communism had to be built and deployed in more ruthless a manner than their communist rivals had done. Not unlike China's violent policies of the Great Leap Forward (1958–61), Cambodia's doctrinaire approach to economic development not only demanded the centralization of society, it also necessitated the categorization of and removal of undesirable members from this society. This is where and when communism and racism as ideologies bled into one another.

The new, imaginary society required new people, so the Khmer Rouge created them, thereby "racializing" the nation. In order to arrive at the "clean" and "pure" people that DK supposedly required, its leaders turned previously mutable categories such as class, ethnicity, and nationality into immutable categories. By manufacturing the invented tradition of Angkar, the Party Organization, the Khmer Rouge created an ideological substitute for the family, which had traditionally served as the social glue in Cambodian relations. By reconstituting all of Khmer society as one highly selective—and unforgiving—family, the regime embarked on one of the most comprehensive racialization projects ever attempted.

This project involved eliminating, literally and figuratively, any traces of pre-DK social relations. "The Khmer Rouge racialized nationality by making every single member of the group the bearer of the same dangerous characteristics."[138] At the bottom of the ladder stood Cambodia's ethnic minorities. They were numerous—some twenty in total—and accounted for more than 15 percent of the country's population. The largest ethnic groups were the Chams (Khmer of Muslim descent), Vietnamese, and Chinese. Although all three groups had coexisted more or less peacefully with Cambodia's Khmer communities for decades, a long-

137. Weitz, *A Century of Genocide*, 144.
138. Weitz, *A Century of Genocide*, 174.

standing undercurrent of resentment toward the Vietnamese minority (and the eastern neighbor whence they originally hailed) took a violent form when the violent Khmer Rouge machine embarked on its utopian project.

Because the majority of victims were ethnic Khmer—like the perpetrators—some scholars have used the term "autogenocide" to label this late twentieth-century example of mass killing. Between 1975 and 1979 the collective dictatorship under the leadership of Pol Pot, also known as Brother Number One, administered killing campaigns that left an estimated 19 percent of the country's eight million inhabitants dead.[139] Some scholars maintain that Cambodia's various genocidal campaigns came about in the absence of an overarching plan of destruction. Notwithstanding outward appearances, they argue, the genocidal state was less unified than is commonly assumed. As Mann claims, "Centralized authoritarianism, provincial warlordism, and guerilla paramilitarism were competing organizational principles within the Khmer Rouge. The combinations of the centralized and the factionalized, the intended and the unintended, escalated killings beyond what any other Communists had perpetrated."[140]

One of the bloodiest Cold War conflicts in Latin America was the war in Guatemala (1962–96), marked by years of intensive, systematic violence against the Mayan population. Between 1981 and 1983, when the armed confrontation between the government and insurgents reached a new level, more than one hundred thousand Guatemalan Maya were killed by the armed forces. As part of a scorched earth counterinsurgency plan, regular and irregular government forces killed, raped, tortured, and forcibly displaced Maya in the rural mountain regions. Beginning in 1983 the army undertook measures to control the survivors, ushering in a second phase of assault marked by a combination of amnesty and intensified militarization of surviving communities. In the worst hit community, Rabinal, 14.6 percent of the population was killed; 99.8 percent of the victims were Maya. This intensive phase ended when the military leaders decided that they had the Maya communities sufficiently under control. Yet the country's long-standing civil war did not come to an end until December 1996, when the interacting adversaries committed to a peace settlement. What Guatemala represents, then, is a case in which genocidal violence was perpetrated over the course of three years but against the background of a civil war that lasted more than thirty.

What explains this transition to and from genocidal violence in the 1980s? The country's genocidal turn coincided with the rise to power of Efraín Ríos Montt. In March 1982 Montt and three co-conspirators established a military dictatorship. Having overthrown the previous government in a military coup, they quickly issued a National Security and Development Plan. As an outgrowth of this comprehensive blueprint for the radical transformation of Guatemala, the military junta came up with Victory 82, a violent campaign directed toward eradicating communism—and the indigenous Mayan population's supposed susceptibility to it—in the countryside, especially in the western highlands. Because the reach of the state had been comparatively limited in this area, a systematic "scorched earth policy" was designed.

139. For a unique account of why ordinary Cambodians participated in the genocidal project of the Khmer Rouge, see Alexander Laban Hinton, "A Head for an Eye: Revenge in the Cambodian Genocide," *American Ethnologist* 25, no. 3 (1998): 352–77. See also Hinton, *Why Did They Kill?*
140. Mann, *The Dark Side of Democracy*, 350.

The policy was adopted in response to what looked like a general popular insurrection in the highlands in 1981.[141] Although the application of large-scale violence against insurgents and civilians in the highlands, which was aimed at destroying the social bases of the guerrillas, had commenced under Romeo Lucas Garcia, who was president of Guatemala from 1978 until 1982, it was only during the subsequent years that the destruction of the Mayan population reached its zenith. Indeed the escalation of the counterinsurgency campaign was a major impetus behind the coup d'état of March 1982.

Increasingly the population, rather than the insurgents, became the preferred targets of destruction under Montt. Among other things, the military government implemented Operation Victory 1982, a comprehensive strategy that combined extermination and indoctrination. One of the most violent components of this strategy was Operation Sofia. Launched on July 8, 1982, by Héctor Mario Lopez Fuentes, Guatemala's army chief of staff at the time, it sanctioned the elimination of "subversives." Throughout, the U.S. and Israeli governments were two of the Montt regime's strongest supporters. The genocidal campaign—which ceased only when Montt, who had become sole head of state, was overthrown in a military coup in October 1983 and because much of the presumed enemy population by then had been annihilated—is said to have led, during the three-year period in question, to the razing of more than four hundred villages, the killing of some seventy-five thousand Maya, and the flight of more than one million people.

That the regime's violent strategies amounted to genocidal violence in the period 1981–83 was demonstrated in no uncertain terms by Guatemala's Commission for Historical Clarification (CEH). Mandated as part of the peace settlement, on February 25, 1999, the CEH released a twelve-volume report, totaling some 3,400 pages, in which it chronicled in systematic and great detail the armed confrontation between the country's incumbents and insurgents over the previous three decades. It identified 669 massacres that took place during this period, the vast majority in the regions of Quiché (344, or 46 percent), Huehuetenango (88, or 16 percent), and Alta Verapaz (61, or 9 percent), all located in the central part of the country.[142] Based on these data and scores of additional evidence, the three-member CEH, which was led by the respected international lawyer Christian Tomuschat, concluded for the three-year period in question "that the reiteration of destructive acts, directed systematically against groups of the Mayan population, within which can be mentioned the elimination of leaders and criminal acts against minors who could not possibly have been military targets, demonstrates that the only common denominator for all the victims was the fact that they belonged

141. For an overview of the intensification and consequences of the counterinsurgency campaign in rural Guatemala, see, most important, Ricardo Falla, *Massacres in the Jungle: Ixcán, Guatemala (1975–1982)* (Boulder, Colo.: Westview Press, 1992); Beatriz Manz, *Paradise in Ashes: A Guatemalan Journey of Courage, Terror, and Hope* (Berkeley: University of California Press, 2004); David Stoll, *Between Two Armies in the Ixil Towns of Guatemala* (New York: Columbia University Press, 1993). For a more general account, see Victoria Sanford, *Buried Secrets: Truth and Human Rights in Guatemala* (New York: Palgrave, 2003).

142. See Guatemalan Commission for Historical Clarification, *Guatemala, Memory of Silence: Report of the Commission for Historical Clarification* (Guatemala City: Guatemalan Commission for Historical Clarification, 1999). A quantitative scholarly investigation reached similar conclusions. See Patrick Ball, Paul Kobrak, and Herbert F. Spirer, *State Violence in Guatemala, 1960–1996* (Washington, D.C.: American Association for the Advancement of Science, 1999).

to a specific ethnic group and makes it evident that these acts were committed with 'intent to destroy, in whole or in part' these groups."[143]

The case of Bosnia, not unlike that of Guatemala, forces us to disentangle the logic of genocide from the larger logic of violence in a web of intersecting civil and interstate wars that tore through the former Yugoslavia. Contrary to much commentary in the early 1990s, when Bosnia was the seat of much collective violence, genocide, by most recent accounts, was not "a national policy."[144] It would be equally misleading, however, to insist that large-scale violence was purely wanton and senseless in Bosnia, primarily the product of roving bandits, and never genocidal.[145] A more accurate reading factors in geographical and temporal variation.

The conflict in Bosnia turned violent when the government of President Alija Izetbegovic, a Muslim, declared independence from rump Yugoslavia following a 1992 referendum.[146] Up until that point, Bosnia-Herzegovina had been one of six republics of the Socialist Federal Republic of Yugoslavia, an artificial federation that Josip Broz Tito had cobbled together in the aftermath of World War II. However, the decline of communism and the rise of nationalism in the waning years of the cold war, combined with rapid declarations of independence by both Slovenia and Croatia, also former socialist republics, in 1991, persuaded Bosnian Serb elites to aggressively push for an imaginary nation-state called Greater Serbia. Conceived as a homeland for Serbs that would unite Serbs residing in Bosnia with those living in Serbia proper, the institutional vision found an ardent advocate in a moderate-turned-nationalist, Slobodan Milošević.

Milošević had become president of Serbia in 1989. He gradually developed an exclusionary brand of nationalism that was in part founded on the realization that, in the likely event of the collapse of the Yugoslav federation, Serbia would be economically less viable on its own than most of the other constituent republics of Yugoslavia. By November 1991, after having violently seized sizable swaths of land from independent Croatia, the Milošević-led Serbia turned its sights on Bosnia, lending military and other support to the Bosnian Serbs, notably with the help of the Yugoslav People's Army (JNA). JNA attacks on Bosnian forces started in April 1992. When the JNA officially withdrew in June, the army of the Republika Srpska and local Serb paramilitaries continued the military onslaught on Muslims, relying on the equipment that the JNA had bequeathed to them. The logic of violence often followed an identical pattern: bombardments were used to weaken military resistance and intimidate local populations; search-and-destroy operations (known as "mopping-up" operations) in local communities delivered more carefully targeted violence. If we believe Mann, however, the intention behind this two-pronged strategy "was not usually genocide, but murderous ethnic cleansing

143. Guatemalan Commission for Historical Clarification, *Guatemala, Memory of Silence*, Conclusions and Recommendations, para. 111.

144. For this argument, see Norman Cigar, *Genocide in Bosnia: The Policy of "Ethnic Cleansing"* (College Station: Texas A&M University Press, 1995), 4–6.

145. Exemplary of this argument is John Mueller, "The Banality of 'Ethnic War,'" *International Security* 25, no. 1 (2000): 42–70.

146. For a journalistic overview of the Bosnian conflict, see Misha Glenny, *The Fall of Yugoslavia: The Third Balkan War*, 3rd edition (New York: Penguin, 1996).

to terrorize Muslims and Croats to flee."[147] Inasmuch as the government in Belgrade "supported Serbian paramilitary violence in Bosnia during 1992–1993, it prevented those same forces from attacking Muslims in Serbia proper."[148]

This empirical irregularity is highly significant because it complicates the conventional genocide narrative, according to which Serbs were intent on annihilating Muslims categorically wherever they encountered them. Instead the changing character of the civil war among interacting adversaries—Serb, Muslim, and Croat—appears to have influenced decision making for and against genocidal violence. Social scientists have shown that large-scale violence was generally concentrated in areas of strategic or economic importance.[149] For example, western Bosnia was heavily affected because it linked Serb territory in Bosnia and Serb territory in Croatia, notably the Krajina region. A similar logic appears to have been at work in northeastern Bosnia, where large-scale violence was also widespread. There the intensity and magnitude of violence can be explained by the area's proximity to Serbia. It was strategically and economically valuable because it connected the Serb-held territories in Croatia and Bosnia with the imaginary homeland, thereby creating a contiguous sphere of violent influence.[150] What many would consider the most horrific sites of genocide during the Bosnian wars—the areas surrounding Prijedor and Srebrenica—were of considerable geopolitical significance to Serb leaders.

Although the elimination of more than seven thousand men in Srebrenica in 1995 has become the touchstone for discussions about genocide in Bosnia, the destruction of parts of Bosnian's Muslim population began in earnest in the municipality of Prijedor, not far from Banja Luka, a Serb stronghold. Prijedor represents the location of the first genocidal campaign against Muslims and also Croats. In late April 1992 the Serbian Democratic Party, a nationalist political party cofounded by Radovan Karadžić, in collaboration with the JNA and paramilitary groups took over the administration of the municipality with the aim of purifying the area. They created a military-led Crisis Staff to govern. Soon after the quasi-military takeover, the new authorities began to violently attack the area's Muslims and Croats. In addition to the shelling of villages and selective executions, a campaign of persecutions was launched. At the end of May the Serbian agents of destruction opened three concentration camps, in Trnopolje, Omarska, and Keraterm. Many members of the targeted populations were forcibly transferred to these sites and tortured and killed there. Proceedings before the International Criminal Tribunal for the former Yugoslavia found a pattern of extermination in Prijedor and environs that amounted to a crime against humanity, causing the death of at least 1,500 people between May and September 1992.[151]

147. Mann, *The Dark Side of Democracy*, 395.
148. James Ron, "Boundaries and Violence: Repertoires of State Action along the Bosnia/Yugoslavia Divide," *Theory and Society* 29, no. 5 (2000): 639.
149. Stathis N. Kalyvas and Nicholas Sambanis, "Bosnia's Civil War: Origins and Violence Dynamics," in Paul Collier and Nicholas Sambanis, eds., *Understanding Civil War: Evidence and Analysis*, vol. 2: *Europe, Central Asia, and Other Regions* (Washington, D.C.: World Bank, 2005), 217–18.
150. Kalyvas and Sambanis, "Bosnia's Civil War," 217–18.
151. See, most important, *Prosecutor v. Milomir Stakic*, Case No. IT-97-24-T, Trial Judgment, International Criminal Tribunal for the former Yugoslavia, July 31, 2003; *Prosecutor v. Milomir Stakic*, Case No. IT-97-24-A, Appeal Judgment, International Criminal Tribunal for the former Yugoslavia, March 22, 2006.

What role did ethnicity play in all of this violence—in Prijedor, Srebrenica, and in the many other spaces of collective violence? Stathis Kalyvas and Nicholas Sambanis, leading scholars of civil war, have rejected arguments that suggest a causal relationship between so-called ancient hatreds and the onset of large-scale violence in Bosnia: "Rather than translating deep division into violent conflict, the anecdotal evidence suggests a situation of rapid 'ethnification' of violence once the war began. Once the war began, it endogenously generated additional waves of violence and further polarization, through the mechanism of revenge; this process consolidated, magnified, and hardened ethnic identities."[152] They insist that we not mistake the form that collective violence takes for its causes. Their interpretation of the Bosnian case is largely consistent with Mann's reading of it.

Although Mann accords a central role to Milošević, he finds no evidence of a long-hatched genocidal plan: "Milosevic's Plan A was a compact Serb-tilting Yugoslav Federation. . . . Milosevic was pressured by repeated failures first to Plan B of militarily aiding cross-border Serbs to achieve a Greater Serbia, then to Plan C of a swift and overwhelming army invasion. Finally, when the army could not achieve this, he plunged into Plan D, combining army artillery bombardments and wild paramilitary/security police assaults that produced the most murderous ethnic cleansing. In Bosnia he moved less far, starting with the Plan C just mentioned, anticipating swift success. Failure then made him escalate quickly to Plan D."[153] The Muslim and Croat populations of Prijedor and Srebrenica were at the receiving end of this escalation. Making ever better sense of their violent fates—and the fates of other groups targeted in the territory of the former Yugoslavia—requires the continued integration of macro-level and micro-level explanations.[154]

The Rwandan genocide, more so than the genocidal campaigns in Bosnia, has generated sophisticated scholarship that combines theoretical reasoning with extensive field research.[155] This research has found that ethnicity played a very different role than previously thought in the one hundred days of slaughter that killed nearly one million Rwandans, mostly from the

152. Kalyvas and Sambanis, "Bosnia's Civil War," 216.

153. Mann, The Dark Side of Democracy, 424. Milošević and the Serb leadership embraced the logic of destruction more readily in the case of Kosovo, where, in 1998 and 1999, the regime in Belgrade launched a violent, increasingly more systematic campaign to expel Kosovar Albanians from their homeland. According to a U.S. Department of State report released at the time, "Death represents only one facet of Serbian actions in Kosovo. Over 1.5 million Kosovar Albanians—at least 90 percent of the estimated 1998 Kosovar Albanian population of Kosovo—were forcibly expelled from their homes. Tens of thousands of homes in at least 1,200 cities, towns, and villages have been damaged or destroyed." See U.S. Department of State, Ethnic Cleansing in Kosovo: An Accounting (Washington, D.C.: U.S. Department of State, 1999), 3.

154. Most recently, see, for example, Nils B. Weidmann, "Violence 'from Above' or 'from Below'? The Role of Ethnicity in Bosnia's Civil War," Journal of Politics 73, no. 4 (2011): 1178–90. For an overview of contending explanations in a sprawling literature on the former Yugoslavia, see Thomas Cushman, "Anthropology and Genocide in the Balkans," Anthropological Theory 4, no. 1 (2004): 5–28; Roumen Daskalov, "The Balkans: Identities, Wars, Memories," Contemporary European History 13, no. 4 (2004): 529–36; David Campbell, "MetaBosnia: Narratives of the Bosnian War," Review of International Studies 24, no. 2 (1998): 261–81; Mark Danner, "America and the Bosnia Genocide," New York Review of Books, December 4, 1997.

155. See, most important, Straus, The Order of Genocide; Lee Ann Fujii, Killing Neighbors: Webs of Violence in Rwanda (Ithaca, N.Y.: Cornell University Press, 2009). Early foundational accounts include Alison Des Forges, Leave None to Tell the Story: Genocide in Rwanda (New York: Human Rights Watch, 1999); Gérard Prunier, The Rwandan Crisis: History of a Genocide, updated edition (New York: Columbia University Press, 1997).

country's Tutsi minority. As Omar McDoom argues, "Ethnic identity—through threat and the underlying emotion of fear—mattered for group polarization but not for individual participation in violence. Ethnicity does not explain why some individuals killed and others not. Rwandans did frame, narrate, and rationalize the violence in ethnic terms however."[156] Nevertheless "the growing body of micro-evidence points to nonethnic motives for killing in group violence."[157] This finding flies in the face of the conventional narratives about the genocide.

Between April 6 and mid-July 1994 Rwanda's Hutu-led government undertook a genocidal campaign that targeted for extermination the country's Tutsi population. It lasted barely longer than one hundred days but killed between 500,000 and 850,000 members of the country's minority population as well as some thirty thousand Hutu, many of whom were suspected of Tutsi ties. The large-scale violence was the immediate outgrowth of a protracted civil war between the Rwandan Patriotic Front (RPF), Rwanda's current ruling party, and the government of the Hutu president Juvénal Habyarimana. For in October 1990 the RPF, then an insurgent army based in neighboring Uganda, had launched an invasion of what it considered its lost homeland. In the rebels' understanding, their homeland was lost in 1959, when Hutu elites with support from the majority seized the commanding heights of the state from the Tutsi minority, who had governed the country from precolonial times. The takeover caused thousands of Tutsi to flee to Tanzania, Uganda, and other neighboring countries. In the decades that followed, Hutu supremacy in politics and life led to an increased marginalization and also repression of Rwanda's remaining Tutsi. Redressing this perceived injustice was the impetus behind the RPF invasion that set off the civil war.

The civil war is a central factor in the 1994 genocide; the war and the international response to it raised the stakes and provoked a radicalization of Hutu hardliners inside Rwanda. When the international community sought in 1991 to broker a settlement to the civil war and encourage democratization, hope was in the air. In August 1993 the diplomatic intervention even resulted in the conclusion of a transitional power-sharing agreement, the Arusha Accord, that the Hutu-controlled government, the country's new opposition parties, and the RPF signed. However, Hutu hardliners in Rwanda rejected the deal struck in Tanzania and mobilized accordingly. On April 6, 1994, they unleashed genocidal violence on their opponents and country. The immediate trigger was the assassination of Rwanda's Hutu president, Juvénal Habyarimana, who had signed the Arusha Accord and was killed when unknown assassins shot down his plane. In the power vacuum that ensued, Rwanda's Hutu hardliners "mobilized the state's civilian and military machinery as well as the Hutu civilian population in a bid to eliminate the Tutsi minority, win the civil war, and maintain Hutu control of the state."[158]

Why did hundreds of thousands of ordinary Rwandans kill their neighbors? Although no serious scholar has ever subscribed to the argument—widely propagated in early coverage by journalists—that ancient hatreds between the "tribes" of Rwanda accounted for the genocide, it is not uncommon to encounter scholarship that posits the centrality of ethnic ha-

156. Omar Shahabudin McDoom, "The Psychology of Threat in Intergroup Conflict," *International Security* 37, no. 2 (2012): 136. For an important analysis of the genocide's long-run antecedents, see Mamdani, *When Victims Become Killers*.
157. McDoom, "The Psychology of Threat in Intergroup Conflict," 136.
158. McDoom, "The Psychology of Threat in Intergroup Conflict," 132–33.

tred.[159] By contrast, Scott Straus, the first scholar who applied a careful research design to the study of the 1994 genocide, has found that "the mechanisms driving individuals to kill were not primarily about ethnic prejudice, preexisting ethnic antipathy, manipulation from racist propaganda, or nationalist commitments. On balance, Hutus did not kill Tutsis because they hated Tutsis in some constant fashion, because they believed Tutsis were no longer human, or because they were deeply committed ideologically to Hutu nationalism or to ethnic utopia. These dimensions of motivation mattered for some perpetrators, but not for the majority."[160] What *did* matter for the majority, says Straus, were the fact that four years of civil war had brought uncertainty and fear to the Hutu population; that neighbors, and Hutu society at large, exerted social pressure to participate in the genocidal campaign; and that ample opportunities existed to secure either power or property (or both) once the genocidal campaign had been set in motion from above. The genocidal campaign in Rwanda was decidedly modern in the sense that it not only involved machete-wielding peasants but saw the deployment of violent specialists, from regular to irregular armed forces, who ensured the early diffusion of genocidal acts. Yet inasmuch as many state officials, especially at the local and provincial levels, encouraged and facilitated the pursuit of destruction, most country specialists do not believe that what transpired in Rwanda in the spring of 1994 was meticulously planned. Most do not deny the significance of localized massacres against Tutsi to the increased group polarization between the two major ethnic groups in the years prior to the genocide, but they cast doubt on arguments that see a straight line running from 1990 to 1994.

One scholar sums up the current state of research on the causes of the genocide in Rwanda thus: "Chaos is not the right model; neither is a carefully constructed, hierarchical 'machine' of killing. Rather a more contingent process happened. . . . After the president was assassinated and the [Tutsi] rebels began advancing, the [Hutu] hardliners let loose. They chose genocide as an extreme, vengeful, and desperate strategy to win a war that they were losing."[161] This portrayal captures a logic of violence in genocide that we have seen in evidence already numerous times in this brief history of destruction: the role of cumulative radicalization. The twenty-first-century conflict in Darfur illuminates this logic yet again.

Like the Holocaust and the Rwandan genocide, the case of Darfur is considerably more complex than conventional wisdom suggests. From early on, news coverage (as well as commentary by NGOs such as Human Rights Watch) invoked the categories "Arabs" and "Africans" to describe the "sides" in the unfolding violence. In addition to being anthropologically and sociologically off the mark, the binary fed into stereotypes about the causes of collective violence in the developing world. "It is scarcely an exaggeration," writes Alex de Waal, perhaps the foremost Western student of Sudan, "to say that the depiction of 'Arabs' killing 'Africans' in Darfur conjures up, in the mind of a non-Sudanese (including in many people in sub-Saharan Africa), a picture of bands of light-skinned Arabs marauding among villages of peaceable black-skinned people of indeterminate religion. In the current context in which 'Arabs' are

159. For one of many examples of the "ancient hatreds" argument in the journalistic coverage of Rwanda, see Tom Masland and Joshua Hammer, "'Corpses Everywhere,'" *Newsweek*, April 18, 1994.
160. Straus, *The Order of Genocide*, 8–9.
161. Straus, *The Order of Genocide*, 272, 12. For the argument that chaos reigned, see, for example, Donatella Lorch, "Anarchy Rules Rwanda's Capital and Drunken Soldiers Roam City," *New York Times*, April 14, 1994.

identified, in the popular western and sub-Saharan press, with the instigators of terrorism, it readily labels Darfur's non-Arabs as victims."[162] Such a categorical statement, however, would be a distortion of how the destruction of many Darfurians (itself an awkward and empirically questionable term) came about in Sudan. In a controversial book on the Darfur conflict, Mahmood Mamdani argues that the clear-cut distinction between "victims" and "killers" depoliticizes the atrocities.[163] A more accurate portrayal would complexify the cast of agents and those affected by the different waves of violence in Darfur.

A second controversy revolved around another aspect of the naming of the conflict: the invocation of the term "genocide." On September 21, 2004, in an address to the UN General Assembly, U.S. president George W. Bush announced his government's conclusion that the atrocities perpetrated in Sudan's Darfur region "are genocide."[164] In January 2005 another investigation called into question the blanket classification of the large-scale violence in western Sudan. The second assessment was undertaken by a high-profile international commission appointed by UN Secretary-General Kofi Annan. Led by the late Antonio Cassese, an eminent international lawyer, the three-person International Commission of Inquiry on Darfur found that "the Government of Sudan and the Janjaweed are responsible for a number of violations of international human rights and humanitarian law. Some of these violations are very likely to amount to war crimes, and given the systematic and widespread pattern of many of the violations, they would also amount to crimes against humanity."[165] Yet the commission concluded, rather controversially at the time, that "the Government of Sudan has not pursued a policy of genocide."[166]

The ongoing debate over labels has distracted from the changing character of the conflict in Darfur. Whereas the period from late 2003 until early 2004 was characterized by a series of genocidal campaigns—involving, among other atrocities, massacres, the burning of villages, and the looting of livestock—undertaken by a combination of regular and irregular armed forces, in early 2005 the conflict in and over Darfur entered into a second, less immediately violent phase. Instead of physical destruction, the pursuit of displacement became the regime's chosen strategy of conflict, not least because a large proportion of Darfur's villages had been destroyed.[167] Or, as two epidemiologists recently noted, "during the second period, from 2006 onwards, the conflict became increasingly complex with the fragmentation of the rebel

162. Alex de Waal, "Who Are the Darfurians? Arab and African Identities, Violence and External Engagement," unpublished paper, December 10, 2004, 19, available at http://conconflicts.ssrc.org/hornofafrica/dewaal. For a historical treatment of identities in Sudan, see Francis M. Deng, *War of Visions: Conflict of Identities in the Sudan* (Washington, D.C.: Brookings Institution Press, 1995).

163. Mahmood Mamdani, *Saviors and Survivors: Darfur, Politics, and the War on Terror* (New York: Pantheon, 2009).

164. Quoted in "President and Secretary of State Characterize Events in Darfur as Genocide," *American Journal of International Law* 99, no. 1 (2005): 266.

165. International Commission of Inquiry on Darfur, *Report of the International Commission of Inquiry on Darfur to the United Nations Secretary-General Pursuant to Security Council Resolution 1564 of 18 September 2004*, 25 January 2005, available at http://www.un.org/News/dh/sudan/com_inq_darfur.pdf, para. 630.

166. International Commission of Inquiry on Darfur, *Report of the International Commission of Inquiry on Darfur*, para. 640.

167. Margie Buchanan-Smith and Susanne Jaspars, "Conflict, Camps and Coercion: The Ongoing Livelihoods Crisis in Darfur," *Disasters* 31, supplement 1 (March 2007): 57–76.

groups, unclear chains of command among both GoS [government of Sudan]–supported militia and the rebels and intensification of banditry."[168] Serious doubt has therefore been cast in recent years on the recurring claim, consistently advanced by human rights advocates as well as by Luis Moreno Ocampo, the first prosecutor of the International Criminal Court, that genocide was "ongoing" in Darfur years after large-scale violence in that part of Sudan had first made international headlines.[169]

Longtime observers of the conflict, including humanitarian agencies and epidemiologists, believe that the genocidal phase of the conflict had effectively come to an end by 2004. Julie Flint, writing in 2007, posited that "the worst violence in Darfur this year has not been caused by aerial bombardment, or by Janjaweed attacks against villages, as it was at the height of the conflict in 2003–4. Darfur in 2007 is not Rwanda. There is a multiplicity of conflicts in Darfur today—government vs. rebel, rebel vs. rebel, former rebel vs. rebel, Arab vs. Arab, Janjaweed vs. Arab, Central Reserve Police vs. Popular Defense Forces, armed bandits vs. anyone with anything to loot. . . . The most lethal battles this year have been caused by fights over land between Arab militias initially armed by Khartoum but now fighting each other. A distant second is attacks on rebel controlled villages by former rebels now aligned with the Sudan government."[170] In 2009 Andrew Natsios, formerly the head of the U.S. Agency for International Development, seconded, with grave concern, Flint's assessment from two years earlier: "Some policymakers continue to call Darfur an ongoing 'genocide,' but in fact, the conflict has descended into anarchy. . . . More civilians died in southern Sudan during the past six months than in Darfur over the past 15 months. Despite such facts and extensive U.N. Security Office reports showing that genocide is not an accurate description, President Obama continues to use that weighted term."[171]

This is not to say that no genocidal violence was committed after 2004. Genocidal destruction comes in many shapes and sizes. It is entirely plausible that all kinds of violence, genocidal and otherwise, were perpetrated in Darfur, and even concurrently, in the first decade of the twenty-first century. Interpreting violence there and elsewhere need not result in dichotomous classifications of genocide/not genocide. The case of Darfur is a prime example of an overdetermined conflict that exhibits phases of genocidal violence but whose origins are irrevocably intertwined with the multiple civil wars that pitted North and South against one another ever since the country's independence in 1956.[172] Not unlike the way Rwanda's civil war led to a cumulative radicalization of hardliners inside the incumbent regime in Kigali, Sudan's so-called Second Civil War (1983–2005) placed enormous pressure on Khartoum.

168. Jens Nielsen, Claudine Prudhon, and Xavier de Radigues, "Trends in Malnutrition and Mortality in Darfur, Sudan, between 2004 and 2008: A Meta-Analysis of Publicly Available Surveys," *International Journal of Epidemiology* 40 (2011): 972.

169. See, for example, Twelfth Prosecutor's Statement to the United Nations Security Council on the situation in Darfur, the Sudan, pursuant to UNSCR 1593 (2005), Office of the Prosecutor, International Criminal Court, December 9, 2010, para. 6.

170. Julie Flint, "Darfur: Stop! Confrontational Rhetoric," *Review of African Political Economy* 34, no. 113 (2007): 537.

171. Andrew S. Natsios, "Obama, Adrift on Sudan," *Washington Post*, June 23, 2009.

172. For the best available overview, see Douglas H. Johnson, *The Root Causes of Sudan's Civil Wars: Peace or Truce*, revised edition (London: James Currey, 2011).

The result, provoked in some respects by insurgents in Darfur's rebel organizations, was an amalgam of collective violence that is still in search of understanding.

A Guide to the Readings

This *Reader* proposes an alternative canon for the study of genocide. By including 150 very diverse selections, it demonstrates that we possess a considerable amount of knowledge about genocide that is worth digesting before presenting solutions for its prevention to the world. We do not tolerate beginners contributing to the prevention of cancer; why do we have lower standards when it comes to the prevention of genocide? Policy interventions without knowledge are a dangerous thing, no matter how morally sound in conviction or compassionate in intention. The readings assembled here form but a very small sample of writings culled from a number of literatures of direct relevance to the study of genocide. This collection does not constitute the only conceivable canon of genocide scholarship. Rather it demarcates the outer boundaries of the field of genocide studies. In order to comprehend the field and what it is capable of achieving intellectually, readers should see its diversity. This collection identifies a number of possible entry points to the field of genocide studies; other entry points exist as well. In the interest of space, a few dozen selections pertaining to the study of both civil war and international war, though indirectly important for rendering genocide more comprehensible, had to be omitted. It is hoped that a future and expanded edition of this *Reader* will give these readings their due.

To familiarize readers with this difficult social phenomenon, and in *all* of its dimensions, the anthology revolves around nine instantly recognizable themes that are central to the phenomenon's study:

> **Concepts:** What is genocide?
> **Causes:** Why does genocide happen?
> **Courses:** How does genocide unfold?
> **Coverage:** How is genocide reported?
> **Consequences:** What happens after genocide?
> **Courts:** Who puts genocide on trial?
> **Coping:** Can one come to terms with genocide?
> **Compensation:** Who makes amends for genocide?
> **Cures:** What can be done about genocide?

Taken together these themes represent the phenomenon of genocide in all its complexity, drawing attention not only to contending terms (Concepts) and explanations of genocidal campaigns (Causes) but also to frequently overlooked differences in the conduct and evolution of these campaigns (Courses) as well as to legal responses to the destruction of targeted groups in domestic and international fora (Courts). Moreover the suffering of individuals and communities (Coping) and the repercussions of large-scale social violence for countries and entire regions (Consequences) is a central concern, as is the ongoing debate over genocide forecasting and prevention (Cures). Of growing salience in debates about genocide are questions at the intersection of money and morals (Compensation): Should victims of genocide or their descendants be entitled to restitution or reparations? If so, under what conditions? Finally, the *Reader* also draws attention to modes of reporting on genocide in various social media (Coverage), for journalists play a significant role in inventing the sticky narratives— including the categories, personalities, metaphors, and tropes—that we often rely on for decades to speak of extremely violent episodes in history, regardless of whether the original depictions were accurate or entirely misleading.

Each of these themes is illuminated by poignant extracts culled from published writings, academic and otherwise, from geographically diverse sources.[173] They are an unorthodox selection of well-known and unknown, classic as well as contemporary writings on an inherently difficult subject. Read in conjunction, these pieces provide a systematic and comprehensive introduction to all dimensions of genocide. Despite important disagreements among many of the authors, each is deserving of serious intellectual engagement. For all of the selections, albeit in different ways and to varying degrees, have advanced the study and history of genocide.

173. A number of key writings are missing on account of various copyright restrictions, notably selections from Kuper, *Genocide*; Hannah Arendt, *Eichmann in Jerusalem: A Report on the Banality of Evil* (New York: Viking, 1964); Slavenka Drakulić, S.: *A Novel about the Balkans*, translated by Marko Ivić (New York: Viking, 2000); Esther Mujawayo, *SurVivantes* (La Tour d'Aigues: Éditions de l'Aube, 2004). Other leading contributions are missing due to space constraints, especially much valuable Holocaust scholarship. For an eminently useful and recent overview of the state of the art in the historiography of the Holocaust, see Stone, *Histories of the Holocaust*.

CHAPTER ONE

Concepts

What is genocide? The term itself has been the source of controversy since its inception. Much of the controversy surrounding the phenomenon of genocide revolves around its conceptual boundaries. The concepts range from Raphaël Lemkin's original definition of genocide, which fused the ancient Greek word *genos* (race, tribe) and the Latin *cide* (killing) to the notion of "genocidalism," as Aleksandar Jokic has termed the practice of employing Lemkin's neologism in instances where it does not apply. The most important reference document, for better or for worse, is still the Convention on the Prevention and Punishment of the Crime of Genocide, which the United Nations General Assembly adopted on December 9, 1948. Because interpretations of that Convention—which is an instrument, first and foremost, of international law—are frequently inaccurate, it is essential to come to terms with it. Perhaps the clearest exposition of the twin requirements of any genocide determination under international law, the *actus reus* (bad act) and *mens rea* (guilty mind), is available in William Schabas's magnum opus on the "crime of crimes." Also included here is the revised legal definition of genocide that appears in the 1998 Rome Statute of the International Criminal Court, which differs in some respects from the earlier international instrument. Among other things, "conspiracy to commit genocide" is not an international crime punishable under the Rome Statute.

Aside from a classic definition by a leading member of the first generation of genocide scholars, Helen Fein, who takes issue with the 1948 Genocide Convention, and a conceptual history by Eric Weitz of the terms *race* and *nation*, this chapter features the work of scholars who have advanced variations on the theme of genocide, mimicking Lemkin's penchant for coining memorable terms. First there is *politicide*, usefully conceptualized by political scientists Barbara Harff and Ted Robert Gurr, both of whom are renowned for their quantitative analyses of international conflict. R. J. Rummel introduced the notion of *democide* because he felt the "killing component" of existing genocide definitions were too limiting for making sense of the real world. Mary Anne Warren, a scholar of gender relations rather than mass murder, came up with the arresting *gendercide* in order to draw attention to the suffering of men and women when they are targeted on the basis of their sex. In a similar vein, Israel Charny refined the original term; he developed the concept of "genocidal massacre" in order to capture in words instances of collective violence that, in his eyes, do not rise to the level of full-fledged genocide on account of their modest scale. More recently Christian Gerlach suggested that we speak of "extremely violent societies" in order to avoid getting bogged down in debates about the boundaries of the noun *genocide*. Nancy Scheper-Hughes coined the notion of the *genocidal continuum* to achieve a similar result.

Then there are genocides with adjectives: *cultural genocide* and *colonial genocide*. Although neither of the authors featured, David Nersessian and David Maybury-Lewis, was responsible for coining these concepts, their pieces illuminate nicely the terms' purposes, for in all instances the terms bespeak a deep dissatisfaction with conventional concepts of genocide, legal or otherwise. The idea of cultural genocide, not recognized under international law and thus contrary to the 1948 Genocide Convention, puts a premium on the violent effects of long-term and nonlethal destruction. The invention of the terms *classical genocide* and *colonial genocide* came in response to the fact that up until very recently, the study of genocide centered primarily on the Holocaust. By clarifying the term *genocide* with adjectives, members of the second generation of genocide scholars highlighted their belief that genocides had already occurred *before* the Holocaust. By so doing they responded with a resounding "No" to the much-debated question of whether or not the Holocaust was a unique event in the history of mankind. Yehuda Bauer reconsiders this question and contemplates the meaning of uniqueness. Opposed to the Holocaust-centered orientation of many early genocide studies, the sociologist Martin Shaw radically reconceptualized genocide as a form of war and a method of politics far more common than ordinarily thought.

Finally, there are the practical implications of contending definitions. David Scheffer, who had ample occasion to contemplate the matter while serving in the U.S. administration of President Bill Clinton, recently concluded that the term *genocide* has done more harm than good. He therefore proposed a replacement, the less memorable concept of *atrocity crimes*, which he elaborates here. Mahmood Mamdani too has found fault with the "G word." In his essay on the Darfur crisis, he is outraged not only by a "pornography of violence" in recent reporting on Sudan but also by the politics of naming and its debilitating effects.

These readings demonstrate that it is far from obvious what exactly we mean when we speak of genocide and that reasonable men and women can disagree about the language that best describes this darkest of human phenomena.

1 • *Genos* and *Cide* (Raphaël Lemkin)

When Nazi Germany invaded Poland in 1939, Raphaël Lemkin (1900–1959), a Polish lawyer of Jewish faith, found refuge in the United States. In his 1944 book Axis Rule in Occupied Europe, *he coined the term genocide, giving a memorable name to the vast destruction that had culminated in the Holocaust and in which some forty members of his family, including his parents, were killed. Committed to uprooting this scourge after World War II, Lemkin successfully lobbied for the creation of an international convention against genocide at the United Nations.*

New conceptions require new terms. By "genocide" we mean the destruction of a nation or of an ethnic group. This new word, coined by the author to denote an old practice in its

SOURCE: Raphaël Lemkin, *Axis Rule in Occupied Europe: Laws of Occupation, Analysis of Government, Proposals for Redress* (Washington, D.C.: Carnegie Endowment for International Peace, 1944), 79–81, 82, 83, 84, 85, 86, 87, 88–90. Reproduced with permission of the publisher.

modern development, is made from the ancient Greek word *genos* (race, tribe) and the Latin *cide* (killing), thus corresponding in its formation to such words as tyrannicide, homicide, infanticide, etc.

Generally speaking, genocide does not necessarily mean the immediate destruction of a nation, except when accomplished by mass killings of all members of a nation. It is intended rather to signify a coordinated plan of different actions aiming at the destruction of essential foundations of the life of national groups, with the aim of annihilating the groups themselves. The objectives of such a plan would be disintegration of the political and social institutions, of culture, language, national feelings, religion, and the economic existence of national groups, and the destruction of the personal security, liberty, health, dignity, and even the lives of the individuals belonging to such groups. Genocide is directed against the national group as an entity, and the actions involved are directed against individuals, not in their individual capacity, but as members of the national group.

The following illustrations will suffice. The confiscation of property of nationals of an occupied area on the ground that they have left the country may be considered simply as deprivation of their individual property rights. However, if the confiscations are ordered against individuals solely because they are Poles, Jews, or Czechs, then the same confiscations tend in effect to weaken the national entities of which those persons are members.

Genocide has two phases: one, destruction of the national pattern of the oppressed group; the other, the imposition of the national pattern of the oppressor. This imposition, in turn, may be made upon the oppressed population which is allowed to remain, or upon territory alone, after removal of the population and the colonization of the area by the oppressor's own nationals. Denationalization was the word used in the past to describe the destruction of a national pattern. The author believes, however, that this word is inadequate because (1) it does not connote the destruction of the biological structure; (2) in connoting the destruction of one national pattern, it does not connote the imposition of the national pattern of the oppressor; and (3) denationalization is used by some authors to mean only deprivation of citizenship. Many authors, instead of using a generic term, use currently terms connoting only some functional aspect of the main generic notion of genocide. Thus, the terms "Germanization," "Magyarization," "Italianization," for example, are used to connote the imposition by one stronger nation (Germany, Hungary, Italy) of its national pattern upon a national group controlled by it. The author believes that these terms are also inadequate because they do not convey the common elements of one generic notion and they treat mainly the cultural, economic, and social aspects of genocide, leaving out the biological aspect, such as causing the physical decline and even destruction of the population involved. . . .

Genocide is the antithesis of the Rousseau-Portalis Doctrine, which may be regarded as implicit in the Hague Regulations. This doctrine holds that war is directed against sovereigns and armies, not against subjects and civilians. In its modern application in civilized society, the doctrine means that war is conducted against states and armed forces and not against populations. It required a long period of evolution in civilized society to mark the way from wars of extermination, which occurred in ancient times and in the Middle Ages, to the conception of wars as being essentially limited to activities against armies and states. In the present war, however, genocide is widely practiced by the German occupant. Germany could not accept the Rousseau-Portalis Doctrine: first, because Germany is waging a total war; and secondly, because, according to the doctrine of National Socialism, the nation, not the state, is the predominant factor. In this German conception the nation provides the biological element for the state. Consequently, in enforcing the New Order, the Germans prepared, waged, and continued a war not merely against states and their armies but against peoples. . . . As classical wars of extermination in which nations and groups of the population were completely or almost destroyed, the following may be cited: the destruction of Carthage in 146 BC; the destruction of Jerusalem by Titus in 72 AD; the religious wars of Islam and the Crusades; the massacres of the Albigenses and the Waldenses; and the siege of Magdeburg in the Thirty Years' War. . . .

The techniques of genocide, which the German occupant has developed in the various occupied countries, represent a concentrated and coordinated attack upon all elements of nationhood. Accordingly, genocide is being carried out in the following fields.

Political

In the incorporated areas, such as western Poland, Eupen, Malmédy and Moresnet, Luxemberg, and Alsace-Lorraine, local institutions of self-government were destroyed and a German pattern of administration imposed. Every reminder of former national character was obliterated. . . . In order to further disrupt national unity, Nazi party organizations were established, such as the Nasjonal Samling Party in Norway and the Mussert Party in the Netherlands, and their members from the local population were given political privileges. Other political parties were dissolved. These Nazi parties were also given special protection by the courts. . . .

Social

The destruction of the national pattern in the social field has been accomplished in part by the abolition of local law and local courts and the imposition of German law and courts, and also by Germanization of the judicial language of the bar. The social structure of a nation being vital to its national development, the occupant also endeavors to bring about such changes as may weaken the national spiritual resources. The focal point of this attack has been the intelligentsia, because this group largely provides national leadership and organizes resistance to Nazification. . . .

Cultural

In the incorporated areas the local population is forbidden to use its own language in schools and in printing. . . . In Lorraine, general compulsory education to assure the upbringing of youth in the spirit of National Socialism begins at the age of six. It continues for eight years, or to the completion of the grammar school (Volksschule), and then for three more years, or to the completion of a vocational school. . . . Not only have national creative activities in the cultural and artistic field been rendered impossible by regimentation, but the population has also been deprived of inspiration from the existing cultural and artistic values. Thus, especially in Poland, were national monuments destroyed and libraries, archives, museums, and galleries of art carried away. . . .

Economic

The destruction of the foundations of the economic existence of a national group necessarily brings about a crippling of its development, even a retrogression. The lowering of the standard of living creates difficulties in fulfilling cultural-spiritual requirements. Furthermore, a daily fight literally for bread and for physical survival may handicap thinking in both general and national terms. It was the purpose of the occupant to create such conditions as these among the peoples of the occupied countries, especially those peoples embraced in the first plans of genocide elaborated by him—the Poles, Slovenes, and the Jews. The Jews were immediately deprived of the elemental means of existence. As to the Poles in incorporated Poland, the purpose of the occupant was to shift the economic resources from the Polish national group to the German national group. Thus the Polish national group had to be impoverished and the German enriched. This was achieved primarily by confiscation of Polish property under the authority of the Reich Commissioner for the Strengthening of Germanism. But the process was likewise furthered by the policy of regimenting trade and handicrafts, since licenses for such activities were issued to Germans, and only exceptionally to Poles. . . .

Biological

In the occupied countries of "people of non-related blood," a policy of depopulation is pursued. Foremost among the methods employed for this purpose is the adoption of measures calculated to decrease the birthrate of the national groups of non-related blood, while at the same time steps are taken to encourage the birthrate of the *Volksdeutsche* living in these countries. Thus in incorporated Poland marriages between Poles are forbidden without the special permission of the Governor (*Reichsstatthalter*) of the district; and the latter, as a matter of principle, does not permit marriages between Poles. The birthrate of the undesired group is being further decreased as a result of the separation of males from females by deporting them for forced labor elsewhere. Moreover, the undernourishment of the parents, because of discrimination in rationing, brings about not only a lowering of the birthrate, but a lowering of the survival capacity of children born of underfed parents. . . .

Physical

The physical debilitation and even annihilation of national groups in occupied countries is carried out mainly in the following ways:

1. *Racial Discrimination in Feeding.* Rationing of food is organized according to racial principles throughout the occupied countries. . . . The following shows the difference in the percentage of meat rations received by the Germans and the population of the occupied countries: Germans, 100 percent; Czechs, 86 percent; Dutch, 71 percent; Poles (Incorporated Poland), 71 percent; Lithuanians, 57 percent; French, 51 percent; Belgians, 40 percent; Serbs, 36 percent; Poles (General Government), 36 percent; Slovenes, 29 percent; Jews, 0 percent. The percentage of pre-war food received under present rations (in calories per consumer unit) is the following: Germans, 93 percent; Czechs, 83 percent; Poles (Incorporated Poland), 78 percent; Dutch, 70 percent; Belgians, 66 percent; Poles (General Government), 66

percent; Norwegians, 54 percent; Jews, 20 percent. . . . The result of racial feeding is a decline in health of the nations involved and an increase in the deathrate. . . .

2. *Endangering of Health*. The undesired national groups, particularly in Poland, are deprived of elemental necessities for preserving health and life. This layer method consists, for example, of requisitioning warm clothing and blankets in the winter and withholding of firewood and medicine. . . . Moreover, the Jews in the [Warsaw] ghetto are crowded together under conditions of housing inimical to health, and in being denied the use of public parks they are even deprived of the right to fresh air. . . . The transfer, in unheated cattle trucks and freight cars, of hundreds of thousands of Poles from Incorporated Poland to the Government General, which took place in the midst of a severe winter, resulted in a decimation of the expelled Poles.

3. *Mass Killings*. The technique of mass killings is employed mainly against Poles, Russians, and Jews, as well as against leading personalities from among the non-collaborationist groups in all the occupied countries. In Poland, Bohemia-Moravia, and Slovenia, the intellectuals are being "liquidated" because they have always been considered as the main bearers of national ideals and at the time of occupation they were especially suspected of being the organizers of resistance. The Jews for the most part are liquidated within the ghettos, or in special trains in which they are transported to a so-called "unknown" destination. The number of Jews who have been killed by organized murder in all the occupied countries, according to the Institute of Jewish Affairs of the American Jewish Congress in New York, amounts to 1,702,500.

Religious

In Luxemburg, where the population is predominantly Catholic and religion plays an important role in national life, especially in the field of education, the occupant has tried to disrupt these national and religious influences. Children over fourteen years of age were permitted by legislation to renounce their religious affiliations, for the occupant was eager to enroll such children exclusively in pro-Nazi youth organizations. . . . Likewise in Poland, through the systematic pillage and destruction of church property and persecution of the clergy, the German occupying authorities have sought to destroy the religious leadership of the Polish nation.

Moral

In order to weaken the spiritual resistance of the national group, the occupant attempts to create an atmosphere of moral debasement within its group. According to this plan, the mental energy of the group should be concentrated upon base instincts and should be diverted from moral and national thinking. It is important for the realization of such a plan that the desire for cheap individual pleasure be substituted for the desire for collective feelings and ideals based upon a higher morality. Therefore, the occupant made an effort in Poland to impose upon the Poles pornographic publications and movies. The consumption of alcohol was encouraged. . . .

The above-described techniques of genocide represent an elaborate, almost scientific, system developed to an extent never before achieved by any nation.

2 • The Legal Definition (United Nations Convention on the Prevention and Punishment of the Crime of Genocide)

The original definition of genocide was adopted by the United Nations General Assembly in 1948 after two years of drafting and redrafting inside the UN bureaucracy. The impetus behind the legalization of the term had come from Cuba, Panama, and India. In late 1946 these countries introduced a draft resolution in the first meeting of the UN General Assembly that called for the recognition of a crime ("peacetime genocide") that developing countries in particular felt had been given short shrift at the International Military Tribunal at Nuremberg, where the Allies had just sat in judgment over Nazi atrocities.

The Genocide Convention put on a legal footing some of Raphaël Lemkin's ideas and ignored others, notably what has become known as cultural genocide. Frequently misunderstood, this first legal definition of genocide fueled discontent in theory and practice alike. Articles II and III of the Convention are the key provisions. The first paragraph of Article II, known as the chapeau, sets out the mens rea, or mental element, of genocide. The remaining paragraphs, labeled (a) to (e), enumerate the five acts of genocide punishable under the Convention. This is the physical element, or actus reus, of genocide. Article III in the main sets out different modes of participation (i.e., ways in which individuals can perpetrate genocide, such as conspiracy and complicity) and describes forms of liability for individuals other than the principal perpetrators (such as accomplices).

Approved and proposed for signature and ratification or accession by
General Assembly resolution 260 A (III) of 9 December 1948
Entry into force 12 January 1951, in accordance with article XIII

The Contracting Parties, Having considered the declaration made by the General Assembly of the United Nations in its resolution 96 (I) dated 11 December 1946 that genocide is a crime under international law, contrary to the spirit and aims of the United Nations and condemned by the civilized world,

Recognizing that at all periods of history genocide has inflicted great losses on humanity, and

Being convinced that, in order to liberate mankind from such an odious scourge, international co-operation is required,

Hereby agree as hereinafter provided:

ARTICLE I

The Contracting Parties confirm that genocide, whether committed in time of peace or in time of war, is a crime under international law which they undertake to prevent and to punish.

ARTICLE II

In the present Convention, genocide means any of the following acts committed with the intent to destroy, in whole or in part, a national, ethnical, racial or religious group, as such:

SOURCE: Convention on the Prevention and Punishment of the Crime of Genocide, adopted by Resolution 260 (III) A of the United Nations General Assembly, December 9, 1948.

(a) Killing members of the group;
(b) Causing serious bodily or mental harm to members of the group;
(c) Deliberately inflicting on the group conditions of life calculated to bring about its physical destruction in whole or in part;
(d) Imposing measures intended to prevent births within the group;
(e) Forcibly transferring children of the group to another group.

actus reus "physical element"

ARTICLE III

The following acts shall be punishable:

(a) Genocide;
(b) Conspiracy to commit genocide;
(c) Direct and public incitement to commit genocide;
(d) Attempt to commit genocide;
(e) Complicity in genocide. *- didn't like but didn't do anything to stop it*

modes of particip- ation

ARTICLE IV

Persons committing genocide or any of the other acts enumerated in article III shall be punished, whether they are constitutionally responsible rulers, public officials or private individuals.

ARTICLE V

The Contracting Parties undertake to enact, in accordance with their respective Constitutions, the necessary legislation to give effect to the provisions of the present Convention, and, in particular to provide effective penalties for persons guilty of genocide or any of the other acts enumerated in article III.

ARTICLE VI

Persons charged with genocide or any of the other acts enumerated in article III shall be tried by a competent tribunal of the State in the territory of which the act was committed, or by such international penal tribunal as may have jurisdiction with respect to those Contracting Parties which shall have accepted its jurisdiction.

ARTICLE VII

Genocide and the other acts enumerated in article III shall not be considered as political crimes for the purpose of extradition.

What does that mean?

The Contracting Parties pledge themselves in such cases to grant extradition in accordance with their laws and treaties in force.

ARTICLE VIII

Any Contracting Party may call upon the competent organs of the United Nations to take such action under the Charter of the United Nations as they consider appropriate for the prevention and suppression of acts of genocide or any of the other acts enumerated in article III.

Thankful!

ARTICLE IX

Disputes between the Contracting Parties relating to the interpretation, application or fulfillment of the present Convention, including those relating to the responsibility of a State for genocide or for any of the other acts enumerated in article III, shall be submitted to the International Court of Justice at the request of any of the parties to the dispute.

ARTICLE X

The present Convention, of which the Chinese, English, French, Russian and Spanish texts are equally authentic, shall bear the date of 9 December 1948.

ARTICLE XI

The present Convention shall be open until 31 December 1949 for signature on behalf of any Member of the United Nations and of any non-member State to which an invitation to sign has been addressed by the General Assembly.

The present Convention shall be ratified, and the instruments of ratification shall be deposited with the Secretary-General of the United Nations.

After 1 January 1950, the present Convention may be acceded to on behalf of any Member of the United Nations and of any non-member State which has received an invitation as aforesaid.

Instruments of accession shall be deposited with the Secretary-General of the United Nations.

ARTICLE XII

Any Contracting Party may at any time, by notification addressed to the Secretary-General of the United Nations, extend the application of the present Convention to all or any of the territories for the conduct of whose foreign relations that Contracting Party is responsible.

ARTICLE XIII

On the day when the first twenty instruments of ratification or accession have been deposited, the Secretary-General shall draw up a procès-verbal and transmit a copy thereof to each Member of the United Nations and to each of the non-member States contemplated in article XI.

The present Convention shall come into force on the ninetieth day following the date of deposit of the twentieth instrument of ratification or accession.

Any ratification or accession effected subsequent to the latter date shall become effective on the ninetieth day following the deposit of the instrument of ratification or accession.

ARTICLE XIV

The present Convention shall remain in effect for a period of ten years as from the date of its coming into force.

It shall thereafter remain in force for successive periods of five years for such Contracting Parties as have not denounced it at least six months before the expiration of the current period.

Denunciation shall be effected by a written notification addressed to the Secretary-General of the United Nations.

ARTICLE XV

If, as a result of denunciations, the number of Parties to the present Convention should become less than sixteen, the Convention shall cease to be in force as from the date on which the last of these denunciations shall become effective.

ARTICLE XVI

A request for the revision of the present Convention may be made at any time by any Contracting Party by means of a notification in writing addressed to the Secretary-General.

The General Assembly shall decide upon the steps, if any, to be taken in respect of such request.

ARTICLE XVII

The Secretary-General of the United Nations shall notify all Members of the United Nations and the non-member States contemplated in article XI of the following:

(a) Signatures, ratifications and accessions received in accordance with article XI;
(b) Notifications received in accordance with article XII;
(c) The date upon which the present Convention comes into force in accordance with article XIII;
(d) Denunciations received in accordance with article XIV;
(e) The abrogation of the Convention in accordance with article XV;
(f) Notifications received in accordance with article XVI.

ARTICLE XVIII

The original of the present Convention shall be deposited in the archives of the United Nations.

A certified copy of the Convention shall be transmitted to each Member of the United Nations and to each of the non-member States contemplated in article XI.

ARTICLE XIX

The present Convention shall be registered by the Secretary-General of the United Nations on the date of its coming into force.

3 • *Actus Reus* and *Mens Rea* of Genocide (William A. Schabas)

The crime of genocide comprises both a physical element (actus reus) *and a mental element* (mens rea). *This important requirement is often overlooked by nonlawyers, prompting misunderstanding of the promise—and limits—of international law. William Schabas's seminal book* Genocide in International Law *(2000) provides a clear discussion of the nature of this requirement. It demonstrates that, legally speaking, for a case of genocide to exist, a defendant must be shown to have perpetrated a punishable genocidal act with a guilty mind. Now available in its second edition, the book has influenced both scholars and law practitioners.*

The "elements of the offense" [of genocide] are fundamental because they set out the ground rules of the trial, determining what must be proven by a prosecution for a case to succeed. If

SOURCE: William A. Schabas, *Genocide in International Law: The Crime of Crimes* (Cambridge: Cambridge University Press, 2000), 172, 177, 256–57, 260, 264–65. Reprinted with permission of the publisher.

the prosecution establishes all the elements of the offense beyond a reasonable doubt . . . of the trier of fact, then a conviction may lie. If the defense casts reasonable doubt on even one "element of the offense," then the accused is entitled to acquittal.

Criminal law analysis of an offense proceeds from a basic distinction between the material elements (the *actus reus*) and the mental or moral element (the *mens rea*). The prosecution must prove specific material facts, but must also establish the accused's criminal intent or "guilty mind": *actus non facit reum nisi mens sit rea*. The definition of genocide in the 1948 Convention invites this analysis, because it rather neatly separates the two elements. The initial phrase or *chapeau* of article II addresses the *mens rea* of the crime of genocide, that is, the "intent to destroy, in whole or in part, a national, ethnical, racial or religious group, as such." The five subparagraphs of article II list the criminal acts or *actus reus*. . . .

Criminal acts, depending upon the definition of the crime, may require proof not only of the act itself, but also of a result. Put differently, the material element includes a result. Three of the five acts defined in article II of the Convention require proof of a result: killing members of the group; causing serious bodily or mental harm to members of the group; forcibly transferring children of the group to another group. Two of the acts do not demand such proof, but require a further specific intent: deliberately inflicting on the group conditions of life calculated to bring about its physical destruction in whole or in part; or imposing measures intended to prevent births within the group. In the three cases where the outcome is an element of the offense, the accused may still be subject to prosecution for attempting to commit the crime even if no result can be proven. Proof of a crime of result also requires evidence that the act itself is a "substantial cause" of the outcome. The *actus reus* of an offense may be either an act of commission or an act of omission. . . .

It is a commonplace to state genocide is a crime requiring "intent." . . . Even without the terms "with intent" in the definition of genocide, it is inconceivable that an infraction of such magnitude could be committed unintentionally. The requirement of intent is reaffirmed in article 30 of the Rome Statute [of the International Criminal Court]. . . . The definition of *mens rea* in the Statute of the International Criminal Court states that a person has intent where, in relation to conduct, that person means to engage in the conduct: in relation to a consequence, that person means to cause that consequence or is aware that it will occur in the ordinary course of events. But the words "with intent" that appear in the *chapeau* of article II of the Genocide Convention do more than simply reiterate that genocide is a crime of intent. Article II of the Genocide Convention introduces a precise description of the intent, namely "to destroy, in whole or in part, a national ethnical, racial or religious groups, as such." The reference to "intent" in the text indicates that the prosecution must go beyond establishing that the offender meant to engage in the conduct, or meant to cause the consequence.

The offender must also be proven to have a "specific intent" (*dolus specialis*). Where the specified intent is not established, the act remains punishable, but not as genocide. It may be classified as a crime against humanity or it may be simply a crime under ordinary criminal law. . . . The degree of intent required by article II of the Genocide Convention can be described as a "specific" intent or "special" intent. This common law concept corresponds to the *dol spécial* or *dolus specialis* of Romano-Germanic systems. . . . A specific intent offense requires performance of the *actus reus* but in association with an intent or purpose that goes beyond the mere performance of the act. Assault with intent to maim or wound is an example drawn from ordinary criminal law. . . .

In practice, proof of intent is rarely a formal part of the prosecution's case. . . . Rather, the intent is a logical deduction that flows from evidence of the material acts. Criminal law presumes that an individual intends the consequences of his or her acts, in effect deducing the existence of the *mens rea* from proof of the physical act itself. . . . The crime [of genocide] must be committed with intent to destroy in whole or in part, a protected group, as such. If the accused accompanied or preceded the act with some sort of genocidal declaration or speech, its content may assist in establishing the special intent. Otherwise, the prosecution will rely on the context of the crimes, its massive scale, and elements of its perpetration that suggest hatred of the group and a desire for its destruction.

4 • The Legal Definition Revised (Rome Statute of the International Criminal Court and Elements of Crimes)

The 1998 Rome Statute of the International Criminal Court and a subsequently adopted document entitled "Elements of Crimes" revised the original legal definition of genocide introduced by the 1948 UN Genocide Convention. Although the Rome Statute has not drastically altered the meaning of the elements of the offense, the Genocide Convention has not been replicated in full in the international treaty adopted by the United Nations Diplomatic Conference of Plenipotentiaries on the Establishment of an International Criminal Court in Rome on July 17, 1998. As a result, differences are discernible, most important, the abolition of conspiracy to commit genocide and additional "other acts" of genocide enumerated in Article III of the Genocide Convention.

Also noteworthy is the fact that the International Criminal Court is guided by the "Elements of Crimes," a unique document adopted by the Preparatory Commission for the International Criminal Court in 2000, that is meant to aid the prosecutors, defense attorneys, and judges of the permanent international court in the interpretation and application of international crimes, including genocide. For example, if a lawyer wants to indict a defendant who stands accused of genocide by killing members of a religious group, she will find in the "Elements of Crimes" an itemized list of all of the elements of that particular offense that must be proven before the defendant can be convicted under the Rome Statute.

Article 6: Rome Statute of the International Criminal Court

For the purpose of this Statute, "genocide" means any of the following acts committed with intent to destroy, in whole or in part, a national, ethnical, racial or religious group, as such:

SOURCE: Rome Statute of the International Criminal Court, adopted by the United Nations Diplomatic Conference of Plenipotentiaries on the Establishment of an International Criminal Court, July 17, 1998; Elements of Crimes, adopted by the Preparatory Commission for the International Criminal Court (Prep-Comm), June 30, 2000.

(a) Killing members of the group;
(b) Causing serious bodily harm to members of the group;
(c) Deliberately inflicting on the group conditions of life calculated to bring about its
     physical destruction in whole or in part;
(d) Imposing measures intended to prevent birth within the group;
(e) Forcibly transferring children of the group to another group.

actus reus

Article 6: Elements of Crimes

With respect to the last element listed for each crime:

—The term "in the context of" would include the initial acts in an emerging pattern;
—The term "manifest" is an objective qualification;
—Notwithstanding the normal requirement for a mental element provided for in Article 30 [of the Rome Statute of the International Criminal Court, which deals with
  the "mental element" of international crimes within the jurisdiction of the ICC], and
  recognizing that knowledge of the circumstances will usually be addressed in proving
  genocidal intent, the appropriate requirement, if any, for a mental element regarding
  this circumstance will need to be decided by the Court on a case-by-case basis.

ARTICLE 6 (A): GENOCIDE BY KILLING

Elements

Manifest Pattern

1. The perpetrator killed[1] one or more persons.
2. Such person or persons belonged to a particular national, ethnical, racial or religious
    group.
3. The perpetrator intended to destroy, in whole or in part, that national, ethnical, racial
    or religious group, as such.
4. The conduct took place in the context of a manifest pattern of similar conduct di-
    rected against that group or was conduct that could itself effect such destruction.

ARTICLE 6 (B): GENOCIDE BY CAUSING
SERIOUS BODILY OR MENTAL HARM

Elements

1. The perpetrator caused serious bodily or mental harm to one or more persons.[2] ✳
2. Such person or persons belonged to a particular national, ethnical, racial or religious
    group.
3. The perpetrator intended to destroy, in whole or in part, that national, ethnical, racial
    or religious group, as such.
4. The conduct took place in the context of a manifest pattern of similar conduct di-
    rected against that group or was conduct that could itself effect such destruction.

---

1. The term "killed" is interchangeable with the term "caused death."
2. This conduct may include, but is not necessarily restricted to, acts of torture, rape, sexual violence or inhuman or degrading treatment.

ARTICLE 6 (C): GENOCIDE BY DELIBERATELY INFLICTING CONDITIONS OF LIFE CALCULATED TO BRING ABOUT PHYSICAL DESTRUCTION

Elements

1. The perpetrator inflicted certain conditions of life upon one or more persons.
2. Such person or persons belonged to a particular national, ethnical, racial or religious group.
3. The perpetrator intended to destroy, in whole or in part, that national, ethnical, racial or religious group, as such.
4. The conditions of life were calculated to bring about the physical destruction of that group, in whole or in part.[3]
5. The conduct took place in the context of a manifest pattern of similar conduct directed against that group or was conduct that could itself effect such destruction.

ARTICLE 6 (D): GENOCIDE BY IMPOSING MEASURES INTENDED TO PREVENT BIRTHS

Elements

1. The perpetrator imposed certain measures upon one or more persons.
2. Such person or persons belonged to a particular national, ethnical, racial or religious group.
3. The perpetrator intended to destroy, in whole or in part, that national, ethnical, racial or religious group, as such.
4. The measures imposed were intended to prevent births within that group.
5. The conduct took place in the context of a manifest pattern of similar conduct directed against that group or was conduct that could itself effect such destruction.

ARTICLE 6 (E): GENOCIDE BY FORCIBLY TRANSFERRING CHILDREN

Elements

1. The perpetrator forcibly transferred one or more persons.[4]
2. Such person or persons belonged to a particular national, ethnical, racial or religious group.
3. The perpetrator intended to destroy, in whole or in part, that national, ethnical, racial or religious group, as such.
4. The transfer was from that group to another group.
5. The person or persons were under the age of 18 years.
6. The perpetrator knew, or should have known, that the person or persons were under the age of 18 years.
7. The conduct took place in the context of a manifest pattern of similar conduct directed against that group or was conduct that could itself effect such destruction.

3. The term "conditions of life" may include, but is not necessarily restricted to, deliberate deprivation of resources indispensable for survival, such as food or medical services, or systematic expulsion from homes.
4. The term "forcibly" is not restricted to physical force, but may include threat of force or coercion, such as that caused by fear of violence, duress, detention, psychological oppression or abuse of power, against such person or persons or another person, or by taking advantage of a coercive environment.

5 • Genocides as Utopias of Race and Nation (Eric D. Weitz)

Virtually all genocidal campaigns in history have been founded on the ideologies of race and nation, albeit in different ways and to varying degrees. Eric Weitz, dean of humanities at City College in New York, offers one of the most eloquent and accessible accounts of these utopias. Drawn from his book A Century of Genocide *(2003), one of the first deeply researched, truly comparative accounts on the topic, this selection provides conceptual buildings blocks that are indispensable for engaging in a meaningful way with genocide as a theoretical, an empirical, and a legal phenomenon. By carefully tracing the emergence of contending categories of difference across five centuries, Weitz demonstrates why the pursuit of utopias of race and nation became so prevalent in the twentieth century. In passing he also sheds light on the difficult concept of ethnicity, another unavoidable term in the study of genocide.*

Race and nation represent ways of classifying difference. The two categories have never been hermetically sealed off from one another; rather, the lines between them are fluid and permeable. Nonetheless, for the sake of analytical clarity, it is important to disentangle them and to define the characteristics of each form of identity. And they have to be defined in relation to a still more general term, "ethnicity."

The members of an ethnic group typically share a sense of commonality based on a myth of common origins (descent from Abraham in the case of Israelites, from Hellen in later Greek accounts), a common language, and common customs. Ethnicity is the most open and permeable form of identity. Whatever the myth of common origins, outsiders are usually able to assimilate into the ethnic group by marriage and acculturation. Ethnic groups develop into nations when they become politicized and strive to create, or have created for them, a political order—the nation-state—whose institutions are seen to conform in some way to their ethnic identity, and whose boundaries are, ideally, contiguous with the group's territoriality. . . .

Race is the hardest and most exclusive form of identity. Race is present when a defined population group is seen to have particular characteristics that are indelible, immutable, and transgenerational. Race is fate; there is no escape from the characteristics that are said to be carried by every single member of the group, bar none. Races can "degenerate" if they become "defiled"; they can go on to still greater accomplishments if they become "pure." But the essential characteristics of each race are seen as immutable, and they are borne "in the blood" by every individual member of that race. While racial distinctions have most often been based on phenotype, race is not essentially about skin color but about the assignment of indelible traits to particular groups. Hence ethnic groups, nationalities, and even social classes can be "racialized" in particular historical moments and places.

Unlike ethnicity, race always entails a hierarchical construction of difference. Racial movements and states understand their creation and defense of a racial order as the great historical task of making the political and social world conform to the reality of nature, with its fixed system of domination and subordination. While ethnicity is often self-defined—and

SOURCE: Eric D. Weitz, *A Century of Genocide: Utopias of Race and Nation* (Princeton, N.J.: Princeton University Press, 2003), 21, 22, 23, 24, 25, 27, 28, 29, 31, 32, 49, 50, 51. Reprinted with permission of the publisher.

this was Max Weber's classic, subjectivist definition of an ethnic group—racial categorizations are most often assigned to a group by an outside power, usually a state, though over time, the group may then develop its own racial consciousness. Ethnicity or nationality by no means always or necessarily takes on racialized forms, but the possibilities are certainly present, all too easily present when modern states seek to limit the pool of citizens and strive actively to shape the very composition of society. Moreover, while biology provided the pseudo-scientific underpinnings for race thinking in its heyday, roughly 1850 to 1945, race can also have a cultural basis. As the French theorist Étienne Balibar writes: "Biological or genetic naturalism is not the only means of naturalizing human behavior and social affinities. . . . *Culture can also function like a nature,* and it can in particular function as a way of locking individuals and groups a priori into a genealogy, into a determination that is immutable and intangible in origin. . . . [This perspective] *naturalizes not racial belonging but racial conduct.*"

While ethnicity has existed since time immemorial, race and nation emerged together historically in the Western world from around 1700 onward. . . . Race was made as European thinkers pondered the meaning of slavery and the world of great diversity. It was also made in colonial societies, in the interactions "on the ground" of Europeans, Native Americans, and Africans. The many sexual relations and even marriages across these lines and the "mulatto" progeny that resulted confounded clear lines of difference and became the flashpoints for establishing far more rigid boundaries designed carefully to demarcate groups from one another. By attempting to place people in fixed categories, colonial legislation and social practices contributed decisively to the making of race. . . . Older environmental and cultural understandings of difference—the kind of understanding that ancient Greeks and Hebrews had articulated—were overthrown with this newer conception that difference was rooted in the body itself and constituted a definable essence, for good or bad. This fatal move had to do with the colonists' perceived need to articulate their differences from—and superiority to—the Native Americans they conquered and the Africans they enslaved. . . . In close connection with the creation of racial slavery, Europeans after 1500 strove to make sense of a world they now knew was much larger and much more variegated than they have ever imagined. . . . The effort to understand this new, exciting, and troubling world unfolded in both political and scientific realms. . . .

But a fully developed theory of race required a new science of humankind. This is what anthropology, an Enlightenment invention, provided. . . . The key figure in the emergence of the new discipline of anthropology was Johann Friedrich Blumenbach (1752–1840), whose *On the Natural Variety of Mankind* insisted on both the unity of the human species and the diversity within it, a diversity that could be accounted for only through rigorous scientific observation. . . . For the next two hundred years, just about down to the present day, scientists would dispute the number and types, but not the effort to define and categorize races. Blumenbach's own collection of skeletons, the raw material of his scientific researches, would be rivaled only by the anthropologists of the nineteenth century who began to collect skulls and measure the cranium as a way of determining race-linked intelligence.

At the same time that Enlightenment thinkers pondered the diverse origins of humankind and located difference in the body, another strain of Enlightenment thought radically postulated equality among men. This is, of course, the Enlightenment that figures so prominently in the language of the American Declaration of Independence and the French Declaration of the Rights of Man and Citizen. By creating republics, the American and French revolutionaries made the nation the critical locus of political rights. In so doing, they dramatically altered the received understanding of "nation." . . . The American and French revolutionaries fused the concepts of nation and people. . . . Most important for the topic [of genocide], both revolutions articulated the nation not only in terms of gendered citizenship, but also as an ethnic and racial community. . . . This "slippage" from the nation as a political community to the nation as a racial community became more prevalent when culture, not political rights, was made the defining element in the formation of the nation—an intellectual move accomplished largely by German theorists. Certainly, it is easy to understand why intellectuals in central Europe, devoid of a nation-state, claimed to find the nation in language, culture, and race, while the French, who had something akin to a single state going back centuries, could formulate a political concept of the nation.

Johann Gottlieb Fichte and Johann Gottfried Herder, two of the key figures in the formulation of a cultural concept of the nation, pursued problems set out by Immanuel Kant but focused more clearly on the relation of the individual to the collective. As an individual "grew into" freedom (in a Kantian sense), moved from the childhood of ignorance and bondage to the adulthood of self-knowledge and freedom, so the political form of the nation-state grew from—and remained organically linked to—the original manifestations of being in language and culture. . . . By the turn into the nineteenth century in the West, race and nation had become established, though not necessarily predominant, ways of understanding human difference. . . . In the course of the nineteenth century, national and racial thinkers further replaced the notion of community based on politics or religion with the idea of the unbreakable national or racial bonds among distinct peoples. Upon that basis physicians and scientists layered a new understanding of the human body and human evolution that seemed to confirm racial categorizations.

Although Darwin's ideas were in eclipse among scientists by the turn into the twentieth century, his revolutionary theories had become immensely popular. Race theorists argued by analogy, substituting races for species and turning all of human history into a struggle among races for the survival of the fittest. Through biology and medicine, race thinking infiltrated the professions and state bureaucracies. . . . Darwinism and then eugenics joined science and medicine to the Enlightenment sense of the perfectibility of humankind—even if Darwin himself posited only a nonteleological progression, not perfectibility. . . . More dangerously, since and medicine had begun to provide the ideas and techniques by which the population could be manipulated, purged of its ailing elements and refined to the lofty stage of pristine purity. . . .

The cataclysm of World War I only intensified the tendency to think in racial and national terms. The first total war in history required the full mobilization of all of society's resources, human and material, for the practice of violence. Total war required total victory; amid the massive death toll, a war of empires and nation-states became a war of nation as race versus the racial enemies. . . . World War I had . . . effects that were decisively related to the subsequent escalation of genocides in the twentieth century. The war established a new model of a powerful interventionist state that tried to manage everything in sight, because only the state had the capacity to mobilize resources on the scale required by total war. . . . World War I also created an aesthetics of violence that reverberated through the postwar period. The massive death toll of the war made violence on such a large scale almost normal and, to some, a necessary, even desirable way of shaping the future society and the character of the new man and new woman who would inhabit it. . . . *I wonder if this is true for Modern West or just Europe — some Civil war had ? deaths*

6 • A Sociological Definition (Helen Fein)

Helen Fein hails from the first generation of comparative scholars of genocide. She was the first president of the International Association of Genocide Scholars, an organization that she helped to found, and she has served for many years as the executive director of the Institute for the Study of Genocide at the City University of New York. Contrary to Lemkin, and more so than Leo Kuper (whose work, unfortunately, could not be included), Fein has been primarily interested in furthering the theory of genocide. In her most important book, Genocide: A Sociological Perspective *(1993), she provides, first and foremost, a critique of the legal definition of genocide and paves the way for a sociological understanding of the phenomenon. By so doing, she elevated the study of genocide to a new level of theoretical rigor. Whereas Leo Kuper had already made important inroads into the analytical study of genocide, it was Fein who challenged her contemporaries to move beyond mere description.*

Social scientists considering genocide have devised varying definitions and typologies, often reflecting consensus on evaluation of specific cases but dissensus on the borderlines of genocide. . . . Because genocide itself occurs in the context of diverse social relations, it is useful to clarify how the term evolved in order to return to the underlying assumptions behind the concept; then I shall suggest a more generic concept, appropriate for sociological usage, paralleling the terms of the UNGC [United Nations Genocide Convention]. . . . Lemkin's conception . . . emerged from an attempt to explain and indict German population policy. Later study has shown that Lemkin overidentified commonalities and implied a coherent and common objective in different countries. . . .

First, we note, the object of genocide was always the defeated national group except for the Jews, conceived by the Nazis as a race or anti-race—non-human, superhuman and menacing. Political groups and classes within the nation who were killed and incarcerated by the German occupiers were conceived as members of a national group. Second, Lemkin conceived of genocide as a set of coordinated tactics or means. *Cultural genocide* was not a term used by Lemkin: cultural discrimination may be a tactic to assimilate or to destroy a group. The objective of genocide was both the social disintegration and the biological destruction of the group. Third, Lemkin recognized grades of genocide: some groups were to be immediately and wholly annihilated (the Jews); others (especially the Poles) were to be slowly destroyed by other means to decimate their numbers and decapitate their leadership. The victims might be observed by contemporaries as destroyed in whole or in part. . . .

Three problems are repeatedly noted by critics of the [UN Genocide] Convention: (1) the gaps in groups covered; (2) the ambiguity of *intent to destroy a group "as such"*; and

SOURCE: Helen Fein, *Genocide: A Sociological Perspective* (London: Sage, 1991), 8, 9, 10, 23–25. Reprinted with permission of the publisher.

(3) the inability of non-state parties to invoke the Convention and the failure to set up an independent enforcement body.... The Convention has been repeatedly criticized for omission of political groups and social classes as target groups....

I believe that the UNGC definition of genocide can be reconciled with an expanded—but bounded—sociological definition if we focus on how the core concepts are related. From the root of *genus* we may infer that the protected groups were conceived (by Lemkin and the UN framers) as basic kinds, classes, or subfamilies of humanity, persisting units of society. What is distinctive sociologically is that such groups are usually ascriptive—based on birth rather than by choice—and often inspire enduring particularistic loyalties. They are sources of identity and value; they are the seed-bed of social movements, voluntary associations, congregations and families; in brief, they are *collectivities*. Further, these collectivities endure as their members tend to reproduce their own kind (to the extent in-group marriage is the norm). But collectivities need not be self-reproducing to be cohesive over a given span of time.

The UNGC implies a universalistic norm: each group has a right to exist and develop its own culture, assuming neither their [*sic*] aim nor methods are criminal; all collectivities should be protected from such crimes against humanity. One can also argue that political, sexual, and class-dominated status groups or collectivities, just like ethnic and religious collectivities, are basic continuing elements of the community.... There is no categorical line, in fact, between the enduring character of ascribed (heritable) identities and elected or achieved identities: both may by constructed or passed on generationally. Being an Italian working-class Communist Party member may be just as heritable a characteristic as being an Italian church-going Roman Catholic. Indeed, church and party could be regarded as counter-congregations or counter-cultures. Both affiliations may be outcomes of election or ascription, conscience or inheritance.

A new sociological definition should include the following elements: (a) it should clearly denote the object and processes under study and discriminate the latter from related processes; (b) it should stipulate constructs which can be transformed operationally to indicate real-world observable events; and (c) the specification of groups covered should be consistent with our sociological knowledge of both the persistence and construction of group identities in society, the variations in class, ethnic/racial, gender, class/political consciousness and the multiplicity and interaction of peoples' identities and statuses in daily life. Further, (d) it should conform to the implicit universalistic norm and a sense of justice, embracing the right of all non-violent groups to co-exist.

Briefly put,

Genocide is sustained purposeful action by a perpetrator to physically destroy a collectivity directly or indirectly, through interdiction of the biological and social reproduction of group members, sustained regardless of the surrender or lack of threat offered by the victim.

To expand on this sociological definition, one can also show how it encompasses the legal definition {terms of the UNGC are noted in these brackets}: *Genocide is sustained purposeful action* (thus excluding single massacres, pogroms, accidental deaths) *by a perpetrator* (assuming an actor organized over a period) *to physically destroy a collectivity* {"acts committed with intent to destroy, in whole or in part a national/ethnical/racial or religious group," Art. 2} *directly* (through mass or selective murders and calculable physical destruction—e.g. imposed starvation and poisoning of food, water, and air—{see Art. 2, a–c}) *or through interdiction of the biological and social reproduction of group members* (preventing births {Art. 2, d} and {"forcibly transferring children of the group to another group," Art. 2, e}, systematically breaking the linkage between reproduction and socialization of children in the family or group of origin).

This definition would cover the sustained destruction of nonviolent political groups and social classes as parts of a national (or ethnic/religious/racial) group but does not cover the killing of members of military and paramilitary organizations—the SA [Nazi Germany's *Sturmabteilung,* or assault detachment, generally translated as "stormtroopers"], the Aryan Nations, and armed guerillas. Documenting genocide or *genocide* demands (at the very least) identifying a perpetrator(s), the target group attacked as a collectivity, assessing its numbers and victims, and recognizing a pattern of repeated actions from which we infer the intent of purposeful action to eliminate them. Such inference is easiest to draw when we can cite both pre-existent plans or statements of intent and the military or bureaucratic organization of a death machine; seldom do we have both kinds of evidence.

7 • Politicide (Barbara Harff and Ted Robert Gurr)

Pioneers of the quantitative study of genocide and related phenomena, Barbara Harff and Ted Robert Gurr offer a succinct definition of politicide, distinguishing the term from genocide in this 1988 journal article. Gurr, an eminent political scientist at the University of Maryland, has been the driving force behind the influential Minorities at Risk data set and also created the Polity data set, whose fourth edition was last updated in 2010. Both Gurr and Harff, the latter a professor at the U.S. Naval Academy, were also instrumental in contributing scholarly expertise to the CIA's State Failure Task Force, first established in 1994, and renamed the Political Instability Task Force in the wake of the terrorist attacks of September 11, 2011. The task force works to understand political fragility in the international system more generally.

Ambiguities still exist as to what distinguishes genocides and politicides from "normal" acts of repression. In the context of warfare, killings of combatants are "normal," whereas widespread killings of civilians are not. Here lies one of the keys to the theoretical and operational identification of genocides and politicides: if unarmed civilians are deliberately and systematically killed, even if they support an opposition group (rebels), then the event is a genocide or politicide. *This seems too broad. Maybe war crime, but not genocide*

et about a state actors?

By our definition, genocides and politicides are the promotion and execution of policies by a state or its agents which result in the deaths of a substantial portion of a group. The difference between genocide and politicide is in the characteristics by which members of the group are identified by the state. In genocides the victimized groups are defined primarily in terms of their communal characteristics, i.e., ethnicity, religion, or nationality. In politicides the victim groups are defined primarily in terms of their hierarchical position or political opposition to the regime and dominant groups. In our definition, geno/politicide is an act of the

SOURCE: Barbara Harff and Ted Robert Gurr, "Toward Empirical Theory of Genocides and Politicides: Identification and Measurement of Cases Since 1945," *International Studies Quarterly* 32, no. 3 (1988): 360. Reprinted with permission of the International Studies Association.

Keep pace w/ Times. ISIS & Yazidis as perfect example

state. This is an accepted principle in the literature on genocides; the term politicide, for which there is as yet no generally accepted definition, is used here in precisely the same way.

Our definitions of genocide and politicide parallel that of the Genocide Convention which, in its points a and c, prohibits "killing members of a group" and "deliberately inflicting on the group conditions of life calculated to bring about its physical destruction in whole or in part." We differ by excluding the convention's point b, which also prohibits actions "causing serious bodily or mental harm to members of the group," because this extends the definition to innumerable instances of groups which have lost their cohesion and identity, but not necessarily their lives, as a result of processes of socioeconomic change. The convention says nothing about political victims, which we do include.

[However,] note that our definitions are not victim-centered. Although the intrinsic characteristics of the victims are important, what is crucial are the characteristics and purposes of the state. Of course the definitions reflect one of our basic theoretical assumptions: whether an episode of mass killing is a genocide or a politicide depends on the combination of a state's objectives, the motives of its ruling elite, the prevailing ideology, and the power relations within its authority structure.

8 • Democide (R. J. Rummel)

• is this a rather clee

For much of his career, R. J. Rummel, professor emeritus of political science at the University of Hawaii, has been concerned with what he calls "death by government." He coined the term demo-cide in an attempt to liken intentional public killing to intentional private killing, or homicide. According to Rummel, democide has claimed more than 262 million victims to date. As such, he says, the death toll from democide is far greater than the death toll from war.

Even when applicable, the concepts of "genocide," "politicide," "mass murder" or "massacre," and "terror" overlap and are sometimes used interchangeably. Clearly, a concept was needed that includes all intentional government killing in cold blood and that is comparable to the concept of murder for *private* killing. . . . I thus offer, as a concept analogous to public murder, the concept of democide, or murder by government agents acting authoritatively. Its one root is the Greek *demos*, or people; the other is the same as for genocide, which is from the Latin *caedere*, to kill.

Democide's necessary and sufficient meaning is the intentional government killing of an unarmed person or people. Unlike the concept of genocide, *it is restricted to intentional killing of people* and does not extend to attempts to eliminate cultures, races, or peoples by other means. Moreover, democide is not limited to the killing component of genocide, nor to politicide, mass murder, massacre, or terror. It includes them all and also what they exclude, as long as the killing is a purposive act, policy, process, or institution of government. In detail, *democide is any action by government:*

Not sure why this term is needed

SOURCE: R. J. Rummel, *Death by Government* (New Brunswick, N.J.: Transaction, 1994), 36–38, 40, 42. Reprinted with permission of the publisher.

1. designed to kill or cause the death of people
    a. because of their religion, race, language, ethnicity, national origin, class, politics, speech, actions construed as opposing the government or wrecking social policy, or by virtue of their relationship to such people;
    b. in order to fulfill a quota or requisition system;
    c. in furtherance of a system of forced labor or enslavement;
    d. by massacre;
    e. through imposition of lethal living conditions; or
    f. by directly targeting noncombatants during a war or violent conflict, or
2. that causes death by virtue of an intentionally or knowingly reckless and depraved disregard for life (which constitutes *practical* intentionality), as in
    a. deadly prison, concentration camp, forced labor, prisoner of war, or recruit camp conditions;
    b. murderous medical or scientific experiments on humans;
    c. torture or beatings;
    d. encouraged or condoned murder, or rape, looting, and pillage during which people are killed;
    e. a famine or epidemic killing during which government authorities withhold aid, or knowingly act in a way to make it more deadly; or
    f. forced deportations and expulsions causing deaths.

[handwritten marginal note: This all just looks lik state genocide]

This definition has the following qualifications and clarifications:

1. "Government" includes de facto governance—as by the Communist Party of the People's Republic of China—or by a rebel or warlord army over a region and population it has conquered—as by the Moslem Turks (East Turkistan Republic) over part of Sinkiang province (1944–46).
2. "Action by governments" comprises official or authoritative action by government officials, including the police, military, or secret service; or nongovernmental action (e.g., by brigands, press-gangs, or secret societies) that has or is receiving government approval, aid, or acceptance.

[handwritten marginal note: what level is "gov"?]

3. Clause [1a] includes, for example, directly targeting noncombatants during a war or violent conflict out of hatred or revenge, or to depopulate an enemy region, or to terrorize civilians into urging surrender. Concrete examples of such instances could include indiscriminate urban bombing or shelling, or blockades that cause mass starvation.
4. "Relationship to such people" [clause 1a] includes relatives, colleagues, coworkers, teachers, and students.
5. "Massacre" [clause 1d] includes the mass killing of prisoners of war and captured rebels.
6. "Quota" system [clause 1c] includes randomly selecting people for execution in order to meet a quota; or arresting people according to a quota, some of whom are then executed.
7. "Requisition" system [clause 1c] includes taking from peasants or farmers all their food and produce, leaving them to starve to death.

8. Excluded from the definition are:
   a. execution for what are internationally considered capital crimes, such as murder, rape, spying, treason, and the like, so long as evidence does not exist that such allegations were invented by the government in order to execute the accused;
   b. actions taken against armed civilians during mob action or riot (e.g., killing people with weapons in their hands is not democide); and
   c. the death of noncombatants killed during attacks on military targets, so long as the primary target is military (e.g., during bombing of enemy logistics). . . .

Democide is meant to define the killing by government, just as the concept of murder defines individual killing in domestic society. Here, intentionality (premeditation) is critical, including *practical* intentionality. If a government causes deaths through a reckless and depraved indifference to human life, the deaths are as though intended. . . . I have to again be absolutely clear on the meaning of democide since so much of the democide that I describe in subsequent chapters takes place in time of war. War-related killing by military forces that international agreements and treaties directly or by implication prohibit is democide, whether the parties to the killing are signatories to the agreements and treaties or not. Killing that is explicitly permitted is not democide. . . . *Does this prove western ideology?*

Pulling all this together, a death constitutes democide if it is the intentional killing of an unarmed or disarmed person by government agents acting in their authoritative capacity and pursuant to government policy or high command (as in the Nazi gassing of the Jews). It is also democide if the death was the result of such authoritative government actions carried out with reckless disregard for the lives of those affected (as putting people in concentration camps in which the forced labor and starvation rations were such as to cause the dearth of inmates). It is democide if government promoted or turned a blind eye to the death even though it was murder carried out "unofficially" or by private groups (as by deaths squads in Guatemala or El Salvador). And the death also may be democide if high government officials purposely allowed conditions to continue that were causing mass deaths and issued no public warning (as in the Ethiopia famines of the 1970s). . . .

I have found in the vast majority of events and episodes, democide is unambiguous. . . . Sad to say, *most cases of government killing in this century are that clear.* The number of deaths will be hazy for many of these cases; the perpetrators and intent will not.

But that isn't true . . .

9 • Gendercide (Mary Anne Warren)

In recent years a number of scholars have emphasized the gender dimensions of genocide, notably the systematic targeting and destruction of a specific sex. Much of this research was inspired by an earlier treatment of gendercide, authored by Mary Anne Warren in 1985. Although Warren is concerned primarily with wrongful forms of sexual discrimination rather than large-scale social vio-

SOURCE: Mary Anne Warren, *Gendercide: The Implications of Sex Selection* (Totowa, N.J.: Rowman and Allanheld, 1985), 1–2, 22, 24–25. Reprinted with permission of the publisher.

lence as conventionally understood, her neologism alerts us to varieties of victimhood in times of genocide.

The idea that millions of women and female children have been killed or allowed to die because of their sex would probably strike most people as false or even paranoid. The further suggestion that sexually discriminatory deaths continue to occur in many parts of the world—including our own society—is apt to be met with ridicule or indignation. Such widespread ignorance is not surprising, given the continuing lack of awareness of the wider phenomenon of sexism. Even many supposedly well-educated people find it easy to dismiss sexism as a relatively trivial problem. . . .

The fact is that sexism is often a matter of life and death for its female victims. Throughout recorded history, in virtually every patriarchal society, innumerable female human beings have been killed, starved, or otherwise abused as a result of the cultural devaluation of the female sex. . . . I use the term "gendercide" to refer to those wrongful forms of sexual discrimination which reduce the relative number of females or males, whether through direct killing or in more indirect ways. . . . Not all gendercide is anti-female gendercide. Millions of men have also died in part because of their sex, e.g., in wars for which only men are conscripted. Wars which decimate the male population of a nation or community may be regarded as a *de facto* form of gendercide. . . . ⟨handwritten: So victims, WWII? The draft? what if women are drafted⟩

Many of the moral issues raised by the prospect of sex selection may usefully be posed through an analogy between the concept of *genocide* and what I call *gendercide*. The *Oxford American Dictionary* defines genocide as "the deliberate extermination of a race or a people." By analogy, gendercide would be the deliberate extermination of persons of a particular sex (or gender). Other terms, such as "gynocide" and "femicide," have been used to refer to the wrongful killing of girls and women. But "gendercide" is a sex-neutral term, in that the victims may be either male or female. There is a need for such a sex-neutral term, since sexually discriminatory killing is just as wrong when the victims happen to be male. The term also calls attention to the fact that gender roles have often had lethal consequences, and that these are in important respects analogous to the lethal consequences of racial, religious, and class prejudice. . . .

If "genocide" means wrongfully killing or otherwise reducing the relative number of persons in a particular race, then "gendercide" means the same thing, except that "sex" is substituted for "race." Like genocide, gendercide need not involve outright murder, although the paradigm examples of it do. Like genocide, gendercide involves actions which are morally objectionable for reasons apart from the mere fact that they may cause an alteration in the numerical ratios between certain groups. Gendercide is no less a moral atrocity than genocide. Those who object to the genocide/gendercide analogy on the grounds that it seems to belittle the genocidal crimes which have occurred in the past, and which continue to occur in our own time, greatly underestimate the severity of gendercidal crimes in both the past and the present. . . . The number of human beings who have been killed because of their sex is probably just as great as the number who have been killed because of their race or religion.

When gendercide involves murder, it is wrong for that reason, but for additional reasons as well. These include the implied insult and threat to all members of the victimized sex, which is always present when gendercidal practices are justified through sexist ideology, and the loss to humanity of contributions which might otherwise have been made by the victims. However, not all actions which happen to reduce the relative number of persons of one sex or the other are gendercidal. Improved medical care has differentially increased the average life span of women in the industrialized nations, thereby reducing the relative number of men alive at the present time; but this is not an instance of gendercide, since it is not morally objectionable to provide people with improved medical care.

Perhaps this is the wrong term

10 • Cultural Genocide (David Nersessian)

A recurring criticism of the 1948 Genocide Convention relates to its glossing over the supposed crime of cultural genocide, *a controversial term that is intended to highlight forms of destruction other than physical death. Despite Raphaël Lemkin's lobbying, the drafters at the United Nations chose to single out only biological forms of destruction. In this 2005 article David Nersessian succinctly chronicles the decline of cultural genocide in the annals of international law, arguing that the present understanding of genocide "preserves the body of the group but allows its very soul to be destroyed."*

Cultural genocide extends beyond attacks upon the physical and/or biological elements of a group and seeks to eliminate its wider institutions. This is done in a variety of ways, and often includes the abolition of a group's language, restrictions upon its traditional practices and ways, the destruction of religious institutions and objects, the persecution of clergy members, and attacks on academics and intellectuals. Elements of cultural genocide are manifested when artistic, literary, and cultural activities are restricted or outlawed and when national treasures, libraries, archives, museums, artifacts, and art galleries are destroyed or confiscated.

The 1948 Convention on the Prevention and Punishment of the Crime of Genocide prohibits physical and biological genocide but makes no mention of cultural genocide. This omission was deliberate. Early drafts of the Genocide Convention directly prohibited cultural genocide. As the treaty was finalized, however, a debate emerged over its proper scope. Many state representatives drafting the treaty understood cultural genocide to be analytically distinct, with one arguing forcefully that it defied both logic and proportion "to include in the same convention both mass murders in gas chambers and the closing of libraries." Others agreed with Lemkin's broader initial conception that a group could be effectively destroyed by an attack on its cultural institutions, even without the physical/biological obliteration of its members.

Cultural genocide ultimately was excluded from the final Convention, except for a limited prohibition on the forcible transfer of a group's children. The drafters acknowledged that the removal of children was physically and biologically destructive but further recognized that indoctrinating children into the customs, language, and values of a foreign group was "tantamount to the destruction of the [child's] group, whose future depended on that next

SOURCE: David Nersessian, "Rethinking Cultural Genocide under International Law," *Human Rights Dialogue*, April 22, 2005, http://www.cceia.org/resources/publications/dialogue/2_12/section_1/5139.html. Reprinted with permission of the Carnegie Council for Ethics in International Affairs.

[handwritten at top: Do we defin genocide in terms of effectiveness? If so, then often (more than bio), cultural destruction fails and pushes a group underground. Plus, cultures are always evolving.]

generation." Despite the limited definition of the offense itself, broader cultural considerations do still play two important roles in prosecuting genocide under the Convention.

First, acts of cultural genocide—conduct violating what the International Criminal Tribunal for the Former Yugoslavia (ICTY) referred to as the "very foundation of the group"—
tend to establish the genocidist's specific intent to destroy the protected group. The ICTY, for
example, held that Serbian destruction of Muslim libraries and mosques and attacks on cultural leaders established genocidal intent against Muslims in the former Yugoslavia. Second,
cultural characteristics are used to help define the contours of the protected groups enumerated in the Convention. Since there are no universally accepted definitions of racial, ethnic,
religious, or national groups, each must be assessed on a case-by-case basis in light of unique
historical and contextual considerations. Cultural concerns, such as a group's social, historical, and linguistic characteristics, help to determine whether a given group of people is protected under the Convention.

Cultural genocide thus plays a subsidiary role in our present understanding of genocide
and group destruction. But this is a product of the political realities of treaty negotiation between states rather than any limitation inherent in the concept. The Convention's drafters
acknowledged the legitimacy of cultural genocide, and indicated that it might be addressed
through other international instruments. Indeed, an individual right to cultural existence was
recognized in the 1948 Universal Declaration of Human Rights and subsequently affirmed in
the International Covenant on Economic, Social and Cultural Rights. And to accommodate
[handwritten in right margin: Is this not a better place to locate it?]
the erosion of traditional geographic and economic boundaries, more recent treaties such as the
Charter of the European Union and the Council of Europe's Framework Convention for the
Protection of National Minorities contain anti-assimilation language and create express obligations to respect cultural diversity. Culture also is protected through such specific-purpose
instruments as the European Cultural Convention and the Convention for the Protection of
Cultural Property in the Event of Armed Conflict. . . .

Human rights jurisprudence lacks sufficient flexibility to properly redress cultural genocide, which differs from other infringements upon cultural rights in both scope and substance.
The existing human rights scheme redresses the intentional and systematic eradication of a
group's cultural existence (for example, destroying original historical texts or prohibiting all
use of a language) with the same mechanisms as it would consider the redaction of an art
textbook. But cultural genocide is far more sinister. In such cases, fundamental aspects of a
group's unique cultural existence are attacked with the aim of destroying the group, thereby
rendering the group itself (apart from its members) an equal object and victim of the attack.
The existing rubric of human rights law fails to recognize and account for these important
differences.

Collective identity is not self-evident but derives from the numerous, inter-dependent
aspects of a group's existence. Lemkin's original conception of genocide expressly recognized
that a group could be destroyed by attacking any of these unique aspects. By limiting genocide
to its physical and biological manifestations, a group can be kept physically and biologically
intact even as its collective identity suffers in a fundamental and irremediable manner. Put
another way, the present understanding of genocide preserves the body of the group but al-
lows its very soul to be destroyed. *[handwritten: When has this happened though? Can it really happen? Is it as bad as death?]*

This is hardly a satisfactory situation, and it is time to revisit the issue put aside by the Convention's drafters through a new treaty dealing specifically with cultural genocide. These efforts should be preceded by a comprehensive analysis of state practice and *opinio juris* to ascertain the current status of cultural genocide under customary international law. The need is patent. Cultural genocide is a unique wrong that should be recognized independently and that rises to the level of meriting individual criminal responsibility. After all, if indeed the highest values of a society are expressed through its criminal laws, what message is being conveyed by not labeling acts of cultural genocide as criminal? Perhaps a message better left unsent. *Who would be prosecuted then? Entire legislative bodies? Courts? Is it possible to criminalize these actions?*

11 • Colonial Genocide (David Maybury-Lewis)

In this 2002 essay the late anthropologist David Maybury-Lewis (1929–2007), who taught at Harvard University until his retirement in 2004, draws our attention to the destruction of indigenous populations at the hands of European colonists from the fifteenth century through the nineteenth. This period of "colonial genocide," according to Maybury-Lewis, was neither the first nor the last period of systematic annihilation in recorded history. In his brief survey of colonial violence, Maybury-Lewis hints at a causal link between "callous developmentalism" and genocide and emphasizes the multiple forms of violence that regularly attended the Western discovery of the non-Western world and which not infrequently led to the extermination of entire strata of conquered societies.

Genocide committed against indigenous populations was a particularly nasty aspect of the European seizure of empires from the fifteenth to the nineteenth centuries, but it was neither invented nor practiced solely by European imperialists. Genocide is in fact a new name, invented in 1944 by Raphael Lemkin, for a very old outrage, namely the massacre or attempted massacre of an entire people. Such annihilation took place in antiquity, such as when the Romans destroyed Carthage and sowed its fields with salt. They were later carried on by conquering peoples such as the Huns and Mongols and countless others. European imperialism and the massacres of indigenous peoples to which it gave rise added a bloody chapter to the history of genocide, which began much earlier and is unfortunately not yet finished. . . .

A discussion of genocide as practiced against indigenous peoples should not . . . focus solely or even principally on deliberate attempts to massacre entire societies. Often the widespread dying resulted not so much from deliberate killing but from the fatal circumstances imposed by the imperialists on the conquered. Where deliberate extermination was the cause, it is useful to refer to [Israel] Charny's distinction between *genocide* and *genocidal massacre*. Indigenous peoples have often been the victims of genocidal massacres, where the slaughter is on a smaller scale and results from a general attitude toward indigenous peoples rather than necessarily being part of a campaign for total elimination of the victim population. On the

SOURCE: David Maybury-Lewis, "Genocide against Indigenous Peoples," in Alexander Laban Hinton, ed., *Annihilating Difference: The Anthropology of Genocide* (Berkeley: University of California Press, 2002), 43, 45–48, 49, 51. Reprinted with permission of the publisher.

other hand, campaigns of extermination are characteristic of those phases of colonization in which the invaders have decided on a course of ethnic cleansing to rid a territory of its indigenous inhabitants and appropriate it for themselves. In the heyday of colonialism such exterminations were often justified in the name of progress. The indigenous populations were stigmatized as savages who ought to make way for civilization.

In his book *The Winning of the West*, for example, Theodore Roosevelt justified the treatment meted out to the Indians of the United States in the following terms: "The settler and pioneer have at bottom had justice on their side; this great continent could not have been kept as nothing but a game reserve for squalid savages." General Roca, the minister for war in Argentina at the end of the nineteenth century, put it even more bluntly when he stated the case of clearing the pampas of their Indian inhabitants. Speaking to his fellow countrymen he argued that "our self-respect as a virile people obliges us to put down as soon as possible, by reason or by force, this handful of savages who destroy our wealth and prevent us from definitely occupying, in the name of law, progress and our own security, the richest and most fertile lands of the Republic." Roca then proceeded to lead a campaign, known in Argentine history as the Conquest of the Desert, whose express purpose was to clear the pampas of Indians. The Indians were not entirely exterminated physically, but they were eradicated socially, ceasing to exist as separate and identifiable peoples.

A similar campaign to exterminate an indigenous population was carried out in Tasmania during the nineteenth century. The settlers tired of acts of resistance committed by the native Tasmanians and therefore organized a drive in which a line of armed men "beat" across the island, as they would do if they were flushing game, only this time the quarry was the remaining Tasmanians.... The line did not, in fact, exterminate the Tasmanians, but it harried and decimated them so severely that it hastened their eventual extinction. A similar line operation had been put into effect earlier in Australia, when General Macquarie organized colonists, soldiers, and constables to drive the aborigines of New South Wales beyond the Blue Mountains, but such organized campaigns increasingly became exceptions in a land where aborigines could be hunted and shot at will....

Alternatively, such killings were carried out as a means of terrorizing people into performing forced labor. The most notorious examples of this were the horrors inflicted on the unfortunate people forced to gather rubber by sadistic overseers in Peru and the Congo.... The Arana brothers in Peru and King Leopold's overseers in the [Belgian] Congo wanted to extract every last ounce of profit from their operations, even if that meant killing their workforce. They seem to have thought there was a limitless supply of native labor to be captured and exploited. Meanwhile the rhetoric of the rulers laid great stress on the fact that they were dealing with savages—either savages to be tamed or savages to be civilized.... It is difficult to tell whether the peoples of the Putumayo region or the considerably larger population in the Congo would have been exterminated if these systems of exploitation had been allowed to run their course. Fortunately, the horrors taking place were publicized and eventually moderated. Estimates of the death toll are more reliable for the Congo, where Roger Casement calculated that the population had been reduced by 60 percent. In terms of sheer numbers, the Congo genocide takes second place only to the loss of African life occasioned by the slave trade. Historians have calculated that fifteen to twenty million Africans were herded overseas as slaves and an equal number were killed in the whole process of slaving, giving a total of up to forty million who were either killed or removed from their homes. Yet the intensity of the killing in the Congo was greater. The slave trade, after all, lasted for centuries, as compared with a few decades for the Congo genocide. . . .

Imperialist genocide against indigenous peoples was thus of two kinds. It was practiced in order to clear lands that invading settlers wished to occupy. It was also practiced as part of a strategy to seize and coerce labor that the settlers could not or would not obtain by less drastic means. It was often inspired furthermore by the rulers' determination to show who was master and who was, if not slave, then at least obedient subject; and it was often put into effect as deliberate policy where the masters felt that their subjects had to be taught a lesson. Acts of resistance or rebellion were often punished by genocidal killings. A classic example of this, out of the scores that might be cited, was the German extermination of the Herero in South West Africa. The German administration of their South West African colony decided that German settlers should pasture their cattle on the best grazing lands in what was by and large an arid region. . . . The Herero did not see it that way, however, and when they were evicted from their grazing lands they fought back. The Germans therefore mounted a punitive expedition in 1904 that massacred thousands of Herero and drove the rest into the waterless desert. . . . The result was the virtual extermination of the Herero, who were reduced to a few thousand landless fugitives.

Genocides against indigenous peoples were not, however, solely a function of colonial policies. Genocidal massacres continued to be committed in the years of decolonization and beyond, only their rationale was different. . . . Dams are built that flood indigenous lands. Timber companies are permitted or actually invited to cut down forests in which indigenous people live. Such development activities destroy the livelihoods of indigenous peoples, disrupt their societies, undermine their health, and leave whole populations in suicidal despair. Loss of life promoted by callous developmentalism [for example] is a slow and insidious form of genocide against indigenous peoples. A more direct form in our present era is the massacre of indigenous peoples for reasons of state. Such genocides were committed in the USSR, where they were inflicted both on nonindigenous and indigenous peoples. In the days when the country was ruled despotically by Stalin, all its constituent peoples could, in whole or in part, be uprooted, relocated, or scattered in remote regions, often with utmost brutality. . . . Such genocides were part of a schizophrenic policy that pretended to guarantee and encourage peoples to cultivate their distinctive ethnicities while simultaneously striving to make sure that local ethnic sentiments were weakened if not destroyed. Soviet genocides were thus a paradoxical result of the Soviet nationalities policy. . . .

It is the idea of the threatened state that is particularly insidious and especially likely to lead to genocide. The Enlightenment idea of the state that has dominated Western thinking until recently stressed the rationality of the modern state, which would treat its citizens equally and guarantee their liberty by protecting their rights. It was thus concerned with the rights of individuals rather than with the rights of groups such as ethnic minorities or indigenous peoples. It was thus supposed instead that ethnicity would evaporate in the modern state as a result of modernization itself. The grim history of the twentieth century and the ethnic conflicts and persecutions that have played such a prominent part in it have shown, however, that ethnicity and ethnic nationalism have not disappeared, nor are they about to.

12 • Genocidal Massacre (Israel W. Charny)

Very much aware of the question of scale in the categorization of collective violence and building on Leo Kuper's work, the psychologist Israel W. Charny introduced the notion of genocidal massacre in a 1994 book chapter. According to Charny, who directs the Institute on the Holocaust and Genocide in Jerusalem, a genocidal massacre shared all the attributes of genocide but involved a smaller number of victims. The question of scale resurfaced in the jurisprudence of the United Nations ad hoc tribunals in The Hague and Arusha, where, pace *Charny, quantitative criteria were deemed inappropriate for determining the existence of genocide in a given context.*

What is needed, I would argue, is a generic definition of genocide that does not exclude or commit to indifference any case of mass murder of any human beings, of whatever racial, national, ethnic, biological, cultural, religious, and political definitions, or of totally mixed groupings of any and all of the above. I propose that whenever large numbers of unarmed human beings are put to death at the hands of their fellow human beings, we are talking about genocide. . . .

I would argue that a *generic definition of genocide* be as follows:

Genocide in the generic sense is the mass killing of substantial numbers of human beings, when not in the course of military action against the military forces of an avowed enemy, under conditions of the essential defenselessness and helplessness of the victims. . . .

At the same time, since there are also a great many important reasons to distinguish between different kinds of genocide, having defined genocide in its generic sense, we also need to create a series of definitions of categories of genocide. Each event of genocide is to be classified into the one or more subcategories for which it qualifies. [Charny distinguishes six such categories: genocidal massacre, intentional genocide (comprising the subcategories specific intentional genocide, multiple intentional genocide, omnicide), genocide in the course of colonization or consolidation of power, genocide in the course of aggressive ("unjust") war, war crimes against humanity, and genocide as a result of ecological destruction and abuse.] It is also to be expected that, over the course of time, there will always emerge new categories, as the complexity of life and reality unfold. . . .

Events of mass murder that are on a smaller scale than mass events may be defined, as Leo Kuper originally proposed, under a category of "genocidal massacre." I would define *genocidal massacre* as follows:

Mass killing as defined above in the generic definition of genocide, but in which the mass murder is on a smaller scale, that is, smaller numbers of human beings are killed.

With this category we are now equipped to describe many pogroms, mass executions, and mass murders that are, intrinsically, no less vicious and no less tragically final for the victims,

SOURCE: Israel W. Charny, "Toward a Generic Definition of Genocide," in George J. Andreopoulos, ed., *Genocide: Conceptual and Historical Dimensions* (Philadelphia: University of Pennsylvania Press, 1994), 74, 75, 76, 77. Reprinted with permission of the publisher.

but in which the numbers of dead are small in comparison to the events of genocide and which even the well-meaning people who do not approve conceptually of the "numbers game" have found it difficult to speak of as genocide. Thus, we would apply the specific concept of genocidal massacre to the government of Sri Lanka's rounding up some five thousand Tamils over a weekend and executing them; and to the government of China's mowing down an estimated similar number in Tiananmen Square. *Debatable*

13 • Genocide as a Form of War (Martin Shaw)

Martin Shaw, research professor in international relations at the University of Sussex, was one of the first scholars to think systematically about the relationship between genocide and war. A sociologist by training, he has been an ardent advocate of bringing social theory to bear on the study of genocide. In his book War and Genocide *(2003), he offers a comparative analysis of war's relationship to genocide in the paradigmatic cases of the twentieth century, from the Armenian genocide to the genocide in Rwanda. Among other things, Shaw posits that genocide is not a phenomenon sui generis but just another form of war.*

The many similarities between war and genocide are hardly coincidences. Most genocides take place during or around interstate and/or civil wars. . . . It is not sufficient, however, to represent the links between war and genocide as external, causal relations. *In no case does war simply cause genocide.* If that was [*sic*] the case, there would be far more major genocidal episodes. Rather, it is the case that when armed military force is being extensively used against organized armed enemies, then it is easier for leaders to take the extraordinary, generally illegitimate steps towards also using armed force against social groups as such. Militaristic and totalitarian ideologies that designate groups as "enemies" are particularly likely to facilitate plans to destroy social groups as such through armed force. . . .

This argument suggests that the links between war and genocide are not simply external or causal but are *internal* to the character of genocide. The simplest way to express this is to say that genocide can best be understood as *a form of war in which social groups are the enemies*. Genocide can be seen on a continuum from war in general, through degenerate war. . . . The core linkages (and differences) between genocide and other forms of war . . . can be described as follows:

1. *Destroying the power of the enemy*. In war in general, the point of organized armed force is to destroy the power of another organized armed enemy together with its ability to resist (Clausewitz's definition). In degenerate total war, the destruction of the organized enemy is extended to include the destruction of the civilian population, but still as a means towards the defeat of the organized enemy. In genocide, organized armed force is used to destroy (social) groups as such (the Convention definition). What destruction means, here, is destroying the social power of a particular group—in economic and cultural as well as political senses—and usually to eliminate or drastically reduce its presence in a particular territory. Destroying the target group's power also involves destroying its ability to resist.

SOURCE: Martin Shaw, *War and Genocide: Organized Killing in Modern Society* (Cambridge: Polity, 2003), 41, 44, 45–47, 48, 49. Reprinted with permission of the publisher.

2. *Killing*. In war, the destruction of an enemy's power involves killing some among its forces (but does not generally involve killing all its forces). In genocide, the deep destruction of the enemy group is defined by the mass killing of some among its members (but does not generally involve killing all of them). In both cases, the extent of killing depends on the precise aims of the parties, the means available and the course of the struggle.

3. *Relationship between killing and other means of coercion*. War is the extension of politics by other means and typically includes economic, ideological and political coercion alongside military action. In genocide, killing is supplemented by other coercive measures. These include discrimination, robbery, expulsion and terror, as well as the transfers of population and control of births specified in the [Genocide] Convention.

4. *Nature of the conflict*. War in general, including degenerate war, is primarily conflict between two or more organized armed forces, although in degenerate war civilians are targeted as well. Genocide is conflict between organized, armed forces, on the one hand, and civilian populations that are largely unarmed, on the other—although some among the latter may offer armed resistance and the group may be more or less linked to an armed force. Many secondary differences of genocide from other forms of war flow from this difference.

5. *Legitimacy*. A crucial difference is that war is generally legitimate. Thus although degenerate war breaches accepted standards of warfare, it masks itself in the general legitimacy of war. But because the enemy in genocide is defined as a civilian group, it is by definition illegitimate. This has all sorts of ramifications—not least that genocide will tend to be presented as war whenever possible. Although perpetrating genocide usually involves special organizations developed for the purpose, it is often carried out mostly by or through the general state machine—especially the army—and other established institutions. Thus it generally utilizes the machinery of war, and other organs of state power, and takes place under their cover. . . .

6. *Preparation*. Like war in general, genocide needs to be understood as a process. Because war is legitimate, long-term war-preparations (e.g., organizing armies, making weapons, advocating military ideas) are generally open and explicit. Genocide is also prepared in complex ways within society, and the institutions and ideas that are mobilized by genocidists are also widely accepted in pre-genocidal periods—indeed they are very much the same institutions and ideas as those mobilized for war. But genocide preparation . . . exists on the margins of social acceptance. The genocidal potentials of armies, ideologies, laws, racism, chauvinism, religious and class hostilities remain, for the most part, abstract. They are not seen as means of genocide. The direct preparation of genocide, in contrast to war, is generally semi-hidden. Therefore the specific machinery of genocide, like the machinery of insurrection in classic revolutions, is usually a novel construction, begun secretively, immediately prior to its use.

7. *Scope*. War is a pervasive and complex social institution, so that we refer to a wide range of practices as *military*, because of their connections with war, without assuming that they are homogenous or that they are simply connected to a maximum case of war like nuclear extermination. Similarly, the broad base of genocide, and the range of its expressions, means that we can also use genocidal as an adjective referring to genocide, without assuming that these are homogenous or involve group extermination. *Genocidal practices* may be defined, therefore, as those that *treat social groups as enemies whose power and lives may have to be destroyed*. Clearly not all hostility towards other social groups, such as racism and chauvinism, is actively

genocidal. However such forms of hostility may be seen in certain contexts as pre- or proto-
genocidal. . . .

8. *Small-scale episodes.* Armed violence may be used against another armed force in a limited context, which does not lead immediately to a fully-fledged war. Likewise such violence
may be used against some members of a group, without leading immediately to an overall
campaign against the group. Moreover we can see now that such episodes, involving relatively
small numbers of killings, often threaten the all-out destruction of a group's power and a much
larger-scale slaughter. As a result of such experience we can now read genocidal dangers in
other movements, even if large-scale genocide may still be some way off. Genocide may be
discerned, therefore, in relatively limited mass killing, short of anything that immediately
threatens the destruction of the whole enemy group.

9. *Extent of killing.* War can often achieve its ends without wholesale killing of the enemy.
Likewise, genocide does not always involve the slaughter of the majority, let alone the entirety, of the "enemy" group. This is because perpetrators can often achieve the destruction
of a group through relatively limited killings, accompanied by other measures. . . .

10. *Conflict.* War is, by definition, conflict between two armed powers. Genocide, likewise, is conflict. Although typically one side is initially unarmed, this may change because
genocide—even when successfully perpetrated in the short term—can never be uncontested.
However unequal the initial struggle between the organized power that wishes to destroy and
the group whose power and lives are attacked, in the end that struggle is likely to become
more balanced. Groups targeted for destruction cannot but resist by whatever means they can
find. However helpless most of the victims may be, much of the time, there are always passive
resisters. There is also usually forcible opposition, sooner or later, either from the population
that is directly attacked, or from other forces that see their interests implicated in what is going
on. Since genocide usually occurs in the context of international political conflict and wider
warfare, victim groups will look for and often find more powerful allies. All-out slaughter may
be avoided because genocidal processes are halted. Indeed, genocide is *generally* ended in war,
by more conventional military forces, as Soviet and Anglo-American armies ended the Holocaust. This is another reason why we should understand genocide as a form of war.

[handwritten margin note, left side:] Just be there is a tendecy to resist/become armed dousn't mean it will happen shaky link thus is it a matter be both sides ARE and or be both will Eventually be

[handwritten note below paragraph:] * Really "war, but like also not 'war'"

14 • Atrocity Crimes (David Scheffer)

In response to perceived limitations of the legal definition of genocide among both scholars and
practitioners, David Scheffer presents a case for abandoning the concept. He introduces the notion
of atrocity crimes as a substitute for genocide. Formerly ambassador-at-large for war crimes in the
administration of U.S. President Bill Clinton, Scheffer, whose very readable, personal reflection on
his time in office, All the Missing Souls, *was published in 2012, argues that a new term is necessary*
in order to overcome the perverse incentives that he believes are associated with the "G word."

SOURCE: David Scheffer, "Genocide and Atrocity Crimes," *Genocide Studies and Prevention* 1, no. 3 (2006):
    229, 230, 231, 232, 236–37, 238–39, 244–45. Reprinted with permission of the journal.

In this article I advance two proposals. First, there is a critical need to liberate governments and international organizations from the genocide factor, by which I mean to enable them to readily identify precursors of genocide without being constrained by the legal requirements that must be met to properly identify the crime of genocide. Second, I believe it is essential that we transform the terminology used in scholarship, public documents, and public dialogue regarding the crime of genocide, crimes against humanity (including ethnic cleansing), and war crimes into a more acceptable and accurate vehicle for the collective description of these crimes, and that the relevant term should be "atrocity crimes" while the associated discipline should be described as "atrocity law." . . . *but wouldn't we need def for?*

Raphael Lemkin recognized the need for a new term to describe the type of human destruction that no other legal term had adequately covered up through World War II, and his introduction of the term "genocide" filled a gap in terminology that had a profound impact on law, culture, history, and politics since the late 1940s. But the term "genocide" has proved insufficient and even, at times, counterproductive. The range of criminal conduct that involves assaults on civilian populations and the misuse of military power in armed conflict extends far beyond the relatively narrow confines of the crime of genocide. Yet the term has been commonly used, particularly in political dialogue to describe atrocities of great diversity, magnitude, and character. *Perhaps we just need new def, not a different one*

Political officials and observers have reached a stage where every mass killing, whether immediate or drawn out over long periods, soon evokes the language of genocide and its all too often intimidating brake on effective responses. As an almost perverse methodology, governments and institutions seem incapable of responding effectively to atrocities because these have not yet been determined to be genocide. If and when such events are painstakingly defined as genocide, the same governments and organizations are paralyzed, prevented from acting by the presumption that any action will trigger that nation's or organization's legal responsibility to commit enough personnel and resources, and stay the course long enough, to defeat the forces of genocide. . . . *So how would new def change this?*

Governments, as opposed to prosecutors and courts, need to understand and apply the term "genocide" largely in a preventive rather than a criminal context. . . . Governments should be liberated to describe quickly and publicly the *precursors of genocide* that may ultimately establish the crime of genocide but, at a minimum, should alert the world to the need to react in a timely manner to prevent further destruction of innocent human life, whether in times of armed conflict or in times of internal repression. . . . Governments, international and regional organizations, and the media should regard the term "precursors of genocide" as significant on a political, not legal, level. The term is useful, pragmatic, and sufficiently diplomatic to be employed without necessarily triggering some of the intimidating consequences of charges of genocide. . . . The term "precursors of genocide" refers to those events occurring immediately prior to and during possible genocide that can point to an ultimate legal judgment of genocide but which should be recognized and used in a timely manner to galvanize international action to intervene, be it diplomatically, economically, or militarily. My primary concern is to employ a term that stimulates, rather than retards, effective action by governments and international organizations, particularly the United Nations, to stem the tide of genocide (whether or not, as a matter of law, what unfolds in the field is ultimately concluded to be genocide). . . .

This seems to open door for abuse?

The primary objective in relying on a more liberal understanding of genocide ... is to establish state responsibility far more readily than is currently possible under the criminal-intent requirements of individual accountability. Such an understanding would give policy makers the freedom to point a finger at a state's responsibility for actions that appear genocidal in real time, without having to prove the direct responsibility of any individual leader or military commander for the crime of genocide. ... Thus, once could point to acts of genocide, as defined by articles II and III of the UNGC [United Nations Genocide Convention], and express the political point that a government appears to be committing such acts of genocide, which it must be prevented from continuing to commit, regardless of who, within such a government of military or militia force, can be shown to demonstrate the requisite specific intent required to convict an individual for the crime of genocide. The state and the government must be seen to be responsible for the acts of genocide, and the witnesses of these events must, at the governmental and organizational levels, be empowered to allege that at least precursors of genocide are apparent and that they merit strong political and, in all likelihood, military responses. This divide—between the political reality of genocide and the criminal character of genocide—must be more broadly accepted if there is to remain any chance of preventing genocide from continuing once it has erupted in an atrocity zone.

Having argued that governments and organizations should be permitted to apply the more flexible term "precursors of genocide" to certain unfolding atrocities that point to the crime of genocide, I believe that it is imperative that there be introduced an even more adaptable terminology to describe genocide and other atrocities meriting effective governmental and organizational responses. ...

I plead for a new category of crimes called "atrocity crimes" and for a new field of international law that describes the law covering atrocity crimes, both in the realm of state responsibility and in the domain of individual accountability. That body of law I would describe as "atrocity law," which essentially encompasses the law of the international and hybrid criminal tribunals. Just as the term "genocide" originally captured what Raphael Lemkin recognized as the essence of a particular crime against humanity requiring special identification in public, legal, and historical terms, so too does the term "atrocity crimes" describe a basket of particularly heinous crimes that are suitable for criminal prosecution before international tribunals and national courts for which states and certain non-state organizations and groups should be held responsible. Atrocity crimes are also collectively executed crimes of such magnitude and destructive character as to be particularly prominent and logically inconsistent with the protection of human rights and the maintenance of international peace and security in an increasingly interdependent and sophisticated global society.

The word "atrocity" (or "atrocities") derives from Roman military law. It described illegal acts performed pursuant to military orders. ... [But because the term no longer occupies a formal place in international law], ... there is a fairly clean slate upon which to use the word "atrocity" as a legal term, particularly in light of what has occurred since the early 1990s and the popular usage of the term "atrocity" by governments, intergovernmental and non-governmental organizations, and the media. Atrocity crimes fit the following profile of cumulative definitional characteristics, *all* of which must exist for the term to be used accurately:

1. The crime must be of significant magnitude, meaning that its commission is widespread or systematic or occurs as part of a large-scale commission of such crimes. The crime

must involve a relatively large number of victims (e.g., a fairly significant number of deaths or casualties), or impose other very severe injury upon noncombatant populations (e.g., massive destruction of private property), or subject a large number of combatants or prisoners of war to violations of the laws and customs of war.

2. The crime may occur in time of war, or in time of peace, or in time of violent upheaval of some organized character, and may be either international or non-international in character.

3. The crime must be identifiable in conventional international criminal law as the crime of genocide, a violation of the laws and customs of war, the crime of aggression (if and when it is defined so as to give rise to clear individual criminal culpability), the crime of international terrorism, a crime against humanity (the precise definition of which has evolved in the development of the criminal tribunals), or the emerging crime of ethnic cleansing.

4. The crime must have been led, in its execution, by a ruling or otherwise powerful elite in society (including rebel or terrorist leaders) who planned the commission of the crime and were the leading perpetrators of the crime. *So what about those that are actual actors in atrocity crime?*

5. The law applicable to such crime, while it may impose state responsibility and even remedies against states, is also regarded under customary international law as holding individuals criminally liable for the commission of such crime, thus enabling the prosecution of such individuals before a court duly constituted for such purpose. *Can these crimes be committed by rogues?*

A crime that marks all five of these criteria would, in my view, be an atrocity crime. In non-legal terms, these are high-impact crimes of severe gravity that are of an orchestrated character, that shock the conscience of humankind, that result in a significant number of victims, and that one would expect the international media and international community to focus on as meriting an international response holding the lead perpetrators accountable before a competent court of law. . . .

Getting the terminology right is part of the accuracy and integrity of the process, and it is part of the job of selling to the public the credibility and utility of these judicial institutions. If public support for international prosecution and military responses to atrocity crimes is lost because what is described appears threatening or incomprehensible to the average person, then the entire venture will be undermined.

15 • Extremely Violent Societies (Christian Gerlach)

In his 2010 book Extremely Violent Societies, *Christian Gerlach, a historian of the Holocaust, advocates a methodological departure from what he calls the "genocide approach." Finding major fault with the conventional way of studying genocide, Gerlach introduces an alternative approach that he terms the "extremely violent societies" approach. His principal objective is to counter the state-centrism that continues to mar much of the literature on genocide. Although Gerlach presents as unified a field that is anything but, his proposal to complement the "dominant political histories" in the field with "a social history of mass violence" is laudable and important. In fact it mirrors ef-*

SOURCE: Christian Gerlach, *Extremely Violent Societies: Mass Violence in the Twentieth-Century World* (Cambridge: Cambridge University Press, 2010), 1–2, 3, 4, 5–6, 7–8. Reprinted with permission of the publisher.

forts in political science that commenced over a decade ago with research on the microfoundations of civil war.

Violence is a fact of human life. Some people may be lucky enough not to experience it. But no society is free of violence, or murder, rape, or robbery. This book, however, deals with extraordinary processes that entail unusually high levels of violence and brutality, which is why I speak of "extremely" violent societies. . . . By extremely violent societies I mean formations where *various population groups* become victims of massive physical violence, in which, acting together with organs of the state, *diverse social groups participate for a multitude of reasons.*

Simply put, the occurrence and the thrust of mass violence depends on broad and diverse support, but this is based on a variety of motives and interests that cause violence to spread in different directions and in varying intensities and forms. This phenomenon differs from what many scholars and other observers see in mass violence—briefly put, a state's attempt to destroy a population group, largely for a certain reason, and often called "genocide."

To begin with, the problem goes beyond the assault of just *one* victim group. Under Nazi Germany, for example, Jews were targeted for killings, but so also were disabled people, Roma and Sinti, political opponents, Soviet prisoners of war, the Polish leadership—broadly defined, and "guerilla-suspect" rural dwellers; perhaps twelve million foreign nationals were deported to Germany as forced labor, and millions of Eastern Europeans, Greeks, and Dutch were plunged into famine. During World War I, Armenians, Greeks, Assyrians, Chaldeans, and Kurds in the Ottoman Empire died in forced resettlement and massacres, and many Turks were also killed. Under Soviet rule from the 1930s to the 1950s, wealthier peasants or individuals with suspicious "bourgeois" origin, people uprooted by the collectivization of agriculture, political opponents, foreign prisoners of war, and citizens belonging to ethnicities who became collectively suspect, were arrested, banished, resettled, or killed. While the treatment of these various groups, and the time, duration, and manner of their persecution may have differed, as did their mortality figures and ratios and their fates afterwards, I suggest that in many ways their suffering should be examined as a whole. . . . Whereas many scholars insist on strictly distinguishing between the different phenomena of violence, I am interested precisely in the links between the different forms. . . .

As a historian, I seek to complement the dominant political histories in the field by a social history of mass violence. . . . By focusing more widely than just on government intentions, the extremely violent societies approach enables us to study far more actors and to take all of their intentions into account, including social and political groups, officials from various ministries, agencies, etc. The agendas of non-state actors often have a major impact on determining the targets, timing, and forms of assault. In the case of such participatory violence, it may become difficult to assign *sole* responsibility for physical violence to one authority or figure, but it is possible to assess each group's contribution. In any case, assigning responsibility for mass violence is no zero-sum game—if there is popular participation, and public-popular cooperation in violence, this need not diminish the guilt of either officials or non-officials. . . . My approach is designed to take into account every sort of actor, from top to bottom levels, within or outside an official apparatus. . . .

This section explains why I do not find "genocide" a useful framework for exploring some of the phenomena at hand, and why I think an alternative framework may be fruitful. For "genocide" marks an approach—one of several imaginable ways to think about mass violence—that lays specific emphasis on the history of ideas and of political systems. A state turns against a group in society that is mostly ethnically defined—this is the story mostly told in genocide studies. The genocide approach focuses on regimes vulnerable to turning to "genocidal" acts, such as Nazi Germany, the Soviet Union, Rwanda, or Cambodia. Many argue that a turn to "genocide" happens in a crisis of the state or of government. Genocide scholars concentrate on how such regimes mobilize bureaucratic machineries, armed formations, and citizens or subjects for violence, mostly through manipulation, propaganda, legislation, and orders; how a persecuted population group, on the basis of an idea of hierarchical otherness, is being excluded, discriminated, stripped of rights, denied its human character, or declared immoral and a threat to the nation. It is excluded from the "universe of obligation."

Using the genocide approach, scholars try to show what grounds are found or invented for rationalizing the destruction of that group (often thought of as premeditated), how mass murder is organized, and how the immoral character of the slaughter is later denied on the basis of the earlier determined rationalizations. Genocide, then, is seen as originating from a failure of a political and judicial system, as well as of public opinion. Genocide scholars often try to isolate one core motive for extermination that is frequently found in the "ideology" of such a regime, mostly pertaining to racism, more rarely to class hatred or religious fanaticism. . . . But thinking in terms of "genocide" means using a framework that restricts the analysis. Genocide scholars have never agreed what "genocide" actually means. The term is used arbitrarily. . . . If genocide scholars agree on one thing, it is that "intent" constitutes "genocide." This also applies to the UN Genocide Convention, and to Raphael Lemkin, the field's founding father. This emphasis on "policy" has led to a state focus in genocide studies, for it is the state to which the "intent" is attributed and that devises policy. . . . As a result, genocide studies have tended to construct a monolithic actor out of people (officials and others) that to me seem to have very contradictory intentions. The focus on government rule and state intent makes it difficult to analyze the particular processes at work within societies. . . .

The biggest problem of genocide studies is the lack of an empirical foundation. This emptiness is obvious at every genocide conference. It may in part be due to the reductionist genocide approach with its emphasis on "proving" "genocide" (however defined) and therefore official "intent." It may also have to do with the high level of abstraction in the work of political scientists and sociologists who have had a strong position in the field. Whatever progress has been made on the topic in the past fifteen years has resulted from empirical work. For a dense description that helps overcome preconceived perceptions of incidents of mass violence, however, it is indispensable to work with a large pool of primary documents as well as secondary sources. The extremely violent societies approach is derived from empirical observations and made for analytical purposes. . . . State-oriented as it is, the genocide approach—while having made important contributions—still captures only some of the causations and developments relevant to mass violence.

16 • The Genocidal Continuum (Nancy Scheper-Hughes)

Rejecting conventional definitions of genocide, notably the 1948 legal definition, Nancy Scheper-Hughes, a professor of anthropology at the University of California, Berkeley, presents a case for the broad conceptualization of the darkest of human phenomena. Inspired by social theorists from Pierre Bourdieu to Michel Foucault, Scheper-Hughes claims, rather controversially, that "invisible genocides" have been perpetrated in ordinary social spaces such as public schools, emergency rooms, nursing homes, city halls, jails, and public morgues. In order to capture the entire universe of genocide, she introduces the notion of a "genocidal continuum" in this 2002 work.

This chapter revisits a key theme in my work, which is derived from a radical tradition of social science: a concern with popular consent to everyday violence. By everyday violence I mean the legitimate, organized, and (above all) routinized violence that is implicit in particular social and political-economic formations. The everyday violence to which I refer is related to but distinct from Pierre Bourdieu's notion of "symbolic violence"; it is perhaps closest to what [Michael] Taussig, citing [the German literary theorist and critic Walter] Benjamin, calls "terror as usual." I want to suggest here that everyday violence—"peace-time crimes"—makes structural violence and genocide possible. So perhaps an alternative sub-title to this chapter might be "toward a genealogy of genocide." Nothing that I say here has not already been said before and more eloquently by those more expert in the field of genocide. My sole contribution lies in weaving together disparate threads of everyday life and everyday practice that participate in sanctioning genocidal-like behaviors toward certain *gens*—classes of people who are seen as dispensable.

Since his early work on the military destruction of Algerian villages Bourdieu became less interested in explaining how violence operates when it is expressed directly and crudely and more in the way that violence structures quite ordinary and "peaceful" social (and gender) relations. Bourdieu saw domination and violence in the least likely places—in the architecture of the home, in the exchange of gifts, in systems of classification, in village matrimonial rituals, in all the ambiguous uses of culture. Violence, he suggests, is everywhere in social practice. It is mis-recognized because its very familiarity renders it invisible. Once could interpret Bourdieu's move toward a symbolic theory of violence as analogous to Freud's decisive turning away from the real and bloody facts of child sexual abuse, which he encountered during his studies in Paris and his familiarity with the published research of Ambroise Tardieu, the leading French forensic pathologist, in order to consider the universal symbolic violence of unconsciously sexualized family relations.

Following Antonio Gramsci, Michel Foucault, Jean-Paul Sartre, Hannah Arendt, and other modern theorists of power and domination Bourdieu treats direct physical violence as a crude, uneconomical, and unnecessary mode of domination. It is less efficient and, following Arendt, it is certainly less legitimate. The Foucauldian narrative, for example, suggests that over the past two hundred years torture as a legitimate tool of the state officially disappeared

SOURCE: Nancy Scheper-Hughes, "The Genocidal Continuum: Peace-Time Crimes," in Jeannette Mageo, ed., *Power and the Self* (Cambridge: Cambridge University Press, 2002), 30–34. Reprinted with permission of the publisher.

in civilized countries. More refined methods for extracting consent were developed and implemented by modern "technicians of the social consensus," including labor and management specialists, urban planners, entertainment and media technicians, educators and, of course, doctors, counselors, psychiatrists, and social workers. . . . Meanwhile, anthropologists of violence have begun to address the shocking rebirth of late modern forms of genocide in Central Africa, Central America, South Asia, and Eastern Europe—the resurgence of what we naively thought (after the Holocaust) simply could not happen again. And so I return here to a question that vexed a generation of post-Holocaust social theorists: what makes genocide possible? How do we explain the alarming complicity of otherwise ordinary "good people" to outbreaks of radical violence perpetrated by the state, police, military, and ethnic groups?

Adorno and his Frankfurt School colleagues suggested that the seemingly willing participation of ordinary people in genocidal acts requires strong childhood conditioning in mindless obedience to authority figures in addition to powerful ideologies, such as anti-Semitism. But [Daniel Jonah] Goldhagen, relying on compelling testimony, argues that millions of ordinary Germans participated willingly, even eagerly, in the Holocaust not for fear of the authorities but because of race hatred. Alternatively, I have suggested a kind of genocidal continuum, made up of a multitude of "small wars and invisible genocides" conducted in the normative, ordinary social spaces of public schools, clinics, emergency rooms, hospital charity wards, nursing homes, city halls, jails, and public morgues.

The question—what makes genocide possible?—has guided a radical tradition of social science inquiry ever since the Holocaust made it impossible for students of human behavior to deny that a great many people, at different times and places, have been capable of perceiving (and disposing) of certain designated "others" as despicable and dirty things, as disposable rubbish, as worthy only (and ultimately) of extinction. Under radical political conditions, and often with broad social consent, policies of mass destruction under the guise of "social hygiene" and "ethnic cleansing" come into play. . . . Another element is necessary, however: the capacity to reduce other humans to non-persons, to things.

An analysis of this terrifying radical estrangement between self and other that I have elsewhere called "basic strangeness" has motivated much of my anthropological work on the structures, meanings, and practices of "everyday violence." It seems essential that we recognize in our species and in ourselves a genocidal capacity and that we exercise a defensive hyper-vigilance and hyper-sensitivity to the less dramatic and far more mundane (and normative) act of violence (sometimes masked as "sacrifice") directed against certain "classes" of humans—whether the farm-inheriting last-born sons in rural Irish farm families who are virtually forbidden to reproduce or the angel-babies of Brazilian shantytowns whose premature deaths are naturalized and spiritualized at one and the same time, or street children of Rio de Janeiro, Salvador, and Reife who are exterminated in the name of public hygiene, or the "oldest old" in America who are consigned to social death in nursing homes that bear resemblance to concentration camps. . . .

The genocidal *capacity* to which I refer has nothing to do with institutionalized drives but refers to the "purely" social sentiments of exclusion, dehumanization, depersonalization, pseudo-speciation, and reification which normalize and routinize behavior toward another or a class of others that would otherwise be seen as atrocious and unthinkable. In referring to "invisible genocides" I realize that I am walking on thin ice, while my suggestion of a "genocidal continuum" flies in the face of a noble tradition within genocide studies that argues for a strict and legalistic definition of genocide so as to prevent the absurd dilution of the term in rhetorical arguments against abortion, drug addiction, and the spread of AIDS in the African-American community, to mention but a few common metaphorical extensions and misuses of the term. Within the context of world courts and genocide tribunals an extremely specific definition of genocide is called for. But I am raising a very different set of questions that have nothing to do with legalities or justice-seeking and more to do with normalities and soul-searching. What is lost, what is gained in noting certain troubling institutional analogies among families, hospitals, schools, and prisons, or between nursing homes and concentration camps?

What is lost, obviously, is an understanding of the absolute uniqueness of genocide and of the Holocaust as the prototype of all genocides. . . . Because the slaughter of the Jews was "for nothing," the Holocaust [in the eyes of some] presents a paradigm of "pure" and gratuitous human suffering. Woe to those who would reduce or trivialize the horror and the exceptional nature of the Holocaust by comparing (and thereby equating) it with other lesser forms of social suffering. And yet I do make such comparisons, though I proceed cautiously and join others who have called attention to forms and spaces of hitherto unrecognized, gratuitous, and useless social suffering.

If there is a moral and political risk—and there is—in extending as powerful a concept as "genocide" into other hitherto unrecognized public and private/domestic spaces, the benefit lies in the ability to draw connections, to make predictions, to sensitize people to *genocidal-like* practices and sentiments hidden within the perfectly acceptable and normative behavior of ordinary, good-enough citizens. Why are we surprised at how easy it seems to be for ordinary people to cooperate in mass killings and genocide once the foundation has been laid in the many ordinary betrayals, the small wars and invisible genocides, already perpetrated against certain classes of sub-citizens[?]

Denial is a prerequisite of genocide. . . . Here, Bourdieu's partial and unfinished theory of evidence is useful. By including the softer, symbolic forms of violence hidden in the minutiae of "normal" social practices, Bourdieu forces us to reconsider the broader meanings and status of violence, especially the links between "everyday violence" and more explicit forms of political terror.

17 ◆ Is the Holocaust Unique? (Yehuda Bauer)

One of the most contested questions in the historiography of genocide is whether the Holocaust constitutes an event sui generis or is a genocide like any other. In his balanced book on the debate in 2001, the eminent Holocaust historian Yehuda Bauer, professor of Holocaust studies at Hebrew University of Jerusalem, concludes that the Holocaust is unprecedented but not unique in the sense of being nonrepeatable. For Bauer, the Holocaust represents an extreme form of genocide, but not one that sets it apart from the flow of history. Although perhaps not the first genocide ever witnessed,

SOURCE: Yehuda Bauer, *Rethinking the Holocaust* (New Haven, Conn.: Yale University Press, 2001), 14, 16, 17, 20, 22, 39, 47, 48, 49, 50. Reprinted with permission of the publisher.

the Holocaust was, in Bauer's estimation, at the time of its perpetration, novel in its global reach and total character.

Absolute uniqueness . . . leads to its opposite, total trivialization: if the Holocaust is a onetime, inexplicable occurrence then it is a waste of time to deal with it. . . . Some historians (including myself), social scientists, theologians, and other specialists have come to the conclusion that the Holocaust can be repeated, even though it is in some ways the most extreme form of genocide known to us to date and the first known occasion for certain types of murderous crimes or criminal thinking. . . .

Indeed, the basis for intelligible historical writing is [the] comparability of human experience. If there are recognizable patterns in the unrolling of human history, then there is a point in examining them. . . . The uniqueness—I shall henceforth use the term *unprecedentedness* despite its awkwardness—of the Holocaust does not lie . . . in the level of brutality reached by the Nazis and their helpers, although that was undoubtedly a peak. The genocide of the Jews was neither better nor worse than any other. . . . As far as brutality, the will to murder, and sadism are concerned, little is unique about the Nazis except that they went further than their predecessors. . . .

The only way to clarify the applicability of definitions and generalizations is with comparisons. The question of whether the Holocaust had elements that have not existed with any other form of genocide (whereas there are no major elements of other genocides that cannot be found in yet other genocides) is extremely important if we want to find out more about social pathology in general. When one discusses unprecedented elements in a social phenomenon, the immediate question is, Unprecedented in comparison with what? The very claim that a historical event is unprecedented can be made only when that event is compared with other events of a presumably similar nature with which it shares at least some qualities. Unless one finds a measure of comparability, unprecedentedness can mean only that the event is not human—in other words, is not historical—in which case it is useless to talk about it except in putative theological or mystical contexts. . . .

One major difference between the Holocaust and other forms of genocide is . . . that pragmatic considerations were central with all other genocides, abstract ideological motivations less so. With the Holocaust, pragmatic considerations were marginal. . . . No genocide to date had been based so completely on myths, on hallucinations, on abstract, nonpragmatic, ideology—which then was executed by very rational, pragmatic means. . . . A second reason why the Holocaust is unprecedented is its global, indeed, universal character. All other genocides were limited geographically; in most cases, the targeted group lived in a reasonably well defined geographic locale (Indian peoples in the Americas, Khmer and Cham in Cambodia . . . , Tutsi mainly in Rwanda, Uganda, Burundi, and Zaire; and so on). The Turks targeted Armenians in ethnically Turkish areas; they did not care about Armenians elsewhere. . . .

A third element sets the Holocaust apart from other genocides: its intended totality. The Nazis were looking for Jews, for all Jews. According to Nazi policy, all persons with three or four Jewish grandparents were sentenced to death for having been born. Such a policy has never been applied in human history before and would have undoubtedly been applied universally if Germany had won the war. If we compare this to other genocides—for instance, the case of the Caribs, who were indeed totally exterminated by Spanish policies—we find that there were never plans to achieve that aim, nor was it express state policy to do so, although that was the practical outcome. . . .

If this analysis is correct, then the Holocaust is an extreme form of genocide. It is important to restate what is meant by "extreme." The suffering of the victims of this genocide was in no sense greater than the suffering of victims of other genocides—there is no gradation of suffering. . . . What is meant by "extreme" is expressed by the three elements described above: the ideological, global, and total character of the genocide of the Jews. The extremeness of the Holocaust is what makes it unprecedented.

18 • The Politics of Naming (Mahmood Mamdani)

In this 2007 contribution to the London Review of Books, *Mahmood Mamdani, the author of, most recently,* Saviors and Survivors, *highlights the difficulties involved in representing the Darfur crisis in Sudan. Focusing on issues ranging from atrocity statistics to the classification of collective violence, Mamdani, professor of anthropology and political science at Columbia University, finds fault with the reporting of Nicholas Kristof, the* New York Times *columnist, as well as the Save Darfur campaign waged in the United States. He chastises both for misunderstanding the causes of the conflict, and for prescribing impossible cures.*

A full-page advertisement has appeared several times a week in the *New York Times* calling for intervention in Darfur now. It wants the intervening forces to be placed under "a chain of command allowing necessary and timely military action without approval from distant political or civilian personnel." That intervention in Darfur should not be subject to "political or civilian" considerations and that the intervening forces should have the right to shoot—to kill—without permission from distant places: these are said to be "humanitarian" demands. In the same vein, a *New Republic* editorial on Darfur has called for "force as a first-resort response." What makes the situation even more puzzling is that some of those who are calling for an end to intervention in Iraq are demanding an intervention in Darfur; as the slogan goes, "Out of Iraq and into Darfur." ← western savior complex mixed w/ guilt over Holocaust?

What would happen if we thought of Darfur as we do of Iraq, as a place with a history and politics—a messy politics of insurgency and counter-insurgency? Why should an intervention in Darfur not turn out to be a trigger that escalates rather than reduces the level of violence as intervention in Iraq has done? Why might it not create the actual possibility of genocide, not just rhetorically but in reality? Morally, there is no doubt about the horrific nature of the violence against civilians in Darfur. The ambiguity lies in the politics of the violence, whose sources include both a state-connected counter-insurgency and an organized insurgency, very much like the violence in Iraq.

The insurgency and counter-insurgency in Darfur began in 2003. Both were driven by an intermeshing of domestic tensions in the context of a peace-averse international environment defined by the War on Terror. On the one hand, there was a struggle for power within the

SOURCE: Mahmood Mamdani, "The Politics of Naming: Genocide, Civil War, Insurgency," *London Review of Books*, March 8, 2007. Reprinted with permission of the publisher.

political class in Sudan, with more marginal interests in the west (following those in the south and in the east) calling for reform at the center. On the other, there was a community-level split inside Darfur, between nomads and settled farmers, who had earlier forged a way of sharing the use of semi-arid land in the dry season. With the drought that set in towards the late 1970s, cooperation turned into an intense struggle over diminishing resources. As the insurgency took root among the prospering peasant tribes of Darfur, the government trained and armed the poorer nomads and formed a militia—the Janjawiid—that became the vanguard of the unfolding counter-insurgency. The worst violence came from the Janjawiid, but the insurgent movements were also accused of gross violations. Anyone wanting to end the spiraling violence would have to bring about power-sharing at the state level and resource-sharing at the community level, land being the key resource.

Since its onset, two official verdicts have been delivered on the violence, the first from the U.S., the second from the UN. The American verdict was unambiguous: Darfur was the site of an ongoing genocide. The chain of events leading to Washington's proclamation began with "a genocide alert" from the Management Committee of the Washington Holocaust Memorial Museum; according to the *Jerusalem Post*, the alert was "the first ever of its kind, issued by the U.S. Holocaust Museum." The House of Representatives followed unanimously on 24 June 2004. The last to join the chorus was Colin Powell. The UN Commission on Darfur was created in the aftermath of the American verdict and in response to American pressure. It was more ambiguous. In September 2004, the Nigerian president Olusegun Obasanjo, then the chair of the African Union, visited UN headquarters in New York. Darfur had been the focal point of discussion in the African Union. All concerned were alert to the extreme political sensitivity of the issue. At a press conference at the UN on 23 September Obasanjo was asked to pronounce on the violence in Darfur: was it genocide or not? His response was very clear:

> Before you can say that this is genocide or ethnic cleansing, we will have to have a definite decision and plan and program of a government to wipe out a particular group of people, then we will be talking about genocide, ethnic cleansing. What we know is not that. What we know is that there was an uprising, rebellion, and the government armed another group of people to stop that rebellion. That's what we know. That does not amount to genocide from our own reckoning. It amounts to of course conflict. It amounts to violence.

By October, the Security Council had established a five-person commission of inquiry on Darfur and asked it to report within three months on "violations of international humanitarian law and human rights law in Darfur by all parties," and specifically to determine "whether or not acts of genocide have occurred." Among the members of the commission was the chief prosecutor of South Africa's TRC [Truth and Reconciliation Commission], Dumisa Ntsebeza. In its report, submitted on 25 January 2005, the commission concluded that "the Government of the Sudan has not pursued a policy of genocide . . . directly or through the militias under its control." But the commission did find that the government's violence was "deliberately and indiscriminately directed against civilians." Indeed, "even where rebels may have been present in villages, the impact of attacks on civilians shows that the use of military force was manifestly disproportionate to any threat posed by the rebels." These acts, the commission concluded, "were conducted on a widespread and systematic basis, and therefore may amount to *crimes against humanity*" (my emphasis). Yet, the commission insisted, they did not amount to acts of genocide: "The crucial element of genocidal intent appears to be missing. . . . It would seem that those who planned and organized attacks on villages pursued the intent to drive the victims from their homes, primarily for purposes of counter-insurgency warfare." At the same time, the commission assigned secondary responsibility to rebel forces— namely, members of the Sudan Liberation Army and the Justice and Equality Movement— which it held "responsible for serious violations of international human rights and humanitarian law which may amount to *war crimes*" (my emphasis). If the government stood accused of "crimes against humanity," rebel movements were accused of "war crimes." . . .

The journalist in the U.S. most closely identified with consciousness-raising on Darfur is the *New York Times* op-ed columnist Nicholas Kristof, often identified as a lone crusader on the issue. To peruse Kristof's Darfur columns over the past three years is to see the reduction of a complex political context to a morality tale unfolding in a world populated by villains and victims who never trade places and so can always and easily be told apart. It is a world where atrocities mount geometrically, the perpetrators so evil and the victims so helpless that the only possibility of relief is a rescue mission from the outside, preferably in the form of a military intervention.

Kristof made six highly publicized trips to Darfur, the first in March 2004 and the sixth two years later. He began by writing of it as a case of "ethnic cleansing": "Sudan's Arab rulers" had "forced 700,000 black African Sudanese to flee their villages" (24 March 2004). Only three days later, he upped the ante: this was no longer ethnic cleansing, but genocide. "Right now," he wrote on 27 March, "the government of Sudan is engaged in genocide against three large African tribes in its Darfur region." He continued: "The killings are being orchestrated by the Arab-dominated Sudanese government" and "the victims are non-Arabs: blacks in the Zaghawa, Massalliet and Fur tribes." He estimated the death toll at a thousand a week. Two months later, on 29 May, he revised the estimates dramatically upward, citing predictions from the U.S. Agency for International Development to the effect that "at best, 'only' 100,000 people will die in Darfur this year of malnutrition and disease" but "if things go badly, half a million will die."

The UN commission's report was released on 25 February 2005. It confirmed "massive displacement" of persons ("more than a million" internally displaced and "more than 200,000" refugees in Chad) and the destruction of "several hundred" villages and hamlets as "irrefutable facts"; but it gave no confirmed numbers for those killed. Instead, it noted rebel claims that government-allied forces had "allegedly killed over 70,000 persons." Following the publication of the report, Kristof began to scale down his estimates. For the first time, on 23 February 2005, he admitted that "the numbers are fuzzy." Rather than the usual single total, he went on to give a range of figures, from a low of 70,000, which he dismissed as "a UN estimate," to "independent estimates [that] exceed 220,000." A warning followed: "and the number is rising by about ten thousand a month."

The publication of the commission's report had considerable effect. Internationally, it raised doubts about whether what was going on in Darfur could be termed genocide. Even U.S. officials were unwilling to go along with the high estimates propagated by the broad alliance of organization that subscribe to the Save Darfur campaign. The effect on American diplomacy was discernible. Three months later, on 3 May, Kristof noted with dismay that not

only had "Deputy Secretary of State Robert Zoellick pointedly refused to repeat the administration's past judgment that the killings amount to genocide": he had "also cited an absurdly
low estimate of Darfur's total death toll: 60,000 to 160,000." As an alternative, Kristof cited the
latest estimate of deaths from the Coalition for International Justice as "nearly 400,000, and
rising by 500 a day."

In three months, Kristof's estimates had gone up from 10,000 to 15,000 a month. Six
months later, on 27 November, Kristof warned that "if aid groups pull out . . . the death toll
could then rise to 100,000 a month." Anyone keeping a tally of the death toll in Darfur as reported in the Kristof columns would find the rise, fall and rise again very bewildering. First he
projected the number of dead at 320,000 for 2004 (16 June 2004) but then gave a scaled down
estimate of between 70,000 and 220,000 (23 February 2005). The number began once more
to climb to "nearly 400,000" (3 May 2005), only to come down yet again to 300,000 (23 April
2006). Each time figures were given with equal confidence but with no attempt to explain
their basis. Did the numbers reflect an actual decline in the scale of killing in Darfur or was
Kristof simply making an adjustment to the changing mood internationally?

In the 23 April column, Kristof expanded the list of perpetrators to include an external
power: "China is now underwriting its second genocide in three decades. The first was in Pol
Pot's Cambodia, and the second is in Darfur, Sudan. Chinese oil purchases have financed
Sudan's pillage of Darfur, Chinese-made AK-47s have been the main weapons used to slaughter several hundred thousand people in Darfur so far and China has protected Sudan in the
UN Security Council." In the Kristof columns, there is one area of deafening silence, to do
with the fact that what is happening in Darfur is a civil war. Hardly a word is said about the
insurgency, about the civilian deaths insurgents mete out, about acts that the commission
characterized as "war crimes." . . .

Newspaper writing on Darfur has sketched a *Powerful* pornography of violence. It seems fasci-
nated by and fixated on the gory details, describing the worst of the atrocities in gruesome
detail and chronicling the rise in the number of them. The implication is that the motivation
of the perpetrators lies in biology ("race") and, if not that, certainly in "culture." This voyeuris-
tic approach accompanies a moralistic discourse whose effect is both to obscure the politics
of the violence and position the reader as a virtuous, not just a concerned observer. Journalism gives us a simple moral world, where a group of perpetrators face a group of victims, but
where neither history nor motivation is thinkable because both are outside history and context. Even when newspapers highlight violence as a social phenomenon, they fail to understand the forces that shape the agency of the perpetrator. Instead, they look for a clear and
uncomplicated moral that describes the victim as untainted and the perpetrator as simply
evil. . . .

The conflict in Darfur is highly politicized, and so is the international campaign. One of
the campaign's constant refrains has been that the ongoing genocide is racial: "Arabs" are trying to eliminate "Africans." But both "Arab" and "African" have several meanings in Sudan.
There have been at least three meanings of "Arab." Locally, "Arab" was a pejorative reference
to the lifestyle of the nomad as uncouth; regionally, it referred to someone whose primary
language was Arabic. In this sense, a group could become "Arab" over time. This process,
known as Arabization, was not an anomaly in the region: there was Amharization in Ethiopia
and Swahilization on the East African coast. The third meaning of "Arab" was "privileged and

exclusive"; it was the claim of the riverine political aristocracy who had ruled Sudan since independence, and who equated Arabization with the spread of civilization and being Arab with descent.

"African," in this context, was a subaltern identity that also had the potential of being either exclusive or inclusive. The two meanings were not only contradictory but came from the experience of two different insurgencies. The inclusive meaning was more political than racial or even cultural (linguistic), in the sense that an "African" was anyone determined to make a future within Africa. It was pioneered by John Garang, the leader of the Sudan People's Liberation Army (SPLA) in the south, as a way of holding together the New Sudan he hoped to see. In contrast, its exclusive meaning came in two versions, one hard (racial) and the other soft (linguistic)—"African" as Bantu and "African" as the identity of anyone who spoke a language indigenous to Africa. The racial meaning came to take a strong hold in both the counter-insurgency and the insurgency in Darfur.

The Save Darfur campaign's characterization of the violence as "Arab" against "African" obscured both the fact that the violence was not one-sided and the contest over the meaning of "Arab" and "African": a contest that was critical precisely because it was ultimately about who belonged and who did not in the political community called Sudan. The depoliticization, naturalization and, ultimately, demonization of the notion "Arab," as against "African," has been the deadliest effect, whether intended or not, of the Save Darfur campaign. The depoliticization of the conflict gave campaigners [two] advantages. First, they were able to occupy the moral high ground. The campaign presented itself as apolitical but moral, its concern limited only to saving lives. Second, only a single-issue campaign could bring together in a unified chorus forces that are otherwise ranged as adversaries on most important issues of the day: at one end, the Christian right and the Zionist lobby; at the other, a mainly school- and university-based peace movement. Nat Hentoff of the *Village Voice* wrote of the Save Darfur Coalition as "an alliance of more than 515 faith-based, humanitarian and human rights organizations"; among the organizers of their Rally to Stop the Genocide in Washington last year were groups as diverse as the American Jewish World Service, the American Society for Muslim Advancement, the National Association of Evangelicals, the U.S. Conference of Catholic Bishops, the U.S. Holocaust Memorial Museum, the American Anti-Slavery Group, Amnesty International, Christian Solidarity International, Physicians for Human Rights and the National Black Church Initiative. . . .

If many of the leading lights in the Darfur campaign are fired by moral indignation, this derives from two events: the Nazi Holocaust and the Rwandan genocide. After all, the seeds of the Save Darfur campaign lie in the tenth-anniversary commemoration of what happened in Rwanda. Darfur is today a metaphor for senseless violence in politics, as indeed Rwanda was a decade before. Most writing on the Rwandan genocide in the U.S. was also done by journalists. In *We Wish to Inform You That Tomorrow We Will Be Killed with Our Families*, the most widely read book on the genocide, Philip Gourevitch envisaged Rwanda as a replay of the Holocaust, with Hutu cast as perpetrators and Tutsi as victims. Again, the encounter between the two seemed to take place outside any context, as part of an eternal encounter between evil and innocence. Many of the journalists who write about Darfur have Rwanda very much in the back of their minds. . . .

With very few exceptions, the Save Darfur campaign has drawn a single lesson from Rwanda: the problem was the U.S. failure to intervene to stop the genocide. Rwanda is the guilt that America must expiate, and to do so it must be ready to intervene, for good and against evil, even globally. That lesson is inscribed at the heart of Samantha Power's book, *A Problem from Hell: America and the Age of Genocide*. But it is the wrong lesson. The Rwandan genocide was born of a civil war which intensified when the settlement to contain it broke down. The settlement, reached at the Arusha Conference, broke down because neither the Hutu Power tendency nor the Tutsi-dominated Rwanda Patriotic Front (RPF) had any interest in observing the power-sharing arrangement at the core of the settlement: the former because it was excluded from the settlement and the latter because it was unwilling to share power in any meaningful way.

What the humanitarian intervention lobby fails to see is that the U.S. did intervene in Rwanda, through a proxy. That proxy was the RPF, backed up by entire units from the Uganda Army. The green light was given to the RPF, whose commanding officer, Paul Kagame, had recently returned from training in the U.S., just as it was lately given to the Ethiopian army in Somalia. Instead of using its resources and influence to bring about a political solution to the civil war, and then strengthen it, the U.S. signaled to one of the parties that it could pursue victory with impunity. This unilateralism was part of what led to the disaster, and that is the real lesson of Rwanda. Applied to Darfur and Sudan, it is sobering. It means recognizing that Darfur is not yet another Rwanda. Nurturing hopes of an external military intervention among those in the insurgency who aspire to victory and reinforcing the fears of those in the counter-insurgency who see it as a prelude to defeat are precisely the ways to ensure that it becomes a Rwanda.

19 • Genocidalism (Aleksandar Jokic)

Although the 2004 article from which this excerpt is taken is in the main an impassioned critique of scholars who have classified (some of) the atrocities committed in Bosnia Herzegovina in the 1990s as genocide, Aleksandar Jokic, an associate professor of philosophy at Portland State University, also makes a useful contribution to the study of genocide more generally by introducing the notion of genocidalism into the debate. By so doing, Jokic, like Mahmood Mamdani, highlights the politics of naming, in particular the inappropriate use of the term genocide *for the pursuit of political ends.*

I define "genocidalism" (stipulatively) as follows: (i) The purposeful neglect to attribute responsibility for genocide in cases when overwhelming evidence exists, and (ii) the energetic attribution of "genocide" in less than clear cases without considering available and convincing, opposing evidence and argumentation. We may call the first manifestation "genocidalism of omission," while the second represents . . . "genocidalism of commission." If we were to

SOURCE: Aleksandar Jokic, "Genocidalism," *Journal of Ethics* 8, no. 3 (2004): 251–97, 251, 252, 254, 296, 297. Reprinted with permission of Kluwer Academic Publishers.

explore the relationship between the two manifestations of genocidalism, we would uncover, I suspect, that the latter often functions in a way that strengthens the former. . . .

Genocidalism is a more widespread phenomenon in the contemporary discourse on international affairs that one might initially think. The parties guilty of genocidalism can be found in a broad range of partakers in this discourse, among journalists, human rights activists, celebrities, politicians, international law experts, and other academics such as psychologists, historians or political scientists. While genocide is undoubtedly the highest crime of which humans are capable, quite a lot of harm can be achieved by morally irresponsible uses of the word "genocide." . . .

As far as the modes of presentation scholars have available to them in addressing the subject of genocide there exists a certain gradation at play that one must be extremely careful about. . . . Whatever may be wrong with giving genocide "too little attention," it ought to be even clearer that giving it too much attention is also a wrong because it amounts to applying the category of genocide where the facts do not warrant it. . . .

Activists on behalf of "international justice" would do much more good if they took up the cause of achieving accountability for genocidalism rather than their preoccupation with genocide. . . . Once the nature of genocidalism of commission is truly appreciated, that is, once it becomes a properly understood and well-researched social phenomenon, it should be recognized as a criminal act. This could be done quite effectively by making it a part of the Genocide Convention or by building the ban on the practice of genocidalism into municipal law not unlike the so-called hate crime legislation in the United States.

CHAPTER TWO

Causes

What causes genocide? This chapter assembles the most important answers generated to date, drawing attention to the various levels of analysis and methodological perspectives that scholars have adopted to make sense of the onset of genocide. It includes notable examples of rationalist, structuralist, and cultural explanations of genocide.

Rationalist explanations are typically founded on assumptions about costs and benefits. Such explanations tend to emphasize the centrality of genocidal planning and cost-benefit analysis. For the purpose of illustration, consider the extract from Vahakn Dadrian's article on the Young-Turk Ittihadist Conference in the late Ottoman Empire. According to Dadrian, the destruction of Armenia's Christians was, in the main, a carefully calibrated and meticulously orchestrated—and in many respects rational—response to the decline of empire. Manus Midlarsky too emphasizes the rational logic of destruction, suggesting that a combination of risk minimization and loss compensation has historically been at fault. Also concerned with the rationality of genocide are Götz Aly and Susanne Heim, for whom Nazi technocrats set in motion genocidal thinking when they attempted to rationally solve the problem of overpopulation in Germany and its occupied territories.

All of these explanations revolve around genocidal agents and their preferences and are complemented here by the contributions of Gerald Scully (who writes about politicide and genocide in terms of rents) and Benjamin Valentino (who develops a strategic model of mass violence).

Zygmunt Bauman's influential argument that modernity was indispensable for making the Holocaust work, Robert Melson's emphasis on the significance of revolution, and Stanley Milgram's finding that authority structures enable individuals when it comes to the application of violence, not to mention Val Percival and Thomas Homer-Dixon's inquiry into the environmental dimensions of genocidal violence, exemplify the structuralist tradition in genocide studies (i.e., the tendency to invoke macro-level explanations such as ones focusing on the importance of modernity or war). Such accounts are featured here alongside the more culturally focused explanations of Patrick Brantlinger (who analyzes the discourse on the extinction of primitive races), Omer Bartov and Phyllis Mack (who inquire into the contribution of religion to genocide), and Daniel Goldhagen, who puts forth the contention that a deep-rooted cultural predisposition toward anti-Semitism caused ordinary Germans to participate in the Holocaust.

Other writings in this chapter point to the causal significance of colonialism (Dirk Moses, Mahmood Mamdani), war (Christopher Browning, René Lemarchand), and psychology (Ervin Staub, James Waller) for making sense of genocide. Together with the other essays, these authors typify the range of approaches and perspectives characteristic of contemporary genocide scholarship.

20 • The Discourse on the Extinction of Primitive Races (Patrick Brantlinger)

In his 2003 study of racism and imperialism in the period 1800–1930, Patrick Brantlinger, professor of English and Victorian studies at Indiana University, draws our attention to the role of language as a harbinger of destruction. Focusing in particular on cases of colonial genocide, he chronicles the lethal consequences of what he terms "extinction discourse" in the nineteenth and twentieth centuries.

Extinction discourse is a specific branch of the dual ideologies of imperialism and racism—a "discursive formation," to use Foucauldian terminology. Like Orientalism and other versions of racism, it does not respect the boundaries of disciplines or the cultural hierarchies of high and low; instead, it is found wherever and whenever Europeans and white Americans encountered indigenous peoples. A remarkable feature of extinction discourse is its uniformity across other ideological fault lines: whatever their disagreements, humanitarians, missionaries, scientists, government officials, explorers, colonists, soldiers, journalists novelists, and poets were in basic agreement about the inevitable disappearance of some or all primitive races. This massive and rarely questioned consensus made extinction discourse extremely potent, working inexorably toward the very outcome it often opposed. . . .

Shadowing the romantic stereotype of the Noble Savage is its ghostly twin, the self-exterminating savage. It is no exaggeration to include this Gothic stereotype among the causes—and not just effects—of the global decimation of many indigenous peoples. The belief that savagery was vanishing of its own accord from the world of progress and light mitigated guilt and sometimes excused or even encouraged violence toward those deemed savage. Even when savagery was not identified as causing its own extinction, it was frequently held that some races could not be civilized and were thus doomed to fall by the wayside no matter what customs they practiced. . . .

The pervasive concept of race reinforced assumptions of biological necessity while lending a supposedly scientific legitimacy to Western ideas about non-Western peoples. Race also homogenized the great diversity of peoples—into the uncivilized stages of savagery and barbarism but also into the stereotypic models of separate, radically unequal types of mankind. Thus, for example, the Incas and the Iroquois, the Hopis and the Kwakutls constituted one "red race" with one ultimate destiny. Throughout its unifications of widely divergent cultures and societies, racial theory and its subset, extinction discourse, downplayed or ignored the possibility that there might be many degrees, levels, or types of progress toward (or degenera-

SOURCE: Patrick Brantlinger, *Dark Vanishings: The Discourse on the Extinction of Primitive Races, 1800–1930* (Ithaca, N.Y.: Cornell University Press, 2003), 1–2, 3, 6, 9, 10, 15, 17, 18, 190. Reprinted with permission of the publisher.

tion away from) civilization—or, more radically yet, that there were diverse cultures and civilizations pursuing different but equally legitimate histories. . . .

Between the early 1800s and the 1930s the belief that most or all primitive traces were doomed, rarely contested even by would-be saviors of indigenous peoples, became a mantra for the advocates of British imperial expansion and American manifest destiny. . . . Especially on colonial frontiers in Australia, New Zealand, South Africa, and North America, there were many rationalizers and even advocates of the extermination of native populations. . . . The rationalizers and sometimes proponents of genocide, however, included many who were humane on other issues such as slavery. . . .

[For example,] in 1872, Anthony Trollope wrote that the "doom" of the Australian aboriginals "is to be exterminated; and the sooner that their doom be accomplished—so that there be no cruelty—the better it will be for civilization." And in his 1870 essay "The Noble Red Man," Mark Twain denied any nobility to the ordinary "Indian," declaring him to be "nothing but a poor, filthy, naked scurvy vagabond, whom to exterminate were a charity to the Creator's worthier insects and reptiles." . . .

Before the publication of Darwin's *Origin of Species* (1859), three types of supposedly scientific discourse dealt with the extinction of primitive races. The first was "natural history," a broad rubric that embraced both geology and biology. . . . The second, emergent science that contributed to extinction discourse was economics. Especially in the second, 1803 edition of his *Essay on Population*, the Reverend Thomas Robert Malthus offers a wide range of information and speculation about the population dynamics of both civilized and primitive societies. Although he does not emphasize race, Malthus has, for good reason, been called "the founding father of scientific racism." . . . The third, at least nascent science concerned with racial extinction was anthropology. All three of these supposedly scientific, often overlapping discourses supported a view of savagery as a Hobbesian state of nature, a *bellum omnium contra omnes* in which the strong exterminated or enslaved the weak. . . . Nevertheless, the Darwinian view of the future of primitive races was just as grim as that of most of the pre-Darwinians. Social Darwinists argued that nature's constant laws mandated the extinction of all unfit creatures and species to make room for new, supposedly fitter ones. . . .

The most lethal aspect of extinction discourse has probably been its stress on the inevitability of the vanishing. The sense of doom has often been rendered all the more powerful by the combination of three elements: belief in the progress of at least some (chosen) peoples from savagery to civilization; the faith that progress is either providential or natural—God's or Nature's wise plan; and the idea that the white and dark races of the world are separated from each other by biological essences that, translated into Darwinian terms, equal "fitness" versus "unfitness" to survive. In all these ways extinction discourse forms a powerful nexus of ideas that has been hegemonic for countless European explorers, colonists, writers, artists, officials, missionaries, humanitarians, and anthropologists. . . .

Today indigenous peoples, whether primitive or not, perhaps number 357 million. . . . Many belong to societies and cultures that have been subjected to genocide in one form or another over the last three centuries. Many continue to be victims of genocidal practices. . . . What now seems inexorably destructive is not the auto-genocide of savagery nor the biological (racially determined) demise of the unfit, but the juggernaut of economic development,

which to peoples trying to maintain traditional ways of life can be just as destructive as armed
massacres.

21 • The Origins of the Genocidal Moment in the Colonization of Australia (A. Dirk Moses)

*Dirk Moses, a historian at the European University Institute, was among the first scholars to explore
issues of colonial genocide in his native Australia. In this widely read essay from 2000, he offers a
succinct account of how the British colonization of Australia in the nineteenth century led to "exterminatory policies" and the destruction of Aboriginal society. Yet rather than assuming that the colonization of Australia was genocidal from the outset and in its entirety, Moses highlights the political
economy of destruction. He illustrates his subtle argument about the cumulative radicalization of
settler behavior with particular reference to the colonization of Queensland, thereby highlighting
important differences between the center (i.e., London and Sydney) and the periphery of an empire.*

Since the release of an Australian government report, in 1996, about the government policies
of forcibly removing indigenous children from their families, genocide has been a prominent
issue in the nationwide discussion about compensation, an official apology, and "reconciliation" with Aborigines. At the same time, the historical scholarship of the 1970s and 1980s,
which highlighted the hitherto repressed issue of the violent settlement of the Australian continent in the 19th century, became a public issue, especially in relation to the land rights issue,
about which the Australian High Court made two landmark rulings in the 1990s.

The ensuing debate has become starkly polarized. Many Aborigines believe that they
were the object of genocidal policies, and historians on the Left tend to agree with them.
Conservative commentators and the current federal government, for their part, vehemently
reject this proposition. There is an unfortunate if understandable tendency in the former
camp to comb the Australian past in search of evidence of genocide, and a proclivity to interpret any such evidence in the worst light. The latter camp do not deny the killings, but it ab-
solves the colonial and national governments of responsibility, and it insists that while the
policies of child removal may have been misguided by today's standards, they were well inten-
tioned. One side claims that the European colonization of Australia was genocidal; the other
denies it. These undifferentiated terms hinder rather than help the attempt to understand the
character of this particular colonization experience. The issue is so intractable, perhaps, because it concerns a complex and unplanned process of colonization, which began, in the im-
mortal words of Sir Robert Seeley, "in a fit of absence of mind."

Seeley's was an intuitive insight because it identified the salient issue that underlies the
controversy over genocide in Australia: the vexed question of intention in such processes. As
is well known, intention is the key element in the United Nations definition of genocide. . . .
The difficulty in applying the UN definition of genocide to colonial cases of mass death rests

SOURCE: A. Dirk Moses, "An Antipodean Genocide? The Origins of the Genocidal Moment in the Colonization of Australia," *Journal of Genocide Research* 2, no. 1 (2000): 89, 90, 91–92, 93, 94, 95–96, 97, 99, 100–102.
Reprinted with permission of Taylor & Francis.

on the fact that most of the indigenous fatalities were not usually the direct consequence of an intended policy of extermination. Disease, malnutrition, alcohol, a decreased birth-rate, and increased intertribal warfare accounted, in the main, for the catastrophic decline in the Aboriginal population in colonial Australia, as it did in indigenous populations in other sites of European colonialism. And yet the destruction of Aboriginal civilization was inevitable once the Europeans determined to occupy the country and develop a pastoral economy. The colonization process undeniably had, so to speak, a "genocidal effect" on Aborigines. Indeed, the destruction of Aboriginal society as a nomadic form of life was in fact an explicit aim of the British colonizers; this is what they meant by "civilizing" the Aborigines. But can processes per se be genocidal? Does not genocide require an agent, or agents, that makes conscious choices and decisions?

. . . The British Colonial Office certainly did not possess a genocidal intention when it sent out the first fleet of convicts and soldiers in 1787. Yet, the assumptions and practice of European settlement—the denial of prior Aboriginal land ownership, the naive Enlightenment assimilation hope, and the rapid spread of a pastoral economy—resulted inevitably in the mass death of Aborigines. In the terminology of the day, they "melted away" and constituted a "dying race." To be sure, such metaphors obscured concrete white behavior against Aborigines, but the fact remains that most Aboriginal deaths and the drastic population decline were attributable to the unintended side-effects of colonization. The objective and inherent character of the British occupation of the Australian continent necessarily entailed the destruction of Aboriginal society as a culture (ethnocide) and vast numbers of Aborigines, even if mass death was not its aim. But this is not genocide.

But how did policy makers respond when Aborigines did not "melt away" and put up sufficient resistance to pastoralists and pastoralism, which was the key sector of the economy, such as to threaten the viability of one of the colonies? The answer is that governments in the metropolis, under intense pressure from the periphery, were prepared to entertain "final solutions" to the "Aboriginal problem." Instead of arguing statically that the colonization of Australia was genocidal *tout court*, or insisting truculently that it was essentially benevolent and progressive, albeit with unfortunate ramifications, it is analytically more productive to view it as a dynamic process with genocidal potential that could be released in certain circumstances. The place to look for genocidal intentions, then, is not in explicit, prior statements of settlers or governments, but in the gradual evolution of European attitudes and policies as they were pushed in an exterminatory direction by the confluence of their underlying assumptions, the demands of the colonial and international economy, their plans for the land, and the resistance to these plans by the indigenous Australians.

I argue, in other words, that the British colonization of Australia was *objectively* and *inherently* ethnocidal and fatal for Aborigines, and potentially genocidal. Only after the initial illusions of peaceful coexistence had been dispelled with increasing contact between the two sides did the deadly implications inherent in the process become apparent to all, and, in a particular constellation of circumstances, its objective intention become subjectively located in the consciousness of the colonial agents themselves. . . .

In the first stage of what might be called the "apparent innocence of initial contact," the subjective intentions of the leaders of the first fleet of convicts and their keepers were relatively benign by the standards of imperialism. Regarding the "natives," the first governor of the colony in Sydney, Arthur Phillip, had instructions from London to "conciliate their affections," to enjoin everyone to "live in kindness with them," and to punish those who would "wantonly destroy them, or give them any unnecessary interruption in the exercise of their several occupations." The British believed in an optimistic Enlightenment anthropology whereby all humans shared a common nature, even if they occupied different levels on the ladder of human development.... The subjective intention of the colonizers was rarely malicious because of the European ignorance of Aboriginal culture, and because the British thought it was possible to share the land as a society of small-scale peasants. In a country as large as Australia there appeared room enough for everyone. Little did the first occupiers realize that within 40 years, extensive pastoralism would come to dominate, and that it would be incompatible with the hunter-gatherer economy of the Aborigines.

The competition for land characterizes the second stage of the conflict. As more convicts and free settlers arrived and pushed into the interior in search of grazing land, they inevitably came into conflict with the local Aboriginal clans.... Where London and the Australian metropolitan authorities wanted an orderly procedure in which the interests of the Aborigines would be protected, the local Europeans simply marched inland to select the property they wanted. And where troops were called in, they inevitably sided with the colonists, because their interests had to prevail.... In all, 200,000 immigrants arrived in Australia between 1832 and 1850, and by 1860, 4,000 Europeans with 20 million sheep occupied 400 million hectares of land from Southern Queensland to South Australia. Not surprisingly, the Aborigines resisted: cultivating and fencing land, and grazing new and strange breeds of animals interfered with their hunter-gatherer economy. Guerilla warfare ensued, and the government authorized self-policing.... Insofar as Aborigines were prepared to submit to the new order and lay down their weapons, they were issued with passes and allowed to move around freely. Insofar as they obstructed the new order, the settlers on the frontier were determined to subdue and even exterminate them, despite government warnings against massacres. Exterminatory attitudes undeniably developed in the frontier milieu....

The genocidal attitude of the settlers was evidence of a keener sense of the reality of the situation than those of the optimistic humanitarians in the metropolis.... The conflict on the frontier had become an existential struggle for survival. It was a direct confrontation between international market forces, incarnated in the pastoralists, and the hunter-gatherers. But is this genocide? Where whole Aboriginal peoples were exterminated by bands of settlers, the requirements of genocide on a local basis are clearly met. But such genocidal massacres were sporadic and unsystematic and do not license the broader claim that the colonization of the country was "a genocide" per se. The situation is complicated by the posture of the state. The killing of Aborigines, except in self-defense, remained a crime, and where colonial authorities, which jealously guarded the state's monopoly on violence, attempted to prosecute the white murderers of Aborigines, they were invariably frustrated by the solidarity of the settlers. In most parts of Australia, the colonization venture was able to proceed without state-sponsored genocidal measures. Even the harsh measures of the native police in the Port Phillip district were retaliatory rather than exterminatory.... Could the colonial state find itself developing and implementing genocidal policies?...

The colony of Queensland, which achieved independence from New South Wales in 1859, was the purest incarnation of the colonization process. Its government represented the interest of the squatter—that is, the priorities of the frontier—without the mollifying factor of control from Sydney or London. . . . The debt-ridden colony, whose far-flung frontiers— Queensland is about 2.5 times the size of Texas—were beyond the resources of the state to police with white troops. The evolution of a genocidal government policy to deal with the frontier crisis can be observed with regard to the Native Police. Comprising units of non-local Aborigines of six to twelve men and led by a white officer, the Native Police was formed in the southern colonies in the 1830s and 1840s to keep law and order on the frontier and prevent the undeclared war that sometimes obtained between settlers and Aborigines. A northern force of about 70 troopers was established for pre-independence Queensland in 1848. . . .

The frontier settlers made no bones about their priorities: "Let us at once extermi- nate these useless and obnoxious wretches. It seems that nothing short of extermination will check their animosity to the whites and all that is theirs." "Desperate diseases call for strong remedies and while we would regret a war of extermination, we cannot but admit that there exists a stern, though maybe cruel necessity for it." . . . Northern pastoralists successfully in- trigued with the "hawks" in the government in Sydney to . . . wrest control of the Native Police from Sydney and transfer it to local, northern magistrates, who were, of course, themselves pastoralists. . . .

The fear grew among the Europeans that Aborigines conspired at their large ceremonial meetings to attack isolated settlements in concerted actions. Consequently, a year later, the official instructions of the Native Police were redefined. The force was not just to patrol the frontier and apprehend law-breakers: it was to become proactive; it was "at all times and op- portunities to disperse any large assemblage of blacks; such meetings, if not prevented, invari- ably lead to depredations or murder."

Like the term "collision," "dispersal" was a euphemism that officers and politicians em- ployed to describe their violent encounters with Aborigines. . . . One observer in 1875 de- scribed a dispersal in the following terms: "The usual method adopted by the Native Police is to find out the 'camp' of the blacks . . . and attack them at the break of day, the troopers stripping themselves of everything but their forage caps and cartridge belt, and leave their horses, etc., in charge of the officer in command, and fire a volley into the camp, and after- wards follow up and shoot as many more of the blacks as they can, and the trooper who kills the most is considered the 'best man' by his comrades, until the 'next hunt,' when some of the others may shoot a greater number. The forage cap is kept on to prevent the troopers shooting one another in the scrub." . . .

The Native Police operated on the nether side of the law and was highly secret. Aborigi- nes were, after all, British subjects and could not legally be shot on sight or subjected to group punishment. And it was precisely the rule of law that the pastoralists insisted got in the way of securing their foothold on the frontier. The Queensland government was regularly attacked by humanitarian lobby groups and the liberal press, which had no doubts that the Native Police was an instrument of an extermination policy. . . . The sheep and cattle industry would have been unthinkable without the "pacification" of the Native Police. . . . The genocidal mo- ment of colonization passed when the Aborigines were either wiped out or submitted to the new order. . . . Because of the secrecy of the force, it is difficult to determine how many people it killed, and the disappearance of relevant files from the Queensland State Archives makes impossible the decoding of the official reports.

The argument has been made by some historians that the presence of the Native Police on the frontier actually prevented even more Aboriginal deaths. This was certainly how the government presented its policy. . . . Even if it is true that the numbers of deaths on both sides were reduced by the terror and massacres of the Native Police, it is equally true that the use of government terror transformed local genocidal massacres by settlers into an official state-wide policy. Was this a genocidal policy in terms of the UN definition? The limited resources of the Queensland state meant that the capacity did not exist to exterminate 100,000 Aborigines. Nor was it possible to justify a policy of explicit extermination, even in the Queensland public sphere. But the government's explicit approval of the Native Police and its proactive "dispersal" policy, which persisted until 1896, indicate a continuing intention to kill Aborigines in large numbers on the frontier until they disappeared or were subdued.

The small size of the Native Police should not draw attention away from the fact that they were "mobile death squads aimed at eradicating Aborigines." Neither does the extended nature of the killing tell against a genocidal intention. It was, according to Alison Palmer, a "piecemeal" rather than a "wholesale" destruction. The intention to destroy part of a group, it should be recalled, is sufficient to establish the necessary *mens rea* for genocide according to the UN definition. And so is the intention to destroy a local people. Nowhere else in Australia did the objective and inherent implication of colonization become so consciously embodied in government policy.

22 • Genocide before the Holocaust (Cathie Carmichael)

Cathie Carmichael, professor of Eastern European history at the University of East Anglia, does two things in this passage from her 2009 book, Genocide before the Holocaust. *First, she argues that the notion of genocide was a "living concept" even before World War II. By so doing, she calls for a comparative historical analysis of the Holocaust. Second, she draws our attention to macrohistorical developments as explanatory factors for the genocidal violence that preceded the Holocaust. According to Carmichael, most important among these factors were the often violent contests over questions of citizenship that attended the disintegration of Europe's most powerful empires—the Ottoman Empire, the Habsburg Empire, and Romanov Empire—in the period 1912–23.*

The modernization of Europe was accompanied by enormous suffering and dislocation. . . . While this process took a few generations in western Europe, in the east of Europe and Eurasia the rapidity of modernization in the late nineteenth and early twentieth centuries was staggering. . . . In western Europe, the powerful states of France, Britain and Spain were unified between the sixteenth and eighteenth centuries through expropriation, violence and forced homogenization. The West then experienced increased diversity from the nineteenth century onward as a result of "counter-flows to colonialism." . . . Eastern Europe was a different story; it remained dominated by large dynastic states until the early twentieth century. The Habsburg

SOURCE: Cathie Carmichael, *Genocide before the Holocaust* (New Haven, Conn.: Yale University Press, 2009), 1–3, 4, 5, 6, 9, 124. Reprinted with permission of the publisher.

monarchy had been ruled by the same dynasty since the late Middle Ages. The Ottoman Empire was ruled by a series of sultans for centuries until 1908; for the last fourteen years of its existence it was ruled as a constitutional monarchy. The Russian Empire had come into existence as the result of the expansion of Muscovy in the early modern period and had been ruled by the Romanovs since 1613. . . .

The long disintegration of the Ottoman Empire, which had been one of the most durable political structures in history, was marked by violence and insecurity. The last years of the over-extended Romanov Empire before its collapse were also marred by violence. Both empires had failed to modernize sufficiently to withstand reformist forces within the state and the territorial revisions of neighboring states. In addition to long-term instability, both states also experienced sporadic outbursts of extreme violence against minority religious communities— outbursts which have been variously described as pogroms or massacres. The Habsburg monarchy showed signs of increasing violence in the immediate years before its collapse, with the brutal treatment of its Balkans neighbors during the First World War. . . . I argue that [the aforementioned] pogroms or massacres of the nineteenth and early twentieth centuries represented a pre-genocidal phase before the clear genocidal crisis of 1912–23. The years between the First Balkan War of 1912 and the treaty of Lausanne of 1923 saw the wholesale destruction of minorities in the Balkans, Black Sea and Anatolia. . . .

Tragically, the idea that questions of nationality and citizenship could be solved by brutal population elimination inspired a generation of the most toxic extremists, or what I have referred to here as "eliminationists." Of course, local variants were extremely important, but as a definable political group these shared a belief in the desirability of population homogenization and the removal of targeted minorities. . . . The contestation over the nature of citizenship was one of the great battles fought in the nineteenth and twentieth centuries in Europe and Eurasia, and it led directly to genocide and population elimination both "from below" and as state policy. . . . Even when the notion of wiping a whole people out was repudiated in its entirety as morally repulsive, it was still something that could be *conceptualized*. . . .

Even before the Second World War, the notion of genocide was not a remote but rather a living concept, even though the word had yet to be set down. . . . Everything changed, from the shapes of villages and fields to the languages people spoke and the religions they followed. The collapse of empires from 1912–1923, predicted in some respects by the pre-genocidal situation in Ukraine, Anatolia and parts of the Balkans before 1912, led to hitherto unknown levels of chaos and dislocation in the whole of Europe. Not only were the empires wiped off the map, but with them the identities of many religions and ethnicities who had owed their continued existence to Ottoman, Habsburg or Romanov protection. The mental, political and human landscape could hardly have altered more in the space of a few years, and the following generation was to pay the price for the collapse of empires with the rise of eliminationist groups across the continent of Europe.

State collapse / political instability → genocide

23 • Revolution and Genocide in the Ottoman Empire
(Robert Melson)

A member of the first generation of genocide scholars, Robert Melson, in Revolution and Genocide
*(1992), examined the causal relationship between revolutionary situations and genocidal outcomes.
In what direction does the causal arrow run? Do revolutionary situations give rise to genocidal outcomes, or do genocidal outcomes give rise to revolutionary situations? By examining side by side the
cases of the Armenian genocide and the Holocaust, Melson in the early 1990s provided tentative
answers. Here he depicts the revolutionary upheaval following the 1908 coup against Sultan Abdul
Hamid as a principal cause of the Young Turks' subsequent destruction of large parts of the Armenian population in the Ottoman Empire.*

The decline of the Ottoman Empire accelerated throughout the nineteenth century. During
this period it was caught between the jaws of Great Power military pressure from abroad and
the demand for self-determination of newly conscious national minorities from within. In
response to Great Power pressures, the various sultans attempted to play the great game of
international balance of power politics, while at the same time they tried to modernize the
empire, especially its armed forces, in a manner that would strengthen their hand and preserve Muslim and Ottoman identity. In response to the minorities the sultans vacillated between, on the one hand, reforms that at least nominally extended equality and some measure
of self-administration, and, on the other hand, policies of repression, including wide-scale
massacre.

By the end of the century the empire's apparent incapacity to deal with the Great Powers
and the minorities helped to precipitate the coup of 23 July 1908 against Sultan Abdul Hamid.
The coup initiated a series of events that brought the Young Turks to power and propelled the
empire along a path of nationalist revolution, war, and genocide. In the period between the
Great War and the founding of the Turkish Republic in 1923, well over a million Armenians
were killed by mass shootings, massacres, deportations, and induced starvation.... At the
end of this period the Armenian community was destroyed as a viable community in Anatolia. Significantly, its destruction was so intended by the Committee of Union and Progress that
had come to power in the revolution of 1908....

The explanation advanced in this chapter finds the primary causes of the genocide in the
revolutionary situation following the events of 1908 and in the Pan-Turkish ideology of the
CUP.... The Turkish revolution destroyed Ottomanism and Pan-Islam, two conceptions of
state and society that would have permitted Armenians to continue to exist as a separate
community of the Ottoman Empire and replaced these with the political myth of Turkish
nationalism. The new political and social construction of "Turk" excluded all minorities, but
especially the Armenians from the new dispensation. When the Great War broke out and the
Ottoman Empire joined Germany against Russia, the excluded Armenians came to be viewed

SOURCE: Robert Melson, *Revolution and Genocide: On the Origins of the Armenian Genocide and the Holocaust*
(Chicago: University of Chicago Press, 1992), 141–43, 157–58, 159, 160–62. Reprinted with permission of
the publisher.

as internal enemies, threatening the continue existence of Turkey, and for that reason had to be destroyed. . . .

What about Armenian reactions at the start of the Great War? If there had been a mass uprising against the Turks, this might have justified, if not genocide, then at least some extraordinary measures to protect the security of Ottoman forces on the Eastern front. But no such uprising occurred. Certainly there were Armenian troops in the Russian armies, some of which were led by Armenian commanders, and there were Armenian irregulars who were also active in the area. . . . But these activities were not commensurate with a conclusion that the Armenian population as a whole needed to be deported and exterminated and the Armenian community destroyed in Turkey. . . . It is safe to say, therefore, that between the revolution of 1908 and the genocide of 1915 Armenians were not a major threat to the integrity of the Ottoman Empire, but it is also true that increasingly they came to be perceived by some members of the CUP as a deadly enemy. Since the radical change in the perceptions of the Young Turks cannot be derived only from Armenian behavior, it is entirely possible that this transformation had its origins in the altered worldview and perspectives of the CUP itself. Such alterations in the worldview of the Young Turks were themselves directly related to the fate of the Turkish revolution following the coup against Sultan Abdul Hamid II and the start of the Great War.

The Armenians did not realize that, through no fault of their own, the identity of the Ottoman state and its political myth of legitimation had been drastically altered by the Young Turks, and that their self-conception as a component millet of that state was no longer shared by the Pan-Turkish leadership of Turkey. We come closer to the truth why the Armenians were seen as a deadly threat, leading to genocide, when we move away from the intentions [of the perpetrators] and alleged provocative actions of the victims and examine, on the one hand, the context of Armenian-Turkish relations, and, on the other hand, the experiences and views of the perpetrators. Both the context of relations and the views of the CUP were drastically altered when between 1908 and 1915 the Young Turks were not able to stem further defeat in battle or the secession of minorities. . . .

On 5 October 1908 [for example], some three months after the Young Turk revolution, Bulgaria proclaimed her complete independence, and, on the following day, Austria annexed Bosnia and Herzegovina, which she had occupied since 1878. Due to the rapaciousness of the Great Powers and Turkey's military weakness, the empire experienced still more extensive losses: in 1911, the Italians occupied Libya, and the next year the Balkan states effectively eliminated Turkey from Europe. Out of a total area of approximately 1,153,000 square miles and from a population of about 24 million, by 1911 the empire had lost about 424,000 square miles and 5 million people. . . . The military failures of the regime had crucial consequences for the situation of the Armenians and for the evolution of the ideology of the Young Turks. Of profound significance for the Armenians was the fact that the loss of the European provinces, in effect, reduced the multinational and multireligious character of the Ottoman Empire. The Greeks and then the Balkan Christians had seceded, leaving the Armenians as the last of the great Christian minorities still under Ottoman rule. . . .

The coming of the Young Turks with their emphasis on Turkish renewal and modernization seemed like a new opportunity to the Armenians, and they invested their energies in the new regime. Ironically and tragically for them, however, by 1912, as the Young Turks became

increasingly more nationalistic, xenophobic, and intolerant, the very aptitude of the Armenians for modernization only worked to emphasize their apparent threat to the new regime.
In sum, the disastrous loss of territory and population that the empire experienced between
1908 and 1912 isolated the Armenians and made them more salient and exposed than they
wished to be. Meanwhile, their talent for modernization challenged Turkish and Muslim supremacy, exacerbating fears that non-Turks were a threat to the Turkish national revolution.
But this was not all, even the location of the Armenians conspired to endanger their lives.
Recall that the great mass of Armenian peasants lived in Eastern Anatolia, an area claimed to
be the heartland of Turkey, bordering on Russia, Turkey's traditional enemy. Across the border was a sizable Armenian population among whom were parties that evinced irredentist
sentiments. Under these circumstances even a benign regime devoted to pluralism and the
rule of law might have cast an uneasy glance in the direction of the Armenians. But by 1912,
certainly by 1915, the Young Turks were not particularly benign or dedicated to pluralism.
They had become xenophobic integral nationalists for whom the identity and situation of
the Armenians were sufficient proof of their treachery and potential threat to the continuity
of the empire. This was the decisive factor in the genocide.

24 • The Secret Young-Turk Ittihadist Conference
(Vahakn N. Dadrian)

*Vahakn Dadrian, a prominent historian of the Armenian genocide, in this 1993 article interprets a
historical document that is believed to have been drawn up by leading representatives of the Young
Turk regime some time during World War I. Dubbed by British authorities in the early twentieth
century the "The Ten Commandments," the document in question has been cited by some as evidence
of a genocidal mindset among the regime. In fact, according to Dadrian, the document is not merely
about mindset; it illuminates the minutiae of genocidal decision making in the Ottoman Empire in
the run-up to the massacres of Armenians during World War I. If we believe Dadrian, the policy
draft was an operative plan meant to implement the decision to destroy the targeted group, in whole
or in part.*

Genocide is today widely viewed as the ultimate crime in the evolution of modern human
conflict. The nature of the crime requires conspiratorial secrecy by the perpetrators, who wish
to avoid personal implication. Moreover, the perpetration of genocide requires decision-
making at the highest levels of the perpetrator group. This decision of necessity follows deliberations on costs, benefits, and risks, and measures are planned to reduce costs and risk.
Therefore, the implementation of a decision to commit genocide requires both an operational
blueprint and a plan of concealment and cover-up. . . . The document presented and analyzed
below, dubbed by British authorities "The Ten Commandments," represents a stage in the

SOURCE: Vahakn N. Dadrian, "The Secret Young-Turk Ittihadist Conference and the Decision for the World
    War I Genocide of the Armenians," *Holocaust and Genocide Studies* 7, no. 2 (1993): 173–76, 178, 179. Re-
    printed with permission of Oxford University Press.

Turkish deliberations which resulted in the decision to murder the Armenians in the Ottoman empire.

Although it is difficult to pinpoint the exact date of the meeting at which this document was developed, it seems to reflect one of a series of secret meetings of top level Ittihad leaders during the early part of World War I. This ten point document reflects an advanced stage of deliberation and its fairly extensive detail warrants addressing it as an example of genocidal decision-making. The document outlines administrative measures, types of lethal violence, incitement of the masses, and measures for deception and maintaining secrecy. All this came on the background of the opportunity for radical measures and massive murder afforded by World War I. *war provides covers/distractions for genocide* [handwritten]

The document was apparently translated from Turkish into English by the British, as indicated by the note inserted by the British High Commissioner's Office in Istanbul after the tenth instruction: "Above is a verbatim translation—dated December 1914 or January 1915." ... The document itself is headed: "DOCUMENTS RELATING TO COMITE UNION AND PROGRES ORGANIZATION IN THE ARMENIAN MASSACRES." The subtitle is, "The 10 Commandments of the COMITE UNION AND PROGRES." The British translation of the text follows:

1. Profiting by the Arts: 3 and 4 of Comite Union and Progres, close all Armenian Societies, and arrest all who worked against Government at any time among them and send them into the provinces such as Bagdad or Mosul, and wipe them out either on the road or there.

2. Collect arms.

3. Excite Moslem opinion by suitable and special means, in places as Van, Erzeroum, Adana, where as a point of fact the Armenians have already won the hatred of the Moslems, provoke organized massacres as the Russians did at Baku.

4. Leave all executive to the people in provinces such as Erzeroum, Van, Mamuret ul Aziz, and Bitlis, and use Military disciplinary forces (i.e., Gendarmerie) ostensibly to stop massacres, while on the contrary in places as Adana, Sivas, Broussa, Ismidt and Smyrna actively help Moslems with military force.

5. Apply measures to exterminate all males under 50, priests and teachers, leave girls and children to be Islamized.

6. Carry away the families of all who succeeded in escaping and apply measures to cut them off from all connection with their native place.

7. On the ground that Armenian officials may be spies, expel and drive them out absolutely from every Government department or post.

8. Kill off in an appropriate manner all Armenians in the Army—this to be left to the military to do.

9. All action to begin everywhere simultaneously, and thus leave no time for preparation of defensive measures.

10. Pay attention to the strictly confidential nature of these instructions, which may not go beyond two or three persons. ...

The Turkish source was Ahmed Essad, who had been the wartime head of the Ottoman Interior Ministry's Department II, Intelligence, which was under the jurisdiction of the office of Public Security (*Emniyeti Umumiye*). Essad had served as secretary to the conference, and two of the four documents acquired by the British from him, including the Ten Commandments, are in his own handwriting. He tried to sell the British these four documents for £10,000. Instead the British had him arrested through the Turkish Court Martial authorities then investigating the Armenian genocide. . . .

The Ten Commandments is a draft of the plan to dislocate, deport, and destroy the Armenians of the Ottoman Empire. The conditions under which this was to be done were spelled out in general terms so as to allow local discretion based on specific local circumstances. Three of the five participants at the conference which produced this document were the ultimate decision-makers in wartime Turkey: Talat, and Doctors Nazim and Behaeddin Şakir. Talat was the omnipotent party boss and prime mover of Ittihad's Supreme Directorate which controlled the destiny of Ottoman Turkey. He also served formally as Interior Minister at the time of the meeting, and as Grand Vizier after February 1917. The two physicians worked jointly with Talat behind the scenes. The prominent role played by these three in the planning and implementation of the Armenian genocide has been documented and discussed elsewhere.

The other two participants in this conference were Ismail Canbolat and Colonel Seyfi, both of whom functioned as the actual organizers of the mass murder. Canbolat was head of Public Security in the Interior Ministry (roughly equivalent to the American FBI today) at the time of the meeting. He later served as Prefect of the Ottoman capital, Constantinople, then as the Interior Minister's Undersecretary, and then briefly as Interior Minister in 1918. Seyfi was head of Department II, Intelligence, in the Ottoman General Headquarters, as well as Director of the Political Section of the General Staff and was a close associate of War Minister Enver. He was in charge of the Special Organization's operational units who were assigned the task of massacring multitudes of deportees en route to "relocation" centers in the Mesopotamian deserts. . . .

The so-called Ten Commandments are not so much a case of decision-making as a byproduct of decision-making. The actual decision preceded the framing of the draft on genocide. Therefore, the draft is an operative plan meant to implement the decision. Both the decision and the blueprint reflect the fact that the crime committed against the Armenians was premeditated and the intent was the wholesale extermination of the victims. . . . The 1909–14 period was the embryonic stage of the genocide idea, with two Ittihadist gatherings in 1910 being most significant: Interior Minister Talat's August 6 speech before a top secret preconvention conclave of Ittihadist leaders in Saloniki, in which the beginnings of a future policy of homogenizing Turkey by force of arms were outlined; and the secret consultations and decisions taken outside the formal sessions of Ittihad's annual convention in Saloniki on October 18–19 [October 31, in the old style]. . . .

The sinister plans for the Armenian population of the Ottoman empire projected at these secret meetings were revealed a year later by Galib Bey, Director of Post and Telegraph in Erzurum (eastern Turkey) and a participant at the convention. He confided to his close friend Dikran Surabian, a Catholic Armenian and official interpreter at the French Consulate in Erzurum, that these plans "make one's hair stand on end (*faire dresser les cheveux sur la tête*)."

25 • Explaining the Holocaust: Intentionalism versus Structuralism (Ian Kershaw)

In this 2000 essay, Sir Ian Kershaw, formerly a professor of modern history at the University of Sheffield and the author of the massive two-volume Hitler, *provides a succinct overview of a long-standing debate among historians of the Holocaust, that between "intentionalist" and "structuralist" (also known as "functionalist") explanations of the Nazi genocide. At issue in this debate is the question of the relative significance of individuals (such as Hitler) to genocidal outcomes. Although the relationship between human agents and societal structures has been exhaustively studied in the historiography of the Holocaust, it has received less attention in explanations of genocidal campaigns elsewhere.*

Studies founded upon the centrality of Hitler's personality, ideas, and strength of will to any explanation of Nazism take as their starting-point the premise that, since the Third Reich rose and fell with Hitler and was dominated by him throughout, "National Socialism can indeed be called Hitlerism" [referencing Karl Dietrich Bracher, the influential German historian]. Behind such an interpretation is in general a philosophy which stresses the "intentionality" of the central actors in the historical drama, according full weight to the freedom of action of the individual and the uniqueness of his action.... The contrasting approach, variously described as "structuralist," "functionalist," or (more disparagingly) "revisionist," offers a fundamentally different interpretation of the Third Reich—concentrating, as the epithets suggest, more on the "structures" of Nazi rule, the "functional" nature of policy decisions, and "revising" what is taken for an unjustifiable overemphasis of the personal role of Hitler in "orthodox" historiography....

Explaining the Holocaust stretches the historian to the limits in the central task of providing rational explanation of complex historical developments.... The central issue remains ... how Nazi hatred of the Jews became translated into the practice of government, and what precise role Hitler played in this process.... The interpretational divide on this issue brings us back to the dichotomy of "intention" and "structure" which we have already encountered. The conventional and dominant "Hitlerism" approach proceeds from the assumption that Hitler himself, from a very early date seriously contemplated, pursued as a main aim, and strived unshakeably to accomplish the physical annihilation of the Jews. According to such an interpretation, the various stages of the persecution of the Jews are to be directly derived from the inflexible continuity of Hitler's aims and intentions; and the "Final Solution" is to be seen as the central goal of the Dictator from the very beginning of his political career, and the result of a more or less consistent policy (subject only to "tactical" deviation), "programmed" by Hitler and ultimately implemented according to the Führer's orders.

In contrast, the "structuralist" type of approach lays emphasis upon the unsystematic and improvised shaping of Nazi "policies" towards the Jews, seeing them as a series of *ad hoc*

SOURCE: Ian Kershaw, *The Nazi Dictatorship: Problems and Perspectives of Interpretation*, 4th edition (London: Arnold, 2000), 70–71, 74, 93, 94, 95–96, 102, 104–5, 116, 132–33. Reprinted with permission of the publisher.

responses of a splintered and disorderly government machinery. Although, it is argued, this produced an inevitable spiral of radicalization, the actual physical extermination of the Jews was not planned in advance, could at no time before 1941 be in any realistic sense envisaged or predicted, and emerged itself as an *ad hoc* "solution" to massive, and self-induced, administrative problems of the regime. . . .

We now turn to a brief evaluation of these positions and an appraisal of some of the available evidence on which an interpretation must be based. . . . A problem with the "intentionalist" position—in particular with its extreme "grand design" variant—is an implicit teleology which takes Auschwitz as a starting-point and looks backwards to the violent expression of Hitler's early speeches and writing, treating these as a "serious declaration of intent." Because Hitler frequently spoke about destroying the Jews, and the destruction of the Jews actually took place, the logically false conclusion is drawn that Hitler's expressed "intention" must have *caused* the destruction. In the light of hindsight, it is easy to attribute a concrete and specific meaning to the barbarous, but vague and fairly commonplace, generalities about "getting rid" (*Entfernung*) or even "extermination" (*Vernichtung*) of Jews, which were part and parcel of Hitler's language (and that of others of the *völkisch* Right) from the early 1920s onwards. . . . If "program," "plan," or "design" in the context of anti-Jewish policy are to have real meaning, then they ought to imply something more than the mere conviction, however fanatically held, that somehow the Jews would be "got rid of" from German territory and from Europe as a whole, and the "Jewish Question" solved. Before 1941, the evidence that Hitler had more than such vague and imprecise convictions is slender. . . .

The "structuralist" type of interpretation also has some weaknesses. The empirical data are seldom good enough to allow detailed reconstruction of the processes of decision-making, on which much of the argument resides. And the emphasis upon contingency, lack of planning, absence of coordination, governmental chaos, and the ad hoc "emergence" of policy out of administrative disorders seems at times potentially in danger of neglecting the motive force of intention (however vaguely expressed) and distorting the focus of the regime's ideologically rooted thrust and dynamic drive. However, the "structuralist" approach does provide the opportunity of *locating* Hitler's "intentions" within a governmental framework which allowed the bureaucratic implementation of a loose ideological imperative, turning a slogan of "get rid of the Jews" into a program of annihilation. And concentrating on the historical question of how "the Holocaust" happened rather than, implicitly or explicitly, seeking to allocate guilt makes the issue of whether Hitler took the initiative at every turn, or whether a particular decision was his alone, seem less relevant and important. . . .

Hitler did not need to issue directives or take clear initiatives in order to promote the process of radicalization in the "Jewish Question" between 1939 and 1941. Rather . . . the momentum was largely stimulated by a combination of bureaucratic measures emanating from the Reich Security Head Office (whose administrative consequences were not clearly envisaged), and *ad hoc* initiatives "taken on the ground" by individuals and agencies responsible for coping with an increasingly unmanageable task. Typical of Hitler's stance was his wish, expressed towards the end of 1940, that his Gauleiter in the East should be accorded the "necessary freedom of movement" to accomplish their difficult task, that he would demand from his Gauleiter *after 10 years* only the single announcement that their territories were purely German, and would not inquire about the methods used to bring it about. His own direct role was largely confined to the propaganda arena—to public tirades of hatred and dire but vague prognostications about the fate of the Jews. . . .

[In conclusion,] the lengthy but gradual process of depersonalization and dehumanization of Jews, together with the organizational chaos in the eastern territories arising from the lack of clear central direction and concept, the hoarding together in the most inhumane circumstances of increasing masses of "non-persons," provided the context in which mass killing, once it had been instigated in the Russian campaign, was applied *ad hoc* and extended until it developed into full-scale annihilation. At the same time, the "Final Solution" did not simply emerge from a myriad of "local initiatives": however falteringly at first, decisive steps were taken at the center to coordinate measures for total extermination. Such central direction appears for the most part to have come from the Reich Security Head Office, though undoubtedly the most important steps had Hitler's approval and sanction. Hitler's "intention" was certainly a fundamental factor in the process of radicalization of anti-Jewish policy which culminated in extermination. But even more important to an explanation of the Holocaust is the nature of "charismatic" rule in the Third Reich and the way it functioned in sustaining the momentum of escalating radicalization around "heroic," chimeric goals while corroding and fragmenting the structure of government.

26 • Eliminationist Anti-Semitism as Genocidal Motivation (Daniel Jonah Goldhagen)

No book in genocide studies is more controversial than Daniel Jonah Goldhagen's Hitler's Willing Executioners, *published in 1996. It caused a great deal of controversy by claiming that the kind of anti-Semitism that Goldhagen believed was the principal cause of the Holocaust had been unique to Germany and deeply embedded in that country's culture. Although scores of general readers (especially in Germany) embraced the provocative text, virtually no historian of the Holocaust (or scholar of genocide) has had anything positive to say about Goldhagen's argument and evidence concerning the causal role of "eliminationist antisemitism" in the Holocaust. The criticisms were plentiful, calling the argument unoriginal, ahistorical, intemperate, and "exceptionally wrong" (Raul Hilberg). Notwithstanding important shortcomings,* Hitler's Willing Executioners *reinvigorated the public debate over the Holocaust, in Germany and elsewhere. As such it is deserving of critical engagement rather than condemnation alone.*

My explanation—which is new to the scholarly literature on the perpetrators—is that the perpetrators, "ordinary Germans," were animated by antisemitism, by a particular *type* of antisemitism that led them to conclude that the Jews *ought to die*. The perpetrators' belief, their particular brand of antisemitism, though obviously not the sole source, was, I maintain, a most significant and indispensable source of the perpetrators' actions and must be at the center of any explanation of them. Simply put, the perpetrators, having consulted their own

SOURCE: Daniel Jonah Goldhagen, *Hitler's Willing Executioners: Ordinary Germans and the Holocaust* (London: Little, Brown, 1996), 14, 416, 417, 419, 425, 428, 442–43, 449. Reprinted with permission of the publisher.

convictions and morality and having judged the mass annihilation of Jews to be right, did not *want* to say "no." . . .   But what about Hungary?

That the perpetrators approved of the mass slaughter, that they willingly gave assent to their own participation in the slaughter, is certain. That their approval derived in the main from their own conception of Jews is all but certain, for no other source of motivation can plausibly account for their actions. This means that had they not been antisemites, and antisemites of a particular kind, then they would not have taken part in the extermination, and Hitler's campaign against the Jews would have unfolded substantially from how it did. The perpetrators' antisemitism, and hence their motivation to kill, was, furthermore not derived from some other non-ideational source. It is not an intervening variable, but an independent one. It is not reducible to any other factor. . . .

A presumption of coercion, social psychological pressure from assenting comrades, and the occasional opportunities for personal advancement, in different measures, were at times real enough [during the Holocaust]; yet they cannot explain . . . the actions in *all* of their varieties of the perpetrators *as a class*, but only some actions of some individuals who might have killed despite their disapproval, or of others who might have needed but a push to overcome reluctance, whatever its source. . . .

The Holocaust was a *sui generis* event that has a historically specific explanation. The explanation specifies the enabling conditions created by the long-incubating, pervasive, virulent, racist, eliminationist antisemitism of German culture, which was mobilized by a criminal regime beholden to an eliminationist, genocidal ideology, and which was given shape and energized by a leader, Hitler, who was adored by the vast majority of the German people, a leader who was known to be committed wholeheartedly to the unfolding, brutal eliminationist program. During the Nazi period, the eliminationist antisemitism provided the motivational source for the German leadership and for rank-and-file Germans to kill Jews. . . .

Whatever the antisemitic traditions were in other European countries, it was only in Germany that an openly and rabidly antisemitic movement came to power—indeed was elected to power—that was bent upon turning antisemitic fantasy into state-organized genocidal slaughter. This ensured that German antisemitism would have qualitatively different consequences from the antisemitisms of other countries, and substantiates the *Sonderweg* [special path] thesis that Germany developed along a singular path, setting it apart from other western countries. . . .

The antisemitism of no other European country came close to combining *all* of the following features of German antisemitism (indeed, virtually every other country feel short on *each* dimension). No other country's antisemitism was at once so widespread as to have been a cultural axiom, was so firmly wedded to racism, had as its foundation a pernicious image of Jews that deemed them to be a mortal threat to the *Volk*, and was so deadly in content, producing, even in the nineteenth century, such frequent and explicit calls for the extermination of the Jews, calls which expressed the logic of racist eliminationist antisemitism that prevailed in Germany. The unmatched volume and vitriolic and murderous substance of German antisemitic literature of the nineteenth and twentieth centuries alone indicate that German antisemitism was *sui generis*. . . .

The road to Auschwitz was not twisted [as some "structuralist" historians such as Hans Mommsen have claimed]. Conceived by Hitler's apocalyptically bent mind as an urgent, though future, project, its completion had to wait until conditions were right. The instant that they were, Hitler commissioned his architects, [Heinrich] Himmler and [Reinhard] Heydrich, to work from his vague blueprint in designing and engineering the road. They, in turn, easily enlisted ordinary Germans by the tens of thousands, who built and paved it with an immense dedication born of great hatred for the Jews whom they drove down that road. When the road's construction was completed, Hitler, the architects, and their willing helpers looked upon it not as an undesirable construction, but with satisfaction. In no sense did they regard it as a road chosen only because other, preferable venues had proven to be dead ends. They held it to be the best, safest, and speediest of all possible roads, the only one that led to a destination from which the satanic Jews are absolutely sure never to return. . . .

The eliminationist antisemitism, with its hurricane-force potential, resided ultimately in the heart of German political culture, in German society itself. . . . Just as the evidence is overwhelming that eliminationist antisemitism was ubiquitous in Germany during the Nazi period, it is equally clear that it did not spring forth out of nowhere and materialize first on January 30, 1933, fully formed. The great success of the German eliminationist program of the 1930s and 1940s was, therefore, owing in the main to the preexisting, demonological, racially based, eliminationist antisemitism of the German people, which Hitler essentially unleashed, even if he also continually inflamed it. As early as 1920 Hitler publicly identified that this was the character and potential of antisemitism in Germany, as he himself at the time explained in his August 13 speech to an enthusiastically approving audience. Hitler declared that the "broad masses" of Germans possess an "instinctive" (*instinktmässig*) antisemitism. His task consists in "waking, whipping up, and inflaming" that "emotional" (*gefühlsmässig*) antisemitism of the people until "it decides to join the movement which is ready to draw from it the [necessary] consequence." . . .

[In other words,] genocide was immanent in the conversation of German society. It was immanent in its language and emotion. It was immanent in the structure of cognition. And it was immanent in the society's proto-genocidal practice of the 1930s. Under the proper circumstances, eliminationist antisemitism metastasized into its most virulent exterminationist form, and ordinary Germans became willing genocidal killers.

27 • Toward a Definition of Anti-Semitism (Gavin I. Langmuir)

The late historian Gavin Langmuir (1924–2005), unlike Goldhagen, did not believe in a straight path leading from anti-Semitism to the Holocaust. In this chapter from Toward a Definition of Antisemitism *(1990), he pointed to the multiple and changing meanings of anti-Semitism in Germany. Langmuir, who for many years was a professor of history at Stanford University, contended that conventional definitions of anti-Semitism fall short and therefore distort the role of anti-Jewish ideology in the Holocaust. In response to this malaise, he distinguished among three types of asser-*

SOURCE: Gavin I. Langmuir, *Toward a Definition of Antisemitism* (Berkeley: University of California Press, 1990), 311, 313, 314, 315, 327–28, 329, 330, 331, 334–35, 336, 341–42, 351–52. Reprinted with permission of the publisher.

tions about "outgroups," notably Jews: realistic, xenophobic, and chimeric. According to Langmuir, only chimeric assertions constitute anti-Semitism properly understood.

Whatever most who now use the term "antisemitism" mean by it, they do not use it in its original and explicitly defined sense, and I will argue that as presently used it impedes rather than aids understanding of hostility against Jews. "Antisemitism" was invented about 1873 by Wilhelm Marr to describe the policy toward Jews based on "racism" that he and others advocated. Although elements of the racist theory can be traced back to the eighteenth century, if not earlier, the theory itself was only fully elaborated in the latter half of the nineteenth. It proclaimed that humans were divided into clearly distinguishable races and that the intellectual, moral, and social conduct and potential of the members of these races were biologically determined. As elaborated in the Aryan myth, it maintained that Jews were a race and that, not only were they, like other races, inferior to the Aryan race, but also that Jews were the most dangerous of these inferior races.

If the meaning of "antisemitism" for its original proponents is clear, their use of the term is empirically meaningless for us because the Aryan myth on which it depended is now recognized as obviously false.... Since the best present knowledge so obviously invalidates the Aryan theory, it follows that we cannot use "racism," the central and false concept of that myth, to explain the hostility toward Jews—or Blacks—displayed by the propagators of the myth. The Aryan myth was *their* (false) rationalization of their hostility, but since we do not believe that biological differences were the cause of their hostility, "racism" cannot be *our* explanation of the myth or of their hostility.... Despite the biological propensities of early anthropologists, "race" is not a term proper to the social sciences. Social scientists use the term either as it is defined by contemporary biologists or in their descriptions of the thoughts of the people they study. In the latter case, "race" refers not to a process of nature but to an artifact of human consciousness which, like phlogiston or centaurs, may have no existence outside the mind of the people studied.

And if the best contemporary biological knowledge forces social scientists to accept that someone who rationalized his hostility by "race," for example, Alfred Rosenberg [author of the Nazis' "racial theory" and creator of, among other things, the *Lebensraum* idea], was wrong in his beliefs about "race," then they must conclude that the biological fact of race (so far as it is a fact) did not cause Rosenberg's beliefs and hostility. They must then look to other features of human nature, such as irrational or wishful thinking, that fall within the purview of their own disciplines to explain why Rosenberg was so hostile to Jews and embraced that error about "race." And as they develop their explanation of such hostility, they should use terms that distinguish their own explanation clearly from the rationalizations they are trying to explain. To typify and explain the process that produced the erroneous thought of believers in the Aryan myth as "racism" is to confuse a symptom with a cause, a confusion that enables the Aryan myth to contaminate our scientific thinking....

In its original meaning, "antisemitism" is as erroneous an explanation of hostility toward Jews as the racism from which it emerged in 1873. And in its present use, "antisemitism," like "racism," has given hostage to the Aryan myth. Of course, because of Hitler, the term has been transvalued. Not only are Jews good in their own eyes, but they are now seen as no worse than, or as good as, anyone else by many others in the West. Consequently, "antisemitism" is now understood as a highly pejorative term both by Jews and many non-Jews—which is what makes the charge of "antisemitism," loosely defined, so useful a weapon in political discourse. So long as memories of the "Final Solution" remain vivid, the use of that special term of dark origin implies that there is something unusually and uniquely evil about any serious hostility toward all Jews.

But the common use of "antisemitism" now to refer to any hostility against Jews collectively at any time has strange implications. Although it transvalues the original meaning of the term and rejects the categorization of Jews as a race, it nonetheless carries over from the Aryan myth the implication that hostility toward Jews is an enduring (if bad) reaction of non-Jews to some unique and unchanging (if now good) real characteristics of Jews. It also implies, in agreement with that myth, that the hostility that made possible Hitler's "Final Solution" was no different in fundamental nature, only in intensity and the technology applied, from the riots in ancient Alexandria in the first century of the Common Era or from any other hostility Jews have ever had to face. The usage thus implies that there was nothing uniquely evil in quality about the Final Solution, only a quantitative difference. . . . Like the Aryan myth, this conception of "antisemitism" depends, I would argue, on the fallacy of misplaced concreteness or illicit reification, in this case of the unproven assumption that for centuries, and despite innumerable changes on both sides, there has been a distinctive kind of reaction of non-Jews directed only at Jews that corresponds to the concept presently evoked by the word "antisemitism." . . . Such a perspective might fairly be called ethnocentric; and, not surprisingly those who accept it have not felt any need to examine non-Jews carefully to see whether the quality of their hostility to Jews has in fact been unique and unchanging. . . .

If the primary function of verbal behavior is to communicate with and influence other humans, the primary questions to ask about assertions some of whose words refer to outgroups are: What is their function? What is the person who makes the assertion trying, consciously our subconsciously, to communicate? And is that intention realized by the recipient? . . . The definitions that follow are an effort to distinguish between assertions referring to outgroups on the basis of their intrinsic structure when viewed in context, and thereby to discover their intended function. . . . I will try to isolate formal characteristics intrinsic to the assertions—or vehicles of communication—themselves. I will then interpret the intention or function of assertions with these different formal characteristics.

Realistic assertions [emphasis added] about outgroups are propositions that utilize the information available about an outgroup and are based on the same assumptions about the nature of groups and the effect of membership on individuals as those used to understand the ingroup and its reference groups and their members. *Xenophobic assertions* are propositions that grammatically attribute a socially menacing conduct to an outgroup and all its members but are empirically based only on the conduct of a historical minority of the members; they neglect other, unthreatening, characteristics of the outgroup; and they do not acknowledge that there are great differences between the individuals who compose the outgroup as there are between the individuals who compose the ingroup. *Chimeric assertions* are propositions that grammatically attribute with certitude to an outgroup and all its members characteristics that have never been empirically observed. . . . For reasons that I hope will become apparent, I would reserve use of the term "antisemitism," if it should be used at all, for socially significant chimerical hostility against Jews. . . .

The most obvious characteristic of xenophobic assertions (for example, "Jews are Christ-Killers") is that they impute to all people labeled as members of an outgroup the actions of some members that have been considered a threat to the ingroup. All Jews are the same and do what those Jews did; individual Jews are no more than bearers of the outgroup's characteristics. In this way, the group is presented as the fundamental reality of which its members are no more than expressions. Yet a group of any size such as "the Jews" cannot be tangibly experienced: for centuries no one has been able to encounter "the Jews" as a whole or all individual Jews. The concept of "the Jews" is an abstraction. And what xenophobic assertions do is to make the abstraction more real than any individual components. How then is the abstraction constituted?

The characteristics ascribed to it are those ascribed by the ingroup to some members of the outgroup—for example, to some Jews whose real, observed conduct has been interpreted as a threat to the ingroup. Xenophobic assertions thus fit the "kernel of truth" theory of prejudice; and here it is well to remember that, so long as it was safe to do, Jews readily asserted that they had killed Christ, and Jews indeed engaged disproportionally in moneylending in the Middle Ages. Yet if we think of Jews as Christ-killers or moneylenders, it is obvious that these were not the only characteristics of the Jews who were involved in such threatening conduct, much less of Jews who were never involved in producing those threatening situations. . . . An obvious feature of these assertions is that they link the abstraction of the outgroup label with another abstraction denoting a social menace, whether a threat from without or an internal weakness of the ingroup, which causes anxiety in the speaker. . . . The reason for the absence of any reference to individual variation or to inoffensive characteristics of "the Jews" is that xenophobic assertions are not intended to function as empirical descriptions of Jews, and that the abstraction does not refer primarily to Jews. . . .

We may deal with chimerical assertions much more briefly. I have introduced the neologism "chimeria" because "prejudice" has such a wide range of meanings in common usage, and because I wish to make a distinction that is not recognized in the social scientists' conception of "ethnic prejudice." The Greek root of "chimeria" makes it a fitting companion to "xenophobia," but, more important, the ancient use of "chimera" to refer to a fabulous monster emphasizes the central characteristic of the phenomenon I wish to distinguish from senophobia. In contrast with xenophobic assertions, chimerical assertions present fantasies, figments of the imagination, monsters, that, although dressed syntactically in the clothes of real humans, have never been seen and are projections of mental processes unconnected with the real people of the outgroup. Chimerical assertions have no "kernel of truth." This is the contrast which distinguishes the hostility that produced Auschwitz from that manifested against Jews in ancient Alexandria.

The clearest example is the assertion that Jews commit ritual murder. Had ritual murder occurred, that conduct would have been so corporeal that it could have been directly observed. But not only do we have no satisfactory evidence that Jews ever—to say nothing of a habit—committed ritual murder; a careful examination of the evidence makes it apparent that those who initiated the accusation had never observed that conduct themselves. . . . A much less obvious example, because it is about an incorporeal quality not susceptible of direct observation and is still widely believed, is the chimerical assertion that blacks are innately inferior in mental potential to whites—an allegation strangely resembling assertions about the mental inferiority of females as compared with males. . . . Chimerical assertions thus attribute with certitude to outgroups characteristics that have never been empirically observed. Another characteristic of chimerical assertions that sharply distinguishes them from xenophobic assertions is that they apply to all real individuals who can somehow be identified as members of the outgroup. Here we may think of the Nuremberg laws and their consequences. . . .

Can we now construct a dynamic model, however schematic, to describe how belief in chimerical assertions—in the inhumanity or subhumanity of some outgroups—developed in a society from which it was previously absent? The moment we pose that question, we realize that there is no necessary relation between xenophobia and chimeria. If we think about European culture and its extensions outside of Europe from 500 to the present, it is obvious that many or most Europeans have made frequent xenophobic assertions about many groups within their society and about most external societies with which they have come in contact. There is, therefore, nothing at all unusual about xenophobic hostility against Jews. Like every other major group, Jews have unique characteristics, a unique history, and their own particular goals. It is also true that Jews have maintained a very distinctive identity for millennia. And since they have maintained their identity for centuries as a minority within a larger society and refused, or not been allowed, to assimilate, it is not surprising that the xenophobia against them has been millennial and often intense. Yet the endurance and intensity of xenophobic hostility against Jews does not mean that it has been different in kind—in basic nature and causes—from xenophobia directed against any other major group, including Jewish xenophobia against other groups. Consequently, there seems no good reason to distinguish xenophobic hostility against Jews from that directed against other groups by giving it a special term, "antisemitism."

"Antisemitism" implies that there has been something peculiar about hostility against Jews, something more than a matter of duration and intensity. Of course, for Jews, any hostility against them is of particular importance just because it is directed against them and their values, but that is their value judgment, not an objective argument about humanity in general. Nonetheless, as the "Final Solution" indicated all too clearly, Jews do seem to have been the object of an unusual hostility; and provided that we refuse to regard xenophobia against Jews as peculiar, it can indeed be argued on objective grounds that Jews have also been the object of an unusual, if not unique, form of hostility for which a special term may seem in order. In addition to xenophobic hostility, Jews have also been a primary target for socially significant chimerical hostility. If we look for chimerical assertions of any frequency that have been general in European culture, we realize that they have been directed above all against Jews and blacks, save for a short period against the individuals labeled as witches. . . .

The need to define antisemitism and the definition toward which I have been moving should now be clear. Taken literally, "antisemitism" is most misleading and thoroughly contaminated with the erroneous presuppositions of the racists. I have sought to demonstrate that neither the theories of "racism" nor those of "ethnic prejudice" enable us to distinguish what has been unusual about some hostility toward Jews. Yet "antisemitism" is still used, as it was by racists, to refer to any hostility at any time against Jews collectively, and to imply that there has always been something special about that hostility. That usage depends on a value judgment about Jews but is no longer based on any empirical theory. . . . The theory I have advanced does identify an unusual quality of hostility toward Jews: there has been socially significant chimerical hostility. . . . If "antisemitism" is meant to refer to an unusual hostility against Jews, then that hostility can be termed "antisemitism."

It might be argued that since socially significant chimeria has not been directed only against Jews, there is no reason to give it a special name when directed against Jews. Nonetheless, socially significant chimeria is an aberration that has seriously affected very few groups but has afflicted them terribly. The use of a special name to designate the peculiarly horrifying example that marked European culture for seven centuries and killed millions of victims during the "Final Solution" therefore seems justifiable. Yet if we continue to use that literally most misleading term, we, as social scientists, should free "antisemitism" from its racist, ethnocentric, or religious implications and use it only for what can be distinguished empirically as an unusual kind of human hostility directed at Jews.

If we do so, we may then be able to distinguish more accurately between two very different kinds of threats to Jews. On the one hand, there are situations in which Jews, like any other major group, are confronted with realistic hostility, or with that well-nigh universal xenophobic hostility which uses the real conduct of some members of an outgroup to symbolize a social menace. On the other hand, there may still be situations in which Jewish existence is much more seriously endangered because real Jews have been irrationally converted in the minds of many into a symbol, "the Jews," a symbol whose meaning does not depend on the empirical characteristics of Jews yet justifies their total elimination from the earth.

28 • The Origins of the "Final Solution" (Christopher R. Browning)

Christopher Browning ranks among the leading historians of the Holocaust, and The Origins of the Final Solution *is his magnum opus. Published in 2004, it is the culmination of a lifetime of research and writing on the causes of Nazi genocide. Browning shares two major findings: that the onset of the "Final Solution" was causally related to a (misplaced) "euphoria of victory" that came about as a result of German military advances in the Soviet Union, and that Hitler participated in the background rather than in the foreground of genocidal decision making. Hitler's exhortations about the destruction of the European Jews were vague and inexplicit; they required deciphering by others, notably Heinrich Himmler, the influential head of the Gestapo (Secret State Police) and the SS (Protection Squadrons) in Nazi Germany.*

In the five weeks between September 18 and October 25, 1941, events had moved rapidly. Hitler had reversed his earlier decision not to permit the deportation of Jews from the Third Reich until after the war and instead sought the unrealizable goal of a *judenfrei* Germany by the end of the year. The sites of the first extermination camps were selected. The testing of various methods of killing by poison gas were conducted. Jewish emigration from the Third Reich was forbidden. And the first 11 Jewish transports had departed for Lodz as a temporary

SOURCE: Christopher R. Browning, *The Origins of the Final Solution: The Evolution of Nazi Jewish Policy, September 1939–March 1942*, with contributions by Jürgen Matthäus (Lincoln: University of Nebraska Press, 2004), 424–25, 427, 432–433. Reprinted with permission of the publisher.

holding station. This vision of the Final Solution—a program aimed at murdering every last Jew in the German grasp—had crystallized in the minds of the Nazi leadership and was henceforth being turned into reality. If the last pieces in the decision-making process came together quickly in the end, this fateful cluster of decisions itself was the climax of a long process stretching over a period of 25 months from September 1939 to October 1941.

The commitment to some kind of final solution to the Jewish question had been inherent in Nazi ideology from the beginning. Thus Jewish Nazi policy had evolved through a series of final solutions, which first envisaged a *judenfrei* Germany through emigration and then a *judenfrei* Germany through expulsion. This process of radicalization culminated in 1941 in the ultimate Final Solution of systematic mass murder. Jewish policy could evolve no further in concept. It remained only to be implemented through action. What was Hitler's role in this fateful evolution? As the ultimate embodiment of Nazi ideology as well as the constant inciter and mobilizer of the party faithful, Hitler had certainly legitimized and prodded the ongoing search for final solutions. His obsession with the Jewish question ensured that the Nazi commitment would not slacken, that the search for a solution *one way or another* to this self-imposed problem would not fade into obscurity or be indefinitely postponed.

No leading Nazi could prosper who did not appear to take the Jewish question as seriously as Hitler did himself. Thus Hitler, simply by his existence, exerted a continuing pressure on the political system, which included a competition among the faithful and ambitious to advance ever more radical proposals and to carry out Jewish policy in an ever more brutal and comprehensive manner. For many—the "true believers"—this commitment to the Final Solution was a deeply felt conviction. For the unquestioning loyalists, it was a matter of completely identifying with Hitler. For eugenicists and planning experts, it was the opportunity to realize an agenda of their own that overlapped with that of Hitler. For technicians of many sorts, it was a chance to display their skills. And for countless others, it was a cynical exercise in political careerism, opportunism, and accommodation. In the end the results were the same. The commitment to some kind of final solution permeated the entire regime, and acceptance of such a priority on the part of the regime characterized much of the German population at large.

But Hitler's role was also more immediate. From September 1939 to October 1941 he was an active and continuing participant in the decision-making process. Indeed, not a single significant change in Nazi Jewish policy occurred without his intervention and approval. Two basic conclusions can be drawn about this participation. The first concerns Hitler's mode of operation. To make his wishes known, he would give signals in the form of relatively vague and inexplicit statements, exhortations, and prophecies. Others, especially Heinrich Himmler, responded to these signals with extraordinary alacrity and sensitivity, bringing to Hitler more specific guidelines for his approval. . . . If one continuity above all others emerges in this regard, it is the close and sympathetic relationship between Hitler and Himmler during this period. If one wants to know what Hitler was thinking, one should look at what Himmler was doing.

A second rather consistent pattern is the chronological correlation between victory and radicalization, indicating that the emergence of the Final Solution was influenced and shaped not only by Hitler's enduring obsession with the Jewish question but also by the changing circumstances and the periods of elation and victory euphoria in which the Third Reich found itself. . . . Nazi racial policy was radicalized at points in time that coincided with the peaks of German military success, as the euphoria emboldened and tempted an elated Hitler to dare ever more drastic policies. With the "war of destruction" in the Soviet Union underway and the imminent prospect of all Europe at his disposal, the last inhibitions fell away. Hitler's final hesitations in August 1941—to wait [before destroying the European Jews] until after the war—were overcome in late September and early October, with the last great military encirclements that still promised an early victory.

But Germany's string of military successes finally came to an extraordinarily abrupt end in late October. The bad weather, terrible roads, shortage of supplies, exhaustion of German troops, and stubborn retreat of the remnants of the Red Army all combined to bring the Wehrmacht to a halt. There was no open road to Moscow. But the tide of war turned too late for European Jewry. The Soviet Union was saved but the Jews of Europe were not. The Nazis were now committed to a program of mass murder which, though conceived in the euphoria of victory, would be implemented in defeat. . . .

German anti-Semitism was not static but intensified with the changing historical context. In the 1930s growing enthusiasm for Hitler and the Nazi regime was due primarily to the restoration of political order, the return of economic prosperity, and the revival of national grandeur. There was no similar popular acclamation for the persecution of German Jews, but likewise no solidarity with the victims, who were increasingly isolated and deprived of their rights and property by a succession of legal and administrative measures. As of 1938, aside from a minority of party activists, most Germans were not yet ready or willing to visit physical violence upon their Jewish neighbors but neither were they interested in coming to their defense. With the outbreak of war and commencement of racial empire building, first in Poland but above all on Soviet territory, that situation changed.

Two vicious circles were set in motion. For the decision makers at the top, each victory and territorial expansion was a setback in solving their self-imposed Jewish problem, as the number of Jews within the German sphere swelled inexorably. For the occupiers in the east, each measure taken brought a solution no closer but instead contributed to "untenable circumstances" (or at best a precarious stabilization) that dehumanized the Jews yet further and at the same time disposed the German occupiers to expect and advocate yet more radical measures. The solution to the Jewish problem through the eventual disappearance of the Jews—sometime, somehow—was taken for granted. Within the context of the murderous "war of destruction" against the Soviet Union, the leap from disappearance of Jews "sometime, somehow" to "mass murder now" was taken in the summer of 1941. Once underway on Soviet territory, this ultimate or Final Solution beckoned to the Nazi regime as a solution for the rest of Europe's Jews as well. Already in the midst of committing mass murder against millions of Jews as well as non-Jews on Soviet territory, "ordinary" Germans would not shrink from implementing Hitler's Final Solution for the Jews of Europe as well.

29 • Demography and the Holocaust
(Götz Aly and Susanne Heim)

In their highly controversial book Architects of Annihilation *(2002), historian Götz Aly and journalist Susanne Heim focus on the role of technocrats in genocide. Based on an analysis of experts' roles in various branches of the Nazi state—from agriculture to trade—the authors advance the argument that, "to a very large extent," the Holocaust was "the product of rational argument taken to a mercilessly logical conclusion." In this view, Nazi genocide was in the main a policy response to the problem of overpopulation that young Nazi technocrats perceived to bedevil the Reich economy.*

When we began, back in 1985, to examine German economic policy and planning in occupied Poland, we discovered two phenomena that have come to influence our analysis of National Socialism far more than we initially anticipated. First of all there was the activity—hardly touched upon in the secondary literature—of those intellectual experts who acted as advisers both to the civilian administration and to the SS in occupied Poland: young academics who did not match the stereotype of the zealous, narrow-minded Nazi ideologue, and who argued their case objectively and dispassionately—aside from the occasional racist remark. And as we read their reports and reviews we noted a recurrent paradigm, time and time again the argument came back to the "overpopulation problem."

Whatever their area of expertise—be it agricultural policy, the "Jewish question," specific branches of trade and commerce or the way ahead for colonization and resettlement policy—and whatever their territorial focus—the Government General, south-east Europe or the occupied portions of the Soviet Union—the assumption that there is an underlying "overpopulation problem" or "population pressure" runs like a red thread through the secret reports and published works alike of these political advisers. And in nearly every case the exposition of this "problem" was followed by calls for an early "solution," in the shape of a fundamental change in population structure.

The post-war critical literature about National Socialist policy in eastern and south-east Europe, however, contains virtually no references to this line of argument. Yet the belief that the central problem in eastern and south-east Europe was massive overpopulation was just as much taken for granted in the 1930s as the well-known eugenic and racial-biological positions. While the link between eugenic theories and eugenic practice, in the form of compulsory sterilization leading on eventually to the "euthanasia" killing programs, is not disputed, the link between the theory of overpopulation and the policy of mass murder as a radical form of demographic engineering is not even up for discussion. . . .

Demography is an interdisciplinary undertaking. Sociologists, anthropologists and political scientists all have their contribution to make, along with public health experts, economists, statisticians, agrarian planners and regional planners. The deliberate and systematic

SOURCE: Götz Aly and Susanne Heim, *Architects of Annihilation: Auschwitz and the Logic of Destruction*, translated by A. G. Blunden (Princeton, N.J.: Princeton University Press, 2002), 283–285, 286, 287, 288, 289, 290. Reprinted with permission of the publisher.

sorting of people, based on "qualitative" criteria as well as quantitative ones, was one of the cornerstones of the "new order." . . .

In their drafts and plans for a modernized and "realigned" Europe the German technocrats concerned indicated that the quickest and cheapest way to attain their goals was to "adjust" the "population factor" in order to "optimize" the population. Population policy was not conducted for its own sake, but was seen as an instrument of economic rationalization: it was a matter of minimizing the "dead costs" and increasing the productivity of society as a whole. The planners were absolutely convinced that massive population shifts throughout Europe were the prime prerequisite for the conduct of an effective continental policy. That inevitably entailed a process of selection. And relocation or resettlement was only the first recourse of this so-called "negative population policy." Other methods followed: deportation for forced labor, ghettoization, the displacement of people into artificially created famine regions, attempts at birth control—and mass murder. . . .

What were the distinguishing features of this German technocracy? In many respects these young German academics were no different from their colleagues in other countries and in other times. They were interested in securing steady funding for their research projects, privileges for themselves, and the fullest possible translation of their theoretical findings into social practice. They saw themselves as professionals and specialists in their field—not Party creatures, carrying out research to order, but men who wished to place their expertise in the service of the modernizing project that would transform society.

And yet the careers of these young academics were marked out by special historical circumstances, which favored their social advancement and catapulted them into positions of astonishing political influence within a relatively short space of time. . . . It was the youngest and most flexible academic elite that had ever come to power in Germany. They swept away "outmoded" structures, and in the first five years of the Third Reich they acquired considerable freedom to maneuver and scope for the exercise of authority, while the links between the scientific-academic community and the seats of political power became ever more tightly interwoven. . . . These academics felt free to turn their utopias into reality. . . .

It was only when ideology came together with modern scientific rationalism that a series of vague program headings became concrete, realizable projects. Traditional concepts like "race," "blood" and "soil" were gradually imbued with new meaning by social scientists, economists and agrarian experts. . . . When it came to the reordering of economic and social life in occupied Poland, racism and modernization were not conflicting tendencies but complementary ones. This only served to ensure that the resettlement schemes, deportations of forced laborers and plans for annihilation were conducted on an even larger scale than might otherwise have been the case. . . .

It could be objected that [the technocrats] were simply opportunists who exploited the policy of annihilation—already planned and approved by others—for their own purposes and projects, legitimizing the murder of minorities after the event as an economic necessity. But this is belied by the fact that the planners themselves created the stalemate in resettlement policy, knowing full well—because they had done the studies themselves—that there was basically nowhere left for forcibly displaced "ethnic national groups" to go. . . . To a very large extent the policy of annihilation was the product of rational argument taken to a mercilessly logical conclusion.

30 • Why Modernity Matters (Zygmunt Bauman)

With the publication in 1989 of Modernity and the Holocaust, *the Polish sociologist Zygmunt Bauman contributed pathbreaking insights to our understanding of genocide's causes, in Germany and elsewhere. While up until that point, sociologists had largely abdicated responsibility for examining the Nazi genocide, Bauman brought social theory to bear on the problem. His principal insight was that, far from being an aberration of progress, the Holocaust was its twentieth-century epitome. The pillars of modernity—rationality, technology, industry, bureaucracy—were not incidental but integral to the destruction of the European Jews.*

There are two ways to belittle, misjudge, or shrug off the significance of the Holocaust for sociology as the theory of civilization, of modernity, of modern civilization. One way is to present the Holocaust as something that happened to the Jews; as an event in *Jewish* history. This makes the Holocaust unique, comfortably uncharacteristic and sociologically inconsequential. . . . Another way—apparently pointing in an opposite direction, yet leading in practice to the same destination—is to present the Holocaust as an extreme case of a wide and familiar category of social phenomena; a category surely loathsome and repellent, yet one we can (and must) live with. . . . Whichever one of the ways is taken, the effects are very much the same. The Holocaust is shunted into the familiar stream of history. . . . The overall result is theoretical complacency. . . .

Without revising some of the essential yet tacit assumptions of sociological discourse, one cannot do anything other than . . . conceive of the Holocaust as a unique yet fully determined product of a particular concatenation of social and psychological factors, which led to a temporary suspension of the civilizational grip in which human behavior is normally held. . . . Having processed the facts of the Holocaust through the mill of that methodology which defines it as a scholarly discipline, orthodox sociology can only deliver a message bound more by its presuppositions than by the facts of the case: the message that the Holocaust was a failure, not a product, of modernity. . . .

The unspoken terror permeating our collective memory of the Holocaust . . . is the gnawing suspicion that the Holocaust could be more than an aberration, more than a deviation from an otherwise straight path of progress, more than a cancerous growth on the otherwise healthy body of the civilized society; that, in short, the Holocaust was not an antithesis of modern civilization and everything (or so we like to think) it stands for. We suspect (even if we refuse to admit it) that the Holocaust could merely have uncovered another face of the same modern society whose other, more familiar, face we so admire. . . .

The truth is that every "ingredient" of the Holocaust—all those many things that rendered it possible—was normal; "normal" not in the sense of the familiar, of one more specimen in a large class of phenomena long ago described in full, explained and accommodated (on the contrary, the experience of the Holocaust was new and unfamiliar), but in the sense of being fully in keeping with everything we know about our civilization, its guiding spirit, its priorities, its immanent vision of the world. . . . Richard L. Rubenstein has drawn what seems

SOURCE: Zygmunt Bauman, *Modernity and Holocaust* (1989; Ithaca, N.Y.: Cornell University Press, 2000), 1, 2, 3, 4, 5, 8, 9, 13, 17. Reprinted with permission of the publisher.

to me the ultimate lesson of the Holocaust: "It bears," he wrote, "witness to the *advance of civilization*." It was an advance, let us add, in a double sense. In the Final Solution, the industrial potential and technological know-how boasted by our civilization has scaled new heights in coping successfully with a task of unprecedented magnitude. And in the same Final Solution our society has disclosed to us its heretofore unsuspected capacity. Taught to respect and admire technical efficiency and good design, we cannot but admit that, in the praise of material progress which our civilization has brought, we have sorely underestimated its true potential. . . .

The Hobbesian world of the Holocaust did not surface from its too shallow grave, resurrected by the tumult of irrational emotions. It arrived (in a formidable shape Hobbes would certainly disown) in a factory-produced vehicle, wielding weapons only the most advanced science could supply, and following an itinerary designed by scientifically managed organization. Modern civilization was not the Holocaust's sufficient condition; it was, however, most certainly its necessary condition. Without it, the Holocaust would be unthinkable. It was the rational world of modern civilization that made the Holocaust thinkable. The Nazi mass murder of the European Jewry was not only the technological achievement of an industrial society, but also the organizational achievement of a bureaucratic society. . . .

[In this context,] the department in the SS headquarters in charge of the destruction of European Jews was officials designated as the Section of Administration and Economy. . . To a degree much too high for comfort, the designation faithfully reflected the organizational meaning of activity. Except for the moral repulsiveness of its goal (or, to be precise, the gigantic scale of the moral odium), the activity did not differ in any formal sense (the only sense that can be expressed in the language of bureaucracy) from all other organized activities designed, monitored and supervised by "ordinary" administrative and economic sections. Like all other activities amenable to bureaucratic rationalization, it fits well with the sober description of modern administration offered by Max Weber. . . . At no point of its long and torturous execution did the Holocaust come in conflict with the principles of rationality. The "Final Solution" did not clash at any stage with the rational pursuit of efficient, optimal goal-implementation. On the contrary, *it arose out of a genuinely rational concern, and it was generated by bureaucracy true to its form and purpose.*

We know of many massacres, pogroms, mass murders, indeed instances not far removed from genocide, that have been perpetrated without modern bureaucracy, the skills and technologies it commands, the scientific principles of its internal management. The Holocaust, however, was clearly unthinkable without bureaucracy. The Holocaust was not an irrational outflow of not-yet-fully-eradicated residues of pre-modern barbarity. It was a legitimate resident in the house of modernity; indeed, one who would not be at home in any other house.

31 • The Ideology of Total Revolution in Pol Pot's Cambodia (Karl D. Jackson)

In the late 1980s Karl Jackson, the Starr Distinguished Professor of Southeast Asia Studies at Johns Hopkins University's Paul H. Nitze School of Advanced International Studies, authored what remains the most comprehensive and careful analysis of Khmer Rouge ideology. He traces the evolution of beliefs in the run-up to and throughout the reign of the genocidal regime in Cambodia. Jackson subtly dissects the leading tenets of Democratic Kampuchea in the period 1975–79 and goes on to compare and contrast the intellectual lifeworld of the Pol Pot regime with that of other communist regimes, including China, the Soviet Union, and neighboring Vietnam. By so doing, Jackson corrects a great many misunderstandings about the reclusive revolutionaries in Phnom Penh.

Understanding the political phenomenon of Democratic Kampuchea requires moving beyond moral condemnation to an attempt to envision the kind of Kampuchea that the Khmer Rouge leadership was trying to create. It is only by understanding their ideology and comprehending how these totalitarian goals actually found expression in the context of revolutionary upheaval that we can arrive at a balanced evaluation of one of history's most grisly events....

In essence, the revolution's ideology was dominated by four interrelated themes: (1) total independence and self-reliance; (2) preservation of the dictatorship of the proletariat; (3) total and immediate economic revolution; and (4) complete transformation of Khmer social values. Each theme can be found in both official statements and actual policies during the 1975–1979 period.... Virtually every revolutionary movement emphasizes nationalism. The theme of national sovereignty and self-reliance, however, was raised to extraordinary prominence by the Khmer Rouge, who identified this goal as the number one priority of the Khmer revolution. In his three-hour address on September 27, 1977, Pol Pot stated that correcting Cambodia's relations with the outside world by expelling the imperialists and their economic and cultural influences was the fundamental priority of the party from its inception in 1960.... In reviewing the weaknesses of Kampuchean progressive movements, Pol Pot emphasized the need for indigenous goals and methods. Interestingly, this injunction itself is an echo of the Maoist doctrine of people's war....

Self-reliance and complete independence meant no formal alliances with any outside power. Even the relationship with China received relatively muted reference in Kampuchean public statements, and nothing analogous to the November 1978 treaty between Vietnam and the Soviet Union was ever signed between Democratic Kampuchea and the People's Republic of China.... They [the Khmer Rouge] feared not only established enemies such as the United States, Vietnam, and Thailand but also more amorphous kinds of dependency resulting from international economic and cultural relations.... Just how complete was the Khmer Rouge elite's sense of cultural alienation from [especially] the Western accoutrements of the Phnom Penh lifestyle is indicated by the following official description of what they found when they captured Phnom Penh on April 17, 1975....

SOURCE: Karl D. Jackson, "The Ideology of Total Revolution," in Karl D. Jackson, ed., *Cambodia 1975–1978: Rendezvous with Death* (Princeton, N.J.: Princeton University Press, 1989), 38–39, 41, 42, 44, 45, 48, 49–50, 51, 54–55, 56–58, 62, 63, 65, 66, 71, 72, 73, 74, 77–78. Reprinted with permission of the publisher.

"Upon entering Phnom Penh and other cities, the brother and sister combatants of the revolutionary army . . . sons and daughters of our workers and peasants . . . were taken aback by *the overwhelming unspeakable sight of long-haired men and youngsters wearing bizarre clothes making themselves undistinguishable [sic] from the fair sex* [emphasis in the original]. . . . Our traditional mentality, more, traditions, literature, and arts and culture and tradition were totally destroyed by U.S. imperialism and its stooges. . . . Our people's traditionally clean, sound characteristics and essence were completely absent and abandoned, replaced by *imperialistic, pornographic, shameless, perverted, and fanatic traits*" [emphasis in the original]. . . .

The set of principles integrating dependency theory with Marxism has become fairly standard among aspiring radical elites in the Third World. The truly extraordinary aspect of the Khmer revolution is the doctrinaire literalism with which they applied these abstract principles without regard for the awesome costs to Cambodia in terms of diplomatic isolation, and massive human suffering. . . . The outside world after April 17, 1975, reacted with a combination of shock and incredulity when the revolutionary elite emptied its cities, destroyed Western consumer goods, burned books and libraries, partially liquidated its Westernized elite, severed most of its diplomatic relations, abolished money, markets, and foreign exchange, established state control over all foreign and domestic trade, and cut almost all trade links with the outside world. . . . Because of its doctrinaire application of the concept of self-reliance, very substantial numbers of the people perished from lack of food. Acceptance of international assistance, especially from the West, would have been an admission of Lon Nol–like weakness, and this was an unacceptable ideological price for the Kampuchean elite to pay. . . .

The development of the Khmer Rouge between 1970 and 1979 falls into two distinct stages: the national front stage, from March 1970 to the capture of Phnom Penh in April 1975, and the stage of power consolidation, from April 1975 to the fall of Phnom Penh to the Vietnamese in January 1979. When the Khmer Rouge were mobilizing their forces to oust the Lon Nol government they divided Cambodian society [in the words of Pol Pot] "into five distinct classes: the working class, the peasant class, the bourgeoisie, the capitalist class, and the feudal class." They concentrated their attack [once again in the words of Pol Pot himself] "against imperialism and the feudal landowner class" and sought to win over all other groups including "the workers, peasants, bourgeoisie, intellectuals, students, national capitalists, Buddhist monks and patriotic and progressive personalities." . . . As Pol Pot himself later admitted, these alliances were tactical, and after the capture of Phnom Penh in April 1975, the Khmer Rouge immediately adopted a very exclusive definition of what constituted a loyal Cambodian. . . . Within days of the capture of the capital, many who were supposed to be amnestied were rounded up for execution, and by the time of the first anniversary in April 1976, "the people" in Khieu Samphan's [initially deputy prime minister and minister of defense, then president of Democratic Kampuchea] speech included only "workers and peasants and the revolutionary army."

Rather than running the state with existing personnel for at least a transition period (as Lenin had done), the Khmer Rouge immediately applied massive doses of terror to atomize or eliminate all potential competitors and institute a nonbureaucratic, decentralized, radically Maoist state controlled by a small army and party for the benefit of the lowest status members of the old society, namely the poor peasants. . . . Terror was the chief instrument of the dictatorship of the proletariat which sought, as quickly as possible, to liquidate: all officers, as well as most noncommissioned officers, and many enlisted men in Lon Nol's army; many bureaucrats of the ancient regime; all royalty (with the exception of Sihanouk); large and medium size landowners; those engaged in commercial enterprise (primarily the Vietnamese-Khmers and Sino-Khmers); skilled laborers who had worked in factories in the Lon Nol area; many Western-educated professionals; all Khmer Moslems (Chams); and many Buddhist monks. . . . The most important motive for the elite [to use such violent means] was a sincere desire to create a new type of egalitarian revolution the likes of which the world had never witnessed, one that would raise up the poor to positions of genuine prominence rather than merely elevate the middle class representatives of the poor and thereby create a "new class." . . . A second motive articulated by the revolutionaries was their moral revulsion toward the old ruling elite and its institutions. . . .

Not only were the goals of the revolutionaries extreme, given the Cambodian stage of social and economic development, but in addition the revolutionaries lived in constant fear that their revolution would either be co-opted by the former ruling classes or crushed from without by traditional enemies such as Vietnam and Thailand. . . . This vision of a revolution in constant jeopardy was not entirely fanciful. Not only were the Vietnamese an ever-present threat, but the Khmer Rouge at the moment of victory in 1975 were probably too small and too weak to dominate the country unless they immediately reorganized it and destroyed or paralyzed the old elite and its supporters. The Khmer Rouge in 1975 were a relatively small communist movement directing a military establishment of approximately sixty thousand largely illiterate peasants. The failure of the Khmer Rouge to penetrate the administrative organs of Phnom Penh before victory, when combined with the illiteracy of their own cadres, made it virtually impossible for them to control the old administration by merely supervising it from above. . . . Hence, the ferocity of the purges conducted in the name of preserving the dictatorship of the proletariat were related both to the weakness of the movement itself and to its ideological goal of creating a revolution genuinely controlled by workers and peasants. Because of the difficulties inherent in such a goal, Pol Pot and his confederates followed a policy of permanent purge that [in the words of exiled Prince Sihanouk] "strove to create a society with no past [and] no alternatives." . . .

It is superficial to describe the Khmer Rouge as intent on returning to the pastoral simplicity of the Angkor era of Cambodian greatness between the ninth and fourteenth centuries. According to this interpretation, the Khmer Rouge emptied the cities because they rejected modern, city-based civilization and sought to transform Cambodia into the kind of largely rural society that predated both colonialism and capitalism. This interpretation misrepresents the aims of the Khmer Rouge elite. The Cambodian revolutionaries despoiled cities populated by their archenemies, the Westernized commercial and governing elites, but they also, almost immediately, began a limited program of repopulation, bringing "the sons and daughters of poor peasants" to run the existing factories and other modern establishments. Likewise, although they abhorred capitalist forms of modernization, the Khmer Rouge were, if anything, radical proponents of forced-draft industrial and agricultural modernization. . . .

The Khmer Rouge sought not to turn back the pages of time to an earlier era of Khmer greatness but to rush forward at a dizzying pace regardless of the consequences. By combining the idealism and heroic virtue extolled by Maoism with a Fanonist [derived from Frantz Fanon, the author of, among other works, *The Wretched of the Earth* (1961), a hugely influential treatise on the nature of national liberation] or Stalinist reliance on wholesale terror, the Khmer Rouge sought to stimulate the Khmer people to participate in a forced march toward a vision of communist modernity. In the same way that Mao, during the Great Leap Forward, sought to move ahead simultaneously to greatly increase rice production, irrigation, and back-yard steel production, the Khmer Rouge vision of modernization emphasized extreme haste, the critical importance of rice, and the simultaneous pursuit of industrial advancement, especially through cottage industries located in self-sufficient communes. . . . With the total mobilization of the nation's labor resources they expected to achieve diverse developmental ends simultaneously and immediately. . . .

Over the entire period, officials' statements are peppered with the language of Mao's Great Leap Forward. Economic tasks were depicted as military offensives and battlefronts, and it was expected that Democratic Kampuchea would leap forward. . . . The small elite of Democratic Kampuchea was distinguished by its nearly unlimited hubris. It made no secret of the contempt felt for the Soviet and Vietnamese models of modernization. In addition, the elite set out to achieve its goals at "a great leap forward pace" in spite of the catastrophic failure of the Great Leap Forward in China itself. Direct warnings from experienced Chinese communist leaders did not deter the Khmer Rouge. . . . Haste, revolutionary optimism, and the rhetoric of simultaneous agricultural and industrial modernization were the symbols of total revolution. . . .

In addition, the Khmer revolution altered completely and immediately the most basic aspects of Cambodian social life such as language, religion, family life, and work habits. To an extraordinary degree the Khmer Rouge sought to replace the slack ways of traditional Cambodia with iron discipline, corruption in high places with unswerving devotion to the interests of the lowly, a hierarchical society with an egalitarian one, and a remote bureaucratic regime with an intrusive, omnipresent but antibureaucratic revolutionary organization. To accomplish a permanent revolution they instituted a new moral code, disestablished Buddhism, romanticized revolutionary struggle and violence, and emphasized ideological militancy and heroic labor as crucial values for Cambodia. In doing so, the revolutionaries sought to alter fundamentally the Khmer value system and way of life. . . .

That the Khmer Rouge resorted to violence very frequently throughout their four-year rule has become an acknowledged fact. Although the scale of the bloodbath under the Khmer Rouge was unprecedented, violence itself was no stranger to Cambodian society before 1970. The murder rate in rural areas was sufficiently high to warrant government suppression of the homicide statistics. . . . The fact that massive amounts of blood were shed by the Khmer Rouge diverged from Khmer norms in scope rather than in kind. In addition, the Khmer Rouge publicly glorified revolutionary violence and blood sacrifice and celebrated them in the country's most important official documents. The blood sacrifices of the revolution became a sanctifying symbol attached to the constitution, the National Assembly, and the national anthem. Virtually every line of the national anthem mentions bloodshed. It as if the revolutionaries sought to harness the darker, more violent side of Khmer national character by giving violence a new cultural and political legitimacy. . . . In a sense, the French-educated Khmer Rouge elite echoed Fran[t]z Fanon's thesis that true liberation cannot come without violence and that the only true revolutionaries are those who participate directly in the shedding of blood. . . .

The Khmer Rouge, like their Chinese counterparts, felt they could replace machines and technical solutions with political militancy and thereby transcend normal developmental obstacles. . . . The revolutionaries relied disproportionately on raw physical coercion rather than on party organization, reeducation, or the mass media to accomplish their ends. In sharp contrast to their Vietnamese communist contemporaries, the Khmer Rouge ruled almost exclusively with the sword rather than the pen, the loudspeaker, or the school. . . . According to refugees, whenever the Khmer Rouge were faced with lack of comprehension or passive resistance, they chose to exterminate rather than reeducate. Formal schools were closed immediately after liberation, newspapers were nearly nonexistent, and radio listening was restricted largely to Khmer Rouge cadres. The special camps for former officials and army personnel who had not been immediately executed, resembled deaths camps rather than institutions in which hard labor and intensive study might hold the prospect of enlightenment and eventual reintegration into Cambodian society.

32 • The Politics of National Homogeneity in Serbia (Ivo Banac)

Ivo Banac, a professor of history at Yale University, explains in this 2006 article how the politics of national homogeneity—the pursuit of statehood without minorities—seized the elites of Serbia in the late 1980s, when it was a constituent unit of communist Yugoslavia. Focusing in particular on the role of Slobodan Milošević, the former president who subsequently stood trial for international crimes at the UN International Criminal Tribunal for the former Yugoslavia at The Hague, Banac illustrates the causal role of ideas in the development of an ethnic cleansing campaign. For example, he shows how the manipulation and appeal of the notion of "Greater Serbia" served to legitimate contempt for and hatred of any groups standing in the way of Serb unity.

There is an underlying pattern that continues across the conflicts in the former Yugoslavia, from the attack on Slovenia [in 1991] right the way through to the campaign in Kosovo [in 1996–98] and even its spill-over into Macedonia in 2001, namely that ethnic cleansing and the construction of nationally homogenous states were not the consequence of but rather the aim of war.

This proposition might not have been obvious to all parties in the encounter at the beginning of the war, but it became their common stock in the course of the conflict. The leaders of Serb, Croat, Bosniac, Kosovar, Albanian and other national communities, with variations, evidently believed that national homogeneity, that is, statehood without minorities, constituted political stability and offered the only genuine chance for peace. In order to illustrate this it is necessary to investigate the behavior of the national leaderships. . . .

As in all other matters, Milošević led the way. Although taciturn in public statements, he was explicit in defense of national homogenization as early as January 1989 in the following

SOURCE: Ivo Banac, "The Politics of National Homogeneity," in Brad K. Blitz, ed., *War and Change in the Balkans: Nationalism, Conflict and Cooperation* (Cambridge: Cambridge University Press, 2006), 30–32, 38, 39, 42. Reprinted with permission of the publisher.

statement at the Twentieth Session of the League of Communists of Yugoslavia Central Committee:

> I . . . ask the critics of homogenization, why are they disturbed by the homogeniza-
> tion of peoples and human beings in general if it is carried out on the basis of just,
> humane, and progressive ideas, in one's own interests, and is of no harm to others?
> Is this not the meaning, the aim, to which humanity has always aspired? Surely the
> sense of human community is not to be inhomogeneous, divided, even when its
> aspirations are progressive and humane?

But had Milošević not been so forthcoming in reconciling the communist notions of unity with national homogenization, his political behavior would have told the story. It was Milošević who turned the propaganda machinery of [the] Serbian party-state through his appointees . . . into vehicles of national ideologization. The Serbian press and electronic media promoted national stereotypes, systematically dehumanized Kosovar Albanians, Croats and Bosnian Muslims, insinuated notions of Serb historical victimization, and aggrandized the role of Serbia and its historical mission in the Balkans. The Serbian media created the preconditions for an ethnically pure Great Serbia that could be accomplished only by war.

Another instrument of national homogenization and war were the paramilitaries, permitted and encouraged by Milošević, and who were given logistical support by Serbia's security apparatus. Such notorious units as Arkan's Tigers, Seselj's Chetniks, and the White Eagles of the Serbian Renaissance Movement were responsible for carefully orchestrated massacres, "strategic rape" and the introduction of terrorist regimes in various Croatian and Bosnian localities that were meant to spread panic and intimidation and compel whole national communities to go into exile. The "regular" armies of Serb parastates—Krajina and Republika Srpska[—]then followed their work.

But even where paramilitaries were not directly involved, where peace prevailed throughout the war, as in Banja Luka, the largest Bosnian city under Serb control, ethnic cleansing was practiced from the beginning. The usual pattern was to create symbolic delegitimation of non-Serb communities (systematic destruction of mosques or occasional razing of Catholic churches), followed by the recruitment of the non-Serbs into units for forced labor, followed by arrests and removal into concentration camps (Manjaca, Omarska) and ending with the expulsion of survivors.

The goal of Serbian policy, which was originally shared by Milošević's ex-communists and groups far to their right, was the establishment of an ethnically cleansed Great Serbia, which would include Serbia and most of Bosnia-Herzegovina, certainly its inner rim. When this goal became untenable, Milošević shifted to a more realistic policy of holding to the lands conceded to the Serbs by the international community. That meant the abandonment of dependencies in Croatia and a certain cooling to the most extreme pretensions of [Radovan] Karadžić [formerly supreme commander of the Bosnian Serb armed forces and, from 1992 to 1996, president of the National Security Council of the Republika Srpska]. When the Croat offensive commenced in 1995, Serbia offered no military help to Milan Martić's Krajina parastate. Milošević's generals only prepared an orderly retreat.

In fact, the exodus of Serbs from Croatia also aided the cause of Serbia's homogenization, by however backhanded means. The inflow of Serbs from Croatia and Bosnia was interpreted as the strengthening of Serbian national juices in a setting destabilized by Albanian, Muslim, Hungarian and other minorities. The loss of Kosovo in 1999, however unanticipated, and the possibility of Montenegro's independence, however resisted, nevertheless offered a possibility of Serbia's greater homogenization. Little Serbia may not be preferable to Great Serbia, but it would certainly be more homogenous.

Milošević's backpedaling in Great Serbianism can be appreciated in terms of his paramount need to maintain himself in power. Because of general disillusionment and the crisis of Great Serbian ideology, Milošević's tactical inventiveness generated new ideological constructs. . . . Milošević was able to run the whole gamut of Serbian political options. He had the option of being "leftist," "rightist" or anything in between. He was "Yugoslav" or narrowly Serbian, as he chose. More importantly, he could be a partner of the West or the greatest enemy of the "new world order." But, whatever the option, he had to dominate. . . .

The politics of national homogeneity were played out in a larger international context in which international entanglements played an increasingly more important role, frequently pursued by affinities that were not necessarily enthusiastic or even logical. Serbia's cause was frequently aided by Russia and Greece, and more distantly by some of the other Eastern Orthodox states, as well as by India and China, but also Libya and Iraq. At key points some of the West European powers (Britain, France, Italy and Spain) also found understanding for Serbia, or better, sought to prevent its collapse. Bosnia's cause was championed, however lukewarmly, by the West in general, but especially by the United States. Turkey, Iran and the other Islamic countries (including some distant ones, such as Pakistan and Malaysia) had their own reasons for the support of various processes in Bosnia (Turkey supported secularized Bosnia nationalism whereas Iran and Saudi Arabia promoted imported strains of nationalized Islam). . . .

American policy wedded Washington to the maintenance of anything that was counterproductive about Yugoslavia. When Slobodan Milošević appeared on the scene, [U.S.] Ambassador John Scanlon represented him as a reformer precisely because Milošević embarked on a seemingly ameliorative recentralization project. . . . It is possible to assess the early stages of Yugoslavia's demise variously, but the fact remains that American non-intervention in the fall of 1991, when Serbian paramilitaries and the JNA [Yugoslav Armed Forces] tore into Croatia, encouraged Milošević's new adventures in Bosnia. . . .

The politics of national homogeneity, however "typically European" in the interpretation of various partitionists, did not establish more legitimate patterns of statehood in the successor states of Yugoslavia and never were successfully countered by the international community. If anything, the discrepancy between statehood and ethnicity, which was the source of Yugoslavia's ills, was continued in every tiny part of the broken state, just as in Hans [Christian] Andersen's tale of the broken mirror that distorted beauty and goodness, and exaggerated ugliness. . . .

The degrees of illegitimacy in post-Yugoslav statehood and the inability of the new states to address the question of minorities in a successful way demonstrate the great potential for new conflicts in the former Yugoslavia. Ethnic cleansing can be read to mean a simpler ethnic map, but it does not promote non-ethnic (or civic) nationhood. . . . The demise of Yugoslavia perhaps came too late from the point of view of European national-state integration and too early in the shaping of a cross-national European identity.

33 • In God's Name (Omer Bartov and Phyllis Mack)

The role of religion in the perpetration of genocidal campaigns has received a fair amount of atten-tion in Holocaust historiography, but less so in genocide studies. Historians Omer Bartov of Brown University and Phyllis Mack of Rutgers University, in the introduction to their collection of original scholarship, In God's Name *(2001), highlight "the centrality of religion for contemporary geno-cide." They pay particular attention to the cases of World War I Armenia and post–cold war Bosnia. By briefly comparing and contrasting these two prominent cases from the twentieth century, Bartov and Mack alert us not only to the importance of taking religion into account as an explanatory fac-tor, but also to the importance of truly understanding how, when, and why religious norms and institutions make a difference in times of collective violence. Religion often matters in genocide, but never quite in the same way as before.*

Violence and religion have been closely associated in a variety of intricate, often contradictory ways, since the earliest periods of human civilization. Institutionalized religions have prac-ticed violence against both their adherents and their real or imagined opponents. Conversely, religions have also been known to limit social and political violence and to provide spiritual and material comfort to its victims. Religious faith can thus generate contradictory attitudes, either motivating aggression or constraining it. Individual perpetrators and victims of vio-lence can seek in religious institutions and personal faith [either] a rationale for atrocity, a justification to resist violence, or a means to come to terms with the legacy of destruction by integrating it into a wider historical or theological context.

Despite the widespread trends of secularization in the twentieth century, religion has played an important role in several outbreaks of genocide since World War I. And yet, not many scholars have looked at the religious aspects of modern genocide, or at the manner in which religion has taken a position on mass killing. . . . What was the importance of religion as an institution, as theology, and as personal experience? Were specific theological ideas particu-larly important to the perpetrators of genocide, or to those who tried to come to terms with their own or other peoples' destruction? Was Christian universalism, or Jewish exclusivity, important in energizing Christian persecutors of Jewish victims? Did religion help to normal-ize genocide by providing myths of ultimate redemption or rationales for annihilation? Since the Enlightenment, religion has been attacked as encouraging impulses toward fanaticism. Do modern acts of genocide bear this out? How much *religious* fanaticism do we see here? . . .

The chapters in this book concern only cases of genocide involving one or several of the three main monotheistic religions: Judaism, Christianity, and Islam. . . . At first glance, what strikes the reader of these essays is the apparent irrelevance or marginality of religious ideas in the history of modern genocide. Certainly, specific religious traditions and concepts had no intrinsic power to influence either genocidal behavior or the responses of rescuers and victims. Muslims were (and are) victims of Orthodox Christians in Bosnia, while in the Otto-man Empire, Muslims drowned Armenian Christian babies and forcibly converted women and children. Indeed, perpetrators of genocide define religious groups in racial and cultural terms,

SOURCE: Omer Bartov and Phyllis Mack, introduction to *In God's Name: Genocide and Religion in the Twentieth Century* (New York: Berghahn Books, 2001), 1–4, 7–8, 17. Reprinted with permission of the publisher.

not in terms of ideas or beliefs of individual perpetrators or victims. People were murdered because they were Jews or Armenians or Bosnian Muslims, regardless of whether or not they (or their killers) actually believed in Jewish, Christian, or Muslim precepts. . . .

The Christian churches were involved on several levels in preparing the theological, moral, political, and mythical groundwork for genocide in this century. That this was part and parcel of European political, social, and religious structures, can be seen from the rather different case of the Ottoman Empire. . . . As long as collective identity in this Muslim-dominated empire was defined according to religious affiliation rather than ethnic or modern national criteria, it was possible for religious minorities to maintain a more or less tolerable existence. Thus, while Islam was the preferred religion, Christian Armenians could rise to positions of relative economic and political prominence in the Ottoman state.

Indeed, it was precisely the disintegration of the old order and the rise of modern nationalism—among Turks just as much as among Armenians, Arabs, or Kurds—which made the existence of an Armenian population in Anatolia appear increasingly intolerable to the new Turkish nationalists. . . . Consequently, just as Armenians began defining themselves more as a people than as members of their church, the Turkish leadership began thinking of the empire in exclusionary nationalist terms. Here religious fanaticism increased precisely at a time when religion was being replaced by strident nationalism as the focus of collective identity; in the multi-ethnic Ottoman Empire it was this process that generated the genocidal policies against the Armenians. . . .

The centrality of religion for contemporary genocide can also be seen in the case of Bosnia. To be sure, we know that during World War II many hundreds of thousands of Orthodox Serbs were massacred by Catholic Croats while the Vatican looked on. In the genocide of the Muslims in Bosnia, it was the turn of the Serbs to turn their wrath upon those they identified with their historical enemies, the Turks. . . . The genocide in Bosnia was not "merely" a case of what Serbs called "ethnic cleansing"—a euphemism for genocidal policies—but also a reenactment of the Serbian myth of that nation's defeat by the Ottoman army six hundred years earlier. Hence the atrocities in Bosnia were seen as part of the liberation of the Serbs from a Muslim occupation that ended a century earlier and as a reassertion of Serbian nationalism, couched in religious-mythical rhetoric and imagery.

Indeed the highly placed Serbian bishops thought the Milosevic government was not militant enough in promoting religious nationalism. Along with organized crime and the secret police, they were the main basis of support for the militias. "Ethnic cleansing" was sometimes planned in local Serbian Orthodox churches, while religious rituals were held to celebrate "successful" cleansing. Serbian Christians also allied their notion of chosenness to a specific mythology of victimhood, reenacting the stories of ancient martyrs to energize their own policy of retaliation. . . . The most extreme example . . . of Serbian religious nationalism is the assertion that Slavic Muslims suffer from a "defective gene." In this manner, religion becomes a racial attribute, and its adherents must therefore be "cleansed" by murder or expulsion, since they cannot be transformed even by conversion. As we know, in the past conversion served as one means of avoiding persecution or massacre, although precisely for religious societies conversion evoked fears of divine punishment and social exclusion, and martyrdom was endowed with the highest moral value. Modern genocide has often tended to relate religion to race, thereby preventing escape through conversion. . . .

We can conclude that by looking at the relationship between religion and genocide in the twentieth century we learn a great deal about the manner in which humanity has both legitimized mass murder and resisted it, repressed past crimes and tried to come to terms with them, justified the perpetuation of existing social, political, and religious structures and subjected them to scrutiny and criticism. There is, of course, something almost obscene in speaking about genocide and spirituality in the same breath, for one is about savagery and cruelty, the other about love and humanness. Yet in both practice and philosophical and theological contemplation, genocide and spirituality are different aspects of the *human* spirit, the former a manifestation of its lower depths, the latter an expression of its transcendental aspirations. Both, then, are human and only human, which is why it is so difficult for us to reconcile them.

34 • Environmental Scarcity and the Genocide in Rwanda (Val Percival and Thomas Homer-Dixon)

What is the relationship between genocide and the environment? Although scholars in recent decades have generated important theoretical and practical insights into the environmental dimensions of civil and international war, we still know very little about the causal role of environmental factors in the onset of genocide. Val Percival, assistant professor of international affairs at Carleton University, and Thomas Homer-Dixon, professor at the Centre for Environment and Business at the University of Waterloo, illuminate this research agenda, focusing on the case of Rwanda. Despite the presence in the 1990s of severe environmental stressors—from low soil fertility to depletion of forests and overpopulation—the authors conclude that environmental factors played but a peripheral role in the genocide of 1994. The findings are of relevance because they contradict a widely held assumption that environmental scarcity significantly contributed to genocide in the case of Rwanda. Percival and Homer-Dixon, for example, find no compelling evidence to suggest that perpetrators in pre-genocide Rwanda were pushed to extremes as a result of economic suffering from years of structural scarcity (exacerbated by the collapse of international coffee prices in 1989).

As renewable resources, such as arable cropland, fish stocks, fuel wood, and potable water supplies, become ever more scarce, attention has focused on the potential relationship between these scarcities and the outbreak of civil strife. . . . When Rwanda exploded into genocidal anarchy in April of 1994, some commentators claimed that environmental and demographic factors were powerful forces behind this violence. On first impression, the recent genocide in Rwanda appears to be a clear case of environmental and population pressures producing social stress, which in turn resulted in violent conflict. . . . Closer study reveals, however, that environmental factors do not provide an adequate explanation of the genocide in Rwanda.

Environmental degradation and high population levels contributed to migrations, declining agricultural productivity, and the weakening of the legitimacy of President Juvenal

SOURCE: Val Percival and Thomas Homer-Dixon, "Environmental Scarcity and Violent Conflict: The Case of Rwanda," *Journal of Environment and Development* 5, no. 3 (1996): 270–72, 276, 277, 278, 280, 281, 288–89. Reprinted with permission of Sage Publishers, Inc.

Habyarimana's regime. Still, a correlation between the scarcities of renewable resources and the outbreak of violence is not adequate proof that violence was caused primarily by resource scarcity. Analysts must trace carefully how environmental factors contribute to the forces that produce violence. Although environmental scarcities have proven to be powerful factors in other cases [e.g., El Salvador], careful analysis demonstrates that environmental scarcities had at most a limited, aggravating role in the civil strife within Rwanda. . . .

The environmental effects of human activity are a function of two factors: the vulnerability of the ecosystem and the product of the total population and that population's physical activity per capita in the region. Homer-Dixon uses the term "environmental scarcity" to refer to scarcity of renewable resources, and he identifies scarcities of agricultural land, forests, water, and fish as the environmental problems that contribute most to violence. These scarcities, however, contribute to violence only under certain circumstances; there is no inevitable or deterministic connection between these variables. The nature of the ecosystem, the social relations within society, and the opportunities for organized violence all affect causal linkages.

Environmental scarcity arises in three ways: Demand-induced scarcity is a result of population growth in a region, supply-induced scarcity arises from the degradation of resources, and structural scarcity occurs because of the unequal social distribution of resources. These three types of scarcity are not mutually exclusive: They often occur simultaneously and interact with one another. Environmental scarcity produces four principal social effects: decreased agricultural potential, regional economic decline, population displacement, and the disruption of legitimized and authoritative institutions and social relations. These social effects, either singly or in combination, can produce and exacerbate conflict between groups. Most such conflict is subnational, diffuse, and persistent. For conflict to break out, the societal balance of power must provide the opportunity for grievances to be expressed as challenges to authority. When grievances are articulated by groups organized around clear social cleavages, such as ethnicity or religion, the probability of civil violence is higher. Under situations of environmental scarcity, in which group affiliation aids survival, intergroup competition on the basis of relative gains is likely to increase. . . .

Until the recent civil violence and mass refugee flows, Rwanda had a high population density and growth rate. In 1992, Rwanda's population was 7.5 million, with a growth rate estimated at 3.3% per year from 1985 to 1990. The population density was roughly 290 inhabitants per square kilometer, among the highest in Africa; the hectare density was 3.2 people in 1993. If lakes, national parks, and forest reserves are excluded from this calculation, the figure increases to 422 people per square kilometer. . . . Before the recent violence, most Rwandans relied almost exclusively on renewable resources, such as agricultural land, to sustain themselves. Ninety-five percent of the population lived in the countryside, and 90% of the labor force relied on agriculture as its primary means of livelihood. . . .

With a large and dense population dependent for its livelihood on extraction from natural resources from a deteriorating resource base, Rwanda clearly exhibited both demand- and supply-induced environmental scarcity; structural scarcity was not serious, primarily because land was evenly distributed throughout the population. Supply-induced scarcity resulted from falling levels of soil fertility, degradation of watersheds, and depletion of forests. Demand-induced scarcity was caused by too many people relying on Rwanda's low supply of land, fuelwood, and water resources.

Prior to the recent conflict, soil fertility had fallen sharply in some parts of Rwanda. Half of the farming in Rwanda occurred on hillsides with slopes of more than 10%; these areas were vulnerable to erosion, particularly under conditions of intense cultivation. On the steepest slopes, heavy rainfall eroded more than eleven tons of soil per hectare per year, with 12 million tons of soil washing into Rwanda's rivers every year. . . . Forest and water scarcity were also serious. Forests cover only 7% of the country. Although deforestation rates have decreased in recent years, in 1986 the Forestry Department estimated that Rwanda was annually using 2.3 million cubic meters of wood, more than the amount its forests produced. Ninety-one percent of wood consumption was for domestic use. . . . These environmental factors began to cause the social effects Homer-Dixon identifies: Agricultural production started to decrease, migrations out of areas of intense environmental stress were commonplace, and the state began to lose legitimacy.

By the late 1980s, environmental scarcity caught up with Rwandan agriculture. Supply- and demand-induced scarcity gravely stressed the ability of food production to keep pace with population growth. . . . In terms of per capita food production, Rwanda was transformed from one of sub-Saharan Africa's top three performers in the early 1980s to one of its worst in the late 1980s. . . . Environmental scarcity [also] caused people to move to ecologically fragile upland and arid areas. . . . Migrants had little choice but to move to and settle in hillside areas, low-potential communes adjacent to western parks and forests, wetlands requiring drainage, and eastern communes near Akagera [National] Park. . . . The government's increasing inability to solve the country's problems created a crisis of legitimacy. Opposition parties formed and organized peaceful protests against the regime. Much of this opposition was based in the southern and central parts of the country, the areas most affected by environmental scarcity and least aided by the government. . . .

Clearly, environmental scarcity was correlated with conflict in Rwanda, but to establish environmental scarcity's causal role, it is not enough to demonstrate that high levels of environmental scarcity were accompanied by conflict. To avoid spurious claims about causation, all factors contributing to the Rwandan conflict must be analyzed and the interaction of environmental scarcity with these factors must be examined. . . .

The Rwanda case tells us important things about the complexity of causal links between environmental scarcity and conflict. Scarcity did play a role in the recent violence in Rwanda, but, given its severity and impact on the population, the role was surprisingly limited. The role also was not what one would expect from a superficial analysis of the case. Although the levels of environmental scarcity were high and conflict occurred, the connection between these variables was mediated by many other factors. This complexity makes the precise role of environmental scarcity difficult to determine.

[Yet] the Rwanda examples teaches us key lessons for the future study of cases exhibiting a strong correlation between environmental scarcity and violence. If our analysis had focused solely on environmental scarcity and the social effects it produced, then its contribution to the conflict would have appeared powerful. By carefully tracing the effects of environmental scarcity and by seriously analyzing competing explanations of the conflict, a more accurate explanation of both the conflict and environmental scarcity's roles was established. If researchers are to understand complex conflicts like the Rwandan genocide, they must be acutely aware of the issues motivating the conflict's actors. They must examine not only the actors' actions and physical environment but also their motivations. A conflict motivated by different political issues could have occurred in Rwanda in which environmental scarcity played a central role. Although the recent violence occurred in conditions of severe environmental scarcity, the Arusha Accords and regime insecurity were the key factors motivating the Hutu elite; environmental scarcity played a peripheral role.

35 • When Victims Become Killers (Mahmood Mamdani)

In a controversial account of the antecedents of the 1994 genocide, Mahmood Mamdani extends the theoretical framework first developed in his book Citizen and Subject *to the case of Rwanda. His dense argument revolves around the politics of indigeneity, notably the ever-changing meaning of settler and native in precolonial, colonial, and postcolonial Rwanda. He contends that the gradual racialization of difference between Hutu and Tutsi, and the legacies thereof, represents an overlooked, remote cause for the genocidal campaign that devastated the tiny country in the late twentieth century.*

In its motivation and construction, I argue that the Rwandan genocide needs to be understood as a natives' genocide. It was a genocide by those who saw themselves as sons—and daughters—of the soil, and their mission as one of clearing the soil of a threatening alien presence. This was not an "ethnic" but a "racial" cleansing, not a violence against one who is seen as a neighbor but against one who is seen as a foreigner; not a violence that targets a transgression across a boundary into home but one that seeks to eliminate a foreign presence from home soil, literally and physically. From this point of view, we need to distinguish between racial and ethnic violence: ethnic violence can result in massacres, but not genocide. Massacres are about transgressions, excess; genocide questions the very legitimacy of a presence as alien. For the Hutu who killed, the Tutsi was a settler, not a neighbor.

Rather than take these identities as a given, as a starting point of analysis, I seek to ask: When and how was Hutu made into a native identity and Tutsi into a settler identity? The analytical challenge is to understand the historical dynamic through which Hutu and Tutsi came to be synonyms for native and settler. . . . My analysis of Hutu and Tutsi as identities differs from the mainstream literature on Rwanda in two important ways. First, whatever other disagreements they may have, historians and political analysts of Rwanda have been preoccupied with finding a *single* answer to the question: Who is a Hutu and who is a Tutsi? In contrast, I argue that Hutu and Tutsi have changed as political identities along with the state that has enforced these identities. There cannot therefore be a single answer that pins Hutu and Tutsi as transhistorical identities. Second, unlike those preoccupied with the *search for origins*— whether biological or cultural—of Hutu and Tutsi, I argue that the clue to Hutu/Tutsi violence lies in two rather contemporary facts. The origin of the violence is connected to how Hutu and Tutsi were constructed as political identities by the colonial state, Hutu as indig-

SOURCE: Mahmood Mamdani, *When Victims Become Killers: Colonialism, Nativism, and the Genocide in Rwanda* (Princeton, N.J.: Princeton University Press, 2001), 14, 34, 74, 75, 80, 87, 101, 102, 134–35, 138, 231, 233. Reprinted with permission of the publisher.

enous and Tutsi as alien. The reason for continued violence between Hutu and Tutsi, I argue, is connected with the failure of Rwandan nationalism to transcend the colonial construction of Hutu and Tutsi as native and alien....

Ancestors of Hutu and Tutsi most likely had separate historical origins. Hutu did not exist as an identity outside the state of Rwanda; it emerged as a transethnic identity of subjects in the [precolonial, Tutsi-dominated] state of Rwanda. The predecessors of the Hutu were simply those from different ethnicities who were subjugated to the power of the state of Rwanda. Tutsi, in contrast, *may* have existed as an ethnic identity before the establishment of the state of Rwanda.... With the Tutsi identity sufficiently porous to absorb successful Hutu through ennoblement and Hutu clearly a transethnic identity of subjects, the Hutu/Tutsi distinction could not be considered an ethnic distinction. Neither could it be considered a socioeconomic distinction, one between exploiters and exploited or rich and poor.... It was also not a distinction between pastoralists and agriculturalists ... because the *petits* Tutsi were usually as cattle-less as the majority of Hutu, and the "*moyens* Tutsi" tended to combine herding a few cattle with cultivating a modest garden.

To be a Tutsi was thus to be in power, near power, or simply to be identified with power—just as to be a Hutu was more and more to be a subject.... It was toward the end of the nineteenth century, as [Tutsi King] Rwabugiri's rule was drawing to a close, that the Hutu/Tutsi distinction clearly began to appear as a political distinction that divided the subject population from those identified with power. Yet, when contrasted with Belgian [colonial] rule which was soon to follow, one is struck by two mitigating features. *First*, the Hutu continued to be present at lower levels of officialdom. *Second*, the boundary between Hutu and Tutsi was softened by a degree of social mobility....

If Hutu/Tutsi evoked the subject-power distinction in the precolonial Rwandan state, the colonial state gave it an added dimension: by racializing Hutu and Tutsi as identities, it signified the distinction as one between indigenous and alien.... The idea that the Tutsi were superior because they came from elsewhere, and that the difference between them and the local population was a *racial* difference, was an idea of colonial origin. It was an idea shared by rival colonists, Belgians, Germans, English, all of whom were convinced that wherever in Africa there was evidence of organized state life, there the ruling groups must have come from somewhere else. These mobile groups were known as the Hamites, and the notion that they were the hidden hand behind every bit of civilization on the continent was known as the "Hamitic hypothesis."...

What then were the institutions that undergirded the identity "Tutsi"? *To begin with*, there was the *political regime* that issued official identities confirming every individual as Hutu or Tutsi, thereby seeking to naturalize a constructed political difference between Hutu and Tutsi as a legislated racial difference. After the 1993 census, Hutu and Tutsi were enforced as legal identities. This has had a crucial social effect: neither *kwihutura* (the social rise of an individual Hutu to the status of a Tutsi) nor *gucupira* (the social fall from a Tutsi to a Hutu status) was any longer possible. For the first time in the history of the state of Rwanda, the identities "Tutsi" and "Hutu" held permanently. They were frozen. Then, *second*, there was the *administrative regime*, which at its lowest rungs, was inevitably a Tutsi power. *Finally*, there was the *legal regime* whereby a Tutsi had a special relationship to the sphere of "customary" law.... It underlined that to be a Tutsi was to have a privileged relationship to power, to be treated preferentially, whether as part of power, in proximity to power, or simply to be identified with power—but in all cases, to be exempt from its worst exactions. In addition, colonialism branded Tutsi privilege, which had existed under Rwabugiri, as *alien* privilege. . . .

To the late nineteenth-century dynamic whereby Tutsi symbolized power and Hutu subject, a new and truly volatile dimension was added. This was the dimension if indigeneity: for the first time in the centuries-long history of the Rwandan state, Tutsi became identified with an alien race and Hutu with the indigenous majority. . . . The big change was that from being at the top of the *local* hierarchy in the precolonial period, the Tutsi found themselves occupying the bottom rung of a hierarchy of *alien* races in the colonial period. . . .

For the postrevolutionary power that was the First Republic [which lasted from 1962 until 1973], Rwanda was exclusively a Hutu state. The rationale for this was disarmingly simple, disarmingly so because it simply turned upside down the logic of the colonial state: the Hutu were indigenous, the Tutsi were alien. Whereas the Tutsi had been treated preferentially by the colonial state as a nonindigenous civilizing influence, the First Republic considered this claim reason enough to treat them as politically illegitimate. The Tutsi thus continued to be officially defined as a "race," never as an "ethnic group." The implication was crucial. The language of race turned around the distinction "indigenous/alien": a racial difference could only be with foreigners, whereas an ethnic difference was with locals. . . .

The Second Republic [which lasted from 1973 until 1994] claimed to complete the "national" revolution of 1959 [a Hutu uprising that led to the dismantling of Tutsi domination] through a "moral" revolution. The change from the First to the Second Republic—a change that seems to have gone unnoticed by many an observer of Rwandan politics—was a shift in the political identity of the Tutsi from a race to an ethnic group. While the First Republic considered the Tutsi a "race," the Second Republic reconstructed the Tutsi as an "ethnicity" and therefore as a group *indigenous* to Rwanda. We have seen that the language of race turned around the distinction between indigenous/nonindigenous. The political distinction between a majority and a minority had little relevance within the domain of "race." For, as a race, Tutsi were simply foreign. Their numbers were of little significance. Once reconstructed as an ethnicity, however, the Tutsi became Rwandan and their numbers became significant, just as the minority/majority distinction also became of great relevance. As a "race" under the First Republic, the Tutsi had been confined to the civic sphere and barred from the political sphere; as an "ethnicity" under the Second Republic, however, they were allowed participation in the political sphere, but limited to a scope said to befit their minority status. . . .

The life of the Second Republic was cut short by the RPF [Rwandan Patriotic Front] invasion of 1990. The invasion [which caused a civil war inside of Rwanda] literally reversed the dynamic of the Second Republic. . . . It once again *polarized* Hutu and Tutsi as political identities. Key to this shift, this repolarization of Hutu and Tutsi as political identities, was the growing realization that the real objective of the RPF invasion was not rights but power—specifically Tutsi power. The assassination of the newly elected Hutu president, Melchior Ndadaye, in Burundi in 1993 by a Tutsi army merely confirmed this realization as a truism. It is, after all, defeat in civil war, and the specter of [renewed] Tutsi Power, that provided the context in which a tendency born of Hutu Power [a conglomeration of radical Hutu political parties and organizations]—the *génocidaire*—chose to embrace death in preference to life. . . .

If it is the struggle for power that explains the motivation of those who crafted the genocide, then it is the combined fear of a return to servitude and of reprisals thereafter that energized the footsoldiers of the genocide. The irony is that—whether in the Church, in hospitals,
or in human rights groups, as in fields and homes—the perpetrators of the genocide saw
themselves as the true victims of an ongoing political drama, victims of yesterday who may
yet be victims again. That moral certainty explains the easy transition from yesterday's victims
to killers the morning after.

36 • Unsimplifying Darfur (René Lemarchand)

*René Lemarchand, professor emeritus of political science at the University of Florida, is known
primarily for his in-depth knowledge of the Africa's Great Lakes region. That he is also deeply familiar with the contemporary history of Sudan is evident in this essay. His is a plea, first and foremost, for studying the dynamics of collective violence in Darfur and elsewhere from the perspective
of the longue durée, for as he points out in this blog post from 2005, the causes of the Darfur crisis
are multiple and complex.*

Not even the most casual observer of Darfur's agony can remain insensitive to the scale of the
human sufferings unfolding in this forbidding dystopia. But it takes more than a superficial
acquaintance with the history, geography and politics of the region to appreciate how radically different from that of Rwanda is the context of the killings in Darfur. Unlike Rwanda
(26,000 sq. kms) Darfur covers a huge expanse of territory, about the size of Texas. In a space
of some 450,000 sq. kms, approximately ten times the size of Rwanda, the population is estimated to be between 3.5 to 4 million, i.e., half that of Rwanda, much of it distributed among
scores of small village communities. This basic fact speaks volumes about the enormous logistical difficulties facing the 4,000-strong AU [African Union] peace-keeping force in its
Sisyphean efforts to stop the hemorrhage . . .

As in the case of Rwanda, no single factor analysis will do to explain the cause of the
tragedy. We are confronted with an array of forces and circumstances that go far beyond the
boundaries of Sudan. Most observers would agree that the triggering factor was the surprise
attack on El Fasher, in April 2003, by the Sudan Liberation Army (SLA), resulting in the destruction of seven military aircraft and the death of about 100 people. But El Fasher was only
the symptom of more fundamental factors. Of these perhaps the most consequential has to
do with the steady advance of desertification through much of northern Darfur, resulting in
devastating famine. . . . What is known locally as the maja'a al-gutala ("the famine that kills")
caused the death of an estimated 95,000 people from August 1984 to November 1985. With
the massive population movements from north to south—and with Arab cattle herders moving in ever increasing numbers into those areas of the south less affected by the drought—a
whole series of local clashes over land erupted, first between Fur and Arabs in the Jebel Mara
area (1987–89), then between Massalit and Arabs (1996–98). Each time the parties to a con-

Isn't this a difficult term?

SOURCE: René Lemarchand, "Unsimplifying Darfur," December 2, 2005, http://coalitionfordarfur.blogspot
  .com. Reprinted with permission of the author.

flict reached out to the Arab-dominated provincial government for a fair settlement, the government consistently sided by the Arabs.

The spread of a stridently pro-Islamic ideology did little to diminish the government's blatant favoritism displayed towards Arabs. The roots of what [the anthropologist Alex] de Waal calls "an Arab supremacist ideology" are to be found in part in ideas indigenous to the Sudan—generally associated with Hasan al-Turabi's National Islamic Front (NIF) and later his Popular Congress (PC). Just as important, however, has been the export of "Arabism" from Chad and Libya. The Chadian side of the story, in a nutshell, involves a warlord named Acyl Ahmed, who, as head of the *Armée du Volcan*, in the late 1970s and early '80s, was able to mobilize a large number of Chadian Arabs against Hissene Habre's *Forces Armées du Nord* (FAN). Of all the Trojan horses produced by Colonel Gaddafi's stable, Acyl was by far the most faithful. Although Acyl died in 1982, his pro-Arab ideology is still alive and well. For this, much of the credit goes to Gaddafi. After suffering a major defeat in northern Chad at the hands of Hissène Habre in 1987, the Libyan leader turned his attention to Darfur. To carve out for himself another sphere of influence and hold aloft the banner of the "Arab Gathering" (Al tajammu al-arabi)—a "militantly racist and pan-Arabist organization," [historian Gérard] Prunier informs us—some 2,000 Islamic Legion troops were sent to Darfur in 1987. The ideological seeds of the present conflict, in short, were planted long before the attack on El Fasher.

Exactly how the southern rebellion has affected its counterpart in Darfur is not entirely clear. Through the years, going back to the Federal Democratic Alliance of the former Darfur Governor Ibrahim Deraige, the Southern Peoples Liberation Army (SPLA) has given moral and financial support to the African resistance in Darfur, but in so doing it has unwittingly stimulated factional disputes about the distribution of arms and money. If the SPLA struggle in the south served as an example to emulate, this doesn't mean that it has always been to the advantage of the Darfurian rebels. Again, considerable ambiguity surrounds the fall-out of the Comprehensive Peace Agreement (CPA) between Khartoum and the SPLA in the south in January 2005. The effect has been to encourage the insurgents to make every effort to wrest a similar agreement from Khartoum, while at the same time contributing to hardening the position of the central government on meeting their demands: after virtually giving up the monopoly of the ruling party, in line with the CPA, it is now dead set against any further erosion of its executive power. . . .

The fragmentation of the insurgency into rival factions, though rarely mentioned in the media, let alone explicated, is not the least of the obstacles to peace. Only recently has Nicholas Kristof [of the *New York Times* editorial page]—the most insistent and articulate critic of Western policies in Darfur—grudgingly recognized that "some responsibility attaches to the rebels in Darfur" as "they have been fighting each other instead of negotiating a peace with the government that would end the bloodbath." Yet there has been bitter infighting among rebels almost from the beginning. No sooner was the Sudan Liberation Army (SLA) created, in early 2003, than a violent struggle for the leadership of the movement began to surface.

Today those who form the bulk of the insurgents are drawn from the Zaghawa, Fur and Massalit "tribes," with the Zaghawa straddling the boundary between Chad and Darfur. Each is divided into subgroups, with the Zaghawa, for example, split between Tuer, Bideyat and Kobe, and each sub-group in turn divided into clans. If the Zaghawa have been the driving force behind the insurgency, this is because many "had acquired professional military training in the Chadian or Sudanese armies, a fact that has caused them to predominate in the upper ranks of the insurgency to this day." Which also helps explain why they came to be seen with considerable suspicion by Fur and Massalit elements—but leaves unanswered the question of why they ended up fighting each other. Part of the answer lies in the multiplicity of sub-ethnic and clanic fissures among the Zaghawa. The really critical factor, however, has to do with the impact of Chadian politics on the rebellion. Just as Darfur has had a significant backlash effect in Chad, the reverse is equally true.

The insurgents are divided into two principal rival armed factions, the SLA and the Justice and Equality Movement (JEM), the latter, the weaker of the two, drawing much of its support from Zaghawa Kobe, and the former from Tuer and Bideyat as well as Fur and Massalit. The SLA, founded in February 2003, is decidedly secular in orientation, while the JEM remains highly receptive to Hasan al-Turabi Islamic ideology. The SLA, moreover, claims a more diversified ethnic membership, which is also why it is more vulnerable to internal dissensions. The early history of the SLA provides a dramatic illustration of the potential for disintegration inherent in its ethnic composition.

At first, every effort was made to include representatives of each major ethnic group in its leadership. Thus, while the chairmanship of the movement was given to a Fur (Abdel Wahid Mohammed el-Nur), the deputy chairmanship went to a Massalit (Mansour Arbab) and the military command to a Zaghawa (Abdallah Abakar, replaced after his death by Minni Arko Minnawi). After receiving substantial support from Zaghawa elements in the Chadian military, Minnawi's Zaghawa scored a number of military successes against the Khartoum government, only to raise the anxieties of Fur elements. A bitter struggle for leadership ensued between Fur and Zaghawa. In the words of a recent International Crisis Group report, "The rapid expansion and intensification of the conflict overwhelmed the leaders and their nascent structures. Over time the animosity between Minni and Abdel Wahid grew as they jostled for primacy. Whereas Minni considers that Zaghawa military strength should be reflected in the leadership, Abdel Wahid and other non-Zaghawa insist on the original tribal allocations of positions, including a Fur as chairman." . . .

By then, however, the JEM had already emerged as a powerful challenger to the SLA, militarily and ideologically. It shares Hasan al-Turabi's Islamic ideas and is said to have received financial and military assistance from Turabi's Popular Congress. In part for that reason, and because it is solidly Kobe, its relationship with President Idriss Deby of Chad, a Bideyat, is fraught with tension. It is indeed widely rumored that Deby was instrumental in stimulating the rise of a breakaway faction, the National Movement for Reform and Development (NMRD). Another split emerged in April 2005 following a trial of strength between field commander Mohammed Salih Harba and JEM's top leader, Khalil Ibrahim, leading to the creation of a Provisional Revolutionary Collective Leadership Council. Some observers do not hesitate to see in this latest defection the evil hand of Idriss Deby. As the crisis spills deeper into Chad, Deby could find himself drawn into a dangerous trial of strength between different Zaghawa subgroups, notably Bideyat (pro-Deby) vs. Kobe.

The Chadian connection is likely to remain a critical dimension of the crisis in Darfur, if only because each of the insurgent factions, as well as the *janjawids*, include a substantial number of Chadians. One well-informed Chadian observer told this writer that the majority of the *janjawids* were Chadian Arabs, many of Juhaina origins. Their expectation, presumably, is that Khartoum will return the favor and help them overthrow Deby, in a replay of the scenario that brought Deby to power in 1990. Today Deby finds himself in a cleft stick: by refusing to give assistance to the SLA—which, as noted earlier, includes a fair number of Zaghawa from his own tribe, the Bideyat—he could seriously antagonize the Bideyat of his own Presidential Guard, who could turn against him; on the other hand, should he get actively involved on the side of the SLA, the likelihood is that Khartoum would immediately retaliate. The worst-case scenario would be a Khartoum-sponsored alliance between Darfurian and Chadian Arabs directed against Deby's regime. No less threatening would be a Kobe-instigated coup within the Chadian army—a scenario that almost became reality in March of [2005]. . . .

There is a curious disconnect between the enormous complexity of the forces at work in the Darfurian killing fields and the readiness with which genocide is invoked by human rights advocates. For some, the question of establishing the evidence of genocide is irrelevant; more important is to use the G-word as a tool to mobilize public opinion. For others, however, whether we are dealing with genocide or something else—e.g., ethnic cleansing or the use of force to crush a rebellion—is the crucial issue. . . . What seems increasingly clear is that the ongoing debate about Darfur's "ambiguous genocide," to use [Gérard] Prunier's expression, is, in practical terms, extremely counterproductive.

37 • Obedience to Authority (Stanley Milgram)

The "Milgram experiment," as it is commonly known, remains one of the most memorable psychology experiments ever conducted. It asked unsuspecting participants ("teachers") to administer what they believed were live electric shocks to underperforming "learners." The initial experiment took place at Yale University in the early 1960s and involved ordinary men of the New Haven community, ages 20 to 50. The study, described by Stanley Milgram, the lead psychologist, in this extract from his 1974 book, revealed a high degree of obedience to authority among the participants—a degree of obedience that persisted even in the face of apparent suffering of another. Milgram conceived the experiment at the time of the 1961 trial of Adolf Eichmann, the infamous Nazi defendant, in Jerusalem. He sought to find out whether Nazi perpetrators were likely to have shared a "mutual intent" during the Holocaust or whether their actions could have been the result of obedience rather than moral conviction. What, if anything, can the Milgram experiment teach us about genocide in the real world?

The Nazi extermination of European Jews is the most extreme instance of abhorrent immoral acts carried out by thousands of people in the name of obedience. Yet in a lesser degree this type of thing is constantly recurring: ordinary citizens are ordered to destroy other people, and they do so because they consider it their duty to obey orders. Thus, obedience to authority, long praised as a virtue, takes on a new aspect when it serves a malevolent cause; far from appearing as a virtue, it is transformed into a heinous sin. Or is it? . . .

SOURCE: Stanley Milgram, *Obedience to Authority: An Experimental View* (New York: Harper and Row, 1974), 2–6. Reprinted with permission of the publisher.

In order to take a close look at the act of obeying, I set up a simple experiment at Yale University. Eventually, the experiment was to involve more than a thousand participants and would be repeated at several universities, but at the beginning, the conception was simple. A person comes to a psychological laboratory and is told to carry out a series of acts that come increasingly into conflict with conscience. The main question is how far the participant will comply with the experimenter's instructions before refusing to carry out the actions required of him.

But the reader needs to know a little more detail about the experiment. Two people come to a psychology laboratory to take part in a study of memory and learning. One of them is designated as a "teacher" and the other a "learner." The experimenter explains that the study is concerned with the effects of punishment on learning. The learner is conducted into a room, seated in a chair, his arms strapped to prevent excessive movement, and an electrode attached to his wrist. He is told that he is to learn a list of word pairs; whenever he makes an error, he will receive electric shocks of increasing intensity.

The real focus of the experiment is the teacher. After watching the learner being strapped into place, he is taken into the main experimental room and seated before an impressive shock generator. Its main feature is a horizontal line of thirty switches, ranging from 15 volts to 450 volts, in 15-volt increments. There are also verbal designations which range from "slight shock" to "danger—severe shock." The teacher is told that he is to administer the learning test to the man in the other room. When the learner responds correctly, the teacher moves on to the next item; when the other man gives an incorrect answer, the teacher is to give him an electric shock. He is to start at the lowest shock level (15 volts) and to increase the level each time the man makes an error, going through 30 volts, 45 volts, and so on. The "teacher" is a genuinely naïve subject who has come to the laboratory to participate in an experiment. The learner, or victim, is an actor who actually receives no shock at all. The point of the experiment is to see how far a person will proceed in a concrete and measurable situation in which he is ordered to inflict increasing pain on a protesting victim. At what point will the subject refuse to obey the experimenter?

Conflict arises when the man receiving the shock begins to indicate that he is experiencing discomfort. At 75 volts, the "learner" grunts. At 120 volts he complains verbally; at 150 he demands to be released from the experiment. His protests continue as the shocks escalate, growing increasingly vehement and emotional. At 285 volts his response can only be described as an agonized scream. Observers of the experiment agree that its gripping quality is somewhat obscured in print. For the subject, the situation is not a game; conflict is intense and obvious. On one hand, the manifest suffering of the learner presses him to quit. On the other, the experimenter, a legitimate authority to whom the subject feels some commitment, enjoins him to continue. Each time the subject hesitates to administer the shock, the experimenter orders him to continue. To extricate himself from the situation, the subject must make a clear break with authority. The aim of this investigation was to find when and how people would defy authority in the face of a clear moral imperative. . . .

A reader's initial reaction to the experiment may be to wonder why anyone in his right mind would administer even the first shocks. Would he not simply refuse and walk out of the laboratory? But the fact is that no one ever does. Since the subject has come to the laboratory to aid the experimenter, he is quite willing to start off with the procedure. There is nothing very extraordinary in this, particularly since the person who is to receive the shocks seems initially cooperative, if somewhat apprehensive. What is surprising is how far ordinary individuals will go in complying with the experimenter's instructions. Indeed, the results of the experiment are both surprising and dismaying. Despite the fact that many subjects experience stress, despite the fact that many protest to the experimenter, a substantial proportion continue to the last shock on the generator.

Many subjects will obey the experimenter no matter how vehement the pleading of the person being shocked, no matter how painful the shocks seem to be, and no matter how much the victim pleads to be let out. This was seen time and time again in our studies and has been observed in several universities where the experiment was repeated. It is the extreme willingness of adults to go to almost any lengths on the command of an authority that constitutes the chief finding of the study and the fact most urgently demanding explanation.

A commonly offered explanation is that those who shocked the victim at the most severe level were monsters, the sadistic fringe of society. But if one considers that almost two-thirds of the participants fell into the category of "obedient" subjects, and that they represented ordinary people drawn from working, managerial, and professional classes, the argument becomes very shaky. Indeed, it is highly reminiscent of the issue that arose in connection with Hannah Arendt's 1963 book, *Eichmann in Jerusalem*. Arendt contended that the prosecution's effort to depict Eichmann as a sadistic monster was fundamentally wrong, that he came closer to being an uninspired bureaucrat who simply sat at his desk and did his job. For asserting these views, Arendt became the object of considerable scorn, even calumny. Somehow, it was felt that the monstrous deeds carried out by Eichmann required a brutal, twisted, and sadistic personality, devil incarnate.

After witnessing hundreds of ordinary people submit to the authority in our own experiments, I must conclude that Arendt's conception of the *banality of evil* comes closer to the truth than one might dare imagine. The ordinary person who shocked the victim did so out of a sense of obligation—a conception of his duties as a subject—not from any peculiarly aggressive tendencies. This is, perhaps, the most fundamental lesson of our study: ordinary people, simply doing their jobs, and without any particular hostility on their part, can become agents in a terrible destructive process.

38 • Difficult Life Conditions (Ervin Staub)

Ervin Staub, a psychologist at the University of Massachusetts at Amherst, was among the first psychologists to take seriously the study of comparative genocide. In The Roots of Evil *(1989), the first book dedicated to the subject, Staub introduced readers to the gamut of psychological knowledge about genocide, which remains scant. Among other things, he emphasized the importance of pre-existing histories of hardship for the rise of genocidal dynamics. The proposed logic is as follows: When difficult life conditions combine with certain cultural preconditions (e.g., feelings of inferiority), affected groups may see incentives to turn against presumed competitors, notably groups deemed*

SOURCE: Ervin Staub, *The Roots of Evil: The Origins of Genocide and Other Group Violence* (Cambridge: Cambridge University Press, 1989), 13–14, 15–16, 18–19, 23. Reprinted with permission of the publisher.

inferior to themselves. For Staub, structural inequalities of the kind described here have a powerful hold on the psyche of individuals and groups alike. Once unleashed, says Staub, it is probable that "initial acts of harm-doing will be followed by further steps along the continuum of destruction."

I believe that tragically human beings have the capacity to come to experience killing other people as nothing extraordinary. Some perpetrators may feel sick and disgusted when killing large numbers of people, as they might feel in slaughtering animals, but even they will proceed to kill for a "good" reason, for a "higher" cause. How do they come to this? In essence, difficult life conditions and certain cultural characteristics may generate psychological processes and motives that lead a group to turn against another group. The perpetrators change, as individuals and as a group, as they progress along a continuum of destruction that ends in genocide. . . .

Human beings often face hard times as individuals or as members of a group. Sometimes a whole society or substantial and potentially influential segments of society face serious problems that have a powerful impact and result in powerful motivations. Economic conditions at the extreme can result in starvation or threat to life. Less extreme economic problems can result in prolonged deprivation, deterioration of material well-being, or at least the frustration of expectations for improved well-being. Hostility and violence threaten and endanger life, whether political violence between internal groups or war with an external enemy. . . . Rapid changes in culture and society—for example, rapid technological change and the attendant changes in work and social customers—also have the psychological impact of difficult life conditions. They overturn set patterns of life and lead to disorganization. The meaning assigned to life problems, the intensity of their impact, and the way groups of people try to deal with them are greatly affected by the characteristics of cultures and social organizations. By themselves, difficult life conditions will not lead to genocide. They carry the potential, the motive force; culture and social organization determine whether the potential is realized by giving rise to devaluation and hostility toward a subgroup. . . .

Difficult life conditions give rise to powerful needs and goals demanding satisfaction. People need to cope with the psychological effects of difficult life conditions, the more so when they cannot change the conditions or alleviate the physical effects. Hard times make people feel threatened and frustrated. Threats to the physical self are important, but so are the threats to the psychological self. All human beings strive for a coherent and positive self-concept, a self-definition that provides continuity and guides one's life. Difficult conditions threaten the self-concept as people cannot care for themselves and their families or control the circumstances of their lives. . . . When their group is functioning poorly and not providing protection and well-being, people's respect for and valuing of the group diminish; their societal self-concept is harmed. Because people define themselves to a significant degree by their membership in a group, for most people a positive view of their group is essential to individual self-esteem—especially in difficult times. The need to protect and improve societal self-concept or to find a new group to identify with will be powerful. . . .

The cultural self-concept of a people greatly influences the need to protect the collective psychological self. A sense of superiority, of being better than others and having the right to rule over them, intensifies this need. Collective self-doubt is another motivation for psychological self-defense. When a sense of superiority combines with an underlying (and often unacknowledged) self-doubt, their contribution to the potential for genocide and mass killing can be especially high. . . . The combination of difficult life conditions and certain cultural preconditions makes it probable that motives will arise that turn a group against one another. This combination makes it probable that initial acts of harm-doing will be followed by further steps along the continuum of destruction. The behavior of bystanders can facilitate or inhibit this progression. Genocide arises from a pattern, or gestalt, rather than from any single source.

39 • Becoming Evil (James Waller)

James Waller, the Cohen Chair of Holocaust and Genocide Studies at Keene State College, takes issue with the concept of evil, which is frequently invoked in the context of genocide. Borrowing from evolutionary psychology, in his 2007 book, Waller rejects "moralistic" conceptions of evil and elaborates a behavioral definition instead. He believes that genocidal perpetrators should be described not as being evil but as becoming evil.

Despite its universality in human affairs, "evil" is not a frequently studied construct with a generally accepted definition. . . . Even those relatively few scholars, most housed in religion and philosophy, who write frequently of evil often shy away from a precise conceptual definition. Why?

To specifically define the "judgmental" and "moralistic" concept of evil seems to threaten the academic ideal of ethical and value neutrality. To be sure, any definition includes, in part, a value statement reflecting one's own perspective. . . . To be equally sure, however, this relativistic ethos has meant that evil has ceased to be a meaningful term. This definitional phobia is a convenient cop-out that keeps us mired on the sidelines of a discussion in which we should be full participants. Though evil may be difficult to define conceptually, we all are aware of its existence and pervasiveness at a concrete level. We know what it looks like, what it feels like, and how it can irrevocably alter our lives. As the late Susan Sontag said, "We have a sense of evil," but we no longer have "the religious or philosophical language to talk intelligently about evil." . . .

I define human evil as the deliberate harming of humans by other humans. This is a behavioral definition that focuses on how people act toward one another. This definition judges as evil any human *actions* leading to the deliberate harming of other humans. . . . Within the broad range of acts defined as human evil, I have chosen to focus . . . on *extraordinary* human evil. . . . The center of my attention is on the deliberate harm we perpetrate on each other under the sanction of political, social, or religious groups—in other words, the malevolent human evil perpetrated in times of collective social unrest, war, mass killings, and genocide. . . . I am referring to the deliberate harm inflicted against a defenseless and helpless group targeted by a political, social, or religious authority—human evil *in extremis*. . . .

In reality, a purely evil person is just as much an artificial construct as a person who is purely good. Perpetrators of extraordinary evil are extraordinary only by what they have done,

SOURCE: James Waller, *Becoming Evil: How Ordinary People Commit Genocide and Mass Murder*, 2nd edition (Oxford: Oxford University Press, 2007), 11, 12, 13–14, 20, 21, 139–40, 142, 148, 149, 154, 158–59, 160. Reprinted with permission of the publisher.

not by who they are. We must not consider them so irrational, so atavistic, as to be beyond human understanding. We must go beyond our tendency to focus on such evil as a peculiar property or characteristic of despicable individuals and come to focus on the ways in which ordinary individuals become perpetrators of extraordinary evil. Recognizing their ordinariness does not diminish the horror of their actions. It increases it. At the same time, it neither excuses their deeds nor minimizes the threat they pose. On the contrary, it reminds us . . . "how fragile are the bonds of civility and decency that keep any kind of human community from utter collapse." . . .

Understanding that ordinary people commit extraordinary evil still begs an explanation. *What factors lead some of us to perpetrate extraordinary evil while others of us stand by indifferently or, occasionally, resist such evil?* In other words, if we are *all* capable of extraordinary evil, why don't we *all* perpetrate extraordinary evil when given the opportunity? How, *exactly*, do ordinary people come to commit genocide and mass killing? . . .

[My] model emphasizes three proximate, here-and-now constructions that converge interactively to impact individual behavior in situations of collective violence. The cultural construction of worldview examines the influence of cultural models—related to collectivist values, authority orientation, and social dominance—that are widely shared by the members of a perpetrator group. The psychological construction of the "other" analyzes how victims of genocide and mass killing become simply the "objects" of perpetrators' actions through the processes of us-them thinking, moral disengagement, and blaming the victims. Finally, the social construction of cruelty explores the influence of professional socialization, group identification, and the binding factors of the group in creating an immediate social context in which perpetrators initiate, sustain, and cope with their cruelty. Underlying these three proximate constructions, however, are other ultimate influences—flowing from the deep evolutionary streams of human nature—which give us a more thorough understanding of individual behavior in situations of collective violence. We have a "developmental spec sheet," given [to] us by nature, which includes innate capacities that can be activated by proximate cultural, psychological, and social constructions to influence our immediate behavior. It is these ultimate influences that reveal the nature of human nature and, in so doing, help us understand the "why" behind the "how" ordinary people commit genocide and mass killing. . . .

How do modern social scientists respond to the question of the nature of human nature? . . . To be sure, there remains a gulf between humans and animals that is far from closed. The edges of this gulf, though, continue to move closer together. As they do, the concept of a human nature has returned to the front of of the academic conversation in the social sciences. . . . Leading this charge into the twenty-first century is the field of *evolutionary psychology*— a hybrid of the natural (evolutionary biology) and social (cognitive psychology) sciences. What is evolutionary psychology, and what does it have to say about the nature of human nature? . . .

The specific goal of EP is to discover and understand the design of the human mind in terms of the Darwinian revolution. In EP, the mind is *not* the brain; rather, the mind refers to what the brain does—that is, information processing or computation. EP is really engineering in reverse. In forward engineering, we design a machine to do something. In reverse engineering, we figure out what a machine—in this case, the human mind—was designed to do. The research of EP, in describing the psychological mechanisms that give rise to our instincts or tendencies, cuts straight to the heart of the nature of human nature. In EP . . . human behavior is driven by a set of *universal reasoning circuits* that were *designed by natural selection* to solve *adaptive problems* faced by our *hunter-gatherer ancestors.* . . .

While natural selection continues its glacial process of building circuits that are more suited to a modern environment, our ability to solve other kinds of more modern problems is best seen as a side effect or by-product of circuits that were designed to solve the adaptive problems of our hunter-gatherer ancestors. I want to restate this point because it is vital to our understanding of why ordinary people commit genocide and mass killing. Human behavior in the *present* is generated by universal reasoning circuits that exist because they solved adaptive problems in the *past.* As a result, these past-oriented circuits will not always necessarily generate adaptive behavior in the present. In some cases, what the circuits were designed to accomplish in the hunter-gatherer context even can lead to maladaptive behavior in response to contemporary environmental contexts. In other words, our minds, like our appendix, are adapted to a world that no longer exists. . . .

In short, we have been endowed by evolution with a host of needs and desires, such that it is often difficult for one person to pursue his or her needs and desires without coming into conflict with other people. However deeply buried, the capacities for evil are within all of us. We have a hereditary dark side that is universal across humankind. Acts of evil are not beyond, beneath, or outside ordinary humanness. Natural selection has left deep traces of design in our minds, and at least some of those designs leave us evolutionarily primed with the capacity for evil—including the perpetration of genocide and mass killing. As William James [the pioneering American psychologist and philosopher] wrote, "We, the lineal representatives of the successful enactors of one scene of slaughter after another, must, whatever more pacific virtues we may also possess, still carry with us, ready at any moment to burst into flame, the smoldering and sinister traits of character by means of which they lived through so many massacres, harming others, but themselves unharmed." . . . EP says that human nature is not blank at all; it consists of a large number of evolved psychological mechanisms. . . . We are obligated to examine the impact of *what* we are on *who* we are in understanding how ordinary people commit genocide and mass killing. To not seek such evidence is like failing to search a suspect for a concealed weapon.

EP, in spite of its youth, is lending substantial credibility to the perception of a fundamental unity among human beings. . . . There *is* something "beneath" socialization or prior to history which serves to define the human—and that something is the long reach of human nature shaped by natural selection. . . . While the roots of genocide and mass killing cannot be distilled solely to natural selection, we can no longer dismiss as an unsupportable theological or philosophical assumption the idea that human nature has a dark side. . . . [Yet] understanding the powerful, innate, "animal" influences lying at the core of human nature is only the first step in understanding how ordinary people commit genocide and mass killing. . . . While EP describes the ultimate evolutionary capacities common to all of us, this understanding must be couched in the context of the more proximate and immediate cultural, psychological, and social constructions that activate these capacities.

40 • Democide and Genocide as Rent-Seeking Activities
(Gerald W. Scully)

In the pursuit of scientific rigor some scholars have begun to build mathematical models of geno-
cide. The late Gerald Scully, formerly emeritus professor of economics at the University of Texas at
Dallas, conceived of democide (which he defines as state murder of members of the general popula-
tion) and genocide (which he defines as state murder of minorities) as rent-seeking activities in this
1997 article. He reports an inverse relationship between the amount of state-sponsored killing of the
domestic population and the price of the people being killed. On this argument, democide and geno-
cide are more prevalent in settings where per capita income is low because authoritarian governments
are more likely to consider life as being cheap—and thus expendable. Tho seems logical

In the twentieth century, some 170 (perhaps 360) million people have been murdered by
their governments. These deaths are more than four times [as numerous as] those from civil
and international wars. The USSR, China (PRC) [People's Republic of China], and Nazi Germany killed on an appalling scale. But, often sight is lost that state-sponsored murder is quite
common. When the state murders some of the general population, the term is democide;
when it murders minorities, the term is genocide. . . .

All communist states have committed democide and some have practiced genocide. . . .
More than a third of the African states [have done so]. Sudan, Uganda, Nigeria, and Rwanda
(1994) killed on a large scale. Fifteen Latin and Central American countries are represented.
Brazil, Guatemala, and Colombia practiced it on a large scale. In Asia and the Middle East,
Pakistan and Indonesia were the leaders, with most of the killing being genocide. Thirteen
nations in the region have committed democide. In Europe, besides Nazi Germany state-
sponsored murder has occurred in Cyprus, France (mainly during the German occupation),
Greece, Italy (again during the fascist period), Spain, Turkey (mainly against the Armenians,
but the Kurds, as well), and the United Kingdom (Ireland, Northern Ireland). Overall, about
a third of the non-communist nations have practiced democide through terror and by genocide in the post–World War II era. . . .

A rough negative correlation exists between the level of state killing and per capital real
gross domestic product. Latin and Central American nations, which have modest levels of
democide, have higher income levels than many of the African and Asian nations that have
killed on a larger scale. This suggests that where per capita income is low, life is viewed by the
authorities as cheap. Where per capita income is higher, states may be constrained, because
killing the population is costly. This suggests that price (measured by a unit of real gross domestic product per capita destroyed) constrains the amount of state-sponsored murder. Terror [inflicted by the state] is a signal to opponents that the price of opposition is high. The
benefit of democide is continued rule. The cost of terror [inflicted by the state] is destroyed
output. A cold calculus suggests that a rational dictator or ruling group will practice democide
or genocide up to the point where the marginal benefit equals the marginal cost. Marginal benefit in this context is continued rule and a share in the rents that dictators [or ruling groups]

Or is N that
stable econs/
politics => ?
GDP o econ
=> ↓ so genocide?

I'm not sure econ loss is ever much considered
in genocidal actions

SOURCE: Gerald W. Scully, "Democide and Genocide as Rent-Seeking Activities," *Public Choice* 93, nos. 1–2
(1997): 77–78, 81–82, 83, 84, 87–89, 93, 96. Reprinted with permission of Kluwer Academic Publishers.

generate through their centralized political and economic control plus any "pleasure" obtained from inflicting terror. Marginal cost is the incremental national output lost from the killing. Civilized people would view government-sponsored murder as demented, the acts of sociopaths. But, many aspects of life that we judge as bad, nevertheless, are governed by the law of demand.

Does democide obey the law of demand? To explore this relationship I estimated a crude demand function. I took the mid-year of the period over which democide occurred and obtained the value of the real gross domestic product per capita (in 1985 dollars) for that year. . . . I confined the sample to nations that killed 10,000 or more of their citizens. The sample consists of 31 nations. The regression in logarithmic form was:

Small sample
Size

$$\text{Log DEMOCIDE} = 22.2153 - 1.4411 \text{ Log RGDP}, \bar{R}^2 = .488$$
$$(11.59) \quad (5.44)$$

The result is highly significant. The sign is as expected. There is an inverse relationship between the amount of state-sponsored killing of the domestic population and the price of the people being killed. The coefficient estimate suggests that a one percent increase in RGDP [real gross domestic product] "buys" about a 1.4 percent decline democide. . . . Then, there is some evidence that democidal governments in higher per capita income nations exercise some self-restraint. This may even help our understanding of the slowdown in the pace of killing in the Soviet Union and China. During the Stalin era (1929–53) about 42.7 million [people] were murdered. About 8.1 million were killed in the 34-year period after Stalin (1954–87). While still a large amount, if Stalin's pace of killing had been maintained, there would have been 63.5 million deaths. Despite the poor performance of socialism, there had been economic growth in the Soviet Union. Comrades were getting more expensive to liquidate. This explanation of the slowdown in the pace of killing seems more tractable than any notion that the post-Stalin communist leadership was more civilized.

When we turn to China, the 28-year rule of Mao Tse-tung (1949–76) yielded 34.4 million killed. In the post-Mao era (1977–87), 874,000 have been killed. The post-Mao era has been characterized by rapid economic growth. Again, the slowdown in the rate of murder may be due to the economic fact that the population [became] more productive (valuable). . . . On the whole, although the evidence [from previous centuries] is very crude, it appears that as per capita incomes have risen with industrialization, there has been a decline in the relative incidence of democide through the centuries.

Humans prefer to dominate rather than to be dominated. They tend to distrust and dislike people who are different. Antipathy may be official government policy or it may arise spontaneously and be tolerated. Its extreme form is murder; its less pernicious form is discrimination. . . . Enmity has economic implications. Among groups of equal productivity majority group per capita income usually exceeds that of the minority. Discrimination transfers incomes from the minority to the majority, and is a form of rent-seeking. . . . The domination and rent-seeking by one group over another may be associated with restrictions on occupational choice, denial of educational opportunities, preferences in the licensing of trade, confiscation of land, nationalization of business, restrictions on property and exchange, mobility restrictions, and so on. The dominant groups earn rents from these sanctioned restrictions . . . and have a vested interest in maintaining them. . . .

My purpose is to estimate the rents associated with democide [and genocide]. It is quite impossible to know the value (not necessarily pecuniary) of those activities to the officials who have practiced [democide or genocide]. But, it is possible to crudely calculate lost national output arising from democide [and genocide]. Democide [and genocide] make life and property insecure. Such insecurity lowers savings. Reduced capital formation lowers the rate of economic growth. I hypothesize that the path of per capita income in nations that practice democide [or genocide] is below the path of income in nations that do not engage in it. By making comparisons of the paths of per capita income it is possible to estimate the order of magnitude of this form of rent-seeking activity. . . .

To make comparisons of the growth paths of nations that practice democide [or genocide] and those that do not a comparison sample is required. These nations should be more or less similar in stage of economic and political development. In most instances the nations that have practiced democide are less developed and autocratic. My comparison sample of non-democidal, less-developed, and mainly autocratic nations consists of twenty-three countries. A composite index of real gross domestic product per capita was obtained by weighing each RGDP by its population and summing. There are thirty-three democide nations in my sample. I converted these thirty-three nations into a representative democidal nation by weighing each nation's RGDP by its population share, summing, and, then converting the RGDP into an index ($1960 = 100$).

Figure 5 [omitted] compares the indexes of the paths of real gross domestic product per capita. Clearly, the path of income in the democidal nations is below that of the non-democidal, autocratic nations. Dividing the index of real per capita gross domestic product of the democidal nations by that of the non-democidal nations yielded an average value of .81. Democidal rent-seeking then is estimated at 19.2 percent of gross domestic product ($1 - .808$). To make sure that the result is not a figment of the twenty-three nations chosen for the comparison sample, I constructed a sample of eleven other mostly freer, less developed, non-democidal nations. Observe that the composite index for these eleven freer nations is above that of the twenty-three autocratic nations. This result is not surprising, since it is known that nations with freer institutions grow more rapidly than nations with less freedom. . . .

[Yet] the scale of democide may differ, people's attitudes toward it may vary (e.g., some may be more stoic; genocide may be less disagreeable to the dominant group than terror). . . . Figures 7–9 [omitted] compare the composite indexes of the democidal nations of Africa, Latin America, and Asia with that of the twenty-three non-democidal nations. There is a ranking among the groups, but it is not very strong. Africa has suffered the most. Democidal rent-seeking is estimated at 24.7 percent of real gross domestic product per capita in Africa, 18.6 percent in Asisa, and 18.0 percent in Latin America. . . .

[Singling out Africa,] terror was the principal form of democide in Algeria and Angola. In Burundi and Rwanda it was genocide. Democidal rents averaged 19.1 percent over the period 1960–90 in Algeria and 61.6 percent in Angola over the period 1975–89. About 50,000 were murdered by the Algerian state in the late 1950s and early 1960s, but democidal terror continued at a lower level thereafter. In Angola, about 125,000 people were murdered between 1975 and 1987. Democidal rents averaged 54.8 percent in Burundi over the period 1965–90. About 150,000 were murdered, mainly in the Hutu genocide. Democidal rents averaged 27.0 percent in Rwanda over the period 1962–90. About 15,000 were murdered in genocide campaigns over the period 1962–73. About 500,000 people were murdered in Rwanda, in 1994. . . .

Democide and genocide are seemingly activities of majority group domination and authoritarian rule. State-sponsored murder on a large scale has a long history. Despite crude weaponry, the Chinese emperors from the Chin dynasty (221 BC) to the Ching (1911), exclusive of the Mongols, murdered about 35.5 million [people]. The Mongols in the fourteenth and fifteenth century killed about 30 million. But, exclusive of communist democide, there has been a historical decline in the rate of state-sponsored murder. I hypothesized that this was due to the historical rise in the productivity of humans, which made the costs in terms of lost GNP [gross national product] too high to continue the killing on a grand scale. A demand function for democide was estimated for a sample of nations in the post–World War II period. The relationship between the quantity of killing and per capita output was found to be highly significant. To estimate rent-seeking losses associated with democide I compared the growth paths of the democidal nations with those of a selected group of non-democidal nations. On average, democide is associated with about a 20 percent loss of wealth.

41 • The Strategic Logic of Mass Killing
(Benjamin A. Valentino)

Benjamin Valentino, an associate professor of government at Dartmouth College, believes that a rationalist approach is the most promising option when it comes to explaining the causes of genocide. In his 2004 book Final Solutions, *he sketches a strategic model that emphasizes the instrumental logic of mass killing. He distinguishes six types of mass killing, but here he is concerned only with the three most salient and destructive of these types: communist, ethnic, and counterguerrilla. According to Valentino, communist mass killings refer to the pogroms, purges, and massacres carried out in an attempt to overhaul the foundations of politics and society so as to bring them in line with communist doctrine. Ethnic mass killings are distinguished from communist mass killings by the explicitly racist or nationalist motives of the perpetrators. Finally, counterguerrilla mass killings are a calculated military response to the unique challenges posed by guerrilla warfare.*

To identify societies at high risk for mass killing, . . . we must first understand the specific goals, ideas, and beliefs of powerful groups and leaders, not necessarily the broad social structures or systems of government of the societies over which these leaders preside. A few leaders cannot implement mass killing alone, but perpetrators do not need widespread social support in order to carry it out. A tiny minority, well armed and well organized, can generate an appalling amount of bloodshed when unleashed upon unarmed and unorganized victims. Levels of hatred, discrimination, or ideological commitment common to many societies are sufficient to recruit the relatively small number of active supporters needed to carry out mass killing and to encourage the passivity of the rest of society. These conclusions suggest that we will best

SOURCE: Benjamin A. Valentino, *Final Solutions: Mass Killing and Genocide in the 20th Century* (Ithaca, N.Y.: Cornell University Press, 2004), 66–67, 69, 73, 74, 75–76, 81, 82. Reprinted with permission of the publisher.

understand the causes of mass killing when we study the phenomenon from a "strategic" perspective.

Rather than focusing on the social structures or psychological mechanisms that might facilitate public support for mass killing, a strategic approach seeks to identify the specific situations, goals, and conditions that give leaders incentives to consider this kind of violence. I contend that mass killing occurs when powerful groups come to believe it is the best available means to accomplish certain radical goals, counter specific types of threats, or solve difficult military problems. From this perspective, mass killing should be viewed as an instrumental policy calculated to achieve important political and military objectives with respect to other groups—a "final solution" to its perpetrators' most urgent problems.

Because mass killing is a means to an end, it is rarely a policy of first resort. Perpetrators commonly experiment with other, less violent or even conciliatory means in the attempt to achieve their ends. When these means fail or are deemed too costly or demanding, however, leaders are forced to choose between compromising their most important goals and interests or resorting to more violent methods to achieve them. Regardless of perpetrators' original intentions or attitudes toward their victims, the failure or frustration of other means can make mass killing a more attractive option.

It is important to emphasize that a strategic understanding of mass killing does not imply that perpetrators always evaluate objectively the problems they face in their environment, nor that they accurately assess the ability of mass killing to resolve these problems. Human beings act on the basis of their subjective perceptions and beliefs, not objective reality. Indeed, the powerful role that small groups and individuals play in the conception and implementation of policies of mass killing can amplify the influence of misperceptions in promoting such violence.... A strategic approach to mass killing, therefore, suggests only that perpetrators are likely to employ mass killing when they perceive it to be both necessary and effective, not when it is actually so. In many cases, the threat posed by the victims of mass killing is more imagined than real....

I have identified six specific motives—corresponding to six "types" of mass killing—that, under certain specific conditions, appear to generate strong incentives for leaders to initiate mass killing. These six motives can be grouped into two general categories. First, when leaders' plans result in the near complete material disenfranchisement of large groups of people, leaders are likely to conclude that mass killing is necessary to overcome resistance by the groups or, more radically, that mass killing is the only practical way to physically remove these groups or their influence from society. I refer to this general class as "dispossessive" mass killings. Second, mass killing can become an attractive solution in military conflicts in which leaders perceive conventional military tactics to be hopeless or unacceptably costly. When leaders' efforts to defeat their enemies' military forces directly are frustrated, they face powerful incentives to target the civilian populations they suspect of supporting these forces. I refer to this class of mass killing as "coercive" mass killings.... Of the six types of mass killings [communist, ethnic, territorial, counterguerrilla, terrorist, and imperialist], three have accounted for the majority of episodes of mass killing as well as the greatest number of victims in the twentieth century: communist mass killings, ethnic mass killings, and counterguerrilla mass killings....

The most deadly mass killings in history have resulted from the effort to transform society according to communist doctrine. Radical communist regimes have proven so exceptionally violent because the changes they have sought to bring about have resulted in the nearly complete material dispossession of vast numbers of people. . . . Faced with the choice between moderating their revolutionary goals to allow for voluntary change and forcing change on society by whatever means necessary, communist leaders like Stalin, Mao, and Pol Pot opted for mass killing over compromise. Mass killings associated with the collectivization of agriculture and other radical communist agricultural policies provide the most striking examples of this process. . . . In addition to violence associated with communist agricultural policies, communist mass killings have also taken the form of bloody intraparty purges and attacks on social and cultural elites, intellectuals, and members of opposition political parties. The Great Terror in the Soviet Union and the Cultural Revolution in China represent the most notorious examples of this kind of communist political terror. . . .

Ethnic, national, or religious groups may become preferential targets in any of the types of mass killing described in this book. In these pages, however, "ethnic mass killings" are distinguished from the other types of mass killing by the explicitly racist or nationalist motives of the perpetrators. Ethnic mass killing, I argue, is not simply the result of perpetrators' bitter hatred of other ethnic groups, or of a racist ideology that calls for the extermination of these groups as such. Ethnic mass killing has deeper roots in perpetrators' fears than in their hatreds. I find that mass killing is most likely to occur when perpetrators believe that their ethnic opponents pose a threat that can be countered only by physically removing them from society, in other words, by implementing a policy of ethnic cleansing. . . . The decision to engage in ethnic cleansing, however, is not always a decision to perpetrate mass killing. Ethnic cleansing and mass killing are often conflated in popular parlance, but they are not synonymous. Ethnic cleansing refers to the removal of certain groups from a given territory, a process that may or may not involve mass killing. . . . The bloodiest episodes of ethnic mass killing occur when leaders conclude that they have no practical options for the physical relocation of victim groups. . . . At the most extreme, perpetrators may conclude that systematic extermination is the only available means to counter the threat. Ethnic mass killing, therefore, is best seen as an instrumental strategy that seeks the physical removal or permanent military or political subjugation of ethnic groups, not the annihilation of these groups as an end in itself. . . .

Mass killing can become an attractive strategy for governments engaged in counterguerrilla warfare. Although many observers have characterized mass killing in counterguerrilla warfare as the result of the actions of undisciplined, frustrated, or racist troops, the strategic approach suggests that counterguerrilla mass killing is a calculated military response to the unique challenges posed by guerrilla warfare. Unlike conventional armies, guerrilla forces often depend on the local civilian population for food, shelter, and supplies. . . . Civilian support can be a major source of strength for guerrilla armies, but it can also be a weakness. Regimes facing guerrilla opponents either at home or abroad have sometimes been able to turn the guerrillas' dependency on the local population to their own advantage. Unlike the guerrillas themselves, the civilian support network upon which guerrillas rely is virtually defenseless and impossible to conceal. Some regimes have found it easier, therefore, to wage war against a guerrilla army by depriving it of its base of support in the people than by attempting to target the guerrillas directly. In the terms of Mao's analogy, this strategy seeks to catch the fish by draining the sea. Not surprisingly, this strategy of counterinsurgency has frequently resulted in mass killing.

42 • The Killing Trap (Manus Midlarsky)

In his 2005 book, The Killing Trap, Manus Midlarsky of Rutgers University, an influential scholar of international relations, presented a realpolitik model of genocide that is founded on insights from prospect theory. If we believe Midlarsky, the experience of loss, real or remembered, causes a risk of acceptance that realpolitik tells us should be minimized to protect the increasingly insecure state. According to this argument, the combination of risk minimization and loss compensation, often exacerbated by a hostile international environment, yields genocidal outcomes.

In the broadest sense, this book is about threat (the fear of potential loss) and vulnerability, two necessary conditions for the occurrence of genocide. The targeted population needs to be perceived as threatening, or at least have a tenuous connection to external threatening agents, whatever the reality of the perception, and the targeted population must be vulnerable to mass murder. At the same time, the potential perpetrators of genocide also must experience some vulnerability to generate their real or fantasized images of threatening civilian populations. Any process that simultaneously increases both the threat to the state and its vulnerability, as well as vulnerability of a targeted civilian population, also increases the probability of genocide. . . .

Genocide, I argue, is a contingent event, one made more probable by [an] earlier experience of loss and its consequences. . . . It is the *experience* of massacre that is crucial. . . . What is required is that perpetrators be aware that there have occurred massacres of elements of the victim population in the recent past, and that they identify with the political goals and mindset of the earlier perpetrators. Identification can provide a bridge between the recent past and present, and makes subsequent mass murder more likely to occur. . . . [For example,] in the Ottoman Empire and Rwanda, many of the same people who had earlier participated in the massacres, or the descendents of those people, participated in the genocide at the local level. . . . Continuity presupposes proximity in time of similar acts, committed by like-minded perpetrators, acting in roughly comparable circumstances. Thus, the *Einsatzgruppen* [mobile death squads] are exemplars of the German continuation of earlier reactionary Russian barbarism in Ukraine and Belorussia in 1918–20, but of course on a much larger scale. The near-elimination of the Herero and Nama tribes by German colonial authorities in South West Africa around the turn of the [twentieth] century also provides an earlier element of continuity in German policy toward "alien" people whom the Germans perceived to be "troublesome." Continuity establishes a temporal causal nexus via the identification of genocidal leaders with the policies of earlier prototypes of the same nationality or at least similar ideological disposition. . . . Thus Nazi leaders could identify with the eliminationist policies of earlier German colonial authorities, as they could with the virulent and murderous anti-Semitism of anti-Bolshevik Ukrainians and White Russians. . . .

We turn directly to theory development. Realpolitik as management of threats to the state and losses as signals of state vulnerability now occupy our attention. Realpolitik is un-

SOURCE: Manus Midlarsky, *The Killing Trap: Genocide in the Twentieth Century* (Cambridge: Cambridge University Press, 2005), 4, 6, 43, 44, 61–62, 83, 84–85, 86, 167, 168. Reprinted with permission of the publisher.

derstood as policies that preserve and strengthen the state, while loss is the experience of either (1) transfer of territory, population, authority, or some combination thereof to another political entity, or (2) military defeat or significant casualties in political violence (e.g., war) that either are about to be or have already been incurred. Concrete expectations of loss in the near term can yield outcomes similar to those of loss itself. . . . Under conditions of extreme threat, the traditional quid pro quo of realpolitik (as in negotiated settlements) can be transformed into a loss compensation akin to revenge that is genocidal.

Prospect theory suggests reasons for the salience of loss aversion with its associated risk taking. By the tenets of prospect theory, the domain of losses—a condition of either experiencing loss or the dominance of the memory of loss—gives rise to a risk acceptance that, in turn, realpolitik tells us, should be minimized to protect the increasingly insecure state. The combination of risk minimization and loss compensation . . . yields the genocidal outcome. . . . The emphasis on losses, principally to other states or societies, and realpolitik, reverses the understandable tendency to view genocide as mainly a domestic enterprise. . . . Clearly, not all states experiencing loss are expected to be genocidal. As noted, . . . vulnerability of a targeted group with a real or purported connection with state security (e.g., ethnic kin in an enemy state) is a necessary condition for the genocide to occur. . . .

The shrinkage of empire and the loss of state strength are both situated within the domain of losses and compromise international sources of state insecurity. In two of the three cases of genocide [under extended investigation in this book]—Germany and the Ottoman Empire—the empires were contracted as the results of defeat in war. . . . In the third, Rwanda, state insecurity was amplified by ongoing conflict that began with the virtual inception of the modern state, followed by territorial losses to the invading Rwandese Patriotic Front (RPF) after 1990, and entailed serious economic weaknesses as well. . . .

By combining elements of realpolitik and prospect theory, we more completely understand the transition from hatred to sporadic killing to the systematized mass murder associated with genocide. This transition depends on the international setting and especially on its increasing threat to the potential perpetrator. Although ideological justification for the genocide is clearly necessary, it is not sufficient for the onset of genocide, since events in the immediate international environment are critical harbingers of the mass killing. A history of losses sets the entire process in motion in which the practice of realpolitik—politics without reference to any standard above politics—is invoked to protect the threatened state and minimize the risk, made far more acceptable by the experience of loss. In this process, millions of people were doomed for extinction. . . . Because realpolitik and the principles underlying prospect theory are continuing elements of the human condition, we have no guarantees that genocide will not occur in the future.

43 • The Dark Side of Democracy (Michael Mann)

In recent years numerous scholars have advanced increasingly sophisticated theories of genocide. Among the first to do so was Michael Mann, an influential sociologist at the University California, Los Angeles. In The Dark Side of Democracy (2005), Mann develops a number of hypotheses about the onset of collective violence, notably what he terms murderous and nonmurderous ethnic cleansing. Central to the book is the argument that the latter phenomenon is somehow associated with democracy, representing its "dark side." Put differently, Mann contends that ethnic cleansing has been far more common than we care to admit. His objective is to account for the tipping point when ordinary cleansing turns into violent cleansing. Although some scholars, such as the political scientist David Laitin of Stanford University, have termed this argument "massively misguided" and found the empirical evidence wanting, Mann's tome remains required reading for students of comparative genocide.

Ethnic cleansing is one of the main evils of modern times. We now know that the Holocaust of the Jews—though unique in important ways—is not unique as a case of genocide. The world's genocides remain thankfully few, but they are flanked by more numerous cases of less severe but nonetheless murderous cleansing. This book offers an explanation of such terrible atrocities. For the sake of clarity, I lay it out up front now, in the form of eight general theses. These proceed from the very general to the very particular, from the macro to the micro, successively adding parts of an overall explanation. . . .

1. My first thesis concerns the broad historical era in which murderous cleansing becomes common. *Murderous cleansing is modern, because it is the dark side of democracy.* This thesis has two parts, concerning modernity and democracy. Ethnic cleansing is essentially modern. Though not unknown in previous history . . . , it became more frequent and deadly in modern times. The 20th-century death toll through ethnic conflict amounted to somewhere over 70 million, dwarfing that of previous centuries. . . . Murderous ethnic cleansing is not primitive or alien. It belongs to our civilization and to us. Most say this is due to the rise of nationalism in the world, and this is true. But nationalism becomes very dangerous only when it is politicized, when it represents the perversion of modern aspirations to democracy in the nation-state. Democracy means rule by the people. But in modern times the people has come to mean two things. The first is what the Greeks meant by their word *demos*. This means the ordinary people, the mass of the population. So democracy is rule by the ordinary people, the masses. But in our civilization the people also means "nation" or another Greek term, *ethnos*, an ethnic group—a people that shares a common culture and sense of heritage, distinct from other people. . . . I clarify this first thesis with some subtheses.

1a. Murderous ethnic cleansing is a hazard of the age of democracy since amid multiethnicity the ideal of rule by the people began to entwine the *demos* with the dominant *ethnos*, generating organic conceptions of the nation and the state that encouraged the cleansing of minorities. . . . 1b. In modern colonies, settler democracies in certain contexts have been truly

SOURCE: Michael Mann, *The Dark Side of Democracy: Explaining Ethnic Cleansing* (Cambridge: Cambridge University Press, 2005), 2, 3, 4, 5, 6, 7, 8, 9. Reprinted with permission of the publisher.

murderous, more so than more authoritarian colonial governments. The more settlers controlled colonial institutions, the more murderous the cleansing.... 1c. Regimes newly embarked upon democratization are more likely to commit murderous ethnic cleansing than are
stable authoritarian regimes. When authoritarian regimes weaken in multiethnic environ-
ments, *demos* and *ethnos* are most likely to become entwined.... 1d. Stably institutionalized
democracies are less likely than either democratizing or authoritarian regimes to commit ethnic cleansing.... 1e. Regimes that are actually perpetrating murderous cleansing are never
democratic, since that would be a contradiction in terms.... The dark side of democracy is
the perversion through time of either liberal or socialist ideals of democracy....

    2. *Ethnic hostility rises where ethnicity trumps class as the main form of social stratification, in
the process capturing and channeling classlike sentiments toward ethnonationalism....* Ethnonationalism is strongest where it can capture other senses of exploitation....

    3. *The danger zone of murderous cleansing is reached when (a) movements claiming to repre-
sent two fairly old ethnic groups both lay claim to their own state over all or part of the same territory
and (b) this claim seems to them to have substantial legitimacy and some plausible chance of being
implemented....* Ethnic differences are worsened to serious hatreds, and to dangerous levels
of cleansing, by persistent rival claims to political sovereignty....

    4. *The brink of murderous ethnic cleansing is reached when one of two alternative scenarios
plays out.... The less powerful side is bolstered to fight rather than to submit ... by believing that
aid will be forthcoming from outside.... The stronger side believes it has such overwhelming military
power and ideological legitimacy that it can force through its own cleansed state at little physical or
moral risk to itself....*

    5. *Going over the brink into the perpetration of murderous ethnic cleansing occurs where the
state exercising sovereignty over the contested territory has been factionalized and radicalized amid
an unstable geopolitical environment that usually leads to war....* Ethnic cleansings are in their
most murderous phases usually directed by states, and this requires some state coherence and
capacity....

    6. *Murderous cleansing is rarely the initial intent of perpetrators.* It is rare to find evil geniuses
plotting mass murder from the very beginning. Not even Hitler did so. Murderous cleansing
typically emerges as a kind of Plan C, developed only after the first two responses to a perceived ethnic threat fail. Plan A typically envisages a carefully planned solution in terms of
either compromise or straightforward repression. Plan B is a more radically repressive adapta-
tion to the failure of Plan A, more hastily conceived amid rising violence and some political
destabilization. When these both fail, some of the planners radicalize further. To understand
the outcome, we must analyze the unintended consequences of a series of interactions yield-
ing escalation.... [Ethnic cleansing] is eventually perpetrated deliberately, but the route to
deliberation is usually a circuitous one.

    7. *There are three main levels of perpetrator: (a) radical elites running party-states; (b) bands
of militants forming violent paramilitaries; and (c) core constituencies providing mass though not majority popular support....* In all my cases particular elites, militants, and core constituencies are
linked together in quite complex ways, forming social movements that (like other social movements) embody mundane power relations. Power is exercised in three distinct ways: top-down
by elites, bottom-up by popular pressures, and coercively sideways by paramilitaries....

8. Finally, *ordinary people are brought by normal social structures into committing murderous ethnic cleansing, and their motives are much more mundane.* To understand ethnic cleansing, we need a sociology of power more than a special psychology of perpetrators as disturbed or psychotic people—though some may be.

sociology of power

CHAPTER THREE

Courses

How do genocidal campaigns unfold? Figuring out *how* people kill is as relevant for understanding genocide as finding out *why* they kill. As the anthropologist Christopher Taylor writes, "Killing one's adversaries while communicating powerful messages about them and oneself are not mutually exclusive." The writings in this chapter illuminate, from various disciplinary perspectives, the many different ways genocidal campaigns have been waged against targeted populations over the millennia.

Particular emphasis is placed on modes of destruction that have not yet received the attention that they deserve, namely diseases (David Stannard, Guenter Lewy, Tzvetan Todorov), famines (Cecil Woodham-Smith, Andrea Graziosi), labor (Nikolaus Wachsmann), deportations (Norman Naimark), child removal (Robert Manne), time (Wolfgang Sofsky), and discrimination (Martha Nussbaum). Reasonable people differ on the question of whether the violence inflicted in some of the cases of destruction considered by these authors should ever be thought of as genocidal in nature. Take, for example, the disagreement between Stannard and Lewy concerning the eradication of Native Americans; whereas Stannard considers the uninhibited spread of disease a strategy of genocide, Lewy categorizes this form of destruction as a natural disaster, an unintended consequence of colonialism, nothing more and nothing less.

But even in instances where there is widespread agreement that we are dealing with a clear-cut case of genocide, scholars disagree about the temporal onset of destruction, which in turn raises important questions about the course of destruction (across both time and space). The Holocaust is a case in point. For some, the destruction of the European Jews got under way in the initial euphoria that accompanied Nazi Germany's invasion of the Soviet Union; for others, the beginning of the Holocaust comes months later. Martha Nussbaum and Robert Collins consider the temporal and spatial diffusion of collective violence in the less well-known cases of Gujarat and Darfur, respectively.

Innovative theoretical and methodological contributions by, among others, Christopher Browning, Gerald Feldman and Wolfgang Seibel, Alexander Hinton, and Christopher Taylor shed further light on important differences in the unfolding of genocidal campaigns. In order to better comprehend a particular mode of destruction employed during the Holocaust— German police battalions operating in the territory of the Soviet Union, for example— Browning, a historian, scrutinized legal documents that had featured in postwar trials of Nazi perpetrators in German courts. By taking seriously as historical sources documents that other scholars eyed with suspicion, he unearthed a great deal of information about the evolution of destruction and the minutiae of its administration.

In a rare interdisciplinary collaboration, Feldman, a historian, and Seibel, a political scientist, brought the methodological tools of network analysis to the study of genocide. They point to an important avenue for future research by illustrating the utility of this approach to the structure of social interaction in the case of the Holocaust. Finally, Hinton and Taylor, in the cases of Cambodia and Rwanda, respectively, demonstrate the power of ethnographic research methods. Based on years of extensive field research, each contributed unexpected insights into the local meanings and mechanics of genocidal violence. By so doing they, and the other authors featured in this chapter, help to make sense of the many different paths to genocide that are logically conceivable and empirically verifiable.

44 • The First Genocide: Carthage, 146 BC (Ben Kiernan)

How old is this phenomenon that we have come to call genocide? According to the Yale historian Ben Kiernan in his 2004 article, the first recorded genocide took place in 146 BC, when some 150,000 Carthaginians perished in the course of Rome's three-year siege. Conceived by Cato and orchestrated by Scipio Aemilianus, Cato's ally, the Roman campaign not only brought about the physical destruction of Carthage—at the time the world's most prosperous city—but also enslaved some fifty-five thousand survivors. The ancient episode raises the question of whether classical and modern genocides are at all comparable.

Delenda est Carthago ("Carthage Must Be Destroyed!") may be the first recorded incitement to genocide. These were the words of Marcus Porcius Cato, the Censor. Plutarch tells us that Cato's call ended his every speech in the Roman Senate, "on any matter whatsoever," from 153 BC to his death aged 85 in 149. Scipio Nasica—son-in-law of Scipio Africanus, conqueror of Hannibal in the Second Punic War (218–202 BC)—would always reply: "Carthage should be allowed to exist." But such challengers were silenced. Rome decided on war "long before" it launched the Third Punic War just prior to Cato's death. One of his last speeches in the Senate, before a Carthaginian delegation in 149, was critical: "Who are the ones who have often violated the treaty? . . . Who are the ones who have waged war most cruelly? . . . Who are the ones who have ravaged Italy? The Carthaginians. . . ." The Carthaginian delegates were accorded no right of reply.

Rome soon began a three-year siege of the world's wealthiest city. Of a population of 2–400,000, at least 150,000 Carthaginians perished. Appian described one battle in which "70,000, including non-combatants," were killed, probably an exaggeration. But Polybius, who participated in the campaign, confirmed that "the number of deaths was incredibly large" and that the Carthaginians were "utterly exterminated." In 146, Roman legions under Scipio Aemilianus, Cato's ally and brother-in-law of his son, razed the city, and dispersed into slavery the 55,000 survivors, including 25,000 women. Plutarch concluded: "The annihilation of Carthage . . . was primarily due to the advice and counsel of Cato. . . ."

Its policy of "extreme violence," the "annihilation of Carthage and most of its inhabitants," ruining "an entire culture," fits the modern legal definition of the 1948 United Nations

SOURCE: Ben Kiernan, "The First Genocide: Carthage, 146 BC," *Diogenes* 51, no. 3 (2004): 27, 28, 31, 32, 33. Reprinted with permission of Sage Publishers, Inc.

Genocide Convention: the intentional destruction "in whole or in part, [of] a national, ethnical, racial or religious group, as such." It would be as unfair to condemn ancient Roman violations of 20th-century international criminal law, as to ignore the spirited opposition Cato's policy provoked in Rome itself. But what ideology demanded the disappearance of a disarmed mercantile city? . . .

Despite "the amazing regularity with which Rome went to war" in this era, the policy to destroy Carthage was unusual. It was both decided in advance and pursued after the city's surrender. Authors differ on the threat Carthage posed, and whether Rome's demands were calculated to minimize it, or resulted from "extreme power hunger." But to Cato, the danger was as much internal. . . . He was a straight-talking veteran of the Second Punic War—when he had first criticized Scipio Africanus for profligacy. With relentless corruption allegations, Cato hounded Scipio until his death in 183. . . . And he insisted on Roman military domination. "The Carthaginians are already our enemies; for he who prepares everything against me, so that he can make war at whatever time he wishes, he is already my enemy even though he is not yet using arms." . . .

Cato's military career had ended in 191 after a fearless feat of arms that clinched Rome's victory in Greece. But at home "he never stopped taking on feuds for the sake of the republic." He became a pugnacious prosecutor and "vigorous opponent of the nobility, of luxurious living, and of the invasion into Italy of Greek culture." . . . According to Cato, exotic corruption threatened Roman culture: "We have crossed into Greece and Asia (regions full of all kinds of sensual allurements) and are even laying hands on the treasures of kings—I am the more alarmed lest these things should capture us instead of our capturing them." At that time, explained Plutarch, "Rome was, on account of its size, unable to preserve its purity; because of its domination over many lands and peoples it was coming into contact with various races and he was exposed to patterns of behavior of every description." . . . The Roman aristocracy "were surrounded by, they floated upon, a sea of products and artifacts and daily usages that had originated in the east." This inevitably provoked the reaction led by Cato. . . .

Racial prejudice, as we know it, was relatively uncommon in the ancient world, but Cato focused on Rome's lineage, as distinct from those of its enemies, and the secrets of its success— husbandry, morals and discipline. Rome, he wrote, followed the mores of the Sabines—Cato's forbears—who claimed descent from hardy Spartans. The Ligurians, by contrast, were "illiterate and liars." The Greeks of Cato's day were an "utterly vile and unruly race." . . . He condemned "all Greek literature across the board" and promoted a series of repressive measures, including expulsion of teachers of Epicureanism and destruction of Greek philosophical works. . . . [According to Cato,] Greek "luxury and laxity," even culture, like colored clothing and Libyan figs, fostered Roman extravagance and decline. Cato was convinced that "the city [of Rome] was in need of a great purgation."

Cato's view of Carthage was merely his most sustained response to a panorama of perils. His perception of the combination of foreign and domestic subversion helps explain Cato's determination to destroy Carthage. . . . Cato's broader notions of culture and politics fostered a violent, vindictive hostility towards Carthage, not applied to other regions. . . . Cato's thinking underlines the connections between domestic and transnational aspects of genocidal policies— ancient and modern.

45 ◆ Extermination, Hyperexploitation, and Forced Deportation in Premodern Times (Mark Levene)

Like other scholars who have called into question the uniqueness of the Holocaust, Mark Levene, a reader in comparative history at the University of Southampton, has focused his research on tracing continuities and discontinuities in the use of mass violence throughout history. In The Meaning of Genocide *(2005), the first volume of his four-volume history of genocide,* Genocide in the Age of the Nation State, *Levene offers a far-ranging argument in support of the claim that genocidal violence is hardly a modern phenomenon. Drawing on illustrative evidence from Athens to India and from Genghis Khan to Shaka Zulu, he insists that premodern societies, stateless and otherwise, were as capable of genocidal destruction as modern ones.*

A prevailing feature of much contemporary culture and society is the assumption that our ancestors, lacking the technological sophistication we possess or even the same degree of social organization, were quite incapable of accomplishing systematic mass murder on the scale of our achievement. Avers one Holocaust study: "Within certain limits set by political and military power considerations, the *modern* state may do anything it wishes to those under its control"—as if traditional states did not have this capacity. This is all the more peculiar when those the modern mind does sometimes remember for mass murders on a significant scale appear not to be states at all but hordes of apparently disorganized, rampaging Huns, Mongols, Zulus or other "barbarians." In so doing, we set up . . . [a] dichotomy: that between civilization and barbarism, almost the very starting point of Lemkin's thesis [that genocide cannot be isolated or pinned down to a specific sequence of mass killing]. As if to turn the problem yet again on its head, if the population of states—i.e., civilized societies—are not exactly incapable of mass murder, then they are socialized in such a way that any proclivity to killing has been ironed out, at least from their "normal," everyday behavior.

To be fair to "civilization" in the pre-modern record, it does, at least superficially, seem as if the "barbarians" have the edge in the murdering stakes. For instance the Mongol conqueror, Genghis Khan, on the estimation of one historian, was responsible in the early thirteenth century for the eradication of some four-fifths of the population along the belt of Arabic Iranian civilization, while his latter-day successor, Timur, better known in the West as Tamerlane, in his great rampage across the great cultural and commercial centers of Central Asia and Northern India between 1379 and 1403, sufficiently excited Arnold Toynbee, another great comparativist, to comment that in the span of these twenty-four years Timur perpetrated as many horrors as the last five Assyrian kings had achieved in the space of 120. Yet it is arguable whether Timur can really be described as a barbarian at all, while his descendants were to found India's great Mogul civilization, before this too was brought to an apparent terminus in 1739, when the forces of another central Asian adventurer, Tamas Kuli Khan (Nadir Shah), concluded his campaign by putting the entire population of Delhi to the sword.

The paradox here should be obvious. Genghis, Timur, Nadir Shah or the Zulu leader, Shaka—primarily responsible for the great waves of extermination know as the *Mfecane*, the

SOURCE: Mark Levene, *Genocide in the Age of the Nation State*, vol. 1: *The Meaning of Genocide* (London: I. B. Tauris, 2005), 145–48.

Great Crushing in which upwards of a million people were killed in southern Africa in the early nineteenth century—may have started their murderous careers as archetypal "barbarians." But the havoc and depredations which they wrought, far from being intended for their own sake, were their chosen route to the achievement of supremely strong, centralized imperial polities. . . . If the barbarian-civilized dichotomy, thus, is largely a false one . . . , a common argument deployed to defend the distinction of twentieth-century "totality" in genocide is the notion that in the past perpetrators rarely, if ever, set out to kill everybody in the target group. Men would be killed or enslaved but at least the younger women and (male as well as female) children would often be spared and even assimilated into the victor's population as chattel or spouses. This was certainly the case in Shaka's wars. But even in some of the best documented cases of unmitigated mass murder in antiquity, like the Athenian onslaught on the Aegean island of Melos, in 416 BC, or the Roman destruction of its great rival, Carthage, in 146 BC, enslavement rather than extermination seems to have been the fate of many female and child survivors. The issue, in such instances, thus becomes whether this would constitute a distinction between genocide now and then. It is true that slavery in the classical world, as well as being the economic underpinning of the social fabric, and, therefore, a practice considered perfectly functional and normal, did not *necessarily* have to lead to either a short and brutish life or painful death.

With this in mind it is hardly surprising that Steven Katz [a Jewish philosopher and genocide scholar at Boston University] has been particularly at pains to stress these least unpleasant contours in order to reinforce his case that there can be no comparison with the sort of hyper-exploitation practiced against Jews in the Holocaust. . . . Yet if this highlights the extremity of the Holocaust it does not invalidate the general rule that enslavement and hyper-exploitation on the one hand, combined with the separated treatment of males and females on the other, have provided an effective tool for emasculating and indeed dissolving targeted national or communal groups *throughout* history. While hyper-exploitation has been mostly conducted for entirely venal purposes, resulting, as in the wake of European conquest and spoliation of the Americas in millions of Amerindian and African deaths, most infamously in the Bolivian mines at Potosi and Huancavelica, and in the "Middle Passage" of the Atlantic slave trade, it has also been part of a consistent battery of methods utilized by polities for the extirpation of perceived ethno-national threats. From this perspective, the labor camps of the Soviet Gulag, or the Nazi *Zwangsarbeitslager für Juden* (ZALs) [forced labor camps for Jews], while undoubtedly statements of modernity in terms of scope and scale, do not in themselves represent a major rupture with the past. . . . Indeed, the context in which these latter mass violations took place—namely, the mass deportation of a people from their settled homelands to another distant and inhospitable frontier—has been practiced, particularly in this Middle (or Near) Eastern region, against rebellious, recalcitrant, or militarily subjugated peoples on a regular basis by Ottomans, Safavids, Byzantines, or, for that matter, by Babylonians, Assyrians and Akkadians, for thousands of years.

True, deportation itself does not have to lead—as in the case of the Ottoman Armenians— to a total genocide. In the ancient, as in the modern [world], the nature and severity of the deportation process is at least partially dependent on the degree to which the perpetrating state seeks to punish or revenge itself on the deportees. But the fact that the very process of uprooting and forced migration cannot but lead to mass mortality underscores the fact the perpetrators' motivation has always been in the broadest sense genocidal. That it is nearly always accompanied by efforts to erase the human topography of the ethnically cleansed region—as if those people never existed—is further confirmation of this intent, while the historically consistent ability to carry out both deportation and culture-obliteration should, incidentally, remind us of the military-bureaucratic power and organizing outreach of *premodern* states.

46 • American Holocaust (David E. Stannard)

In his provocative book American Holocaust *(1993), David Stannard, professor of American studies at the University of Hawaii, likened the suffering of colonial peoples in the Americas to the destruction of the European Jews. He describes the manner in which one particular people, the Cherokee, became victims of colonial genocide. Stannard explains why the effects of expropriation, relocation, and disease are comparable to the effects of industrial annihilation in the Holocaust.*

Just twenty years after Columbus's first landing in the Caribbean, the vastly populous island that the explorer had re-named Hispaniola was effectively desolate; nearly 8,000,000 people—those Columbus chose to call Indians—had been killed by violence, disease, and despair. It took a little longer, about the span of a single human generation, but what happened on Hispaniola was the equivalent of more than fifty Hiroshimas. And Hispaniola was only the beginning.

Within no more than a handful of generations following their first encounters with Europeans, the vast majority of the Western Hemisphere's native peoples had been exterminated. The pace and magnitude of their obliteration varied from place to place and from time to time, but for years now historical demographers have been uncovering, in region upon region, post-Columbia depopulation rates of between 90 and 98 percent with such regularity that an overall decline of 95 percent has become a working rule of thumb. What this means is that, on average, for every twenty natives alive at the moment of European contact—when the lands of the Americas teemed with numerous tens of millions of people—only one stood in their place when the bloodbath was over. To put this in a contemporary context, the ratio of native survivorship in the Americas following European contact was less than half of what the human survivorship ratio would be in the United States today if every single white person and every single black person died. The destruction of the Indians of the Americas was, far and away, the most massive act of genocide in the history of the world. . . .

The extraordinary outpouring of recent scholarship that has analyzed the deadly impact of the Old World on the New has employed a novel array of research techniques to identify introduced disease as the primary cause of the Indians' great population decline. . . . It is true, in a plainly quantitative sense of body counting, that the barrage of disease unleashed by the Europeans among the so-called "virgin soil" populations of the Americas caused more deaths than any other single force of destruction. However, by focusing almost entirely on disease, by

SOURCE: David E. Stannard, *American Holocaust: The Conquest of the New World* (New York: Oxford University Press, 1993), x, xii, 121–23, 124, 254, 255. Reprinted with permission of the publisher.

displacing responsibility for the mass killing onto an army of invading microbes, contemporary authors increasingly have created the impression that the eradication of those tens of millions of people was inadvertent—a sad, but both inevitable and "unintended consequence" of human migration and progress. . . . In fact, however, the near-total destruction of the Western Hemisphere's native people was neither inadvertent nor inevitable.

From almost the instant of first human contact between Europe and the Americas firestorms of microbial pestilence *and* purposeful genocide began laying waste the American natives. Although at times operating independently, for most of the long centuries of devastation that followed 1492, disease and genocide were interdependent forces acting dynamically—whipsawing their victims between plague and violence, each one feeding upon the other, and together driving countless numbers of entire ancient societies to the brink—and often over the brink—of total extermination. . . .

How these deadly phenomena interacted can be seen clearly by examining the case of the Cherokee. After suffering a calamitous measure of ruination during the time of their earliest encounters with Europeans, the Cherokee population continued to decline steadily and precipitously as the years unfolded. During the late seventeenth and [a] major part of the eighteenth century alone, for example, the already devastated Cherokee nation endured the loss of another three-fourths of its population. Then, just as the colonies were going to war in their quest for liberation from the British, they turned their murderous attention one more time to the quest for Indian liquidation; the result for the Cherokee was that "their towns is all burned," wrote one contemporary, "their Corn cut down and Themselves drove into the Woods to perish and a great many of them killed." . . . Thus, the attempt at straightforward extermination. Next came expulsion.

From the precipice of non-existence, the Cherokee slowly struggled back. But as they did, more and more white settlers were moving into and onto their lands. Then, in 1828 Andrew Jackson was elected President. The same Andrew Jackson who once had written that "the whole Cherokee Nation ought to be scurged." The same Andrew Jackson who had led troops against peaceful Indian encampments, calling the Indians "savage dogs," and boasting that "I have on all occasions preserved the scalps of my killed." The same Andrew Jackson who had supervised the mutilation of 800 or so Creek Indian corpses—the bodies of men, women, and children that he and his men had massacred—cutting off their noses to count and preserve a record of the dead, slicing long strips of flesh from their bodies to tan and turn into bridle reins. The same Andrew Jackson who—after his Presidency was over—still was recommending that American troops specifically seek out and systematically kill Indian women and children who were in hiding, in order to complete their extermination: to do otherwise, he wrote, was equivalent to pursuing "a wolf in the hammocks without knowing first where her den and whelps were." . . .

Almost immediately upon Jackson's ascension to the Presidency, the state of Georgia claimed for itself enormous chunks of Cherokee property, employing a fraudulent legal technique that Jackson himself had once used to justify dispossession. . . . Soon the forced relocation, what was to become known as the Trail of Tears, began under the direction of General Winfield Scott. In fact, the "relocation" was nothing less than a death march—a Presidentially ordered death march that, in terms of the mortality rate directly attributable to it, was almost as destructive as the Baathan Death March of 1942, the most notorious Japanese atrocity in all of the Second World War. . . . All told, by the time it was over, more than 8,000 Cherokee men, women, and children died as a result of their expulsion from their homeland. That is, about half of what then remained of the Cherokee nation was liquidated under Presidential directive, a death rate similar to that of other southeastern peoples who had undergone the same process—the Creeks and the Seminoles in particular. Some others who also had been expelled from the lands of their ancestors, such as Chickasaw and the Choctaw, fared better, losing only about 15 percent of their populations during their own forced death marches. For comparative purposes, however, that "only" 15 percent is the approximate equivalent of the death rate for German combat troops in the closing year of World War Two, when Germany's entire southern front was collapsing and its forces were being overwhelmed and more than decimated. The higher death rate of the Creeks, Seminoles, and Cherokee was equal to that of Jews in Germany, Hungary, and Rumania between 1939 and 1945. . . .

The *purpose* of genocide is to do away with an entire people, or to discriminately consume them, either by outright mass murder or by creating conditions that lead to their oblivion. Thus, the slave labor projects that worked people to death in the synthetic rubber factory at Auschwitz, or in the nearby coal mines, were no less genocidal than the gas chambers there and in other camps. . . . The same is true of the anti-Indian genocide in the Americas. Just as those Jews and others who died of exploitation and disease and malnutrition and neglect in "countless other, terrible ways"—other, that is, than straightforward cold-blooded butchery— would not have died when and where they did, but for the genocide campaign that was swirling furiously all about them, so too in the Indies and the Americas: the natives of Hispaniola and Mexico and Peru and Florida and Virginia and Massachusetts and Georgia and Colorado and California and elsewhere who died from forced labor, from introduced disease, from malnutrition, from death marches, from exposure, and from despair were as much victims of the Euro-American genocidal race war as were those burned or stabbed or hacked or shot to death, or devoured by hungry dogs.

47 • Were American Indians the Victims of Genocide? (Guenter Lewy)

In his 2004 article Guenter Lewy, a retired professor of political science at the University of Massachusetts, engages with the argument put forth by David Stannard in American Holocaust. *Unlike Stannard, Lewy finds unpersuasive the claim that genocide was committed on American soil. According to Lewy, the large number of Indian casualties from diseases that transpired in the course of colonialism cannot be considered genocide because those diseases were introduced inadvertently.*

That American Indians suffered horribly is indisputable. But whether their suffering amounted to a "holocaust," or to genocide, is another matter. . . . To address this issue properly we must begin with the most important *reason* for the Indians' catastrophic decline—namely, the spread of highly contagious diseases to which they had no immunity. This phenomenon is known by

SOURCE: Guenter Lewy, "Were American Indians the Victims of Genocide?" *Commentary* 118, no. 2 (2004): 56, 57–58, 59, 61, 62–63. Reprinted with permission of the journal.

scholars as a "virgin-soil epidemic"; in North America, it was the norm. The most lethal of the pathogens introduced by the Europeans was smallpox, which sometimes incapacitated so many adults at once that deaths from hunger and starvation ran as high as deaths from disease; in several cases entire tribes were rendered extinct. Other killers included measles, influenza, whooping cough, diphtheria, typhus, bubonic plague, cholera, and scarlet fever. . . .

To some . . . this is enough in itself to warrant the term genocide. . . . As an example of actual genocidal conditions, Stannard [for example] points to Franciscan missions in California as "furnaces of death." . . . It is true that the cramped quarters of the missions, with their poor ventilation and bad sanitation, encouraged the spread of disease. But it is demonstrably untrue that, like the Nazis, the missionaries were unconcerned with the welfare of their native converts. No matter how difficult the conditions under which the Indian labored—obligatory work, often inadequate food and medical care, corporal punishment—their experience bore no comparison with the fate of the Jews in the ghettos. The missionaries had a poor understanding of the causes of the diseases that afflicted their charges, and medically there was little they could do for them. By contrast, the Nazis knew exactly what was happening in the ghettos, and quite deliberately deprived the inmates of both food and medicine; unlike in Stannard's "furnaces of death," the deaths were meant to occur. . . .

European settlers came to the New World for a variety of reasons, but the thought of infecting the Indians with deadly pathogens was not one of them. As for the charge that the U.S. government should itself be held responsible for the demographic disaster that overtook the American-Indian population, it is unsupported by evidence of legitimate argument. The United States did not wage biological warfare against the Indians; neither can the large number of deaths as a result of disease be considered the result of a genocidal design. Still, even if up to 90 percent of the reduction in Indian population was the result of disease that leaves a sizable death toll caused by mistreatment and violence. Should some or all of these deaths be considered instances of genocide?

We may examine representative incidents by following the geographic route of European settlement, beginning in the New England colonies. . . . The Pequot tribe in particular, with its reputation for cruelty and ruthlessness, was feared. . . . This revulsion accounts at least in part for the ferocity of the battle of Fort Mystic in May 1637, when a force commanded by John Mason . . . surprised about half of the Pequot tribe encamped near the Mystic River. The intention of the colonists had been to kill the warriors "with their Swords," as Mason put it, to plunder the village, and to capture women and children. But the plan did not work out. About 150 Pequot warriors had arrived in the fort the night before, and when the surprise attack began, they emerged from their tents to fight. Fearing the Indians' numerical strength, the English attacker set fire to the fortified village and retreated outside the palisades. . . . When the battle was over, the Pequots had suffered several hundred dead, perhaps as many as 300 of these being women and children. . . . A number of recent historians have charged the Puritans with genocide: that is, with having carried out a premeditated plan to exterminate the Pequots. The evidence belies this. The use of fire as a weapon of war was not unusual for either Europeans or Indians, and every contemporary account stresses that the burning of the fort was an act of self-protection, not part of a pre-planned massacre. . . .

A second famous example from the colonial period is King Philip's War (1675–76). This conflict, proportionally the costliest of all American wars, took the life of one in every sixteen men of military age in the colonies; large numbers of women and children also perished or were carried into captivity. . . . Before long, both colonists and Indians were dismembering corpses and displaying body parts and heads on poles. . . . The hatred kindled by King Philip's War became even more pronounced in 1689 when strong Indian tribes allied themselves with the French against the British. In 1694, the General Court of Massachusetts ordered all friendly Indians confined to a small area. A bounty was then offered for the killing or capture of hostile Indians, and scalps were accepted as proof of a kill. . . . Here, too, genocidal intent was far from evident; the practices were justified on grounds of self-preservation and revenge, and in reprisal for the extensive scalping carried out by Indians. . . .

Lastly, we come to the wars on the Great Plains. Following the Civil War, large waves of white migrants, arriving simultaneously from East and West, squeezed the Plains Indians between them. In response, the Indians attacked vulnerable white outposts. . . . To force the natives into submission, Generals Sherman and Sheridan, who for two decades after the Civil War commanded the Indian-fighting units on the Plains, applied the same strategy they had used so successfully in their marches across Georgia and Shenandoah Valley. Unable to defeat the Indians on open prairie, they pursued them to their winter camps, where numbing cold and heavy snows limited their mobility. There they destroyed the lodges and stores of food, a tactic that inevitably resulted in the deaths of women and children. Genocide? These actions were almost certainly in conformity with the laws of war accepted at the time. . . . In any event, there was never any order to exterminate the Plains Indians, despite heated pronouncements on the subject by the outraged Sherman and despite Sheridan's famous quip that "the only good Indians I ever saw were dead." . . .

The crucial role played by intentionality in the Genocide Convention means that under its terms the huge number of Indian deaths from epidemics cannot be considered genocide. The lethal diseases were introduced inadvertently, and the Europeans cannot be blamed for their ignorance of what medical science would discover only centuries later. Similarly, military engagements that led to the death of non-combatants, like the battle of the Washita, cannot be seen as genocidal acts, for the loss of innocent life was not intended and the soldiers did not aim at the destruction of the Indians as a defined group. By contrast, some of the massacres in California, where both the perpetrators and their supporters openly acknowledged a desire to destroy the Indians as an ethnic group, might indeed be regarded under the terms of the convention as exhibiting genocidal intent. . . .

Finally, even if some episodes can be considered genocidal—that is tending toward genocide—they certainly do not justify condemning an entire society. . . . Even if some elements in the white population, mainly in the West, at times advocated extermination, no official of the U.S. government ever seriously proposed it. Genocide was never American policy, nor was it the result of policy. . . . In the end, the sad fate of America's Indians represents not a crime but a tragedy.

48 • The Conquest of America (Tzvetan Todorov)

Tzvetan Todorov, a Franco-Bulgarian literary theorist, illuminates the courses of colonial genocide in his 1999 book by focusing on the encounters of Spanish conquistadors with the proverbial "other" in South America. What makes this argument compelling is the fact that Todorov attributes the pull of destruction—what he calls "atheistic murder"—to a lack of moral and institutional control in the colonial periphery of European empires. For him, the "barbarity" of destruction is a sign not of regression but of progress.

[Hernando] Cortés [the Spanish conquistador] understands relatively well the Aztec world that appears before him—certainly better than [the Aztec emperor] Montezuma [today known as Moctezuma II] understands the Spanish realities. And yet this superior understanding does not keep the conquistadors from destroying Mexican civilization and society; quite the contrary, we suspect that destruction becomes possible precisely because of this understanding. There is a dreadful concatenation here, whereby grasping leads to taking and taking to destruction. . . . The paradox of the understanding-that-kills might be readily resolved if we observed at the same time, among those who understood, an entirely negative value judgment of the Other; if success in knowledge were accompanied by an axiological rejection. . . . Yet if we read the conquistadors' writings, we find that this is anything but the case, and that on certain levels at least, the Aztecs provoke the Spaniards' admiration. [For example,] the Mexicans' cities, Cortés believes, are as civilized as those of the Spaniards. . . . [In other words,] not only did the Spaniards understand the Aztecs quite well, [but] they admired them—and yet they annihilated them; why?

Let us reread Cortés's admiring observations. One thing is striking about them: with very few exceptions, they all concern objects: the architecture of houses, merchandise, fabrics, jewelry. . . . Cortés goes into ecstasies about the Aztec productions but does not acknowledge their makers as human individualities to be set on the same level as himself. . . . Cortés is interested in the Aztec civilization, and at the same time remains altogether alien to it. Nor is he the only one; this is the behavior of enlightened men of his time. . . . To formulate matters differently: in the best of cases, the Spanish authors speak well of the Indians, but with very few exceptions they do not speak to the Indians. Now, it is only by speaking to the other (not giving orders but engaging in a dialogue) that I can acknowledge him as subject, comparable to what I am myself. Hence we can now specify the relation among the words that form the title of this chapter ["Understanding, Taking Possession, and Destroying"]: unless grasping is accompanied by a full acknowledgment of the other as subject, it risks being used for purposes of exploitation, of "taking"; knowledge will be subordinated to power.

What remains still obscure, then, is the second relation: why does taking lead to destroying? For there is certainly destruction, and in order to answer this question, we must review its principal elements. Let us examine the destruction of the Indians in the sixteenth century on two levels, quantitative and qualitative. . . . Without going into detail, and merely to give a

SOURCE: Tzvetan Todorov, *The Conquest of America: The Question of the Other*, translated from the French by Richard Howard (Norman: University of Oklahoma Press, 1999), 127, 128, 129, 130, 132, 133, 134, 135, 138, 141, 143, 144–45. Reprinted with permission of Harper Collins Publishers.

general idea (even if we do not feel entirely justified in rounding off figures when it is a question of human lives), it will be recalled that in 1500 the world population is approximately 400 million, of whom 80 million inhabit the Americas. By the middle of the sixteenth century, out of these 80 million, there remain ten. Or limiting ourselves to Mexico: on the eve of the conquest, its population is about 25 million; in 1600, it is one million. If the word genocide has ever been applied to a situation with some accuracy, this is here the case. It constitutes a record not only in relative terms (a destruction on the order of 90 percent or more), but also in absolute terms, since we are speaking of a population diminution estimated at 70 million human lives. None of the great massacres of the twentieth century can be compared to this hecatomb. It will be understood how vain are the efforts made by certain authors to dissipate what has been called the "black legend" of Spain's responsibility for this genocide. . . .

But it may be objected that there is no point in attempting to establish responsibilities, or even to speak of genocide rather than of a natural catastrophe. The Spaniards did not undertake a direct extermination of these millions of Indians, nor could they have done so. If we examine the forms taken by the diminution of the population, we realize that there are three, and that the Spaniards' responsibility is inversely proportional to the number of victims deriving from each of them: [1] By direct murder, during the wars or outside of them: a high number, nonetheless *relatively* small; direct responsibility. [2] By consequence of bad treatment: a higher number; a (barely) less direct responsibility. [3] By diseases, by "microbe shock": the majority of the population; an indirect and diffused responsibility. I shall return to the first point, examining the destruction of the Indians on the qualitative level; first let us look at the Spaniards' responsibility in the second and third forms of death.

By "bad treatment" I mean chiefly the labor conditions imposed by the Spaniards, especially in the mines, but not only there. The conquistador-colonists have no time to lose, they must become rich at once; consequently, they impose an unendurable rhythm of labor, with no concern to preserve the health, hence the life, of their workers; the average life expectancy of a miner of the period is twenty-five years. Outside the mines, the tribute and taxes are so extreme that they lead to the same result. . . . Certainly the question is one of economic murder in all these cases, for which the colonizers bear the entire responsibility. . . . Matters are less clear-cut with regard to diseases. Epidemics decimated the European cities of the period, as they did those in America, though on another scale. . . . [But] we cannot consider . . . these murderous epidemics as a purely natural phenomenon. . . . It is certain that the conquistadors see the epidemics as one of their weapons: they do not know the secrets of bacteriological warfare, but if they could, they would not fail to make use of disease quite deliberately; we can also assume that in most cases they did nothing to prevent the spread of epidemics. . . .

Now let us return to the qualitative aspect of the destruction of the Indians. . . . I mean by it the particularly impressive and perhaps modern character this destruction assumes. . . . Here now is an account concerning the expedition of Vasco Nuñez de Balboa, transcribed by someone who has heard many conquistadors telling their own adventures: "The Spaniards cut off the arm of one, the leg or hip of another, and from some their heads at one stroke, like butchers cutting up beef and mutton for market. Six hundred, including the cacique, were thus slain like brute beasts. . . . Vasco ordered forty of them to be torn to pieces by dogs. . . ." Time passes but habits remain: as we observe from the letter which the monk Jerónimo de San Miguel sent to his king on August 20, 1550: "Some Indians they burned alive; they cut off the hands, noses, tongues, and other members of some; they threw others to the dogs; they cut off the breasts of women." Everything occurs as if the Spaniards were finding an intrinsic pleasure in cruelty, in the fact of exerting their power over others, in the demonstration of their capacity to inflict death.

Here we ... might evoke certain immutable features of "human nature," for which the psychoanalytic vocabulary reserves terms such as "aggression," "death instinct," or even *Bemächtigungstrieb*, instinct for mastery.... We might also assert that each people, from the beginning of time to our own day, sacrifices its victims with a kind of murderous madness.... But it would be a mistake to erase all differences in this way.... [Instead] we may speak of sacrifice-societies and massacre-societies, of which the Aztecs and the sixteenth-century Spaniards would be the respective representatives. Sacrifice from this point of view is a religious murder: it is performed in the name of official ideology and will be perpetrated in public places, in sight of all and to everyone's knowledge. The victim's identity is determined by strict rules.... The sacrifice is performed in public and testifies to the power of the social fabric, to its mastery over the individual. Massacre, on the other hand, reveals the weakness of this same social fabric, the desuetude of the moral principles that once assured the group's coherence; hence it should be performed in some remote place where the law is only vaguely acknowledged; for the Spaniards, America or even Italy.

Massacre is thus intimately linked to colonial wars waged far from the metropolitan country. The more remote and alien the victims, the better: they are exterminated without remorse, more or less identified with animals. The individual identity of the massacre victim is by definition irrelevant (otherwise his death would be a murder): one has neither time nor curiosity to know whom one is killing at that moment. Unlike sacrifices, massacres are generally not acknowledged or proclaimed, their very existence is kept secret and denied. This is because their social function is not recognized, and we have the impression that such action finds justification in itself: one wields the saber for the pleasure of wielding the saber, one cuts off the Indian's nose, tongue, and penis without this having any ritual meaning for the amputator.

If religious murder is sacrifice, massacre is an atheistic murder, and the Spaniards appear to have invented (or rediscovered; but not borrowed from their immediate past, for the Inquisition's stakes were more closely related to sacrifice) precisely this type of violence, which we encounter in our own recent past, whether on the level of individual violence or that of violence perpetrated by states. It is as though the conquistadors obeyed the rule of Ivan Karamazov [one of the three major protagonists in Fyodor Dostoyevsky's nineteenth-century novel *The Brothers Karamazov*]: "everything is permitted." ... Far from the central government, far from royal law, all prohibitions give way, the social link, already loosened, snaps, revealing not a primitive nature, the beast sleeping in each of us, but a modern being, one with a great future in fact, restrained by no morality and inflicting death because and when he pleases. The "barbarity" of the Spaniards has nothing atavistic or bestial about it; it is quite human and heralds the advent of modern times.

49 • The Ontological Destruction of Canadian Aboriginal Peoples (Andrew Woolford)

By charting the contours of destruction among Canadian aboriginal peoples, Andrew Woolford makes a case in his 2009 article for rereading the 1948 Genocide Convention. Yet instead of rejecting outright that international instrument, as most critics are wont to do, he chides its users for interpreting it too narrowly. He argues that a strictly legalistic reading of the Genocide Convention risks misunderstanding the meaning (in an anthropological sense) of genocide. In response to this misunderstanding, Woolford, a professor of sociology at the University of Manitoba, reinterprets the terms group, destruction, *and* intent *from the vantage point of Canada's indigenous peoples.*

The terms "cultural genocide" and "ethnocide" have often been used to describe the destruction perpetrated against Canadian Aboriginal peoples. In such cases, one senses that these terms are not intended to invoke one of the categories of genocide created by Raphael Lemkin when the United Nations Secretariat retained him in 1946 to help draft an international convention but, rather, are used as qualifiers to describe processes different from and less severe than genocide proper, which some suggest must involve the attempted physical annihilation of the targeted group. However, to characterize the harms produced by Canadian colonialism as cultural genocide is problematic on at least three grounds.

First, the varied path of attempted Aboriginal destruction in Canada is misrepresented by attempts to reduce Canadian colonialism to a singular event and Aboriginal Canadians to a single "group." To put it simply, Canadian Aboriginal peoples are culturally and regionally diverse and experienced colonialism in different ways. Second, while all Aboriginal groups experienced at least some degree of attempted assimilation, some also experienced high levels of physical destruction through settler violence, disease, and deadly residential-school conditions, as well as biological interference with reproductive processes. Finally, the separation between "cultural" and "physical" forms of destruction—a modernist contrivance that contends that such neat categories in fact exist—collapses under a more detailed investigation of Aboriginal experiences of destruction. This third problematic is the primary focus of this article.

While the assumption that Canadian Aboriginal peoples experienced only cultural genocide is commonplace, in my research on land claims and reparations for Aboriginal peoples in British Columbia, I have come across many Aboriginal persons who describe their experiences of colonialism as "genocide." At first, I took this to be a politicized use of the term—an attempt to harness its symbolic power to the task of advancing Canadian Aboriginal justice claims. Surely they meant cultural genocide or ethnocide. . . . [But] I begin this article from the premise that these people are neither strategically misinterpreting the term "genocide" nor employing it solely for political purposes. In doing so, I argue that a re-reading of the 1948 United Nations Convention on the Prevention and Punishment of Genocide (UNCG) through a lens sensitive to Aboriginal realities lends greater validity to these claims. . . . My project is not to relativize or to broaden the concept of genocide to the extent that it loses all meaning.

SOURCE: Andrew Woolford, "Ontological Destruction: Genocide and Canadian Aboriginal Peoples," *Genocide Studies and Prevention* 4, no. 1 (2009): 81, 82, 83, 85, 86, 88, 89, 90, 91, 92–93. Reprinted with permission of the journal.

Instead, the UNCG will continue to serve as a guiding framework for constituting acts of genocide, but key components of its definition will be interrogated and opened up so that they move beyond modernist and Eurocentric meaning horizons. The goal is to employ the UNCG in a manner more sensitive to cultural specificity, rather than in a strictly legalistic sense. To this end, I will seek to destabilize what it means to be a "group," to show "intent," and to experience "destruction," all terms specified in art. 2 of the UNCG. . . .

Despite the early presence of European traders and missionaries, settlers were few at the onset of Canadian colonization. Indeed, Aboriginal peoples would have been in a secure position to maintain their power, territories, traditions, and trade had it not been for the spread of European diseases. Since Aboriginal peoples had established little resistance to diseases such as smallpox, these diseases provided "biological power" to facilitate European control. Carried along these trade routes, diseases often preceded Europeans into Aboriginal communities and decimated their populations. At least half the Aboriginal population of between 200,000 and 300,000 people was killed by disease between the beginning of the seventeenth century and the end of the nineteenth. This devastating death toll opened vast areas of land to European settlement and exploitation. The destructive effect of colonialism intensified as Europeans began to seek possession of Aboriginal territories for settlement and resource exploitation. . . . The combined effects of land appropriation, violated or ignored treaties, legal domination, and forced assimilation were devastating for Aboriginal peoples. . . .

The complexity of this historical narrative, even in such a simplified form, makes any application of the concept of genocide to the circumstances difficult. . . . These issues must be acknowledged in addressing Canadian Aboriginal claims of genocide. However, they also distract us somewhat from grappling directly with Aboriginal experiences of attempted colonial destruction. . . . The remainder of this article is devoted to re-reading the opening sentence of art. 2 of the UNCG in a manner informed by Canadian Aboriginal experiences of colonialism. The objective is to illustrate how we must first open our evaluative tools to localized Aboriginal understandings of group identity and collective destruction before we can attempt to adjudicate whether or not genocidal intent was evident in the Canadian case. . . .

[First,] the restrictions placed on group identity by the UNCG are inappropriate and potentially encourage a "totalization" of community life that is itself a danger to Aboriginal group identities. In other words, by seeking to impose clear community parameters upon Canadian Aboriginal groups, interpreters of the UNCG may miscategorize these communities in a way that obstructs their attempts to exist as "becoming communities"—that is, communities engaged in an ongoing and daily process of self-definition and redefinition that never suggests a point of community closure. . . . The UNCG further implies that a group consists solely of its human members, but this may be quite contrary to the group identity of collectivities adhering to or built upon animist belief systems that include their environs and local wildlife as part of the group. . . . To fully acknowledge the Aboriginal experience of attempted destruction, we need to understand land and environment not simply as means of sustaining group life, but as key components of group life. . . .

[Second,] what does it mean to "destroy" a group? . . . Genocide carries with it notions of harm that are artifacts of a specific (in particular, modernist) viewpoint that may not reflect how harms are experienced and understood by different collectivities. . . . The UNCG is often read within a modernist framework that assumes a stark divide between nature and culture.

Thus, the five forms of destruction highlighted in art. 2—"killing members of the group; causing serious bodily or mental harm to members of the group; deliberately inflicting on the group conditions of life calculated to bring about its physical destruction in whole or in part; imposing measures intended to prevent births within the group; forcibly transferring children of the group to another group"—all presume a decidedly social strategy of elimination. The problem with this presumption, in terms of understanding the attempted destruction of Canadian Aboriginal peoples, is that it allows the colonizer to avoid responsibility for hybridic assaults on Aboriginal peoples. Disease is conveniently removed as relevant evidence because it is classified as a natural process. But diseases such as smallpox and tuberculosis, and industrial ailments such as mercury poisoning, were experienced by Aboriginal peoples as consequences of enforced contact with non-Aboriginal peoples, and as part of a structured set of destructive relations, that cannot simply be categorized as "natural." If we are to contend adequately with these experiences, we must not exclude certain forms of destruction from consideration; instead, genocide scholars must be ready to interrogate the modernist oppositions that shape our ways of knowing and being in the world. . . .

[Third,] one of the most vexing issues in discussions about genocide in Canada is that of intent. As in debates about genocide in other settler societies (the United States, Australia, and New Zealand), questions are raised about whether the perpetrators clearly formulated an intent to eliminate Aboriginal peoples. Some argue that because the Canadian colonial government's assimilation policies were based on humanitarian and welfare-oriented concerns, they cannot be considered genocidal, since they do not evince a clear malevolent intent. Others point to the fact that functionaries and settlers operating at a distance from government were often the key agents of Aboriginal destruction. Missionaries, gold miners, settlers, and others carried with them no government mandate to impinge upon Aboriginal lifeworlds. However, Lemkin's work on Aboriginal genocides suggests that centrally coordinated planning is not required for an event to be categorized as genocide. Indeed, Lemkin's work shows great awareness of the networked character of Aboriginal destruction, acknowledging that various "genocidists" possessing different motives might each play a role in the wider process of Aboriginal destruction. . . .

The source of destruction may lie less in an "unambiguous 'intent to destroy' a human group, than in the presumption that there was not much *to* destroy." Thus, to better understand the Aboriginal experience of destruction, we must move beyond a legalistic notion of intent that seeks to identify specific calculations of destruction on the part of the perpetrator; instead we must understand intent as a catastrophic form of misrecognition, which so devalues a population that assimilation is assumed to be a matter of their general welfare. In many ways, Europeans imagined Aboriginal peoples to be destitute, backward, uncivilized, and savage, and these assumptions facilitated their choice to impose a "liberal humanism" that denied Aboriginal ontologies.

50 • The Irish Potato Famine, 1845–1849
(Cecil Woodham-Smith)

In 1996 a report commissioned and distributed by the New York–based Irish Famine/Genocide Committee asserted that the Irish Potato Famine, which in the mid-nineteenth century claimed upwards of one million lives, had been deliberately engineered by the British government and thus amounted to a case of genocide. Years earlier the historian A. J. P. Taylor had noted that in the wake of the famine "all Ireland was Belsen," likening the consequences of British rule to that of the Holocaust. The British historian Cecil Woodham-Smith, in her classic and evenhanded account The Great Hunger *(1962), considers this line of argument but ultimately finds it wanting. Although economists and others have since conducted a great deal of more sophisticated empirical research on the conflagration in the mid-nineteenth century, Woodham-Smith's account remains a useful starting point.*

At the beginning of the year 1845 the state of Ireland was, as it had been for nearly seven hundred years, a source of grave anxiety to England. Ireland had first been invaded in 1169; it was now 1845, yet she had neither assimilated nor [been] subdued. The country had been conquered not once but several times, the land had been confiscated and redistributed over and over again, the population had been brought to the verge of extinction—after Cromwell's conquest and settlement only some half million Irish survived—yet an Irish nation still existed, separate, numerous and hostile. . . .

On January 1, 1801, an event of enormous importance had taken place—the Act of the Union between Ireland and England became operative. The countries were made one, the economy of Ireland was assimilated into the economy of England, the Irish Parliament at Dublin disappeared and the Parliament at Westminster henceforward legislated for both countries. . . . [Yet] the Union was bitterly opposed [by the Irish]; contemporaries described it not as a marriage but as a "brutal rape." . . . An Irish people united and controlled was an ominous spectacle, and the British Government, seized with something near panic, began to prepare "as if in hourly expectation of civil war." Troops were hastily brought from England, barracks were fortified and provisioned to withstand a siege. . . . On the eve of the famine, the Government of Ireland was admittedly a military occupation, and the garrison of Ireland was larger than the garrison of India. . . .

The hostility between England and Ireland, which six centuries earlier had failed to extinguish, had its roots first of all in race. After the first invasions, the first conquests, the Irish hated the English with the hatred of the defeated and the dispossessed. Nevertheless, eventually the English and the Irish might have fused, as the English and the Scots, the English and the Welsh have, for practical purposes, fused, had it not been that in the sixteenth century racial animosity was disastrously strengthened by religious enmity. The crucial event was the Reformation. The ideas of liberty which the English cherish and the history of their country's rise to greatness are bound up with Protestantism, while Ireland, alone among the countries

SOURCE: Cecil Woodham-Smith, *The Great Hunger: Ireland, 1845–1849* (1962; London: Penguin, 1991), 15, 16, 17, 18–19, 29, 31, 32, 35–36, 37, 38, 41, 54, 75, 118, 146, 165, 187, 411–12, 407, 408, 410. Reprinted with permission of the publisher.

of northern Europe, was scarcely touched by the Reformation. The gulf which resulted could never be bridged.

In the political division of Europe which followed the Reformation, England and Ireland were on opposing sides. Henceforward, Irish aspirations could only be fulfilled, Irish faith could only flourish, through the defeat of England and the triumph of her enemies. Freedom for Ireland meant Philip of Spain and the Inquisition in place of Elizabeth I, it meant James II instead of William III, it even meant, since misery and oppression make strange bedfellows, the victory of Napoleon. . . . In Ireland the name of Elizabeth I stands only for the horrors of her Irish conquest; in the defeat of the Armada, Ireland's hopes of independence went down; above all, with the name of William III and the glorious revolution of 1688, the very foundation of British liberties, the Catholic Irishman associates only the final subjugation of his country and the degradation and injustice of the penal laws. Freedom for the one meant slavery for the other; victory for the one meant defeat for the other; the good of the one was the evil of the other. Ireland, resentful and hostile, . . . in every crisis of England's history she seized the moment of weakness to stab her enemy in the back. It is the explanation, if not the excuse, for the ferocity with which the English have treated Ireland. . . .

A hostile, lawless, oppressed and poverty-stricken population in Ireland was already giving signs of future tragedy when a new development made catastrophe inevitable. Between sixty and seventy years before the famine the population of Ireland began and continued to increase at a rate previously unknown in the history of Europe. . . . For this closely-packed and rapidly-increasing people the only outlet—with the exception of Ulster—was the land. . . . The consequence was the doom of Ireland. The land was divided and sub-divided, again and again, and holdings were split into smaller and smaller fragments, until families were attempting to exist on plots of less than an acre, in some cases half an acre. . . . The possession of a piece of land was literally the difference between life and death. . . .

The whole of this structure, the minute subdivisions, the closely-packed population existing at the lowest level, the high rents, the frantic competition for land, had been produced by the potato. The conditions of life in Ireland and the existence of the Irish people depended on the potato entirely and exclusively. The potato, provided it did not fail, enabled great quantities of food to be produced at a trifling cost from a small plot of ground. Sub-division could never have taken place without the potato: an acre and a half would provide a family of five or six with food for twelve months, while to grow the equivalent grain required an acreage four to six times as large and some knowledge of tillage as well. . . . Yet it was the most dangerous of crops. It did not keep, nor could it be stored from one season to another. Thus every year the nearly two and a half million laborers who had no regular employment more or less starved in the summer, when the old potatoes were finished and the new ones had not come in. . . .

Yet the British Government felt no apprehension about the potato crop. . . . There were, however, voices crying the wilderness. . . . In the forty-five years since the Union no fewer than 114 Commissions and 61 Special Committees were instructed to report on the state of Ireland, and without exception their findings prophesied disaster; Ireland was on the verge of starvation, her population rapidly increasing. . . . [This notwithstanding,] the British Government's mind was made up. The property of Ireland must support the poverty of Ireland, and a menace to England must be removed. . . . The British Government . . . continued to contemplate the condition of the Irish people with "imperturbable apathy." Meanwhile, in 1844, a report was received that in North America a disease, hitherto unknown, had attacked the potato crop. . . .

[By September 1845,] the potato disease . . . had undeniably appeared in Ireland [via England]. Now the question was, how far would it spread? . . . The influence of [English] *laissez faire* on the treatment of Ireland during the famine is impossible to exaggerate. Almost without exception the high officials and politicians responsible for Ireland were fervent believers in non-interference by Government, and the behavior of the British authorities only becomes explicable when their fanatical belief in private enterprise and their suspicions of any action which might be considered Government intervention are borne in mind. . . .

In the long and troubled history of England and Ireland no issue has provoked so much anger or so embittered relations between the two countries as the indisputable fact that huge quantities of food were exported from Ireland to England throughout the period when the people of Ireland were dying of starvation. . . . All over Europe the harvest of 1846 was wholly or partially a failure. The wheat crop was scanty, oat and barley "decidedly deficient," rye and potatoes a total loss, and "general famine" followed. . . . The British Government could not have foreseen the general failure of the harvest in Europe, but it might have led them to modify their Irish relief plans. No modification was attempted, the scheme stood as drafted. No orders for food were to be placed abroad; no Government food depots were to be established, except in the west; all importing was to be left to private enterprise. . . . The British Government did not suggest how people who were without food of any kind were to keep alive until next year's harvest. . . .

The British Government had started Irish relief with a millstone round its neck—the 2,385,000 persons who, as the Poor Inquiry Commission reported, starved, more or less, every year in Ireland, whether the potato failed or not. This hopeless, wretched, multitude . . . swamped every scheme, and formed a hard core of destitution whose numbers could be reduced only by death. . . . [And] as if starvation were not enough, a new terror assailed the Irish people in [the fall of 1846]. . . . Fever, on a gigantic scale, was now beginning to ravage Ireland. . . .

How many people died in the famine will never precisely be known. It is almost certain that, owing to geographical difficulties and the unwillingness of the people to be registered, the census of 1841 gave a total smaller than the population in fact was. Officers engaged in relief work put the population as much as 25 percent higher. . . . In 1841 the population of Ireland was given as 8,175,124; in 1851, after the famine, it had dropped to 6,552,385, and the Census Commissioners calculated that, at the normal rate of increase, the total should have been 9,018,799, so that a loss of at least 2½ million persons had taken place. The figures available, however, must be regarded as giving only a rough indication; vital statistics are unobtainable, no record was kept of deaths, and very many persons must have died and been buried unknown. . . .

The treatment of the Irish people by the British government during the famine has been described as genocide—race murder. The British Government has been accused, and not only by the Irish, of wishing to "extirpate" them, as Hitler wished to exterminate the Jews. The eighteen-forties, however, must not be judged by the standards of today; and whatever parsimony and callousness the British Government displayed towards Ireland, was paralleled seven years later by the treatment of their own soldiers which brought about the destruction of the British Army in Crimea.

The conduct of the British Government during the famine is divided into two periods. During the first, from the partial failure in 1845 until the transfer to the Poor Law in the summer of 1847, the Government behaved with considerable generosity. An elaborate relief organization was set up, public works were started on a scale never attempted before, and what was, for the time, a very large sum of money indeed, more than eight million pounds, was advanced. . . . But during the second period, after the transfer of the Poor Law in the summer of 1847, the behavior of the British is difficult to defend. . . . They knew that Ireland was, at the moment, in the grip of a major famine . . . yet with these facts before them, the Government threw the hordes of wretched destitute on their local Poor rates, refusing assistance when the second total failure of the potato occurred. . . . Neither during the famine nor for decades afterwards were any measures of reconstruction or agricultural improvement attempted, and this neglect condemned Ireland to decline. . . .

[However,] these misfortunes were not part of a plan to destroy the Irish nation; they fell on the people because the [British] government of Lord John Russell was afflicted with an extraordinary inability to foresee consequences. It has been frequently declared that the parsimony of the British Government during the famine was the main cause of the sufferings of the people, and parsimony was certainly carried to remarkable lengths; but obtuseness, short-sightedness and ignorance probably contributed more.

51 • From Native Policy to Genocide in South West Africa (George Steinmetz)

George Steinmetz, in pursuit of what "colonial genocide" really entailed, provides glimpses into the development of "native policy" in South West Africa, today's Namibia. Seized by Wilhelmine Germany in the scramble for Africa, the rather resource-poor colony became the site of a genocidal campaign against the indigenous Herero population in 1904–7. Steinmetz, a sociologist at the University of Michigan, explains the function of ideas—notably German ethnographic visions of the Herero—in the transition from colonialism to destruction in his 2007 book, The Devil's Handwriting.

Historians have debated whether there was a premeditated Ovaherero revolt [in German Southwest Africa] in 1904 or whether their uprising was a response to an unprovoked German assault. . . . The war [against the Herero] effort was initially conducted by [Theodor] Leutwein, whose position as governor [of the colony] made him commander of the *Schutztruppe* [the colonial army]. But he became entangled in disagreements with the Colonial Department [in Berlin] because of his "moderate" stance. Leutwein wrote in February: "I cannot agree with those imprudent voices which would now like to see the Herero completely de-

SOURCE: George Steinmetz, *The Devil's Handwriting: Precoloniality and the German Colonial State in Qingdao, Samoa, and Southwest Africa* (Chicago: University of Chicago Press, 2007), 191, 192–93, 194, 195, 197–98, 200, 201–2, 203. Reprinted with permission of the author and the publisher.

stroyed [*vernichtet*]. Aside from the fact that a people with sixty to seventy thousands souls is not so easy to annihilate, I would consider such a measure a grave mistake from an economic point of view. We still need the Hereros as breeders of small livestock and especially as workers. We only have to kill them politically." . . .

The decision to dismiss Leutwein altogether was made after he withdrew from a battle with the massed Ovaherero warriors at Oviumbo on April 13 to await reinforcements from Germany. In May the [German] emperor appointed General Lothar von Trotha as supreme commander of the war effort, although he gave von Trotha no specific instructions. Von Trotha declared martial law in the colony on June 11, 1904, and he was effectively in charge of the colony until August 1905, when a new governor was appointed. . . . Pursuing his plan to crush Ovaherero military resistance in a single blow, von Trotha waited until he had received massive reinforcements from Germany and then encircled the Ovaherero at the Waterberg plateau, where tens of thousands of Ovaherero were gathered, including men, women, and children, along with all of their livestock. Von Trotha launched his attack on August 11, 1904, with as many as two thousand troops, including three machine-gun batteries (against an estimated five to six thousand Ovaherero warriors). Most of the Ovaherero escaped through a gap in the German encirclement that channeled them into the parched Omaheke Desert. There they were pursued by German patrols for almost two months, which drove them deeper and deeper into the sand plains. An unknown number, but probably tens of thousands, perished. The decision to create a fanlike troop formation to cut off Ovaherero lines of escape and to continue pushing them farther into the Omaheke marked a shift toward an explicitly genocidal strategy, since "death from thirst did not distinguish between men, women, and children" (all Ovaherero warriors were men). . . .

General von Trotha has gone down in history as the author of the *Vernichtungsbefehl*, or "order of annihilation," against the Ovaherero, which he issued on October 2, 1904. . . . Von Trotha stated his goal bluntly in a letter to the chief of the Great General Staff, Count von Schlieffen: "to annihilate the nation as such, or when this proves impossible through tactical blows, to expel it from the country." If there was any ambiguity at all, he added, "I think it is better if the nation as such perishes." . . . Although von Trotha arrived at his exterminationist policy independently after the Waterberg battle, it was approved at the highest levels. In a letter to the chancellor [of Wilhelmine Germany] on November 23, Count von Schlieffen wrote that "one can concur with [General von Trotha] that the entire nation should be exterminated or driven from the country." Von Schlieffen offered as possible alternative for the Ovaherero a "permanent state of forced labor, that is, a form of slavery," adding that "the race war, once it has broken out, can only be ended by the extermination [*Vernichtung*] or the complete subjugation of one of the parties." . . .

The Ovaherero were not entirely exterminated. They continued to be exploited severely in slavelike forced labor after 1904, and as "free" laborers after 1907. The fact remains that von Trotha sought deliberately to wipe out the Ovaherero in 1904, and that he was supported in this by his officers and soldiers and by many of the highest authorities in Berlin. This concerted movement beyond native policy into an unambiguous policy of genocide calls for an explanation. It cannot be dismissed as a historical aberration. . . . To account for the genocide, we need to [adopt a] triple analytic focus on ethnographic discourse, symbolic competition, and imaginary identification with the colonized as determinants of native policy. With respect to the first, the Ovaherero had been demonized for decades, and fantasies of extermination had been rife. If the massacre was a caesura in terms of actual policy, the destruction had deep roots in German ethnographic visions. Von Trotha was no more disparaging of Ovaherero culture than earlier German officials or precolonial missionaries. . . . The demonization of black Africans in general and the Ovaherero in particular was a necessary but not a sufficient condition for the shift to genocide. After all, Leutwein had not attempted to massacre even a fraction of the rebellious Ovaherero in 1896.

The constellation of the colonial state field was a second necessary factor. The extreme polarization between Leutwein and von Trotha [who, prior to Leutwein's dismissal, had been commander of the *Schutztruppe*] crystallized in highly exaggerated form the class hostility that arose "naturally" in Wilhelmine Germany between a military aristocrat and a pastor's son who flaunted his classical education. . . . Von Trotha's hostility to Leutwein led him to adopt an even harsher "ethnographic" approach, and this spiraling clash had dire consequences for the Ovaherero. Von Trotha relished the dual resonance of the term *Vernichtung*. In conventional German military language, *vernichten* meant "to deal a devastating blow" to the enemy, breaking his resistance. Von Trotha's language in the second half of 1904 increasingly evoked the connotations of that term that were tied specifically to the colonial context. . . . The traditional European military concept of the *Vernichtungskrieg* would never have been associated with images of "rivers of blood" or "blatant terrorism and cruelty"—these were colonial amendments. Von Trotha was reasserting the specific cultural capital of Prussian and German nobility, its specialization in the arts of domination and violence, under conditions that a European imagination perceived as lying outside the borders of civilization. . . .

A third source of von Trotha's genocidal policy was his sadistic imaginary identification with an imago of the colonized. . . . The image of the viciously cruel Ovaherero, already widespread after 1870, became almost universal among colonial Germans in 1904. Ovaherero physically beat to death German settlers and soldiers and mutilated some of their bodies. . . . But are hatred and revenge sufficient to explain the lynchings, the removal of body parts and skulls for scientific study, and the attempt to exterminate an entire people? It is difficult to understand von Trotha's "irrational" course without attending to his self-image as the "great general of the German soldiers" exercising "terrorism," shedding "rivers of blood," and driving women and children to their death. This self-perception suggests an identification with a European imago of the "cruel Herero," recalling Kaiser Wilhelm's eagerness to identify himself and his soldiers with the "Huns." Challenged by men like Leutwein who seemed to embody the inexorable demise of noble privilege, von Trotha cross-identified with a caricatured image of the enemy and redirected his savage "Herero" wrath against both the soft opinions of German liberals and the African military opponent. . . .

Von Trotha's genocidal turn was multiply overdetermined. The first moving force was the weight of ethnographic discourse. Second was his paradoxical identification with an imago of extreme cruelty. This was powered by von Trotha's positioning in a competitive field facing an embodiment of the educated, liberal middle class that threatened Germany's old noble elite. Von Troth exploded this field, producing a situation of mutual nonrecognition and heightening the aggressive energy of the situation. The result for the Ovaherero was a policy of "colonialism without the colonized." . . . [Yet] von Trotha did not accomplish his goal of exterminating the entire Ovaherero population or driving them out of the colony. With the appointment of von Lindequits as governor in August 1905, the colony began to move slowly back toward a focus on Ovaherero native policy, although this was combined with ongoing deadly negligence in the concentration camps that quietly continued the genocide through 1907.

52 • Aboriginal Child Removal and Half-Castes in Australia (Robert Manne)

Scholars who claim that genocide was committed in colonial Australia use the removal of aboriginal children to document the course of destruction. In his 2004 essay, Robert Manne considers the genocide claim through the lens of a 1997 Australian government report entitled Bringing Them Home. *He shows who was involved in transforming from paternalistic cruelty into genocidal policy the colony's long-standing practice of removing half-caste children (i.e., children of mixed descent, usually the offspring of white colonists and Aborigines) from their families.*

Bringing Them Home, the findings of the federal government inquiry into the removal of thousands of Aboriginal children from their mothers, families, and communities [in Australia] in the first two-thirds of the twentieth century, was published in 1997. It argued that the Commonwealth government and the governments of several Australian states were guilty of the crime of genocide.

The basic argument was straightforward. According to the United Nations Convention on the Prevention and Punishment of the Crime of Genocide, ratified by Australia in 1949, genocide is defined as the intentional destruction of a racial, religious, national, or ethnic group. Not only does the convention make it clear that genocide can be committed without killing, for example, by the use of methods to prevent births, it also explicitly mentions the forcible removal of children of a group as a means by which the crime may occur. In *Bringing Them Home,* it is argued that the idea of the crime of genocide was introduced into international law by a resolution of the United Nations in December 1946. From that date, the argument continues, with the forcible removal of Aboriginal children, the Commonwealth government and the government of the states were engaged in unambiguously genocidal acts.

Following the publication of *Bringing Them Home,* a small number of scholars prominent in the field of indigenous history and politics offered broad support for the position it had argued on the question of genocide. One of these scholars, Robert van Krieken, saw the policy and practice of Aboriginal child removal, both before and after the Second World War, as a clear instance both of "cultural genocide" and of the barbarous face of the "civilising process" when set within a colonial frame. In general, however, the genocide conclusion of *Bringing Them Home* was treated by the Australian government, by the popular media, and by the right-wing intelligentsia with levity and derisive contempt. Nor was such an attitude restricted to the right. One of Australia's most admired liberal historians, Inga Clendinnen, the author of

SOURCE: Robert Manne, "Aboriginal Child Removal and the Question of Genocide, 1900–1940," in A. Dirk Moses, ed., *Genocide and Settler Society: Frontier Violence and Stolen Indigenous Children in Australian History* (New York: Berghahn, 2004), 217–18, 220, 221, 222, 225–26, 227, 231, 232, 235, 237–38. Reprinted with permission of the publisher.

Reading the Holocaust, described the argument about genocide and Aboriginal child removal as nothing less than "a moral, intellectual and . . . political disaster."

Between the supporters and opponents of the genocide conclusion of *Bringing Them Home*, a third position has emerged, one that distinguishes between the prewar ideas about the biological absorption of mixed-descent Aborigines and postwar ideas about the possibility of their assimilation. . . . Russell McGregor argues persuasively that the charge of genocide with regard to Aboriginal child removal in the post–Second World War era, when Aboriginal policy was driven by the ambition for the social and cultural assimilation of the indigenous population of Australia, is misconceived. It is the purpose of the present chapter to assess whether claims about the genocidal character of Aboriginal child removal in the era before the Second World War are more soundly based. . . .

In 1899, the Chief Prosecutor in Western Australia, Henry Prinsep, issued the following warning in his annual report to parliament:

> The intercourse between the races is leading to a considerable increase of half-castes. Many of them find their way into the missions, but a far greater number are probably reared in native camps, without any sort of education, except a vicious one. Each half-caste, so brought up, is a menace to the future moral safety of the community. . . .

According to the old Aboriginal Act of 1865, the police in Queensland were able to bring any Aboriginal or half-caste child before a magistrates' court, to charge them with being neglected simply on the evidence that their mother was an Aborigine. They would then be transferred to a reformatory or what was called, at the time, an Industrial School. Moreover, according to the new Aboriginal Act of 1897, the Prosecutors were able to remove, under warrant from the Home Minister, any Aboriginal or half-caste Aboriginal adult or child to any location in the state. . . .

There can be little doubt that conspicuous cruelty was involved in the removal of these half-caste children. . . . Yet acts of cruelty are not, of course, evidence of genocidal intent. In his voluminous monthly and annual reports to the Minister and the Queensland parliament, [Walter] Roth's intentions in the removal of the half-caste children become clear. Dr. Roth [the northern protector of Aborigines in Queensland] removed the children, in part, because he believed the conditions in and around the Aboriginal camps spoke of such human degradation that they were altogether unsuitable for any half-European child. . . .

In 1904, . . . Western Australia's first comprehensive Act concerning Aborigines was passed. In one of its provisions, the Chief Protector became guardian of all Aboriginal and half-caste children up to the age of sixteen. Although the legal situation with regard to Aboriginal child removal was not completely clear until certain amending legislation of 1911, which made it explicit that the Chief Protector's guardianship overrode the rights of the mother to her illegitimate child, for some time it appeared as if there was no legal impediment to the collection of the half-castes. . . .

The system of half-caste child removal, as it had developed by the late 1920s in Queensland, Western Australia, and the Northern Territory, was deeply paternalistic in its blithe indifference to the wishes of the Aborigines and its certainty that only the administrators knew what was for the best. It was racist in its most fundamental assumption, namely, that it was

unconscionable to allow "part-European" children to grow up in what was commonly regarded as the filthy, immoral, superstitious, and degraded Aboriginal world. For the human
beings whose lives were frequently shattered by these policies—for both the Aboriginal
mothers and the children—the policy was exceedingly cruel. Yet, scrutinized from the point
of view of the intentions of the administrators, the removal policies were not yet genocidal
in any recognizable sense. . . . It was only when the policy and practice of child removal was
resituated by administrators and intellectuals into a more general framework as part of a supposed solution to the problem of the half-caste—that is to say, when the administrators began
to make plans for the elimination of the half-castes and to see in child removal one instrument
by which this purpose could be achieved—that the genocidal dimensions of Aboriginal child
removal emerged. . . .

At this time, Aboriginal administrators, like most Australians, still believed that the full-
blood Aborigine was unlikely to survive. The "doomed race" theory, as it has been called, was
grounded, in part at least, in nineteenth-century scientific thought. As early as 1846, in his
influential Oxford lectures, Herman Merivale argued that for aboriginal peoples "the mere
contact of Europeans is fatal in some unknown manner." . . . While administrators felt obliged
to accept that the full-blooded Aborigines were destined to die out as a consequence of contact with a superior civilization as a kind of melancholy scientific fact, by the early 1930s their
minds were far more actively exercised by a demographic problem of an altogether different
kind—the seemingly inexorable rise in the number of half-castes. In 1901, at the birth of the
Commonwealth, there were fewer than eight thousand half-castes in Australia; by the early
1930s, more than twenty thousand. . . . Many were convinced that if the half-caste population
was allowed to grow, Australia would eventually be confronted by a serious racial problem, of
the kind faced by the United States or South Africa. . . . What then was to be done?

On one occasion in 1934, a senior government official, William Gall, the Under-Secretary
at the Home Department in Queensland, argued that the only feasible solution was the sterilization of all half-castes. Sterilization, however, had no serious support, probably because it
was not a policy tradition in Great Britain. Far more significant, as we shall see, was another
proposed solution—the biological absorption into the white of the half-caste population
through a state-engineered program of encouraged miscegenation. . . . On the day the Pre-
mier's Conference of June 1933 convened, supposedly to discuss as one item of a national
policy for breeding out the color of the Aborigines, the Chief Prosecutor in Western Australia,
A. O. Neville, issued an official statement to the press expressing his support for the Commonwealth government's scheme:

> The decision made by the Commonwealth Government to adopt as definite policy
> the encouragement of marriages of white men and half-caste women with a view to
> raising the standard of mixed blood to that of whites, is nothing new in this State. I
> have foreseen it for years, and sponsored it as the only outcome of the position. The
> blacks will have to go white. . . .

In April 1937, administrators of Aboriginal policy from the Northern Territory and each of
the states (with the exception of Tasmania) met for the first time since the formation of the
Commonwealth to discuss matters of common concern. The most important issue at the conference was the problem of the half-caste. . . . The balance of opinion at the April 1937 confer-

ence on the question of the future of the Aborigine can best be summarized as follows. The Aborigines could and should be absorbed, both culturally and biologically, into the white population. In the short term, absorption policy would concentrate solely on the half-castes. Eventually, the full-bloods would most likely become extinct. The half-caste descendants of the current full-blood population would, however, also have to be absorbed. This whole process would take fifty years or more. After this time, in Neville's words, everyone would be able "to forget that there were every any aborigines in Australia." The conference had produced a long-term plan for the elimination of the Aboriginal people.

53 • Absolute Destruction as Strategy: Wilhelmine Germany and the Ottoman Empire (Isabel V. Hull)

In her discussion of the relationship between German military culture and the Armenian genocide, the historian Isabel Hull not only inquires into the cultural dimensions of genocide but also explores its transnational dimensions. This section of her 2004 book contributes to our understanding of the cultural dimensions by charting the rise of the maxim of "absolute destruction" in Germany military theory and practice. She contributes to the scholarship on the transnational dimensions of genocide by exploring the diffusion of the behavioral norm of absolute destruction and the concomitant doctrine of "military necessity." She does so by tracing the salience of these manifestations of Wilhelmine Germany's military culture in the Ottoman Empire, where German military officers were dispatched to aid the Young Turk regime during World War I.

This is a study of institutional extremism. It examines the German conduct of war from 1870 through 1918. In engagements large and small, in Europe and in the colonies, the Imperial German military repeatedly resorted to terrific violence and destruction in excess of Germany's own security requirements or political goals, in contravention of international norms, and even contrary to ultimate military effectiveness. Routine German military operations developed a dynamic of extremism that could, and did, lead to extermination of civilian populations in the colonies and that characterized German practices in occupied Europe during the First World War. . . .

Germany's military culture developed a constellation of mutually reinforcing characteristics that enhanced tactical efficacy. Unleashed in war, however, these characteristics propelled the army to ever greater, and in the end, dysfunctional extremes of violence. [This book] analyzes these interactive and self-generating characteristics, which include risk-taking; the dogmatic conviction that annihilation was the sole goal of war (*Vernichtungskrieg*); resulting prescriptions for correct fighting (the offensive, concentration of forces, use of reserves, hectic speed) that all greatly increased casualties; minutely technical planning; focus on the tactical and operative rather than the strategic; disregard of logistics and thus growing unrealism; the conviction (indeed requirement) of one's qualitative superiority over one's enemies; a

SOURCE: Isabel V. Hull, *Absolute Destruction: Military Culture and the Practices of War in Imperial Germany* (Ithaca, N.Y.: Cornell University Press, 2004), 1, 2–3, 4, 93–94, 110, 117, 119, 126, 127, 129, 130, 165–66, 263, 265, 269–70, 271, 275, 276, 278, 290, 326, 327. Reprinted with permission of the publisher.

romantic ruthlessness and actionism (exaggerated drive for action [*Aktionismus*]) on the part of officers in order to bridge the gap between risk and reality; and finally the acceptance of self-destruction (and thus the willingness to destroy everyone else, as well). Some of these qualities were expressed in doctrine, but many more were buried inside organizational routines and the unexamined expectations of the officer corps. . . . Perceived "military necessity" removed one protective limit after another. Ubiquitous forced labor, deportation, and widespread death spread across occupied Europe. In the Ottoman Empire, Germany's Turkish ally claimed "military necessity" as it exterminated its Armenian civilians.

. . . The terrible violence, immense destruction, and mass death caused by the operation of military culture were indeed large-scale disasters, but they had small, literally routine beginnings. Seemingly goal-irrational, the practices of military culture were eminently institutional-rational; they were the product of intelligent professionals working in the finest army of its time. We will now enter their world, a place where, in the words of Norman Maclean, writing about a small forest fire that suddenly turned deadly, "the ordinary can suddenly become monstrous." . . . "Military culture" is a way of understanding why an army acts as it does in war. Unlike military sociology, which mostly has focused on military organizations in peacetime, a military-cultural perspective concentrates on practices during war. By "practice" I mean two things: the actions that result consciously from applied doctrine and training, and the habitual actions that seem obvious by virtue of unquestioned assumptions or necessary by virtue of the unintended consequences of regular military procedure. Two fields analyze practices in this sense: anthropology and the sociological subfield of organizational culture. Using both one can develop a conception of military culture that will help explain how and why a particular military behaved as it did in wartime. . . .

Prussia entered the mid-nineteenth century with a formidable military tradition. It was the product of self-contradictory parentage: the pragmatic "absolutism" of Frederick the Great, the liberal reforms of the Napoleonic period (epitomized in the writings of Carl von Clausewitz), the hostile revisions of those reforms that accreted after the post-Napoleonic restoration, and the antiliberal but technically modernizing "reform" of King Wilhelm I in the early 1860s. These doctrinal, institutional, and cultural inheritances were galvanized and transformed during the three wars of German unification in 1864 (against Denmark), in 1866 (against Austria and the other German states), and in 1870–71 (against France). The Franco-Prussian War of 1870–71 set the model for the subsequent standard practices of the German army. . . .

The practices that developed in 1870–71 were codified in army regulations that remained substantially the same down to 1914, because no European war occurred to challenge them and because the colonial punitive expeditions, which were Germany's main military experience from 1871 to 1914, seemed to confirm their aptness. Furthermore, the basic interpreter of the lessons of 1870 was the General Staff, and its subsequent hegemony over doctrine, planning, and preparation ensured that its interpretation became canonical. . . . The year 1870 deserves the epithet "traumatic" because it was literally "existential"—the future of Germany hung in the balance—and also because its course was unexpected and supremely frustrating to the self-understanding [of] the army. . . . The significance of the 1870 war lies . . . in the precedents it set. Chancellor Otto v. Bismarck recognized the harshness of military conduct as something new in Germany's history. The new methods deemed acceptable after 1870 related mostly to the treatment of enemy civilians, who were pulled into the vortex of war and who were less protected from severe treatment than were prisoners of war. . . .

Among the premises contained in the German position as it developed after 1870 are several fundamental assumptions that had major implications for military practice. First, . . . war, all war, was existential, which meant it contained no limits and tended to develop its capacity for violence and destruction to the extreme. Second, the counterpart to this unsettling picture was a conception of equally extreme order, which the military was instantly to establish in the occupied areas. Order in this conception was practically lifeless, for it required an extreme self-abnegation (of emotional loyalty to one's land or people, of self-preservation) that could hardly exist in real life. . . . Third, the unrealistic expectation of perfect order artificially produced occasions for disorder, which turned enemy civilians into criminals subject to harsh military law. In short, "order" encouraged reprisals when it inevitably failed. Punishment thus became a major military duty, and civilians became as dangerous as enemy soldiers. . . . A fourth basic assumption concerned international law, the only limit to the violence of war. Some writers, heady with the success of German arms in 1870–71, opined immediately thereafter that international law simply did not exist: there could be no limits to the sovereignty of the nation-state. . . . We turn now to a final basic assumption, a collective self-understanding that repeatedly emerged in Germany's argumentation at the international conferences. . . .

The German government thought of itself as always victorious, and of victory as always territorial (and probably aggressive), that is, as involving the movement of German troops into other lands. . . . The official German point of view was thus military, not civilian; bellicose, not peaceful; and utterly devoted to victory. . . . For our purposes, the most important point is the premium on victory, which was so powerful that defeat was inconceivable, and thus could never be factored into decision making or planning as a (regrettable) possibility. The self-generated pressure to succeed at all cost was one of the chief parameters influencing officers' decisions in actual wars. . . . The Schlieffen Plan, as the retiring chief of staff set it down in 1906, gives us the clearest distillation in a single source of the army's organizational knowledge and thus represents a summary at the doctrinal level of Wilhelmine military culture. It clearly shows how the dynamic toward extremes was (unintentionally) built into the system, and it reflects and accounts for the actual conduct of Germany's wars in the colonies and during the First World War. . . .

In the spring of 1915 [the Ottoman Empire,] Germany's new Turkish ally, began systematically murdering its Armenian population. The most radical reformers in the ruling Committee of Union and Progress (CUP) used the cover of war to "deport" the Armenians from their homes in Anatolia. . . . In the end, Anatolia's three-thousand-year-old, 1.5–2 million-strong Armenian community was gone. That was the CUP's goal—to build a nation-state around a homogenous Turkic-Islamic population, stripped of its Christians (Armenians, Greeks, Nestorians, and some Syrians) and Jews. This genocidal project killed at least eight hundred thousand Armenians, most likely a million or more. United States and Allied commentators quickly suspected German involvement. . . . Like contemporaries, scholars today remain divided on Germany's role. . . . Germany's role in the Armenian genocide was, in fact, complicated and riddled with contradiction. . . .

When Turkey entered the war, the influence of German military officers increased because military operations were being conducted; the disastrous campaign of 1914–15 and the attack on Suez were both German ideas, for example. But the war also decreased German officers' power in several ways. With three exceptions, no German officer commanded troops. . . . [However,] the Turkish interpretation of the treacherous Armenians and Greeks and of the requirements of "military necessity" became for many German officers simply facts that formed the basis of their own reckoning. . . . The credulity of many German officers toward the prodigious Turkish propaganda campaign . . . came from several sources . . . [notably] the similarity between the story that Turkish officers told and their own military-cultural assumptions about a world of enemies and traitors, the instrumentalization of civilians for military purposes, and the necessity of using force to the end. . . .

Did German staff officers initiate the deportations in eastern Anatolia? And if they did, what did they mean by deportation? We know that some German staff officers did indeed advise the Turkish army to deport Armenian civilians. But the timing of their advice is unclear. . . . It is possible, in my judgment likely, that [Friedrich] Bronsart [von Schellendorf, the German chief of the Ottoman General Staff], [Lieutenant Colonel Felix] Guse, and [Lieutenant Colonel Otto von] Feldmann [who served as head of operations in the Ottoman General Staff] (who all accepted the standard Turkish stories of Armenian perfidy) recommended clearing the rear echelon of the [Ottoman] 3rd Army by deportation in late winter and early spring 1905. That advice inadvertently gave Enver [Pasha, the CUP's minister of war and leader of the 1913 military coup that had brought the Young Turk movement to power in the Ottoman Empire] and [Mehmet] Talât [the CUP's minister of the interior] the cover they wanted to pursue the CUP's ideologically driven "final solution" [to the "Armenian problem"], whose first steps they had already taken. . . .

Feldmann and Guse explained the standard logic behind the German recommendations: the military necessity to save the weak Turkish army required removing all potential threats and, without hesitation, instrumentalizing civilians. This thinking was consistent with standard assumptions of [German] military culture as we have seen them operate elsewhere. Enver cloaked the provisional [Ottoman] law of 27 May 1915, which was the legal cover for the genocide, in the mantle of military necessity. . . . Although the documentary evidence will only permit us to speculate about whether German officers' recommendations helped precipitate the shift in CUP policy from provocative killings to mass murder via deportation, it clearly shows that a few officers advised deportations even after they knew that deportation meant death. It is impossible to tell if they actively approved of the consequences . . . or were simply indifferent to them. "Military necessity" covered both positions. And Guse, Feldmann, . . . and Bronsart all continued to cite military necessity to justify the genocide in the 1920s and beyond. . . . The standards of existential military struggle that Germany applied to itself, its troops, civilians, and those in its occupied zones, it also applied to Turkey, where going to extremes took the form of genocide. As long as German leaders, civilian and military, acted from these premises, they could not take effective action. . . .

The processes I have described as issuing from military culture are organizational, meaning that they are not personal or idiosyncratic; furthermore, they are products of bureaucratic functioning. If one regards bureaucracy as a modern phenomenon (which one need not do),

then they are "modern." . . . The [German] military's default program of escalating violence
was positively reinforced from inside Germany, as well. Military culture, for all its autism, was
enmeshed in a dialectical relationship with government and political culture. The incapacities
of Wilhelminian government (to rein [in], correct, or guide the military) intensified military
culture, making it seem stronger and more reliable than mere "politics." That encouraged
civilian leaders to rely more and more on the military and to submit to its perceptions of and
solutions to problems, which increased the pressure on the army to succeed, which in turn
encouraged more extremes in its institution and its culture. . . . This is the reason, in abstract
terms, why the victory of annihilation, the tendency to "final solutions," was so predominant
in pre-war German military culture.

54 • Cumulative Radicalization and the Armenian Genocide
(Donald Bloxham)

*In this controversial 2003 intervention into the debate over the Armenian genocide, Donald Blox-
ham argues that deportation and depredations were the principal modes of destruction in the crum-
bling Ottoman Empire. Yet he insists that the genocidal campaign waged by the embattled Young
Turk regime was the consequence of a cumulative radicalization of policy, not the realization of a
long-standing plan of destruction. According to Bloxham, a professor of modern history at the University of Edinburgh, a confluence of structural developments—imperialism, nationalism, and war—
accounts for the peculiar evolution of the genocidal campaign.*

From late summer 1914, Armenian settlements on either side of the Ottoman borders with
Persia and the Caucasus were plundered by Ottoman forces, and the Armenian menfolk were
killed. From 24 April 1915, prominent members of the Ottoman Armenian community
were incarcerated en masse in Constantinople. From late March to late May, arrest and limited deportations from Armenian communities were also conducted in the Cilicia region to
the south-east, around the Gulf of Alexandretta. Thereafter, in a wave spreading westwards
and southwards throughout the empire from the provinces of eastern Anatolia—the areas of
heaviest Armenian population—the Turkish government, led by *Ittihad ve Terakki Cemiyeti*
(Committee of Union and Progress: CUP), implemented an increasingly radical program of
deportation and murder.

Communal leaders and civilian men were incarcerated and/or murdered outright. The
women, children and elderly were forced to emigrate to the southern desert regions, in modern-day Syria and Iraq, and along the way their numbers were decimated by depredations—
rape, kidnap, mutilation, outright killing and death from exposure, starvation and thirst—at the
hands of gendarmes and soldiers, irregulars, and Muslim tribespeople. Many surviving this
process then perished from privation or disease in desert concentration centers, where they

SOURCE: Donald Bloxham, "The Armenian Genocide of 1915–1916: Cumulative Radicalization and the
Development of a Destruction Policy," *Past and Present*, no. 181 (November 2003): 141–43, 146, 148, 149,
150, 152, 176, 179, 181–82, 190. Reprinted with permission of Oxford University Press.

were left without provision and, in mid-1916, subjected to a further spate of massacres. A total of at least one million Armenians died, more than two-thirds of those deported. Many of the kidnapped, some of the other surviving women, and an indeterminate number of orphans were forcibly converted to Islam—in total 5 to 10 percent of the Ottoman Armenians. . . .

The historiography of this carnage is marked by crude controversy. Besides the denial that the fate of the Armenians constituted genocide, at the heart of the Turkish nationalist literature is the untenable claim that whatever was done was justified by national security in the face of Armenian insurgency. Conversely, opposing scholars, particularly those from the Armenian diaspora, have sought to explain the killing entirely in terms of the prior genocidal intent of the CUP, and to this end have sometimes employed dubious evidence to suggest destruction "plans" conceived well in advance of the genocide. The polemical battle has centered upon a false dichotomy of "ideology" versus "pragmatism" as the basis for governmental measures. On the one hand, the thesis that Armenian revolt objectively "provoked" the CUP to their actions makes no sense if it is accepted that widespread indiscriminate massacre occurred (and the weight of neutral documentation demands it must be). Armenians as a whole were ultimately targeted on the basis of their group identity, and this can only be explained by the CUP's increasingly radical ideology of ethnic exclusivity. On the other hand, just as Nazi racism is insufficient to explain why the "final solution" happened where, when, and how it did, circumstance in 1914–15 was crucial to the development of the most radical of all policies.

For the "Armenian" side, fighting the Turkish apologist line has involved downplaying any notion of Armenian agency, lest it be read as "justifying" CUP action as a pragmatic response. Yet Armenian nationalist activity within and beyond the Ottoman empire was one important catalyst for the destruction process. This was a catalyst (or rather a series thereof) in the proper sense: an element that alters by its introduction the situation to which it is introduced, therefore not a "pretext" or legitimating excuse, as some contend. This article examines the proximate causes of the genocide. Space precludes full analysis of the longer-term causes, which include the history of Turkish-Armenian relations and particularly the nature of the CUP regime. The radicalism of that regime will, to a certain extent, have to be taken as a given, and can be examined in detail elsewhere. The article contends, however, that there was no a priori blueprint for genocide, and that it emerged from a series of more limited regional measures in a process of cumulative policy radicalization. Among other things, this article is a plea for the *normalization* of the study of state-sponsored mass murder, and for a recognition that it emerges, like many other governmental policies, in a spectrum of regimes, often piecemeal, informed by ideology but according to changing circumstances.

Several interconnected developments affected Muslim-Christian, and especially Turkish-Armenian, relations: the rise of nationalism among the subject peoples of the empire; the territorial disintegration of the Ottoman polity; and hegemonic Great Power intervention in its affairs—all key elements of the "eastern question." . . . As Ottoman control over the European provinces was eroded, Turkish nationalists looked eastwards to see Anatolia as an indivisible whole, the seedbed for Turkic-Muslim national renewal. Though no ethnie comprised an absolute majority of the inhabitants of eastern Anatolia, Armenians formed a plurality, alongside Kurds. These Armenians would come to be seen as an internal obstacle to ethnoreligious homogeneity, and, the other side of the coin, with their development of a greater national consciousness during the nineteenth century, as a potentially disloyal or separatist Christian community in these "imagined" heartlands. . . .

The late nineteenth century brought in an era of violent and often deadly repression of the Armenians. Between 1894 and 1896, 80,000–100,000 were killed in the eastern provinces in a series of sustained massacres during the regime of the ruthless and paranoid Abdülhamid II, and certainly with his quiescent knowledge. Though not a genocide, since the victims were generally adult males and the killings had a regional pattern, this was an attack on the Armenians as a whole, combining elements of pogrom against a minority and calculated use of force against a protonational group—a sort of "cull." In 1909, the year following the coup that introduced the second Ottoman constitutional period, CUP forces were implicated in the massacre of around 20,000 Armenians in the Adana province in Cilicia, supposedly to repress increasingly forthright calls for Armenian separatism, during a crackdown on a reactionary counter-revolt. . . . [It followed] a consolidation of power under a more radical and explicitly Turkish nationalist leadership in an internal coup by the previously discredited CUP. The new ruling triumvirate consisted of Talât, Minister of the Interior and subsequently Grand Vizier; Enver, Minister of War; and Cemal, Minister of the Marine and Governor of Syria, backed behind the scenes by the party's central committee. The CUP leadership cadre consisted of ruthless activists as well as more "theorized" ethnonationalists . . . , informed by half-digested notions of social Darwinism. These would be the driving force behind the genocide and the other population policies enacted during the First World War. . . .

[Yet], the construction of a potential apparatus of destruction throughout 1914 is not a "smoking gun," as has been suggested by one influential scholar. The *Teshkilati Mahsusa*, or Special Organization, an irregular military force, was mobilized again for the world war. At its height between 1914 and 1918 it consisted of 30,000–40,000 men, drawn from the ranks of the Turkish gendarmerie and Muslim bands, including *muhacirler* and criminals specially released from prison. It was staffed by young army officers, but civilians from the CUP were integrally involved at the highest level. However ruthlessly it behaved prior to the spring of 1915, as in the pre-war harassing of Greek communities, the development of the Special Organization in 1914 is not a reliable indicator of genocidal intent. It originated as a means of forwarding the ethnic war outside Turkish boundaries by irredentist agitation, guerilla warfare and assassination, including of prominent Armenians. . . . The precise time of its change to a dedicated instrument of indiscriminate mass murder is unclear. . . .

If general deportation was not itself a long-planned move, that does not mean there was no pressure from different Turkish quarters for extreme measures and a final reckoning. Talât freely admitted to [U.S. Ambassador Henry] Morgenthau that the decision arose out of great deliberation in the CUP central committee, but this is less indicative of a plan than of the ongoing search for a "solution" of the correct nature and magnitude. . . . A plausible explanation for the absence of comprehensive anti-Armenian measures up to this point is Talât's own claim that he feared the international condemnation general deportation would bring. . . . By late May [1915], after a series of stages of radicalization in Turkish policy, the move to a decision for general deportation was probably not a question of the shedding of any vestige of moral restraint. It was more a matter of logistics, of concern for Turkey's image, even perhaps of imagination, in terms of finally seizing the moment to "solve the Armenian question." At the same time, we should not, conversely, imagine that as soon as Talât and Enver opted for general measures they decided that each and every Armenian should die. First, the death of every single Armenian was not crucial for the fulfillment of the aim of destroying the Armenian national presence in Anatolia and Cilicia. . . . Secondly, it is unlikely that the CUP leaders instantly developed a precise template of how their inherently murderous scheme would unfold across the empire. A discrete decision for total murder, as endlessly debated in the historiography of the Nazi "final solution," is a product of the *ex post facto* ruminations of genocide scholars. . . .

Pinpointing the precise time within that period of radicalization at which a state framework that is demonstrably permissive of murder and atrocity becomes explicitly genocidal is extremely difficult and unlikely ever to be achieved definitively. One scholar of a new wave to have debunked the idea of a unilinear progression from idea to act via a "Führer order" in the Jewish genocide is Peter Longerich. To borrow from his analysis of the development of the "final solution," if we think more along the lines of a "policy of annihilation" we get the idea of a general consensus of destruction of the Armenian national community, a consensus which developed and was augmented over time around broad principles of discrimination and xenophobia, progressing from notions of removal by dilution and/or assimilation to physical removal by deportation and/or murder. Thus phases of acceleration and radicalization become more appropriate terms of reference than discernable, discreet shifts in intent.

55 • Hunger by Design: *Holodomor* in Ukraine (Andrea Graziosi)

A topic insufficiently addressed in genocide studies is the role of man-made disasters, including famine. In this 2008 essay, Andrea Graziosi attends to the topic for an insufficiently covered historical period: Soviet-era communism. Just as in the case of the Irish Potato Famine of the mid-nineteenth century, the politics of starvation demand further scrutiny in the Soviet Union as well. A professor of history at the University of Naples, Graziosi asks whether the series of famines that wrecked havoc in the USSR in the 1930s can legitimately be considered instances of genocide. He distinguishes with great care interlocking events, revealing a temporal and spatial complexity that sheds new light on the course of what has become known as the Holodomor *("death by hunger").*

Between the end of 1932 and the summer of 1933, famine in the USSR killed, in half the time, approximately seven times as many people as the Great Terror of 1937–1938. It was the peak of famines that had started in 1931, and it constituted the turning point of the decade as well as a Soviet prewar history's main event. With its approximately five million victims . . . , compared to the one to two million victims of 1921–1922 and 1946–1947, this also was the most severe famine in Soviet history and an event that left its mark for decades. . . . Since 1987–1988,

SOURCE: Andrea Graziosi, "The Soviet 1931–1933 Famines and the Ukrainian Holodomor: Is a New Interpretation Possible, and What Would Its Consequences Be?" in Halyna Hryn, ed., *Hunger by Design: The Great Ukrainian Famine in Its Soviet Context* (Cambridge, Mass.: Harvard Ukrainian Research Institute, 2008), 1–2, 3–4, 6, 7, 8, 10–12. Reprinted with permission of the publisher.

the rediscovery and interpretation of the Famine have played a key role in Ukraine in discussion between supporters of the democratization process and those who still adhere to a pro-communist ideology. The *Holodomor* (the word coined to mean hunger-related mass extermination, implying intentionality) thus moved to the center of the political and cultural debate, becoming part of the process of state and nation building in Ukraine....

On one side [in this debate] there are what we could call "A" people. They support the genocide thesis and see in the Famine an event artificially organized in order to: (a) break the peasants and/or (b) alter (destroy) the Ukrainian nation's social fabric, which obstructed the transformation of the USSR into a despotic empire. On the other side we have "B" people, who, though fully recognizing the criminal nature of Stalin's policies, deem it necessary to study the Famine as a "complex phenomenon," in which many factors, from the geopolitical situation to the modernization effort, played a role in Moscow's intentions and decisions. I believe that today we have most of the elements needed for a new, and more satisfactory, interpretative hypothesis, capable of taking into account both the general and complex Soviet picture and the undeniable relevance of the national question....

In order to formulate this new interpretation, we need to first define the object of our investigation. As should be clear by now, we are in fact dealing with what it would be more correct to call, on a pan-Soviet level, the *1931–1933 famines*, which had of course common causes and common background, but included at least two very different and special phenomena: the Kazakhstan famine-*cum*-epidemics of 1931–1933 and the Ukrainian-Kuban (the latter area, though belonging to the Russian republic's province of Northern Caucasus, being mostly inhabited by Ukrainians) Holodomor of late 1932 to early 1933. Many past misunderstandings have been caused by the confusion between these two national tragedies and the general phenomenon that provided their framework.... A very clear distinction between the general phenomenon and its republic-level or regional manifestations should therefore be introduced in the Soviet case. However, most "A" supporters are in fact speaking specifically of the Holodomor, while many of the "B" proponents think on a pan-Soviet scale.... The second step toward a new interpretation consists of yet another analytic distinction. We must separate the 1931–1932 "spontaneous" famines—they, too, of course, were direct, if undesired consequences of choices made in 1928–1929—from the post-September 1932 Famine, which took on such terrible features not least because of human decision.... Finally, the third step we need to take is to gather and combine useful elements from both "A" and "B" and drop their unsatisfactory parts....

If one analyzes the Famine's origins and pre-autumn 1932 developments on a pan-Soviet level, it seems arduous to claim that famine was the conscious goal of those policies, as it is maintained by those who support the hypothesis that famine was willfully implemented to break the peasant resistance or to execute a Moscow- (sometimes meaning Russian-) planned Ukrainian genocide. However, the intensity, course, and consequences of the phenomenon, which new studies and new documents allow us to analyze, were undeniably and substantially *different* in different regions and republics. Out of the six to seven million victims (demographers now impute to 1930–1931 part of the deaths previously imputed to 1932–1933), 3.5 to 3.8 million died in Ukraine; 1.3 to 1.5 million in Kazakhstan (where deaths reached their peak in relation to the population size, exterminating 33 to 38 percent of the Kazakhs and 8 to 9 percent of the Europeans); and several hundred thousand in Northern Caucasus and, on a lesser scale, in the Volga, where the most harshly hit area coincided with the German autonomous republic.... The extreme figures for Ukraine are explained by the Famine's different course there, for which different Moscow policies were largely responsible.

In Ukraine, as elsewhere, in the spring of 1932 local officials, village teachers, and republican leaders noted the spreading of hunger and the beginning of a mass rural exodus. Stalin, urged by the Ukrainian party, which asked for a reduction in procurements, acknowledged in early June that this [suffering and starvation as a consequence of hunger] was indeed necessary, at least in the most hard-hit areas, also out of a "sense of justice." . . . When, as it was to be expected, procurement proved unsatisfactory throughout the grain-producing lands, [Viacheslav] Molotov, [Lazar] Kaganovich, and Pavel Postyshev were sent to Ukraine, Northern Caucasus, and the Volga to redress the situation. The decision to *use the famine*, thus enormously and artificially strengthening it, in order to impart a lesion to peasants who refused the new serfdom was . . . taken in the fall of 1932, when the crisis caused by the first five-year plan peaked.... The punishment was tragically simple: he who does not work—that is, does not accept the kolkhoz system [a system of collective farming instituted in the wake of the October Revolution of 1917]—will not eat. . . . Most of the stricken areas were not extended any help until the spring of 1933. . . . The fact that . . . the decision to use the Famine took on very specific traits in Ukraine and Kuban is confirmed by measures that were, at least in part, very different from those taken on a pan-Soviet scale. . . . The decision . . . opened the way for the repression of local officials who had helped out starving peasant families by distributing grain to them. Hundreds of such officials were shot and thousands arrested, often on the charge of "populism." . . . Famine thus took on forms and dimensions much bigger than it would have if nature had followed its course. It was less intense, in terms of both drought and the area it affected, than the 1921–1922 Famine (the 1932 crop, though quite low, was still higher than the 1945 crop, when there were no comparable mass hunger-related deaths), yet it caused three to four times as many victims—essentially because of political decisions that aimed at saving the regime from crisis to which its very policies had led and at assuring the victory of the "great offensive" launched four years previously. . . .

The adoption of the term Holodomor seems therefore legitimate, as well as necessary, to mark a distinction between the pan-Soviet phenomenon of 1931–1933 and the Ukrainian Famine *after* the summer of 1932. . . . The number of victims makes the Soviet 1931–1933 famines into a set of phenomena that, in the framework of European history, can be compared only to later Nazi crimes. . . . *Was there also* a Ukrainian genocide? The answer seems to be *no* if one thinks of a famine conceived by the regime, or—this being even more untenable—by Russia, to destroy the Ukrainian people. It is equally *no* if one adopts a restrictive definition of genocide as the planned will to exterminate all the members of a religious or ethnic group, in which case only the Holocaust would qualify. In 1948, however, even the rather strict UN definition of genocide listed among possible genocidal acts, side by side with "killing members of the group, and causing serious bodily or mental harm to members of the group," *"deliberately inflicting on members of the group conditions of life calculated to bring about its physical destruction in whole or in part."* . . . I believe that the answer to our question, "Was the Holodomor a genocide?" cannot but be positive.

Between the end of 1932 and the summer of 1933 . . . Stalin and the regime he controlled and coerced . . . consciously executed, as part of a drive directed at breaking the peasantry, an anti-Ukrainian policy aimed at mass extermination and causing a genocide. . . . This genocide was the product of a famine that was not willfully caused with such aim in mind, but was willfully maneuvered towards this end once it came about as the unanticipated result of the regime policies. . . . It took place within a context that saw Stalin punishing with hunger, and applying terror to, a number of national and ethnosocial groups he felt to be actually or potentially dangerous. . . . From this perspective, the relationship between the Holodomor and the other tragic punishments by repression of 1932–1933 do in a way recall the already-mentioned relationship between Nazi repressions and the Holocaust. It did not aim at exterminating the *whole* nation, it did not kill people *directly*, and it was motivated and constructed theoretically and politically—might one say "rationally"?—rather than ethnically or racially. . . . From this perspective, the Holocaust is exceptional because it represents the purest, and therefore qualitatively different, genocide imaginable. It thus belongs in another category. Yet at the same time it represents the apex of a multilayered pyramid, whose steps are represented by other tragedies, and to whose top the Holodomor is close.

56 ◆ The Soviet Deportation of the Chechen-Ingush (Norman N. Naimark)

Like the question of the Holodomor, the Soviet deportation of the Chechen-Ingush has received only scant attention in the annals of genocide. Whether or not we agree that the 1944 ethnic cleansing of the Chechen and Ingush peoples in the Caucasus amounts to genocide (as we now use the term), it behooves students of the phenomenon to acquaint themselves with the dynamics of destruction. What was peculiar about Stalin's campaign, says Norman Naimark, a professor of history at Stanford University, in his 2001 book was the will to destroy the Chechen and Ingush nations without necessarily eliminating their peoples.

New concepts are consistently being invented to describe, classify, and arrange events of the past in order to understand them in the present. In this sense, "ethnic cleansing," which was used with increasing frequency after May 1992, is little different from the term "genocide," which derived its meaning from Rafael [*sic*] Lemkin's writings during World War II. . . .

A new term was needed because ethnic cleansing and genocide are two different activities, and the differences between them are important. As in the case of determining first-degree murder, intentionality is the critical distinction. Genocide is the intentional killing off of a part or all of an ethnic, religious, or national group; the murder of a people or peoples (in German, *Völkermord*) is the objective. The intention of ethnic cleansing is to remove a people and often all traces of them from a concrete territory. The goal, in other words, is to get rid of the "alien" nationality, ethnic, or religious group and to seize control of the territory they had formerly inhabited. At one extreme of its spectrum, ethnic cleansing is closer to forced deportation or what has been called "population transfer"; the idea is to get people to move, and the

SOURCE: Norman M. Naimark, *Fires of Hatred: Ethnic Cleansing in Twentieth-Century Europe* (Cambridge, Mass.: Harvard University Press, 2001), 3–4, 89–90, 91–92, 94, 95–97, 98, 104–5. Reprinted with permission of the publisher.

means are meant to be legal and semi-legal. At the other extreme, however, ethnic cleansing and genocide are distinguishable only by the ultimate intent. Here, both literally and figuratively, ethnic cleansing bleeds into genocide, as mass murder is committed in order to rid the land of a people.

Further complicating the distinction between ethnic cleansing and genocide is the fact that forced deportation seldom takes place without violence, often murderous violence. People do not leave their homes on their own. . . . The result is that forced deportation often becomes genocidal, as people are violently ripped from their native towns and villages and killed when they try to stay. Even when forced deportation is not genocidal in its intent, it is often genocidal in its effects. . . .

In addition to making a useful distinction from genocide, the term "ethnic cleansing" is also valuable because of its associated meanings. In its Slavic form *chishchenie* in Russian and *ciscenja* in Serbo-Croatian, cleansing often refers to political elimination or the purging of enemies. The [Stalinist] purges in the Soviet Union [in the 1930s], for example, were called *chistki*. The German word for cleansing, *Säuberung*, has the same kind of meaning, especially in the history of communism, but is also tied to the development of racial "science" in Germany at the turn of the [twentieth] century. . . . Although the phrase ethnic cleansing itself was not used in the German or Slavic context, as far as I know, at the beginning of the century, German racial thinking did create the term *völkische Flurbereinigung*, which uses a metaphor from agriculture to indicate the cleansing, in this case of alien ethnic elements from the soil. . . .

Ethnic cleansing and genocide often take place against the background of war or during the transition from war to peace. World War II exacerbated in every way Stalin's fears regarding national enemies at home and abroad. . . . Stalin looked at his role as that of a Russian tsar, conflating his own Soviet and Russian identity as *vozhd*—leader. . . . The new Soviet man and woman was to look like a Russian (Belorussian or Ukrainian), speak like a Russian, and—if not actually be Russian or Slavic—to recognize the inherent superiority of the Russians in the historical development of the lands in which he or she lived and in contemporary affairs. . . . Any nation that stood in the way of this melding of Soviet and Russian patriotism was imperiled. The deportations of Chechen-Ingush and of the Crimean Tatars in 1944 can be understood only as part of this story. . . .

The history of these peoples in the northern Caucasus goes back almost six thousand years. . . . Known in the period up to the 1917 revolution simply as *gor'tsy* or "mountaineers," the Chechens and Ingush operated as clans and groups of clans, sometimes more closely tied to other "nations" in the region than to their own "people." . . . With the Russian penetration of the Caucasus in the first half of the nineteenth century, Chechens and Ingush—like other Muslim mountaineers—found themselves the object of Cossack raids and incursions into what they thought was their homeland, and they fought bitterly to preserve the integrity of their customs and law. . . .

World War II provided the immediate background for the deportations of the Chechen and Ingush peoples. The official justification for the deportations emphasized the collaboration of the Chechens [with Nazi Germany] during the fighting. . . . Although hardly the collaborators portrayed by the Soviets, the Chechens and Ingush were unquestionably a thorn in the side of Moscow authorities. . . . The attachment of the Chechen and Ingush to their homelands, the difficulty of imposing modern state forms on a resilient traditional society, and the ability of the Chechens and Ingush to resist both direct pressures from Moscow and the modernization expected from the granting of national institutional forms made the Soviet leadership determined to deal with them once and for all. This was a Soviet-style final solution to an ongoing and scabrous problem of national antagonism. . . .

[Lavrenty] Beria [as deputy head, later head, of the NKVD (Soviet People's Commissariat for Internal Affairs), the notorious ministry coordinating all security affairs in the 1930s, in command of the Soviet security and secret police apparatus] was in full charge of the operation in the northern Caucasus. When the Red Army liberated the Caucasus from the last *Wehrmacht* units in January and February 1943, Beria initiated the first discussion of operation *Chechevista*. . . . On the night of February 23–24, 1944, Beria ordered the operation to start. He called in Chechen party leaders and told them about the fate of their people. . . . Troops went from house to house informing the residents that they had half an hour . . . to get themselves ready for transport. . . . Troops assembled villagers and townspeople, loaded them onto trucks—many deportees remembered that they were Studebakers, fresh from Lend-Lease deliveries over the Iranian border—and delivered them at previously designated railheads. Anyone who resisted was shot, but the NKVD reported only sporadic cases of resistance. From the railway stations, the Chechen and Ingush nations were loaded into boxcars and sent off to Kazakhstan and Kirghizia, which were to be their domiciles until the mid-1950s.

The NKVD ordered all Chechens and Ingush out of their homelands. No exceptions were allowed. . . . Those who could not be moved were shot. . . . The entire Chechen and Ingush nations, 496,460 people, were deported from their homeland. . . . As in every case of ethnic cleansing and forced deportation of peoples, large numbers of Chechens died in the process. Some 3,000 perished even before being deported. . . . One can extrapolate . . . that roughly 10,000 died from disease, hunger, and cold. The rail cars were sealed; there was no food or water; sanitation was nonexistent. Typhus left thousands dead and dying. The trains stopped periodically to dispose of corpses, but the locals were forbidden to help. . . . The largest death toll came in the days and months after arrival—roughly 100,000 in the first three years (again extrapolating from NKVD statistics). . . .

Some Chechen and Ingush historians assert that the deportations of 1944 constituted genocide against their nations. But if it was genocide, it was genocide with a particular Soviet twist. Stalin and Beria's goal—as best we can tell—was to destroy the Chechen and Ingush nations without necessarily eliminating their peoples. Certainly, the fate of the Chechen-Ingush Autonomous Republic [which Moscow had established in 1934] leads one to think that the Soviet leaders were in search of a permanent solution to the Chechen question. The region was officially dissolved in 1944, and neighboring Daghestan, northern Ossetia, Georgia, and Stavropol region eagerly seized and absorbed their designated sections of the Chechen and Ingush lands. . . . No one spoke of the deportations in the newspapers, in meetings, or in public. Post-deportation records of Grozny *obkom* meetings never mention the peoples who had once lived there. They disappeared even from history books and encyclopedias. . . .

The deportations of the Chechens-Ingush . . . fit the definition of ethnic cleansing as it has been developed in this book. Stalin, Beria, and the Soviet leadership intentionally and forcibly removed these peoples from their homelands and deported them to regions from which they were allowed no escape. That tens of thousands died during the deportations and after they [the Chechen-Ingush] arrived at their destinations did not overly concern Soviet authorities, though killing off these nations in a genocidal attack was clearly not the Soviets' intention. Instead, policies were implemented to reeducate the Chechen-Ingush ... to force them to forget their homelands and their cultures. The "human material" was salvageable; just the nations—as nations—were slated to disappear through assimilation and detachment from their homelands. This was different from Hitler's [genocidal] attack on the Jews and gypsies, where humans themselves were [deemed] inherently tainted and therefore doomed to extinction.

57 • Bloodlands: Europe between Hitler and Stalin
(Timothy Snyder)

A historian of East Central Europe based at Yale University, Timothy Snyder, in his book Blood-
lands (2010), challenges his audience to reconsider their preconceived notions of the nature of Nazi
and Soviet atrocities. By adopting a uniquely pan-European lens, Snyder drives home the frequently
overlooked point that both Hitler and Stalin killed most of their millions of victims far away from
either Germany or Russia. Most of the killing sites were on the periphery of both empires, in what
Snyder terms the "bloodlands," by which he means the swath of land that stretches from central
Poland to western Russia and includes Ukraine, Belarus, and the Baltics. If we neglect the singu-
lar importance of the bloodlands, says Snyder, we misunderstand "the horror of the twentieth
century."

In the middle of Europe in the middle of the twentieth century, the Nazi and Soviet regimes murdered some fourteen million people. The place where all of the victims died, the blood-lands, extends from central Poland to western Russia, through Ukraine, Belarus, and the Baltic States. During the consolidation of National Socialism and Stalinism (1933–1938), the joint German-Soviet occupation of Poland (1939–1941), and then the German-Soviet war (1941–1945), mass violence of a sort never before seen in history was visited upon this region. The victims were chiefly Jews, Belarusians, Ukrainians, Poles, Russians, and Balts, the peoples native to these lands. The fourteen million were murdered over the course of only twelve years, between 1933 and 1945, while both Hitler and Stalin were in power. Though their homelands became battlefields midway through this period, these people were all victims of murderous policy rather than casualties of war. ...

Auschwitz is the most familiar killing site of the bloodlands. Today Auschwitz stands for the Holocaust, and the Holocaust for the evil of a century. Yet the people registered as laborers at Auschwitz had a chance of surviving: thanks to the memoirs and novels written by survivors, its name is known. Far more Jews, most of the Polish Jews, were gassed in other German death factories where almost everyone died, and whose names are less often recalled: Treblinka, Chelmno, Sobibór, Belzec. Still more Jews, Polish or Soviet or Baltic Jews, were shot over ditches and pits. Most of these Jews died near where they had lived, in occupied Poland,

SOURCE: Timothy Snyder, *Bloodlands: Europe between Hitler and Stalin* (New York: Basic Books, 2010), vii–ix, x, xi–xiv. Reprinted with permission of the publisher.

Lithuania, Latvia, Soviet Ukraine, and Soviet Belarus. The Germans brought Jews from else-where to the bloodlands to be killed. Jews arrived by train to Auschwitz from Hungary, Czechoslovakia, France, the Netherlands, Greece, Belgium, Yugoslavia, Italy, and Norway, German Jews were deported to the cities of the bloodlands, to Lódz or Kaunas or Minsk or Warsaw, before being shot or gassed. . . . The German mass murder of Jews took place in oc-cupied Poland, Lithuania, Latvia, and the Soviet Union, not in Germany itself. Hitler was an anti-Semitic politician in a country with a small Jewish community. Jews were *fewer than one percent* of the German population when Hitler became chancellor in 1993, and *about one quarter of one percent* by the beginning of the Second World War. . . .

The Soviet Union defeated Nazi Germany on the eastern front in the Second World War, thereby earning Stalin the gratitude of millions and a crucial part in the establishment of the postwar order in Europe. Yet Stalin's own record of mass murder was almost as imposing as Hitler's. Indeed, in times of peace it was far worse. In the name of defending and modernizing the Soviet Union, Stalin oversaw the starvation of millions and the shooting of three quarters of a million people in the 1930s. Stalin killed his own citizens no less efficiently than Hitler killed the citizens of other countries. Of the fourteen million people deliberately murdered in the bloodlands between 1993 and 1945, a third belong to the Soviet account. . . .

The bloodlands were where most of Europe's Jews lived, where Hitler and Stalin's impe-rial plans overlapped, where the Wehrmacht [German army] and the Red Army fought, and where the Soviet NKVD [Soviet secret police] and the German SS [German paramilitary unit] concentrated their forces. Most killing sites were in the bloodlands: in the political geography of the 1930s and early 1940s, this meant Poland, the Baltic States, Soviet Belarus, Soviet Ukraine, and the western fringe of Soviet Russia. Stalin's crimes are often associated with Russia, and Hitler's with Germany. But the deadliest part of the Soviet Union was its non-Russian periphery, and Nazis generally killed beyond Germany. The horror of the twen-tieth century is thought to be located in the camps. But the concentration camps are not where most of the victims of National Socialism and Stalinism died. These misunderstand-ings regarding the sites and methods of mass killing prevent us from perceiving the horror of the twentieth century.

Germany was the site of concentration camps liberated by the Americans and the British in 1945; Russian Siberia was of course the site of much of the Gulag, made known in the West by Alexander Solzhenitsyn. The images of these camps, in photographs or in prose, only sug-gest the history of German and Soviet violence. . . . Ninety percent of those who entered the Gulag left it alive. Most of the people who entered German concentration camps (as opposed to the German gas chambers, death pits, and prisoner-of-war camps) also survived. The fate of concentration camp inmates, horrible though it was, is distinct from that of those many millions who were gassed, shot, or starved. The distinction between concentration camps and killing sites cannot be made perfectly: people were executed and people were starved in camps. Yet there is a difference between a camp sentence and a death sentence, between labor and gas, between slavery and bullets. The tremendous majority of the mortal victims of both the German and the Soviet regimes never saw a concentration camp. . . . The German and Soviet concentration camps surround the bloodlands, from both east and west, blurring the black with their shades of gray.

At the end of the Second World War, American and British forces liberated German concentration camps such as Belsen and Dachau, but the western Allies liberated *none* of the important death facilities. . . . American and British forces reached *none* of the bloodlands and saw *none* of the major killing sites. It is not just that American and British forces saw none of the places where the Soviets killed, leaving the crimes of Stalinism to be documented after the end of the Cold War and the opening of the archives. It is that they never saw the places where the *Germans* killed, meaning that understanding of Hitler's crimes has taken just as long. The photographs and films of German concentration camps were the closest that most westerners ever came to perceiving the mass killing. Horrible though these images were, they were only hints at the history of the bloodlands. They are not the whole story; sadly, they are not even an introduction.

58 • Mass Murder Technologies (Jacques Semelin)

As the founder of the useful Online Encyclopedia of Mass Violence, the French social scientist Jacques Semelin has done his share to explore the similarities and differences in historical and contemporary instances of genocide. In his book Purify and Destroy (2007), *Semelin, who is also a professor at the Institut d'Études Politiques in Paris and a researcher with France's Centre National de la Recherche Scientifique, draws attention to, among other things, the ways perpetrators kill. Comparing and contrasting cases, he points out that the perpetration of mass violence always involves a multitude of methods. What follows from this observation is the imperative to explain and understand what factors determine the choice of "mass murder technologies."*

To analyze killing methods, we must first manage to overcome the horror and repulsion which their description arouses. . . . I will limit myself here to insisting on the fact that methods of killing should be viewed as a human activity: certainly not one that is really like any other . . . but one that is *also* like others. These methods always reflect to some extent a country's economic and technical development, its modes of cultural expression, etc. If the economy is predominantly rural, it is no surprise that farming and field tools (machete, knife, hatchet) are used to kill, and are wittingly involved as the tools used by extremist propaganda. Similarly, the perfection of the process of murder by gassing developed in Germany proclaims the particular level of scientific and technological development attained by that country.

Some killing methods can be common to several countries, like for example, the execution by machine gun or firing squad. Used for the first time during the American Civil War, and for repressing the Communards of the Paris Commune, the machine gun proved formidably efficient when it came to "mowing down" the adversary and terrorizing survivors. It also gave Westerners crushing superiority in their conquest of Africa at the end of the nineteenth century. The use of this portable and powerful weapon thus became widespread: it crops up again and again in the majority of twentieth-century mass murders, from the Armenians to Rwanda

SOURCE: Jacques Semelin, *Purify and Destroy: The Political Uses of Massacre and Genocide* (New York: Columbia University Press, 2007), 233–34, 235, 236. Reproduced with permission of the publisher.

and including the mass massacres of Jews by the *Einsatzgruppen* [mobile death squads during the Holocaust].

Once again it should be pointed out that like any other form of collective action, methods of destruction sometimes borrow from tradition, and in other respects constitute an innovation. So in Bosnia ethnic cleansing operations in the 1990s made partial use of procedures resorted to during the Balkan Wars at the start of the twentieth century, such as the burning of houses (to drive out inhabitants declared to be undesirable). Analyzing these forms of violence obliges us to distinguish between those that stem from tradition and those that derive from modernity or a re-invented tradition. When on 2 May 1991 [Vojislav] Seselj's men set about massacring Croatian policemen at Borovo Selo [near Vukovar in northeastern Croatia], going so far as to pluck out their eyes and cut off their ears, they rekindled in a single stroke the painful past that some fifty years earlier had seen the Chetnicks [usually spelled "Chetnik," a movement of Serbian nationalist and monarchist paramilitary organizations that collaborated with Nazi Germany and fascist Italy during World War II] and Ustashis [commonly known as the "Ustaše," a Croatian fascist movement that violently aided the Axis powers in the occupation of Yugoslavia, notably much of the territory of what today is Croatia and Bosnia and Herzegovina as well as parts of modern-day Serbia] massacring Croatians and Serbs respectively. And once again they were not alone, because Germans, Italian fascists and Tito Partisans alike had done the same. Against a background of nationalist revivals in the early 1990s, this event could not fail to arouse immediate and impassioned invective on Serbian and Croatian television screens, contributing just a little more to tipping the conflict over into war.

On the other hand there is no doubt that the development of the gas chambers, principally installed in Poland, is an unprecedented event in the history of mass murders. The first gas lorries (carbon monoxide) came into operation in Chelmno in November 1941, and then during 1942 several Zyklon B gas chambers were put into service at Belzec, Sobibor, Treblinka, Auschwitz-Birkenau and Majdanek—constituting an incredible and terrifying "advance" in the domain of techniques for putting large numbers of people to death. . . . What is literally stupefying is how massacre from this point on took on the character of an industrial activity of "waste" disposal. . . . Nevertheless, for the Nazis killing by gas was only an additional method of destroying the Jews: shootings had not ceased any more than the slower extermination techniques in the camps. And when these camps had to be evacuated (when the Russian arrived) the Nazis organized "death marches" in which tens of thousands of prisoners died.

All too often we tend to boil down the history of the mass murder process to a single killing method. It is absurd, for instance, to state that the killings in Rwanda in 1994 were all done with machetes, as some Westerners have intimated. Numerous reports claimed that the Tutsis were also killed with other instruments (cudgels, hoes, hammers), grenades and other firearms, not to mention when victims were burnt in churches where they had hoped to find refuge. . . . In Bosnia knives were also used, along with grenades and machine guns as in Srebrenica. It was convenient to also make use of the steep terrain in this region, for example to dispose easily of bodies by throwing them into ravines or deep river gorges. In general mass murder combines several methods of killing—often complementary—that evolve depending on the circumstances, the killers' experience and the means at their disposal at the time.

59 • Ordinary Men: Reserve Police Battalion 101 in Poland (Christopher R. Browning)

With Ordinary Men *(1992), Christopher Browning produced one of the most frequently cited and most widely admired books in genocide studies. Browning, a professor of history at the University of North Carolina, zeroes in on the micro-organizational dynamics of the Holocaust. By reconstructing in painstaking detail, chiefly from German court documents, the activities—genocidal and otherwise—of Reserve Police Battalion 101 on the territory of the Soviet Union, Browning finds that most of the perpetrators were "ordinary men." Why was it that these unremarkable individuals committed extraordinary atrocities? After weighing a number of explanations, Browning concludes that their involvement in the destruction of Jews was, more than anything, a consequence of group socialization and the collective norms that Reserve Police Battalion 101 developed in enemy territory. Put differently, rather than arriving in the Soviet Union with either a desire or a motive for murder, most of the individuals in his study turned violent in response to the real and imagined expectations of their peers. Participation in group destruction became socially appropriate.*

In mid-March 1942 some 75 to 80 percent of all victims of the Holocaust were still alive, while 20 to 25 percent had perished. A mere eleven months later, in mid-February 1943, the percentages were exactly the reverse. At the core of the Holocaust was a short, intense wave of mass murder. The center of gravity of this mass murder was Poland, where in March 1942, despite two and a half years of terrible hardship, deprivation, and persecution, every major Jewish community was still intact, and where eleven months later only the remains of Polish Jewry survived in a few rump ghettos and labor camps. In short, the German attack on the Jews of Poland was not a gradual or incremental program stretched out over a long period of time, but a veritable blitzkrieg, a massive offensive requiring the mobilization of large numbers of shock troops. This offensive, moreover, came just when the German war effort in Russia hung in the balance. . . .

How had the Germans organized and carried out the destruction of this widespread Jewish population? And where had they found the manpower during this pivotal year of the war [with the Soviet Union] for such an astounding logistical achievement in mass murder? The personnel of the death camps was quite minimal. But the manpower needed to clear the smaller ghettos—to round up and either deport or shoot the bulk of Polish Jewry—was not. . . . Ultimately, the Holocaust took place because at the most basic level individual human beings killed other human beings in large numbers over an extended period of time. The grass-roots perpetrators became "professional killers."

The historian encounters numerous difficulties in trying to write about a unit of such men, among them the problem of sources. In the case of Reserve Police Battalion 101 [a unit of the German Order Police; the majority of its nearly five hundred members hailed from Hamburg], in contrast to many of the killing units operating in the Soviet Union [the Ein-

SOURCE: Christopher R. Browning, *Ordinary Men: Reserve Police Battalion 101 and the Final Solution in Poland*, new edition (New York: Harper Perennial, 2001), xv, xvi, xvii, xviii, 38–39, 41–42, 44–45, 47–48, 121, 142, 159, 161, 162, 164, 165, 169, 170, 171, 176, 184–86, 188–89. Reprinted with permission of the publisher.

satzgruppen], there are few contemporary documents and none that deal explicitly with its killing activities. . . . In writing about Reserve Police Battalion 101, therefore, I have depended heavily upon the judicial interrogations of some 125 men conducted [in Germany] in the 1960s. . . .

When Germany invaded Poland in September 1939, Police Battalion 101, based in Hamburg, was one of the initial battalions attached to a German army group and sent to Poland. . . . On December 17, 1939, the battalion returned to Hamburg, where about a hundred of its career policemen were transferred to form additional units. They were replaced by middle-aged reservists drafted in the fall of 1939. In May 1940, after a period of training, the battalion was dispatched from Hamburg to the Warthegau, one of the four regions in western Poland annexed to the Third Reich as the incorporated territories. . . . In May 1941, the battalion returned to Hamburg and was "practically dissolved." All remaining prewar recruits beneath the rank of noncommissioned officer were distributed to other units, and the ranks were filled with drafted reservists. The battalion had become, in the words of one policeman, a "pure reserve battalion." . . . In June 1942, Reserve Police Battalion 101 was assigned another tour of duty in Poland. . . .

The battalion consisted of 11 officers, 5 administrative officials (in charge of financial matters relating to pay, provisioning, lodging, etc.), and 486 noncommissioned officers and men. . . . The battalion was divided into three companies, each of approximately 140 men at full strength. Two companies were commanded by police captains, the third by the senior reserve lieutenant in the battalion. Each company was divided into three platoons, two of them commanded by reserve lieutenants, and the third by the platoon's senior sergeant. Each platoon was divided into four squads, commanded by a sergeant or corporal. The men were equipped with carbines, the noncommissioned officers with submachine guns. Each company also had a heavy-machine gun detachment. . . .

Of the rank and file, the vast majority were from the Hamburg area. About 63 percent were of working-class background, but few were skilled laborers. The majority of them held typical Hamburg working-class jobs: dock workers and truck drivers were most numerous, but there were also many warehouse and construction workers, machine operators, seamen, and waiters. About 35 percent were lower-middle-class, virtually all of them white-collar workers. Three quarters were in sales of some sort, the one-quarter performed various office jobs, in both the government and private sector. The number of independent artisans and small businessmen was very small. Only a handful (2 percent) were middle-class professionals, and very modest ones at that, such as druggists and teachers. The average age of the men was thirty-nine; over half were between thirty-seven and forty-two, a group considered too old for the army but most heavily conscripted for reserve police duty after September 1939. Among the rank and file policemen, about 25 percent (43 from a sample of 174) were [Nazi] Party members in 1942. Six were *Alte Kämpfer* who had joined the Party before Hitler came to power; another six joined in 1933. . . . Another six men who worked aboard ships were admitted by the Party section for members living overseas. Sixteen joined in 1937. . . . The remaining nine joined in 1939 or later. . . .

By mid-November 1942, following the massacres at Józefów, Łomazy, Serokomla, Końskowola, and elsewhere, and the liquidation of the ghettos in Międzyrzec, Łuków, Parczew, Radzyń, and Kock, the men of Reserve Police Battalion 101 had participated in the outright execution of at least 6,500 Polish Jews and the deportation of at least 42,000 more to the gas chambers of Treblinka. Still their role in the mass murder campaign was not finished. Once the town and ghettos of the northern Lublin district had been cleared of Jews, Reserve Police Battalion 101 was assigned to track down and systematically eliminate all those who had escaped the previous roundups and were now in hiding. In short, they were responsible for making their region completely *judenfrei* [free of Jews].... For a battalion of less than 500 men, the ultimate body count was at least 83,000 Jews....

Why did most men in Reserve Police Battalion 101 become killers, while only a minority of perhaps 10 percent—and certainly no more than 20 percent—did not? A number of explanations have been invoked in the past to explain such behavior: wartime brutalization, racism, segmentation and routinization of the task, special selection of the perpetrators, careerism, obedience to orders, deference to authority, ideological indoctrination, and conformity. These factors are applicable in varying degrees, but none without qualification....

Wartime brutalization through prior combat was not an immediate experience directly influencing the policemen's behavior at [for example] Józefów. Once the killing began, however, the men became increasingly brutalized. As in combat, the horrors of the initial encounter became routine, and the killing progressively easier. In this sense, brutalization was not the cause but the effect of these men's behavior.... No one confronted the reality of mass murder more directly than the men in the woods of Józefów. Segmentation and routinization, the depersonalizing aspects of bureaucratized killing, cannot explain the battalion's initial behavior there.... By age, geographical origin, and social background, the men of Reserve Police Battalion 101 were least likely to be considered apt material out of which to mold future mass killers.... In short, Reserve Police Battalion 101 was not sent to Lublin to murder Jews because it was composed of men specially selected or deemed particularly suited for the task....

Many studies of Nazi killers have suggested a different kind of selection, namely self-selection to the Party and SS [*Schutzstaffel*, or Defense Guard] by unusually violence-prone people.... If Nazi Germany offered unusually numerous career paths that sanctioned and rewarded violent behavior, random conscription from the remaining population—already drained of most of its most violence-prone individuals—would arguably produce even less than an average number of "authoritarian personalities." Self-selection on the basis of personality traits, in short, offers little to explain the behavior of the men of Reserve Police Battalion 101.... Among the perpetrators, of course, orders have traditionally been the most frequently cited explanation of their own behavior.... But as a general rule, even putative duress does not hold up for Reserve Police Battalion 101.... The [judicial] testimonies are filled with stories of men who disobeyed standing orders during the ghetto-clearing operations and did not shoot infants or those attempting to hide or escape. Even men who admitted having taken part in firing squads claimed not to have shot in the confusion and melee of the ghetto clearings or out on patrol when their behavior could not be closely observed....

To what degree ... did the conscious inculcation of Nazi doctrines shape the behavior of the men of Reserve Police Battalion 101? ... The men of Reserve Police Battalion 101, like the rest of German society, were immersed in a deluge of racist and anti-Semitic propaganda. Furthermore, the Order Police provided for indoctrination both in basic training and as an ongoing practice within each unit.... Influenced and conditioned in a general way, imbued with a particular sense of their own superiority and racial kinship as well as Jewish inferiority

Stanley Milgram would be proud

and otherness, many of them undoubtedly were; explicitly prepared for the task of killing Jews they most certainly were not.

Along with ideological indoctrination, a vital factor . . . [to explore is] conformity to the group. The battalion had orders to kill Jews, but each individual did not. Yet 80 to 90 percent of the men proceeded to kill, though almost all of them—at least initially—were horrified and disgusted by what they were doing. To break ranks and step out, to adopt overtly nonconformist behavior, was simply beyond most of the men. It was easier for them to shoot. Why? First of all, by breaking ranks, nonshooters were leaving the "dirty work" to their comrades. Since the battalion had to shoot even if individuals did not, refusing to shoot constituted refusing one's share of an unpleasant collective obligation. It was in effect an asocial act vis-à-vis one's comrades. Those who did not shoot risked isolation, rejection, ostracism—a very uncomfortable prospect within the framework of a tight-knit unit stationed abroad among a hostile population, so that the individual had virtually nowhere else to turn for support and social contact. . . . Coping with the contradictions imposed by the demands of conscience on the one hand and the norms of the battalion on the other led to many tortured attempts at compromise: not shooting infants on the spot but taking them to the assembly point; not shooting on patrol if no "go-getter" was along who might report such squeamishness; bringing Jews to the shooting site and firing but intentionally missing. Only the very exceptional remained indifferent to taunts of "weakling" from their comrades and could live with the fact that they were considered to be "no man." . . .

manliness peer pressure

The behavior of any human being is . . . a very complex phenomenon, and the historian who attempts to "explain" it is indulging in a certain arrogance. When nearly 500 men are involved, to undertake any general explanation of their collective behavior is even more hazardous. What, then, is one to conclude? Most of all, one comes away from the story of Reserve Police Battalion 101 with great unease. This story of ordinary men is not the story of all men. The reserve policemen faced choices, and most of them committed terrible deeds. But those who killed cannot be absolved by the notion that anyone in the same situation would have done as they did. For even among them, some refused to kill and others stopped killing. Human responsibility is ultimately an individual matter. At the same time, however, the collective behavior of Reserve Police Battalion 101 has deeply disturbing implications.

There are many societies afflicted by traditions of racism and caught in the siege mentality of war or threat of war. Everywhere society conditions people to respect and defer to authority, and indeed could scarcely function otherwise. Everywhere people seek career advancement. In every modern society, the complexity of life and the resulting bureaucratization and specialization attenuate the sense of personal responsibility of those implementing official policy. Within virtually every social collective, the peer group exerts tremendous pressures on behavior and sets moral norms. If the men of Reserve Police Battalion 101 could become killers under such circumstances, what group of men cannot?

60 ◆ Belonging and Genocide: Hitler's Community (Thomas Kühne)

Thomas Kühne, a professor of history and the Strassler Family Chair in the Study of Holocaust History at Clark University, describes the consequences of genocidal violence for identity formation on the part of perpetrators in his 2010 book. With particular reference to a small group of Nazi perpetrators stationed in Lithuania during World War II, he illustrates why a sense of belonging is often both cause and consequence of a genocidal campaign. Focusing on these performative aspects of the Holocaust, that is, the nonverbal forms of behavior that also contributed to its development, Kühne offers a glimpse into what he calls a national brotherhood of mass murder, "Hitler's community." By tracing methods of nonlethal destruction such as humiliation and degradation back to this community of belonging, Kühne makes a major contribution to our understanding of the courses of genocide.

Genocidal violence, the destruction of Them, can also bolster the love between Us. When Germans carried out genocidal war against the Jews and other "undesirables" in order to realize the utopia of a purified nation, they not only destroyed what they considered to be dirty and dangerous. They experienced togetherness, cohesion and belonging, and they deluded themselves into believing they would attain a homogenous and harmonious social body, cleansed of pollution, conflict, and inner enemies. The Nazis called this social body a *Volksgemeinschaft*, a people's community. The entire nation would feel as a family or a group of friends, providing closeness, safety, and warmth. Nobody would be alone, everyone would be taken care of, all would feel connected to each other—and all would act in concert. Through committing the Holocaust, Germans gained a feeling for this grand utopia of belonging.

Historians have often deemed this vision nothing more than propaganda. In fact, they have argued, German society never really changed its class and religious cleavages, at least not during the Nazi period. Although this view carries some truth, it leaves one question unanswered. If German society really was so divided, if its unity had been only a façade, why then did it not fall apart, especially after 1942, when Germany's downfall became obvious? My answer is that the Nazis managed to include and utilize even strong anti-Nazi support to support a grand brotherhood of crime—one that left practically no backdoor to escape. . . . And although understood as a community based on criminal conduct, complicity, and cognizance, it was yet presented as morally sacrosanct. The regime propagated a revolutionary ethos that assured Germans that their murderous activities were morally good. . . .

Repudiating the Judeo-Christian traditions of mercy toward the weak and the Enlightenment principles of universalism, individualism, and egalitarianism, Nazi ethics demanded that charity, kindness, and pity be restricted to Aryan Germans. [Claudia] Koonz and other historians have focused on the exclusionary side of pre-1939 Nazi ethics. By contrast, I show how these racially limited ethics worked within the in-group and propelled powerful senti-

SOURCE: Thomas Kühne, *Belonging and Genocide: Hitler's Community, 1918–1945* (New Haven, Conn.: Yale University Press, 2010), 4–5, 68, 74, 75, 76, 77–78, 167–68, 169–70, 171. Reprinted with permission of the publisher.

ments of belonging, togetherness, and community even more during the war and genocide that started in 1939. . . .

From 1941 to 1944, some twenty to thirty officers of the Border Police Station in Nowy Sącs (in German, Neu-Sandez), fifty miles southeast of Krakow in West Galicia, managed to murder thousands of Jews and send another 15,000 or more to Belzec and other death camps. Although these policemen were by no means equally eager to perform genocide, they did not need orders to do so. They developed a murderous dynamic that created a microcosm of the Holocaust, located between mobile death squads and stationary camp guards. . . . In late August 1942, the decisive step of the [so-called] Final Solution was enacted in Nowy Sącs. . . . More than fifteen thousand Jews were made to walk to the next train station where they would be sent to the Belzec death camp. A third group of more than three thousand Jews were deemed too weak to walk. Over the next couple of days, [Joachim] Hamann's [an SS unit leader of Einsatzkommando 3 in Lithuania] unit killed all of them at four different villages, leaving each a site of barbarian cruelty. The largest of these actions took place in Mszana-Dolna. Hamann decided that its entire Jewish population, about nine hundred persons, was not able to walk in the summer heat and thus should be shot on the spot. . . . The local mayor Gelb, a *Volksdeutscher* (an ethnic German who had lived in Poland before 1939), felt particularly responsible for the well-being of the German police officers and bizarrely provided them with a picnic of alcoholic beverages and sandwiches. . . . When the job was finished . . . , the perpetrators could relax. Following an invitation by Mayor Gelb, they joined a feast at the local restaurant. An orchestra played dance music. . . .

What happened in Nowy Sącs occurred in innumerable other places in Nazi-occupied Europe as well. . . . Terror in the East often served as entertainment. In Zhitomir, soldiers could attend special performances of revenge. SS *Einsatzkommando* 4a was in charge of mass shootings in the area. . . . Photos taken at such events do not reveal ashamed spectators but amused ones. They celebrated their splendid community. The "Us" had triumphed over the "other." Kept like trophies, photos of atrocities also illustrated, and were intended to illustrate, the dichotomous social reality of genocide. On the one hand, we see the triumphant group of perpetrators, enjoying themselves committing or watching cruelty. They stick together, they act together, and they feel together. They experience belonging, the epitome of "humanity"— a special notion of "humanity," to be sure. On the other hand there are the isolated, humiliated, naked victims—frightened and freezing, robbed of the signs of their personal identity, all looking alike, no longer retaining their humanity. Cynically, members of the Einsatzgruppen [mobile killing squads] referred to the manner they piled hundreds of corpses in graves [as] "sardine procedure." First isolated and then thrown together, they [the victims] were no longer social beings in the eyes of the perpetrators. "Dissociation" of the victims enhanced "association" of the perpetrators.

The Holocaust did not consist solely of killing the Jews. Before the perpetrators murdered them, they felt compelled to humiliate these victims. They mocked them, and they made them stage grotesque ceremonies. This was not just about sadistic pleasure. In the Holocaust, humiliation was arranged as theater. Degradation carries meaning. It is constructive. According to the sociologist Harold Garfinkel, it binds perpetrators to a collectivity and reinforces their solidarity. By destroying the symbols, the bonds, and the identities of their victims, the perpetrators strengthened their ethics of hardness and thus their own social identity.... Comradeship radiated belonging, togetherness, and security but only the one who conformed, joined in, and was ready to trade in his individual identity for a collective identity gained the benefits of comradeship. Comradeship meant searching for, identifying, and excluding the Other.

The moral grammar of comradeship obeyed one rule: anything was allowed that intensified the group's social life and secured its cohesion. The best way to unite people was to make them commit crimes together, as Hitler knew well.... Small communities like the Border Police Station in Nowy Sącs, Police Battalion 101, the Auschwitz camp guards, *Einsatzkommandos*..., requisitioning corps, the bawling and murdering crow of rank-and-file... all these communities provided evidence that the *Volksgemeinschaft* really existed on a daily basis....

But the joy of belonging in the Third Reich was permeated by pressure and compulsion. Although the Nazi dictatorship was not able to suppress freedom of action completely, taking advantage of the remnants of freedom was risky. You could refuse to participate in acts of brutality, but you would pay for it by being ridiculed, humiliated, and ostracized by your comrades and superiors. Only a few people were able to stand such pressure. And the same was true for the pressure to participate in murder at least once, after which you knew you could no longer turn back.

In fact, the consequences of refusing to participate were limited. You could not be completely excluded, let alone shot or jailed. Instead you would be disgraced and subordinated. The hierarchic fabric of the group needed the "shirker" as an in-built outsider just as it needed the bully. The sociology of inclusion was perfidious. The gang did not leave the apostates alone but made them do the preliminary work such as rounding up the victims, or they made them at least witness the crime, thus evoking in them too a sense of complicity. Indeed, only wearing the same uniform as the actual perpetrators sufficed to cause that sense of complicity....

The Nazi genocide was thus doubly paradigmatic: it developed the logistics necessary to spread genocide over an entire continent and—as this book has argued—it made an entire, civilized nation feel complicit in that genocide. It was the knowledge of having perpetrated or supported the Holocaust that launched a completely new kind of nation building. Its outcome was the national brotherhood of mass murder—Hitler's community.

61 • War of Annihilation on the Eastern Front, 1941 (Geoffrey P. Megargee)

What role did the German Armed Forces, the Wehrmacht, play during the Holocaust? For decades, ordinary wisdom held that Hitler's conventional soldiers were bystanders to genocide but not active participants in it. This interpretation was recently overturned by a vast body of scholarship. As Geoffrey Megargee of the U.S. Holocaust Memorial Museum points out in his 2007 book, the attitude in the upper echelons of the armed forces ranged from nervous resignation to enthusiastic support. Moreover, the Einsatzgruppen (mobile killing units) were regularly aided by Wehrmacht forces. Yet,

SOURCE: Geoffrey P. Megargee, *War of Annihilation: Combat and Genocide on the Eastern Front, 1941* (Lanham, Md.: Rowman and Littlefield, 2007), 33, 34, 35–36, 43, 67, 68–69, 70, 71, 92–94, 96, 97, 150, 153. Reprinted with permission of the publisher.

argues Megargee, the culpability of Nazi Germany's military extends even further, for it actively
encouraged their soldiers to disregard the value of Jewish life and to impose the harshest occupation
regime conceivable, including starvation and forced labor as strategies of destruction.

In the past, many histories have treated the Germans' military and economic plans separately
from the criminal designs that came into being at the same time, but in reality they were inseparable. The nature of German military operations [during World War II], the need for—
and assumption of—a quick victory, the difficulties to supply and of securing the vast territories [in the Soviet Union] through which the supplies would have to flow: these factors were
bound up with broader German strategic, political, and economic goals, racist attitudes, and
the concept of total war to an even greater extent than had been the case in Poland [which
Nazi Germany had invaded in 1939]. The result would be depredation, suffering, and death
on a level nearly unequaled in history.

Germany's senior military leaders could hardly have been surprised at the brutality of the
campaign to come. Hitler had expounded several times on the nature of the war in the east,
and certainly the events in Poland could have left little doubt in the mind of any astute observer as to the regime's goals and methods. Further indications were not lacking. On March
30, 1941, less than two months before the eastern campaign began, Hitler explained his intentions again, even more explicitly, to the most important commanders and staff officers who
would lead the Wehrmacht [the German military] into the USSR. The war against the Soviet
Union would be a war of extermination, he said. . . .

Absolute ruthlessness was the rule by which the Germans intended to conquer and "pac-
ify" their new realm. Perhaps the most cynical of the Germans' plans is also the least known;
it concerned food supplies. Not only would the army's logistical apparatus be unable to bring
food forward to the troops in sufficient quantities, but the Reich Food Ministry was also
worried about food shortages in Germany itself. Arguments of "military necessity" now combined with concerns about civilians' morale; obviously the troops had to eat, and no one
wanted to see a repetition of the hunger and unrest that had weakened home-front morale in
the First World War. Over the longer term, as well, Hitler wanted the resources of eastern
Europe and European Russia to support an extended conflict with Britain and, in all likelihood, the United States. As a result, representatives of the regime and the military met and, in
early May 1941, agree upon what historians have come to call the "hunger plan." According
to this plan, the Germans would take the "surplus" food from the more agriculturally productive southern regions of the USSR to feed the Wehrmacht's troops and the Reich. "Surplus,"
in this context, referred to food that normally went to feed people in the cities and the USSR's
less productive northern zone. By agreeing to this plan, German military and civilian authorities quietly accepted that up to thirty million Soviet citizens would starve to death. . . .

Other measures aimed to ensure security and promote Nazi racial goals in the occupied
territories by actively eliminating partisans, potential partisans, and anyone else whom the
Germans saw as a near- or long-term threat to their overlordship. These policies grew from
two overlapping imperatives: that of the military, which did not want problems in the rear
areas to slow its advance, and that of the civilian authorities, who needed to maintain strict
control in order to exploit the conquered lands and who also wanted to eliminate Jews and
other supposedly inferior people outright, as a matter of principle.

Hitler began laying the groundwork for these measures early in 1941.... The OKW [Oberkommando der Wehrmacht, or Armed Forces High Command], the OKH [Oberkommando des Heeres, or Army High Command], and the SS [Schutzstaffel, or Protective Squadron] worked out a series of plans and orders that corresponded to Hitler's wishes. One of these, which the OKW issued on March 13 as a supplement to the basic order for *Barbarossa* [the code name for the Nazi war against the Soviet Union], delineated the respective spheres of responsibility for the army and the SS, in general terms. It stated that Hitler had given the *Reichsführer-SS* [the head of the SS, Heinrich Himmler] certain "special tasks," tasks that "arise from the legal struggle between two opposing political systems," and that Himmler would deal with [these] "independently and on his own authority." Negotiations began that very same day ... on the nature of army-SS cooperation. ...

A draft agreement was ready on March 26 and [Walther] von Brauchitsch [commander in chief of the army] signed the resulting order on April 28. According to this order, "special detachments" of the Security Police and SD [Sicherheitsdienst, or Security Service] would carry out "special tasks" within the army's zone of operations, tasks that would fall outside the jurisdiction of the troops. Although the order did not name them as such, these "special detachments" were the SS *Einsatzgruppen* [mobile killing units], the same kinds of units that had carried out "special tasks" in Poland. ... No preinvasion order with any mention of liquidations has surfaced, after the war ... senior [military] officers would claim that they did not know what the *Einsatzgruppen* were going to do. However, given the groups' activities in Poland, and especially in light of the other orders that the military was preparing at this time, that claim is nearly impossible to credit. ...

By the morning of June 22, 1941, the Germans had amassed a force of over three million of its own soldiers and another half million of its allies for the start of the invasion. The attack opened at 0315, when a small force of bombers struck key Soviet air bases at the same time that the ground campaign began with an artillery bombardment up and down the long border with the USSR. At dawn, more than 1,200 German aircraft—part of a total force of over 2,700—crossed the Soviet border and began bombarding additional Red Army airfields. ... Operation Barbarossa, which would grow into the most destructive military conflict of all time, had begun. ... Debate continues among historians to this day over the point at which Hitler decided to eliminate the Jews of the Soviet Union physically, whether before or during the campaign, but the fact of the decision is plain. The Jews would be the first target for abuse, forced labor, and, ultimately, extermination.

The execution of policies against Jews was, first and foremost, the province of the SS *Einsatzgruppen*, along with police and Waffen-SS [the heavily-armed, special combat detachment of the SS] units. ... The *Einsatzgruppen* used a couple of different tactics in their war on the Jews, one of which was to trigger or intensify pogroms—massacres—by local inhabitants against their Jewish neighbors, preferably without leaving any evidence of German involvement. This tactic had two purposes: first, to take some of the workload of the Einsatzgruppen themselves, and, second, to place a major part of the responsibility for the killings on the locals and simultaneously "prove" how unpopular the Jews were. ... All told, thousands of Jews and others fell victim to German-inspired pogroms. On the whole, however, the Germans were disappointed with many local citizens' unwillingness to attack their Jewish neighbors, and the victim count remained lower than the instigators had hoped. The other, and predominating, tactic was to simply enter a town, round up the intended victims, take them to a more-or-less remote area nearby, and shoot them. . . .

Where was the army in all this? To a greater or lesser extent depending on the circumstances, its attitude, at least in the upper echelons, varied between nervous resignation and enthusiastic support. In any case there was usually no lack of cooperation with the Einsatzgruppen and the other killing squads. . . . The cooperation took several forms. The army provided the murder squads with their supplies, ammunition, transport, and housing, without which they could hardly have carried out their missions. During the killings themselves, the army usually remained "neutral" at best, as in the case of Kaunas [in Lithuania], when hundreds of Wehrmacht soldiers and officers watched as the slaughter took place; those who objected were told not to intervene. At other times the army took a more active role. Army units, such as security divisions under the command of the army group rear area headquarters, sometimes identified, segregated, and guarded the victims; at other times, they cordoned off the areas where shootings occurred. In Lvov [in Ukraine], the local commander went so far as to help instigate a pogrom himself. . . . In some areas the army also played a leading role in setting up ghettos in which to segregate and control the Jews. . . .

Within the army itself, the effects of its cooperation with the SS were insidious. There were, all along, a few army commanders who attempted to prevent their troops from taking part in, or even observing, the killing actions. The commanders' concern, though, just as had been true of von Brauchitsch during the planning process, and before that in connection with SS activities in Poland, was usually with troop discipline, rather than with fundamental moral questions. The officer corps did not want their troops running amok. . . .

August and September marked a period of change in the German campaign to eradicate the Jews. Not only did the killing squads begin shooting ever greater numbers of victims, but they now included whole communities, rather than killing mostly young men. Whereas the killing of women and children had been merely allowed before, now it was encouraged and even ordered. The reasons for that change, and its timing, are still subject to debate. Some historians believe that Hitler made the decision to eradicate the Jews completely before the [Barbarossa] campaign even started, and that only tactical considerations, such as shortage of shooters, limited the killings in the first few weeks. Others maintain that he decided on extermination while the campaign was going on and communicated it to the units in the field through Himmler. Still others emphasize the role of field commanders themselves in instigating actions that Himmler and Hitler then approved and encouraged. There is no way to settle the debate with any degree of certainty—we have no written order, for example, and the various testimonies and other pieces of evidence are often contradictory. We can safely say, however, that whether the impetus for the killings came from the top down, the bottom up, or some combination of the two, there was no lack of enthusiasm at any level. Hitler was fully informed and certainly approved of the new measures, at the very least. Himmler made inspection tours to observe and encourage the men and their commanders, and often the killings increased in scale after his visits. . . .

This was also the time when plans were moving forward for a broader Holocaust. On September 10 Himmler met with several key subordinates, apparently to draw up plans for camps at Belzec, Majdanek, and Auschwitz/Birkenau in Poland. . . . By midmonth Hitler had decided to empty the Reich of Jews as soon as possible. . . . Moreover, by September the SS was developing the carbon monoxide poisoning techniques with which they would kill hundreds of thousands of Jews and other victims in the east, building upon the Nazis' earlier experience in killing handicapped Germans. . . . By the end of September the tone of war in the east was clear to both sides, and that tone was shaping the military outcomes. This was no ordinary campaign. . . . In order to ensure their victory, the generals . . . helped lay the plans for Hitler's vision of an exterminationist war. Later they would claim that the SS was solely responsible for the crimes in the east, but in fact the military's role was crucial. At the most basic level, the crimes could never have taken place if the Wehrmacht had not conquered the ground, but the generals' culpability extends well beyond that fact. They encouraged their soldiers in an attitude that placed little or no value on the life of Soviet civilians; in fact they ordered their men to use the harshest conceivable means to establish German dominance. They planned for the deliberate starvation of millions of people and for forced labor by millions more. . . .

We can see, for one thing, that the events in the Soviet Union were a strong influence upon the decision for the so-called Final Solution of the Jewish question (or at least its European stage; the Nazis had plans for other regions too). On the one hand, the relative success with which the Nazis rounded up and shot hundreds of thousands of innocent people helped to convince Germany's leaders that extermination was a real option, while the prolongation of the war helped close out deportation as an alternative and encouraged a sense of urgency, a belief that the solution could not wait until after final victory. At the same time, the Germans could also see the limitations in the killing units' operations; their search for other methods led them to the gas chamber and the death camp.

62 • Networks of Nazi Persecution
(Gerald D. Feldman and Wolfgang Seibel)

Gerald Feldman and Wolfgang Seibel of the University of Konstanz explore the utility of network analysis for the study of the Holocaust. Generally speaking, the methodology enables scholars to depict social structures, such as perpetrator groups, as pictorial graphs. By mathematically manipulating these network representations, Feldman and Seibel seek to reveal the mechanisms and processes of social interaction, including genocidal interaction. Their 2005 chapter concentrates on the division of labor in the perpetration of the Holocaust.

Modernity is key

Organized mass crime is unthinkable without division of labor. The Holocaust is no exception to this rule but, rather, its most horrifying manifestation. Evidence related to the role of government bureaucracy was, to be sure, already part of classic Holocaust research. Meta-theories of the Holocaust have drawn on the nature and consequences of modern bureau-

SOURCE: Gerald D. Feldman and Wolfgang Seibel, "The Holocaust as Division-of-Labor-Based Crime— Evidence and Analytical Challenges," in Gerald D. Feldman and Wolfgang Seibel, eds., *Networks of Nazi Persecution: Bureaucracy, Business, and the Organization of the Holocaust* (New York: Berghahn Books, 2005), 1–3, 4, 5–6. Reprinted with permission of the publisher.

cracy as a tool of persecution and mass murder, the most prominent being Hannah Arendt's banalization theory.

Both the planning and the implementation of [the Nazi] genocide were carried out in accordance with conventional division-of-labor principles. From 1939 on, the Amt IV, *"Gegnererforschung und Bekämpfung"* (Researching and Combating the Enemy) of the *Reichssicherheitshauptamt* (Reich Security Main Office) with its Department IV B 4, run by Adolf Eichmann, was in charge of anti-Jewish policy. The enforcement of the persecutory measures was delegated to the *Staatspolizeileitstellen* (State Police Head Offices) or, in the German occupied territories outside the Reich, to the *Befehlshaber der Sicherheitspolizei und des Sicherheitsdienstes* (SD) (Commanders of the Security Police and Security Service) (BdS). These core institutions, however, were dependent on numerous other institutions and individual participants, state and private, German and, in the occupied territories, domestic agents, for the implementation of the "final solution."

In the occupied territories in particular, anti-Jewish policy implied resource dependency of the occupation administration and the Berlin central offices. Vertical division of labor was eclipsed by the rivalry between different agencies, both German and domestic, resulting in "polycracy" or even "organized chaos." Thus, anti-Jewish policy and the persecution apparatus were obviously not just an SS [Schutzstaffel, or Defense Guard] and Gestapo [Geheime Staatspolizei, or Secret State Police] matter. What is more, coordination of the complex persecution apparatuses could not be accomplished in an exclusively hierarchical manner. . . . Coordination took place in a hierarchical as well as a cooperative way and, just as the differentiation of power within the regime or between the occupying power and domestic authorities played a role, so did the interdependence of a variety of agencies beyond formal rules of cooperation. To a large extent, the persecution apparatus was made up of inter-organizational networks as they have been described in political science and [the] organization[al] sociology literature. This perspective is supported by three strands of recent Holocaust research findings.

The first aspect concerns the situation of the SS and police apparatus, without question the core institution of the persecution apparatus. The degree of hegemony of the SS and police apparatus—abundantly described in the literature—as it had been emerging in Germany since 1933 through the fusion of party organizations (SS, SD) with the state police and its independence vis-à-vis the general public administration, was, in the occupied territories, again dependent on the formal structure of the occupation regime. This, in turn, was shaped by the strategic goals of the occupying power, but it did not follow a standardized plan within these goals as is revealed by the situation even in a region so highly homogenous as German occupied Western Europe. In one way or the other, . . . division of labor meant collaboration of indigenous institutions and individuals.

The second aspect concerns the range of the anti-Jewish measures, mainly the relationship between economic and repressive police persecution. The "Aryanization" of Jewish-owned businesses was not controlled by the SS and Gestapo but instead took place under the jurisdiction of the *Gauwirtschaftsberater* (Regional Economic Advisors) of the *Nationalsozialistische Deutsche Arbeiterpartei* [National Socialist German Workers' Party] (NSDAP) in cooperation with the self-administrative chambers of industry and commerce and the free professions, as well as the local governments, law firms, banks and insurance companies. In German-occupied territories, the jurisdiction for "Aryanization" and the spoliation of Jewish assets in general lay with the regular civil or military occupation administration, which was again decisively dependent on domestic agencies.

Finally, the destruction of . . . economic existence was inseparably connected to the physical extermination of the Jews. Although organization of the deportations was the exclusive domain of the Gestapo, the plundering of the last personal assets and belongings prior to deportation required cooperation with a large number of regular authorities, for instance, as has been reported for Germany proper, with the residential registration offices (*Einwohnermeldeämter*), fiscal authorities, housing offices, district courts, employment offices, and further with the chambers of trade and commerce, trade guilds, savings banks and other banks, and, last but not least, with the *Reichsbahn* (state railroad). In the German occupied territories, this pattern was repeated, despite considerable regional differences. In the final phase of the victims' complete defenselessness, there was a downright "enrichment race" in both the "Aryanization" and the plundering of household and other personal belongings between the Gestapo and the finance administration and, under the supervision of public authorities, between companies, private individuals, and banks. . . .

However overwhelming the diversity of actors and institutions involved in the persecution [of European Jewry], the ways in which [this] division of labor was linked to perpetrator agency have, by and large, remain unexplored. . . . One important fact to be acknowledged is that the formal status of [the] division of labor varied substantially. It ranged from highly formalized and tightly coupled relationships between participating agencies to ephemeral and loosely coupled linkages between individual actors. Weberian bureaucracy with rigid rules and hierarchies did play a crucial role in the preparation and execution of persecution and mass murder. . . . It would be misleading to assume, however, that the machinery of public administration always acted in accordance with the conventional rules of hierarchy and regulated cooperation as far as the persecution of the Jews was concerned.

A striking phenomenon is the self-initiative of local and regional authorities, which often took independent steps of anti-Jewish discrimination and persecution years ahead of central Reich regulations, and then asked for central coordination for the sake of homogeneity. . . . While this largely reflects the influence of local Nazi leaders in municipal administration, state administration [at the subnational level of the German *Länder*], too, rigidly implemented anti-Jewish regulation without central initiation or coordination. Moreover, public authorities and the Nazi party organization were not just acting as law-abiding agencies. Bribery and corruption were an integral part of the persecution. . . .

What made those networks stable and effective was, above all, the mutual benefit of those involved. Networks and the presumptive source of their formation and stability make us aware that, although individuals persecuted the Jews in obedience to orders and in accordance with their own anti-Semitism, neither hierarchy nor ideology was an indispensable prerequisite for the active involvement in mass crime. . . . Individuals contributed to the racialization of anti-Jewish policy without following orders or a particular commitment to anti-Semitism. Apparently, the motivation basis of persecution was much more encompassing. However extended the variety of motives of persecutors and their helpers, motivation was not just contingent. . . .

Regardless of its uniqueness in history, the Holocaust shares crucial characteristics with organized mass crime in general, of which the present volume stresses networks and division

of labor as predominant structural features. Organized crime is obviously a structural phenomenon, but a merely structural perspective entails obvious risks of misinterpretation. Criminal
action, like any kind of human agency, is embedded in social structures in the sense of regu-
larities of interindividual relationship, but crime as such is committed by responsible individuals. Assessing the degree of personal responsibility is what the structural analysis of organized
crime should be ultimately aiming at. . . . The evidence presented in this volume, both empirical
and theoretical in nature, supports the assumption that informal, network-type mechanisms
of governance on the one hand and traditional bureaucracies on the other hand were equally
effective in mobilizing human resources for evil purposes during the Holocaust. . . .

   It is precisely *not* the willingness to cooperate for the sake of common goals which
makes organizations stable, powerful, and effective. Rather, individuals use organizations for
personal purposes such as income, career promotion, etc. The decoupling of organizational
performance from personal commitment to organizational goals makes organizations much
more effective than cooperation on the basis of shared goals, the reason being the enormous
diversification of motivational sources. Networks, reaching far beyond the boundaries of formal organization, even enlarge this diversity. . . .

   The very ambivalence of organizations as such makes the structure of organized mass
crime robust and vulnerable at the same time. The robustness stems from the decoupling of
individual motivation from organizational goals, which makes "organized evil" decisively more
dangerous than mobilization through shared goals or beliefs. . . . The opacity and blurriness of
networks do not help reduce those risks. The fact, however, that individuals (accomplices,
"willing executioners," "collaborators," etc.) in spite of all their selfishness, remain aware of
organizational goals implies, first, that accomplices remain accountable for what they are doing
even when they act in networks that are fluid and opaque in nature and, secondly, that the
separation of organizational goals and individual motivation is limited by the quest for legitimacy and identity.

63 • Annihilation of State Prisoners through Labor
(Nikolaus Wachsmann)

*In his 1999 article Nikolaus Wachsmann, a lecturer of history at Birkbeck College, draws our atten-
tion to one of the lesser studied aspects of the Holocaust, namely the genocidal campaign waged
against "asocials" or "community aliens," ranging from the Roma and Sinti (a loose collection of
communities, found predominantly in East Central Europe, that share a number of cultural, linguistic, and ethnic attributes) to slave laborers and the disabled. By focusing in particular on the
extermination of certain state prisoners, Wachsmann sheds new light on the multiple ways in which
Germany's Nazi regime went about destroying "unworthy" life. He helpfully supplements the sizable
literature on the destruction of the European Jews with an account of smaller-scale annihilation poli-*

SOURCE: Nikolaus Wachsmann, "'Annihilation through Labor': The Killing of State Prisoners in the Third
     Reich," *Journal of Modern History* 71, no. 3 (1999): 624, 625, 628, 629–31, 634, 636, 637, 638, 641–42, 645,
     646, 649–51. Reprinted with permission of the University of Chicago Press.

cies. Most important, he contradicts, with evidence from the Mauthausen concentration camp, the still widespread view that Nazi genocide was chiefly an industrial killing spree.

One of the most distinctive features of Nazi society was the increasingly radical division of its members into "national comrades" and "community aliens." . . . With the start of the Second World War, various nonlethal forms of discrimination against these "community aliens" were gradually replaced by policies geared to physical annihilation, culminating above all in the extermination of the European Jews. . . . From late 1942 onward, over twenty thousand offenders classified as "asocial" were taken out of the state penal system and transferred to the police for "annihilation through labor." At least two-thirds of them perished in concentration camps. But in the historical literature this program has either been dealt with in passing or completely ignored. . . .

On August 20, 1942, Adolf Hitler appointed Otto-Georg Thierack as his new Minister of Justice. He used the opportunity to spell out privately to Thierack his vision of the role of the legal system in the Nazi state. For instance, Hitler complained that during the war a prison sentence was no longer adequate punishment for criminals, as war inevitably led to a "negative selection": while "the bravest" were killed at the front, the criminal survived in state penal institutions. . . . To avert such a catastrophe, Hitler concluded, he had to "ruthlessly exterminate the vermin." . . . Thierack was quick to turn Hitler's vague if forcibly expressed views into reality. Already in late August or early September 1942 he met with leading officials in the Ministry of Justice in Berlin. . . . Thierack had to determine which of the more than 190,000 inmates of German's state penal institutions were to be selected for annihilation. . . . Following Hitler's table talk, only those prisoners deemed a serious threat were to be killed. Thierack also had to decide how these prisoners, once selected, should be murdered. After all, they had all been legally sentenced to imprisonment and no more. . . .

On September 18, 1942, Thierack met with Heinrich Himmler, head of the SS [Schutzstaffel, or Defense Guard] and the German police, in Himmler's Field Headquarters in Zhitomir, west of Kiev. One of the issues settled was the "transfer of asocial elements from the prison service to the *Reichsführer SS* [i.e., Himmler] for annihilation through labor (*Vernichtung durch Arbeit*)." This transfer was to be accomplished under two separate policies, which can be termed "general transfer" and the "individual transfer." In the "general transfer," all Jews, Sinti and Roma, Russians, and Ukrainians in state penal institutions were to be handed over to the police without exception. The same was agreed for Poles with sentences of no more than three years. Also, all state prisoners sentenced to security confinement (*Sicherheitsverwahrung*) were to be transferred to the police. . . . The policy governing "individual transfer" of state prisoners was crucially different. It covered all German and Czech inmates with penitentiary sentences of more than eight years. They were not to be transferred automatically to the police. Rather, they would be examined individually by a commission of the Ministry of Justice as to their "asociality."

The transfer of "asocial" state prisoners from late 1942 onward was part of a wider vision, which aimed at a division of labor between the state penal system and concentration camps. The state penal service was to be limited to "reformable" inmates only, while the police were to be given jurisdiction over all "incorrigible criminals" and "racial aliens." Concerning the latter category, Thierack explained in a letter to Martin Bormann [head of the Party Chancellery from 1941 and secretary to the Führer from 1943] on October 13, 1942, that the judiciary "could only contribute on a small scale to the extermination of members of these races" (poles, Russians, Jews, Sinti and Roma). Handing them over to the police would "produce much better results." . . .

The transports to the camps started in November 1942, and by summer 1943 most prisoners had been transferred. Overall, more than 17,300 state prisoners were turned over to the police as part of the "general transfer." . . . It included a total of 6,242 Poles. . . . In comparison to Poles, the number of Jewish prisoners (1,078) handed over to the police was rather small. . . . [This was so because] the majority of so-called offenses by Jews never reached the courts but were dealt with directly by the police or SS. . . . The largest single group of prisoners handed over to the police as part of the "general transfer" were prisoners sentenced to security confinement. In the statistics of April 24, 1943, they made up more than half (8,813) of all the transferred inmates. These prisoners were often characterized by Nazi legal officials as dangerous violent criminals, sex offenders, and professional confidence tricksters. . . .

While the program of "general transfer" was slowing down by mid-1943, the process of "individual transfer" went on until almost the end of the war. . . . The prisoners individually examined were different in two ways from the ones transferred to the police as part of the "general transfer." First, they included a large number of political prisoners, who had been almost absent in the "general transfer." . . . Second, a number of criminal offenders who were part of the "individual transfer" were serving very lengthy sentences for violent crimes, such as murder, rape, and robbery, rather than petty property offenses, as in the case of many prisoners in the "general transfer." . . . In late 1942, the German prison governors reported the results of their first examinations to the Ministry of Justice. At the time, there were around fourteen thousand inmates with sentences of security confinement. The governors classified only 593 as "reformable." Approximately 95 percent of the inmates were reported as "asocial." How can this level of support be explained?

The Ministry of Justice in Berlin encouraged the "annihilation (*Vernichtung*) of these alien elements." On January 1, 1943, Thierack in his monthly "judges' letter" (*Richterbrief*) to the German courts reminded the officials to "exclude the asocial criminal ruthlessly from the community through imposition of the death penalty." Their "annihilation" was vital not just for security reasons, Thierack stated, but also as a contribution to the racial-hygienic aim of "cleansing the racial body" from all "degenerates." These developments clearly radicalized prison officials, not least because executions were carried out within the walls of state penal institutions. . . .

Overall, more than twenty thousand state prisoners were handed over to the police as part of the "general" and "individual" transfers. At a very conservative estimate, around two-thirds of them died in the camps; the real total may well have been higher. All Jewish inmates were transported to Auschwitz. . . . The majority of former state prisoners was transported to the concentration camp in Mauthausen near Linz [in Austria], which according to SS guidelines was reserved for the most dangerous inmates. . . . For most of the former state prisoners, mainly German inmates with sentences of security confinement, the transport to Mauthausen was a death sentence. They were savagely beaten when they arrived on the trains, so that often the first inmates were already dead before the transport had even reached the camp. Once inside, the torture continued. . . . Many of those inmates who survived the beatings and shootings of the first weeks faced "annihilation through labor" in the main camp's quarry (*Wiener Graben*), which was notorious for its murderous conditions. The Wiesbaden State Prosecutor described this torture in 1949, based on several testimonies:

> In a completely mindless way, without any obvious economic use for the war effort, the inmates had to perform the hard labor of cutting big blocks of stone, weighing up to 50 kilograms, which they had to carry up and down 186 steps. In all cases, this had to be performed at a running pace. Weakened by insufficient nutrition, many inmates broke down under the weight of the stones and plunged into the quarry. If they did not die instantly, they were either shot by SS-guards or beaten to death by *Kapos* [concentration camp inmates who served low administrative functions]. Many inmates were simply thrown down into the quarry from a height of 30 to 40 meters. Also, inmates at the top of the site were often forced to empty their trucks of stones, thus striking dead many prisoners working beneath them in the quarry. A great number of prisoners also voluntarily jumped down into the quarry to put an end to the agony, which they had to endure again and again.

This brutal treatment, senseless labor, and murder of the former state prisoners in Mauthausen, all of whom were non-Jews and predominantly German, contradicts recent claims [made, notably, by Daniel Jonah Goldhagen] that the "Germans . . . gave senseless work almost exclusively to Jews." . . .

Most former state prisoners did not survive for long in Mauthausen. By March 1943, only a few months after the "transfer" had started, 3,306 of the 7,587 state prisoners transported to Mauthausen were already dead. By February 1944, 10,231 state prisoners had been taken to Mauthausen. Three out of four of them had died since their arrival. Often, they were murdered with unimaginable brutality. This direct, physical violence stands in sharp contrast to the still widespread image of Nazi genocide as a factory-like, anonymous, and largely bureaucratic process.

64 • Nazi Concentration Camps (Wolfgang Sofsky)

During the early years of the "Third Reich," fifty-nine concentration camps were in existence. During World War II twenty-three Stammlager, or main camps, were operating alongside some 1,300 subcamps. In his highly influential book The Order of Terror *(1993), the German sociologist Wolfgang Sofsky explicates the nature of everyday life—and death—in Nazi Germany's concentration camp system. In particular, he explains how the structuring of time contributed to the order of terror.*

The present study does not investigate the social history of the German concentration camp system and of the murder of the Jews. Rather, it analyzes the concentration camp as a distinc-

SOURCE: Wolfgang Sofsky, *The Order of Terror: The Concentration Camp*, translated by William Templer (1993; Princeton, N.J.: Princeton University Press, 1997), 13, 14, 73, 74–75, 78, 79–80, 81. Reprinted with permission of the publisher.

tive system of power. It proceeds from the thesis that in the camps, a social form of power crystallized that was essentially different from the familiar types of power and domination. Absolute power should not be confused with asymmetrical relations of exchange or with primitive power. Nor should it be confused with modern disciplinary power or with relations of domination founded on obedience. It is not based on exploitation, sanction, or legitimacy, but rather on terror, organization, and excessive violence. The focus of the following study is on the processes typical of this power, the structuring of space, time, and sociality in the camps, and the excessive and organized intensification of the power to kill. How can we grasp the way this power functioned? How can it be described? . . .

As important as social history may be for the question of why the camps were originally set up, it is of little use for the analysis of the system of power. That approach adds little or nothing to our knowledge about the structures of absolute power and their effects on the microcosm of everyday life in the camps. By contrast, if one foregrounds the psychology of perpetrators and their victims, social reality is reduced to the motivations and experiences of the individuals involved. The processes of sociation and dissociation, organization and violence, are thus overlooked. In order to penetrate to an internal view of the *univers concentrationnaire*, the present study adheres to three general rules:

1. The social reality of the camp cannot be equated with the aims and objectives planned (or proclaimed) by the top organizational echelon of the SS [*Schutzstaffel*, or Protective Squadron]. The camp system was a focus of differing (and at times opposed) interests, an object for dispute and negotiation, a bone of contention between numerous offices and agencies. As in any social system, organization here was not a means to an end, but a dynamic field of action. The self-preservation of the system, the processes of power and terror, often had little if anything to do with the plans of the terror managers. . . .

2. Within society, the concentration camp was a closed system. Nowhere is the theory of the closed social system more pertinent than in the case of the concentration camp. Its boundaries could not be crossed; its inmates were isolated and locked into a world of terror in which the camp personnel enjoyed a free hand. . . .

3. Organized terror takes place in situations of action and suffering. Ultimately, even absolute power targets the social situations in which human beings live and function. Here, it breaks their resistance, herds them together, sheds social ties; it dissolves action; it devastates life. Any investigation of the camps is shortsighted and flawed if it fails to include the power that micrologically pervades the structures of space and time, sociality and identity. For that reason, a methodological close-up on the typical situations of the world of the concentration camp is indispensable. Consequently, the present study not only employs a battery of concepts drawn from the general sociology of power, but also is indebted to work on the analysis of social institutions.

The aim of the investigation is a "thick description" of the universe of power in the concentration camp. In methodological terms, thick descriptions are analyses of meaning. They do not provide protocols of events but rather interpretations of actions and situations; not reports but explications of structures and processes. Thick descriptions present a reading of the meaning of what has happened. They are interpretive and microscopic, not deductive and generalizing. Their quality criterion is neither the stringency of a deductive theory nor the presumably correct mapping of a model. Thick description succeeds to the extent that it expands the understanding of a strange and alien world. . . .

[To better understand the function of absolute power in the concentration camp system, consider, for instance, the example of "camp time."] Social time is an objective, imposed standard time of organization, but power can arbitrarily expand, slow down or accelerate it. Camp time was more than the external compulsion characteristic of all social time. Camp power permeated inner time-consciousness, sundering the internal band that laces together memory, expectation, and hope. Absolute power far surpasses the familiar forms of organized temporal control. It is not satisfied simply with the synchronization and coordination of events. It destroys the continuity of inner time and severs the ties between past and future, locking people into an external present. Far from being satisfied with controlling human bodies, it seizes hold of biographical time and the motions of the mind.

The planning of time is one of the proven tools of social power. Scheduling fixes chains of events and determines change and duration; it generates repetitions and habits. Schedules mark beginning points, end points, phases, transitions, linear sequences or cyclical returns. Schedules are programs of succession. They prescribe when something should be done; they define times for action and pauses, directing future events into predetermined paths. Through them, social action becomes predictable and amenable to social integration. . . . But absolute power has only a limited interest in a rigid institutionalization of time. It regularly departs from the standardized time tracks it has instituted. . . . With a rigid time structure, terror would abrogate itself. Its intrusions and attacks would be predictable; the victims could take countermeasures; power would degenerate into a mere means for order. Nothing of the kind existed in the concentration camp.

Terror alternates between planning and disorder, between regulation and assault. It installs a temporal order that assures a minimal degree of organization, but builds phases of acceleration and hesitation into that time path. By reserving for itself the choice of deviations and special times, power secures its rule over time. The temporal law of absolute power is not calculability, but the free variation of tempo, the shift between duration and abrupt suddenness, hectic rush and waiting, rest and shock. The camp's standard time was deceptive. Within the external framework of cyclical repetition, time pulsated irregularly. Consequently, no prisoner was able to devise long-term plans for action. . . . It is a fundamental mistake to confuse the temporal structure in the camp with the time that predominates in modern disciplinary institutions. Camp time was not goal oriented. . . .

The course of the dense day obeyed a recurrent schema. The prisoners were awakened at 4:00 or 4:40 a.m. by changing bells, whistles, or sirens. . . . In a hectic rush, beds had to be made, the block cleaned, clothing put on, breakfast distributed, and a visit paid to the latrine. Inmates had half an hour, or at most forty-five minutes, from the crack of reveille until they formed up for the morning roll call. . . . Whoever dallied was punished by beating, or shoved along by fellow prisoners. Even before the SS made its appearance, the day commenced with a brutal, frenetic scramble. This rush was followed by a period of waiting. The prisoners marched out by block to the *Appellplatz* [roll call square] and waited there for the SS to appear. . . . Despite the fixed time for morning roll call, the SS was often late. . . . Their entrance was a carefully calculated show of power. To leave thousands waiting is always a demonstration of total power. And time was something the camp masters had plenty of. Inmates did not march off to their places of work until it was light. Consequently, morning roll call in the winter months could drag on for more than ninety minutes. . . .

After work, the morning rhythm was repeated in the opposite direction. . . . After entering the camp [returning from locations of forced labor], there was a renewed time of terror: the evening roll call. Like every mass assembly, evening roll call was held for one ostensible purpose: a bureaucratic check on numbers. This procedure could have been completed in less than hour, despite the changes during the day—the transports, new arrivals, changes in work units, cases of illness, prisoner deaths. But evening roll call was far more than just a technical administrative affair. It constituted the high-water mark of the daily tide of power. Prisoner society was fully assembled down to the last person; thousands stood in rigid formation, confronted by a handful of SS men to whom they were compelled to show respect. Even the dead and dying had to be present for roll call. They were laid on the ground next to their respective block formations. The fact that the dead could not be brought to the morgue until after roll was not just a question of record keeping, of quantitative completeness. All the prisoners were meant to witness time's ravages: just how many victims the day had claimed. . . . Those who collapsed during roll call were placed right next to the dead. Although far outnumbering their guards, the prisoners were forced to watch the spectacle of dying. They could do nothing. They were merely a collective body, a conglomerate bereft of internal unity. The evening roll call staged the lethal contrast between the powerless mass and absolute sovereignty. . . .

A few guards roamed through the formations, on the lookout for any irregularity. There was always something: a foot extended a few centimeters over the line, a missing cap, eyes not looking rigidly straight ahead. . . . Since the mass formation was one single collective body, the slightest deviation was noticed immediately. . . . The roll call often lasted for several hours, but power scanned this period with the microtime of the most minute gesture. Absolute power binds individuals together into a mass, shaping its structures. It synchronizes the collective anatomy, whose movements can be measured in mere fractions of a second. Unlike other inspections, the evening roll call did not have any time limit. After work, the roll call could be extended at will. Every minute it lasted meant a minute less for the prisoners; it was subtracted from their time for eating, relaxation, and sleep. It prolongation was a temporal sanction, a mode of punishment that used time itself as a means.

If a single prisoner was missing among the many thousands, a lengthy procedure was initiated. Each number was called; interpreters read the foreign names in all languages represented in the camp. If an attempted escape was suspected, search parties were sent out. . . . During the search, all the others had to remain standing. . . . The collective sanction of time pitted the massed society against the individual. Everyone had an interest in hoping that none was absent or had attempted to escape. In the large main camps, the normal evening roll call usually lasted one and a half to two hours; in the event of public punishment or execution, it went on a bit longer. However, the punitive roll call was occasionally extended into a roll call of extermination, dragging on into the night. During cold winter months, the SS left the prisoners standing until they froze [to death] by the dozens or had collapsed in exhaustion. . . . Murder was here committed with truncheons or firearms. The SS used an everyday procedure in order to kill—because absolute power always has time, it can take its time. . . .

The sequence from waking to lights out was repeated day after day.... The recurrent rhythm of feverish commotion and waiting, duration and abruptness, gradually ravaged one's sense of time.... Camp time, to be sure, had a standard form, but the time norms provided terror only with an armature. Absolute power is not subject to time. Rather, it manipulates time by expansion and acceleration, sudden incursions and attacks, and the torment of duration. The multiple time destroyed the security that cyclical time structures otherwise guarantee. The camp forced its inmates into an eternal present, a constancy of uncertainty and horror.

[handwritten margin notes: I.l ravages One s humanity and mastery over nature that we pride our humanity on]

65 • Genocide as Transgression (Dan Stone)

Dan Stone, professor of history at Royal Holloway, University of London, argues that people regularly kill one another—in genocidal campaigns and otherwise—because they can, and because they enjoy doing so. This is what he calls "violence as transgression." According to Stone, in the killing process perpetrators experience a heightened sense of belonging and eventually form "ecstatic communities." He motivates his argument by drawing on the literary theories of Dominick LaCapra, Roger Caillois, and Georges Bataille. More specifically Stone elaborates on LaCapra's observations about the carnivalesque nature of some of the violence perpetrated in the Holocaust, deepens this insight by tying it to Caillois's writings about the human frenzy of festivals, and finds, with Bataille, that participation in genocide may allow, among other things, individuals and groups to release what the French theorist termed "excess energy."

When one undertakes genuinely comparative genocide studies and not just work which lists other genocides only to dismiss them in the face of the Holocaust—it quickly becomes apparent that the murder of the Jews shares many features with many other of this century's most gruesome events. One feature in particular, what I have called "genocide as transgression," is especially noteworthy in all examples of genocide.... Although this shared characteristic could be felt too broad an interpretive tool, too axiomatic, to be of use to the person seeking to understand what leads to genocide as a form of human behavior, I argue that violence is, quite simply, the norm in society, a natural urge of human beings that can be mobilized by certain ideologies under certain conditions, and that what we call "civilization" is the exception, though one no less worth striving for.

I argue that people kill one another when they have been granted leave to do so or otherwise feel that they are safe to do so, for the main reason that they can, and because they enjoy doing so.... In each example we see, as well as the unspeakable sufferings of the victims, what can only be called the "high" of the perpetrators. Massacres, genocides, and the perpetration of atrocities create what ... I call "ecstatic communities," that is communities of perpetrators who experience a heightened sense of belonging to their own group by virtue of the fact that they have transgressed together. This apocalyptic, orgiastic experience of

SOURCE: Dan Stone, "Genocide as Transgression," *European Journal of Social Theory* 7, no. 1 (2004): 47, 48–51, 52–53, 54, 55–57. Reprinted with permission of Sage Publishers, Inc.

participation—which refers not only to the actual moment of killing—has been termed *Rausch* ("ecstasy" or "high") by Saul Friedländer [the influential Holocaust historian], and I will adopt this term. . . .

After examining the numerous acts of mass murder or genocide that have occurred in this century . . . , it is the similarities that are striking just as much as the differences. . . . I want to show that, even given all these differences, there is a level at which these genocides and massacres can be seen to stem from something in common: the creation of "ecstatic communities" based on a radical form of exclusion that occurs under sociologically and anthropologically explicable circumstances. . . . Here we come to the notion of transgression. What is it that is being transgressed, and why does this form of excessive behavior seem to take place with such alarming regularity in the modern world? Although I have criticized the distinction between "pre-modern" and "modern" societies, I do so because of the false distinction that is usually made between societies based on feelings, rituals, and charismatic attachments to a leader and societies based on means-end rationality and purposive, goal-oriented action. The fact is that especially in the latter ("modern societies") massacres and genocides take place, not because of the "dialectic of enlightenment," in which the domination of nature ends in the domination over human beings . . . , but because the refusal to recognize the need for non-purposive activity ends in outbursts of affect on a grand scale, dressed up as ideology or *raison d'état* these may be. In other words, the modern age, contrary to the expectations of sociologists of modernity, is an age of great, if disguised, passions. Modern "hyper-rationality" can end in ultra-violence just as "primitive barbarism" can, a fact implied a century ago by William James [the famed American psychologist and philosopher] when he argued . . . that "our esteem for facts has not neutralized in us all religiousness. It is itself almost religious." . . .

For [the literary theorist] Dominick LaCapra, the transgressive nature of the Holocaust is firmly tied to the actual killings themselves, not just what they stand for. In particular, he borrows a term from the Russian literary theorist Mikhail Bakhtin that has become common currency among students of literary theory: the "carnivalesque." . . . LaCapra, in particular, highlights aspects of the murders that require further elaboration: contamination, sacrificialism, the carnivalesque, scapegoating. All of these suggest ways of thinking derived from anthropology, in particular from the study of the rituals that mark societies at moments of extreme joy (festival) or crisis (war). There is of course, in terms of content, no comparison between festivities and warfare, but formally, in terms of the place they occupy in society, they are remarkably similar. . . . LaCapra's highly theorized attitude to genocide is given more concreteness by Roger Caillois. . . . Caillois's description of the festival is . . . highly instructive when considering the place of genocide in modern society.

Contemporary societies do not, as a rule, permit the useless squandering of energy and goods, since they are goal-oriented and profit-seeking. . . . In primitive societies, such squandering was, according to Caillois, built into the calendar in the form of the festival. His descriptions reveal his fear of and his attraction to the festival, and his implicit criticism of the drabness of modern life, which lacks such an outlet. But what he describes sounds very much like a description of genocide, especially of the frenzy of the massacre. In an analysis shared with his colleague (and fellow member of the influential Collège de sociologie) Georges Bataille, who wrote about the need for societies to squander their "excess energy" and the inability of modern societies to recognize this need, with the result that such energies risk being expended "catastrophically," Caillois wrote, in *Man and the Sacred* (1939, and in the appendices added in the 1950 edition) that all societies require periods of "collective effervescence" in order to break free from the monotony of everyday life. In modern societies, the vacation does not fill this role, since it is devoted to relaxation, quite the opposite of intoxicated exudation. The closest analogy in the modern world that he could find to the primate society's festival was war.

How does Caillois understand the festival to function in primitive societies? . . . It is described as a time of intensity, of intoxication, of the useless and excessive destruction and squandering of energies, possessions, and wealth. It turns established social, moral, and sexual relations on their heads, breaking all taboos (for example, incest or hierarchical relationships). . . . Many participants would therefore be shocked by what they had done when recalling it later in calm reflection. Yet festivals do not take place in complex civilizations such as modern industrial societies; their functioning simply does not permit such a shutting down of institutions and a destruction of the infrastructure. . . . War, then, is truly the modern equivalent of the festival, for it is [as Caillois puts it] a "monstrous societal brew and climax of existence, a time of sacrifice but also of violation of every rule, a time of mortal peril but yet sanctifying, a time of abnegation and also of licence." . . .

This anthropological theory of Caillois's, broad and untenable though it may be on close scrutiny, is highly suggestive for understanding the use of such terms in the literature on the Holocaust like "carnivalesque," "contamination," or "sacrificialism" by LaCapra, or *Rausch* by Friedländer. Indeed, although Caillois confined his analysis to war (he was of course writing only shortly after the term "genocide" had been coined by jurist Raphaël Lemkin . . .), it has obvious application to genocide in general. . . . Explaining the origins of genocide solely with Caillois's theory of transgression is clearly far too reductive. Yet if one thinks of genocide as a grand project, undertaken for (ill-perceived) reasons of state, it becomes clear that if leaders wish to involve their people in participating in acts of mass murder, such a project has to be presented as being beneficial to the well-being of the community that is ostensibly under threat and that requires purifying. Such participation—under conditions of war, or in a highly-charged ideological atmosphere—may itself be said to represent a legitimate transgression of the law for the sake of the community; the actual killing-process makes this sense of "ecstatic belonging" quite plain. . . .

Rwanda offers many examples of such "collective effervescence." Hutu Power's infamous "ten commandments" reveal a vicious and paranoid sexual and social transgression at work aimed at "purifying" the Hutu community from the "pollution" of Tutsis. . . . Similarly, the murder of the Jews permitted a heightened sense of belonging among the perpetrators, just as the absence of Jews from Germany and other parts of Europe was key to the formation of the racially pure *Volksgemeinschaft* [people's community], a community to which the *Volksgenossen* [people's comrades] were to be bound by affective ties deriving from an awareness of shared biology. . . . Just as war involves the massive squandering of resources with no commensurate utilitarian gain, and just as it legitimizes the furor of killing, so genocide concentrates all of its resources solely on mass murder. It is also a time of sacrifice. Of "psychic vigor," of the "joy of destruction." It too takes perpetrators (in the cases of Cambodia, Rwanda or the Holocaust, whole societies) out of the realm of the everyday and enjoins them to participate in the holy task of renewing the community. Whether this explosion should be regarded as the using up of excess energy is debatable; that it is a time of "collective effervescence" (a term that actually seems rather coy to define genocide) seems clear.

66 • A Head for an Eye: "Disproportionate Revenge" in the Cambodian Genocide (Alexander Laban Hinton)

Alexander Hinton, professor of anthropology at Rutgers University, draws attention to the cultural dimensions of genocide, focusing in particular on what he calls the model of "disproportionate revenge" in Cambodia. It is important to appreciate the meaning of revenge in pregenocidal Cambodia, says Hinton in this 1998 article, because it sheds light on both the motives and manners of genocidal perpetrators. According to Hinton, the model of disproportionate revenge became a template for part of the genocidal violence that the Khmer Rouge inflicted on Democratic Kampuchea in the 1970s. If we believe Hinton, the model of disproportionate revenge goes a long way toward explaining why ordinary Cambodians often killed in the extreme manner that they did.

In this article which is based on 15 months of fieldwork in Cambodia, I provide an example of how anthropological insights can be applied to large-scale genocide. In particular, I will show how the Cambodian cultural model of disproportionate revenge (*karsângsoek*) contributed to the genocidal violence that occurred during DK [the regime known as Democratic Kampuchea]. In contrast to a biblical concept of revenge that is premised on the talion principle of "an eye for an eye," the Cambodian model of disproportionate revenge involves disproportionate retaliation against one's enemy, what I call "a head for an eye." . . .

I should note, however, that the cultural model of disproportionate revenge does not guide Cambodian behavior in a deterministic manner. Cultural models may be differentially internalized, vary in their distribution and saliency across contexts, and have disparate degrees of motivational force for people. Moreover, when a person acts, he or she has a variety of available options. Cambodians who are insulted will therefore not automatically seek disproportionate revenge. Drawing on an alternative set of Buddhist norms, they may choose "to block/control [their] hearts" (*tuap chett*) or "disperse [their] anger" (*rumsay komhoeng*). . . . Such choices, however, are not made in a vacuum. Human behavior is both enabled and constrained by sociocultural structures—including cultural models that are an important part of what scholars have variously termed "habitus" [as originated by Pierre Bourdieu], "practical consciousness" [Anthony Giddens], "discourse" [Michel Foucault], and "hegemony" [Raymond Williams]. . . . Such cultural knowledge constitutes a crucial site upon which genocidal regimes can work. . . . This is exactly what happened during DK, as the exponents of Khmer Rouge ideology invoked the Cambodian model of disproportionate revenge. . . .

One of the most chronic and volatile sources of violence in Cambodia is a "grudge" (*kum, kumkuon, kumnum, kongkuon*) that leads to the desire for "disproportionate revenge" (*karsângsoek*). . . . While such a grudge most often arises when another person (or group) makes the

SOURCE: Alexander Laban Hinton, "A Head for an Eye: Revenge in the Cambodian Genocide," *American Ethnologist* 25, no. 3 (1998): 353, 355, 356–57, 358, 359, 361, 362–63, 364, 365, 366, 367, 369. Reprinted with permission of the author and publisher.

individual in question (or that person's group) suffer (e.g., by murdering a family member), lose power (e.g., by deposing that person from office), and/or lose face (e.g., by dishonoring that person by a slight), it almost always involves anger, shame, and the desire to defeat (*chneah*) a foe. Vengeance has a distinct moral basis in Cambodian culture. The root of the word *sângsoek*, *sâng*, refers to the moral obligation "to return (an object), to pay back (debt), to pay for damage." One of the greatest virtues in Cambodia is repaying (*sâng*) the "kindness" (*kun*) of others. Thus, Cambodians are morally obliged to "repay the good deeds" (*sângkun*) that their parents, relatives, teachers, and patrons have done for them. An ingrate who ignores this debt (*romilkun*) is widely detested. Whereas in many Judeo-Christian societies such moral debts are often viewed as analogous to a commercial transaction, in Cambodia they frequently create a personalized relationship between the two parties involved. . . .

By extension, we can see that revenge is the moral inverse of gratitude. Just as people must return a good deed, so too are they morally obliged to repay a bad deed. The word *sângsoek* literally means "to pay back" (*sâng*) "the enemy" (*soek*). Moreover, the injured party's obligation to repay an enemy for whatever the latter has done creates a bond between them. A Cambodian bearing malice is often said to be "tied, linked" (*châng*) to an enemy by anger or a grudge (*châng komhoeng*, *châng kumnum*). During the post–Khmer Rouge communist period . . . , for example, the government sponsored a national holiday on May 20 that was popularly known as the "Day to Remain Tied in Anger" (or, sometimes, the "Day of Hate").

A Cambodian who has a big grudge is sometimes said to want to "eat the flesh and sip the blood" (*si sach hot cheam*) of the enemy. Despite this strong desire to take revenge, however, Cambodians recognize that it is often not propitious to repay a bad deed immediately. A grudge thus contains an element of latent potentiality and is frequently long-lasting. . . . To maintain an element of surprise or to prevent a powerful adversary from taking the initiative, Cambodians bearing malice will often try to hide their animosity from their foes. . . . Those who are unable to seek revenge in person may decide to hire a killer or order a subordinate to perform the deed. . . .

[One] reason why a Cambodian grudge results in disproportionate revenge is the view that a person must "completely defeat the enemy" (*phchanh phchal*) in order to deter further retaliation. The phrase *phchanh phchal* literally means "to defeat, vanquish" in such a manner as "to cause [the opponent] to be afraid and not dare to repeat the same act." . . . The extreme form of *phchanh phchal* consists of killing one's enemy and possibly their family lines as well. . . . The origins of this tradition go far back in Cambodian history to times when, after winning a war, a victorious Cambodian king would sometimes attempt to kill the opposing king and his entire family line. As we shall see, much DK violence can be viewed as a modern example of "cutting off a familial line." . . .

In early 1967 hundreds of peasants from the Samlaut subdistrict in Battambang province revolted. Fed up with the government's new policy of directly purchasing the rice crop from farmers at prices far below the black market rate, high levels of debt, heavy-handed treatment by local soldiers, corruption, and the reallocation of their land, peasant rebels murdered two soldiers and stole their weapons on the morning of April 2. . . . During the next few weeks, the revolt quickly expanded. . . . While the Samlaut rebellion did not overthrow the Sihanouk government, it illustrated the existence of a substantial base of disaffected peasants who could potentially be incited to join the Khmer Rouge movement. . . . Khmer Rouge ideology took the resentment stemming from all these sources and gave it a common focus (class struggle) and target (the urban population). Political education sessions were geared . . . to "create class ardor and fury."

Khmer Rouge ideologies attempted to focus the "burning rage" . . . upon the urban centers, the bastions of capitalism. This goal was often not difficult to achieve given the initial resentment many of the poor felt toward rich city people who allegedly looked down upon them, enjoyed a much easier life, and supported Lon Nol, who was responsible for the overthrowing of [Prince] Sihanouk and the carpet bombing of the countryside. Khmer Rouge propaganda employed slogans such as "trees in the country, fruit in the town." . . . By drawing on preexisting resentment and focusing it on the city, Khmer Rouge ideology effectively fostered a rural class grudge (*kumnum vonnah*) against the urban population. The city people had done "something bad" to the poor by making them suffer and lose face. One or more of these "happenings" led the poor to be "seized with painful anger" (*chheu chap*), which they stored inside themselves. The Khmer Rouge inflamed this hidden resentment into a class grudge that motivated many of the poor to want to "eat the flesh and sip the blood" of their enemies. . . .

This hatred was quickly directed at the first targets of revenge, the Lon Nol government and military. Leading officials were rounded up and executed. . . . Urbanites being evacuated out of the cities were asked to give background information about their former occupations. Many who told the truth were taken away to be killed. Others were sent to be "re-educated" in special camps or through rural peasant life. Up to two hundred thousand people may have been killed during this first wave of DK killing. . . . Instead of ending the vengeance after this initial period of violence, the Khmer Rouge attempted to keep the class grudge inflamed. . . . Realizing to whom such ideology would have the greatest appeal, the Khmer Rouge placed the extreme poor and the young in local-level positions of power during DK. These individuals had the greatest reason to hate their "class enemies" and to be loyal to their powerful new patron, Ângkar. . . .

The family of a young woman named Gen experienced a similar tragedy, which I will recount in detail. When local officials began researching people's backgrounds, her family could not hide the fact that her father, Tak, had been a teacher during the Lon Nol period. . . . Tak eventually went to the local hospital because his stomach had become swollen because of lack of food. A few days later, Tak was told to gather his things because he was being transferred to the regional hospital. Instead of going there, Tak was taken to an area behind the hospital and killed. . . . Perhaps two months later, Gen's mother went to the hospital to get an injection to make her feel better. Before administering the shot, the doctor, Khon, supposedly asked, "Are you Tak's wife?" When she responded affirmatively, Khon filled the syringe with a white liquid. Gen's mother died immediately after receiving the shot. . . . Three of Gen's sisters were the next to be killed. . . . A few days later, Gen and her younger sister made a dramatic escape from the village. Unfortunately, Gen's four younger brothers were still in the area living with an uncle. [The subdistrict head] sent for them and had them work the local pagoda, which was being used by the Khmer Rouge as a prison. Their job was to carry out the prisoners' excrement. Just before the end of DK, the boys were all executed after being forced to dig their own graves.

The destruction of Gen's entire family illustrates how the Khmer Rouge attempted to take disproportionate revenge in such a manner as to "destroy completely" (*phchanh phchal*) their class enemies. Because the Khmer Rouge were so powerful, they were able to engage in the most extreme form of *phchanh phchal*—killing off the enemy's line. Gen sadly explained, "The Khmer Rouge had a grudge against my family because my father had been a government worker during the previous regime. They were seized with painful anger and wanted to take revenge against 'new' people like us. They wanted to cut off our entire familial line so no one would be left to seek revenge against them on a later day." Many other Cambodian family lines were similarly destroyed during the DK. . . .

I have attempted to provide an example of how anthropology can contribute to our understanding of large-scale genocide. In particular, I have demonstrated how the Cambodian cultural model of disproportionate revenge served as a template for part of the genocidal violence that occurred in DK. It is crucial for anthropologists to point out how cultural models come to serve as templates for violence, since such implicit cultural knowledge often provides fodder for genocidal ideologies. . . . Khmer Rouge ideology about class struggle, which played upon traditional suffering and humiliation of the poor, served to transform the anger and resentment of many of the regime's followers into a class struggle. These cadres and soldiers in turn used the traditional cultural model of disproportionate revenge as a template for committing genocidal atrocities. The result was the death of hundreds of thousands of "enemies" and, often, of their families.

67 • Who Were the *Génocidaires* of Rwanda? (Scott Straus)

Why did ordinary Rwandans participate in the 1994 genocide, and how? And who were they? In his book The Order of Genocide *(2006), Scott Straus, professor of political science at the University of Wisconsin, Madison, reports findings gleaned from 210 interviews with convicted perpetrators. Aside from basic demographic data, we learn about the educational and occupational background of the perpetrator sample and the varieties in which—and the degrees to which—Rwanda's Hutu partook in the genocidal campaign. Straus concludes that the number of perpetrators was likely considerably lower than previously assumed.*

We know little about the basic facts of the perpetrator population [during the 1994 genocide in Rwanda] in terms of who the perpetrators were, how they compare to the rest of the Rwandan population, and how many perpetrators there were. . . . I focus on the attacks themselves. I discuss who led the attacks against Tutsis, as well as how large the attacks were. I use my findings here to estimate how many perpetrators there were in the genocide. Overall, the chapter helps clarify the dynamics of genocide at the local level. . . .

I decided that the best method for generating theoretically relevant information about perpetrators was to interview them. . . . In total, I interviewed 210 detainees in fifteen central prisons during a six month period, and the survey represents the largest study of perpetrators of which I am aware. . . . With that background in mind, let me now turn to the findings. I start

SOURCE: Scott Straus, *The Order of Genocide: Race, Power, and War in Rwanda* (Ithaca, N.Y.: Cornell University Press, 2006), 97, 99, 100, 103, 104, 105, 106–8, 109–10, 111, 112, 113, 114–15, 116, 117–18. Reprinted with permission of the publisher.

with the basic demographic profile of the perpetrators: age, level of education, paternity rate, and so forth. Where possible, I compare my findings to national census figures before the genocide in order to determine how and whether perpetrators differed from the rest of the population.

How old were Rwanda's *génocidaires*? Many observers claim that young men and "unemployed city youth" were the genocide's main perpetrators. . . . The results clearly show that my sample of perpetrators is not predominantly youthful. To the contrary, the perpetrators were primarily adult men: 89 percent were 20 to 49 years old and the greatest concentration were men 30 to 39 years old. The median age was 34. . . . The results for paternity rates are similar. Most perpetrators in my sample—some 77 percent—were fathers: they were not unattached youths. . . . I also asked each respondent to identify his occupation. . . . Overall[,] the sample's occupation profile is broadly similar to the national population. The main difference is an overrepresentation of professionals, administrative cadre, and specialized workers in the sample. . . . The findings on education and literacy show the same. . . . Overall, the perpetrators appear to be slightly better educated than the average Rwandan man, but the differences are slight and may reflect a skew in the census. Again, this evidence indicates that Rwandan perpetrators were representative of the adult male Hutu population at the time of the genocide and certainly were not undereducated. Taken together, the findings . . . have important implications. Some theories posit that genocide perpetrators are different in some fashion. They might be sadistic, socially deviant, or otherwise predisposed to violence. Or perpetrators might be ignorant or deprived in some fashion. My findings run squarely against these arguments. Rwanda's perpetrators as represented in my random sample of sentenced confessors were quite ordinary. . . .

In addition to questions about demographic data, I also asked respondents about their social affiliations and networks. Here I wanted to find out both whether perpetrators came from particular political parties and whether preexisting social networks were the primary conduits for mobilization. . . . I start with political party affiliation. . . . The responses appear credible, and they suggest that party affiliation alone did not determine who became a perpetrator. Perpetrators belong to every major party in the country. During the interviews, I also asked a series of questions relating to civic and state involvement. . . . The strongest positive finding here concerns the *umuganda* community labor program: some 88 percent of respondents took part in the program. Without comparable data, I cannot say whether participation in the program predisposed men to commit genocide or whether the program itself was widespread. But at a minimum the finding demonstrates that a large number of genocide perpetrators had already complied with state orders to participate in unpaid labor *before the genocide*. . . . Nothing stands out among the other findings. Some respondents had family members in the government but most did not. . . . The same is true for associational membership. . . .

Not all perpetrators were alike in their degree of participation. Some killed many Tutsis; others led the killing in their areas; others killed one person; still others joined attacks against Tutsis but did not kill. . . . Measuring degree of participation matters for evaluating whether differences in participation correlate to differences in the characteristics discussed above. To look for these relationships, I use two different statistical procedures. . . . The regression analyses indicate that the younger perpetrators, those with fewer or no children, and those with lower levels of education tended to be the most violent during the genocide. The findings thus support some common wisdom about the genocide: namely, that Rwanda's killers were un-attached youths and poorly educated. In other words, my primary finding . . . is that most perpetrators were ordinary men who broadly reflected the society in which they lived. How-ever, the statistical analysis reveals that among perpetrators the most violent appear to have been younger, less well educated, and with fewer children, often no children. . . .

Occupation also matters. The self-described leaders were all administration officials, non-state rural elites, or farmers who had other ways to earn income (one was a tailor, the other a brickmaker). However, of those who killed two or more people, nearly 90 percent had preexisting firearms training (as in the case of an army reservist or a forest guard) or were farmers. These patterns suggest that the leaders of the violence tended to have some preexist-ing social status, while the most violent persons tended to be trained in firearm use or were young farmers. These statistical results have important implications. They confirm a general pattern. . . . In particular, there was a core group of perpetrators at the local level. These in-cluded local elites who tended to take charge during the genocide, whether they held govern-ment posts or not. Working with them were the "thugs": a small group of younger men or those who had firearms. The thugs were political party youths, angry young men, reservists, and, in one case, a forest guard. They were local specialists in violence or those who used their youth and strength to their advantage, and they did the lion's share of killing. The stereotype of the unattached youthful militia may not characterize the perpetrator population as a whole but rather those who were most violent at the local level. Otherwise, ordinary Hutu men formed the mass of perpetrators. . . .

I also asked respondents to describe attacks against Tutsis in some detail. . . . The evi-dence is consistent with the patterns seen elsewhere: the leaders of attacks tended to have preexisting social status—they were local authorities or local elites—or else they were offi-cials in the army or the gendarmerie. . . . The evidence also shows how during the genocide, non-state authorities could opportunistically seize the initiative and lead the violence in their areas. . . . Armed militias [such as the notorious Interahamwe] also played an important role, but their presence was less pervasive than is often claimed: they were present only in about a quarter of attacks. Moreover, according to the respondents, armed militias were in the attacks *without* civilian authorities or soldiers in only 3 percent of the cases. The perpetrators also indicate that Burundians were not strongly present in most attacks, a finding that runs con-trary to the claim that Burundi refugees were key instigators of the violence. . . .

I also asked respondents about the magnitude of the attacks in which they partici-pated. . . . First, violence during the genocide happened almost exclusively in groups. Of all the respondents I interviewed, only one said he launched an attack of his own. The genocide was a group-perpetrated activity. Second, perpetrator groups varied in size, but many were quite large. Nearly 20 percent of all reported attacks had one hundred or more perpetrators, and some attacks exceeded a thousand persons. As for the size of the perpetrator population, I estimate 5,852 *cellules* [or cells, the lowest administrative unit] where genocide occurred, a number that I multiply by the estimate of the average number of perpetrators per cellule. The product of these numbers is 128,744 persons [as opposed to estimates claiming figures from tens of thousands to several million perpetrators], which is a base estimate for the number of perpetrators (22 persons x 5,852 *cellules*). . . . If we assume a baseline standard of thirty per-petrators per cellule, the total number of perpetrators would be about 175,000, whereas if we

242 THREE • Courses

assume thirty-five perpetrators per cellule, then the total number of perpetrators would be about 210,000. . . .

If the figure of 175,000 to 210,000 perpetrators holds up as more evidence becomes available, the estimate has two important implications. First, the numbers run counter to allegations that the current authorities are governing a "criminal population." The Rwandan census defines "active adults" as eighteen to fifty-four years old. As such, my estimate of the number of perpetrators equals 7 to 8 percent of the active adult Hutu population and 14 to 17 percent of the active adult male Hutu population at the time of the genocide. It was not all Hutus who participated in the genocide, nor all Hutu men. It was only a minority who did. Second, even if not all Hutu men participated in the genocide, a very significant number did. Rarely do governments succeed in mobilizing 14 to 17 percent of an adult male population to participate in state-sanctioned behavior. . . .

Some scholars argue that in most genocides direct participation in the murdering of civilians is limited to a very small minority of the population. If true, then the magnitude of civilian participation in the Rwandan genocide would be anomalous when compared to other cases of genocide. . . . All this points to the importance of civilian participation in the genocide and the need to explain it.

68 • The Cultural Face of Hutu Terror (Christopher C. Taylor)

In this 2002 book chapter, the anthropologist Christopher Taylor argues that knowledge about how people kill can tell us something about why they kill. If we believe him, the destruction of a targeted individual or group in times of genocide is often about much more than mass murder. Taylor finds that many of Rwanda's Hutu perpetrators communicated powerful messages about themselves by killing Tutsi victims in ways that invoked (although perhaps not always consciously) Rwandan symbolism and tradition. Taylor illustrates his innovative argument with particular reference to the role of "flow/blockage" imagery in the course of the genocidal campaign. Put simply, he maintains that in keeping with local symbolism, Tutsis came to be portrayed, and eventually seen, as "obstructing beings" who were interrupting the natural flow of life in the body politic. Taylor explains that because this particular cosmology—defined as the beliefs, interpretations, and practices that collectivities invent and, over time, turn into templates for making sense of the place of humans in the universe— has for a long time had a strong hold on Rwanda's rural population, the "removal" of the human blockage from the body politic took on a cultural significance above and beyond the destruction of a mere enemy.

The violence that occurred in Rwanda cannot be reduced solely and simply to the competition for power, dominance, and hegemony among antagonistic factions. Much of the violence, I maintain, followed a cultural patterning, a structured and structuring logic, as individual

source: Christopher C. Taylor, "The Cultural Face of Terror in the Rwandan Genocide of 1994," in Alexander Laban Hinton, ed., *Annihilating Difference: The Anthropology of Genocide* (Berkeley: University of California Press, 2002), 139, 141, 146, 147, 148, 158–59, 160, 161, 163, 164, 165, 166, 168, 169, 171. Reprinted with permission of the publisher.

Rwandans lashed out against a perceived internal other who threatened, in their imaginary, both their personal integrity and the cosmic order of the state. It was overwhelmingly Tutsi who were sacrificial victims in what in many respects was a massive ritual of purification, a ritual intended to purge the nation of "obstructing beings," as the threat of obstruction was imagined through a Rwandan ontology that situates the body politic in analogical relation to the individual human body. . . .

But there was no simple cultural determinism to the Rwandan genocide. I do not advance the argument that the political events of 1994 were in any way caused by these symbols, or by Rwandan "culture," conceived of in a cognitively determinist way in the manner of [Daniel Jonah] Goldhagen's controversial analysis of the Nazi genocide. These representations operated as much during times of peace as during times of war. The "generative schemes"— the logical substrate of oppositions, analogies, and homologies—upon which the representations were based constituted for many Rwandans a practical, everyday sense of body, self, and others. Because these "generative schemes" were internalized during early socialization, they took on a nearly unconscious or "goes without saying" quality. Although many Rwandan social actors embodied this knowledge, they never explicitly verbalized it. . . .

In order to make . . . forms of violence comprehensible in terms of local symbolism, it is first necessary to understand . . . that social systems inscribe "law" onto the bodies of their subjects. . . . Based on Rwandan popular medical practices that I observed during the 1980s, I have elsewhere advanced the hypothesis that a root metaphor underlies conceptualizations of the body. Basically, these conceptualizations are characterized by an opposition between orderly states of humoral and other flows to disorderly ones. Analogies are constructed that take this opposition as their base and then relate bodily processes to those of social and natural life. In the unfolding of human and natural events, flow/blockage symbolism mediates between physiological, sociological, and cosmological levels of causality. . . . Pathological states are characterized by obstructed or excessive flows. . . . Despite an apparently less than conscious quality in Rwanda, flow/blockage metaphors are imagined and enacted in a diverse array of domains. Although they may be most commonly encountered in popular healing, my research has revealed that similar representations are also present in myths, legends, and the rituals of sacred kingship, and that they involve potencies of various types. . . .

The construction of the moral person among rural Rwandans is contingent upon the social attestation that the person properly embodies the physiological attributes that analogically evoke the capacity to reciprocate. This entails the capacity to ingest and the capacity to excrete. . . . By analogical extension the concern with unobstructed connection and unimpeded movement characterizes earlier Rwandan symbolic thought about the topography of the land, its rivers, roads, and pathways in general. . . . In Rwanda of 1994 torturers manifested a certain proclivity to employ violent methods with specific forms. These forms betrayed a preoccupation with the movement of persons and substances and with the canals, arteries, and conduits along which persons and substances flow: rivers, roadways, pathways, even the conduits of the human body, such as the reproductive and digestive systems. . . .

Although in the postcolonial Rwandan state . . . rivers appear to have lost their previous ritual significance, Rwanda's rivers were conscripted into the genocide. . . . Rwanda's rivers [into which perpetrators dumped the bodies of their victims] became part of the genocide by acting as the body politic's organ of elimination, in a sense "excreting" its hated internal other.

It is not much of a leap to infer that Tutsi were thought of as excrement by their persecutors. Other evidence of this is apparent in the fact that many Tutsi were stuffed into latrines after their deaths. Some were even thrown while still alive into latrines; a few of them actually managed to survive and to extricate themselves.

Among the accounts of Rwandan refugees that I interviewed in Kenya during the late spring and early summer of 1994, there was persistent mention of barriers and roadblocks. . . . These were the most frequent loci of execution for Rwanda's Tutsi and Hutu opponents of the regime. Barriers were erected almost ubiquitously and by many different groups. There were roadblocks manned by Rwandan government forces, roadblocks of the dreaded *Interahamwe* militia, Rwandan communal police checkpoints, barriers set up by neighborhood protection groups, opportunistic roadblocks erected by gangs of criminals, and even occasional checkpoints manned by the Rwandan Patriotic Front in areas under their control. For people attempting to flee Rwanda, evading these blockades was virtually impossible. . . . Barriers were ritual and liminal spaces where "obstructing beings" were to be obstructed in their turn and cast out of the nation. The roadblocks were the space both of ritual and of transgression. . . . There were scenes of inordinate cruelty. . . .

If the movement of people could be obstructed with barriers, it could also be hindered by directly attacking the body. The parts of the body most frequently targeted to induce immobility were the legs, feet, and Achilles tendons. Thousands of corpses discovered after the violence showed evidence of one or both tendons having been sectioned by machete blows. . . . As with barriers on paths and roadways, there is a deeper generative scheme that subtends both the killers' intentionality and the message inscribed on the bodies of their victims, even though these techniques of cruelty also involve a degree of improvisation. Power in this instance, in symbolic terms, derives from the capacity to obstruct. . . .

In addition to the imagery of obstruction, numerous instances of the body as conduit can be discerned in the Rwandan violence of 1994. This imagery tends to center on two bodily foci: the digestive tract and the reproductive system. . . . Perhaps the most vivid example of this during the genocide was the practice of impalement. . . . Rwandan Tutsi men in 1994 were . . . impaled from anus to mouth with wooden or bamboo poles and metal spears. Tutsi women were often impaled from vagina to mouth. . . . In precolonial and early colonial times, Rwandans impaled cattle thieves. . . . The torturers [in 1994] not only killed their victims; they transformed their bodies into powerful sins that resonated with a Rwandan habitus even as they improvised upon it and enlarged the original semantic domain of associated meanings to depict an entire ethnic group as enemies of the Hutu state.

Among other violence reported during the Rwandan genocide, there were frequent instances of emasculation of Tutsi males, even those too young to reproduce. Attackers also slashed off the breasts of Tutsi women. These techniques of cruelty had also been employed during earlier periods of Rwandan history. Both emasculation and breast oblation manifest a preoccupation with the reproductive system, and specifically with parts of the body that produce fertility fluids. In both cases, the symbolic function interdigitates with and reinforces the pragmatic function, but the symbolic function cannot simply be reduced to the pragmatic one of destroying the future capacity of a group to reproduce. . . . In order to convince themselves that they were ridding the polity of a categorical enemy and not just assaulting specific individuals, they first had to transform their victims' bodies into the equivalent of "blocked beings." . . . There were also cases of forcing adult Tutsi to commit incest with one of their children before killing them. Here the image of misdirected flows is quite clear, for incest causes blood and semen to flow backward upon one another in a closed circuit within the family rather than in an open circuit between families. Not only were the victims brutalized and dehumanized by this treatment but, in addition, their bodies were transformed into icons of asociality. . . .

Methodological individualists might very well object that atrocities occur in all violent conflicts, and that they are at their worst in fratricidal disputes and civil wars. The Rwandan atrocities would then have followed an instrumental logic based on maximizing the number of enemies killed, or maximizing the psychological effect by the sheer horror of atrocity. Such an explanation might concur with what the authors of the atrocities themselves claim was the reasoning behind their acts. Although such an explanation is not inexact, it is incomplete. It cannot explain the depth of passion that clearly lay behind the Rwandan violence, nor the fact that it assumed specific forms. One type of logic to the cruelty does not preclude all others; pragmatism and symbolism in a general way are not necessarily conflictual. Killing one's adversaries while communicating powerful messages about them and oneself are not mutually exclusive.

69 • Genocide in Gujarat (Martha C. Nussbaum)

Was genocide committed in the state of Gujarat, India, when several thousand Muslims were mutilated and killed in the aftermath of a mysterious train fire in 2002? If so, how? Martha Nussbaum, professor of law and ethics at the University of Chicago, takes on both questions in her 2003 article. She contends that the campaign waged against Muslims was indeed genocidal in nature and the result of the long and deliberate construction of hatred by the Hindu nationalist party, Bharatiya Janata. In Nussbaum's reading of the facts, the intent to destroy Gujarat's Muslims was present "in all the ways" the 1948 Genocide Convention specifies.

On February 27, 2002, the Sabarmati express train arrived in the station of Godhra, in the state of Gujarat, bearing a large group of Hindu pilgrims who were returning from the alleged birthplace of the god Rama at Ayodhya (where some years earlier, angry Hindu mobs had destroyed the Babri mosque, which they claim is on top of the remains of Rama's birthplace). The pilgrimage, like many others in recent times, aimed at forcibly constructing a temple over the disputed site, and the mood of the returning passengers, frustrated in their aims by the government and the courts, was angrily emotional. When the train stopped at the station, passengers got into arguments with Muslim vendors and passengers. At least one Muslim vendor was beaten up when he refused to say *"Jai Sri Ram"* ("Hail Ram"), and a young Muslim girl narrowly escaped forcible abduction. As the train left the station, stones were thrown at it, apparently by Muslims.

SOURCE: Martha C. Nussbaum, "Genocide in Gujarat," *Dissent* 50, no. 3 (2003): 15–20. Reprinted with permission of the University of Pennsylvania Press.

Fifteen minutes later, one car of the train erupted in flames. Fifty-eight men, women, and children died in the fire. Most were Hindus. Attempts to determine what really happened by reconstructing the event have shown only that a large amount of a flammable substance must have been thrown from inside the train. We will never know who threw it. Because the area adjacent to the tracks contained Muslim dwellings, and because a Muslim mob had gathered in the region to protest the treatment of Muslims on the train platform, blame was immediately put on Muslims. (One former chief minister of Gujarat, Amarsinh Chaudhary, argued that the blaze was set by Hindu nationalists. Many others agree, especially in light of later evidence that the subsequent rioting had been elaborately prepared.) No evidence has been found linking alleged Muslim perpetrators to any organized movement or group.

In the days that followed, wave upon wave of violence swept through the state. The attackers were Hindus, many of them highly politicized, shouting Hindu-right slogans, such as *"Jai Sri Ram"* and *"Jai Hanuman"* (an aggressive monkey god), along with "Kill!" "Destroy!" "Slaughter!" There is copious evidence that the violence was planned before the precipitating event. The victims were almost all Muslims (with an occasional Christian or Parsi thrown in). There was no connection between victims and the alleged perpetrators; attacks took place, for the most part, far from the original site. Many families of the original dead implored the mobs to stop the violence. Nonetheless, more than two thousand Muslims were killed in a few days, many by being burned alive in or near their homes. Nobody was spared: young children were immolated along with their families. Particularly striking were the mass rapes and mutilations of women. Typically, a woman would be raped or gang-raped, often with gruesome tortures, and then set on fire and killed. Historian Tanika Sarkar, who played a leading role in investigating the events, has argued that the evident preoccupation with destroying women's sexual organs reveals "a dark sexual obsession about allegedly ultra-virile Muslim male bodies and overfertile Muslim female ones, that inspire[s] and sustain[s] the figures of paranoia and revenge." This sexual obsession is evident in the hate literature circulated during the carnage, of which the following "poem" is a typical example:

> Narendra Modi [chief minister of Gujarat] you have fucked the mother of [Muslims]
> The volcano which was inactive for years has erupted
> It has burnt the arse of [Muslims] and made them dance nude
> We have untied the penises which were tied till now
> Without castor oil in the arse we have made them cry. . . .
> Wake up Hindus, there are still [Muslims] alive around you
> Learn from Panvad village where their mother was fucked
> She was fucked standing while she kept shouting
> She enjoyed the uncircumcised penis
> With a Hindu government the Hindus have the power to annihilate [Muslims]
> Kick them in the arse to drive them out of not only villages and
> Cities but also the country. [The word rendered "Muslims" (*miyas*) is a word
>   meaning "mister" that is standardly used to refer to Muslims.]

As Sarkar says, the incitement to violence is suffused with anxiety about virility, and the treatment of women seems to enact a fantasy of sexual sadism far darker than mere revenge. During the violence, many Muslim cities and villages were burned to the ground. Muslims of all social classes fled for their lives. One former chief justice of the Rajasthani High Court, living in retirement in Gujarat, fled, later commenting to an investigative tribunal that there was "a deliberate conspiracy to stifle criminal law." What this witness meant was that the carnage was aided and abetted both by the police and by local politicians. . . . Meetings were held between police and local government leaders, at which Hindus were called "we" and Muslims "them," and pleas of some officers to take action against rioters were rejected. Meanwhile, local leaders of the Hindu-right were seen shouting slogans and inciting the mob to further violence.

Particularly upsetting was the active participation of tribal and lower caste Hindus, *adivasis* and *dalits*, in the violence against equally poor Muslims. The Hindu nationalist party, Bharatiya Janata (BJP), has succeeded all too well in its strategy of getting many lower caste Hindus to put religion ahead of caste and class and to fear as their enemies not the wealthy and upper caste Hindus who have long oppressed them, but the Muslims who in most cases share their economic misery.

The events of March 2002 emerged from a long history of deliberate construction of hate. For some time, a lot of money (whose sources I shall discuss later) has been poured into the creation of camps for young Hindu men, where they are taught hatred and fear of Muslims and partisan fervor is cultivated. For older folks, the Vishwa Hindu Parishad (VHP), the cultural wing of the Hindu nationalist movement, organizes pilgrimages to Ayodyha, which invariably stir up sectarian emotion. But the history of the episode goes back much further. We need to consider the origins of the BJP (the political arm of Hindu nationalism) and its allied organizations, the umbrella Rashtriya Swayamsevak Sangh (RSS), the Bajrang Dal (para-military), and the VHP (cultural). When we examine this history, we see that the tensions between Hindus and Muslims expressed here are not "ancient" or even indigenous hatreds. They result from a borrowed fascist ideology of purity, which has gradually been imposed, transforming a Hinduism that in its origins is plural, diverse, and tolerant.

The ideologue whose views were central in the formation of the RSS and BJP, M. Golwalkar, derived many of his views from German romantic nationalism, and especially from its National Socialist formation. In his 1939 tract *We, or Our Nationhood Defined*, Golwalkar argues that only Hindus are true Indians, and that Muslims, Christians, Parsis, and Jews are all foreigners, who should stay in the territory only on terms set by the Hindus. . . . Golwalkar portrays the Muslims, particularly, as outsiders and "despoilers" who must now finally be "shake[n] off." Expressing his sympathy with the Nazi program, he writes:

> To keep up the purity of the Race and its culture, Germany shocked the world by her purging the country of the Semitic Races—the Jews. Race pride at its highest has been manifested here. Germany has also shown how well nigh impossible it is for Races and cultures, having differences going to the root, to be assimilated into one united whole, a good lesson for us in Hindusthan to learn and profit by.

As late as 1966, Golwalkar repeated the same views, calling Jews and Parsis "guests," and Muslims and Christians "invaders." And he explicitly attacked the Indian Constitution (drafted in 1950) for its pluralism and secularism. . . . Such attitudes have nothing to do with the history of the Hindu religion or with any religious doctrines dating from before the 1930s. Hinduism, rather like ancient Greek religion, has traditionally been plural, loosely organized,

regional, and highly varied. The very idea that Rama is the one central god in the Hindu pantheon is itself a BJP political construct. In some regions Rama was important, in others not,
and in some he was not even thought of as an admirable deity. Hindus and Muslims have
traditionally borrowed a lot from one another, and it is futile to inquire into the origins of a
given practice. Most salient differences that studies of human well-being measure (for example, differences regarding the status of women) are regional rather than religious; that is, Hindus and Muslims in a given region have similar practices in many important matters. Over the
years, however, the BJP has worked very successfully to create the public perception that Hinduism really is what the BJP says it is, and that Islam is very different, dedicated to violence
and subversion and to the oppression of women. . . .

Gujarat has been unusually prone to outbreaks of both anti-Christian and anti-Muslim
violence, and its elected BJP officials ran on a strong Hinduization platform. Why should
tensions run high in Gujarat, the state that gave birth to Gandhi's campaign of nonviolence,
the state that saw the birth of Ela Bhatt's now world-famous movement to organize female
workers? One plausible conjecture is that the Muslims of Gujarat play a somewhat different
role in society than Muslims elsewhere in India. Elsewhere, Muslims are on average poor, ill-
educated, downtrodden. In Gujarat, although most Muslims are very poor, a significant number have been a merchant class, well off and socially prominent. They can thus be compared
to the Jews in Europe: as successful people they more easily arouse fear and resentment. Still,
before the advent of the BJP and RSS, Hindus and Muslims for the most part lived side by side
in amity. . . .

How should concerned citizens of the world think about these terrible events [in Guja-
rat]? . . . It is an undisputed fact about Gujarat that there were mass killings and rapes on
grounds of religion. Muslims were sought out not because of any even imagined complicity
in the precipitating event at Godhra, but simply because they were Muslims. Slogans shouted
by the mob indicate that their intent was to assert Hindu superiority, to exterminate Muslims,
and to destroy Muslim society: for example, "Kill them all, destroy their society." "Finish off
all Muslims; our people were not spared by them, don't have mercy." In light of these facts, it
seems beyond dispute that the violence in Gujarat meets the definition of genocide offered in
the UN Convention on Genocide. . . . Indeed, given the centrality of rape in the events that
took place, usually rape followed by murder, we can say that the intent to destroy the group is
enacted in all the ways the Convention specifies—with the exception of the removal of children to another group, since children were murdered here along with their parents. Moreover,
the evidence of long and deliberate construction of hatred undermines any claim that these
events were just the acts of a mob that got out of control.

70 ▸ Insurrection in Darfur (Robert O. Collins)

*A longtime historian of Darfur, Robert Collins in his 2008 book analyzes the convoluted history of
insurrection in western Sudan, focusing on the interplay between incumbents in Khartoum and*

SOURCE: Robert O. Collins, *A History of Modern Sudan* (Cambridge: Cambridge University Press, 2008),
    287–90, 291–92, 293. Reprinted with permission of the publisher.

insurgents in Darfur. Against this background, he recounts the typical course of destruction in the countryside. The story that emerges is one considerably more complex than the conventional narrative, according to which the government in Khartoum pursued a straight path to genocide.

On 26 February 2003 some 300 rebels calling themselves the Darfur Liberation Front (DLF) and led by 'Abd al-Wahid Muhammad al-Nur seized the town of Gulu, capital of Jabal Marra Province in western Darfur, and raided scattered police and army posts before retiring to their training camps in Jabal Marra. Two weeks later, the DLF, now called the Sudan Liberation Movement/Army (SLM/A), briefly recaptured Gulu in a fierce firefight, killing 195 government soldiers and forcing the garrison to flee. Secretary-General of the SLM, the political arm of the movement, Minni Arku Minnawi, released its Political Declaration to the press in which the SLM/A opposed the policies of Arabization, political and economic marginalization, and "the brutal oppression, ethnic cleansing, and genocide sponsored by the Khartoum Government."

The second insurgency organization in Darfur, the JEM [Justice and Equality Movement], was very different from the secular SLM/A and more of a rival than an ally in the struggle against the Sudanese government in Darfur. Unlike the indigenous African Fur origins of the SLM/A, the JEM's beginnings were among the "riverized" Darfuris, a patronizing term used by traditionalists to describe those from Darfur living in Khartoum who had adopted many of the customs and characteristics of the riverine Arabs. Like their country cousins, however, many had become increasingly embittered by marginalized treatment and discrimination toward them, despite their partial integration into the urban life of the capital. In the early 1990s they had embraced with considerable enthusiasm the Islamist revolution engineered by Hasan al Turabi and were, paradoxically, stalwart members of the NIF [National Islamic Front]. . . . Unlike the members of the SLM, they were not about to abandon their Arabic Islamic beliefs, but instead they sought to reform the NIF from within to give the *awlad al-gharib* ["people of the west"] the proper recognition in the central and now regional government that had been denied to them ever since the British left Sudan in 1956. . . .

Khartoum university students have always been compulsive organizers. And the Darfuri graduates were no exception. They formed a committee of twenty-five in 1997 who began to collect the appalling statistics of their economic and political marginalization, culminating in the publication of the *Black Book* in May 2000 which convinced its members that reform from within had to be replaced by a more active program of reform from without. It remains unclear how many were willing to abandon their Islamist principles, but they no longer believed they were the answer to the Darfur Problem, which only an armed insurrection, appropriately called *the Justice and Equality Movement*, could resolve.

In August 2001 Dr. [Khalil] Ibrahim [Muhammad, formerly Minister for Education in the old Darfur province] grandly announced the founding of the JEM at a press conference in the Netherlands and called for "a comprehensive congress to redress injustices perpetuated by 'a small group of autocratic rulers.'" The JEM sought a utopian solution in Sudan whereby all Sudanese, not just Darfuris, would have equal rights, basic services, and economic development in every region, from which social injustice and political tyranny would be extirpated. Unlike the SLM/A, who demanded the separation of church and state, the leaders of the JEM could not entirely discard their Islamist roots and somewhat ambiguously agreed that shari'a

should not be imposed upon non-Muslims, but that "believers in other faiths must not oppose Muslim attempts to apply the laws of religion for themselves."

Within a few days of the SLA victory at Gulu the government security committee for
western Darfur swiftly opened negotiations with the SLM and arranged a fragile cease-fire. It
soon collapsed. On 18 March 2003 an Arab militia assassinated a respected Masalit leader,
Shayk Salih Dakoro, near Geneina. This was followed by Sudanese air force Hind helicopter
gunships destroying the town of Karnoi. The SLA retaliated on 25 March, seizing the strategic
Masalit town of Tiné on the Chad frontier and capturing large stocks of arms and equipment
from its garrison. Thereafter, fighting raged throughout West Darfur State during which the
easy victories of the SLA dramatically revealed that the several thousand government troops
stationed in Darfur were ill-prepared and inadequate to contain a major insurgency.

Consequently, on Friday 25 April 2003, a combined SLA/JEM force, sometimes spe-
ciously called the "Opposition Forces," with thirty-three "technicals" staged a hit-and-run attack
on the airport outside El Fasher during which they destroyed helicopters and Antonov bombers, occupied army headquarters, and captured air force Major-General Ibrahim Bushra, while
another SLA unit seized four tanks in clashes outside Kutum and captured Colonel Mubarak
Muhammad al-Saraj, chief of intelligence for public security in Aynshiro, north of Jabal Marra.
In late May the SLA destroyed a Sudanese battalion, killing 500 and taking 300 prisoners
north of Kutum. In mid-July they attacked Tiné again, inflicting heavy losses, and on 1 August
2003 took Kutum and seized large quantities of arms and ammunition before retiring.

Since the army could not suppress the insurgency, Khartoum hastily rearmed [they had
already served Khartoum in 1999 by crushing a Masalit insurgency] and unleashed the *janjawiid* to rescue the army, just as Sadiq al-Mahdi and Burma Nasr had unleashed the *murahiliin*
[Arab militias] Baqqara on the Bahr al-Ghazal Dinka in 1986, with similarly devastating results. The *janjawiid* had begun their ethnic cleansing as early as October 2002 from their
camps in Jabal Kargu, Boni, and Idalghanam in southern Darfur, with some 5,000 *janjawiid*
each equipped and trained by the Sudanese army. The Fur, whom Salah 'Ali Alghali, the Governor of southern Darfur, had openly vowed to exterminate, were the primary targets for the
mounted *janjawiid* commandoes, usually comprised of 100 raiders who would sweep down
on a village just before dawn.

The pattern of destruction was the same. The men were killed, often mutilated, the women
raped, and the children sometimes abducted or killed. The village was burnt, livestock seized,
fields torched, and the infrastructure—wells, irrigation works, schools, clinics—methodically
destroyed in a systematic scheme to drive the African population from their ancestral lands—
ethnic cleansing for Arab colonization. By January 2003 hundreds of Fur had been killed,
thousands wounded, and tens of thousands had fled from the wasteland left behind by the
janjawiid, more units of which were now being trained in camps in North Darfur State.

Supported by helicopter gunships and Antonov bombers, the *janjawiid*'s killing and displacement of Fur, Masalit, and Zaghawa escalated throughout the summer and autumn of
2003, while the Sudan army defeated the SLA north of Kutum in late August with heavy
losses, including two of its leading commanders. In order to regroup and regain the initiative
the SLM/A signed a cease-fire in September, but it was short-lived. Throughout the remainder of 2003 fighting raged on, particularly in western Darfur, with rhetorical claims of victory
by both sides and occasionally a reliable report. On 27 December the JEM ambushed a *jan-*

jawiid column moving against the rebel-held town of Tiné on the Chad border, inflicting very heavy losses, and in January 2004 the JEM repulsed another attempt to take Tiné, once more inflicting heavy losses. Increasingly *janjawiid* columns would pursue and kill those they had evicted, even crossing into Chad to hunt down fleeing refugees. By February 2004 the army had lost all hope of suppressing the insurgency after some 25,000 Darfuri officers and soldiers in the regular army, whose loyalty was highly suspect, were purged and replaced by units from the ineffectual PDF [People's Defense Force], leaving the *janjawiid* free to plunder.

Unrestrained, the *janjawiid* pursued their ethnic cleansing and displacement of African *zurqa* [referring to Sudan's black African population], which conservatively claimed 30,000 lives and forced 1 million people from their lands as IDPs [internally displaced persons] and another 200,000 as refugees to camps in Chad. Another 350,000 Darfuris were expected to die within the following nine months from famine and disease before the rains arrived in late spring. . . . [On 9 February 2004,] President ['Umar Hasan Ahmad al-]Bashir [of Sudan] announced that the Sudan army and militias had crushed the rebellion. On 12 February 2004 the rebel forces, now numbering 27,000 men, shot down two army helicopters. In the succeeding weeks they launched hit-and-run attacks near El Fasher and cut the road from Khartoum to Nyala, the capital of South Darfur State.

In late March, President Idriss Déby of Chad, who was deeply concerned about the influx of Sudanese refugees and the violence in Darfur spilling into Chad, offered to mediate in N'Djamena, and on 8 April 2004 a forty-five day cease-fire was signed, to be followed on 25 April by a political agreement to seek a comprehensive final solution, which the SLM and JEM promptly disavowed, claiming their delegations had exceeded instructions. This revealed internal schisms within each movement—tensions between Zaghawa and Fur/Masalit in the SLM, and disagreements between the political wing of the JEM led by Dr. Khalil Ibrahim and his military commander, Jibril 'Abd al-Karim, whom he accused of being in the pay of Sudan Military Intelligence. Both the SLM and JEM would have nothing to do with an all-inclusive conference of Darfuris, insisting on direct political talks with the government to reach "a comprehensive settlement." . . .

Despite its humanitarian rhetoric, the political response from the West was ambivalent. . . . Both the United States and the EU [European Union] sought to resolve this dilemma by urging the African Union (AU) and the UN to intervene. By August 2004 the AU Ceasefire Committee of 125 monitors under the Nigerian Brigadier General Okonkwo was in Darfur supported by 305 troops from Rwanda and Nigeria, which constituted the African Union Mission to Sudan (AMIS). They were limited to protecting only the UN monitors and providing security so that IDPs could avail themselves of humanitarian assistance; the AMIS was not a peacekeeping force. By mid-July the UN had established the Joint Implementation Mechanism (JIM) to monitor events in Darfur. The JIM's reports to the [UN] Security Council, combined with pressure from the United States, resulted in Security Council Resolution 1556 demanding that the Sudan government immediately cease all offensive military operations, disarm the *janjawiid*, arrest their leaders, and report back to the Security Council, but on 30 August UN Secretary-General Kofi Annan dutifully reported that Sudan had "not met its obligation" to stop "attacks against civilians and ensur[e] their protection." . . .

By February 2005 the ethnic devastation caused by the *janjawiid razzias* [raids] was so widespread and consistent that the humanitarian agencies began to declare a genocide in

Darfur. In July the U.S. Congress passed a unanimous resolution declaring the carnage in Darfur "genocide," but officials in the [George W.] Bush administration, the UN, EU, and AU were more restrained. After their visit to Darfur at the end of June 2004, both [U.S. Secretary of State] Colin Powell and Kofi Annan had been reluctant to declare the situation in Darfur "genocide." In July the heads of the AU concluded there was no genocide in Darfur, as did the Arab League and the influential Organization of the Islamic Conference. The personal representative of Kofi Annan in Sudan, Jan Egeland, used the more sanitary "ethnic cleansing," which soon became fashionable. The reaction of the NIF Islamist government was complete denial. On 9 September 2004, however, Colin Powell, in testimony before the [U.S.] Senate Foreign Affairs Committee, concluded that "genocide has been committed in Darfur, and that the government of Sudan and the Janjawiid bear responsibility—and genocide may still be occurring." . . . The declaration by the United States of genocide in Darfur intensified the debate of this terrible tragedy, but the Sudan government remained inviolate behind its denials, assured that the threat of international intervention would dissipate, leaving them to practice their own diplomacy of "splendid isolation."

CHAPTER FOUR

Coverage

Most of us become aware of unfolding genocidal campaigns because of the stories filed by journalists. This is reason enough to celebrate the art of reporting, but also to take pause and consider problems of genocide coverage, whether it appears in newspapers, on television, or in blogs. To facilitate both celebration and critique, this chapter brings together a series of noteworthy news stories, features, essays, and commentary relating to genocide. Because space constraints disallow a comprehensive sampling under this rubric, I have included noteworthy pieces by journalists. They are noteworthy either because they got things right (e.g., David Rohde's Pulitzer Prize–winning reporting on the genocide in Srebrenica; Samantha Power's reporting on the Christian dimensions of U.S. foreign policy toward Darfur) or because they got things wrong (e.g., the *New York Times*'s relative neglect of the Holocaust; the same paper's early reporting on the 1994 genocide). Both types of journalism ought to be studied, albeit for different reasons. In addition to these writings by journalists, this chapter includes pieces about journalists by both scholars (Laurel Leff, Barbie Zelizer, Deborah Murphy) and one journalist (Conor Foley).

The Holocaust, somewhat surprisingly, was relegated to the back pages of most the world's newspapers while it occurred. Even the *New York Times* distinguished itself with silence. Leff explains why. Inasmuch as U.S. coverage of the Holocaust was scant, it also produced haunting accounts like that by Martha Gellhorn, who filed one of the first stories from the liberated concentration camps, originally published in *Collier's Weekly*, on June 23, 1945.

At the end of the twentieth century the coverage of genocidal campaigns in the former Yugoslavia and Rwanda was far more comprehensive, but not always more perceptive than the coverage of the Holocaust had been fifty years earlier. Take, for instance, the news report from the *New York Times*, "Tribes Battle for Rwandan Capital." The reporting in this piece, as in many others from the period, is replete with stereotypes about "ancient hatreds" that gravely misrepresent the causes of the violence that was being perpetrated in 1994. Not only the *New York Times* got it wrong. The coverage of virtually *all* news sources was a disservice to their readers, listeners, and viewers. The case of Darfur is a case in point. Numerous studies have drawn attention to the frequently simplistic coverage of the Darfur crisis, with its regular invocation of misleading, essentializing labels such as "Africans" and "Arabs." It does not look as if the news media, notably in the United States, has learned the lessons of Rwanda. Yet exceptions do exist, a selection of which is included here.

From the former Yugoslavia there is, first, the fine journalism of Laura Silber and Allan Little, who report on the beginnings of "ethnic cleansing." The next piece is by David Rohde, who won a Pulitzer Prize for his dispatches from Srebrenica, where some seven thousand

Muslim men and boys became the targets of genocidal destruction. From Rwanda, Philip Gourevitch tells a disturbing story on roving dogs, written in the aftermath of the carnage. His piece is exemplary of an entirely different type of genocide coverage: literary journalism. Rather than merely documenting, like a detached beat reporter, the political goings-on in Rwanda, his penchant for reflection and stylistic strategies traditionally associated with fiction has elevated genocide reportage to a distinct journalistic form. Samantha Power, in the style of more conventional journalism, reveals the Christian dimensions of the U.S. response to the Darfur crisis. All of these journalistic pieces are characterized by an emotional attachment to the subjects rather than the emotional detachment that defines leading scholarship.

The final three contributions take a step back from the day-to-day reporting and offer reflections on the coverage of genocide. They analyze trends and patterns in journalistic op-ed commentary on Darfur (Deborah Murphy), raise concerns about the uses of photography in Holocaust journalism (Barbie Zelizer), and caution about the rise of e-journalism in the twenty-first century (Conor Foley). It is important not to overlook this public dimension of genocide, for the "framing" of genocide (in addition to the "naming" of genocide discussed in chapter 1) has an immediate impact on the courses and consequences of genocide as well as the cures available for it.

Taken together, the writing in this chapter shows the varied ways in which we encounter word of this darkest of human phenomena.

71 • Dachau (Martha Gellhorn)

Martha Gellhorn (1908–98) was one of the most influential journalists of her time, rising to fame in the wake of her reporting from the theaters of World War II. She was one of the first journalists to set foot in concentration camps liberated by the Allies. Her 1945 account from the grounds of Dachau concentration camp, near Munich, remains one of the most haunting pieces of genocide coverage. Radioed in from Paris, it appeared in the long-defunct lifestyle magazine Collier's Weekly. *With a circulation of 2.5 million during the war years, the half-tone magazine ensured that Gellhorn's eyewitness account was widely read in the United States.*

Behind the barbed wire and the electric fence, the skeletons sat in the sun and searched themselves for lice. They have no age and no faces; they all look alike and like nothing you will ever see if you are lucky. We crossed the wide, crowded, dusty compound between the prison barracks and went to the hospital. In the hall sat more skeletons, and from them came the smell of disease and death. They watched us but did not move; no expression shows on a face that is only yellowish, stubby skin, stretched across bone.

What had been a man dragged himself into the doctor's office; he was a Pole and he was about six feet tall and he weighed less than a hundred pounds and he wore a striped prison

SOURCE: Martha Gellhorn, *The Face of War* (New York: Simon and Schuster, 1959), 235, 238, 239, 240, 241–42. Excerpts from *The Face of War*, copyright © 1936, 1988 by Martha Gellhorn. Used by permission of Grove/Atlantic, Inc.

shirt, a pair of unlaced boots and a blanket which he tried to hold around his legs. His eyes were large and strange and stood out from his face, and his jawbone seemed to be cutting through his skin. He had come to Dachau from Buchenwald on the last death transport. There were fifty boxcars of his dead traveling companions still on the siding outside the camp, and for the last three days the American Army had forced Dachau civilians to bury these dead. When this transport had arrived, the German guards locked the men, women and children in the boxcars and there they slowly died of hunger and thirst and suffocation. They screamed and they tried to fight their way out; from time to time, the guards fired into the cars to stop the noise. This man had survived; he was found under a pile of dead. . . .

Then, because I could listen to no more, my guide, a German socialist who had been a prisoner in Dachau for ten and a half years, took me across the compound to the jail. In Dachau, if you want to rest from one horror you go and see another. The jail was a long clean building with small white cells in it. Here live the people whom the prisoners called the NN. NN stands for *Nacht und Nebel*, which means night and [fog]. Translated into less romantic terms, this means that the prisoners in these cells never saw a human being, were never allowed to speak to anyone, were never taken out into the sun and the air. They lived in solitary confinement on water soup and a slice of bread, which was the camp diet. . . .

It is not known how many people died in this camp in the twelve years of its existence, but at least forty-five thousand are known to have died in the last three years. Last February and March, two thousand were killed in the gas chamber, because, though they were too weak to work, they did not have the grace to die; so it was arranged for them. The gas chamber is part of the crematorium. The crematorium is a brick building outside the camp compound, standing in a grove of pine trees. . . . "You will put a handkerchief over your nose," the guide said. There, suddenly but never to be believed, were the bodies of the dead. They were everywhere. There were piles of them inside the oven room, but the SS had not had time to burn them. They were piled outside the door and alongside the building. They were all naked, and behind the crematorium the ragged clothing of the dead was neatly stacked, shirts, jackets, trousers, shoes, awaiting sterilization and further use. The clothing was handled with order, but the bodies were dumped like garbage, rotting in the sun, yellow and nothing but bones, bones grown huge because there was no flesh to cover them, hideous, terrible, agonizing bones, and the unendurable smell of death.

We have all seen a great deal now; we have seen too many wars and too much violent dying; we have seen hospitals, bloody and messy as butcher shops; we have seen the dead like bundles lying on all the roads of half the earth. But nowhere was there anything like this. Nothing about war was ever as insanely wicked as these starved and outraged, naked, nameless dead. Behind one pile of dead lay the clothed healthy bodies of the German soldiers who had been found in this camp. They were shot at once when the American Army entered. And for the first time anywhere one could look at a dead man with gladness. . . .

I have not talked about how it was the day the American Army arrived, though the prisoners told me. In their joy to be free, and longing to see their friends who had come at last, many prisoners rushed to the fence and died electrocuted. There were those who died cheering, because that effort of happiness was more than their bodies could endure. There were those who died because now they had food, and they ate before they could be stopped, and it killed them. I do not know words to describe the men who have survived this horror for years, three years, five years, ten years, and whose minds are as clear and unafraid as the day they entered.

I was in Dachau when the German armies surrendered unconditionally to the Allies. The same half-naked skeleton who had been dug out of the death train shuffled back into the doctor's office. He said something in Polish; his voice was no stronger than a whisper. The Polish doctor clapped his hands gently and said, "Bravo." I asked what they were talking about. "The war is over," the doctor said. "Germany is defeated." We sat in that room, in that accursed cemetery prison, and no one had anything more to say. Still, Dachau seemed to me the most suitable place in Europe to hear the news of victory. For surely this war was made to abolish Dachau, and all the other places like Dachau, and everything that Dachau stood for, and to abolish it forever.

72 • Buried by the *Times* (Laurel Leff)

Why did the New York Times, *the world's most venerable newspaper, largely ignore the Holocaust? According to Laurel Leff, professor of journalism at Northeastern University, the* Times's *owner and publisher, Arthur Hays Sulzberger, played a critical role. Leff contends that it was Sulzberger's Jewish identity that persuaded him to bury stories concerning the persecution of Jews and the unfolding of the Holocaust deep inside the paper. In other words, America's leading newspaper, if we believe Leff, failed to prominently feature the Holocaust because of Sulzberger's concern that the publication, which his father, Adolph Ochs, had bought in 1896, could be seen as a Jewish newspaper.*

That the *New York Times* and other newspapers did not consider what was happening to the Jews [during the Holocaust] important is to some extent self-evident. Because only 44 front-page stories had anything to do with Jews, a little more than half of which directly concerned their fate in Europe, appeared during the war, the *Times* obviously did not perceive the news to be important, or at least not as important as the other approximately 24,000 stories it put on page one. The reasons for that determination, however, are not at all obvious. As with believability, some currents pushed journalists to conclude the information did not have much value, whereas other currents suggested it did. . . .

To some extent, journalists' priorities mirrored those of other bystanders. During the war years, the war itself dominated the minds of most Americans. Their sons were fighting and dying, and all Americans faced the terrifying prospect of living under Nazi domination. . . . For 6 years, the world war dominated the news like no event before or since: ship battles in the Pacific, air fights over Britain, hand-to-hand combat in the cities of the Soviet Union. Harried editors had to sort through the stories, while planning maps and charting future coverage. . . . The Jews' persecution was judged in relation to the conflict and found to be of lesser significance, because of their numbers (9 million compared with hundreds of millions of people caught up in the conflagration) and the supposed reason for their persecution. Be-

SOURCE: Laurel Leff, *Buried by the* Times: *The Holocaust and America's Most Important Newspaper* (Cambridge: Cambridge University Press, 2005).

fore the war, and during its first 2 years, the press portrayed their persecution as part of the Nazis' quest for domination of first Germany and then other Axis countries.... So news about Jews was perceived as a footnote to a larger narrative that fit comfortably on an inside page alongside continuations of front-page European stories....

In 1942, what was happening to the Jews could not be dismissed as just more Jewish persecution. The extermination centers had gone into operation in Poland, and the Einsatz-gruppen's murderous onslaught in the Soviet territories had claimed at least 1 million Jews. Yet, at the same time, the war's "larger carnage" had grown, too, and engulfed the United States. In the wake of Pearl Harbor, American forces beat a steady retreat in the Pacific. The German drive in the Soviet Union met ferocious resistance that left millions of Russians, including civilians, dead. The killing of millions of Jews could have been lost in the midst of this apoca-lyptic news. Indeed, some stories, particularly out of the Soviet Union, did not differentiate the Jewish dead from Russian, Ukrainian, or Polish dead. Nor did they specify the method of their execution.... Most journalists, it seems, did not so much acknowledge the Jews' de-struction, and then discount its importance; they determined as a matter of the first order that the Jews' fate had relatively little news value no matter what had happened to them. Ques-tions about believability, from the prosaic to the profound, made it easier to maintain that indifference.... Most American journalists simply did not focus on what was happening to the Jews.

But the *New York Times* did. For conventional journalistic reasons—its extensive network of foreign correspondents, its commitment to international news, its larger number of pages for news, and its substantial Jewish audience who identified to some extent with the plight of their European brethren the *Times* had more reasons than most American newspapers to pay attention to what was happening to Europe's Jews. In addition, the *Times*' publisher, who set the tone for the newspaper, identified with the plight of European Jews, as evidenced by his efforts to help distant relatives, a Bucharest correspondent, and total strangers; by his sup-port of refugee havens in the Dominican Republic and Australia, and rescue schemes in Hun-gary; and by his intense, if acrimonious, involvement in the American Jewish community.

Yet, Arthur Hays Sulzberger had reasons he did not want his public pronouncements to match his private gestures, why he did not want his newspaper to recognize fully and forth-rightly the significance of what was happening to the Jews. Philosophically, he considered singling out Jews to be a concession to Hitler's racial views and a contravention of his Reform Jewish convictions that the Jews were not a race or a people. To retreat from that ideal would have meant acknowledging that his place in America and his identity as an American were not as secure as he resolutely asserted. Although other Jews might have felt torn between their roles as Americans and their roles as Jews—between supporting their nation's leaders and maintaining ties to their community—Sulzberger professed no such conflict. America, as he reputedly stated, came first.

Besides, Sulzberger maintained that the only hope for European Jews was if their plight could be linked to that of other groups, because, as he said repeatedly, a minority could not save itself. His idealism (Jews should not be recognized as a separate group) and his pragma-tism (Jews could not be saved as Jews) meshed perfectly. This particularly potent combina-tion also made him less likely to alter his convictions throughout the war and even afterward. So his newspaper's opinion page published editorials about refugees, about persecution in

Poland, about mass slaughter in Russia, and even about the Warsaw ghetto uprising, that never referred to Jews. . . . The irony is that the *Times* was reluctant to lead for the same reason that the government and the press looked to it for leadership—its Jewish ownership.

73 • Covering Nazi Atrocities in Photographs (Barbie Zelizer)

In her book Remembering to Forget *(1998), Barbie Zelizer, a professor of communication at the University of Pennsylvania, identifies important problems associated with atrocity photographs. Considering images taken upon the liberation of Nazi concentration camps, Zelizer warns of the pitfalls of relying uncritically on photographs as historical sources. By examining strategies of composition and presentation, she demonstrates that the representation of genocide in photographs is beset with danger.*

Like reporters, photographers [operating in World War II Europe] found the [concentration] camps a horrifying experience. Photographers struggled with their own necessary intrusion on the dignity of their cameras' targets. Whether depicting victims or survivors, dead or living, perpetrators or traumatized, the photographers' normally prying behavior proceeded with a certain insensitivity to the boundaries between public and private that was intensified by the challenge posed by the scenes of the camps to common standards of decency and civility. Certain photographers associated with recording the camps' liberation—Margaret Bourke-White, George Rodger, John Florea, Lee Miller, Dave Scherman, and William Vandivert of *Life* are among the best known—later claimed that the experience had irrevocably changed them as professionals. . . .

The atrocity photos taken by the U.S. and British photographers streamed in so quickly that the press back home had little time to debate their impact. Turning out roll after roll of black-and-white film, photographers relentlessly depicted the worst of Nazism in stark, naturalistic representations of horror: bodies turned at odd angles to each other, charred skulls, ovens full of ashes, shocked German civilians alongside massive scenes of human carnage. Within days of photographers' arrival in the camps, the wires were flooded with scenes of explicit and gruesome snapshots of horror, the likes of which had never before been presented on the pages of the U.S. and British popular press. . . .

From the beginning, the photos appeared in both Britain and the United States without much attention to the content of the stories at their side. While the reporters' narratives had progressed chronologically from camp to camp, photographs were presented with little regard for when they had been taken. . . . This lack of attentiveness to the actual day on which an image had been taken suggests that time, as referential data, was not particularly relevant to an atrocity photo's presentation. Rather, the story's visualization was primarily nonsequential. That nonsequentiality facilitated the use of visuals to illustrate the broader strokes of the atrocity story rather than the contingent details of one specific instance of violence.

SOURCE: Barbie Zelizer, *Remembering to Forget: Holocaust Memory through the Camera's Eye* (Chicago: University of Chicago Press, 1998), 87, 89, 92–93, 94, 97, 100, 108, 110–11, 114, 115, 117–18, 123, 125, 126, 127, 132, 139, 140. Reprinted with permission of the publisher.

Atrocity photos were similarly presented with little attention to the place where they had been taken. Photos documenting one camp were appended to stories of another camp. *Time*, for instance, ran one article on the camps that was illustrated with a picture of Nordhausen, which was not discussed. Often, the public was told little or nothing about the place being depicted, leaving the photo to function instead as a generalized spot of Nazi horror. . . . In negating the usual linkages to time and space that were typical of news photos, images were presented differently than were the words of news reports. An individual photo's status as evidence mattered less than the ability to simply document what the Nazis had done. Photography thereby provided a collective body of visual documentation that facilitated the act of bearing witness to Nazi brutality, even if photos were not given specific captions and were not presented in association with the times and places in which they had been taken. . . .

The atrocity photos accommodated a broader story about atrocity through a wide range of presentational strategies. Primary among them was photography's ability to supersede reporters' preferred chronicle of documentation—the eyewitness report. . . . Images addressed the territory and witnessing activity that had been so central to the eyewitness report, but they did so via visual equivalents that at times appeared to supplant the verbal cues supplied by reporters. The most frequent early objects of depiction were among those that later resurfaced as Holocaust iconography—skulls and corpses, barbed-wire fences separating survivors and victims from the outside world, camp courtyards, accoutrements of atrocity such as crematorium chimneys and furnaces, the victimized mother and child, and abandoned possessions. . . .

Images captured the camps' territory in a way that had not been possible with words. . . . Each camp produced its own degradation of public space—the wagons of Buchenwald, the pits of Belsen, the train tracks of Dachau. . . . Territory appeared to work most effectively when its visualization was unnamed, and the press provided scores of shots of unidentified camps. . . . Each concentration camp was interchanged with other localized sites to tell a broader story about suffering under the Nazis. Depictions of camps' territory thus moved the atrocity story onto a different level of telling, which suggested not only the detail of human suffering but also its magnitude and scope. . . . The press also provided links between each photo and the larger atrocity story through practices of composition and presentation. Each set of practices helped consolidate the images of the camps as symbols of atrocity. . . . While varying the depiction—by changing the camera position, camera angle, focal length of the lens, light, and length of exposure—might have lent an individualized signature to the photos [as far as composition was concerned], this was generally not characteristic of these photos. . . .

[Turning to composition,] the decision of where to place evidence of atrocity in a photo created a layering between the atrocity photos' foreground and background, for the two often communicated different levels of specificity about what was being depicted. Witnesses and bodies were depicted in many of the images, and one was used as context for the other. . . . A second practice of composition had to do with the numbers of people who were depicted in the atrocity photos. The photos oscillated between pictures of the many and pictures of the few. Pictures of the many portrayed mass graves, where bodies had been thrown together so indiscriminately that it was difficult, if not impossible, to discern which appendage belonged to which body; pictures of the few portrayed single individual bodies frozen in particularly horrific poses—a starved man stretched out in rigor mortis on the grounds of one of the camps.

Taken together, the images portrayed both individual agony and the far-reaching nature of mass atrocity, suggesting that the depiction of each individual instance of horror represented thousands more who had met the same fate. The photos functioned not only referentially but as symbolic markers of atrocity in its broadest form. . . .

Yet a third compositional practice had to do with the gaze of those being depicted. The gaze of emaciated, near-dead survivors, whose eyes seemed not to comprehend the target of vision, tended to be frontal and appeared to signify frankness. . . . Other photos portrayed the unseeing eyes of the dead. . . . German perpetrators generally were depicted in side views or three-quarter gazes, their eyes averted and narrowed. Often they were depicted looking sideways at a survivor or soldier, who nearly always stared either directly at them or toward the camera. . . . In composition, then, the published photos depicted a level of horror that went beyond one specific instance of brutality so as to present it as a representative incident. . . .

A similar movement toward the broader atrocity story was achieved in presentation. Many atrocity photos lacked basic identifying attributes, and they were as patterned in the type of information they neglected to provide as in that which they provided. Captions gave little information about what was being depicted. . . . They generally omitted any definitive detail about the victims, about which camp had claimed their lives, or about the circumstances in which they died. Detail about the taking of the photograph itself was also often missing, about who had taken the photos, when, or where. In some cases, no name of photographer or photographic agency was given. . . . The image's referentiality was thus undermined even as the image's symbolic force was underscored. . . .

Yet another way of cuing the broader atrocity story through images was via layout. In the press, photos often appeared in photographic spreads or so-called pictorial pages, a presentational format made familiar by the picture-magazine, with four to eight images separated from the verbal text. . . . Paradoxically, the usefulness of such images [displayed in photographic spreads] depended on their anonymity. The anonymity through which they made claim to authenticity in fact provided strong visual evidence of atrocity at a generalized level, but uneven documentation of the particular events they were brought in to depict. . . . But using photographs as symbolic markers of atrocity inverted journalistic modes of news representation. Rather than provide more cues when the information was most unbelievable, less cues were provided when the information stretched belief. Here the more horrific the images, the less detailed the anchoring of the text that accompanied it. . . .

In using many of the shots already presented in the daily press, the picture-magazines were instrumental in recycling a certain visualization of atrocity. This was central to consolidating the importance of photography, even if picture-magazines played a secondary role. The combined presentation of many familiar images renewed their power. Impact, then, had as much to do with the repeated presentation of certain photographs as with the informative news value of any one image. . . . In representing atrocity in this fashion, photographs challenged traditional journalistic modes of representation and enhanced an alternative aim— that of bearing witness.

The more horrific the image, the less detailed the images' anchoring needed to be. . . . The transformation of atrocity photos from definitive indices of certain actions to symbolic markers of the atrocity story had to do with a general and urgent need to make sense of what had happened. When images were particularly graphic, the press needed less to explain them and more to link them with broader interpretive themes that lent meaning to the depictions. Images were thus a more effective means of bearing witness than words. . . . While bearing witness took journalism beyond itself by requiring an alternative mode of journalistic practice—one that emphasized cooperation over professional prowess and competition—the reliance on photographs to do so made images the main event of the camp's coverage. . . . It was no surprise that photography's triumph would permeate the heart of the atrocity story as it was recycled into collective memory.

74 • The Invention of "Ethnic Cleansing" in Yugoslavia (Laura Silber and Allan Little)

When the former Yugoslavia disintegrated in the early 1990s, Laura Silber was the Balkans correspondent for the Financial Times *and Allan Little reported for the BBC. Together they conceived a pathbreaking multipart documentary and one of the earliest and most perceptive accounts of the multifaceted conflicts that ensued,* The Death of Yugoslavia. *In their 1995 book they chronicle the unfolding of "ethnic cleansing" in towns and cities of northern Bosnia, from Bihac to Čelinac.*

They arrived in Croatia by the thousands with tales which, at first, the world did not believe: tales of harassment and torture, of mass killings and deportations, of the burning of villages and towns, of wanton, sadistic, gratuitous cruelty so base that they found themselves accused of fabrication to discredit their enemy. Then, in May, a new term entered the international political vocabulary, a term that has proved the enduring lexicographical legacy of the Yugoslav war: *etničko čišćenje*, ethnic cleansing. It had been practiced the year before in Croatia; in Bosnia it became the defining characteristic of the conflict.

The columns of refugees that spilled into Croatia in April and May 1992 were not fleeing the war zones. They had been driven from their homes on the grounds of their nationality. They were not the tragic byproduct of a civil war; their expulsion was the whole point of the war. In a systematic campaign, Serb paramilitary hit-squads swept through northern and eastern Bosnia in the spring and summer months and, municipality by municipality, seized control of the region without, in most places, encountering real military opposition. Sometimes the cleansing was orderly and achieved without resort to open conflict. The village of Orašac, just south of Bihać in north-eastern Bosnia, was one such example.

Serb paramilitaries first surrounded the village and then closed in on it. There was token resistance from a handful of armed Muslims. Five were killed in gun battles and the village fell in less than twenty-four hours. Two hundred Serb paramilitaries entered the village while others blocked the entrances and exits. House by house they ordered the people out into the main street. The men were separated from the women and children; and the women and children, after being robbed of their money and jewelry, were allowed to go—north towards Bihać town—while their homes were looted, blown up or burned. The men—180 of them—were taken to the village primary school, and held there for two days. On the second day a

SOURCE: Laura Silber and Allan Little, *The Death of Yugoslavia* (London: BBC Books, 1995), 269, 270–71, 273. Reprinted by permission of The Random House Group Ltd.

Serb officer, whom none of the village men knew, arrived with a list of six names. . . . It contained the names of prominent local Muslims. . . . They were then separated from the rest. Their fate was never recovered.

A common characteristic of the cleaning operation was this systematic elimination of community leaders—prominent people, intellectuals, members of the SDA [Party for Democratic Action], the wealthy. The existence of such lists of names was in itself an instrument of cleansing. The terror it instilled in neighboring communities, once news of the atrocities spread, encouraged many of those who feared they might be targeted to flee even before they were attacked. It was the conscious elimination of an articulate opposition, and of political moderation. It was also the destruction of a community from the top down.

After two days, the men of Orašac separated into smaller groups. About seventy were interned in a disused tractor-repair plant in the neighboring village of Ripač. . . . They were subject to random beatings by their captors, some of whom were former neighbors. They were held there until they could be safely moved to one of the larger detention centers, the existence of which was eventually [documented] by an ITN television crew [from Great Britain] in early August. Elsewhere, the cleansing was violent and accompanied by mass killing. On 20 July, the village of Biščani was singled out for a cleansing sweep. Here the paramilitaries entered and began a killing spree that left dozens dead. More than a hundred were rounded up and marched out of town. The paramilitaries argued among themselves about whether to kill, or detain, the survivors. Two men were shot dead in cold blood. The others were beaten with clubs or rifle butts before being driven to the detention camp at Trnopolje.

Humiliation, terror and mental cruelty were almost universally deployed. Captured men would be told that they were to be executed the following day. At dawn they would be taken out, convinced that they were to be killed, only to be thrown into a new detention camp. They were forced to sing Serb nationalist songs to entertain their jeering tormentors, and to avoid being beaten. They were told that their wives had been raped and then killed, that their children were dead. Frequently, they were forced, on pain of death, to perform atrocities against each other—mutilation, physical and sexual, and, often, mutual killing. They were forced to dig mass graves and collect and bury the bodies of their families and neighbors. Sometimes, those on grave detail would themselves be killed and thrown on top of the bodies they had just delivered. The technique had a clear political purpose that went far beyond the sadistic gratification of the perpetrators, beyond, even, the desire to send hundreds of thousands of people fleeing. It was designed to render the territory ethnically pure, and to make certain, by instilling a hatred and fear that would endure, that Muslims and Serbs could never again live together. . . .

The cleansing of the towns and cities of northern Bosnia presented a different challenge to that of the countryside. Here, whole communities could not be rounded up so easily, because the three nationalities tended to live side by side, as in Sarajevo. Here, the lives of the non-Serbs were rendered unlivable. They were sacked from their jobs. They were harassed in the street. Their homes were attacked and their businesses blown up at night. In some areas, rigid restrictions, that were hauntingly reminiscent of the early Nazi curbs on the activities of Jews, were imposed on the freedom of movement of non-Serbs. At Čelinac, near Prijedor, Muslims were forbidden, by a decree issued by the Mayor's office, to drive or travel by car, or to make phone calls other than from the post office. They were forbidden to assemble in groups larger than three, or to leave without the permission of the authorities. By August, Muslim households began to fly white flags from their balconies: it was a signal that they were prepared to go quietly and make no trouble. . . .

Every major population center in northern Bosnia acquired during these months a "Bureau for Population Exchange." It was a euphemism. They were, in fact, the agents of this form of ethnic cleansing—ethnic cleansing by eventual consent. Most Muslims and Croats were not allowed to leave without first signing documents surrendering all future rights to their property. Hundreds of thousands of people willingly gave up their homes, cars, business premises, money, luxury goods, fearing for their lives at the hands of Serb local authorities and the paramilitary terror squads. They would, as a final indignity, be charged a fee for being driven out of town, robbed, and sent into exile in Croatia or government-held areas of Bosnia. . . .

The international aid agencies found themselves the unwitting accomplices to ethnic cleansing. In July, having been assured by the local Bosnian Serb authorities that these Muslims were leaving voluntarily to be reunited with families elsewhere, UNPROFOR [UN Protection Force] troops and UNHCR [UN High Commissioner for Refugees] aid-workers escorted 7,000 of the cleansed from northwestern Bosnia across the Serb-controlled UN Protected Area to the Croatian city of Karlovac. Only on arrival did the UN workers realize the scale of the terror from which the refugees were fleeing. . . . When Croatia slammed the door on refugees, circumstances deteriorated further still for the desperate Muslims still trapped in northern Bosnia. Their escape route now led south into Government-held central Bosnia. Columns of those fleeing the cleansing would take to the mountain roads. Those with vehicles soon lost them to pillaging Serb militiamen at checkpoints along the way. They were abused and intimidated as they marched south, carrying whatever belongings they had the strength to bring with them. They were shot at and beaten. Some were killed. . . . So much for the women, children and elderly. For the men it was worse still.

75 • Srebrenica (David Rohde)

David Rohde, a reporter for the New York Times, *received the 1996 Pulitzer Prize for International Reporting for his coverage of Serb atrocities perpetrated in Srebrenica, a town in the eastern part of Bosnia-Herzegovina, a selection of which is reprinted here, drawn from his 1997 book. In it he tells with precision and without fanfare the story of the genocidal campaign waged against Muslim men and boys in that city. At the conclusion of the campaign, some seven thousand victims were dead. What makes Rohde's work on Bosnia an example of strong journalism is his in-depth reporting, coupled with a hard-earned knowledge of the region, grounded in a foundation of restrained (rather than crusading) moralism.*

The town of Srebrenica is shaped like a long, thin finger. . . . Driving from one end to the other takes only fifteen minutes. A thin strip of houses, schools and stores runs at the bottom of a

SOURCE: David Rohde, *Endgame: The Betrayal and Fall of Srebrenica: Europe's Worst Massacre since World War II* (New York: Farrar, Straus and Giroux, 1997), xiii–xvi. Reprinted with permission of the publisher.

two-mile-long, half-mile-wide ravine. Steep hills rise on either side of Srebrenica, giving one a sense of being sheltered—or trapped. . . .

The border with Serbia is only ten miles away and many teenagers left town for jobs or universities in Belgrade, the capital of Serbia and [the former] Yugoslavia, instead of Sarajevo, the capital of Bosnia. . . . After World War II, Yugoslavia's Communist government built car battery, car brake and zinc processing factories in Potočari, a village two miles north of Srebrenica. Bauxite and zinc mines to the south and northeast flourished. Nearly every miner or factory worker had an apartment, car and summer cottage. By the 1990s, most households had a TV, VCR, washing machine and a host of modern appliances. Movie theaters and supermarkets opened. Srebrenicans enjoyed a standard of living that rivaled that of the United States and Western Europe. According to the last census conducted before the war, 37,211 people lived in Srebrenica *opština* or municipality, which consisted of the town and approximately fifty-square-mile area around it. Seventy-three percent described themselves as Muslims, 25 percent as Serbs and 2 percent as "Yugoslavs" or part of no ethnic group.

Soon after fighting broke out [in Bosnia-Herzegovina] in April 1992, nationalist paramilitary groups from Serbia seized control of Srebrenica with the aim of expelling the town's Muslims as they had throughout Bosnia. Muslims fled to nearby forests. Three weeks later Muslims led by Naser Orić, a charismatic twenty-six-year-old policeman, retook the town. The heavily armed Serbs had suffered one of their first major defeats of the lopsided war, but they still surrounded the town. Orić then led Muslim forces from Srebrenica to a series of stunning victories in 1992, which more than doubled the size of the island of Muslim territory. By January 1993 the enclave was only five miles from linking with Muslim-held central Bosnia. But Bosnian Serbs, backed by troops, tanks and artillery from neighboring Serbia, quickly launched a counteroffensive. With the Serbs blocking UN food convoys, U.S. Air Force planes dropped food into the area by parachute. Muslim-held towns and villages continued to fall. By mid-March 1993, over 60,000 Muslim civilians packed the town of Srebrenica and a small area around it.

Fearing the collapse of Srebrenica, the UN commander in Bosnia, French general Philippe Morillon, set off for the teetering enclave without the permission of his superiors in New York. Morillon bluffed his way through Serb lines and entered Srebrenica. Surrounded by Muslim women and children when he tried to leave a day later, Morillon made an impromptu announcement that would cost him his job and change the course of the war. "You are now under the protection of the United Nations," the fifty-seven-year-old, white-haired general with a flair for the dramatic proclaimed from a post office window on March 12. "I will never abandon you." The UN flag was raised over Srebrenica.

The Serbs allowed a few food convoys into the enclave but just over a month later they attacked again. As the town's defenses crumbled on April 15, Srebrenica's leaders requested that surrender negotiations begin. Under intense pressure to act, a divided UN Security Council passed Resolution 819 and declared Srebrenica and a thirty-square-mile area around it the world's first United Nations "safe area" on April 16. When UN Secretary General Boutros Boutros Ghali later requested 34,000 peacekeepers to police Srebrenica and five other newly declared safe areas [Bihać, Goražde, Sarajevo, Tuzla, and Žepa], the United States and other countries balked at sending their own troops. A second proposal, sarcastically referred to as "safe areas lite" by UN officials, was adopted and only 7,600 peacekeepers were sent to the six new safe areas.

First Canadian and the Dutch peacekeepers were deployed in Srebrenica. Seven hundred and fifty lightly armed UN peacekeepers were responsible for disarming Srebrenica's Muslim defenders and "deterring" Bosnian Serb attacks against the safe area. Two years later, a Serb flag flew where the UN's once did and 7,079 Muslim men were missing. . . .

76 ◆ Tribes Battle for Rwandan Capital (*New York Times*)

Virtually all media reporting on the 1994 genocide in Rwanda misinterpreted the origins of the violence there, as exemplified by this story from the New York Times, *published more than one week into the genocide. Instead of appreciating that the collective violence that swept across the landlocked country was decidedly modern in nature as far as both its causes and courses were concerned, reporters invoked a supposed "centuries-old feud between Rwanda's majority Hutu and minority Tutsi ethnic groups." However, this recourse to explanations revolving around ostensible "ancient hatreds" was not unique to Rwanda. It was a staple of media coverage at century's end and recently resurfaced in the reporting on the Darfur crisis.*

New reports of massacres emerged today from Rwanda, including an account of nearly 1,200 men, women and children shot and hacked to death in a church where they sought refuge.

Gangs of youths armed with machetes roamed the streets of Kigali again today, adding new bodies to the piles of decaying corpses in the capital. A United Nations spokesman, Moctar Gueye, said Rwanda's Hutu-dominated Government and predominantly Tutsi rebels had agreed to direct talks that United Nations officials hoped would lead to a cease-fire. But the two sides continued to fight for control of Kigali. Belgian news media reported that nearly 1,200 Tutsis, more than half of them children, were massacred Wednesday at a church in Musha, 25 miles east of Kigali. It was the largest reported massacre so far in the fighting. Mr. Gueye said the United Nations had received reports of the massacre but had not been able to confirm it.

About a third of the capital's 300,000 people are believed to have fled, many on foot. Thousands of people were still trying to flee Kigali today. The International Rescue Committee, a humanitarian organization, reported an eight-mile-long column of people streaming out of the city. Thousands more remained huddled in hiding with little or no food. "There are hundreds of thousands of people cut off from anything decent or human," Mr. Gueye said. "People are starving to death in their own houses. Babies have starved to death in their own homes. People are in hiding and cannot find food. Hospitals are not functioning."

Tens of thousands of people are estimated to have died in a week of fighting rooted in the centuries-old feud between Rwanda's majority Hutu and minority Tutsi ethnic groups. Many have been hacked to death by gangs with machetes, knives and spears. The United Nations

SOURCE: "Tribes Battle for Rwandan Capital: New Massacres Reported," *New York Times*, April 16, 1994. Reprinted with permission of the publisher.

peacekeepers were sent in last year to monitor a fragile peace accord between the Government and the rebels after almost three years of civil war. The cease-fire fell apart in the fighting that followed the death of President Juvenal Habyarimana, a Hutu, in a plane crash on April 6. At least 12,000 people were under United Nations protection in Kigali at the national stadium and at the main King Faisal Hospital. But Mr. Gueye said that the lightly armed United Nations peacekeepers did not have the resources to cope with the refugees.

Radio Vlaanderen Internationaal in Belgium and reporters in Kigali for the Belgian newspapers *Het Volk* and *De Morgen* said the Hutu-dominated presidential guard was being blamed for the church killings. "At 6:30 Wednesday morning, they suddenly came into our church," the pastor, Danko Litrick, told *Het Volk*. "They kicked in the door and immediately opened fire with semi-automatic weapons and threw grenades. Afterwards, they attacked the defenseless people with knives, bats and spears. Only a few could have survived this massacre. There were 1,180 bodies in my church, including 650 children."

In a separate massacre, Polish missionaries said they could hear the slashing of machetes and moans and calls for help when marauders slaughtered about 80 Tutsis at a Roman Catholic church in Kigali last Saturday. Mr. Gueye said that after the withdrawal of 428 Belgian soldiers protecting Kigali's airport, there would be about 2,090 foreign soldiers left in the country. A Belgian military spokesman, Gilbert Hertoghe, said in Brussels that it would take most of the day to complete the evacuation of foreign civilians. The United Nations Security Council met behind closed doors to decide whether to leave peacekeepers in Rwanda.

77 • Shooting Dogs (Philip Gourevitch)

Philip Gourevitch's memorably titled We Wish to Inform You That Tomorrow We Will Be Killed with Our Families *(1998) ranks among the most popular books on the Rwandan genocide of 1994. It is not difficult to see why. Gourevitch, a staff writer at the* New Yorker *and former editor of the* Paris Review, *is a keen observer and has a talent for recording arresting images. Here he writes compellingly about the genocide and its bystanders—by focusing on dogs.*

The dead at Nyarabuye were, I'm afraid, beautiful. There was no getting around it. The skeleton is a beautiful thing. The randomness of the fallen forms, the strange tranquility of their rude exposure, the skull here, the arm bent in some uninterpretable gesture there—these things were beautiful, and their beauty only added to the affront of the place. I couldn't settle on any meaningful response: revulsion, alarm, sorrow, grief, shame, incomprehension, sure, but nothing truly meaningful. I just looked, and I took photographs, because I wondered whether I could really see what I was seeing while I saw it, and I wanted also an excuse to look a bit more closely. We went on through the first room [of Nyarabuye Church, located in eastern Rwanda] and out the far side. There was another room and another and another and another. They were all full of bodies, and more bodies were scattered in the grass, and there

SOURCE: Philip Gourevitch, *We Wish to Inform You That Tomorrow We Will Be Killed with Our Families: Stories from Rwanda* (New York: Farrar, Straus and Giroux, 1998), 19, 23–24, 147–49. Reprinted with permission of the publisher.

were stray skulls in the grass, which was thick and wonderfully green. Standing outside, I heard a crunch. The old Canadian colonel stumbled in front of me, and I saw, though he did not notice, that his foot had rolled on a skull and broken it. For the first time at Nyarabuye, my feelings focused, and what I felt was a small but keen anger at this man. Then I heard another crunch, and felt a vibration underfoot. I had stepped on one, too. . . .

As I traveled around the country, collecting accounts of the killing, it almost seemed as if, with the machete, the *masu*—a club studded with nails—a few well-placed grenades, and a few bursts of automatic-rifle fire, the quiet orders of Hutu Power had made the neutron bomb obsolete. "Everyone was called to hunt the enemy," said Theodore Nyilinkwaya, a survivor of the massacres in his home village of Kimbogo, in the southwestern province of Cyangugu. "But let's say someone is reluctant. Say that guy comes with a stick. They tell him, 'No, get a *masu*.' So, OK, he does, and he runs along with the rest, but he doesn't kill. They say, 'Hey, he might denounce us later. He must kill. Everyone must help to kill at least one person.' So this person who is not a killer is made to do it. And the next day it's become a game for him. You don't need to keep pushing him." At Nyarabuye, even the little terracotta votive statues in the sacristy had been methodically decapitated. "They were associated with Tutsis," Sergeant Francis explained. . . .

The nights were eerily quiet in Rwanda. After the birds fell silent, there were hardly even any animal sounds. I couldn't understand it. Then I noticed the absence of dogs. What kind of country has no dogs? I started to keep watch in the markets, in the streets, in the countryside, in churchyards, schoolyards, farmyards, graveyard, junkyards, and the flowering yards of fine villas. Once, far out in the hills, I thought I spotted a boy leading a dog on a tether down a dirt lane. But it was a goat at the end of the rope. Village life without dogs? Children without dogs? Poverty without dogs? There were plenty of cats—the first pets to disappear in a famine, but famine was not Rwanda's problem—and I began to wonder whether, in Rwanda, cats had won their eternal war with dog-kind.

During my first three months in the country, between May and August of 1995, I kept a list of the dogs I saw: A Belgian lady at the Hôtel des Milles Collines had a pair of toy poodles that trotted beside her on her morning strolls through the garden around the swimming pool; the French landlady of a Dutch aid worker I knew had a fat golden retriever; a team of American and Belgian sappers had some German shepherds who assisted them in land-mine removal; and once I saw a scrawny bitch gnawing a fish skeleton behind a restaurant in the northwestern town of Gisenyi, but that dog might have just slipped over the border from Zaire a few hundred yards away, and after a moment a cook spotted her and chased her away with loud cries and the whack of a long wooden spoon. Studying this list, you might conclude that dog ownership corresponded to skin color: white people had dogs and Africans did not. But Africans are generally as fond of dogs as the rest of humanity, so the impressive doglessness of Rwanda perplexed me.

I made inquiries, and I learned that right through the genocide dogs had been plentiful in Rwanda. The words people used to describe the dog population back then were "many" and "normal." But as the RPF [Rwandan Patriotic Front] fighters had advanced through the country, moving down from the northeast, they had shot all the dogs. What did the RPF have against dogs? Everyone I asked gave the same answer: the dogs were eating the dead. "It's on film," someone told me, and I have since seen more Rwandan dogs on video monitors than I ever saw in Rwanda—crouched in the distinctive red dirt of the country, over the distinctive body piles of that time, in the distinctive feeding position of their kind. . . .

Even the blue-helmeted soldiers of UNAMIR [UN Assistance Mission in Rwanda] were shooting dogs on sight in the late summer of 1994. After months, during which Rwandans had been left to wonder whether UN troops knew how to shoot, because they never used their excellent weapons to stop the extermination of civilians, it turned out that the peacekeepers were very good shots. The genocide had been tolerated by the so-called international community, but I was told that the UN regarded the corpse-eating dogs as a health problem.

(78) • Dying in Darfur (Samantha Power)

Known primarily for her Pulitzer Prize–winning book, A Problem from Hell, *Samantha Power in recent years turned to the plight of Darfuris affected by the crisis in Sudan. In her 2004* New Yorker *article, she elaborates the Christian dimensions of U.S. responses to the conflict as well as the complicated run-up to the insurgency in Darfur and Khartoum's scorched earth policy. On account of her antigenocide activism, Power, who is a professor of practice at Harvard University's John F. Kennedy School of Government, was asked to join the U.S. administration of President Barack Obama, where she became senior director for multilateral affairs on the staff of the National Security Council. In 2013 she was appointed U.S. Ambassador to the United Nations.*

Two days before the 2000 Presidential election, George W. Bush met the Reverend Billy Graham for breakfast in Jacksonville, Florida. They were joined by Graham's son Franklin, the president of Samaritan's Purse, a Christian relief-and-development organization that has worked in Sudan since 1993.

Sudan, the largest nation in Africa, had been mostly mired in civil war since it won independence from Britain, in 1956. The central conflict, between Muslim government forces in the North and rebels in the South, began in 1955, abated in 1972, and resumed in 1983. Some two million people died because of the war, and many of them were Christians. The situation was deeply troubling to American evangelicals, and Franklin Graham had led an effort to raise money for victims. During the breakfast meeting, Graham told me, he urged Bush to turn his sights to the suffering of Christians in Africa. "We have a crisis in the Sudan," Graham said. "I have a hospital that's been bombed. I hope that if you become President you'll do something about it." Bush promised Graham that he would.

Sudan had already attracted an unusually formidable constituency in Washington. In the nineties, the Clinton White House imposed successive sanctions against the Sudanese government. Sudan had become a haven for terrorists—including Osama bin Laden, who had settled there in 1991—and had repressed religious minorities in the South; in addition, it had failed to crack down on a slave trade that had emerged there. Backed by Christian and African-American constituencies, many U.S. lawmakers had traveled to Sudan. Senator Bill Frist, a sur-

SOURCE: Samantha Power, "Dying in Darfur: Can the Ethnic Cleansing in Sudan Be Stopped?" *New Yorker*, August 30, 2004, 59–62, 68. Reprinted with permission of the author.

geon, made several short trips there, serving as a volunteer doctor at the hospital in southern Sudan that had been bombed shortly before Graham's meeting with Bush.

President Clinton's approach was largely confrontational. In 1996, he withdrew the U.S. Ambassador, citing terrorist threats against American officials. (There is still no U.S. Ambassador in Khartoum.) The same year, the United States and Saudi Arabia pressured Sudan to expel bin Laden, who subsequently left for Afghanistan. In 1998, after Al Qaeda's attacks on the American Embassies in Kenya and Tanzania, Clinton ordered a Tomahawk-missile strike on the Al Shifa pharmaceutical factory, which was suspected of producing chemical weapons. (This suspicion remains unproved.) Meanwhile, the Administration made little progress in curtailing Sudan's civil war. In 1999, Clinton announced the appointment of a special envoy to Sudan, but then never met with the person who filled the post.

President Bush was more attentive. He rejuvenated a multilateral peace process that had been hosted by Kenya since 1993. On September 6, 2001, he appointed John Danforth, an ordained Episcopal minister and a three-term senator from Missouri, his special envoy for peace in Sudan.

During the 2000 campaign, Bush frequently invoked the values of Midland, the Texas town where he and his wife, Laura, grew up, telling the *New York Times*, "People—if they want to understand me—need to understand Midland." Midland is home to several churches with sister congregations in southern Sudan. In November 2001, Midland hosted the International Day of Prayer for the Persecuted Church, an annual evangelical event. Some forty Midland churches participated, and many of them passed out leaflets on Sudan and devoted part of their Sunday services to the civil war and the slave trade there. A half-dozen Sudanese refugees spent the weekend in Midland and shared their stories. "They took us out of our comfort zones," Deborah Fikes, one of the event's organizers, said, "We Christians in the U.S. have to use our resources not to build bigger churches, and not to be even more concerned with being pro-life, but to show how we value life by protecting the lives that are being lost every day because of war, disease, and starvation." Midland's churches raised money for Sudanese schools, and local religious and civic leaders petitioned the White House and wrote letters to the government in Khartoum. The Chief of Mission at the Sudanese Embassy in Washington deemed "the town of George Bush" important enough to respond personally to these letters.

In 2002, Fikes and other activists invited thirteen Sudanese exiles to visit Midland during its annual Christian-music festival, and paired them with local youths to construct two portable "Sudanese villages." The first had seven wooden huts with grass roofs, a large thatch-roofed church, and a market, modeled on that of a typical southern Sudanese town. The second consisted of six huts that had been burned or partly demolished. Fikes had ordered some plastic skeletons from a Halloween Web site and set them aflame ("with the town fire marshal on hand!"), so that they could be displayed as charred corpses. The American evangelical community's intense interest in Sudan put Danforth and the rest of the U.S. government team under considerable pressure.

The Bush Administration was also aware that Sudan's oil reserves yield two billion dollars in annual revenue, although just a fraction of the oil has been tapped. (Oil was discovered in Sudan, by Chevron, in the nineteen-seventies, but it has been exported only since 1999.) These reserves, which were being exploited by China, Canada, and Sweden, were off limits to

American companies, because of a 1997 executive order barring U.S. oil companies from operating in Sudan. Before U.S. companies could legally begin prospecting Sudan would have to end its civil war.

Danforth's overtures were surprisingly well received. The Sudanese government, a U.S. diplomat told me, was desperate to end U.S. sanctions and to court American oil investors, and in the wake of September 11th and the war in Afghanistan it wished to avoid being added to the Administration's target list. The southern rebels, who saw that they stood little chance of dislodging the government, were also ready to negotiate.

Thanks largely to the sudden surge in U.S. involvement, the peace talks moved forward. Both sides agreed to allow the posting of a small team of civilian protection monitors. Fighting in the South abated, and Sudan's rival parties inched closer to a long-term political agreement that they hoped would end the civil war. The President, Omar al-Bashir, provisionally agreed to share about half the oil revenues with the South, and to permit Christians in the North to escape punishments dictated by Sharia—traditional Islamic law. Bashir even offered to give the South the right to secede from Sudan six years from the signing date, if irreconcilable divisions remained. In return, the rebel leader, John Garang, said he would be willing to serve as Vice-President in a postwar government. By December 2003, negotiators were so certain that a deal was imminent that two seats were reserved for Bashir and Garang at Bush's 2004 State of the Union address. The stage was set: Bush would delight his Christian constituency; U.S. businesses would gain access to Sudan's oil; and Sudanese civilians would stop dying. Moreover, at a time when the U.S. was isolated and mistrusted abroad, Bush would prove that he was capable of making peace as well as war—and in the process be seen as uniting Arabs and Americans, Christians and Muslims.

There was a difficulty with this scenario, however: . . . Darfur had caught fire. At the same time that the Sudanese government was offering autonomy and oil profits to southern Sudanese, people in another neglected region, whose leaders had been excluded from the U.S.-backed peace talks, had risen up and demanded political reform and economic assistance. Just when Bashir's regime seemed poised to stop its raids in southern Sudan, it had launched a bombing campaign in western Sudan. Washington had a problem—and the people of Darfur had a far greater one. . . .

At 5 A.M. on Friday, April 25, 2003, a blast shook a tiny, one-runway airport in El Fasher. . . . It was followed by six rapid detonations. Sleeping Sudanese soldiers, who were encamped in a nearby garrison, awoke and scrambled out of their barracks toward an ammunition depot across the street. Many of the soldiers, some still in their nightclothes, were picked off by machine-gun fire as they ran. Rebel Darfurian marksmen were perched high in the trees. The attackers, members of a then obscure group, the Sudanese Liberation Army, did damage far greater than their numbers or their reputation. Employing two hundred and sixty men, forty Toyota Land Cruisers, four trucks, and mainly small-arms fire, they managed to take over a vital military outpost. Because the attack occurred on a Friday, the day of prayer in Sudan, when many soldiers are home with their families, the Sudanese military had mounted few patrols around the airport, and the rebels sneaked unchallenged onto the tarmac.

The raid, which lasted several hours, killed around a hundred soldiers. Five Antonov airplanes and two helicopter gunships were destroyed. (The government is said to have fewer than a hundred attack aircraft.) The rebels at first tried to disable the planes with haphazard gunfire; then someone shouted, "Hit the fuel tank," and the aircraft erupted in flames. The rebels also seized nineteen Land Cruisers and six trucks, and emptied several warehouses that were filled with weapons. (They almost made away with eight tanks, but they couldn't find the keys.) When the rebels left El Fasher, around midday, they had lost only nine men, and had kidnapped the head of the Sudanese Air Force, General Ibrahim Bushra Ismail, whom they released forty-five days later, after protracted negotiations with tribal leaders.

The rebel group, which was formed in February 2003, had legitimate complaints. Darfur's inhabitants felt that the region was being ignored. The Sudanese government rarely paid for road building and repair, schools, hospitals, civil servants, or communications facilities in Darfur. Those who considered themselves ethnically African were angered by the government's practice of awarding most of the top posts in the region to local Arabs, even though they were thought to be the minority there. Disgruntled Darfurians had appealed to the government to include their concerns on the agenda of the U.S.-backed peace process. This effort failed, and many concluded that, if they ever wanted to see their needs met, they would have to do what John Garang had done in the South: take up arms against the Sudanese government and try to get the world's attention.

The Sudanese Liberation Army's founding manifesto, which was posted on the Internet and circulated by hand in Darfur, invited Arabs and Africans alike to join in protesting Khartoum's "policies of marginalization, racial discrimination, exclusion, exploitation, and divisiveness." The group's objective, it said, was "to create a united democratic Sudan on a new basis of equality, complete restructuring and devolution of power, even development, cultural and political pluralism and moral and material prosperity for all Sudanese." All regions should have significant autonomy and work together under the banner of "Sudanism"—a shared identity for Arabs, Africans, Christians, and Muslims. The S.L.A. attempted to demonstrate its inclusiveness by appointing an Arab, Ahmed Kabour Jibril, to be its commander in South Darfur.

At first, the Sudanese government did not take the S.L.A. seriously, and dismissed its demands. At a rally in El Fasher on April 12, 2003, President Bashir downplayed the rebellion, calling it "acts of armed banditry." Two weeks later, after the devastating airport raid, the government decided to treat the rebels as a major threat. During the conflict with the rebels based in the South, the Sudanese military had honed a strategy for combating insurgents: the Air Force bombed from the sky, while Arab tribesmen, armed by the government, launched raids on the ground. In Darfur, the Sudanese Army needed to rely even more heavily upon local Arab militias. A majority of the Army's rank-and-file soldiers were from Darfur, and they could not be trusted to take up arms against their neighbors and kin. (Many Darfurians had served with the Army in the war against Garang's rebels.) By July 2003, the government was appealing to Darfur's Arab tribal leaders to defend their homeland against rebels whom they branded as "tora bora" (an allusion to the terrorist fighters based in the caves of Afghanistan). . . .

Neither President Bush nor Kofi Annan, the Secretary-General of the United Nations, spoke publicly about the killings in Darfur before March of this year [2004], by which time some thirty thousand people had died as a result of ethnic cleansing. Thanks to the relentless efforts of Andrew Natsios and Roger Winter, two officials at the United States Agency for International Development, the U.S. government had begun attempting to deliver humanitarian aid to Darfur in February 2003. But the Administration's top officials remained quiet. Cabinet members were, of course, preoccupied with Iraq, but even Washington diplomats who monitored Sudan chose not to speak out, for fear of upsetting the North-South peace process. By this time, some hundred thousand Darfurians had fled to Chad, in addition to the million or so people who had been displaced within Darfur—yet the North-South negotiations continued, as if nothing unusual were happening elsewhere in Sudan.

Last March, the U.N.'s humanitarian coordinator for Sudan, Mukesh Kapila, who had served a year there without denouncing Darfur's horrors, erupted. "The only difference between Rwanda and Darfur is the numbers involved of dead, tortured, and raped," Kapila said at the final press conference he gave before leaving his post. He told the BBC, "This is ethnic cleansing, this is the world's greatest humanitarian crisis, and I don't know why the world is not doing more about it." Kapila's statement was well timed. The following month, the world's leaders were to commemorate the ten-year anniversary of the systematic slaughter of eight hundred thousand Rwandans. Both Bush and Annan would have to issue statements on Rwanda, and the media interest aroused by Kapila's declaration made it impossible for the two leaders to avoid the subject of Darfur. In a statement on April 7th, Bush condemned the "atrocities" in Darfur, saying, "The government of Sudan must not remain complicit in the brutalization of Darfur." Annan went further, raising the possibility of "military action." In May, Natsios and Winter issued a grim mortality survey predicting that, even if world leaders substantially increased aid to Darfur, three hundred thousand people would be dead by December. If world leaders ignored Sudan, they warned, a million could die.

The international media was extremely slow to post journalists to the region. Those who went tended to remain at the Chad border, for the Sudanese government often denied journalists' visa requests. But in May firsthand reports from Darfur began appearing, and the editorial boards of the *Washington Post* and the *New York Times* regularly publicized the crisis. Between April 1st and August 19th, the *Post* ran twelve editorials. The *Times* ran only four, but its columnist Nicholas Kristof traveled twice to the Chad-Sudan border and wrote ten passionate columns about the atrocities.

On Capitol Hill, where interest in Sudan's oppression of Christians had always been high, members of Congress finally shifted their focus to Darfur. "We were late," Frank Wolf, a Republican congressman from Virginia, told me. "We so wanted to get peace in the South that it was like the Simon and Garfunkel song: 'A man hears what he wants to hear and disregards the rest.'" Wolf and Sam Brownback, a Republican senator from Kansas, visited Darfur in June and returned with grim refugee testimonies and video footage of torched villages. In July, Congress passed a resolution, introduced by Donald Payne, a Democratic congressman from New Jersey, to describe the killings in Sudan as "genocide"—the first time that Congress had described an ongoing massacre in such terms.

Bush's evangelical base offered full backing. That same month, Franklin Graham called the White House and told one of Bush's aides, "Just because you've signed a peace deal with the South doesn't mean you can wash your hands of Darfur." Samaritan's Purse, Graham's charity, is now transporting food aid by plane from Khartoum to Darfur. "Killing is wrong, whether you're killing a Jew, a Christian, or a Muslim," Graham told me. "I'm as concerned about what's happening in Darfur as I am about what happened in southern Sudan. It's evil. God made the people there in Darfur. For us to ignore them would be a sin." In August, fifty-one evangelical Christian leaders, representing forty-five thousand churches, called on the President to consider sending troops to Darfur to stop the "genocide."

79 • Narrating Darfur (Deborah Murphy)

In this 2007 essay, Deborah Murphy provides a critical look at patterns in media commentary on the Darfur crisis. Analyzing eighty-three editorials and op-ed pieces published in four daily newspapers in the United States between March and September 2004, she finds that the opinion pieces were largely decontextualized. Instead of situating the dynamics of collective violence within the complex history of Sudan—notably the long-standing North-South conflict—American journalists and commentators focused on the humanitarian situation and called for international action by inserting the goings-on in Darfur into the history of genocide. By imaging similarities between the vastly different situations of Rwanda and Darfur, among other things, these contributors provided representations of collective violence that often only had superficially to do with empirical reality.

This chapter is a review of the eighty-three editorials and op-eds on Darfur appearing in the *New York Times*, the *Washington Post*, the *Wall Street Journal*, and the *Washington Times* from March to September 2004. . . . Darfur began to attract attention in the U.S. press in late March and early April 2004. Twelve editorials on Darfur appeared in April in the selected newspapers—with eight of them appearing in the first half of the month, clustered around the tenth anniversary of the Rwandan genocide on April 7—eight editorials appeared in May, nine in June, sixteen in July, fifteen in August, and nineteen in September. Fourteen of the eighty-three articles described a visit that the authors had made to refugee camps in Chad, or in two cases, to Darfur itself.

The articles appearing in April, May, and June were primarily concerned with explaining the background of the crisis and urging the U.S. and UN to "take action." Later in the summer there was much less emphasis on providing background or even focusing on what was going on in Darfur; instead, the focus shifted to the developments on the international scene that were driving the response. Over April, May, and June, a common description of the conflict quickly emerged: the Arab-dominated Sudanese government had armed local Arab militias (usually called "Janjawiid") to attack civilians (identified either as "African" or "non-Arab"), causing thousands to flee to neighboring Chad and hundreds of thousands more to remain internally displaced in Darfur beyond the reach of relief agencies. Twenty-three of the eighty-three articles also stated that the violence was a response to a local rebellion, which was itself a response to, variously, the government's favoring of the Arab population, the historical neglect of the Darfur region, or the exclusion of Darfurian groups from the North-South peace process. However, little attention was paid to the rebels.

Of the eighty-three articles reviewed, forty-one identified the conflict as one between Arabs and Africans. Several writers used the term "non-Arab" rather than "African" to refer to the victims, but the perpetrators were almost uniformly identified as Arab. [Nicholas] Kristof [of the *New York Times*] and Jerry Fowler (of the U.S. Holocaust Memorial Museum's Committee on Conscience) both identified the victims as primarily members of the Fur, Masalit, and Zaghawa tribes, but no other articles described the role of different ethnic groups in the

SOURCE: Deborah Murphy, "Narrating Darfur," in Alex de Waal, ed., *War in Darfur and the Search for Peace* (Cambridge, Mass.: Global Equity Initiative, 2007), 314–17, 320, 321. Reprinted with permission of the publisher.

conflict. Eleven articles also mentioned how the historical competition between Arab pastoralists and African farmers over scarce land and water resources contributed to the conflict.
Environmental degradation was blamed for causing the rise of these tensions, and the Arab
militias were said to be motivated by a desire for the farmers' land. The Sudanese government
was held to be ultimately responsible for the violence because it had armed the Janjawiid and
also conducted bombing campaigns. It was also assumed to be capable of stopping the violence, if it so desired, by disarming and disbanding the Janjawiid.

Besides depictions of the violence, most descriptions of the crisis emphasized the humanitarian plight of the refugees and the internally displaced people (IDPs), and the criminality of the Sudanese government's refusal to allow adequate access to IDPs in Darfur. Frequent mention was made of the UN's Sudan Coordinator's March description of the conflict
as "the world's most severe humanitarian crisis" and of USAID [U.S. Agency for International
Development] Administrator Andrew Natsios's estimate, in early June, that 300,000 to 1 million people would die in the region before the year's end depending on the international
response. . . .

Occasionally other humanitarian crises—such as the Holocaust, Cambodia, Bosnia, and
Kosovo—were used as points of comparison to urge U.S. intervention. Kosovo was invoked
as the only example of Western intervention stopping a government from committing genocide. . . . One compelling analogy was largely overlooked: The war in southern Sudan, which
had been ongoing for most of the forty-nine years since Sudan's independence then seemed
to be drawing to a close, due in no small part to U.S. diplomatic efforts. The vicious counter-
insurgency tactics seen in Darfur had first been employed against rebels in the South. . . .
These precedents were largely ignored, however; only fifteen of the reviewed articles mentioned the North-South war, with seven articles making explicit comparisons between the
causes and conduct of the wars in the South and Darfur. There was also little attention paid to
the imminent end of the war in South, except for concern that the U.S. diplomatic investment
in Naivasha would hamper strong action on Darfur. In general, Darfur was removed from the
Sudanese context and was instead incorporated into the history of genocide.

80 • Reporting Genocide Is Not Easy (Conor Foley)

An article by the journalist Conor Foley that originally appeared in the Guardian *in the United
Kingdom in 2006 sounds a cautious note, similar to Barbie Zelizer's. Yet unlike Zelizer, Foley addresses problems associated with print rather than visual journalism and turns to the reporting of
genocidal violence in the present, notably in the context of Darfur. As part of his reflections, Foley
critiques the use of modern information technology (e.g., blogs, websites, video feeds) in disseminat-
ing information about unfolding instances of violence. He is concerned about the relationship between new media and antigenocide activism because of the excess of moralism that he has encountered in the writings of intrepid amateur journalists and activists keen to document atrocities. Foley*

SOURCE: Conor Foley, "Reporting Genocide Isn't Easy: The New Generation of Citizen Journalists Are
a Mixed Blessing for Humanitarianism," *Guardian*, December 28, 2006. Reprinted with permission of the
publisher.

bemoans the fact that many of these self-made reporters have come to conflict settings with predetermined views about the causes of collective violence. Supporting causes while reporting is problematic, says Foley, because it runs counter to the ethical imperative of journalism: to report facts as an impartial bystander.

Three years ago a group of U.S. college students recorded a documentary about children in Northern Uganda forced to flee their homes every night to escape abduction by rebels of the Lord's Resistance Army. The film, *Invisible Children*, has been shown in U.S. colleges, schools and churches and has led to the development of a mass movement to raise funds and influence U.S. policy towards the region. The film-makers formed their own non-governmental organization (NGO), touring college campuses to organize solidarity activities.

I met some of them when I was working in Northern Uganda. They came across as nice and sincere people. But it was noticeable that they remained quite distinct from the staff of the more established humanitarian agencies, some of whom were rather dismissive of the amateur nature of their work. The people behind *Invisible Children* are part of a new generation of U.S. activists becoming engaged in international solidarity. Some of these groups are linked to American religious groups, while others are formed by the same type of people that support the work of Amnesty International and Greenpeace. "Stop Genocide Now" [SGN], for example, sent a couple of "citizen journalists" to spend their Christmas holidays in Darfur. SGN claim that "we have entered an age of knowledge which empowers us to protect." But there is actually a long tradition to this type of bearing witness. Their trip to Darfur was preceded by a very similar delegation from Amnesty International.

The use of technology, well-designed websites, video-feeds and talk-boards does, however, give a new feel to this work. There is also some glamour in young volunteers heading off to war zones to bring back stories that the rest of the media are too afraid to cover. Just as blogging is challenging the mainstream media, on-line interactive activism has opened campaigning to a new generation. Yet there are some causes for concern. The SGN's claim to "replace statistics with names, faces and stories," while not exactly new, does reflect an understanding that people, faced with information over-load, want their stories simple, direct and moving. Real life, unfortunately, is often just not like that and there are problems with trying to reduce every conflict to a story of good and evil.

Humanitarian and human rights organizations have sometimes been accused of exaggerating crises, for fund-raising purposes. We have tried to become more professional in the last few years and others now complain that we behave more like a commercial business. The new groups may bring humanitarian aid back to its voluntarist ethic, but they need to learn the lessons from our mistakes. Truth is the first casualty in conflict. In both Iraq and Kosovo international military interventions were justified by claims which turned out not to be true. This clearly raises the stakes for those, like me, who support humanitarian interventions in certain cases and increases our responsibility to get our facts right. Larger organizations, such as Amnesty International, have developed elaborate cross-checking procedures to verify allegations, which mirror the editorial procedures of the mainstream media. Bloggers and citizen journalists are, by definition, subject to fewer constraints.

Bloggers made their mark during last summer's war in the Lebanon, exposing the "enhancing" of a photograph showing smoke above Beirut and alleging that the story of an Israeli military attack on Red Cross ambulances was a hoax. This second claim was rejected by the International Committee of the Red Cross and mainstream media outlets, including the *Guardian*, and ably rebutted by other bloggers. Such reports have an impact though and there is a danger when they are being produced by people who are approaching the issue primarily from an ideologically committed stand-point. One blogger even produced her own YouTube video clip to "prove" Islamic terrorists regularly use UN and Red Cross ambulances to transport weapons. In a context where humanitarian organizations are coming under increasing attack by all sides in conflicts ranging from Sri Lanka to Afghanistan this seems to have been almost deliberately murderous in its intent.

None of this is to knock initiatives such as those taken by SGN and *Invisible Children*. From what I have seen of the SGN website, they are taking their task seriously and avoiding sensationalism. It is unfortunate that their name itself suggests they have some pre-determined view about what is happening in Darfur; if their trip helps them to become better informed then that alone probably makes it worthwhile. It can only be a good thing that people are motivated to want to stop suffering in other countries. But it is also worth remembering the humanitarian dictum: first of all, do no harm.

CHAPTER FIVE

Consequences

What happens in genocide's aftermath? This chapter addresses a number of different aspects of this question, from humanitarian relief to the establishment of stability and security. Suzanne Moranian provides a unique account of the Christian missionary movement in the United States and its contribution to the alleviation of suffering in the context of the Armenian genocide. Sarah Kenyon Lischer accounts for the de facto failure of humanitarian assistance at the end of the twentieth century, focusing in particular on the inappropriate international administration of refugee camps in what was formerly Zaire. Sarah Wagner discusses the role of DNA technology and the cultural dynamics of identification and recovery in Srebrenica, the site of genocide in the former Yugoslavia. Similarly seized by the problem of death are John Hagan and Wenona Rymond-Richmond, who speak of a simple yet fundamentally difficult task: how to count the dead. Dealing with the living and their social and psychological well being are Jeffrey Alexander, Claudia Card, and I.

Alexander elaborates the concept of "cultural trauma," which he defines as collective suffering that leaves indelible marks upon the consciousness of groups, "marking their memories forever and changing their future identity in fundamental and irrevocable ways." He is keen to understand trauma dynamics—the mechanisms and processes that give rise to forms of group consciousness related to victimhood—and therefore insists that scholars pay more attention to the distinction between individual and collective suffering. Card pushes in a similar direction, drawing attention to the question of "social death," a term that the sociologist Orlando Patterson introduced in 1982 in a cross-cultural study of slavery's pernicious long-term effects. Card argues that we similarly must take seriously, in the case of genocide but also more generally, the ways mass violence destroys not just physical lives but also the vitality of cultures in which these lives were lived. On this argument, the deadly effects of genocide go well beyond acts of physical destruction. My article on the trauma of genocide makes a case for integrating insights from the social sciences and the medical sciences when trying to understand the psychological consequences of victimhood in times of genocide.

The remaining articles and book excerpts in this chapter have a somewhat different focus. Rather than engage with the theoretical and methodological dimensions of studying the consequences of genocide, they are concerned with the medium-term and long-term consequences of genocide for national and international peace and security. Evan Gottesman singles out postgenocide Cambodia and traces the emergence of authoritarian rule there under the auspices of neighboring Vietnam. Filip Reyntjens too is concerned with the authoritarian efforts of a liberating power in the wake of genocide, namely the Rwandan Patriotic Front, which, in his eyes, built a postgenocidal dictatorship that in many respects rivals the oppressive character of the pregenocidal regime in Rwanda. Reyntjens's sobering analysis of the domestic consequences of genocide in Rwanda is complemented by the work of Gérard Prunier, who writes critically of postgenocide Rwanda's involvement in death and dying in the Democratic Republic of Congo. There, says Prunier, President Paul Kagame's armed forces have been centrally involved in setting off "Africa's World War." Sumantra Bose, while critical of the Dayton Agreement, finds relative stability in Bosnia. Turning to the present, Roland Marchal comments perceptively on a largely neglected issue: the regional consequences of the crisis in Darfur.

Finally, there is Benjamin Madley, who opens this chapter by considering whether genocidal ideas travel across space and time, in this case from the periphery (South West Africa) to the center (Nazi Germany). Madley wonders whether the Nazis got any ideas for the Holocaust from their experience with the destruction of the Herero some thirty years earlier. His discussion raises an as yet unexplored question: Do genocidal campaigns in one country inspire violent actors elsewhere?

81 • From Africa to Auschwitz (Benjamin Madley)

What is the relationship between Wilhelmine Germany's destruction of the Herero in South West Africa between 1904 and 1907 and Nazi Germany's destruction of the European Jews three decades later? Where previously the two genocidal campaigns were treated as separate events, Benjamin Madley, in his 2005 article, maintains that the case of South West Africa should no longer be overlooked as an important antecedent to Nazi genocide. In fact Madley, a postdoctoral fellow in history at Dartmouth College, suggests that the ideology of Lebensraum *("existence space") and Nazi annihilationist rhetoric borrowed directly—at times verbatim—from Wilhelmine Germany's colonial experiment.*

The German terms *Lebensraum* [existence space] and *Konzentrationslager* [concentration camp], both widely known because of their early use by the Nazis, were not coined by the Hitler regime. They were minted years earlier in reference to German South West Africa, now Namibia, during the first decade of the twentieth century, when Germans colonized the land and committed genocide against the local Herero and Nama peoples. Later use of these borrowed words suggests an important question: did Wilhelmine colonization and genocide in Namibia influence Nazi plans to conquer and settle Eastern Europe, enslave and murder millions of Slavs and exterminate Gypsies and Jews? . . .

German South West Africa was colonial, but not typically so. Its violent subjugation had as much in common with the Holocaust as with other colonial mass murders and may be regarded as a transitional case between these two categories of violence. What distinguishes the German South West African genocide from most other colonial mass murders is the fact that the Germans in colonial Namibia articulated and implemented a policy of *Vernichtung*, or an-

SOURCE: Benjamin Madley, "From Africa to Auschwitz: How German South West Africa Incubated Ideas and Methods Adopted and Developed by the Nazis in Eastern Europe," *European History Quarterly* 35, no. 3 (2005): 429, 430, 436, 438, 439, 440, 441–42, 445, 446, 457–58. Reprinted with permission of Sage Publishers, Inc.

nihilation. Wilhelmine rule in German South West Africa was not the sole inspiration for Nazi policies in Eastern Europe, but it contributed ideas, methods, and a lexicon that Nazi leaders borrowed and expanded. . . .

Comparing the German South West African genocide to similar events in Southern Rhodesia, British Natal, the Belgian Congo, and Italian Ethiopia illustrates that while the articulation of an annihilation policy separates the Namibian catastrophe from these other cases of mass theft and murder, the German South West African experience was one of many violent colonial episodes that may have inspired Nazi conquest and genocide in Eastern Europe. . . . [For example,] German South West African colonists pioneered the implementation of a *Weltanschauung* [ideology], later adopted by the Nazis, in which superior Germans rule over sub-human non-Germans with brutality and slavery. This paradigm provided new ideas and methods for Nazi colonialism that were transferred to Germany and to future Nazis by a variety of vectors, of which colonial literature is one easily documented. . . . Colonial Namibian literature . . . exposed metropolitan Germans to a new form of racism in which non-Germans had the right to exist only insofar as they served Germans and in which some authors even endorsed extermination. . . .

Parallels between German South West African and Third Reich race laws indicate that the colony's legal system provided conceptual and linguistic prototypes from which Nazi lawmakers borrowed extensively. Like the Nazis, Germans in colonial Namibia embedded racism into their legal system. . . . German South West Africa's 1905 law banning *Rassenmischung*, or race mixing, demonstrates how certain race laws and associated rhetoric were pioneered in the colony, received wide exposure in Germany, and were then adopted by the Third Reich. The ban on interracial marriage associated it with the new term *Rassenschande*, meaning racial shame. . . . Given Germans' exposure to these terms and ideas, amplified by seven years of *Reichstag* debates, it is not surprising that Nazis deployed vocabulary nearly identical to German South West African *Rassenmischung* laws and associated *Reichstag* debates when they criminalized marriage and sexual intercourse between Jews and "Aryan" Germans. Linguistic connections indicate wholesale borrowing. . . .

Annihilationist "cleansing" rhetoric developed quickly in the colony. . . . Nazi annihilationist rhetoric sometimes directly echoed German South West African phrases and frequently connected annihilation with colonial goals. Indeed, the Nazis' blueprint for the East broadly replicated the colonization of Herero lands. Nazis envisioned largely emptying the land of sub-humans to create a vast *Lebensraum*. On this tabula rasa they planned to inscribe a new, utopian social order, populated by Aryan farmers ruling over Slavic slaves. Following the 1904 uprising, Germans [had] cleared Herero lands of people they considered sub-human before enslaving survivors. . . .

Historians regularly proclaim Hitler's war in the East unprecedented in ferocity and scale. This is true. However, when one considers the genocidal wars fought against the Herero and Nama, four striking similarities suggest that these colonial campaigns incubated many elements of the *Vernichtungskrieg* [war of annihilation] later waged by Nazi forces [in the Soviet Union]. First German military leaders defined both conflicts as *Rassenkampf*, or race war. Second, both armies articulated a *Vernichtungskrieg* strategy predicated on physically destroying the enemy. Third, as part of this strategy, German military leaders, in both wars, systematically murdered prisoners of war (POWs) and civilians. Finally, in each case, leaders employed the rhetoric of public health in attempts to rationalize mass murder. . . . Although discussions of racial hygiene and eugenics were common in late nineteenth and early twentieth-century Germany, these linguistic overlaps suggest that rhetoric associated with German South West Africa was a source from which Nazis borrowed. . . .

[Next, the] Nazis neither invented the concentration camp nor pioneered its use by Germans. The first German concentration camps were built in colonial Namibia and on 11 December 1904, *Konzentrationslager*, or concentration camp, was introduced into the German language. [Germany's] Chancellor [Bernhard] von Bülow wrote the word in a letter commanding [General Lothar] von Trotha [the German Reich's commanding officer in South West Africa] to rescind the Annihilation Order [or *Vernichtungsbefehl*, which von Trotha had issued on October 2, 1904] and "establish *Konzentrationslager* for the temporary housing and sustenance of the Herero people." Von Bülow likely borrowed the word and institution from the British, who had incarcerated Boer men, women, and children in barbed wire compounds during the 1899–1902 South African War. The British in turn had made use of the concentration camp concept developed by Spaniards in Cuba. . . .

[Furthermore,] Nazi colonialism in Eastern Europe broadly followed patterns set in German South West Africa not by chance, but because Germans in Wilhelmine Namibia had pioneered the implementation of *Lebensraum* theory, the brutal treatment of colonized people as sub-humans, and the use of legally institutionalized racism, all of which were central to later Nazi rule in the East. Likewise, Third Reich leaders borrowed ideas and methods from the German South West African genocide that they then employed and expanded upon. Genocidal rhetoric, a new definition of Vernichtuingskrieg, executing POWs, murdering civilians en masse, and deporting POWs and noncombatants to work and death camps were all introduced to modern German history through the Namibian colonial experience. . . .

The roots of Nazi ideas and policies range well beyond the German South West African experience. However, connections can be drawn from the colony to the Third Reich as one way of understanding the origins of Nazi imperialism and mass murder in Eastern Europe. German South West Africa should no longer be overlooked as an important antecedent to Nazi colonialism and genocide.

82 • The Armenian Genocide and American Missionary Relief Efforts (Suzanne E. Moranian)

From Rwanda to Darfur, humanitarian relief efforts during and after genocide have become a staple of our times. Yet, as Suzanne Moranian convincingly shows, the international administration of aid was already a sophisticated undertaking nearly a century ago. In this essay from 2003, Moranian tells of the sprawling network of American missionaries—assembled under the American Board of Commissioners for Foreign Missions—and their relief efforts in the Ottoman Empire in the course and wake

SOURCE: Suzanne E. Moranian, "The Armenian Genocide and American Missionary Relief Efforts," in Jay Winter, ed., *America and the Armenian Genocide of 1915* (Cambridge: Cambridge University Press, 2003), 185, 192, 194, 195–96, 201, 202, 203, 204, 205, 209–10, 212, 213. Reprinted with permission of the publisher.

[Handwritten margin note:] but also geo-logical and strategic. Question of if Germany could have developed these ideas w/out Namibia before them

of the genocide between 1915 and 1927. She also explains how the U.S. missionary movement—through its relief efforts in Armenia and elsewhere—sought to enhance its role in an increasingly secular United States. This aspect is relevant because it speaks to the often criticized professionalization and politicization of humanitarianism in the twenty-first century.

The largest American missionary organization operating in Turkey at the time [of the genocide] was the American Board of Commissioners for Foreign Missions, headquartered in Boston. Based on reports it received from its missionaries in the Turkish field, the American Board launched a relief drive that broke new ground in the history of American philanthropy. The American missionaries were the most critical figures in the relationship between the United States and the Armenians during the genocide era. They were unmatched in exerting influence and expertise in the Turkish field and on the American home front, as well as in American policy, intellectual, and cultural circles. . . . It was the problem of relief that brought piety into overt partnership with the political, and elevated the missionaries to a position of influence in Washington. In only a few years, through sophisticated fund-raising techniques, the American Protestants eventually created a multimillion-dollar business of Near-East aid. . . .

Appalled at the start by the overwhelming need for assistance, leading American philanthropists joined the American Board, and other mission and religious societies, in founding numerous relief organizations. These included the formation in 1915 of the American Committee for Armenian and Syrian Relief (ACASR), which briefly became the American Committee for Relief in the Near East (ACRNE), and then evolved into the Near East Relief (NER). The United States Congress granted the NER a charter in 1919, thereby infusing it with political prestige. . . . The Rockefeller Foundation made early and large contributions, which it increased as the needs mounted. The unfailing support of the American Red Cross during the war years made it possible to increase greatly Near East relief work. By January 1918, the Red Cross donated $1,800,000, and, with subsequent appropriations, its total gift amounted to $6 million. The Armenian-American community also worked hard to raise money for the relief of their fellow Armenians. . . .

Over the years, the United States government would donate $25 million to the NER in supplies, services, and cash. Herbert Hoover, Franklin D. Roosevelt, and William Howard Taft each served as trustees of the NER. Over fifteen years, the missionary-based NER spent a staggering $116 million in assistance. It helped well over 1, if not 2, million refugees—two-thirds of whom were women and children. More than 132,000 orphans graduated from the Near East Relief orphanage schools. It trained 200 nurses. Of its volunteers, 30 lost their lives, succumbing to illness and the sometimes dangerous environment. Foreshadowing the work of the Peace Corps, the NER built hundreds of miles of roads and well-paved streets. Through irrigation it reclaimed thousands of acres of arable land. It erected permanent buildings and repaired old ones. The NER established new industries. It imported new breeds of cattle and poultry. It planted better seeds of corn, cotton, wheat, other grains, and vegetables. The NER also demonstrated the advantages of such equipment as the modern tractor. . . .

While the missionaries depended on their outreach ministries to recreate Christianity globally, they simultaneously used these foreign programs to enhance their role in an increasingly secular and politically changing United States. The missionary-led relief efforts were part of the larger move by the Protestant progressives towards the mainstream of an urban-industrial America. . . . Ironically, the Protestants' search for power at home would come to depend, in part, on their evangelical and humanitarian programs abroad. [For this reason,] the social Gospelers drew upon the dynamic, twentieth-century ideas of bureaucracy and rationalization. They adopted the rhetoric and meaning of system and efficiency. The American missionary leadership turned fund raising into a modern science. . . . Fund raising for Armenian relief mirrored the methods of a business conglomerate. . . . The relief organizers, from the beginning, held strategy meetings, developed and executed lines of promotional attack, maintained local, state, national, and international levels of organization, intensely pursued government lobbying, and coordinated local and national media outreach. They established and supervised an international network of relief agents. . . . Their progressive, philanthropic efforts incorporated state-of-the-art organizational skills with the ancient zealousness of the Gospel. That is what made them so potent. . . .

The American public regarded the missionaries as the most trustworthy experts on the Armenian Question. This was no accident. The missionaries were unique as global couriers of knowledge. . . . [They] took very seriously the effort to educate their supporting constituencies back home. Evangelists in the United States visiting on furlough crisscrossed the country giving speeches and addresses. . . . The missionary organizations [also] had in-house periodicals and regularly contributed to many others. They also published nondenominational textbooks for readers of all ages describing the geography, history, and political problems of the foreign lands being served. . . . Certainly, the missionaries determined almost everything that the American people knew about the Armenians. From their years in the Anatolian field, the missionaries knew more about the Armenians than did any other Americans. . . . The missionary interest ran an information network and purposely attempted to control public opinion. They did this partly out of a lofty sense of sharing and teaching. They also did this to build a nationwide constituency of support for their programs and concerns. . . .

Laymen with commerce backgrounds came to replace those who had traditionally raised money, such as untrained volunteers or clergy, who were less experienced in business. Since public image was important, these sleek and professional missionary and relief administrators were adept at not just religious but also promotional awakenings. Soliciting money would not depend on children saving up pennies. From the beginning, the relief organizations included appeals to wealthy individuals for donations, community campaigns, gifts from churches, and public information and collection meetings. . . . In building such broad-based support, they became trend setters in American philanthropy.

The relief committee members had voted not to use relief funds to pay for advertising, deciding that expensive advertising would be injurious to the cause. Instead, they depended on the goodwill of the American press. Melville Stone of the Associated Press served as their media consultant. . . . They made contacts with the editorial staff of all of America's leading journals. They furnished special material for editorial purposes. . . . It was a masterful propaganda blitz. . . . Between 1915 and 1928, over twenty different American magazines ran hundreds of stories on the Armenians which by the relief committee's design, were central to raising money. Many of the writers, and often editors, were missionaries, friends of the missionary interests, or relied on missionary information as sources. . . . Major American newspapers gave comprehensive coverage of the Armenian Question, also enhancing the relief effort. Because the American missionaries were usually the only Americans living in the Turkish interior, the news reported often originated with them. The *New York Times* ran 146 pieces in 1915 alone. . . .

Certain themes ran through the articles appearing in the United States concerning the Armenians dating back to the 1896–6 massacres. These motifs had a profound bearing on American understanding of and feelings towards both the Armenians and the Turks. The pieces combined facts with emotion. Even the most straightforward story could become lurid simply by its documentary contents. The reports and commentaries were gripping. They seized the heart and were high human drama. The plot repeated in the American media for years was a basic one: good versus evil. The press championed the underdog fighting the oppressor, who naturally hated his prey. The Armenians were portrayed as the innocent, martyred Christians whom the barbaric Muslim Turks victimized. Americans identified with the Christian Armenians. . . . Indeed, the United States led the world in a massive outpouring of giving towards the Armenians, spearheaded and then delivered on site by the missionaries, with funds raised through the missionary-led NER. "Never since the Civil War has the country been so sympathetically unified in a particular enterprise of Christian fellowship," declared American editor Albert Shaw in 1930. . . .

Americans became the world leaders in the foreign missionary movement by 1920. Activism and donations peaked in the first two decades of the twentieth century. Contributions connected to the secular crisis of the Armenians' plight figured largely in that accomplishment. The First World War, however, raised in the minds of many American Protestants the issue of just who might be the pagans in need of the Gospel. The spectacle of Christian nations involved in such bloody conflict drew outraged criticisms of hypocrisy. It nullified the optimistic pledge to evangelize the world in one's generation. Among its many consequences, the First World War initially expanded and then hastened the decline of the foreign mission movement. It robbed the mission message of its spirit and legitimacy.

83 • Cambodia after the Khmer Rouge (Evan Gottesman)

It is a well-known fact that Vietnam's 1979 intervention in Cambodia put an end to the genocide that Pol Pot's Khmer Rouge regime had been waging there. What is less well known is what happened afterward. Evan Gottesman reconstructs the intended and unintended consequences of genocide termination in his 2003 book, Cambodia after the Khmer Rouge. *He gives a sense of the manifold problems that await intervening forces, particularly if they are intent, as in the case of Vietnam in postgenocide Cambodia, on rebuilding the country in their own image.*

Vietnamese soldiers entered the Cambodian capital on the morning of January 7 [1979], their jeeps roaring down the city's deserted avenues. . . . On January 8 an ostensibly Cambodian news agency announced the composition of a Cambodian government, the Kampuchean People's Revolutionary Council (KPRC), to be headed by Heng Samrin. On January 10 the

SOURCE: Evan Gottesman, *Cambodia after the Khmer Rouge: Inside the Politics of Nation-Building* (New Haven, Conn.: Yale University Press, 2003), 11, 40, 42, 43–44, 45, 48, 49, 50, 60, 78. Reprinted with permission of the publisher.

KPRC officially declared the establishment of a new regime, the People's Republic of Kampuchea, or PRK. . . . The world's image of Cambodia in 1979, conveyed largely by television, was of the tens of thousands of refugees who crossed into Thailand in the first few months of the year. . . . By the end of October 1979 three hundred thousand Cambodians were living along the [Thai-Cambodian] border. For the next twelve years, this exodus divided not only Cambodians but, politically at least, much of the world.

In regional capitals and in Beijing, Washington, and Moscow, the Cambodia conflict was seen and often referred to as a "proxy" for Cold War antagonism. Almost immediately, the dispute over Cambodia pitted Vietnam against Thailand, which in turn matched Moscow and the Eastern Bloc against China, the United States, and the capitalist countries of the Association of Southeast Asian Nations (ASEAN). The [once genocidal] Khmer Rouge, after years of self-imposed isolation, now looked to the international community for diplomatic support while fashioning a message that blended anti-Vietnamese rhetoric with warnings of a global Soviet conspiracy. . . . Although the United States did not directly assist the Khmer Rouge resistance, it condemned neither China's resuscitation of its forces nor China's February invasion of northern Vietnam, an incursion intended as retaliation for the occupation of Cambodia. The U.S. State Department also walked a fine line in its criticism of the Khmer Rouge, carefully avoiding the word "genocide" in order to finesse the judicial and diplomatic implications of the Genocide Convention. The United States attempted to isolate Vietnam and [postgenocide] Cambodia as well. Throughout the summer of 1979, American diplomats lobbied other countries, charities, international aid organizations, the International Monetary Fund, and the World Bank to suspend aid to both countries. . . . On the ground, the West's interaction with Cambodia was limited to the border camps into which Cambodian refugees were herded. The first camps, established under the watchful eye of the Thai military in 1979–80, served as military bases for the Khmer Rouge leadership and for the Cambodians they conscripted. Elsewhere, though, entire new cities were emerging out of refugee camps controlled by noncommunist resistance forces. . . .

Back in Phnom Penh, Vietnamese and Cambodian officials had settled upon words and phrases with which to describe the regime, its enemies, and, ultimately, its legitimacy. The PRK stood in opposition to all "expansionist genocidal Pol Potists," the "reactionary clique," and the "Chinese expansionists." The resistance, both outside and within the country, became the "enemy" or "Pol Pot." As the bellicose lyrics of the PRK's new national anthem made clear, the regime would find purpose and unity in its struggle against a monolithic, genocidal, and as-yet-unidentified opponent. . . . Amidst the diplomatic posturing and revolutionary rhetoric, the PRK was taking shape. Guided by Vietnamese military and civilian advisors, the regime established itself along typical communist lines. . . . The Party leadership, whose members were eventually organized as a Politburo, were, for the moment, grouped into a small Central Committee. An assortment of Khmer Rouge defectors and Hanoi-trained revolutionaries, they were known collectively, by external critics who preferred not to recognize the PRK regime and by Cambodians accustomed to personifying power, as the Heng Samrin regime.

Heng Samrin, the former Khmer Rouge commander whom the Vietnamese selected to be president [of postgenocide Cambodia] and head of state, was virtually unknown to Cambodians. . . . Uneducated and yet rigidly Marxist in outlook, Samrin was politically and ideologically reliable. His background as a former Khmer Rouge cadre also allowed Hanoi to present the new regime as being led by "forces inside the country," as opposed to Hanoi-trained communists. Later, it became apparent that Samrin was dependent on Vietnamese support and that he lacked the political skills necessary to develop a personal power base. . . .

The Cambodian leadership and its Vietnamese advisors sought to replicate the vast, ubiquitous structure of the Vietnamese Communist Party, establishing Party branches in every state institution, from ministries to local government offices, military units, schools, and hospitals. Initially, however, the lack of Party members forced the regime to rely on the next best thing: core groups (*krom snoul*). . . . Yet in April 1979, the Party had managed to field core groups in only a few central ministries and were desperately scouring the state administration, the Cambodian military, and the Front for acceptable cadres. Recruitment was proceeding so slowly in part because of the Party's obsession with political purity. In addition to the dutiful execution of Party orders, core group candidates were expected to have a "clear personal history." . . . [Yet] Cambodians, most of whom were deeply disillusioned with communism, were suspicious of the Party. Even those who were tempted to join out of pure opportunism had reason to balk, aware that the Khmer Rouge had executed thousands of its own Party members. As a result of these misgivings and the restrictive core group qualifications, Party membership remained low, particularly outside Phnom Penh, where, in the summer of 1979, there were fewer than seven members per province. . . .

Communist revolutionaries tend, upon victory, to politicize and gradually restaff the bureaucracies of their predecessors. Both Democratic Kampuchea [as the previous genocidal regime was known] and the PRK were exceptions to this pattern, however—Democratic Kampuchea because it chose to eliminate and to do without a normal administration, the PRK because the Khmer Rouge left nothing behind. In the starkest physical terms, the lack of functioning ministries required that each [incoming] minister and his staff scout the city for a proper physical site, negotiate with Vietnamese officials for each office building, and hire crews to clean up the long-abandoned buildings, collect the trash, and clip overgrown weeds and bushes. The tiny ministry staffs then went out in search of chairs, desks, pens, paper, typewriters, and other supplies. . . . Once the bureaucracy began to function, Cambodian ministers and their Vietnamese advisors encountered confusion over the roles of the various ministries. The Khmer Rouge's extermination of civil servants had nearly erased a national memory of how government worked. . . .

From the beginning, the prospect of relying solely on the core people posed ideological and pragmatic problems. Not only did they lack previous communist training, but, having served neither the pre-Revolutionary regimes nor the Khmer Rouge, they offered no administrative experience. The core people also lacked political connections to the PRK's provincial leadership and thus failed to contribute to the regime's efforts to consolidate power. For strategic and ideological reasons, the Vietnamese had appointed former Khmer Rouge cadres as provincial Party secretaries and governors. Those officials, looking to build patronage networks with family members, friends, and former comrades, naturally appointed other Khmer Rouge veterans to positions in the districts, communes, and villages. Far from offending the Vietnamese, these attempts to establish personal fiefdoms made the PRK's provincial apparatus more cohesive and therefore stronger.

The presence of former comrades in positions of power reassured members of the Khmer Rouge resistance that they could safely surrender and would even be rewarded for throwing their support behind the PRK. With a civil war to fight, the co-optation of the remnants of Democratic Kampuchea became the regime's overriding strategic goal, one that would guide the Party for the next twenty years.... The problem was that the entire justification for the PRK's existence was to serve as a clean break from Cambodia's cruel past.... Whereas the PRK's definition of the noncommunist threat gradually expanded to include an entire culture, its communist enemies, the Khmer Rouge, were reduced to one name: Pol Pot.

84 • Dangerous Sanctuaries in Zaire (Sarah Kenyon Lischer)

An inevitable consequence of genocidal campaigns is flows of internally displaced persons (IDPs) as well as refugees who spill into neighboring countries. Most recently, in Chad hundreds of thousands of Darfuris found shelter from violence. Yet the international administration of refugee camps has been fraught with difficulties, even dangers, as Sarah Kenyon Lischer, a political scientist at Wake Forest University, demonstrates clearly in Dangerous Sanctuaries *(2005). Focusing on the humanitarian response, in many respects disastrous, to the refugee crisis in the wake of the 1994 genocide in Rwanda, Lischer shows how and when humanitarian assistance exacerbates conflict instead of ameliorating it. When the international community failed to adequately administer the millions of refugees that had fled to eastern Zaire, the refugee camps inadvertently became a restaging ground for génocidaires from Rwanda.*

Since the early 1990s, internal conflicts have caused millions of deaths in the Democratic Republic of Congo (formerly Zaire), Rwanda, Burundi, and Uganda. In Congo alone, over three million people died from the effects of war between 1998 and 2003. These many internal conflicts did not remain isolated from each other, but rather spread across national borders, escalating the costs of war. The potent mix of millions of refugees, thousands of rebels, and abundant humanitarian assistance acted as a catalyst for the spread of conflict in the Great Lakes region of Africa. A locus of this regional destabilization was the 1994 Rwandan genocide and the resulting refugee crisis....

The genocide and subsequent defeat of the Hutu forces in 1994 spread massive refugee flows to neighboring states. Nearly two million Hutu refugees fled at the instigation of an estimated 20,000 Hutu soldiers and 50,000 militia members, who joined the refugees in exile.... From the beginning of the crisis, the Rwandan Hutu refugees served a valuable strategic role for the planners and executors of the genocide. The refugees provided international cover for the genocidaires and also served as an indictment of the new Tutsi-led regime in Rwanda. The militants extracted resources from the refugees and used the camps as recruitment pools. The well-funded camps quickly became the launching point for violence directed against the new Rwandan government. Although limited cross-border attacks against Rwandan targets originated from Tanzania and Burundi, the vast majority of the violence emanated from eastern Zaire.

SOURCE: Sarah Kenyon Lischer, *Dangerous Sanctuaries: Refugee Camps, Civil War, and the Dilemmas of Humanitarian Aid* (Ithaca, N.Y.: Cornell University Press, 2005), 73, 75–76, 78, 79, 80, 81, 87, 90, 92, 166. Reprinted with permission of the publisher.

From the camps in Zaire, the refugees organized to destabilize the Rwandan government. Cross-border attacks against Rwanda occurred throughout 1995 and 1996, with Hutu assailants targeting genocide survivors and abducting local men to participate in the militias across the border. The conflict escalated sharply in late 1996, when the Rwandan government and Zairian rebels attacked the refugee camps, dispersing nearly a million people. Since that time, international and civil war have continued nearly unabated in the region. . . .

The Rwandan refugee population in Zaire constituted a state in exile from the early days of the crisis. Numerous sources concur with the Organization for African Union (OAU) [predecessor of the African Union] description of the camps as "a rump genocidal state." The postcrisis UNHCR [United Nations High Commissioner for Refugees] evaluation characterized the refugee flow as "a strategic retreat by the former Government of Rwanda and its armed forces following a genocide." . . . The fleeing refugees took with them to Zaire nearly everything of value in Rwanda, from the entire state treasury down to door handles and window frames. One UNHCR official recalled seeing ex-FAR (former Rwandan army) tanks and two or three warplanes parked at Bukavu airport. Aid workers observed Rwandan public transport buses and old Mercedes being driven around the camps. . . .

In the first few months of the refugee crisis, chaos and violence ruled the camps in eastern Zaire. From July 1994 until about October, a virulent cholera epidemic killed 50,000 refugees, which—to say the least—greatly added to the confusion. During that time, the militants openly battled for control of the refugee population and made no secret of their ambition to invade Rwanda and topple the RPF [the Tutsi-led Rwandan Patriotic Front]. . . . That same month a group of machete-wielding *Interahamwe* dissuaded several hundred refugees from repatriating. Numerous refugees were killed after merely obtaining information about repatriation. Militants set up roadblocks within the camps and instituted neighborhood security patrols to monitor refugee activity. After the initial period of chaos, militant Hutu leaders established complete control over the camps in eastern Zaire, demonstrating a high level of political and military organization. . . .

The same local authority structures that [had] existed in Rwanda [prior to the genocide] now governed the camps in Zaire, enabling the genocidal leaders to maintain tight control. In December 1994, the refugee-run Commission Sociale restructured the Goma camps into *quartiers* (districts), *sous-quartiers* (sub-districts), *cellules* (neighborhoods), and *nyumba kumi* (groups of ten houses). . . . The OAU estimated that around 10 percent of the refugees— over 100,000 people—were actually militants and war criminals. The militants used the relative security of exile to stockpile weapons in and around the camps. Aid workers confirmed that weapon shipments destined for the Hutu military leaders regularly arrived at Goma airport. . . .

In eastern Zaire, virtually all international actors involved in the crisis contributed to the spread of civil war, whether intentionally or not. External support, especially from France, allowed the militant refugees to continue the war and even strengthen their forces. Sudan, China, and the Angolan UNITA rebel movement also aided Mobutu's government [in Zaire]. The Zairian ADFL [Alliance des Forces Démocratiques pour la Libération du Congo-Zaire] rebels gained assistance or sympathy from the governments of Rwanda, Burundi, Angola, Uganda, the United States, and also from the Southern Sudanese rebels. No international force attempted to demilitarize the refugee areas or secure Zaire's borders. As a failing state,

Zaire lacked the capability to prevent external interference in the crisis. As an ally of the Hutu militants, Zaire willingly abetted international involvement on their behalf. . . .

Zaire's weak central government provided little or no oversight of the many UN agencies and hundreds of NGOs that descended on eastern Zaire following the refugee crisis. Major international organizations included [the] UNHCR, the World Food Program (WFP), and the International Committee of the Red Cross and NGOs such as CARE, Médecins sans Frontières, International Rescue Committee, Oxfam, American Rescue Committee Caritas, and Médecins du Monde. The humanitarian organizations competed fiercely for the billions of dollars in aid contracts and for public recognition of their charitable activities. International donors spent $1.4 billion on relief contracts for Goma, Zaire, between April and December 1994. UNHCR alone spent $115 million in Goma between July and October 1994. The chaotic situation and abundant aide provided a windfall for the militants, who used it to support their planned invasion of Rwanda. Humanitarian organizations contributed to the spread of civil war in . . . four ways. . . . Aid agencies provided food directly to militia members and soldiers. The internationally supported camps also sustained the militants' supporters. The billions of dollars of aid contributed to the war economy. And the international images of the refugees as victims legitimated the militants' position in the camps. . . . The genocidaires realized how far they could misuse aid without triggering a withdrawal or public denunciation. . . . Humanitarian organizations were aware of the militarization but took few actions to counter it and did not publicize it. . . .

Current humanitarian responses to militarized refugee crises generally ignore the political context of the crises. By doing so, humanitarian organizations all too often contribute to the spread of conflicts. The numerous excuses for ignoring militarization may seem legitimate, but they provide little consolation when humanitarian aid exacerbates violence. In the long run, if agencies do not leverage their resources to improve security, they risk losing their moral clout when humanitarian assistance contributes to conflict. The humanitarian fiasco in the Rwandan refugee camps highlighted the urgent need to design refugee relief programs with a better understanding of their political and military impacts. In militarized refugee crises, purity of intention cannot prevent the spread of conflict.

85 • The U.S. State Department Atrocities Documentation Survey in Darfur (John Hagan and Wenona Rymond-Richmond with Alberto Palloni and Patricia Parker)

Through a fascinating account of the rise and decline of the U.S. State Department's Atrocities Documentation Survey (ADS), the eminent sociologist John Hagan and his coauthors illuminate the politics of humanitarianism in the international system in their book, Darfur and the Crime of Genocide *(2008). Administered with the support of the State Department and the Coalition for International Justice, the ADS has been at the center of much contentious politics in the debate over*

SOURCE: John Hagan and Wenona Rymond-Richmond, *Darfur and the Crime of Genocide* (Cambridge: Cambridge University Press, 2008), 79, 80, 81–83, 84, 85, 86, 87, 97, 99, 100, 101, 103, 105. Reprinted with permission of the publisher.

the collective violence in Darfur. Participants in the debate disagree fundamentally about the nature of the conflict and sharply about the number of victims. By delving deeply into the machinations surrounding the making of the ADS and its subsequent politicization, Hagan et al. shed a bright light on an insufficiently studied, and far from trivial, aspect of genocide research: how to count the dead.

Documenting Atrocities in Darfur is the title of the eight-page report based on a survey of Darfur refugees in Chad and published by the U.S. Department of State in September 2004. The report's chillingly cogent tables, charts, maps, and pictures—derived from interviews with 1,136 refugees in Chad—speak volumes. Our recording from the Atrocities Documentation Survey (ADS) identified more than 12,000 deaths and many more rapes and atrocities that the respondents personally witnessed or heard about before fleeing. . . . We demonstrate in this chapter that the administration's use of survey evidence, including its own victimization survey, involved flip-flop diplomacy. To understand the confusing politics of these events, it is important to first understand the genesis of the ADS. . . .

Stefanie Frease of the Coalition for International Justice (CIJ) and Jonathan Howard, a research analyst with the State Department's Office of Research, conducted the survey. Howard developed the research design, and Frease assumed the role of field supervisor. The State Department wanted Frease to complete the survey in just two months. . . . The . . . challenge was to develop a survey instrument, recruit interviewers and interpreters, plan the logistics of conducting surveys in nineteen remote locations in eastern Chad, implement a sampling plan, move the research team in and out of the survey locations, and organize the coding and analysis of more than one thousand interviews. . . . The team was able to complete several hundred interviews in time for [U.S. Secretary of State Colin] Powell's appearance before the UN Security Council in July, and it finished the full survey of 1,136 refugees in Chad before Powell's congressional testimony in early September | when, in an appearance before the Senate Foreign Relations Committee, he declared that "genocide has been committed in Darfur"]. . . .

We use the ADS data in this chapter to elaborate a preliminary estimate of mortality in Darfur. . . . Of course, there are other sources of data about the conflict in Darfur. Probably the best-known data collected on this conflict come from surveys conducted by the World Health Organization (WHO) in the internal displacement camps inside Darfur. The breadth of the WHO survey work is important because of the absence of census or hospital data from which to calculate Darfur mortality. However, the difference between the ADS and WHO survey data reflect important distinctions . . . between the crime and health research paradigms. The ADS design is a cutting-edge example of a crime victimization approach, with its emphasis on incident-based reporting of criminal events before and in the refugee camps. In contrast, the WHO survey applies the health research approach to complex humanitarian emergencies, with a subsequent emphasis on mortality linked to disease and nutritional problems inside the displacement camps. The French human rights group Médecins San Frontières (MSF) also conducted surveys in West Darfur. Although the MSF surveys covered a small number of camps, this initiative uniquely combined attention to pre-camp and in-camp deaths. This research is crucial for the conclusion we reach later in this chapter. First, however, it is important to learn more about the findings of the WHO and ADS studies. . . .

Health organizations—especially in a setting such as Darfur—obviously focus on immediate and ongoing challenges of disease and malnutrition. They are less concerned with the past violence that leads displaced persons to flee to camps in the first place. This is a key reason why Powell's State Department and its ambassador on war crimes needed a crime victimization survey and initiated the ADS. At about the same time as the ADS was launched, during the late summer of 2004, the WHO conducted surveys of mortality and other health and nutrition issues with the cooperation of the Sudanese Ministry of Health (hereafter referred to as the WHO/SMH survey). This work allowed estimates of crude relative mortality (CMR) rates. . . . Thus, a WHO retrospective survey conducted during the summer months in 2004 produced a CMR of 2.14 for the states of North and West Darfur. This level of mortality is from four to seven times the "normal or expected" mortality in sub-Saharan Africa. This CMR is a meaningful estimate of mortality (following displacement) due to health problems in the camps, with some added deaths resulting from violence experienced during refugee forays outside the camps to collect firewood or other necessities. . . .

The survey work of [the] WHO led to an early estimate of 70,000 Darfurian refugee deaths in just seven months of 2004, again almost entirely from malnutrition and disease. . . . The death toll probably peaked in the summer months of 2004. [The WHO] concluded that from 5,000 to 10,000 persons died in Darfur per month during this period, but we will suggest that the peak number of deaths per months was even higher. . . . UN emergency relief coordinator Jan Egeland returned from Darfur in March 2005. . . . He extrapolated from the UN's WHO survey by multiplying . . . [the] 10,000 per month figure by eighteen months (i.e., instead of seven). The UN estimate then jumped to 180,000. Even though this latter estimate involved no further data . . . , Egeland's new number took hold. . . .

Among the mortality estimates receiving attention in the media at the beginning of 2005, the projection of 180,000 deaths from the WHO survey work was at the low end. Jan Coebergh, a British physician, noted the absence of violent deaths from the WHO survey and estimated in the British periodical, *Parliamentary Brief*, that the true death toll was nearer 300,000. The scale of this estimate echoed that offered by the American activist-scholar, Eric Reeves of Smith College, who offered similarly large estimates based on parallel assumptions. . . . Coebergh and Reeves' estimates both added deaths from violence recorded in the ADS to the deaths caused by disease and malnutrition in the WHO survey. Thus, these estimates bridged the crime and health paradigms. . . . At about the same time in the spring of 2005, we issued a press release in conjunction with the CIJ detailing a mortality estimate based on a combination of the WHO and ADS surveys. . . . We concluded that as many as 350,000 persons had died, with nearly 400,000 persons either missing or dead in Darfur. . . . A consensus formed that there were hundreds of thousands of deaths ion Darfur, with the estimates ranging from 180,000 to 400,000. . . .

[U.S.] Assistant Secretary of State Robert Zoellick [currently president of the World Bank], the deputy to the new Secretary of State, Condoleezza Rice, paid a personal visit to Darfur in the early spring of 2005. . . . Zoellick first startled reporters in Khartoum by declining to reaffirm Powell's earlier determination of genocide in Darfur. . . . He then disputed the prevailing consensus estimates of hundreds of thousands of deaths in Darfur. Zoellick instead reported a new State Department estimate of as few as 60,000 and at most 146,000 "excess" deaths. The State Department posted a new report on its Web site, *Sudan: Death Toll in Darfur*, which asserted that "violent deaths were widespread in the early stages of this conflict, but a successful, albeit delayed humanitarian response and a moderate 2004 rainy season combined to suppress mortality rate by curtailing infectious disease outbreaks and substantial disruption of aid deliveries." . . .

The reference to as few as 60,000 "excess" deaths indicated that the new State Department estimate tilted toward the public health side of the disciplinary divided and marked a step away from the ADS victimization methodology. It relied on the health paradigm of "complex humanitarian emergencies," rather than the human rights and war crimes framework. In particular, the new estimate relied on the false assumption that the kind of survey work done by the WHO could fully measure the scale of mortality in Darfur. In effect, the State Department was ignoring its own ADS findings. . . . The State Department's new estimate had an immediate impact on major media news outlets. Whereas these sources previously had reported *hundreds of thousands* of deaths in Darfur, the widely reported death toll now shrunk to *tens of thousands*. . . .

Our final estimation is based on a unique study that bridged the concerns of the crime and health perspectives. Médecins San Frontières (MSF) published this study in the journal of medical research, *Lancet,* in October 2004. MSF reported on four displacement camps in West Darfur between April and June 2004. The use of a limited number of sites resulted from the Sudanese government's restrictions of access placed on the researchers. Like the WHO/SMH study, the MSF study found within-camp violence accounting for only 6 to 21 percent of deaths. Yet, the MSF study also asked about the period leading to flight to three of the four camps. Nearly 90 percent of the deaths before and during flight resulted from violence. In these three camps, the village and flight CMRs (5.9–9.5) were much higher than the in-camp CMRs (1.2–1.3). Overall, the average mortality rate was 3.2 across the four MSF camps—with pre-camp violence included in three of the camps. . . . Still, we concluded that it would be more persuasive to develop a new and alternative calculation that estimated mortality in Darfur on a month-by-month basis during different time periods included in the MSF camp surveys. . . . We combined the MSF and WHO/SMH surveys to draw on the strengths of both. We narrowed the focus initially to nineteen months of the conflict and to the state of West Darfur, and later drew broader conclusions. . . . [We found that] the overall rise and decline in estimated deaths in West Darfur follows the classical pattern of complex humanitarian emergencies. Perhaps most interestingly, the peak monthly level of deaths estimated for West Darfur is about 4,000. We argue that there is good reason to believe that deaths are distributed approximately evenly across the three Darfur states. If this is so, the death toll in Darfur peaked in early 2004 at about 12,000 per month. Note that this figure lies between the 10,000 estimate of [the] WHO/SMH and our earlier 15,000 estimate that combined the findings of [the] WHO and ADS. . . .

Using additional data from a subsequent WHO/SMH survey, the death toll reaches 65,296 in West Darfur. This estimate covers thirty-one months of the conflict, which has been underway for more than five years. . . . Largely as the result of the violence, the UN indicates that more than one million individuals are now displaced or affected in West Darfur, with about one million people similarly displaced in each of the adjoining states of North and South Darfur. If the same ratio of death to displacement applies across states, this implies that about 200,000 deaths occurred over thirty-one months in Greater Darfur. . . . Our final estimate of mortality presented in this chapter was published in the journal *Science* in September 2006. The conclusion—that hundreds of thousands rather than tens of thousands died as a result of the conflict in Darfur—appeared in more than 100 newspaper articles worldwide. . . . Oddly, the U.S. Government Accounting Office (GAO) published a review of Darfur death estimates in November 2006 that did not include the *Science* estimate. . . .

The GAO insisted it did not have the time to include the *Science* estimate. However, the two-month interval between the *Science* and GAO publications and the importance of the issue make this explanation implausible. We suggest two alternative explanations. First, the GAO did not want to probe the assumptions of the population health paradigm that guided its report. Second, the GAO did not want to more directly confront the background and timing of the April 2005 State Department estimate and its neglect of its own ADS data. . . . Nonetheless, . . . the State Department's low estimate was ignored when major news organizations reported and adopted our *Science* estimate of 200,000 or more deaths in the fall of 2006. In February 2007, four years after the outbreak of atrocities, the new U.S. Special Envoy to Sudan, Andrew Natsios, corrected the State Department's low mortality estimate and reaffirmed Sudan's genocidal responsibility for hundreds of thousands of deaths in Darfur. "Arming the Janjaweed," Natsios told the U.S. House Committee on Foreign Affairs, "led to the launching of genocide in 2003 and 2004, which resulted in the deaths of hundreds of thousands of innocent civilians and the destruction of their villages and livelihoods."

86 • DNA Technology and Srebrenica's Missing
(Sarah E. Wagner)

With her 2008 book, Sarah Wagner, an assistant professor of anthropology at the University of North Carolina, Greensboro, adds to the growing canon of innovative works founded on observational field research in postgenocidal settings. What makes Wagner's work so compelling is her exploration of the cultural meaning of DNA analysis. Through an investigation of local and international efforts at recovering and identifying the remains of Srebrenica's dead, she provides unusual insights into the dynamics, logistical and otherwise, of accounting for missing citizens in the aftermath of genocide. Among other points, Wagner illuminates the local and international politics that governed the recovery and identification of mortal remains in Bosnia.

From the end of the war in December 1995 to November 2001, fewer than 1 percent of Srebrenica's missing were identified. By the tenth anniversary of the genocide, the mortal remains of 1,938 individuals—nearly 25 percent of the total missing—had been identified and buried in the Srebrenica-Potočari Memorial Center. The breakthrough in the identification process came on November 16, 2001, when DNA laboratory technicians at the International Commission on Missing Persons (ICMP) successfully extracted and matched the genetic profiles from the mortal remains of a sixteen-year-old boy and the blood samples of his surviving family members. . . .

SOURCE: Sarah E. Wagner, *To Know Where He Lies: DNA Technology and the Search for Srebrenica's Missing* (Berkeley: University of California Press, 2008), 82–82, 86–88, 89–90, 93, 97, 105–6, 121, 122. Reprinted with permission of the publisher.

Science assumes a very powerful role in these unfolding events. But the story behind the development of the DNA-based technology used to identify missing persons of Srebrenica and, more generally, those of the conflicts of former Yugoslavia in the 1990s, is not one of reified science as deus ex machina, whose sophisticated instruments of genetic testing impart order in a disorderly postwar society. Rather, it is a story of knowledge production occurring within the specified sociopolitical context of postwar Bosnia and encompassing a range of sources of authority and expertise. Studying how this technology came into being entails assessing the network of actors both supporting and rejecting the knowledge it promised to produce, the political aims behind its creation, and the often competing claims of truth and objectivity underwriting its results. While media representations of the recovery process tend to credit DNA testing with the successful identification of nearly one quarter of Srebrenica's missing, there are other vital aspects of the process frequently overshadowed by the innovative application of this biotechnology. . . .

The notion of identifying persons missing as a result of the war presented Bosnia's dual-entity government with a vexing political objective: to locate, recover, and identify the mortal remains of victims of all ethnic groups. The numbers of missing among the three ethno-national groups at the end of the war were significantly different: 87.8 percent Bosniaks, 2.8 percent Croats, 9 percent Serbs, and .4 percent others. While recovering and identifying Srebrenica's victims were important goals for many Bosniak political and religious leaders, in particular those nationalist politicians from the Podrinje region eager to document claims of Serb aggression with concrete facts and numbers, Bosnia Serb officials were reluctant to support the identification initiatives, especially when it came to dislodging locations of suspected mass graves. Yet their cooperation was imperative—without Bosnian Serb authorities' participation, exhuming and identifying remains, especially those of the Srebrenica missing, would be extremely difficult if not impossible. . . .

As with many aspects of its governance, the political structure of the postwar Bosnian state hampered its ability to undertake the task of identifying its missing citizens. The Dayton Peace Agreement had formally divided the Republic of Bosnia and Herzegovina into two entities—the Federation of Bosnia and Herzegovina and the Republika Srpska—and its federal government consisted of a convoluted equal-representation parliamentary assembly and a rotating tri-presidency. . . . Coupled with the disparity in respective numbers of missing persons and competing moral understandings of victimhood and aggression, . . . separate, entity-specific identification initiatives in the immediate postwar years precluded the kind of collaboration necessary to develop a centralized identification system, let alone one capable of marshaling the resources for DNA analysis.

Given that the divided government of Bosnia and Herzegovina was incapable of accounting for and recovering all of its missing citizens regardless of ethnicity, the task fell to the authority behind the postwar government—that is, the international presences intent on establishing a liberal democracy from the fractured polity of postwar Bosnia [i.e., the Office of the High Representative established in Annex 10 of the Dayton Peace Agreement]. . . . Helping Bosnia acquire and implement [the] cutting-edge application of forensic science advanced the meta-narrative of progress through the transfer of technology and knowledge. It also demonstrated the international community's responsiveness to the surviving families, who held the UN responsible for failing to protect the enclave [of Srebrenica] and who had demanded the technoscientific resource be made available to identify their missing relatives.

Beyond these more limited goals, the DNA-based identification technology provided the international protectorate presence and the Bosniak leadership a means to care for and control Bosnia's living citizens by accounting for the dead. The process of extracting and analyzing human genetic material presented a seemingly apolitical method of identification. . . . Like other mechanisms of counting and categorizing, such as censuses and identity documents, DNA profiles enabled the individual identity of missing persons to be "codified and institutionalized in order to become *socially significant*," thus "making the dead count" by making them "socially legible." On the one hand, the mortal remains of Srebrenica's victims had to be codified and institutionalized for the state of Bosnia and Herzegovina to meet the families' needs, for example to determine eligibility for monetary support as survivors of missing persons. On the other hand, the identification technology developed to recognize those remains was instrumental in assessing wartime culpability by tabulating and "sorting out" the various victims. . . .

Concerned with more than just listing the missing of Srebrenica, several institutions became involved in the recovery and identification of their mortal remains. In the initial postwar period, these included the Federation Commission for Missing Persons, the International Criminal Tribunal for the former Yugoslavia (ICTY), the International Committee of the Red Cross (ICRC), Physicians for Human Rights (PHR), the University Clinical Centre in Tuzla (responsible for issuing death certificates), and an organization just being set up in the region, the International Commission on Missing Persons (ICMP). . . . Begun as a small international organization that contracted the services and expertise of Physicians for Human Rights, ICMP would eventually become the lead international institution working on the identification process. As its efforts expanded, so too did its financial support, especially from the U.S. government, to date its largest donor. . . .

The design and strategy of ICMP's DNA identification program, specifically its blood collection program, is an exercise in mapping genealogies. The blood collection teams and data entry staff at the Identification Coordination Division apply their understanding of genetic inheritance when assessing the availability of relevant blood samples. They question potential donors about family members, their precise relationship to missing persons, and their whereabouts. These staff members work along a genealogical script, and with each question seek out the possibility of a relevant, existent potential donor that might yield the critical genetic material to "close the circle" of a nuclear DNA match. Such interviews take place with each donor (surviving family member) at ICMP facilities or at the person's residence. The mobile blood collection teams are made up of a pair of staff working in tandem to gather not only the necessary blood samples but also the pertinent data.

They collect the blood samples by lightly pricking the donor's finger and pressing four drops onto a bloodstain card. The card is then sealed and they place a matching barcode on it and on the accompanying paperwork (the donor blood sample form). The data entry staff then transfers the information recorded on this form into the database set up for the donor blood samples. The database assigns each donor a numerical value according to the relevancy of the sample in relation to nuclear DNA analysis: 5 points are given to the mother, father, and spouse; sisters, brothers, and children are awarded 2.5 points. For each missing person, a window in the database indicates the total number of points accrued through the collection of blood samples. A missing person with 10 points is considered a strong case. If the body is recovered and DNA successfully extracted, ICMP should be able to generate the necessary genetic profile matches to identify the person. . . . However, there are still hundreds of Srebrenica cases with total values of only 0 or 2.5 points. . . .

The controversy around the Srebrenica genocide has engendered an insistence on facts regarding the historiography of the event and the means of recovering and naming its victims. In a sense, the language of facticity, epitomized by results grounded in genetic science, has transformed the local discourse used to assess wartime losses and culpability. . . . For the truth surrounding the events of Srebrenica in July 1995 represents a hard-fought battle of competing claims—including the names and numbers of its missing. . . . The language of facts, couched in statistics and empirical evidence, forces the competing parties to enter into the same dialogue. It raises the stakes by raising the standards of proof, including lists, names, and numbers of missing persons. In order to arrive at those highly prized kernels of truth, however, the facts must be recognized and accepted by more than simply those who claim them.

87 • The Trauma of Genocide (Jens Meierhenrich)

In postgenocidal settings, talk of trauma is ubiquitous. Yet existing medical research on the salience of suffering is inconclusive. In fact a number of clinical studies have found an overdiagnosis of psychological disorders in survivors, notably of posttraumatic stress disorder (PTSD). In an attempt to advance the debate over the psychological disturbance of genocide survivors, this 2007 journal article distinguishes between psychological trauma, that is, the damage to the psyche of an individual that occurs as the result of a traumatic event, and cultural trauma, that is, the state of collective suffering that arises when members of a collectivity feel they have been subjected to a horrendous event that leaves indelible marks upon their group consciousness. Based on a review of scholarship in medicine and the social sciences, I conclude that scholars and practitioners would be well advised to recognize, more explicitly than they have thus far, the range of suffering (individual and collective) in the context of genocide and the types of trauma (psychological and cultural) that may be manifestations of this range.

Ever since the British physician John Erichsen first identified symptoms of trauma in victims suffering from a fear of railway accidents in the 1860s, the concept of trauma has inspired research projects in the medical sciences and social sciences. Some 13,000 scholarly articles on the subject were published between 1987 and 2001. The concept of trauma has been used widely to make sense of the psychological consequences of disturbing phenomena ranging from natural phenomena . . . to human phenomena. . . . In recent years, the trauma of genocide has received particular attention in the fields of psychopathology and psychotraumatology.

In December 2004, while the first genocidal campaign of the twenty-first century was unfolding in Darfur, Sudan, the International Congress of Ministers of Health for Mental

SOURCE: Jens Meierhenrich, "The Trauma of Genocide," *Journal of Genocide Research* 9, no. 4 (2007): 549, 550–52, 553, 554–55, 558, 564–67, 568. Reprinted with permission of Taylor & Francis.

Health and Post-Conflict Recovery released its long-awaited "Mental Health Action Plan" in Rome, Italy. Dubbed "Project 1 Billion," the historic initiative is the culmination of international cooperation to respond to the trauma of mass violence in the international system. . . . This article places the "Mental Health Action Plan" in theoretical and comparative perspective, and considers its implications for genocidal societies. The principal argument put forth is that we ought to revise the study of genocidal trauma. In pursuit of this argument, the article revisits the concept of trauma—one of the most frequently invoked notions in psychology—and reflects on the challenges facing the medical community and the international community in humanitarian crises, notably genocide. . . .

The *Diagnostic and Statistical Manual of Mental Disorders* of the American Psychiatric Association (APA) defines trauma as a psychological situation that is (1) characterized by an individual's overwhelming fear that he (or a family member or close associate) will be involved in a horrendous event, notably injury or death; and (2) the accompanying belief that this event is beyond the individual's control. . . . The effects of psychological trauma—re-experience, avoidance, arousal—are observable to some degree in all trauma victims, but when strong and persistent they typically lead to a diagnosis of PTSD. In the medical sciences, the concept of PTSD was introduced to describe reactions to trauma in very different situations. In fact, the emergence of the concept in the early 1980s subsumed earlier concepts of psychological disturbance, including "concentration camp syndrome," "post-torture syndrome," and "rape trauma syndrome." What all of the aforementioned concepts have in common is the assumption that "the very 'threat of annihilation' that defined the traumatic moment may pursue the survivor long after the danger has passed." And even though PTSD constitutes but one diagnostic category in the classification of individual suffering in the aftermath of traumatic events, it has dominated international responses in the last decade or so. . . .

[For example,] research conducted at Harvard Medical School and the Harvard Program in Refugee Trauma found significant trauma levels in post-genocidal societies. Data compiled at Site 2, the largest Cambodian refugee camp, located on the Thai-Cambodian border, revealed "levels of acute clinical depression and PTSD of 68 and 37 percent, respectively." . . . Despite an increase in the diagnosis and treatment of PTSD, especially in genocidal societies, a wide variety of research designs, founded on different methodologies (e.g., prevalence studies, comorbidity studies, life course studies), have been brought to bear on the investigation of the phenomenon, and have at times come to different conclusions. These studies (of trauma in contexts ranging from dangerous professions to natural disasters to concentration camps) found that the occurrence of PTSD following a traumatic event was "the exception rather than the rule," notably when individuals were not suffering from other psychiatric disorders. Inasmuch as this research suggested that the prevalence rate of persistent and chronic PTSD was higher in the aftermath of extremely traumatic events (e.g., capture as a prisoner of war; detention in a concentration camp), they challenge the idea of PTSD as a typical response to trauma. . . .

In an attempt to advance the debate over the psychological disturbance of survivors, the concept of *cultural trauma* was recently formed in the social sciences. Whereas the concept of PTSD in particular was designed to describe *individual* manifestations of psychological disturbance, the concept of cultural trauma is meant to capture *collective* manifestations thereof. . . . What is cultural trauma? The empirical meaning of cultural trauma—like psychological trauma—depends, above all, on context. If we believe recent advances in the social sciences, the invention of psychological trauma was based on a "naturalistic fallacy." The counter-argument from the social sciences holds that events are *not* in and of themselves traumatic—as the argument from the medical sciences supposes—but that trauma is the result of structured contingency. . . . Based on this assumption, the sociologist Jeffrey Alexander recently defined cultural trauma in the following terms: "Cultural trauma occurs when members of a collectivity feel they have been subjected to a horrendous event that leaves indelible marks upon their group consciousness, marking their memories forever and changing their future identity in fundamental and irrevocable ways." . . .

What is to be gained by the distinction between psychological trauma and cultural trauma? Let me single out three gains in particular. First, the introduction of cultural trauma as a trauma type allows for a more complete understanding of genocidal trauma, for it sensitizes us to the distinction between individual and collective suffering. Second, the concept of cultural trauma alerts us to the importance of explicating *trauma dynamics*, the mechanisms and processes involved in both the social construction of trauma—and its social experience. Whereas a salient feature of psychological trauma is its embeddedness in the structure of personality, a salient feature of cultural trauma is its embeddedness in the structure of society. We need to understand both personality structures *and* society structures—and the dynamics of their constitution—to fully come to grips with the trauma of genocide. Third, the concept of cultural trauma—unlike the concept of psychological trauma—raises the question of responsibility. For if we assume that trauma is not merely the product of psychological processes, rooted in personality structures, but also of cultural processes, rooted in social structures, the question arises *who* is involved in the construction (in the sense of both causation and representation) of trauma, *how* and *why.* . . .

A complaint that could be heard increasingly in recent years is that a "trauma industry" has cornered the international donor market. "Such is the preoccupation with trauma that over the last decade," according to Vanessa Pupavac, "trauma victims have even replaced famine victims in the Western public's imagination." Given this, responses to material suffering have, in the eyes of those affected by the calamities of collective violence, often been inadequate when compared with responses made available for the treatment of supposed mental suffering. As the British Red Cross reported in the context of the Kosovo crisis at last century's end: "If one matches the needs expressed by refugees, host families and RC [Red Cross] staff . . . with what a PS [psychosocial] programme could provide, there is a relatively modest role for a PS programme." . . .

By ignoring the mutually constitutive relationship between the concept of the medical and the concept of the social in the international administration of trauma recovery, the international community entered what Primo Levi and others have termed the "gray zone." The grayness in Levi's formulation refers to the uncertainty "regarding the degree of an agent's responsibility." For in some instances, the international administration of trauma recovery has led to trauma renewal rather than trauma recovery, as recently pointed out in a study sponsored by Save the Children, which showed that "very serious problems arise if the trauma discourse is used in non-Western societies, or with refugees from such societies, without due regard to the problems involved. Within Western societies there is at least a shared background set of beliefs and assumptions within which this discourse makes some sense. In non-Western settings, idioms of distress are likely to be quite different. Because psychiatry understands itself as scientific and thus culturally neutral, it fails to grasp the cultural specificity of its concepts and interventions. . . ." This finding underlines the principal argument of this article. . . .

Although the data are illustrative and the findings preliminary, tentative conclusions can be derived. First, trauma recovery is a *sui generis* affair. Lessons learned in the treatment of suffering in the context of a given genocide do not easily transfer across geographical and temporal boundaries. This echoes a recommendation by the ISTSS [International Society of Traumatic Stress Studies] which insists that "thorough, integrative understanding of the multiple dimensions of each context is needed to inform training design and implementation" of trauma recovery." Second, the treatment of traumatic disturbances must vary with the severity of the suffering inflicted on the victims in the course of the genocide. In this context, it might even be helpful to distinguish not only between *traumatic stress* (which can be defined, drawing on Hans Selye, as the non-pathological, transitory response of the body to the experience of a traumatic event) and *psychological trauma*, as is common in the medial sciences, but also between *cultural stress* (which could be defined as the non-pathological, transitory response of a society to the experience of a traumatic event) and *cultural trauma*.

The neologism of *cultural stress* might guard against the overdiagnosis of cultural trauma, which is a potential given the penchant for the therapeutic paradigm within the humanitarian community. The term has the advantage of emphasizing the normality (rather than the pathology) of the distress that is being experienced in a given society in the aftermath of a calamity. In light of our experience with the inflationary use of PTSD, it promises to be good sense to avoid conceptualizing the pathological as the norm. Interestingly, the International Rescue Committee's Psychosocial Needs Assessment team, while deployed in Kosovo in the late 1990s, came to a conclusion directly relevant to the conceptual issue at stake here: "Although many people in Kosovo have had traumatic experiences, the complexity and diversity of the situation mitigate against describing the general state of mind as 'mass trauma.'" . . .

Another tentative conclusion, third, is that the concept of the medical is deeply, perhaps intractably, intertwined with the concept of the social. The medical community and international community must acknowledge this relationship—both at the macro- and micro-level— and adapt the international administration of trauma recovery accordingly. "This means there should be no compulsory procedure that imposes a particular model of recovery on victims." . . . This is the crux of the relationship between the concept of the medical and the concept of the social in the aftermath of genocide. It serves as a reminder "that the mental health needs of a people after conflict cannot be hinged on the single psychiatric diagnosis, but are wide and complex: interweaving psychological, social, educational and human rights issues." Or, to paraphrase an influential adage from the social sciences, trauma is what actors—both victims and responders—make of it.

The argument that trauma—as a concept and diagnosis—is socially constructed is not to deny (1) that trauma is psychologically meaningful, or (2) that trauma recovery is socially desirable. . . . Rather, the argument about the social construction of trauma is to remind us— the medical community and international community—that the trauma of genocide cannot "be healed by the magic of counseling alone, but is reparable only by interventions that approach all aspects of the problem, in an integrated manner. This is psychosocial work." And yet, the idea of psychosocial work, too, suffers from shortcomings. As persuasive as arguments about the invention of PTSD and related diagnoses are, we must also acknowledge the limits of social constructivism, and possible implications thereof for responding to the trauma of genocide. . . .

Psychosocial work, properly understood, requires *both* the concept of psychological trauma *and* the concept of cultural trauma. It is for this reason that the medical sciences and social sciences ought to be considered complementary—rather than contending—approaches to trauma recovery. . . . Instead of espousing categorical imperatives about possible—and impossible—solutions to the problem of genocidal trauma, scholars and practitioners would be well advised to recognize, more explicitly than they have thus far, the *range* of suffering (individual and collective) in the context of genocide, and the *types* of trauma (psychological and cultural) that may be manifestations of this range.

88 • Cultural Trauma (Jeffrey C. Alexander)

In this extract Jeffrey Alexander, a professor of sociology at Yale University, elaborates the concept of cultural trauma, distinguishing it from psychological trauma. He has his sights set on what he calls "lay trauma theory," according to which traumas are naturally occurring events that shatter an individual's or a group's sense of well-being. Far from it, challenges Alexander in this essay, published in 2004. He insists that events are not inherently traumatic. Rather trauma is a socially mediated attribution. On this interpretation, psychological trauma does not exist objectively but is a socially invented state of mind and body. As for cultural trauma, it is not the result of a group experiencing pain. For Alexander, cultural trauma is the result of this pain not merely being experienced but also entering into the core of the group's sense of its own identity.

Cultural trauma occurs when members of a collectivity feel they have been subjected to a horrendous event that leaves indelible marks upon their group consciousness, marking their memories forever and changing their future identity in fundamental and irrevocable ways. . . . It is by constructing cultural traumas that social groups, national societies, and sometimes even entire civilizations not only cognitively identify the existence and source of human suffering but "take on board" some significant responsibility for it. Insofar as they identify the cause of trauma, and thereby assume such moral responsibility, members of collectivities define their solidarity relationships in ways that, in principle, allow them to share the sufferings of others. Is the suffering of others also our own? In thinking that it might in fact be, societies can expand the circle of we. By the same token, social groups can, and often do, refuse to recognize the existence of others' trauma, and because of their failure they cannot achieve a moral stance. By denying the reality of others' suffering, people not only diffuse their own responsibility for the suffering but often project the responsibility for their own suffering on these others. . . .

SOURCE: Jeffrey C. Alexander, "Toward a Theory of Cultural Trauma," in Jeffrey C. Alexander, Ron Eyerman, Bernhard Giesen, Neil J. Smelser, and Piotr Sztompka, eds., *Cultural Trauma and Collective Identity* (Berkeley: University of California Press, 2004), 1, 2, 3, 5, 8–9, 10, 11, 12, 15, 22–23. Reprinted with permission of the publisher.

One of the great advantages of this new theoretical concept is that it partakes so deeply of everyday life. . . . The trick is to gain reflexivity, to move from the sense of something commonly experienced to the sense of strangeness that allows us to think sociologically. For trauma is not something naturally existing; it is something constructed by society. . . . [And yet] scholarly approaches to trauma developed thus far actually have been distorted by the powerful, commonsense understandings of trauma that have emerged in everyday life. Indeed, it might be said that these commonsense understandings constitute a kind of "lay trauma theory" in contrast to which a more theoretical reflexive approach to trauma must be erected. According to lay trauma theory, traumas are naturally occurring events that shatter an individual or collective actor's sense of well-being. . . . There are "enlightenment" and "psychoanalytic" versions of this lay trauma theory. The enlightenment understanding suggests that trauma is a kind of rational response to abrupt change, whether at the individual or social level. . . . A psychoanalytic perspective . . . has [also] become central to both contemporary lay common sense and academic thinking. This approach places a model of unconscious emotional fears and cognitively distorting mechanisms of psychological defense between the external shattering event and the actor's internal traumatic response. . . . According to this perspective, the truth can be recovered, and psychological equanimity restored, only, as the Holocaust historian Saul Friedlander once put it, "when memory comes." . . .

It is through these Enlightenment and psychoanalytic approaches that trauma has been translated from an idea in ordinary language into an intellectual concept in the academic languages of diverse disciplines. Both perspectives, however, share the "naturalistic fallacy" of the lay understanding from which they derive. It is upon the rejection of this naturalistic fallacy that our own approach rests. First and foremost, we maintain that events do not, in and of themselves, create collective trauma. Events are not inherently traumatic. Trauma is a socially mediated attribution. The attribution may be made in real time, as an event unfolds; it may also be made before the event occurs, as an adumbration, or after the event has concluded, as a post-hoc reconstruction. Sometimes, in fact, events that are deeply traumatizing may not actually have occurred at all; such imagined events, however, can be as traumatizing as events that have actually occurred.

This notion of an "imagined" traumatic event seems to suggest the kind of process that Benedict Anderson described in his *Imagined Communities*. Anderson's concern, of course, is not with trauma per se, but with the kinds of self-consciously ideological narratives of nationalist history. Yet these collective beliefs often assert the existence of some national trauma. In the course of defining national identity, national histories are constructed around injuries that cry out for revenge. . . . The Serbians inside Serbia, for example, contended that ethnic Albanians in Kosovar did them traumatic injury, thus providing justification for their own "defensive" invasion and ethnic cleansing. The type of case such militarist construction of primordial national trauma was Adolph [*sic*] Hitler's grotesque assertion that the international Jewish conspiracy had been responsible for Germany's traumatic loss in World War I. . . .

Imagination informs trauma construction just as much when the reference is to something that has actually occurred as to something that has not. It is only through the imaginative process of representation that actors have a sense of experience. Even when claims of victimhood are morally justifiable, politically democratic, and socially progressive, these claims still cannot be seen as automatic, or natural, responses to the actual nature of an event itself. . . . At the level of the social system, societies can experience massive disruptions that do not become traumatic. Institutions can fail to perform. Schools may fail to educate, failing miserably even to provide basic skills. Governments may be unable to secure basic protections and may undergo severe crises of delegitimation. . . . Such problems are real and fundamental, but they are not, by any means, necessarily traumatic for members of the affected collectivities, much less for the society at large.

For traumas to emerge at the level of the collectivity, social crises must become cultural crises. Events are one thing, representations of these events quite another. Trauma is not the result of a group experiencing pain. It is the result of this acute discomfort entering into the core of the collectivity's sense of its own identity. Collective actors "decide" to represent social pain as a fundamental threat to their sense of who they are, where they came from, and where they want to go. . . . The gap between event and representation can be conceived as the "trauma process." Collectivities do not make decisions as such; rather, it is agents who do it. . . . They broadcast these representations as members of a social group. These group representations can be seen as "claims" about the shape of social reality, its causes, and the responsibilities for action such causes imply. The cultural construction of trauma begins with such a claim. . . . Such claims are made by what Max Weber, in his sociology of religion, called "carrier groups." Carrier groups are the collective agents of the trauma process. Carrier groups have both ideal and material interests, they are situated in particular places in the social structure, and they have particular discursive talents for articulating their claims—for what might be called "meaning making"—in the public sphere. Carrier groups may be elites, but they may also be denigrated and marginalized classes. . . .

Bridging the gap between event and representation depends upon what [the sociologist] Kenneth Thompson has called, in reference to the topic of moral panics, a "spiral of signification." Representation of cultural trauma depends on constructing a compelling framework of cultural classification. In one sense, this is simply telling a new story. Yet this storytelling is, at the same time, a complex and multivalent symbolic process that is contingent, highly contested, and sometimes highly polarizing. For the wider audience to become persuaded that they, too, have become traumatized by an experience or an event, the carrier group needs to engage in successful meaning work. . . . This representational process creates a new master narrative of social suffering. Such cultural (re)classification is critical to the process by which a collectivity becomes traumatized. . . .

"Experiencing [cultural] trauma" can be understood as a sociological process that defines a painful injury to the collectivity, establishes the victim, attributes responsibility, and distributes the ideal and material consequences. Insofar as [cultural] traumas are so experienced, and thus imagined and represented, the collective identity will become significantly revised. This identity revision means that there will be a searching re-remembering of the collective past, for memory is not only social and fluid but deeply connected to the contemporary sense of the self. Identities are continuously constructed and secured not only by facing the present and future but also by reconstructing the collectivity's earlier life. Once the collective identity has been so reconstructed, there will eventually emerge a period of "calming down." The spiral of signification flattens out, affect and emotion become less inflamed. . . .

As the heightened and powerfully affecting discourse of [cultural] trauma disappears, the "lessons" of the trauma become objectified in monuments, museums, and collections of historical artifacts. The new collective identity will be rooted in sacred places and structured in ritual routines. . . . In this routinization process, the trauma process, once so vivid, can become subject to the technical, sometimes desiccating attention of specialists who detach affect from meaning. This triumph of the mundane is often noted with regret by audiences that had been mobilized by the trauma process, and it is sometimes forcefully opposed by carrier groups. Often, however, it is welcomed with a sense of public and private relief. Intended to remember and commemorate the trauma process, efforts to institutionalize the lessons of the trauma will eventually prove unable to evoke the strong emotions, the sentiments of betrayal, and the affirmations of sacrality that once were so powerfully associated with it. No longer deeply preoccupying, the reconstructed collective identity remains, nevertheless, a fundamental resource for resolving future social problems and disturbances of collective consciousness.

89 • Genocide and Social Death (Claudia Card)

Claudia Card, a professor of philosophy at the University of Wisconsin, Madison, contends that what sets genocidal acts apart from other international crimes is the harm that they inflict on victims' social vitality. She makes the case in her 2003 article, "Genocide and Social Death," where she argues, "When a group with its own cultural identity is destroyed, its survivors lose their cultural heritage and may even lose their intergenerational connections. To use sociologist Orlando Patterson's terminology, in that event, they may become 'socially dead' and their descendants 'natally alienated,' no longer able to pass along and build upon the traditions, cultural developments (including languages), and projects of earlier generations."

This essay develops the hypothesis that social death is utterly central to the evil of genocide, not just when a genocide is primarily cultural but even when it is homicidal on a massive scale. It is social death that enables us to distinguish the peculiar evil of genocide from the evils of other mass murders. Even genocidal murders can be viewed as extreme means to the primary end of social death. Social vitality exists through relationships, contemporary and intergenerational, that create an identity that gives meaning to life. Major loss of social vitality is a loss of identity and consequently a serious loss of meaning of one's existence. Putting social death at the center takes the focus off individual choice, individual goals, individual careers, and body counts, and puts it on relationships that create community and set the context that gives meaning to choices and goals. If my hypothesis is correct, the term "cultural genocide" is probably both redundant and misleading—redundant, if the social death present in all genocide implies cultural death as well, and misleading, if "cultural genocide" suggests that some genocide do not include cultural death. . . .

Centering social death accommodates the position, controversial among genocide scholars, that genocidal acts are not always or necessarily homicidal. . . . Forcibly sterilizing women or men of a targeted group or forcibly separating their children from them for re-education for assimilation into another group can also be genocidal in aim or effect. Such policies can be aimed at or achieve the eventual destruction of the social identity of those so treated. It may

SOURCE: Claudia Card, "Genocide and Social Death," *Hypatia* 18, no. 1 (2003): 63, 64–65, 66, 67, 68, 72, 73, 77–78. Reprinted with permission of Indiana University Press.

appear that transported children simply undergo change in social identity, not that they lose all social vitality. That may be the intent. Yet, parents' social vitality is a casualty of children's forced re-education, and in reality, transported children may fail to make a satisfying transition. The [H]olocaust was not only a program of mass murder but an assault on Jewish social vitality. . . . Jews who had converted to Christianity (or whose parents or grandparents had done so) were hunted down and murdered, even though one might think their social identities had already changed. This pursuit makes a certain perverted sense if the idea was to extinguish in them all possibility of social vitality, simply on grounds of their ancestral roots. . . .

Not all injustices are evils, as the harms they produce vary greatly in importance. Some injustices are relatively tolerable. They may not impact people's lives in a deep or lasting way, even though they are wrong and should be eliminated—unjust salary discriminations, for example, when the salaries in question are all high. An injustice becomes an evil when it inflicts harms that make victims' lives unbearable, indecent, or impossible, or that make victims' deaths indecent. Injustices of war are apt to fall into this category. Certainly genocide does. . . .

The literature of comparative genocide that historian Peter Novick calls "comparative atrocitology" so far includes relatively little published work by philosophers. . . . Yet, philosophical issues run through the literature. . . . They include foundational matters, such as the meaning of "genocide," which appears to be a highly contested concept, and such issues of ethics and political philosophy as whether perpetrators can be punished in a meaningful way that respects moral standards. . . . Controversies over the meaning of "genocide" naturally lead to the closely related question of whether genocide is ethically different from nongenocidal mass murder. . . . If the social death of individual victims is central to genocide, then, arguably, genocide does capture something more. What distinguishes genocide is not that it is has a different kind of victim, namely, groups (although it is a convenient shorthand to speak of targeting groups). Rather, the kind of harm suffered by individual victims of genocide, in virtue of their group membership, is not captured by other crimes. . . .

Genocide is not simply unjust (although it certainly is unjust); it is also evil. . . . It targets people on the basis of who they are rather than on the basis of what they have done, what they might do, even what they are capable of doing. (One commentator says genocide kills people on the basis of *what* they are, not even *who* they are.) Genocide is a paradigm of what Israeli philosopher Avishai Margalit calls "indecent" in that it not only destroys victims but first humiliates them by deliberately inflicting an "utter loss of freedom and control over one's vital interests." Vital interests can be transgenerational and thus survive one's death. Before death, genocide victims are ordinarily deprived of control over vital transgenerational interests and more immediate vital interests. They may be literally stripped naked, robbed of their last possessions, lied to about the most vital matters, witness to the murder of family, friends, and neighbors, made to participate in their own murder, and if female, they are also likely to be violated sexually. Victims of genocide are commonly killed with no regard for lingering suffering or exposure. They, and their corpses, are routinely treated with utter disrespect. These historical facts, not simply mass murder, account for much of the moral opprobrium attaching to the concept of genocide.

Yet such atrocities, it may be argued, are already war crimes, if conducted during wartime, and they can otherwise or also be prosecuted as crimes against humanity. Why, then, add the specific crime of genocide? What, if anything, is not already captured by laws that prohibit such things as the rape, enslavement, torture, forced deportation, and the degradation of individuals? Is any ethically distinct harm done to members of the targeted group that would not have been done had they been targeted simply as individuals rather than because of their group membership? This is the question that I find central in arguing that genocide is not simply reducible to mass death, to any of the other war crimes, or to the crimes against humanity just enumerated. I believe the answer is affirmative: the harm is ethically distinct, although on the question of whether it is worse, I wish only to question the assumption that it is not.

Specific to genocide is the harm inflicted on its victims' social vitality. It is not just that one's group membership is the occasion for harms that are definable independently of one's identity as a member of the group. When a group with its own cultural identity is destroyed, its survivors lose their cultural heritage and may even lose their intergenerational connections. To use Orlando Patterson's terminology, in that event, they may become "socially dead" and their descendants "*natally alienated*," no longer able to pass along and build upon the traditions, cultural developments (including languages), and projects of earlier generations. The harm of social death is not necessarily less extreme than that of physical death. Social death can even aggravate physical death by making it indecent, removing all respectful and caring ritual, social connections, and social context that are capable of making dying bearable and even of making one's death meaningful. In my view, the special evil of genocide lies in its infliction of not just physical death (when it does that) but social death, producing a consequent meaninglessness of one's life and even of its termination. . . .

If social death is central to the harm of genocide, then it really is right not to count as a genocide the annihilation of just any political group, however heinous. Not every political group contributes significantly to its members' cultural identity. Many are fairly specific and short-lived, formed to support particular issues. But then, equally, the annihilation of not just any cultural group should count, either. Cultural groups can also be temporary and specialized, lacking in the continuity and comprehensiveness that are presupposed by the possibility of social death. Some mass murders—perhaps the bombing of September 11, 2001—do not appear to have had as part of their aim, intention, or effect the prior soul murder or social death of those targeted for physical extermination. If so, they are mass murders that are not also genocides. But mass murders and other measures that have as part of their reasonably foreseeable consequence, or as part of their aim, the annihilation of a group that contributes significantly to the social identity of its members are genocidal.

90 • Bosnia after the Dayton Agreement of 1995
(Sumantra Bose)

Focusing on the diplomatic consequences of genocidal acts, Sumantra Bose, a professor of government at the London School of Economic and Political Science, elaborates the principal features of the Dayton Agreement of 1995, a controversial peace agreement that inaugurated the international

SOURCE: Sumantra Bose, *Bosnia after Dayton: Nationalist Partition and International Intervention* (New York: Oxford University Press, 2002), 2–3, 60, 61, 62, 63–64, 65–66, 256, 257, 258, 259. Reprinted with permission of the publisher.

territorial administration of Bosnia, parts of which (such as Prijedor and Srebrenica) had previ-
ously been the setting of genocidal violence. Published in 2002, Bose's book detects in each of the
communities accommodated by the Dayton settlement—Croats, Bosniaks, Serbs—a fair amount
of discontent and even an aggrieved stance toward the very delicate equilibrium that the interna-
tional community created.

For almost four years between April 1992 and January 1996, the war in Bosnia and Herzegovina dominated global headlines and soundbites. Since then, BiH may have ceased to be
"the centre of the world." . . . Yet this small country of perhaps 3.5 million people, located
geographically and otherwise on the margins of Europe, remains an important place to know
and understand.

At the end of 1995, a controversial peace agreement reached after heavy American arm-
twisting on a nondescript air force base in a remote town in the American Midwest ended the
Bosnian war. That accord, initialed in Dayton, Ohio, on November 21, 1995, was formally
signed almost a month later, on December 14, in the somewhat more hallowed precincts of
the Versailles palace near Paris. But "Bosnia" and "Dayton" have ever since come to be used as
thoroughly entangled, almost interchangeable expressions. Every Bosnian child knows about
"Dayton," and one of Sarajevo's more enterprising companies is called "Dayton Import-Export."
For the past six years, the merits and demerits of "Dayton" have been the topic of spirited
debate not just among Bosnians and other former Yugoslavs, but among scholars, politicians,
diplomats and assorted "experts" throughout the Western world.

With good reason. Since the beginning of 1996, "Dayton Bosnia" has been the site of
internationally sponsored political engineering on a remarkable scale. . . . Tens of thousands
of military and civilian staff deployed by a consortium of international organizations—the
North Atlantic Treaty Organization (NATO), the Organization for Security and Cooperation
in Europe (OSCE), the United Nations (UN) and its agencies, the World Bank and International Monetary Fund (IMF), among others—have been engaged in the arduous mission of
transforming this fractured society into a economically and politically viable state. . . .

Bosnia is a state by international design and of international design. Its post-war institutional design reflects the circumstances of the state's birth in March–April 1992, its effective
demise immediately afterwards, and the painful, tentative rebirth engineered at Dayton. . . .
The constitution of BiH is primarily the work of lawyers from the United States' Department
of State. It establishes a fairly skeletal framework of common-state institutions based on
equality and parity representation of Bosniacs, Serbs and Croats as collectively defined communities to a narrow band of competencies. . . . The legislative organ of the Bosnian state . . .
consists of a bicameral Parliamentary Assembly. The first Chamber, the House of Peoples,
has 15 Delegates—five Croats and five Bosniacs from the FBiH [Federation of Bosnia and
Herzegovina, one of the two constitutive entities of the state of Bosnia and Herzegovina] and
five Serbs from the RS [Republika Srpska, the other of the two constitutive entities of the state
of Bosnia and Herzegovina]. The five Serb delegates are nominated by the RS's legislature, the
National Assembly, while the Bosniac and Croat delegates are selected by the Bosniac and
Croat delegations, respectively, to the House of Peoples of the (also bicameral) Federation
parliament. The presence of nine out of 15 delegates constitutes a quorum, with the proviso
that at least three Serbs, three Bosniacs and three Croats must be present. The other Chamber,

the House of Representatives, consists of 42 directly elected Members, 28 from the Federation and 14 from the RS. A simple majority of these 42 members constitutes a quorum in this house. . . .

Two of the four classic features of a "consociational" or group-based power-sharing system [as theorized by Arend Lijphart and Donald Horowitz] are evident in the legislature of the Bosnian state: allocation of seats in a way that takes account of group membership, including a strict parity formula in the House of Peoples, and veto rights for representatives of national segments. The Bosnian state's principal executive organ, the Presidency, includes these two features as well as a third defining element of consociation: central decision making by grand coalition between representatives of the segments. In a replication of the socialist Yugoslav model, the executive is a *collective state presidency* that consists of three members or co-presidents. . . . The co-presidents serve a four-year term, the chair rotates among them every eight months, and they are supposed to "endeavour to adopt all Presidency Decisions by consensus" [according to Article 5.2 of the Dayton constitutional framework]. . . . Not unpredictably, the collective presidency has mostly served as a photo-opportunity for its members, in Sarajevo, at UN headquarters in New York and other transnational forums. . . .

Ironically, the most robust of Bosnia's central institutions is the one on which non-Bosnians play a direct role. This is the country's supreme judicial organ, the Constitutional Court of BiH. The court has nine judges, of whom four are selected by the FBiH's House of Representatives, and two by the National Assembly of Republika Srpska. In effect, this has meant two Bosniacs, two Croats and two Serbs. The other three judges are appointed by the president of the European Court of Human Rights, after consultation with the tripartite BiH presidency. They cannot be citizens of BiH or of any neighboring state. A majority of the nine judges is sufficient to constitute a quorum, and the court issues rulings by majority decision as well. The jurisdiction of the court is wide-ranging. It is the ultimate guarantor of the BiH state constitution. The court [according to Article 6 of the Dayton constitutional framework] has "exclusive jurisdiction to decide any dispute that arises . . . between the Entities, between Bosnia and Herzegovina and an Entity or Entities, or between institutions of Bosnia and Herzegovina." . . .

What a tangled web the international community confronts in Bosnia. . . . The debate over Bosnia and Herzegovina's post-Yugoslav future remains not just unsettled but fiercely contested after six years of intensive international involvement. The underlying cause is that all three of BiH's communities have what might be described as *defensive mentalities*, albeit for different reasons. The Bosnian Serbs, traumatized by the collapse of Yugoslavia and radicalized by the experience of a bitter war, are determined to preserve and protect the entity they ultimately salvaged from a very dark period in their history as a people. . . . The Bosnian Muslims are the single largest national group in Bosnia, at a level probably close to constituting a single majority of the population. This matters a great deal in a region where the relative numbers (and proportions) of groups provide a basic fulcrum and determinant of politics. . . .

The BiH Croats are, in a way, in the most ambiguous and quixotic position of the three groups, which helps explain the viciously defensive posture of considerable elements of the community. It was Serb-Croat antagonism (not disregarding the basic contribution made by the Slovenes) that broke up Yugoslavia, precipitated civil war in Croatia, and led to war in Bosnia, with tragic consequences for all three peoples, especially the Bosnian Muslims. Within

Bosnia, however, the major adversary for the Croats in the armed conflict turned out to be not the Serbs, but the Muslims. Yet in an ironic turn of events, purely because of circumstantial forces and the insistence of the United States that a Croat-Muslim military alliance was the essential linchpin of a successful strategy to roll back the Serbs in both BiH and Croatia, the BiH Croats found themselves corralled into a "federation" with the Muslims, engineered in Washington, D.C., in March 1994 and confirmed at Dayton, Ohio in November 1995. All the assurances and built-in constitutional safeguards of equality, parity, consensus etc. have over the years failed to obviate a dominant perception among BiH Croats that they are the subordinate partner in an accidental marriage which is blighted by mutual suspicion. . . .

Each of the Bosnian communities thus has a *minority syndrome*, albeit in relation to different political-geographical contexts—the Serbs within the territory of Bosnia and Herzegovina, the Muslims within the wider region including Serbia-Montenegro and Croatia, and the Croats within the framework of the Muslim-Croat federation. These variants of the minority syndrome result in each community having a guarded, defensive and at least somewhat aggrieved stance towards the very delicate equilibrium created by the Dayton settlement. . . .

91 • From Genocide to Dictatorship in Rwanda (Filip Reyntjens)

Filip Reyntjens, a professor of law at the University of Antwerp, demonstrates that postgenocidal regimes are not necessarily harbingers of peace. Reviewing ten years of reconstruction and development in Rwanda, Reyntjens's 2004 article paints a bleak picture. He writes of an illiberal regime, led by Paul Kagame and his Rwandan Patriotic Front (RPF), growing more authoritarian by the day. This regime, according to Reyntjens, caused not only moderate Hutu to flee the country but even former Tutsi loyalists to abandon ship. For Reyntjens, postgenocide Rwanda bears a striking resemblance to pregenocide Rwanda, carrying the seed for renewed mass violence in the future.

After its military victory [over the genocidal regime] in early July 1994, the RPF inherited a devastated country. In human terms, the toll was horrendous: about 1.1 million dead, 2 million refugees abroad, over 1 million internally displaced, tens of thousands of deeply traumatized genocide survivors, and over half a million "old caseload" (i.e., Tutsi) refugees returned in a chaotic fashion. . . .

In a context where security concerns were genuine and trade-offs needed to be made between freedom and control, the RPF initially seemed to waver between, on the one hand, political openness and inclusiveness (witness the setting up of a government of national union and the return to Rwanda of a number of non-RPF civilian and military office-holders) and, on the other, a violent mode of management and discriminatory practices (witness the large number of civilians killed by the RPF . . .). However, a strong feeling prevailed in the international community that some latitude needed to be given to a regime facing the colossal

SOURCE: Filip Reyntjens, "Rwanda, Ten Years On: From Genocide to Dictatorship," *African Affairs* 3, no. 411 (2004): 178, 179, 180–81, 182, 184, 187, 188, 191, 192, 203, 208, 209, 210. Reprinted with permission of Oxford University Press.

task of reconstructing the country in human and material terms. . . . At a donors' roundtable in Geneva in January 1995, almost US$600 million was pledged in bilateral and multilateral aid to Rwanda. The failure to tie the pledges to improvements in a rapidly deteriorating human rights situation may well have persuaded the regime that it could act without restraint, and that its impunity was assured. In addition, the RPF was squarely supported by "Friends of the New Rwanda," in particular the U.S., the UK and the Netherlands. These countries were not burdened by much knowledge of Rwanda or the region, and, driven by an acute guilt syndrome after the genocide, they reasoned in terms of "good guys" and "bad guys," the RPF naturally being the "good guys." . . .

Initially a number of politicians, civil servants, judges, and military in place under the old regime either remained in the country or returned from abroad, and indicated their willingness to cooperate with the RPF. The illusion of inclusiveness was soon shattered, however, by the departure into exile of Hutu first, of Tutsi genocide survivors later, and even, eventually, of RPF old hands. From early 1995, Hutu elites became the victims of harassment, imprisonment and even physical elimination. Provincial governors (*préfets*), local mayors, head teachers, clerics and judges were killed in increasing numbers. In most cases, the responsibility of the Rwandan Patriotic Army (RPA, which had become the national army) was well documented. The first watershed came in August 1995, when Prime Minister Faustin Twagiramungu, Interior Minister Seth Sendashonga (one of the rare RPF Hutu) and Justice Minister Alphonse Nkubito resigned. The first two went into exile, while Nkubito stayed and died in early 1997. The many who left in this first wave included government ministers, senior judges, high-ranking civil servants, diplomats, army officers, journalists, leaders of civil society and even players in the national soccer team. As soon as they were out of the country, they made allegations of concentration and abuse of power, outrages by the army and intelligence services, massive violations of human rights, insecurity and intimidation, discrimination against the Hutu and even against Tutsi genocide survivors. A second wave of departures came in early 2000, in part against the background of increasing tensions between Tutsi returnees, those from Uganda in particular, and genocide survivors. The latter felt that they were becoming second-rate citizens who had been sacrificed by the RPF, which was suspected of having been interested in military victory rather than in saving them. . . .

[The] departures of Tutsi, many of them active RPF members, showed the extent of discontent with a regime growing more authoritarian by the day. . . . With the constitutional referendum and the presidential and parliamentary elections in view, the regime crossed the Rubicon in the spring of 2003 and ceased attempting to hide its authoritarian drift. . . . On 15 April, Parliament recommended that the main opposition party, the MDR [Mouvement démocratique républicain], be banned for spreading "divisionism," a recommendation endorsed by the government on 16 May. . . . While it officially rejected ethnic discrimination and even the notion of ethnicity, the RPF rapidly reserved access to power, wealth and knowledge to Tutsi. . . . The "Tutsization," which was also a means of consolidating the hold of the RPF on the system, was quite spectacular at most levels of the state: by 1996, the majority of MPs, four of the six Supreme Court presiding judges, over 80 percent of mayors, most permanent secretaries and university teachers and students, almost the entire army command structure and the intelligence services were Tutsi. . . . [By mid-2000,] out of a total of 169 of the most important office-holders, 135 (or about 80 percent) were RPF/RPA and 119 (or roughly 70 percent) were Tutsi. . . . In a country where Hutu number about 85 percent of the total population, these figures obviously show a strong ethnic bias in favor of a small Tutsi elite. . . .

Over the years, movements opposed to the RPF have proliferated and considerably broadened in scope. While initially the opposition was found mainly among Hutu refugee communities abroad, from the late 1990s onwards new platforms were put in place bringing together Hutu and Tutsi, including former RPF militants who were disillusioned and fled the country in increasing numbers. . . . For the RPF, the emergence of a bi-ethnic opposition constitutes a considerable challenge. Indeed, formerly when Hutu defected, the RPF could accuse them of nurturing an ethnically-oriented project, or could even describe them as "participants in the genocide," but this strategy of discredit can obviously not be used against Tutsi opponents. . . . Even criticisms formulated by UN bodies or international NGOs have been systematically rejected or discredited, sometimes even stifled. In June 1997, the Rwandan government, through a large-scale diplomatic offensive, succeeded in having the mandate of the UN Special Rapporteur René Degni-Ségui abolished, as he had become a nuisance. He was replaced by a Special Representative whose mandate and interest in criticizing the regime was more limited. . . .

There is a striking continuity from the pre-genocide to the post-genocide regime in Rwanda. Indeed, the manner in which power is exercised by the RPF echoes that of the days of single-party rule in several respects. A small inner circle of RPF leaders takes the important decisions, while the Cabinet is left with the daily routine of managing the state apparatus. Under both [former President Juvénal] Habyarimana and [Paul] Kagame [the current president of Rwanda], a clientelistic network referred to as the *akazu* accumulates wealth and privileges. Both have manipulated ethnicity, the former by scapegoating and eventually exterminating the Tutsi, the latter by discriminating against the Hutu under the guise of ethnic amnesia. Both have used large-scale violence to eliminate their opponents, and they have done so with total impunity, which is another element of continuity. . . . Continuity is visible not just in the exercise of power, but also in the nature of the state. An ancient state tradition plays an undeniable role here: a mere two years after the extreme human and material destruction of 1994, the state had been rebuilt. Rwanda was again administered from top to bottom, territorial, military and security structures were in place, the judicial system was re-established, tax revenues were collected and spent. . . .

Rwanda presents the international community with a grave dilemma. . . . After the 2003 [presidential and parliamentary] elections, . . . the donor community, having abandoned Rwanda [the] first time in 1994, attempted to redeem itself by committing another major mistake, becoming, as it did, complicit in the installation of a new dictatorship. By indulging in wishful thinking, the international community is taking an enormous risk and assuming a grave responsibility. While it is understandable that the "genocide credit" and the logic of "good guys and bad guys" should have inspired a particular understanding of a regime born out of the genocide, this complacent attitude has incrementally, step by step, contributed to a situation that may well be irreversible and that contains the seeds for massive new violence in the medium or long run.

92 • Africa's World War (Gérard Prunier)

The consequences of genocide affect not only the country of its setting but also neighboring nations. Few countries have been as adversely affected by regional stabilization in the aftermath of genocide as the former Zaire, now the Democratic Republic of Congo (DRC). In his 2009 book, the French historian Gérard Prunier traces the effects of the 1994 genocide in Rwanda on the DRC. He focuses in particular on the early origins of "Africa's World War," recalling the ongoing military confrontation between the victorious, Tutsi-led Rwandan Patriotic Front and its adversaries, Hutu génocidaires in exile. In September 2006, for example, postgenocide Rwanda intervened in what at the time was still called Zaire. The goal was to uproot the roving génocidaires who had found safe havens in the partially militarized refugee camps that the international community had set up. Although largely successful, this retaliation was the beginning of an ongoing continental war.

Let me be clear: the Rwandese genocide and its consequences did not *cause* the implosion of the Congo basin and its periphery. It acted as a *catalyst*, precipitating a crisis that had been latent for a good many years and that later reached far beyond the original Great Lakes locus. This is why the situation became so serious. The Rwandese genocide has been both a product and a further cause of an enormous African crisis: its very occurrence was a symptom, its nontreatment spread the disease.

In Zaire itself what passed for a government structure was so rotten that the brush of a hand could cause it to collapse. A few mortar shells dislocated it beyond recognition. Paris was stunned for the second time, while Washington gleefully boasted about "New African Leaders." And all the peripheral conflicts started to roll down into the Congo basin like so many overripe toxic fruits. In Burundi the civil war that started in 1993 had never stopped. Sudan and Uganda were still at each other's throats and ready to jump, flailing, into the Congolese ring. The so-called Angola Peace Agreement was but a breathing spell between two periods of military campaigns. In Zimbabwe an ethnopolitical elite that had lost any sense of moderation or financial decency was keen to jump in with bright visions of political investments designed to counter South African economic expansion northward. Even in distant Namibia a weak government afraid of the new South African imperialism was ready to follow its supposedly strong protector in Luanda into the general melee. . . .

The violence of the so-called Congolese conflict, which for a while became a continent-wide war, was the product of unsettled questions that the Rwandese genocide had brushed raw. What is a country in Africa? What is a legitimate government? Who is a citizen? Why do we live together? Whom should we obey? Who are we? Who are the "others," and how should we deal with them? None of these questions had been answered, except by the dry legalistic proviso of the Organization of African Unity charter guaranteeing the intangibility of the former colonial borders. Pretending to answer so many vital questions with one paragraph in a forty-year-old treaty designed for a now obsolete context was unrealistic. . . .

SOURCE: Gérard Prunier, *Africa's World War: Congo, the Rwandan Genocide, and the Making of a Continental Catastrophe* (Oxford: Oxford University Press, 2009), xxxi, xxxii, 24–25, 26–27, 67, 68, 73, 74, 75. Reprinted with permission of the publisher.

The end of the [civil] war and the end of the genocide [in Rwanda] were accompanied by a massive wave of Rwandese refugees fleeing their country toward Zaire, Tanzania, and even conflict-torn Burundi. They did not run far, settling with UN and NGO assistance in enormous refugee camps located almost directly on the border with Rwanda. Contrary to other refugee exoduses from countries at war, this was not the flight of individuals wishing to escape danger; rather, just as the genocide had been, it was an organized system of mass mobilization for a political purpose. The refugees settled in their camps in perfect order, under the authority of their former leaders, ready to be used for further aims. . . .

With about thirty-five camps of various sizes, Zaire was at the core of the problem. The most formidable locations were the five enormous camps of Katale, Kahindo, Mugunga, Lac Vert, and Sake around Goma, the administrative capital of North Kivu province. Together they held no fewer than 850,000 people, including the 30,000 to 40,000 men of the ex-FAR [Forces Armées Rwandaises], the army of the genocide, complete with its heavy and light weapons, its officer corps, and its transport echelon. To the south of Lake Kivu, around Bukavu and Uvira, thirty smaller camps held about 650,000 refugees. . . . Practically all the politicians and military men had gone to Zaire [instead of Burundi and Tanzania], where President Mobutu's sympathy for their fallen regime afforded them greater freedom of movement. . . .

Did this militarization of the camps put the former [Hutu-led] regime in a position to seriously threaten the [Tutsi-led] RPF [Rwandan Patriotic Front] in Kigali? Yes and no. In the short run, the ex-FAR did not have the military capacity to seriously challenge the recent victors. But the future was much more uncertain, as the ex-FAR had started a process of re-arming, practically in full view of the international community. The *génocidaires* had taken with them all of the Rwandese government's official financial resources, and they kept making money out of the camps themselves. In addition they could call on the private resources of corruption money stashed away by their leadership in better times. They also went to their former arms suppliers, particularly in South Africa, and asked for completion of the partially fulfilled contracts they had signed while in power. New suppliers were also found, such as when President Mobutu kindly took along Mrs. [Agathe] Habyarimana [wife of the former, assassinated Rwandan president Juvénal Habyarimana and the linchpin of the so-called *akazu*, or "little house," a network of extremists that wielded enormous power during Rwanda's Second Republic and which was centrally involved in the perpetration of the 1994 genocide] and her brother Séraphin Rwabukumba on a state visit to China in October 1994. They visited Chinese arms factories during their trip and were able to acquire five million [U.S.] dollars' worth of equipment at extremely competitive prices. . . .

The basic cause that led the Rwandese leadership to attack Zaire in September 1996 [thus] was the presence of the large, partially militarized refugee camps on its borders. But there was also a broader view, which was a systematic trans-African plan to overthrow the Mobutu regime in Zaire. Already in November 1994, in the wake of the Rwandese genocide, [President Yoweri] Museveni [of Uganda] had called a meeting in Kampala of all the "serious" enemies of Mobutu to discuss the idea of overthrowing him. The conclusion had been that the time was not yet ripe. In early 1995 former President [Julius] Nyerere [of Tanzania] had relaunched the idea, developing contacts with a number of African heads of state with the purpose of cleaning up what they looked upon as the shame of Africa. The heads of state involved were the presidents of Eritrea, Ethiopia, Rwanda, Uganda, Zimbabwe, and Angola. . . .

His basic reasons for launching this unconventional effort were coherent with his lifelong choices: socialism and pan-Africanism. . . .

Rwanda, because of the refugee question, was of course to be the entry point and the spearhead of the operation. Never mind that General [Paul] Kagame [then vice president of Rwanda] probably had scant regard for the inclusion of Rwanda into either a resurrected version of Deutsche [sic] Ostafrika or a modernized version of the East African Community. In the short run he was satisfied to be able to count on a regional alliance to back him. . . .

When General Kagame sent his army across the Zairian border in September 1996 he had a clear main purpose: countering the military threat posed to the new Rwandese regime by the remnants of the former regime who were rearming under the cover of the refugee camps. Conceivably this could have been a limited operation in the manner of the Israeli army hitting Hezbollah across the border into Lebanon. But the regional environment into which this move was going to take place was radically different from that of the Middle East. Borders were porous, populations were highly heterogeneous, and their distribution did not correspond to the border limits; conflicts overlapped and intermingled in ways that made them influence each other even when they were of a completely different nature. Central to the whole gathering storm was the huge sick blob of Zaire. . . .

The sudden Rwandese assault on the refugee camps was frontal and it was total. But it soon became apparent that it would not be limited to its initial target. The Rwandese invasion was taking place in a regional environment already undermined by years of complex and largely unnoticed conflicts. Force of habit caused the Western powers to consider the Mobutu regime as perhaps unpleasant but something that could stagger on for a while yet. There was still, lingering from the 1960s, the specter of an enormous zone of chaos at the heart of Africa.

The Rwandese assault thus had a dual effect: on the one hand, it exploded the myth of Mobutu as the only possible ruler of Zaire; on the other hand, it brought tumbling down into the vast Congolese basin a multiplicity of particular conflicts, each with its own logic, its own history, and its own independent actors. Once they had all rolled in and meshed with local Congolese problems, disentangling them from their involvement in order to return home became a daunting task. The RPF military elite, with its view of the continent mostly limited to the Great Lakes region and a highly militarized conception of politics, completely failed to realize the size of the Pandora's box it was cracking open.

93 • The Unseen Regional Implications of the Crisis in Darfur (Roland Marchal)

Roland Marchal, a senior research fellow at the National Center for Scientific Research, based at L'Institut d'études politiques in Paris, expertly traces the international dimensions of the conflict in Darfur. Focusing in particular on the role of Chad and the ethnic politics of Zaghawa identity, his 2007 essay provides an important corrective to accounts of the Darfur crisis that are framed solely

SOURCE: Roland Marchal, "The Unseen Regional Implications of the Crisis in Darfur," in Alex de Waal, ed., *War in Darfur and the Search for Peace* (Cambridge, Mass.: Global Equity Initiative, 2007, 173, 175–76, 181, 182, 183, 186, 188, 189, 190, 191, 193–94, 195, 196, 197. Reprinted with permission of the publisher.

in terms of a genocidal narrative. Marchal places the relationship between Chad and Sudan in historical perspective, explaining why the two countries were allies in the 1990s and why they nevertheless became adversaries over Darfur in the twenty-first century. In so doing, he reminds us of the sometimes overlooked consequences of collective violence for countries beyond the immediate location of atrocities. The implication of this perspective is that responses to the specter of genocide in one country should not be contemplated without taking into account possible repercussions for neighboring countries.

Since early 2003, the Darfur crisis has had a high profile in the Western press. Yet its regional dimension has scarcely been mentioned. Even though Eastern Chad and [the] northern Central African Republic (CAR) are increasingly the location of skirmishes, full-scale battles, and abuses against the civilian population, Darfur's war is still overwhelmingly seen as an internal Sudanese crisis. When reports do consider Chad, then the insecurity affecting Wadai (eastern Chad) is usually described as a spillover from the conflict in Darfur. Very few analysts have tried to make sense of this merger of the two different crises in Chad and Sudan that has reconfigured the political setting on both sides of the border, while the CAR is ignored completely. Some analysts have discussed relatively marginal military supplies from the SPLA [Sudan People's Liberation Army]], Eritrea, and some informal yet efficient Chadian and Libyan networks in support of insurgent movements [in Darfur], including the two most important, the SLA [Sudan Liberation Army] and JEM [Justice and Equality Movement]. However, the political implications of such facts have never been fully addressed, perhaps because they challenged the common stance of the international community or raised difficult questions about the mediation process led by the African Union. . . .

This chapter provides background on how Idriss Déby's ethnic group, the Zaghawa, became prominent in Chadian politics, on the linkages between the civil war in Chad and the Darfur crises, and on the crucial role of Libya. Lastly, it explains why the crises in Darfur and Chad are increasingly linked because of the nature of Déby's regime.

Understanding Zaghawa politics is essential to explaining the linkages among Chad, Libya, CAR, and Darfur. Zaghawa is a confederation of a great number of highly individualized clans, with separate habitats connected by religion and language. This cultural, tribal, and geographical diversity is accompanied by multiple names. In Sudan and Chad, they are known as Zaghawa and Bideyat; the latter are a branch of Zaghawa. Mostly nomads, the land of the Bideyat usually lies far from the settled Zaghawa, who enjoy more stability. But the language, customs, and traditions of the two are the same, although the Zaghawa call themselves *Beri*. The Zaghawa are scattered among and migrate between and within these countries, a feature they share with other non-Arab and Arab tribes from Chad and Sudan, such as the Masalit, Tama, Salamat, and Mahamad-Rizeigat. This situation has been exacerbated by distress migrations, occurring for two main reasons. First, drought and desertification provided a push factor over the last century (and especially in the 1960s, 1970s, and 1980s) that created the conditions for massive displacements of people. A second reason for forced migration has been the conflicts and feuds that took place on both sides of the borders since the 1970s.

The Zaghawa today appear to be in a more powerful position than other groups that straddle the eastern Chad basin. They have easy access to the many Gorane who have positions in the Libyan army and in local administration in southern Libya. Likewise, Idriss Déby and his extended lineage and allies monopolize power in Chad, while other members of this extended network associated with him are key leaders in the insurgency in Darfur ... and constitute the backbone of its military apparatus. In the CAR, General Bozizé was able to undertake his coup in March 2003 thanks to Chadian mercenaries and his success was achieved with the armed support of Idriss Déby. . . .

The original export of Chad's war to Darfur in the 1980s had an important impact on the Zaghawa's collective identity. In 1987–1989 conflict in Darfur was sparked by the presence of Arabs who had been against [Hissène] Habré [the president of Chad between 1982 and 1990] for quite a while (Déby was chief of staff of the army and special security adviser in the presidency when major mass killings occurred in Chad against southerners and Arabs). When the Zaghawa began to oppose Habré, war was not only waged in Chad but also in Darfur. Habré armed ethnic groups against the Zaghawa, and he also allowed his troops to cross the border at different times to wage the only form of war they knew, which included burning of villages, raping, looting, and mass killing. Since there was hardly a difference between Sudanese and Chadian Zaghawa settlements, they all became targets in the conflict. . . . To a large extent, Déby's success in Chad was accidental, owing more to the weakness of Habré [whom he deposed] than to his own might. . . .

In the early years of Déby's rule, power was consolidated through brutalities, killings, and authoritarianism. . . . Beyond the brutality of its coercion or, at some points, its accommodation, Déby played his regional and international cards well. . . . [Aside from good and improved relationships with France and Libya in the 1990s,] the new U.S. Pan-Sahel Initiative on counter-terrorism provides Chad and Déby, as other authoritarian regimes in northern Africa, with increased leverage. Relationships between Khartoum [the capital of Sudan] and N'djamena [the capital of Chad] were [also] excellent in the 1990s. . . . There were three main reasons for Khartoum to support the new regime in N'djamena. The relative importance of the factors changed over the years, but all were affected by both the peace negotiations and the Darfur crisis. The factors are: the security issue, an alternative to the containment policy enforced by the U.S. in the late 1990s against Islamist Sudan, and the attempt by the latter to achieve greater influence in west and north Africa through business and proselytism (da'wa). . . .

It is an understatement to say that the Darfur crisis disrupted this whole architecture of collusion and shared interests. . . . Given the earlier amity between the two [Chad and Sudan], when the threat from Darfur first emerged, Khartoum considered N'djamena capable of and responsible for curbing the threat. . . . But while the SLA obtained its first consignment of weapons from the SPLA and Eritrea, the JEM was generously supplied by Zaghawa officers from the Chadian army and presidential guard. Khartoum did not understand why Déby was unable to put his house in order. Sudanese military intelligence [therefore] mobilized would-be militias in Darfur to oppose what was locally described as (and to a certain extent was in fact) a Zaghawa upheaval. . . . Thus, the longer the conflict and survival of the Darfur insurgency, the less trust Khartoum had in Déby and the more bitter discussions with him became.

Déby was certainly not indifferent to preparations for war in Darfur, nor was he only acting for the sake of his Sudanese friends. He also had his own reasons to counter Khalil Ibrahim, the future JEM chairman. . . . As head of state, he considered himself to be at the top of the Zaghawa social and political hierarchy: others were supposed to rely on him. Khalil never did rely on him, for various reasons. . . . Nevertheless, a deal between Déby and the JEM was eventually struck in the summer of 2005. Its reasons had little to do with Darfur and much to do with Chadian politics. . . . The slow disintegration of Déby's regime did not go unnoticed in Khartoum. Beginning in early 2003, many in the Sudan armed forces, military intelligence, and at the presidency were convinced that the Chadian president was playing a double game. . . . Suspecting that the key to the logistics of the rebellion [in Darfur] lay in Chad, Khartoum responded by supporting Déby's adversaries. By the middle of 2005, Chadian opponents who had until then been mostly employed as surrogate forces to fight against the Darfur insurgency were given clearance to set up their camps in Darfur and obtain military hardware. . . . Déby's reaction was to try to reunify the Zaghawa elements of the Darfur insurgency to protect his own regime. . . .

Strong internal differences existed within the Sudan government on the nature of a settlement in Darfur and, by corollary, political changes in Chad. The army and the palace, after having been the Chadian president's main supporters, became adamant in their opposition to Déby and worked to build a more effective opposition, while some in the ruling National Congress Party were still advocating [unsuccessfully] for rebuilding a good relationship with Chad in order to isolate the rebellion and get it to accept an agreement under Khartoum's terms. . . .

A subregional system of wars has developed in . . . Sudan, Chad, and [the] CAR, as armed conflicts resulting from distinct national situations and involving different actors, methods, and issues, have become connected with each other, spilling over the geographical, social, and political borders that originally separated them. Such a subregional conflict nexus has been seen in other parts of the continent, for example, in the Mano River countries (Liberia, Sierra Leone, and Guinea) and the Great Lakes [Rwanda, Burundi, and the Democratic Republic of Congo]. All the conditions exist for such a complex of internal and regional violence to develop encompassing Chad, [the] CAR, and Darfur, and possibly spread further.

CHAPTER SIX

Courts

How can we prosecute genocide? Should we prosecute genocide? One of the most common and controversial strategies for coming to terms with the legacies of genocide, at least in the twentieth and twenty-first centuries, has been adjudication. Domestic and international trials of *génocidaires* have increased in size, scope, and sophistication, notably in the wake of atrocities in the former Yugoslavia and Rwanda. More recently the International Criminal Court (ICC) has begun to turn its attention to the investigation of atrocities in Darfur and elsewhere. This chapter covers noteworthy scholarship on the range of legal responses that have been devised for coming to terms with genocide, as well as selections from international jurisprudence.

The adjudication of international crimes, notably genocide, truly began following World War I, when Turkish military tribunals adjudicated cases from the Armenian genocide. Vahakn Dadrian offers a rare assessment. Hardly less controversial than the Turkish efforts was the Frankfurt Auschwitz Trial of the 1960s. Devin Pendas lends an insightful analysis of that trial.

The next three contributions all revolve around international justice dispensed by the United Nations International Criminal Tribunals for the former Yugoslavia (ICTY) and Rwanda (ICTR). The first selection, from the *Akayesu* trial judgment, a much-debated case heard at the ICTR, draws attention to the deliberation involved in applying aspects of the 1948 Genocide Convention to a case at hand. Catharine MacKinnon advances a forceful critique of the concept of rape as interpreted in the jurisprudence of both UN ad hoc tribunals. Guénaël Mettraux rounds off the section on the ICTY and ICTR with a brief discussion of the similarities and differences between extermination as a crime against humanity and genocide, a distinction that is lost on most nonlawyers. Of relevance to the discussion of international justice for genocide is also the much-anticipated 2007 decision by the International Court of Justice (ICJ) in the case of *Bosnia and Herzegovina v. Serbia and Montenegro*. Sections of the long and controversial (especially in Bosnia, where the findings were condemned by victims of Serb atrocities) decision elaborate the ICJ's finding that the evidence before it did not show that the Serbian state had committed crimes of genocide in Bosnia (other than in Srebrenica) but that the Serbian state had failed to comply with its obligations, pursuant to Article I of the Genocide Convention, to prevent and punish genocide.

Luc Reydams and Lars Waldorf analyze two very different efforts at adjudicating genocidal crimes in domestic courts. Reydams tackles the principle of universal jurisdiction in international law, that is, the progressive idea that states can prosecute foreign individuals for crimes despite the fact that the alleged offenses were not committed in the prosecuting country and did not claim as victims nationals from that country or have any other connection with the country. He does this through the lens of Belgium's successful prosecution of Rwandan genocide perpetrators. Waldorf zeroes in on Rwanda's own genocide trials, notably the country's thousands of *gacaca* jurisdictions, in which hundreds of thousands of laypersons sat in judgment over alleged *génocidaires*. Unlike many observers of said jurisdictions, Waldorf deems the Rwandan effort at "participatory justice" to be a failing experiment in restorative justice, for contrary to expectations, the *gacaca* jurisdictions by and large did not help to restore relations among Hutu and Tutsi. Instead they often exacerbated problems by meting out retribution.

Kelly Whitley then illuminates one of the most recent projects of coming to terms—by way of law—with genocidal acts and omissions: the Extraordinary Chambers in the courts of Cambodia. This hybrid court, comprising both domestic and international elements, in 2007 commenced the adjudication of atrocities that had been perpetrated some thirty years prior during the genocidal Pol Pot regime.

Finally, the chapter turns to the International Criminal Court and the Darfur crisis. Two documents provide useful reference: the UN Security Council's referral of the "situation in Darfur" to the ICC and the much-debated 2009 Decision by a Pre-Trial Chamber of the ICC to issue a warrant for the arrest of Omar Al Bashir, the incumbent president of Sudan. Just how controversial the Bashir prosecution has been becomes apparent very quickly in Julie Flint and Alex de Waal's scathing critique of Luis Moreno Ocampo's handling of the Darfur prosecutions, which concludes the chapter.

What the collected examples of scholarship encourage is a more careful interdisciplinary perspective on the prosecution of genocidal acts. At present the vast majority of writings on domestic and international adjudication is characterized either by an insufficient command of legal doctrine and jurisprudence or by a rudimentary grasp of the nonlegal aspects that also have a bearing on the effectiveness of legal responses to genocide, or both. The selections in this chapter showcase some of the best work from either perspective, but when read in conjunction, they also provide a sense of what the advanced study of courts is still lacking in the context of genocide.

94 • Testimony (Giorgio Agamben)

An Italian philosopher known for his work on the philosophy of language, Giorgio Agamben in his influential book Remnants of Auschwitz *(2002) inquires into the ethical and juridical questions raised by the court-based testimony of Holocaust survivors. He believes that the adjudication of Holocaust-era crimes did not advance our understanding of the Holocaust. Instead, says Agamben, the trials at Nuremberg and elsewhere "are responsible for the conceptual confusion that, for decades, has made it impossible to think through Auschwitz."*

SOURCE: Giorgio Agamben, *Remnants of Auschwitz: The Witness and the Archive*, translated by Daniel Heller-Roazen (New York: Zone Books, 2002), 13, 15, 16, 17, 18, 19, 20, 31–33, 34, 38, 39. Reprinted with permission of the publisher.

Some want to understand too much and too quickly; they have explanations for everything. Others refuse to understand; they offer only cheap mystifications. The only way forward lies in investigating the space between these two options. Moreover, a further difficulty must be considered, one which is particularly important for anyone who studies literary or philosophical texts. Many testimonies—both of executioners and victims—come from ordinary people, the "obscure" people who clearly comprised the great majority of [concentration] camp inhabitants. One of the lessons of Auschwitz is that it is infinitely harder to grasp the mind of an ordinary person than to understand the mind of a Spinoza or Dante.... In its form, this book is a kind of perpetual commentary on testimony....

In the camp, one of the reasons that can drive a prisoner to survive is the idea of becoming a witness.... Primo Levi is a perfect example of the witness. When he returns home, he tirelessly recounts his experience to everyone.... But Levi does not consider himself a writer; he becomes a writer so that he can bear witness. In a sense, he never became a writer.... In Latin there are two words for "witness." The first word, *testis*, from which our word "testimony" derives, etymologically signifies the person who, in a trial or lawsuit between two rival parties, is in the position of a third party (*terstis*). The second word, *superstes*, designates a person who has lived through something, who has experienced an event from beginning to end and can therefore bear witness to it. It is obvious that Levi is not a third party; he is a survivor (*superstite*) in every sense. But this also means that his testimony has nothing to do with the acquisition of facts for a trial (he is not neutral enough fort his, he is not a *testis*). In the final analysis, it is not judgment that matters to him, let alone pardon....

One of the most common mistakes—which is not only made in discussions of the camp—is the tacit confusion of ethical categories and juridical categories.... Almost all the categories that we use in moral and religious judgment are in some way contaminated by law: guilt, responsibility, innocence, judgment, pardon.... This makes it difficult to invoke them without particular caution. As jurists well know, law is not directed toward the establishment of justice. Nor is it directed toward the verification of truth. Law is solely directed toward judgment, independent of truth and justice.... If this is true—and the survivor knows that it is true—then it is possible that the trials (the twelve trials at Nuremberg [thirteen if one also counts the Trial of the Major War Criminals that was conducted prior to the twelve successor trials under Control Council Law No. 10], and the others that took place in and outside German borders, including those in Jerusalem in 1961 that ended with the hanging of [Adolf] Eichmann) are responsible for the conceptual confusion that, for decades, has made it impossible to think through Auschwitz. Despite the necessity of the trials and despite their evident insufficiency (they involved only a few hundred people), they helped to spread the idea that the problem of Auschwitz had been overcome.... With the exception of occasional moments of lucidity, it has taken almost half a century to understand that law did not exhaust the problem, but rather that the very problem was so enormous as to call into question law itself, dragging it to its own ruin....

Several years ago, when I published an article on the concentration camps in a French newspaper, someone wrote a letter to the editor in which, among other crimes, I was accused of having sought to "ruin the unique and unsayable character of Auschwitz." I have often asked myself what the author of the letter could have had in mind. The phenomenon of Auschwitz is unique (certainly in the past, and we can only hope for the future).... But why unsayable?

Why confer on extermination the prestige of the mystical? . . . To say that Auschwitz is "unsayable" or "incomprehensible" is equivalent to *euphemein* [which originally referred to the practice of observing religious silence], to adoring in silence, as one does with a god. Regardless of one's intentions, this contributes to its glory. We, however, "are not ashamed of staring into the unsayable" [and will give testimony]—even at the risk of discovering that what evil knows of itself, we can also easily find in ourselves.

Testimony, however, contains a lacuna. The survivors agree about this. [As Levi writes,] "There is another lacuna in every testimony: witnesses are by definition survivors and so all, to some degreed, enjoyed a privilege. . . . No one has told the destiny of the common prisoner, since it was not materially possible for him to survive." . . . [Or, as Eli Wiesel observes,] "Those who have not lived through the experience will never know; those who have will never tell; not really, not completely. . . . The past belongs to the dead. . . . It is worth reflecting on this lacuna, which calls into question the very meaning of testimony and, along with it, the identity and reliability of the witnesses. [Here again is Levi:] "I must repeat: we, the survivors, are not the true witnesses. . . . We survivors are not only an exiguous but also an anomalous minority: we are those who by their prevarications or abilities or good luck did not touch bottom. Those who did so, those who saw the Gorgon, have not returned to tell about it or have returned mute, but they are the Muslims, the submerged, the complete witnesses, the ones whose deposition would have a general significance. They are the rule, we are the exception."

[Continues Levi:] "We who were favored by fate tried, with more or less wisdom, to recount not only our fate but also that of the others, indeed of the drowned; but this was a discourse 'on behalf of third parties,' the story of things seen at close hand, not experienced personally. The destruction brought to an end, the job completed was not told by anyone, just as no one ever returned to describe his own death." . . . The witness usually testifies in the name of justice and truth and as such his or her speech draws consistency and fullness. Yet here the value of testimony lies essentially in what it lacks; at its center it contains something that cannot be borne witness to and that discharges the survivors of authority. The "true" witnesses, the "complete witnesses," are those who did not bear witness and could not bear witness. They are those who "touched bottom": the Muslims, the drowned. The survivors speak in their stead, by proxy, as pseudo-witnesses; they bear witness to missing testimony. And yet to speak here of proxy makes no sense; the drowned have nothing to say, nor do they have instructions or memories to be transmitted. They have no "story," no "face," and even less do they have "thought."

Whoever assumes the charge of bearing witness in their name knows that he or she must bear witness in the name of the impossibility of bearing witness. But this alters the value of testimony in a definitive way; it makes it necessary to look for its meaning in an unexpected area. . . . It is necessary to reflect on the nature of that to which no one has borne witness, on this non-language. This means that testimony is the disjunction between two impossibilities of bearing witness; it means that language, in order to bear witness, must give way to a non-language in order to show the impossibility of bearing witness. The language of testimony is a language that no longer signifies and that, in not signifying, advances into what is without language, to the point of taking on a different insignificance—that of the complete witness, that of he who by definition cannot bear witness.

95 ◆ The Turkish Military Tribunal (Vahakn N. Dadrian)

While the literature on the International Military Tribunal at Nuremberg is burgeoning, relatively little has been written about the Turkish Military Tribunal that was established following World War I to address the destruction of Armenians in the Ottoman Empire. Among the few available studies is one by Vahakn Dadrian, which appeared in 1997 in Holocaust and Genocide Studies. *Dadrian, an independent scholar, recounts the genesis of the various trials, the challenges involved in mounting them, and their significance. For Dadrian, the principal contribution of the court proceedings lies in the fact that they established "beyond reasonable doubt" that the Young Turk regime had organized and implemented a scheme of genocide.*

The prosecution of dozens of World War I Turkish war criminals by a Turkish Military Tribunal has yet to engage the attention of scholars of legal history, in particular genocide studies. . . . The trials constitute a milestone in Turkish legal history. The post-war Turkish authorities had to reckon with a theocratic system which had an established legacy of severity in dealing with non-Muslim subject nationalities embroiled in conflict with Ottoman authorities. The trials challenged this legacy by introducing a novel element in the handling of nationality conflicts.

For the first time, Ottoman-Turkish authorities of the highest rank were being held accountable for their crimes against these nationalities. To add emphasis to this novelty, the Sultan and his government did so via a Special Military Tribunal, whose work proceeded under a succession of Ottoman governments in the wake of an exhausting war which had ended with the devastating defeat of the Ottoman army. It is most certain that this undertaking was dictated by political expediency. On the one hand, it was hoped that it would be possible to inculpate the Ittihadist Party leadership as primarily, if not exclusively, responsible for the Armenian massacres, thereby exculpating the rest of the Turkish nation. On the other, many representatives of the victorious Allies nurtured a strong belief that the punishment of the perpetrators might induce the victors to be lenient at the Peace Conference. . . .

The task of the Special Military Tribunal was not easy as it faced serious resistance from Ittihadist partisans who continued to dominate the Civil Service, the ministries of War, Interior, and Justice, and, above all, the central and local offices of the powerful Istanbul Police. These tried to impede the work of the Tribunal by temporizing, withholding documents, stalling the transmission of information, and occasionally outright disobedience of court orders. Obstruction was clandestinely abetted by operatives of the residual Special Organization (SO), the outfit which had actually carried out the killing operations of the Armenian genocide. Secret cells of the SO in the Ottoman capital unleashed a campaign of intimidation against the judges, the attorneys-general, and witnesses for the Tribunal, as well as against those organs of the press whose editors exposed details of the Armenian genocide by publishing eye-witness testimonies of Turkish citizens anxious to see the criminals punished. . . .

SOURCE: Vahakn N. Dadrian, "The Turkish Military Tribunal's Prosecution of the Authors of the Armenian Genocide: Four Major Court-Martial Series," *Holocaust and Genocide Studies* 11, no. 1 (1997): 28, 30, 31, 32–33, 44–45, 46–47, 49–50, 53. Reprinted with permission of Oxford University Press.

In addition to this encumbrance, the Tribunal suffered from instability as it underwent four changes in structure and function between December 1918 and November 1920. These changes included revisions of its statutes, a switch from a military-civilian to strictly military court-martial (March 1919), and the enlarging of the scope of the charges to encompass "overthrowing the government" (April 1920) added to the principal charges of "deportation and massacre." Turnover among presiding judges and attorneys-general in charge of the prosecution was considerable; there were at least six of the former and nine of the latter. Parallel to these turnovers, Cabinet and ministerial changes affected the personnel of the Tribunal—there were ten different justice ministers alone. . . .

Despite all these handicaps, however, the Tribunal functioned in the inhospitable milieu as best as it could. It was able to secure, authenticate, and compile an array of documents, including formal and informal orders for massacre, implicating the Ottoman High Command, the ministers of interior and justice, and the top leadership of the Ittihadist Party. The Tribunal's Key Indictment and nearly all of its verdicts are predicated upon these documents rather than courtroom testimony. Owing to the ascendancy of Kemalism first in the interior of the country, then gaining momentum in 1919 and 1920, and eventually prevailing throughout the entire land, displacing and expelling the Sultan's government in Istanbul, the prosecution ultimately faltered. Only a fraction of the 200 suspects (including 150 civilian officials of government and party and 22 military officers) against whom the so-called Mazhar Inquiry Commission had marshaled incriminating evidence and prepared separate files for delivery to the Tribunal could be convicted.

With the fall of the Republic of Armenia in November–December 1920, invaded and demolished by the Kemalist General Kâzim Karabekir, and attendant demise of pro-Sultan Damad Ferid's fifth and last cabinet, the courts-martial were jettisoned. . . . All difficulties notwithstanding, the Tribunal performed its task of investigating the genocide of the Armenians with the help of the Administration's Mazhar Inquiry Commission, adjunct inquiry commissions attached to the Tribunal, and Parliament's Fifth Inquiry Commission. . . . As the series of Verdicts demonstrates, the Tribunal substantiated the key charge of premeditated (ta'ammüden) mass murder organized by the Central Committee of the Ittihadist Party, carried out by the "Special Organization" (Teşkilâti Mahsusa), largely consisting of hard-core criminals released from the empire's prisons for the purpose. . . .

The Court asserted [in the courts-martial series concerned with the war-time cabinet ministers and top Ittihadist leadership] that the deportations and massacres [of Armenians] constituted a comprehensive attempt to radically solve the Armenian question (hall ve fasl). The Indictment points out the dual character of the Ittihad: the external and public, on the one hand, and the covert and secret (mestur ve hâfi) on the other; the latter relied on framing and issuing "oral and secret instructions." To achieve maximum results, the perpetrators used several methods of killing, including drowning in the Black Sea (irkâp ve gark). The Indictment repeatedly underscores the cupidity of the perpetrators, as the ancillary motive of mass murder, citing many examples of self-enrichment through pillaging and profiteering. . . .

The trials [of the war-time cabinet ministers and top Ittihadist leadership] began on April 28, 1919, and (after a series of changes in court statutes and the composition of personnel) ended on July 5, 1919, when the Key Verdict and sentences were pronounced. Altogether fourteen sittings proceeded on the basis of two separate but interrelated indictments. The first seven (April 28–May 17, 1919) covered the trial of a large number of Ittihadist power-wielders and Special Organization chieftains. The Attorney General had argued that the investigation of the Cabinet ministers was not yet completed and that their trial should therefore be deferred. They would be tried in the next round of seven sittings (June 3, 1919–June 26, 1919). . . . On June 3 at the opening of the second series of seven trials a new, amended indictment was read into the record. . . . Even though the deportations and massacres [of Armenians] were the main focus, Attorney General Feridun enlarged the scope to include the charge of "overthrowing the government." The defendants were accused of having created "a fourth instance of power" in the governmental set-up of the Ottoman state. . . . The preamble to the new indictment speaks of "the extermination of an entire people constituting a distinct community," and of "the admission and confession" of the defendants (*kabul ve itiraf*).

The Court also asserted that the deportations had not been dictated by military necessity, and that they did not constitute a disciplinary measure. The amended text of the indictment was even more explicit on these points. These deportations, "conceived and decided upon by Ittihad's Central Committee," had "tragic consequences . . . in almost every corner of the Ottoman Empire." . . . Perhaps the most significant aspect of the new indictment is its re-inculpation of the Special Organization as the main instrument of the genocide, particularly in the eastern provinces. . . . To emphasize premeditation and central organization[,] the indictment points out the "uniform patterns" (*yeknesak harekâti*) in the perpetration of the crimes, and especially utilization of local party organizations by recruiting their "central committees." . . .

Even though this trial series dealt with several aspects of the genocide (premeditation, decision-making, and organization), its main focus was implementation. Those being tried were almost entirely identified with the Executive branch of the Ottoman government, i.e., Cabinet ministers. The ranks of the latter were supplemented by the top leaders of the Ittihad. Some of these leaders were simultaneously Cabinet ministers; others operated behind the scenes to informally and covertly direct the genocide. Most important, many of these representatives of the leadership had been in charge of the Special Organization. The structure and function of this super secret organization came to light during the cross-examination of several of its leaders. . . .

The judgment [in the first sitting of the second part of this trial series] focused on Ittihad as a conspiratorial body which penetrated, subverted, and gained control over the Ottoman government. The Verdict identified the General Assembly [of the Ittihadist political party] as the actual "authors of the crime" since they represented "the moral personality" of the party. . . . Having thus spelled out its grounds, the Court's Verdict focused on the mass murder of the Armenians. The Special Court Martial had "examined" and "verified" (*tahakkuk*) the massacres enacted in various parts of the Ottoman Empire, and established that these crimes were "organized and carried out" (*tertib ve icra*) by "the leaders" (*erkân*) of Ittihad. Accordingly, the Court found many of these leaders guilty of first degree mass murder. It sentenced [Mehmet] Talât [the Committee of Union and Progress's (CUP) minister of the interior], Enver [Pasha, the CUP's minister of war and leader of the 1913 military coup that had brought the "Young Turk" movement to power in the Ottoman Empire], Cemal, and Dr. Nazim to the death penalty—in absentia. Other ministers received prison sentences of various durations. . . .

The most salient feature of the present case is the remarkable chasm between the determination of guilt and the indulgence through which so many of the guilty escaped retribution. A reasonably successful prosecution does not necessarily ensure a reasonably just retribution. A *nation* was murdered in its ancestral territories and the Tribunal could convict and condemn to death only fifteen men, of whom only three—indeed only the most insignificant of the pack—were actually executed; the rest escaped, or were allowed to escape.... Nevertheless, the proceedings of the Turkish Military Tribunal, despite its dismal failure in the area of retributive justice, served a critical purpose as a judicial body. The proceedings demonstrated beyond reasonable doubt that the Ittihad, which had become a monolithic governmental party, intended to destroy the Armenian population of the empire and for that purpose had organized and implemented its scheme of genocide.

96 • Film as Witness at the International Military Tribunal at Nuremberg (Lawrence Douglas)

One of the most original, and least known, contributions to our understanding of court proceedings in the aftermath of genocide comes from Lawrence Douglas, a professor of law, jurisprudence, and social thought at Amherst College. In his 2001 book The Memory of Judgment, *Douglas reflects on the evidentiary value of documentary film, focusing on the screening of* Nazi Concentration Camps *during the Trial of the Major War Criminals at the International Military Tribunal (IMT) at Nuremberg. According to Douglas, the screening amounted to an exercise in "didactic legality," that is, one in which the resort to law serves the purpose of historical edification. By raising serious questions about the cinematography, editing, and narration of the documentary, Douglas emphasizes the limits of film as witness to genocide.*

The Nuremberg trial's most spectacular moments were neither oratorical, adversarial, nor testimonial—but documentary. If the prosecution's embattled paradigm of proof often contributed to the trial's dullness, it also made possible its moments of extraordinary spectacle. One such moment occurred as the trial entered its second week. Following [U.S. Chief of Counsel Robert] Jackson's outstanding opening address, the American prosecution had quickly bogged down. A lengthy and disorganized presentation of evidence concerning the *Anschluß* of Austria had resulted in the tribunal's requiring the prosecution to read documents into the record. Sensing the need to reinfuse drama into the proceeding, the prosecution ended its discussion of the Austrian annexation on the afternoon of November 29, 1945, with an announcement of its intent to interject a brief cinematic interlude.... The Nuremberg prosecution turned to a novel witness—a documentary film laconically entitled *Nazi Concentration Camps*.

This use of film was unprecedented. Crime scene photography was well established in Anglo-American courts; but while the turn to filmic proof was perhaps a logical extension of

SOURCE: Lawrence Douglas, *The Memory of Judgment: Making Law and History in the Trials of the Holocaust* (New Haven, Conn.: Yale University Press, 2001), 20–21, 23–24, 25, 26–27, 29–30, 31, 32, 33, 34–36, 37, 56, 57–60. Reprinted with permission of the publisher.

available technology, it nevertheless marked a wholly new method of documenting criminality. Although motion pictures had been submitted as trial evidence as early as 1913, prior to Nuremberg one can find no records of any court using graphic film of atrocities as proof of criminal wrongdoing. As the prosecution readied the army's documentary for screening, James Donovan, an assistant trial counsel, expressed succinctly the logic behind the turn to the filmic witness. "These motion pictures," he announced, "speak for themselves in evidencing life and death in Nazi concentration camps." As a visual artifact, the film could offer undeniable proof of a reality that might seem invented or exaggerated if recounted through written or spoken testimony.

As the first evidence of extermination and of the larger "concentrationary universe" presented to the Nuremberg courtroom, *Nazi Concentration Camps* tells a great deal about how the Nuremberg trial sought to locate an idiom adequate to the task of representing and judging the extermination of European Jewry. Indeed, a study of what the court saw in this startling documentary, and how the evidence it supplied was assimilated into the prosecution's case and the court's judgment, reveals in exemplary fashion how imperfectly evidence of Nazi genocide was presented and digested [in the Trial of the Major War Criminals] at Nuremberg.

What exactly did the tribunal see when the prosecution screened *Nazi Concentration Camps*? . . . Some eighty thousand feet of tape had been edited into about six thousand feet of film with a running time of a little more than an hour. The accompanying narrative, Donovan noted [in court], had been "taken directly from the reports of the military photographers who filmed the camps." According to the official [trial] transcript, "photographs were then projected on the screen showing the following affidavits [certifying that the images have not been retouched, distorted, or altered] while at the same time the voices of the respective affiants were reproduced reading them." . . . Yet after the dramatic buildup preparing the court for the documentary, the trial transcript suddenly turns laconic:

> (The film was then shown.)
> Col. Storey: That concludes the presentation.
> (The Tribunal adjourned until 30 November 1945 at 1000 hours.)

The morning session on Friday, November 30, began without any mention of the film, as the prosecution turned from its meandering discussion of the *Anschluß* to an equally unfocused presentation of the seizure of the Sudetenland. Yet the absence of any mention of the film should not be taken as a sign that the documentary had left the court unmoved. On the contrary. [Accounts of the screening by observers and lawyers, from prison psychologist G. M. Gilbert to Telford Taylor, involved in the proceedings], despite their differences, share an interesting rhetorical feature. Hardly mentioning the images in the film, they ask us to see the film voyeuristically through they eyes not of just any viewers, but of those allegedly responsible for the very atrocities captured on film. The technique itself partakes of a cinematic logic, as the spectators, caught between voyeurism and revulsion, break their gaze away from the images of atrocity and turn toward the perpetrators. . . .

In focusing on the Nazi defendants, the memoirs leave one in the dark about what the tribunal actually saw in *Nazi Concentration Camps*. This was not accidental, as the authors of the memoirs do not investigate the defendants' legal culpability as much as presuppose it: they ask readers to see the defendants through the reflection of atrocities in their eyes. By neglecting to make clear what the court saw in *Nazi Concentration Camps*, the journalists and memoirists only reinforce an understanding that the images "speak for themselves" as to the defendants' guilt. . . . However minor its explicit evidentiary value, *Nazi Concentration Camps* was hardly a diversion. [It was] an exercise in didactic legality. . . .

To view *Nazi Concentration Camps* today gives an imperfect idea of what the tribunal saw fifty years ago. The horror captured in *Nazi Concentration Camps* is by now so familiar that it is difficult to imagine an *original* screening—that is, a screening that shocks not simply because of the barbarity of the images, but also because of their novelty. . . . *Nazi Concentration Camps* begins by testifying to its own authenticity. The trial transcript . . . notes that pictures of various affidavits supporting the film's accuracy were projected before the Nuremberg court. What the transcript fails to make clear, however, is that these affidavits are part of the film itself, and the voice that reads them aloud is part of the sound track. . . . On a procedural level, this unorthodox submission of affidavits draws attention to the relaxed rules of proof that governed the tribunal's proceedings and permitted the prosecution to introduce film as evidence. The standard of admissibility of filmic proof, at least in Anglo-American jurisprudence, centered on the doctrine of the authenticating witness. This doctrine, which continued to control in certain jurisdictions until well after Nuremberg, maintained that "the motion picture does not of itself prove an actual occurrence but the thing reproduced must be established by the testimony of witness."

Because film was conceptualized as being dependent upon the corroboration of eyewitness testimony, it was often barred not because of its inaccuracy, but because of its redundancy: it offered no more than a needless repetition of information already supplied by the eyewitness. Furthermore, the failure to support filmic evidence with eyewitness testimony was also fatal, as the film would then be barred as hearsay. Without in court corroboration, such evidence would provide no more than a declaration of material fact made by an out-of-court witness unavailable for adversarial cross-examination—the very definition of hearsay. Finally, and crucially to the Nuremberg tribunal, certain American jurisdictions had barred photographic proof not because it was cumulative or hearsay, but because it was "gruesome": graphic pictures of injuries had been declared inadmissible in certain suits because their relevance as evidence was outweighed by their potential for prejudicing a jury. The enabling charter of the International Military Tribunal solved these evidentiary problems by the simplest means possible: it declared that the trial would "not be bound by technical rules of evidence." . . . While the trial was meant to supply a critical precedent for the articulation and defense of principles of international law, the procedures that governed the conduct of the trial were bound by neither the past nor the future. . . .

Although shot entirely in that finely shaded black and white that has powerfully overdetermined our images of the period, *Nazi Concentration Camps* could have been a color film. Technicolor, an expansive process, was available at the time of the liberation of the camps, and [Lt. Col. George C.] Stevens [the director of the film] filmed much of the footage from Dachau with [a] handheld color camera. . . . The army, however fearing that the three-track projectors necessary for showing Technicolor films would be unavailable in courtrooms and movie houses, decide to rely exclusively on monochrome for its documentaries, a decision that proved instrumental in shaping persistent cultural images of the Holocaust as an event that unfolded in black and white. . . .

While it is commonplace today to speak of the camera's exclusions and aggressions, in *Nazi Concentration Camps* the viewer catches glimpses of a more unusual phenomenon: the camera's confusion and embarrassment. . . . The camera functions . . . less as the invisible witness imagined by the prosecution than as a flummoxed provocateur—spectators learn of the survivors' world through their reactions (or lack thereof) to the lens's awkward probings. . . . Close-ups of former inmates [for example] show the twisted facial geometries and afflicted eyes of the demented. Their very obliviousness to the filming eye, the absence of any defense against the camera's intrusions, makes their isolation and despair manifest. . . . At other times, the survivors' awareness of the camera presents moments of inadvertent revelation. In one peculiar shot, three former inmates are caught posing not for the filmmaker, but for a still photographer also captured within the documentary's frame. According to the accompanying soundtrack, these "photographs are [being] made for further documentation of the horrors committed at the Hannover camp." Yet in the shot within the shot, we see the three survivors—two emaciated men, stripped to their waists, seated on either side of a third, standing, clothed in layers of rags—directing gaunt, macabre smiles toward the photographer, like three members of a grotesque reunion. Here it is the absurdity of their efforts to satisfy the roseate expectations of the camera that creates a haunting image.

In another shot, a young woman lifts her skirt to reveal puncture wounds upon her buttocks inflicted by Nazi torturers. She is filmed, for reasons unknown, standing on the rooftop of an apartment building, and as she stares over her shoulder back at the camera, her skirt [is] gathered at her waist. . . . Yet the very effort to document the Nazis' sexual cruelty inadvertently creates a pornographic moment, as the film offers her body as an object to be voyeuristically surveyed. . . . The horrors mount and intensify as the film journeys to Buchenwald, Dachau, and Bergen-Belsen. The camera lingers upon naked, emaciated bodies strewn upon a barrack floor. Suddenly, one twitches, and one realizes that unlike the mounds of corpses, these people are alive. It is a jarring moment, as what appears to be a still turns into a moving image. The camera then shifts to a shot of emaciated men moving like phantoms. "These are the survivors," comments the narrator tersely. The documentary concludes with the now famous footage of British bulldozers pushing a veritable mountain of bodies into a mass grave. As the dead and dirt cascade down the deep pit, the narrator ends with the flat declaration, "This was Bergen-Belsen." The horrific images render any additional comment superfluous. . . .

Just as the documentary calls attention, however, inadvertently, to the camera's intrusions, it relies upon a final, notable technique to authenticate what it has seen: it offers shot after shot of eyewitnesses viewing the very legacy of atrocities that the film records. One watches Generals Eisenhower, Bradley, and Patton grimly examining the camps; one tracks the journey of a delegation of congressmen; one follows the footsteps of GI's filing past rows of bodies. Here, again, the documentary supplies within its own frame witnesses to corroborate the truth of its representations. . . . Many of the most powerful images are shots of Germans forced to bear witness to Nazi barbarity. . . . In his opening statement [of the trial], Jackson declared that the prosecution did not seek to condemn a nation in its entirety: "We have no purpose to incriminate the whole German people"; the film, by contrast, offers no such assurances. It disperses responsibility to those who, through the tacit and cowardly tolerance of places they chose to know nothing about, became complicitous in the crimes that surrounded them. Yet by dispersing responsibility so broadly, the film gives little insight as to who is responsible for the atrocities in a more conventionally legal sense. . . . But the problems lie deeper still. For if the film fails to identify who was responsible for the atrocities it has documented, it also fails to name the crimes whose legacy the viewer has witnessed. Though the film provides a picture of a crime scene so extreme that its horrors have unsteadied the camera's idiom of representation, it does not translate its images into a conventional vocabulary of wrongdoing. . . .

Like most documentary films, *Nazi Concentration Camps* was made up of two principal constitutive elements—images and narration. . . . Close study of *Nazi Concentration Camps*, however, reveals that the narration does not simply strengthen the verisimilitude of the image; on the contrary, the voice of the commentary comes ultimately to assert control over the film's images. . . . The entire text of the hour-long film takes up no more than eleven pages of the tribunal's massive eighteen volume catalogue "Documents and Other Material in Evidence." Indeed, it is the very flatness and terseness of the commentary that most potently creates the impression that the images, not the words, are speaking. Yet this terseness, upon closer inspection, calls attention to certain interesting omissions. The word "Jew," for example is mentioned only once in the entire film, and in such a manner as to obscure any suggestion that Nazi terror was directed against Jews as a group. . . . The film's understanding of its own images is revealed, then, in a small but telling description. As the camera moves across the corpses littered about Buchenwald, the narrator declares, "Pictorial evidence of the *almost* unprecedented crimes perpetrated by the Nazis at Buchenwald Concentration Camp." . . . In the film's own parsing, crimes perpetrated by the Nazis at Buchenwald are "almost" unprecedented not because the final solution has its historical antecedents, but because the film does not understand itself to be a document about genocide against the Jews. . . .

If *Nazi Concentration Camps* does not open a window upon the crimes of the final solution, then what does it show? . . . By its own terms, . . . *Nazi Concentration Camps* is a film about political terrors and the excesses of war. It documents a barbaric campaign to eliminate political enemies of a brutal regime. It exposes the horrific mistreatment of prisoners of war and the enslavement of civilians to service a ruthless war machine. It bears witness to spectacular excesses of cruelty and reveals the administrative and technological apparatus that made possible campaigns of mass murder. It understands mass killing, however, in terms of the harsh logic of political control and military conquest. The crimes it has witnessed are the consequence of aggressive militarism rather than genocide unconnected to the aims of war.

97 • The Frankfurt Auschwitz Trial (Devin O. Pendas)

Less well-known than the 1961 trial of Adolf Eichmann in the District Court of Jerusalem—which centered on the leading role that the nondescript bureaucrat had played in the administration of the Holocaust—is the Frankfurt Auschwitz Trial, which took place in Germany only a few years after

SOURCE: Devin O. Pendas, *The Frankfurt Auschwitz Trial, 1963–1965: Genocide, History, and the Limits of the Law* (Cambridge: Cambridge University Press, 2006), 1–2, 24, 47, 50–51, 53, 54–55, 56, 57, 58, 227, 232–33, 288, 291, 293–94, 300. Reprinted with permission of the publisher.

the proceedings in Israel. Devin Pendas, an associate professor of history at Boston College, provides an exhaustive account of the judicial undertaking in his 2006 book, The Frankfurt Auschwitz Trial, 1963–1965. *Pendas covers the origins of the trial, the unique legal constraints imposed by Germany's Criminal Code, and the controversial verdicts. He finds that the Frankfurt Auschwitz Trial failed to understand the full import of its own evidence.*

This book is a history of the Frankfurt Auschwitz Trial (1963–65), the largest, most public, and most important Nazi trial to take place in West German courts after 1945. It was the most dramatic and politically resonant of the more than 6,000 such trials that took place between 1945 and 1980. Yet if the Auschwitz Trial was unusual among such trials in its drama and significance, in two other respects it was quite typical. First, like all West German Nazi trials after the Federal Republic regained full autonomy in the early 1950s, the Auschwitz Trial was conducted under ordinary statutory (as opposed to international) law. Second, like most such trials after the late 1950s, the Auschwitz Trial was a Holocaust trial, concerned at its core with the Nazi genocide of the Jews. . . .

Twenty-two defendants stood in the dock at the start of the Auschwitz Trial; twenty remained at the end. Of these, seven were convicted of murder, and ten of accessory to murder, and three were acquitted. Sentences ranged from three and one-quarter years to life in prison. Over the course of twenty months and 183 trial sessions, over 350 witnesses testified, including 211 survivors of Auschwitz. Dozens of attorneys, representing the prosecution, the defense, and civil plaintiffs from around the world, argued about the nature and meaning of mass murder, torture, and genocide. In its final judgment—both oral and written—the court attempted to render justice for the crimes of Auschwitz within the limits allowed by the law. And the West German public watched it all with a curious blend of macabre fascination, hostile indifference, and heartfelt shame and remorse. . . .

It was a matter of some luck that the Frankfurt Auschwitz Trial ever took place at all. As with almost all German Nazi trials in the first postwar decades, it was a private allegation, rather than any systematic investigation, that initially brought the case to the attention of authorities. In the spring of 1958, a convicted con man named Adolf Rögner wrote to the Stuttgart prosecutor's office claiming that one Wilhelm Boger, formerly of the Auschwitz Political Section (*Politische Abteilung*, or PA), the camp Gestapo, lived in the vicinity and that he had committed murder and other crimes while at Auschwitz. Initially, the investigation was handled from Stuttgart but was transferred to Frankfurt in 1959. Boger subsequently became one of the "star" defendants in the Auschwitz Trial. Less typical [for the times] perhaps was the enthusiasm with which the Frankfurt authorities, under the guidance of the Hessian attorney general, Fritz Bauer, pursued the case. . . .

From the time they began their investigation until early 1961, the Frankfurt prosecutor's office managed to investigate allegations against at least 290 potential suspects. . . . In the spring of 1961, the prosecutors began preparations for convening an official judicial preliminary investigation (*Voruntersuchung*). In keeping with Bauer's desire for a large, systematic trial, the plan was to convene an investigation against roughly twenty-five persons. . . . After internal review, the prosecution made their motion to convene a judicial preliminary investigation on July 12, 1961. The motion covered twenty-four suspects, seventeen of whom eventually became defendants in the Auschwitz Trial. . . . By the time the trial convened in 1963, an additional five defendants were added to the list of defendants, making for a total of twenty-two defendants at the start of the trial.

Shortly thereafter, Judge Heinz Düx took over the investigation [as is customary in inquisitorial systems of criminal prosecution such as those in Germany, France, Argentina, and Japan]. Judge Düx conducted the investigation with considerable vigor and a level of personal engagement hardly typical of the German judiciary in the early 1960s. Düx questioned more than 1,500 witnesses in the course of his investigation. When he was denied permission [from his superiors] for an official visit to Auschwitz to examine the scene of the crime personally, he requested permission to undertake the visit at his own expense as a private citizen. This request was also denied.... Only after repeated requests was Düx finally given permission to visit Auschwitz as a private citizen....

Finally, on April 16, 1963, a formal indictment was brought against "Mulka and others" for crimes committed at Auschwitz. With this, the preliminary investigation came to an official close and the Auschwitz Trial proper can be said to have begun, although the main proceedings themselves did not convene until December 20.... German criminal law itself formed one of the crucial structures of action for the participants.... Consequently, an understanding of the central features of German criminal law is indispensable for an understanding of the Auschwitz Trial.

The single most important thing to remember about German Nazi trials is that they took place under existing statutory law (*Strafgesetzbuch*, or StGB). This means that, to a much greater extent than trials conducted under either international (e.g., the Nuremberg trial [of the major war criminals]) or under the charge of "crimes against humanity" (e.g., the [Klaus] Barbie trial in France), German Nazi trials, including the Auschwitz Trial, were profoundly dependent on "ordinary" criminal procedure and categories. This led to several serious jurisprudential problems when it came to prosecuting Nazi genocide. In these legal technicalities, we see the ways in which German criminal law was, quite simply, not well equipped—conceptually or procedurally—to deal with genocide, the ways in which it fundamentally lacked the theoretical apparatus to grasp and render judgment on systematic, bureaucratically organized, state-sponsored mass murder....

The specificity of German criminal law becomes particularly clear if one contrasts it with the common law tradition, which conceptualizes many key categories quite differently. Certainly, it is safe to say that the German law of homicide is strikingly different from Anglo-American law in the way it treats the question of motivation and individual [criminal] responsibility. In particular, the key element in the American law of homicide is intention, that "malice aforethought" that Blackstone called the "grand criterion" for establishing murder. Malice aforethought is constituted, in one way or another, by intent. Furthermore, "nearly all states that grade murder by degrees provided that a 'willful, deliberate, premeditated' killing," that is once characterized by a "specific intent to kill" is murder in the first degree. Murders lacking such characteristics are deemed second-degree murder. Other than having murder in mind, then, the specific content of the perpetrator's motives for killing is not relevant to the legal definition of murder under American law. [Incidentally, the same goes for murder as a crime of genocide under international law.] Similarly, under American law, an accomplice is likewise defined by his or her intent. "S is an accomplice of P in the commission of an offense if he intentionally assists P to engage in the conduct that constituted the crime."

In determining whether a given homicide constitutes murder, it is largely a matter of in-difference to American law *why* a murderer intended to commit his or her crime, only that he or she committed it deliberately. . . . Furthermore, intent is generally demonstrated under American law according to the so-called natural-and-probable consequences rule, which holds that a person intended the results of his or her actions (in this case, the death of another human being) if the consequences were natural and probable and could thus have been fore-seen by any ordinary person. Any action that could reasonably be expected to result in the death of another human being will be considered intentional, and hence murder under Amer-ican law. . . . Not so with German law, where murder is defined largely in relation to a specific set of statutorily defined motives.

The second aspect of German criminal law that has proved troublesome during Nazi trials is the distinction between a perpetrator (*Täter*) and an accomplice (*Gehilfe*). Again, un-like American law, where intent remains the defining attribute of an accomplice, this distinc-tion is made in German law largely on the basis of the defendant's specific motives for acting as he or she did. . . .

The first, and from a pragmatic legal point of view, most significant jurisprudential prob-lem confronting the participants in Nazi trials was the distinction between *Mord* (murder) and *Totschlag* (manslaughter). §211 StGB defines *Mord* as follows: "A murderer is anyone who kills a human being out of blood lust, in order to satisfy their sexual desire, out of greed or other base motives, maliciously (*grausam*) or treacherously (*heimtückisch*) or by means dangerous to the public at large or in order to enable or conceal another crime." §212 StGB defines *Totschlag* more simply as anyone who kills another person without being a murderer under the above definition. *Totschlag* is thus a broader category than manslaughter is in Amer-ican law, and encompasses crimes that would be considered second-degree murder in the United States.

The relevance of this distinction is twofold. First, *Totschlag* fell under the statute of limita-tions in 1960. Thereafter, it became necessary for prosecutors to demonstrate that any given Nazi crime [involving the killing of one or more persons] met the specific criteria for *Mord* in order to bring an indictment. This made it considerably more difficult to indict Nazi criminals after 1960, since it was no longer enough simply to demonstrate that they had killed another human being or even that they had killed thousands; the prosecutor also had to prove that it was a specific kind of killing [i.e., one committed out of base motives]. . . . Second, it is im-portant to note that . . . of the various motives listed in §211, only two have really come into question for Nazi crimes: "blood lust" and other "base motives."

Blood lust is defined by the German High Court of Appeals, the *Bundesgerichtshof* (BGH) [usually and officially translated as German Federal Supreme Court], as an act done "on the basis of an unnatural joy at the destruction of human life." The other relevant mo-tive for *Mord* is the statutorily unspecified category of "base motives." These are judged, again according to German legal practice, as those "which according to healthy sensibilities are ethically particularly despicable." . . . In terms of Nazi crimes, it has mainly been possible to demonstrate blood lust for perpetrators from the lower ranks, those who did "the actual killing" (to borrow a phrase from Tolstoy), while base motives have tended to be easier to demonstrate across the board. . . . The most striking thing about both of these motivational determinants of *Mord* is that, since they concern internal states of affairs, they can usually be demonstrated only on the basis of indirect evidence (e.g., laughing while killing someone or acting in excess of one's orders), except in those rare cases where direct statements made by the perpetrators at the time of the crime are available. Ex post facto statements regarding the perpetrator's motives are held to be tainted and/or irrelevant and, hence, inadmissible [as evidence].

On August 19 and 20, 1965, [Presiding] Judge [Hans] Hofmeyer [who replaced Hans Forester when the latter was removed from the helm of the bench in the fall of 1963 due to a possible conflict of interest] announced the verdicts in the Auschwitz Trial and provided the requisite "oral justification" for the judgment. . . . The court's written judgment, drafted immediately after the conclusion of the trial, is an exhaustive 457-page document. It is divided into three main parts: an excursus on the history of the concentration camp system and Auschwitz in particular, a consideration of the cases against the individual defendants, and, finally, a consideration of procedural issues. The consideration of the cases against the individual defendants is by far the most extensive section in the written judgment, consuming 405 pages. The historical excursus, by contrast, is a mere forty pages long. . . .

Did the Auschwitz Trial succeed or fail? In asking this question, one must immediately also ask: On whose terms? The various actors in the trial each brought with them their own, often antithetical standards of success or failure. . . . These criteria [or standards] can be articulated in terms of the claims of justice, on the one hand, and the claims of truth, on the other hand. The Auschwitz Trial can be, and has been, judged to be both a success and a failure under both criteria. . . . It is more useful to think about the Auschwitz Trial in terms of limits and boundaries, rather than relying on the language of success or failure. In other words, rather than first choosing an evaluative criterion—truth or justice—and then applying this to the trial like a yardstick, it makes far more sense to examine what the trial actually *did*, in both the juridical and representational domains, where it drew the boundaries between these two and how the internal dynamic of tension and resolution between them unfolded. . . .

So, what was the trial able to achieve within these boundaries? On the one hand, the trial produced remarkably nuanced treatments of the various defendants, perhaps a bit too nuanced in some instances. . . . On the other hand, it was unable to articulate adequately a historical account of the Holocaust that fully incorporated or even sufficiently acknowledged the extent to which it was a "total social event," one in which every dimension of German society was implicated to one degree or another. It has been remarked by others that by punishing a few particularly egregious Nazi murderers trials such as this functioned as alibis for the remainder of German society. . . .

However, the problem is actually much more complicated than that. It was not simply that German Nazi trials provided an alibi for those disinclined to examine their own histories. More significant was the *kind of historical account* provided by the Auschwitz Trial. What was at stake was not just whether to think about the Nazi past but how to think about it. And in the Auschwitz Trial, the lens through which this past was viewed was carnivalesque, in the sense that like the mirrors in a carnival fun house, it greatly exaggerated one aspect of the truth, while simultaneously minimizing and distorting others. In this case, individual responsibility and individual atrocities were exaggerated and social structures and broader bureaucratic frameworks were diminished. . . . The tragedy of the Auschwitz Trial is not that it distorted an established historical understanding of Nazi genocide but that, in attempting to render criminal justice on that genocide, it failed to understand the full import of its own evidence.

98 • Did Tutsi Constitute an "Ethnical" Group?
(International Criminal Tribunal for Rwanda)

A perennial challenge in the adjudication of genocidal acts lies in the difficulty of determining whether or not a given victim group constitutes a "protected group" under the 1948 Genocide Convention, that is, whether it amounts to a national, ethnical, racial, or religious group under the meaning of the treaty. In the case of the Rwandan genocide, Trial Chamber I of the UN International Criminal Tribunal for Rwanda, better known by its acronym, ICTR, had to ascertain in its influential Akayesu judgment whether or not the Tutsi population of Taba commune comprised an "ethnical" group as defined under international law. The three-judge panel's complete deliberations of the issue are expounded upon in this document. While many observers take it for granted that Tutsi constituted a protected group, in legal terms the question was thornier. For as the judges pointed out, in anthropological terms, Tutsi are indistinguishable from Hutu. This notwithstanding, the Trial Chamber concluded that the long-standing politicization of ethnic identities and the pregenocidal government's official classification of Tutsi as a separate ethnic group were sufficient to extend to it the protection of the Genocide Convention.

Since the special intent to commit genocide lies in the intent to "destroy, in whole or in part, a national, ethnical, racial or religious group, as such," it is necessary to consider a definition of the group as such. Article 2 of the Statute [of the International Criminal Tribunal for Rwanda], just like the Genocide Convention, stipulates four types of victim groups, namely national, ethnical, racial or religious groups.

On reading through the *travaux préparatoires* of the Genocide Convention, it appears that the crime of genocide was allegedly perceived as targeting only "stable" groups, constituted in a permanent fashion and membership of which is determined by birth, with the exclusion of the more "mobile" groups which one joins through individual voluntary commitment, such as political and economic groups. Therefore, a common criterion in the four types of groups protected by the Genocide Convention is that membership in such groups would seem to be normally not challengeable by its members, who belong to it automatically, by birth, in a continuous and often irremediable manner.

Based on the *Nottebohm* decision rendered by the International Court of Justice, the Chamber holds that a national group is defined as a collection of people who are perceived to share a legal bond based on common citizenship, coupled with reciprocity of rights and duties. An ethnic group is generally defined as a group whose members share a common language or culture. The conventional definition of racial group is based on the hereditary physical traits often identified with a geographical region, irrespective of linguistic, cultural,

SOURCE: *Prosecutor v. Jean-Paul Akayesu*, Case No. ICTR-96-4-T, Judgment, September 2, 1998, paragraphs 510–16, 169–71, 702.

national or religious factors. The religious group is one whose members share the same religion, denomination or mode of worship.

Moreover, the Chamber considered whether the groups protected by the Genocide Convention, echoed in Article 2 of the Statute, should be limited to only the four groups expressly mentioned and whether they should not also include any group which is stable and permanent like the said four groups. In other words, the question that arises is whether it would be impossible to punish the physical destruction of a group as such under the Genocide Convention, if the said group, although stable and [whose] membership is by birth, does not meet the definition of any one of the four groups expressly protected by the Genocide Convention. In the opinion of the Chamber, it is particularly important to respect the intention of the drafters of the Genocide Convention, which according to the *travaux préparatoires*, was patently to ensure the protection of any stable and permanent group. . . .

The Chamber finds beyond a reasonable doubt that the acts of violence which took place in Rwanda during this time were committed with the intent to destroy the Tutsi population, and that the acts of violence which took place in [the commune of] Taba [not far from Gitarama in central Rwanda] during this time were a part of this effort. Paragraph 7 of the indictment alleges that the victims in each paragraph charging genocide were members of a national, ethnic, racial or religious group. The Chamber notes that the Tutsi population does not have its own language or a distinct culture from the rest of the Rwandan population. However, the Chamber finds that there are a number of objective indicators of the group as a group with a distinct identity.

Every Rwandan citizen was required before 1994 to carry an identity card which included an entry for ethnic group (*ubwoko* in Kinyarwanda and *ethnie* in French), the ethnic group being Hutu, Tutsi or Twa. The Rwandan Constitution and laws in force in 1994 also identified Rwandans by reference to their ethnic group. Article 16 of the Constitution of the Rwandan Republic, of 10 June 1991, reads, "All citizens are equal before the law, without any discrimination, notably on grounds of race, colour, origin, ethnicity, clan, sex, opinion, religion or social position." Article 57 of the Civil Code of 1988 provided that a person would be identified by "sex, ethnic group, name, residence and domicile." Article 118 of the Civil Code provided that birth certificates would include "the year, month, date and place of birth, the sex, the ethnic group, the first and last name of the infant." The Arusha Accords of 4 August 1993 in fact provided for the suppression of the mention of ethnicity on official documents. . . .

Moreover, customary rules existed in Rwanda governing the determination of ethnic group, which followed patrilineal lines of heredity. The identification of persons as belonging to the group of Hutu or Tutsi (or Twa) had thus become embedded in Rwandan culture. The Rwandan witnesses who testified before the Chamber identified themselves by ethnic group, and generally knew the ethnic group to which their friends and neighbors belonged. Moreover, the Tutsi were conceived of as an ethnic group by those who targeted them for killing. . . .

In the light of the facts brought to its attention during the trial, the Chamber is of the opinion, that, in Rwanda in 1994, the Tutsi constituted a group referred to as "ethnic" in official classifications. Thus, the identity cards at the time included a reference to "*ubwoko*" in Kinyarwanda or "*ethnie*" (ethnic group) in French which, depending on the case, referred to the designation Hutu or Tutsi, for example. The Chamber further noted that all the Rwandan witnesses who appeared before it invariably answered spontaneously and without hesitation the questions of the Prosecutor regarding their ethnic identity. Accordingly, the Chamber finds that, in any case, at the time of the alleged events, the Tutsi did indeed constitute a stable and permanent group and were identified as such by all.

99 • Defining Rape Internationally (Catharine A. MacKinnon)

The Akayesu *trial judgment from 1998 is best known for expressly defining rape as a crime under international law. Catharine MacKinnon, a professor of law at the University of Michigan, points to the long and winding paths of rape cases heard by the UN ad hoc tribunals. In particular she takes issues with changing definitions of rape, faulting international judges for inconsistency and lack of concern for the suffering of women. In addition to her academic work on rape, MacKinnon in* Kadić v. Karadžić *in 2000, with co-counsel, won a damage award of $745 million for Bosnian women survivors of Serbian genocidal sexual atrocities.*

Each time a rape law is created or applied, or a rape case is tried, communities rethink what rape is. Buried contextual and experiential presumptions about the forms and prevalence of force in sexual interactions, and the pertinence and modes of expression of desire, shape public consciousness and judicial determinations of law and fact. The degree to which the actualities of raping and being raped are embodied in law tilt ease of proof to one side or the other and contribute to determining outcomes, which in turn affect the landscape of expectations, emotions, and rituals in sexual relations, both everyday and in situations of recognized group conflict.

Illegal rape is commonly defined to revolve around force and unwantedness in sexual intercourse. Many jurisdictions—by statute, interpretation, or in application—tend to emphasize either compulsion or lack of agreement. Some weigh one to the relative exclusion of the other; some permit one or the other alternately or simultaneously. Many require proof of both. In life, the realities of compulsion and lack of accord in sexual interactions overlap and converge. Force abrogates autonomy just as denial of self-determination is coercive. Although the determinants of desire and techniques of compulsion (and the mutual interactions of the two) are far from simple, anyone who has sex without wanting to was compelled by something, just as someone who had sex they wanted was not forced in the conventional sense. Yet conceptually speaking, emphasis on nonconsent as definitive of rape views the crime fundamentally as a deprivation of sexual freedom, a denial of individual self-acting. Emphasis on coercion as definitive, on the other hand, sees rape fundamentally as a crime of inequality, whether of physical or other force, status, or relation.

Where coercion definitions of rape see power—domination and violence—nonconsent definitions envision love or passion gone wrong. Consent definitions accordingly have proof of rape turn on victim and perpetrator mental state: who wanted what, who knew what when.

SOURCE: Catharine A. MacKinnon, "Defining Rape Internationally: A Comment on *Akayesu*," *Columbia Journal of Transnational Law* 44, no. 3 (2006): 940–47, 949, 950, 951–52, 954, 957–58. Reprinted with permission of the journal.

This crime basically occurs in individual psychic space. Coercion definitions by distinction turn on proof of physical acts, surrounding context, or exploitation of relative position: who did what to whom and sometimes why. This crime basically takes place on the material plane. Accordingly, while consent definitions tend to frame the same events as individuals engaged in atomistic one-at-a-time interactions, coercion definitions are the more expressly social, contextual, and collective in the sense of being group-based.

The statutes of the ad hoc criminal tribunals for Yugoslavia and Rwanda, regions of conflict in the 1990s where sexual atrocities were widely deployed for ethnic destruction, were established to adjudicate international violations of the laws of war and humanitarian law. Rape under these statutes is thus not a free-standing crime but must be charged as an act of war, genocide, or crime against humanity. Expressly defining rape under international law for the first time in 1998, the *Akayesu* [judgment] of Trial Chamber I of the International Criminal Tribunal for Rwanda (ICTR) held that rape, there charged as a crime against humanity, is "a physical invasion of a sexual nature, committed on a person under circumstances which are coercive." As with torture, to which it was analogized, rape was defined by its purpose to the perpetrators in context, together with its specific nature as being sexual. *Akayesu* defined rape as an act of coercion not reducible to narrow bodily description: "The Chamber considers that rape is a form of aggression and that the central elements of rape cannot be captured in a mechanical description of objects and body parts." Crucially, "coercive circumstances need not be evidenced by a show of physical force" but "may be inherent in certain circumstances," such as armed conflict or the military presence of threatening forces on an ethnic basis.

Interpreted in light of the distinction between coercion definitions, on the one hand, and nonconsent definitions, on the other, to be sexually invaded under coercive circumstances, as *Akayesu* terms it, is clearly to be subjected to an unwelcome act, but that did not make nonconsent a matter of proof for the prosecution. Under the conditions of overwhelming force present in a "widespread or systematic attack against any civilian population on national, political, ethnic, racial or religious grounds" that constitute a context of crimes against humanity in acts found to be part of the campaign, inquiry into individual consent was not even worth discussion. Mr. Akayesu was found individually criminally responsible for crimes against humanity for ordering, instigating, aiding, and abetting the sexual violence under his aegis that took place as part of such a widespread and systematic attack on civilians. And, arguably for the first time, rape was defined in law as what it is in life. . . .

In the line of cases that followed, the International Criminal Tribunal for the Former Yugoslavia (ICTY) led in tilting the definition of rape for both tribunals away from the *Akayesu* breakthrough resolution and, step by step, back in the direction of nonconsent. Although the ICTY trial chamber's *Delalic* [judgment] initially embraced *Akayesu*'s definition, in a reversion first publicly visible late in 1998, the ICTY's *Furundzija* trial [judgment] while acknowledging that rape was a forcible act, mentioned the *Akayesu* definition only to ignore it. In nothing other than the "body parts" definition *Akayesu* had expressly rejected as mechanical and missing the whole point three months earlier, the *Furundzija* [trial chamber] required a showing of vaginal or anal penetration by a penis or object, or oral penetration by a penis. "Without the consent of the victim" crept back in at the same time. Five years later, this regression culminated in the ICTR's *Semanza* and *Kajelijeli* trial [judgments] turning rape on nonconsent. The *Furundzija* trial chamber predicated these developments on a lengthy recital of national laws, claiming a need for "specificity" and "accuracy" in definition. . . .

Even before *Furundzija*, the ICTY's rape prosecutions were marked by missteps and missed opportunities. In the first case to be resolved at trial, *Tadic*, brought against a guard at the Omarska camp notorious for systematic rape of a group of women captives, the one count for rape of a woman victim had to be withdrawn, leaving a sexual attack on a man the only sexual assault adjudicated in the case. Particularly women survivors of captivity in Omarska found this to be an insulting, even traumatic misrepresentation, a public mockery of their experiences. Making matters worse, the ICTY's Rule 96, which had originally provided that "consent shall not be allowed as a defense" to charges of rape under the Tribunal's jurisdiction, giving the Tribunal considerable credibility with survivors, was changed by the Tribunal so that it no longer ruled out consent entirely. That the Tribunal could imagine that rapes that were part of war, genocide, or a campaign of crimes against humanity could be consensual outraged many women survivors of that conflict and badly damaged the Tribunal's credibility with that community.

A related and further problem has been the long-term reluctance of the ICTY to charge rape as an act of genocide. Many perpetrators have been indicted for rape and other sexual violence under other rubrics, and for genocide for other acts, but despite *Akayesu* showing the way, only ten ICTY cases have indicted rape as genocide, prominently culminating in the Milosevic indictment in 2001, compared with almost four times as many by the ICTR. Since survivors of rape in the Serb-led genocide against Bosnia-Herzegovina and Croatia typically understood that they had been raped precisely to destroy their ethnic and religious communities, in acts of sexual violence against women because they were not Serbian, the ICTY's seeming reluctance to grasp the entire point of their victimization made survivors unwilling to put themselves in its hands, damaging trust and opportunities for cooperation. . . . In contrast, the Rwanda Tribunal's general clarity that it was facing a genocide to which rape and other sexual atrocities were integral components encouraged a conception of the acts focused not on the absence of individual consent but on the presence of group force. Where extremist Hutu exterminated and raped and otherwise sexually violated Tutsi by the hundreds of thousands, as in Rwanda, the decontextualized interaction of discrete body parts and one-at-a-time mental states were simply irrelevant, otherworldly. Simply put, the ICTR grasped that inquiring into individual consent to sex for acts that took place in a clear context of mass sexual coercion made no sense at all. . . .

Back at the ICTR, which endorsed the *Akayesu* definition in *Musema* and *Niyitegeka*, one trial chamber, following the lead of the ICTY, reverted to the consent-based rape definition that *Akayesu* had already superseded. The *Semanza* ruling in 2003 termed the *Akayesu* definition "broad"; the ICTY's definition—"the non-consensual penetration, however slight, of the vagina or anus of the victim by the penis of the perpetrator or by any other object used by the perpetrator, or of the mouth of the victim by the penis of the perpetrator"—was termed "narrower." It is unclear what these two terms mean except that they imply that some acts included in the *Akayesu* definition are not actually rapes. . . . Instead of foregrounding the larger (and statutory) context of reality in which the acts took place, proof was now to focus on mechanical interactions of specified body parts of individuals and what individual perpetrators were thinking about what their victims were thinking—almost as if the *Interahamwe* were going out on a date with the Tutsi women they hunted down and slaughtered with machetes. In defining rape exclusively by nonconsent, *Semanza* completed the full turn backward to the English common law. No other crime against humanity has ever, once the other standards are met, been required to be proven nonconsensual. With sex, it seems, women can consent to what would otherwise be a crime against their humanity, making it not one. . . .

Charting the beginning of its recovery from the *Semanza* detour, the *Muhimana* trial [judgment] in 2005 marked the ICTR's return to the course *Akayesu* began. In an accurate synthesis of prior rulings with the facts of the cases both tribunals confronted, *Muhimana* applied *Akayesu* toward resolving the definitional debate. It held that "coercion is an element that may obviate the relevance of consent as an evidentiary factor in the crime of rape" and that most international crimes "will be almost universally coercive, thus vitiating true consent." . . . The *Akayesu* approach and the pattern of outcomes in cases since support the suggestion that rape laws fail because they do not recognize the context of inequality in which they operate, focusing as they so often do on isolated proof of nonconsent against a false background presumption of consent in the context of a presumed equality of power that is not socially real. Consent often operates as a flag of freedom flown under the illusion that, if it is instituted as a legal standard, whatever sex women want will be allowed and whatever sex women do not want will be criminal. Legal consent standards do not conform to this fantasy anywhere, wholly apart from the complexities that inequality introduces to what members of powerless groups can want or reject. But an unnoticed slippage in the discussion of the term between social myths of and desires for freedom, on the one hand, and legal discussions of actual rules that tacitly reflect and impose inequalities, on the other, gives the term an appeal it does not earn. . . .

In light of the realism and administrability of the *Akayesu* definition, it is regrettable that the ICC [International Criminal Court] codified rape for its international purposes in the chronological middle of the tribunals' process described here. Taking one page from *Akayesu*'s invasion of a sexual nature under coercive circumstances and one from *Furundzija*'s body parts without consent, the ICC straddles the definitional divide rather than resolves it. Although the ICC's elements lean toward force and coercion in defining sexual assault crimes, the door that *Akayesu* shut so decisively and appropriately was left once more ajar by the ICC's evidentiary code, through which rapists can walk away after rapes that show no sign of stopping.

100 • State Responsibility for Genocide: *Bosnia v. Serbia* (International Court of Justice)

With a landmark, albeit controversial, decision, the International Court of Justice in 2007 settled the long-standing case Bosnia and Herzegovina v. Serbia and Montenegro *over the application of the 1948 Genocide Convention to atrocities committed in the region in the early 1990s. The fifteen judges concluded that the evidence before them showed not that the Serbian state had committed crimes of*

SOURCE: *Application of the Convention on the Prevention and Punishment of the Crime of Genocide (Bosnia and Herzegovina v. Serbia and Montenegro)*, 2007 ICJ, February 26, 2007, paragraphs 231, 370, 371, 379, 395, 396, 397, 412, 413, 415, 425, 429, 430, 431, 438, 439, 442, 447, 448, 449, 450

genocide in Bosnia (other than in Srebrenica) but that the Serbian state had failed to comply with its obligations, pursuant to Article I of the Genocide Convention, to prevent and punish genocide.

In this case the Court is seized of a dispute between two sovereign States, each of which is established in part of the territory of the former State known as the Socialist Federal Republic of Yugoslavia [FRY], concerning the application and fulfillment of an international convention to which they are parties, the Convention on the Prevention and Punishment of the Crime of Genocide. The task of the Court is to deal with legal claims and factual allegations advanced by Bosnia and Herzegovina against Serbia and Montenegro. . . .

In light of its review of the factual evidence before it of the atrocities committed in Bosnia and Herzegovina in 1991–1995, the Court has concluded that, save for the events of July 1995 at Srebrenica, the necessary intent required to constitute genocide has not been conclusively shown in relation to each specific incident. The Application however relies on the alleged existence of an overall plan to commit genocide, indicated by the pattern of genocidal or potentially acts of genocide committed throughout the territory, against persons identified everywhere and in each case on the basis of their belonging to a specified group. . . . The Court notes that this argument of the Applicant moves from the intent of the individual perpetrators of the alleged acts of genocide complained of, to the intent of higher authority, whether within the VRS [Army of the Republika Srpska, i.e., the Bosnian Serb Army] or the Republika Srpska, or at the level of the Government of the Respondent itself. . . .

The Court now must ascertain whether the international responsibility of the Respondent can have been incurred, on whatever basis, in connection with the massacres committed in the Srebrenica area during the period in question. . . . For this purpose, the Court may be required to consider the following three issues in turn. First, it needs to be determined whether the acts of genocide could be attributed to the Respondent under the rules of customary international law of State responsibility; this means ascertaining whether the acts were committed by persons or organs whose conduct is attributable, specifically, in the case of the events at Srebrenica, to the Respondent. Second, the Court will need to ascertain whether acts of the kind referred to in Article III of the [1948 Genocide] Convention, other than genocide itself, were committed by persons or organs whose conduct is attributable to the Respondent under those same rules of State responsibility: that is to say, the acts referred to in Article III, paragraphs (*b*) to (*e*), one of those being complicity in genocide. Finally, it will be for the Court to rule on the issue as to whether the Respondent complied with its twofold obligation deriving from Article I of the Convention to prevent and punish genocide. . . .

The Court . . . finds that the acts of genocide at Srebrenica cannot be attributed to the Respondent as having been committed by its organs or by persons or entities wholly dependent upon it, and thus do not on this basis entail the Respondent's international responsibility. . . . The Court must now determine whether the massacres at Srebrenica were committed by persons who, though not having the status of organs of the Respondent, nevertheless acted on its instructions or under its direction or control. . . . In other words, it is no longer a question of ascertaining whether the persons who directly committed the genocide were acting as organs of the FRY, or could be equated with those organs—this question having already been answered in the negative. What must be determined is whether FRY organs—incontestably having that status under the FRY's internal law—originated the genocide by issuing instructions to the perpetrators or exercising direction or control, and whether, as a result, the conduct of organs of the Respondent, having been the cause of the commission of acts in breach of international obligations, constituted a violation of those obligations. . . .

[The available evidence] does not establish a factual basis for finding the Respondent responsible on a basis of direction or control. . . . The Applicant has not proved that instructions were issued by the federal authorities in Belgrade, or by any other organ of the FRY, to commit massacres, still less that any such instructions were given with the specific intent (*dolus specialis*) characterizing the crime of genocide, which would have had to be present in order for the Respondent to be held responsible on this basis. All indications are to the contrary: that the decision to kill the adult male population of the Muslim community of Srebrenica was taken by some members of the VRS Main Staff, but without instructions from or effective control by the FRY. . . . The Court concludes from the foregoing that the acts of those who committed genocide at Srebrenica cannot be attributed to the Respondent under the rules of international law of State responsibility: thus, the international responsibility of the Respondent is not engaged on this basis. . . .

The Court now turns to the third and last of the questions set out [above]: has the respondent State complied with its obligations to prevent and punish genocide under Article I of the Convention? Despite the clear links between the duty to prevent genocide and the duty to punish its perpetrators, these are, in the view of the Court, two distinct yet connected obligations, each of which must be considered in turn. . . . The Court will . . . [first] confine itself to determining the specific scope of the duty to prevent in the Genocide Convention. . . . It is clear that the obligation in question is one of conduct and not one of result, in the sense that a State cannot be under an obligation to succeed, whatever the circumstances, in preventing the commission of genocide: the obligation of States' parties is rather to employ all means reasonably available to them, so as to prevent genocide so far as possible. A State does not incur responsibility simply because the desired result is not achieved; responsibility is however incurred if the State manifestly failed to take all measures to prevent genocide which were within its power, and which might have contributed to preventing the genocide. In this area the notion of "due diligence," which calls for an assessment *in concreto*, is of critical importance. . . .

A state's obligation to prevent, and the corresponding duty to act, arise at the instant that the State learns of, or should normally have learned of, the existence of a serious risk that genocide will be committed. From that moment onwards, if the State has available to it means likely to have a deterrent effect on those suspected of preparing genocide, or reasonably suspected of harboring specific intent (*dolus specialis*), it is under a duty to make such use of these means as the circumstances permit. . . .

In view of their undeniable influence and of the information, voicing serious concern, in their possession, the Yugoslav federal authorities should, in the view of the Court, have made the best efforts within their power to try and prevent the tragic events then taking shape [in Srebrenica], whose scale, though it could not have been foreseen with certainty, might at least have been surmised. The FRY leadership, and President Milošević above all, were fully aware of the climate of deep-seated hatred which reigned between the Bosnian Serbs and the Muslims in the Srebrenica region. As the Court has noted . . . above, it has not been shown that the decision to eliminate physically the whole of the adult male population of the Muslim community of Srebrenica was brought to the attention of the Belgrade authorities. Nevertheless, given all the international concern about what looked likely to happen at Srebrenica, given Milošević's own observations to [General Ratko] Mladić [chief of staff of the VRS between 1992 and 1995], which made it clear that the dangers were known and that these dangers seemed to be of an order that could suggest intent to commit genocide, unless brought under control, it must have been clear that there was a serious risk of genocide in Srebrenica. Yet the Respondent has not shown that it took any initiative to prevent what happened, or any action on its part to avert the atrocities which were committed.

It must therefore be concluded that the organs of the Respondent did nothing to prevent the Srebrenica massacres, claiming that they were powerless to do so, which hardly tallies with their known influence over the VRS. As indicated above, for a State to be held responsible for breaching its obligation of prevention, it does not need to be proven that the State concerned definitely had the power to prevent the genocide, it is sufficient that it had the means to do so and that it manifestly refrained from using them. Such is the case here. In view of the foregoing, the Court concludes that the Respondent violated its obligation to prevent the Srebrenica genocide in such a manner as to engage its international responsibility. . . .

The Court now turns to the question of the Respondent's compliance with its obligation to punish the crime of genocide stemming from Article I and the other relevant provisions of the [1948 Genocide] Convention. . . . The Court would first recall that the genocide in Srebrenica . . . was not carried out in the Respondent's territory. It concludes from this that the Respondent cannot be charged with not having tried before its own courts those accused of having participated in the Srebrenica genocide, either as principal perpetrators or as accomplices, or of having committed one of the other acts mentioned in Article II of the Convention in connection with the Srebrenica genocide. . . . For the purposes of the present case, the Court only has to determine whether the FRY was under an obligation to cooperate with the ICTY, and if so, on what basis, from when the Srebrenica genocide was committed in July 1995. . . .

From 14 December 1995 at the latest, and at least on the basis of the Dayton Agreement, the FRY must be regarded as having "accepted [the] jurisdiction" of the ICTY within the meaning of Article VI of the [1948 Genocide] Convention. . . . Turning now to the facts of the case, the question the Court must answer is whether the Respondent has fully cooperated with the ICTY, in particular by arresting and handing over to the Tribunal any persons accused of genocide as a result of the Srebrenica genocide and finding themselves on its territory. . . . The Court cannot but attach a certain weight to the plentiful, and mutually corroborative, information suggesting that General Mladić, indicted by the ICTY for genocide, as one of those principally responsible for the Srebrenica massacres, was on the territory of the Respondent at least on several occasions and for substantial periods during the last few years and is still there now, without the Serb authorities doing what they could and can reasonably do to ascertain exactly where he is living and arrest him. . . . It therefore appears to the Court sufficiently established that the Respondent failed in its duty to cooperate with the ICTY. This failure constitutes a violation by the Respondent of its duties as a party to the Dayton Agreement, as a Member of the United Nations, and accordingly a violation of its obligation under Article VI of the Genocide Convention. . . .

It follows from the foregoing considerations that the Respondent failed to comply both with its obligation to prevent and its obligation to punish genocide deriving from the Convention, and that its international responsibility is thereby engaged.

101 • Extermination as a Crime against Humanity versus Genocide (Guénaël Mettraux)

One of the most confusing genocide-related issues for nonlawyers is the difference between genocidal acts and extermination as a crime against humanity. Guénaël Mettraux, a defense counsel at the UN International Criminal Tribunal for the former Yugoslavia and other international courts and tribunals, highlights similarities and differences between these two international crimes in this section from his 2005 book on international crimes. Particularly noteworthy is the fact—rarely appreciated outside of international law—that it can be significantly harder to prosecute extermination as a crime against humanity than genocidal acts. Although any genocide prosecution requires a demonstration of the very demanding special intent requirement (i.e., proof that a defendant committed the genocidal act for which he stands accused with the intent to destroy, in whole or in part, a national, ethnical, racial, or religious group, as such), the number of victims who were affected by the genocidal acts can be very small indeed. In the case of extermination as a crime against humanity, on the other hand, no special intent requirement exists. However, as far as the actus reus (i.e., the physical element of the crime) is concerned, prosecutors must demonstrate not only that the defendant committed the offense as part of a "widespread or systematic attack against a civilian population" but also that a large number of persons died as a result of the extermination.

What distinguishes a crime against humanity from an ordinary crime (or from other international crimes [including genocide]) is the requirement that it must have been committed in the context of a "widespread or systematic attack against a civilian population." This requirement, which constitutes the chapeau or general requirements of crimes against humanity, must be seen as a whole and it sets out the necessary context in which the acts of the accused must be inscribed. . . .

"Extermination" [as a crime against humanity] consists first and foremost of an act or a combination of acts which contributes to the killing of a large number of individuals. Criminal responsibility for extermination therefore only attaches to those individuals responsible for a large number of deaths, even if their part therein was remote or indirect. By contrast, responsibility for one or a limited number of such killings is insufficient in principle to constitute an act of extermination.

Acts of extermination must, therefore, be collective in nature rather than directed towards singled-out individuals. Contrary to genocide, however, the offender need not have intended to destroy the *group* or part of the group to which the victims belong. The large or massive scale of the factual basis that must underlie the crime of extermination is what dif-

SOURCE: Guénaël Mettraux, *International Crimes and the Ad Hoc Tribunals* (Oxford: Oxford University Press, 2005), 155, 176–77, 178, 179, 338, 339. Reprinted with permission of the publisher.

ferentiates it from murder [as a crime against humanity]. Contrary to what might have been said in a number of unsupported decisions [i.e., judgments handed down by the International Criminal Tribunals for the former Yugoslavia (ICTY) and Rwanda (ICTR)], a single killing may not therefore qualify as extermination. . . .

Concerning the requisite *mens rea* [mental element] for that offense, the Prosecution must establish that the offender intended to kill a large number of individuals, or to inflict grievous bodily harm, or to inflict serious injury, in the reasonable knowledge that such act or omission was likely to cause death as in the case of murder. In addition, the accused must also be shown to have known of the vast scheme of collective murders and have been willing to partake therein. . . . Trial Chamber II of the ICTY noted that "the ultimate reasons or motives—political or ideological—for which the offender carried out the acts [of extermination] are not part of the required *mens rea* and are, therefore, legally irrelevant." The Prosecution must only prove that the perpetrator intended to kill the individual victim, with knowledge of the larger murderous context. As such, the perpetrator's motive in selecting his victims is legally irrelevant. . . .

Contrary to genocide, which may be directed at civilians and military alike, extermination (as with any other crime against humanity) may be committed against civilians only. Counter-intuitively, extermination is, from a purely legal sense, more of a crime of scale than even genocide. While . . . a conviction for genocide may occur [as far as the *actus reus* is concerned] even without the accused having killed or taken part in the killing of any one individual, extermination requires that the accused contributed to the killing of a large number of individuals. Also, while genocide may be attempted, it appears that at least in the law of the *ad hoc* Tribunals [i.e., the ICTY and ICTR], extermination only exists if and when a large number of individuals have in fact been killed. . . .

Also, there is generally a more direct link between the acts of the exterminator and the result which he intended to achieve than there may be with genocide: whereas the exterminator intends to kill many, and must, by his act or omission, cause death, the relationship between the acts of the genocidaire and the result sought to be attained (the destruction of the group in whole or in part) is often much more indirect and difficult to establish. How, for instance, can one establish that the transfer of a number of children to another ethnic group was intended to annihilate a group in the longer term, rather than, for example, to have been carried out for medical, social, or economic reasons (even if such reasons would not in themselves be legitimate or even lawful)? This ambiguity between means and ends stems from the fact that while extermination is exclusively a crime of the "murderous" genre, genocide is a more complex sort of crime, for which the route between acts of the accused and the result intended by him is generally much more difficult to trace. . . .

Criminal responsibility for extermination is therefore limited to those individuals responsible for a large number of deaths, even if their part therein has been relatively remote or indirect, while responsibility for one or a limited number of deaths would be insufficient to guarantee a conviction. Such a limitation does not apply in the context of genocidal charges where a single murder could, for instance, constitute genocide, all other conditions being met.

102 • Universal Jurisdiction and the "Butare Four"
(Luc Reydams)

Aside from the international adjudication of genocide, various countries in the past decade or so initiated domestic proceedings against suspected génocidaires. One of these countries was Belgium, which, invoking the principle of universal jurisdiction, in 1995 launched a comprehensive investigation of genocidal acts committed in the monastery of Sovu, Rwanda. The subsequent trial led to the conviction in 2001 of the "Butare Four," among them two nuns. The moniker refers to the location of the crime scene on the outskirts of the city of Butare, Rwanda's intellectual center. In this 2003 journal article, Luc Reydams, who teaches at the University of Notre Dame, puts the municipal trial in perspective. Although he finds merit in the courageous prosecution of foreign nationals in a Belgian court in an effort to combat impunity for international crimes, he chides the authorities for the long delay that accompanied the domestic proceedings. This, says Reydams, was incompatible with the defendants' right—enshrined in the 1966 International Covenant on Civil and Political Rights—to be tried without undue delay.

Prosecutor v. the "Butare Four" marks the provisional end of long drawn-out proceedings in Belgium against persons believed to be responsible for the genocide against the Tutsi and the massacres of moderate Hutu in Rwanda during the armed conflict between government forces (FAR) and the rebel army of the Rwandan Patriotic Front (RPF) from April to July 1994. The accused are the first persons tried and convicted on the basis of the 1993 Act Concerning Grave Breaches of International Humanitarian Law, the interpretation and application of which has led to (ongoing) domestic and international litigation. They were among hundreds of Rwandans from both sides of the conflict who fled to Belgium in 1994. Absent a treaty between Belgium and Rwanda, extradition of any suspect to Rwanda was *a priori* excluded....

The trial in May–June 2001 before a Brussels jury is part of multifaceted proceedings in Belgium and elsewhere [e.g., Switzerland and France] regarding the events in Rwanda. Acting upon an order of the Minister of Justice, in March 1995 an examining magistrate in Brussels launched a sweeping investigation that focused on, but was not limited to, incidents and suspects with a link to Belgium. Rwanda and several other countries lent their support by allowing Belgian investigators on their territory. At the request of the International Criminal Tribunal for Rwanda (ICTR) Belgium deferred its proceedings against a number of suspects and arrested several others. After much procrastination Belgian authorities decided to join the then remaining cases for the purpose of trial. The counts the four defendants were accused of took place for the most part in the southern Rwandan prefecture of Butare. For Tutsi and internally displaced persons, Butare was a source of hope, both as a way station to Burundi and as a refuge in itself since initially the prefecture had been spared violence. This changed with the removal of the Tutsi prefect on 17 April. In the following weeks tens of thousands were massacred.

SOURCE: Luc Reydams, "Belgium's First Application of Universal Jurisdiction: The Butare Four Case," *Journal of International Criminal Justice* 1, no. 2 (2003): 428–30, 431, 432, 433, 434–35, 436. Reprinted with permission of Oxford University Press.

The first defendant, Vincent Ntezimana, was a physics professor at the National University of Rwanda in Butare city. The prosecutor described him as one of the ideologues of the genocide, attributing to him the "Appeal to the Conscience of the Bahutu" [which ends with the notorious "Ten Hutu Commandments," reprinted earlier], an inflammatory manifesto that was published and circulated in Rwanda from 1991 onwards.... However, he was not formally charged with drafting the document, in part because it predated the 1993 [Belgian] statute.... The second defendant, Alphonse Higaniro, according to the indictment, was a member of the *akazu*, the inner circle of power around the presidential family, who had climbed all rungs of the hierarchy, to the level of cabinet minister. At the time of the events he was the director of the *Société Rwandaise des Allumettes* (Sorwal), a partly state-owned match company, as well as a board member of the infamous *Radio et Télévision Libre des Mille Collines*.... The third and fourth defendants, Consolata Mukangango and Julienne Mukabutera, were Benedictine nuns at the Sovu monastery (commune of Huye). During the conflict different groups of refugees, thousands altogether, sought refuge in the convent's compounds. According to the indictment, Mukangango, the convent's superior, discussed the fate of the refugees—whom she referred to as "garbage" (*saleté*)—with the local Interahamwe leader. Most refugees were eventually killed in three consecutive attacks on the compounds....

The prosecutor argued that the defendants were accessories and/or accomplices to murder and assassination under the Belgian and Rwandan penal code and to war crimes. The defendants were thus not charged with crimes against humanity or genocide, perhaps to avoid a possibly controversial retroactive application of the [Belgian] War Crimes Act as amended [in 1999, when crimes against humanity and genocide were added to the Act's list of punishable crimes]. The war crimes counts were brought under the [Belgian] Act Concerning Grave Breaches of International Humanitarian Law ... , under common Article 3 of the 1949 Geneva Conventions, and under Article 4(2)(a) of Additional Protocol II.... Over 100 witnesses testified during the eight-week-long trial.... The jury found all factual allegations against the four defendants to be proven, with the exception of some killings attributed to Ntezimana. The prosecutor asked for the maximum sentence, life imprisonment, citing the defendants' position of trust and authority in a traditional hierarchical society as an aggravating factor. The court after consultation with the jurors, pronounced the following prison sentences: 12 years for Ntezimana and Mukabutera, 15 years for Mukangango, and 20 years for Higaniro. The adjudication of civil claims was postponed....

The trial lends itself to a number of comments. Neither the defendants nor the Republic of Rwanda challenged Belgium's jurisdiction under international law. To be sure, Belgium was under no *obligation* to prosecute the suspects because the mandatory "try and extradite" regime of the 1949 Geneva Conventions does not apply to violations of common Article 3 and Additional Protocol II. Conversely, several facts militate strongly for a right to prosecute. Some pioneering decisions of the [United Nations ad hoc] tribunals for the former Yugoslavia and Rwanda have recognized certain "internal atrocities" as crimes under customary international law. [Furthermore] there were strong links between the armed conflict and Belgium, and extradition to the territorial state was legally impossible. The ICTR, although endowed with primary jurisdiction, declined to take over the proceedings. Belgium was thus faced with the dilemma of granting asylum to persons suspected of the most serious crimes under international law, or prosecuting them. In any event, Rwanda waived its right to protest by fully collaborating with the proceedings. . . . The determination of the forum thus was certainly not arbitrary, and in retrospect the venue was probably to the defendants' advantage. Compared with the sentencing practice of the ICTR and the Rwandan courts they got off lightly. . . .

One of the few legal arguments made by the defense was the objection to the admission of hearsay evidence. The court's decision to admit incriminating statements made by incarcerated witnesses as part of a plea bargain with foreign authorities may make some common law jurists knit their eyebrows. However, that decision does not contravene Belgian rules of evidence, which admit hearsay evidence, although they of course leave to judges the task of evaluating its credibility and probative value. . . . Although, all in all, the action of the Belgian court would seem to be meritorious, the fact remains, however, that after a swift and sweeping investigation by an examining magistrate it took the competent authorities nearly five years to commit the suspects for trial. Such a delay is hardly reconcilable with the right to be tried within a reasonable time. Then again, the delays at the ICTR are even longer. The trial [before the international tribunal in Arusha, Tanzania] of the *"Butare Six,"* which includes two suspects transferred from Belgium to the ICTR in 1996, opened shortly *after* the Brussels trial and was still going on in early 2003.

103 • Rwanda's *Gacaca* Jurisdictions (Lars Waldorf)

Hailed by many, understood by few, Rwanda's gacaca jurisdictions have received a great deal of attention in recent years on account of their ostensible inclusion of ordinary Rwandans in the adjudication of genocidal violence. Lars Waldorf, formerly of Human Rights Watch and now with the University of York, provides a critical introduction to what he describes as Rwanda's failing experiment in restorative justice in this 2006 essay. Although other, more positive assessments of Rwanda's extraordinary legal response to the 1994 genocide exist, Waldorf's critical approach is representative of leading scholarship on the topic.

Eight years after the 1994 genocide, the Rwandan government launched *gacaca* to speed justice and promote reconciliation. As grassroots justice, *gacaca* is appropriately named for the "lawn" where traditional dispute resolution took place. After almost three years as a pilot project, *gacaca* was expanded nationwide in early 2005: some 111,000 elected lay judges are now holding open-air genocide hearings in over 10,000 localities. In March 2005, the first *gacaca* trials commenced with *génocidaires* pleading guilty and receiving reduced sentences.

Several commentators have argued that restorative justice is better suited for postgenocide Rwanda than retributive justice, given the intermingling and interdependence of the majority Hutu and minority Tutsi, as well as the high levels of Hutu participation in the genocide. Generally, they have lauded *gacaca* for promoting a restorative justice model rooted in local, customary practices. In fact, *gacaca* has always been an uneasy mix of restorative and retributive justice: confessions *and* accusations, plea-bargains *and* trials, forgiveness *and* pun-

SOURCE: Lars Waldorf, "Rwanda's Failing Experiment in Restorative Justice," in Dennis Sullivan and Larry Tifft, eds., *Handbook of Restorative Justice: A Global Perspective* (London: Routledge, 2006), 422, 424–26, 429–30, 431, 432. Reprinted with permission of the publisher.

ishment, community service *and* incarceration. Early on, Penal Reform International warned that the implementation of *gacaca* was emphasizing legalistic retribution over socio-political reconciliation. Since then, *gacaca* has become increasingly retributive, both in design and in practice. . . .

Following the genocide, the [Tutsi-led] RPF [Rwandan Patriotic Front, which had ended the Hutu-led collective violence] rejected the idea of a South Africa–style truth commission, insisting that only retributive justice could end a culture of impunity. Soldiers, police, and officials arrested thousands of genocide suspects, often on the basis of vague denunciations. By 2001, approximately 120,000 genocide suspects were crammed into Rwanda's prisons and communal lock-ups under life-threatening conditions. From December 1996 to December 2003, Rwanda's courts managed to try about 9,700 people. The quality of justice has been poor due to political interference and a lack of resources. In an effort to speed up genocide trials and reduce the numbers of detainees, Rwandan officials turned for inspiration to *gacaca*, a traditional method of dispute resolution, where respected male elders (*inyangamugayo*, literally "those who detest disgrace") adjudicated disputes over property, inheritance, personal injury, and marital relations. Traditional *gacaca* did not treat cattle theft, murder, or other serious crimes. *Inyangamugayo* could impose a range of sanctions to achieve restitution and compensation. Punishment was not individualized; rather, family and clan members were also obligated to repay any assessed judgment. The losing party typically had to provide beer to the community as a form of reconciliation. By the late 1980s, *gacaca* had been transformed into a "semi-official and neo-traditional" institution used by local authorities to resolve minor conflicts outside the official judicial system. . . .

In the aftermath of the 1994 genocide, several Rwandan scholars rejected the idea of using *gacaca* to try genocide cases because it had never even been used to judge homicide cases. Instead, they proposed that *gacaca* function as local truth commissions. The government did not adopt that suggestion. . . . The government decided to modernize *gacaca* for use with genocide cases in 1999 and passed a law establishing *gacaca* courts in 2001. The law has been subsequently amended, most recently in June 2004. There is little tradition left in the modernized *gacaca* courts. . . . By contrast, the new *gacaca* system is a formal institution, intimately linked to the state apparatus of prosecutions and incarceration, and applying codified, rather than customary, law. *Gacaca* courts are judging genocide, "the crime of crimes," and meting out prison sentences. Finally, *gacaca* court judges are elected (often after being nominated by local officials). . . .

While the national courts retain jurisdiction over the most serious cases (involving planners, leaders, notorious killers, and rapists), *gacaca* courts will try lower-level perpetrators, as well as property offenses committed during the genocide. Murder, manslaughter, and assault cases are tried by the 1,545 sector-level *gacaca* courts and appeals from those cases will be heard by separate sector-level *gacaca* appeals courts. The 9,201 cell-level *gacaca* courts are responsible for pre-trial fact-finding and for trying property offenses (except where the parties have reached an amicable settlement). Each *gacaca* bench consists of nine elected judges (with seven constituting a quorum). . . .

Both the 1996 genocide law and *gacaca* law adopted the common law practice of plea-bargaining but the *gacaca* law introduced community service. For example, defendants who confess to killings before their names appear on the list of perpetrators compiled by the cell-level *gacaca* court will receive sentences ranging from seven to twelve years, while those who confess after their names are on the list will get twelve- to fifteen-year sentences. Regardless of the timing of their confessions, killers who confess will serve half their sentences doing community service. By contrast, defendants who refuse to confess and are found guilty of killing will be sentenced to prison for twenty-five to thirty years. . . . Persons who plead guilty are eligible to serve half their sentences outside prison doing non-remunerated labor three days a week in public or private enterprises. . . .

From a restorative justice perspective, *gacaca* has four major weaknesses: (1) it is not truly participatory; (2) it provides no compensation to victims; (3) it is "victor's justice"; and (4) it risks imposing collective blame on Hutu. . . .

Gacaca was initially hailed as participatory justice despite the fact that it was imposed on local communities in a top-down fashion by a highly centralized and authoritarian regime. Although early public opinion surveys indicated a high level of popular support for *gacaca*, it quickly became clear during the pilot phase that many Rwandans did not want to participate. . . . During the pilot phase, local officials sometimes coerced attendance. They ordered the local paramilitary forces to close down shops, round up people for *gacaca*, and prevent people from leaving *gacaca* sessions. They also fined, or threatened to fine, people who were absent. . . .

Restorative justice is impossible without reparations for survivors of mass atrocities. Eleven years after the genocide, the Rwandan government still has not created the long-promised compensation fund for survivors. That underscores the political marginalization of the Francophone Tutsi survivors, who have an uneasy relationship with the Anglophone, Ugandan born Tutsi who led the RPF. Until they were largely silenced in 2000, Tutsi survivors voiced disagreement with the RPF over several issues. . . .

Gacaca cannot produce restorative justice as long as it proceeds as victor's justice. The 2004 amendments [to the *gacaca* law] expressly prohibited *gacaca* courts from trying war crimes and crimes against humanity committed by the RPF's predominantly Tutsi soldiers against Hutu civilians in the period 1990 to 1994. The RPF engaged in widespread and systematic killings of an estimated 25,000 to 45,000 Hutu civilians during and immediately after the genocide. . . . Obviously, the RPF's war crimes cannot be equated to the genocide, either in scope or intent. But if the Rwandan government is serious about ending impunity and achieving long-term peaceful coexistence in Rwanda, it should provide some accountability for RPF killings. . . .

The real danger of *gacaca* is that it will wind up ascribing collective guilt to most Hutu. The inclusion of property offenses in the genocide and *gacaca* laws is legally dubious, trivializes genocide, and risks criminalizing many Hutu who engaged in opportunistic looting. Given large-scale participation in roadblocks and patrols during the genocide, a broad interpretation of accomplice liability could lead to mass inculpation. . . . Although *gacaca* was designed to speed genocide trials and reduce the detainee population (approximately 55,000 in September 2005), it is likely to have just the opposite effect: government officials estimate that new confessions and accusations may result in up to a million new suspects. . . .

The preliminary empirical data collected during *gacaca*'s pilot phase suggests that its restorative justice goals are unlikely to be met. In part, this reflects the enormous difficulty of achieving truth-telling, reintegrative shaming, and reconciliation in any society recovering from mass atrocity. However, it also reflects the deliberate choices of an authoritarian government whose commitment to justice and reconciliation for all Rwandans remains half-hearted at best.

104 · The Long History of the Khmer Rouge Tribunal (Kelly Whitley)

In 2007, some thirty years after the event, the Extraordinary Chambers in the Courts of Cambodia commenced in Phnom Penh the prosecution of domestic and international crimes committed by the Khmer Rouge in the mid- to late 1970s. It took almost a decade of negotiations between the United Nations and the government of Cambodia to get the ECCC off the ground. In this 2006 essay, Kelly Whitley, formerly of the Documentation Center of Cambodia, gives an account of the contentious history of the latest so-called mixed criminal tribunal established in the international system. By chronicling the drawn-out international politics of the ECCC's creation, she provides some of the background knowledge that is necessary for understanding why the prosecution of international crimes in Cambodia has been so mired in controversy ever since the ECCC took up its work. Much of this turmoil can be traced back to the imperfect institutional compromise that the UN and the Cambodian government entered into in 2003.

The reign of the Khmer Rouge in Cambodia ranks as one of the most horrific episodes in modern history. Between April 1975 and January 1979, the Democratic Kampuchea (DK) regime employed radical and brutal methods in an attempt to create an agriculturally based, "purely Khmer" society. . . . Flawed attempts to try Khmer Rouge leaders in domestic courts followed, but they had little international participation and did not result in arrest or punishment of any high-level DK officials. In essence, the crimes of Democratic Kampuchea have gone unpunished. Only in 1997, after nearly two decades of relative inaction by the international community on the matter, did the United Nations (UN) and Royal Government of Cambodia (RGC) begin to discuss establishing a tribunal to try the alleged perpetrators. Laborious and sometimes acrimonious debates ensued concerning the type and mandate of the proposed "Khmer Rouge Tribunal." . . .

In April 1997, the UN Commission on Human Rights opened the door for talks between the UN and the Cambodian government. In its annual report on Cambodia, the Commission requested that the UN provide assistance to the Cambodian government in bringing to justice individuals responsible for past human rights abuses. Two months later, co-Prime Minister Hun Sen and Prince Ranariddh issued a letter formally requesting United Nations help in ensuring criminal accountability for Khmer Rouge atrocities. Progress stalled in July 1997, however, when a complex series of events that many analysts have described as a "coup" effectively marginalized Prince Ranariddh and left Hun Sen in power as the country's sole Prime Minister. . . . After a significant delay, the UN Secretary-General appointed a group of

SOURCE: Kelly Whitley, "History of the Khmer Rouge Tribunal: Origins, Negotiations, and Establishment," in John D. Ciorciari, ed., *The Khmer Rouge Tribunal* (Phnom Penh: Documentation Center of Cambodia, 2006), 29, 38, 39, 40, 41, 42, 43, 44, 45, 46–47, 48, 49, 51. Reprinted with permission of the author.

experts to assess the feasibility of bringing former Khmer Rouge leaders to justice and to recommend the best legal process to achieve that goal. . . .

In February of the following year, the [three-person] team issued its report. . . . Of the three possible legal options—international, mixed, or domestic tribunals—the report concluded that the best legal option was to establish an ad hoc international tribunal. . . . Prime Minister Hun Sen, who was in control of the government following the events of 1997, immediately rejected the team's findings and claimed that prosecuting the Khmer Rouge would risk sending the country back to civil war. . . . The impasse between the United Nations and Cambodian government ended at the UNHCHR [UN High Commissioner for Human Rights] session in 1999. With broad international support, the Commission approved a resolution encouraging the Cambodian government to continue its cooperation with the international community. . . . Both the United Nations and Cambodian government appointed legal experts in local and international law to collaborate on drafting the enabling legislation. The UN side was headed by the organization's legal department, the Office of Legal Affairs, and Hun Sen created the Khmer Rouge Tribunal Task Force to lead negotiations for the Cambodian government. The talks between the expert groups began in late August 1999. They ultimately led to the October 2004 adoption by the Cambodian National Assembly of the UN-RGC Agreement and amended ECCC [Extraordinary Chambers in the Courts of Cambodia] Law. . . .

From the outset, the two sides had very divergent views of how the tribunal would be conceived. The differences were apparent with nearly every aspect of the tribunals. The Cambodian task force proposed that the trials take place within the existing domestic court system. The United Nations, however, envisioned that a special tribunal be established. Additionally, both the Cambodian government and the United Nations argued that judges from their respective "sides" should be in the majority. One issue that would be long debated concerned the appointment process for judges and prosecutors. The Cambodian task force proposed that the Supreme Council of [the] Magistracy, the body in Cambodia responsible for the judicial and prosecutorial appointments, would appoint all Cambodian judges, and the Secretary-General would nominate foreign judges after consultation with the Cambodian government. The UN's Office of Legal Affairs, however, held the view that the Supreme Council of [the] Magistracy lacked the necessary independence. . . .

Another obstacle related to personal jurisdiction. Both sides agreed that it was not realistic for the court to try persons from all ranks of the Khmer Rouge regime, but [that it] should focus instead on a limited number of cadres. UN officials argued that the criminal proceedings should include both senior leaders of the Khmer Rouge and those most responsible for the atrocities. A suggested number put forth in the 1999 expert report was between 20 and 30, a figure that Hun Sen adamantly rejected. His view was that the prosecutions would be highly selective, limited to only four or five senior Khmer Rouge leaders. Hun Sen asserted that the inclusion of more than a limited number of accused would guarantee violent reactions from the remaining Khmer Rouge forces. . . . The issue of the court's personal jurisdiction also ignited debate on a related matter: the Ieng Sary [Khmer Rouge cofounder and deputy prime minister as well as foreign minister of the DK regime] pardon. The UN position was clear; the possibility of any amnesties or pardons in cases of crimes against humanity was unacceptable. The Cambodian government, however, was reluctant to formally deny the King one of his constitutional rights. Hun Sen personally rejected the UN position, holding to his long-standing policy of exempting from prosecution Khmer Rouge defectors who had declared themselves loyal to his party. . . .

A draft of the enabling law was finalized and submitted to the Cambodian National Assembly in January 2000, and a copy was forwarded to the UN Secretary-General. Certain issues resurfaced. References to a majority of Cambodian judges remained. The issue of Ieng Sary's pardon was not resolved, and new problems emerged. . . . The perceived intransigence of the Cambodian position [in these and related matters] led to a UN announcement in February 2002 that it would withdraw from negotiations. . . . In a resolution sponsored by Japan and France in December 2002, the UN General Assembly authorized the Secretary-General to renew prior negotiations on the establishment of the tribunal. The resolution also pressed the legal experts to return to Phnom Penh to conclude negotiations on the terms demanded by Cambodia. . . . The two legal teams [of the UN and RGC] met a total of six times during January 2003 but failed to make progress. . . . Under strong public appeals by interested member states—including Australia, Japan, the United States, France, India, and the Philippines—to reach a compromise, the legal team returned for a final round of talks with the Cambodian task force.

On June 6, 2003, the United Nations and Cambodian government signed a draft agreement establishing a tribunal that would operate along the lines of the 2001 ECCC Law, but with modifications such as excluding amnesties or pardons . . . and simplifying the court structure from three chambers to two. . . . Adoption of the UN-RGC agreement and the amendments to the 2001 ECCC Law [was] a foremost government priority. The [Cambodian National] Assembly passed them in October. . . . In addition, UN and RGC negotiators agreed swiftly on the amount of money to be provided by each party to fund the tribunal over an estimated three-year period. The United Nations would provide US$43 million, and Cambodia would contribute US$13 million. . . .

Several years of negotiation led the United Nations and the Cambodian government to compromise on most of the important substantive and procedural questions involved in creating a Khmer Rouge Tribunal. Although both sides made significant concessions, the results of [the] negotiations generally accord more closely with the preferences and interests of the Cambodian government. UN and RGC officials appear to have reached mutually agreeable legal definitions of the crimes to be tried, as well as general agreement on the rules of evidence and a number of other important matters. However, on the most politically contentious issues surrounding the court's jurisdiction, structure and personnel, the Cambodian government has gotten more of what it wanted. . . . The result of negotiation [for example] favor the Cambodian government's interests by placing domestic judges in the majority on the mixed tribunal.

There will be two chambers within the existing Cambodian court system: a trial chamber and an appeal chamber. The *Trial Chamber* will seat three Cambodian judges and two international judges, and the *Appeals Chamber* will seat four Cambodian judges and three international judges. The Supreme Council of [the] Magistracy will appoint all Cambodian judges, as well as international judges nominated by the UN Secretary-General. Both chambers will require a super-majority decision, whereby there must be an affirmative vote of at least four judges at the trial chamber level and an affirmative vote of at least five judges at the appeal chamber level. The super-majority provision represents a considerable safeguard for advocates of stronger international control of the proceedings, but it also ensures that a coalition of international judges and a single "swing" Cambodian judge will be unable to establish a verdict. . . . The Cambodian government also secured relative control over other units within the Extraordinary Chambers. The *Pre-Trial Chamber* . . . will be composed of three Cambodian judges . . . , with one serving as President, and two international judges. . . . The Director of the *Office of Administration* will be a Cambodian appointed by the government, and he or she will be responsible for the overall management of the Office. . . . Prosecutorial duties will be more evenly split in the *Office of the Prosecutor*, comprising two co-Prosecutors, one international and the other Cambodian. . . . One Cambodian and one international Investigating Judge will also serve the tribunal. . . .

The international political forces described above prevented the United Nations or any combination of great powers from exerting enough influence to secure solid international control over the Khmer Rouge Tribunal proceedings. The result is a mixed tribunal that many human rights advocates view as a defeat for international standards of justice, fairness and due process. . . . Throughout the negotiations, the United Nations was resolute in maintaining that any tribunal established to try Khmer Rouge leaders must conform to the highest standards of international law. Nonetheless, Cambodian officials managed to secure their primary objectives at nearly every turn.

105 • Decision on the Prosecution's Application for a Warrant of Arrest against Omar Al Bashir (International Criminal Court)

In the summer of 2008, the Office of the Prosecutor (OTP) of the International Criminal Court requested a warrant for the arrest of Omar Al Bashir, the president of Sudan, on the suspicion that he, as head of state, was individually responsible for the commission of genocide and other international crimes in Darfur. In the spring of 2009, Pre-Trial Chamber I, one of the chambers in the ICC's Pre-Trial Division that deals with all matters in judicial proceedings until the confirmation of charges against an accused, granted the arrest warrant—although in part only. As explicated in the excerpted decision, the majority of the three judges found the genocide charges not tenable in light of the presented evidence. The Decision held that the OTP did not provide reasonable grounds to believe that either President Bashir or the government of Sudan acted with the specific intent to destroy in whole or in part the Fur, Masalit, and Zaghawa groups. On appeal, in February 2010 the ICC Appeals Chamber remanded the case back to the Pre-Trial Chamber I because the latter had applied a too demanding—and thus incorrect—standard of proof. The Appeals Chamber directed the Pre-Trial Chamber to decide anew whether or not the arrest warrant should be extended to cover the charge of genocide. The three-judge panel did so and in July 2010 issued a second, amended arrest warrant for the Sudanese president, noting that there were "reasonable grounds to believe that Omar

SOURCE: *In the Case of the Prosecutor v. Omar Hassan Ahmad Al Bashir ("Omar Al Bashir")*, Case No. ICC-02/05-01/09, Decision on the Prosecution's Application for a Warrant of Arrest against Omar Hassan Ahmad Al Bashir, March 4, 2009, paragraphs 4, 28, 40, 110, 111, 136, 144, 145, 157, 159, 160, 161, 163, 164, 204, 205, 206, 207.

Al Bashir acted with dolus specialis/*specific intent to destroy in part the Fur, Masalit and Zaghawa ethnic groups."*

On 14 July 2008, the Prosecution filed an application under article 58 [of the Statute of the International Criminal Court] . . . requesting the issuance of a warrant of arrest against Omar Hassan Ahmad Al Bashir (hereinafter referred to as "Omar Al Bashir") for his alleged criminal responsibility in the commission of genocide, crimes against humanity and war crimes against members of the Fur, Masalit and Zaghawa groups in Darfur from 2003 to 14 July 2008. . . . The Chamber is of the view that the Prosecution Application for the issuance of a warrant of arrest . . . can only be granted if the Chamber is convinced that the three following questions are answered affirmatively:

 i. Are there reasonable grounds to believe that at least one crime within the jurisdiction of the Court has been committed?

 ii. Are there reasonable grounds to believe that Omar Al Bashir has incurred criminal liability for [one of more] such crime under any of the modes of liability provided for in the Statute?

 iii. Does the arrest of Omar Al Bashir appear to be necessary under article 58(1) of the Statute? . . .

In relation to the jurisdiction *ratione personae* [personal jurisdiction], the Chamber considers that, insofar as the Darfur situation has been referred to the Court by the Security Council [by way of Resolution 1593 adopted on March 31, 2005], acting pursuant to article 13(b) of the Statute, the present case falls within the jurisdiction of the Court despite the fact that it refers to the alleged criminal liability of a State that is not party to the Statute, for crimes which have allegedly been committed in the territory of a State not party to the Statute. . . .

The Prosecution submits that there were reasonable grounds to believe that Omar Al Bashir bears criminal responsibility under article 25(3)(a) of the Statute for the crime of genocide as a result of: (i) the killing of members of the Fur, Masalit and Zaghawa ethnic groups (article 6(a)–Count 1); (ii) causing serious bodily or mental harm to members of the Fur, Masalit and Zaghawa ethnic groups (article 6(b)–Count 2); deliberately inflicting on the Fur, Masalit and Zaghawa ethnic groups conditions of life calculated to bring about the groups' physical destruction (article 6(c)–Count 3). . . . Nevertheless, the Prosecution acknowledges that (i) it does not have any direct evidence in relation to Omar Al Bashir's alleged responsibility for the crime of genocide; and that therefore (ii) its allegations concerning genocide are solely based on certain inferences that, according to the Prosecution, can be drawn from the facts of the case. . . .

The Majority observes that the practice of ethnic cleansing is not referred to in the 1948 Genocide Convention or in article 6 of the Statute. A proposal made [by the Syrian delegation] during the drafting of the 1948 Genocide Convention to include in the definition "measures intended to oblige members of a group to abandon their homes in order to escape the threat of subsequent ill-treatment" was not accepted. [It was rejected at the time by 29 votes to 5, with 8 abstentions.] Moreover, the ICJ [International Court of Justice] has recently emphasized in its [2007] Judgment on Genocide that: "Neither the intent, as a matter of policy, to render an area 'ethnically homogenous,' nor the operations that may be carried out to im-

plement such policy, can as such be designated as genocide: the intent that characterizes genocide is 'to destroy in whole or in part' a particular group, and deportation and displacement of
a group, even if effected by force, is not necessarily equivalent to destruction of that group, nor
is such destruction an automatic consequence of the displacement. As the ICTY [International
Criminal Tribunal for the former Yugoslavia] has observed, while 'there are obvious similarities between a genocidal policy and the policy commonly known as 'ethnic cleansing' . . . yet
'[a] clear distinction must be drawn between physical destruction and mere dissolution of a
group. The expulsion of a group or part of a group does not in itself suffice for genocide.'" . . .

Nevertheless, in the view of the Majority, this does not mean that the practice of ethnic
cleansing—which usually amounts to the crime against humanity of persecution—can never
result in the commission of the crime of genocide if it brings about the commission of the
objective elements of genocide provided for in article 6 of the Statute and the Elements of
Crimes with the *dolus specialis*/specific intent to destroy in whole or in part the targeted
group. . . . In this regard, the Majority recalls that, according to the consistent interpretation
of article 58 of the Statute by this Chamber, a warrant of arrest or a summons to appear shall
only be issued in relation to a specific crime if the competent Chamber is satisfied that there
are reasonable grounds to believe that the relevant crime has been committed and that the
suspect is criminally liable for it under the Statute. . . . As a result, the Majority considers that,
if the existence of a GoS's [government of Sudan] genocidal intent is only one of several reasonable conclusions available on the materials provided by the Prosecution, the Prosecution
Application in relation to genocide must be rejected as the evidentiary standard provided for
in article 58 of the Statute would not have been met. . . .

In the Majority's view, this conclusion, besides being fully consistent with the case law
of the ICTY and ICTR [International Criminal Tribunal for Rwanda] on the matter, is also
required by the application of the general principle of interpretation *in dubio pro reo*, embraced
by article 22(2) of the Statute. Moreover, it constitutes the only interpretation consistent with
the "reasonable suspicion" standard provided for in article 5(1)(c) of the *European Convention
on Human Rights* and the interpretation of the Inter-American Court of Human Rights in
respect of the fundamental right of any person to liberty under article 7 of the *American Convention on Human Rights*. . . . In this regard, the Majority highlights that a different interpretation would result in either an impermissible extension of the applicable law on proof by inference or an impermissible lowering of the standard of proof that, according to article 58 of the
Statute, must be met for the issuance of an arrest warrant. . . .

The Majority observes that the Prosecution, at paragraphs 366 *et seq* of the Prosecution
Application, provides for nine different factors from which to infer the existence of a GoS's
genocidal intent. . . . In the Majority's view, they can be classified into the following categories: . . . the alleged existence of a GoS strategy to deny and conceal the crimes allegedly committed in the Darfur region against the members of the Fur, Masalit and Zaghawa groups; . . .
some official statements and public documents, which, according to the Prosecution, provide
reasonable grounds to believe in the (pre) existence of a GoS genocidal policy; . . . the nature
and extent of acts of violence committed by GoS forces against the Fur, Masalit and Zaghawa
civilian population. . . .

The . . . analysis of the Prosecution's allegations concerning the GoS's genocidal intent
and its supporting materials has led the Majority to make the following findings: i. even if the

existence of an alleged GoS strategy to deny and conceal the crimes committed in Darfur was to be proven, there can be a variety of plausible reasons for its adoption, including the intention to conceal the commission of war crimes and crimes against humanity; ii. The Prosecution's allegations concerning the insufficient resources allocated by the GoS to ensure adequate conditions of life in IDP [internally displaced persons] Camps in Darfur are vague in light of the fact that, in addition to the Prosecution's failure to provide any specific information as to what additional resources could have been provided by the GoS, there existed an ongoing armed conflict at the relevant time and the number of IDPs, according to the United Nations, was as high as two million by mid-2004, and as high as 2.7 million today; iii. the materials submitted by the Prosecution in support of the Prosecution Application reflect a situation within the IDP Camps which significantly differs from the situation described by the Prosecution in the Prosecution Application; iv. the materials submitted by the Prosecution in support of the Prosecution Application reflect a level of GoS hindrance of medical and humanitarian assistance in IDP Camps in Darfur which significantly differs from that described by the Prosecution in the Prosecution Application; v. despite the particular seriousness of those war crimes and crimes against humanity that appeared to have been committed by GoS forces in Darfur between 2003 and 2008, a number of materials provided by the Prosecution point to the existence of several factors indicating that the commission of such crimes can reasonably be explained by reasons other than the existence of a GoS's genocidal intent to destroy in whole or in part the Fur, Masalit and Zaghawa groups; vi. the handful of GoS official statements (including three allegedly made by Omar Al Bashir himself) and public documents relied upon by the Prosecution provide only *indicia* of a GoS's persecutory intent (as opposed to genocidal intent) against the members of the Fur, Masalit and Zaghawa groups; and vii. As shown by the Prosecution's allegations in the case of *The Prosecutor v. Ahmad Harun and Ali Kushayb*, the Prosecution has not found any *indicia* of genocidal intent on the part of Ahmad Harun, in spite of the fact that the harsher language contained in the above-mentioned GoS official statements and documents comes allegedly from him. . . .

In the view of the Majority, when all materials provided by the Prosecution in support of the Prosecution Application are analyzed together, and consequently, the above-mentioned findings are jointly assessed, the Majority cannot but conclude that the existence of reasonable grounds to believe that the GoS acted with a *dolus specialis*/specific intent to destroy in whole or in part the Fur, Masalit and Zaghawa groups is not the only reasonable conclusion that be drawn therefrom. . . . As a result, the Majority finds that the materials provided by the Prosecution in support of the Prosecution Application fail to provide reasonable grounds to believe that the GoS acted with *dolus specialis*/specific intent to destroy in whole or in part the Fur, Masalit and Zaghawa groups, and consequently no arrest warrant for Omar Al Bashir shall be issued in relation to counts 1 to 3. . . .

Nevertheless, the Majority considers that, if, as a result of the ongoing Prosecution's investigation into the crimes allegedly committed by Omar Al Bahir, additional evidence on the existence of a GoS's genocidal intent is gathered, the Majority's conclusion in the present decision would not prevent the Prosecution from requesting, pursuant to article 58(6) of the Statute, an amendment to the arrest warrant for Omar Al Bashir so as to include the crime of genocide.

106 • A Prosecutor without Borders
(Julie Flint and Alex de Waal)

In their journal article published in 2009 anthropologist Alex de Waal, a research professor at Tufts University, and journalist Julie Flint deliver a trenchant critique of Luis Moreno Ocampo, the chief prosecutor of the International Criminal Court, and his handling of the investigation and prosecution of international crimes in Darfur, Sudan. They point to mistrust, mismanagement, and manipulation within the ranks of the Office of the Prosecutor.

Nine months after the Rome Statute [of the International Criminal Court] came into effect, in April 2003, the Argentinian lawyer Luis Moreno Ocampo was elected as the Court's first Prosecutor. He promised a "sexy court" that would dispense swift and telegenic justice comprehensible to faraway and often uneducated victims. Three countries referred themselves to the ICC over the next two years—Uganda, the Democratic Republic of Congo, and the Central African Republic—and in March 2005 the Security Council referred the case of Darfur. But it was not until March 2006 that the ICC took its first suspect into custody, a hitherto obscure Congolese militia leader named Thomas Lubanga Dyilo. . . .

Despite the challenge of building and operating an institution in an uncertain and evolving field of law, Moreno Ocampo had a strong wave to ride—the goodwill of publics across the globe, including a powerful American human rights constituency, and some of the ablest legal minds in the business. But three years into his tenure, many in the Office of the Prosecutor (OTP) were questioning his ability to do the job. A further three years on, and the Court is in trouble—a trickle of resignations has turned into a hemorrhage, and cases under prosecution and investigation are at risk of going calamitously wrong. The Lubanga trial has come to court under a cloud of controversy over the Prosecutor's handling of evidence and charges, and an arrest warrant issued for Sudan's president, Omar al-Bashir, has set in motion a chain of events that threatens a humanitarian disaster for the victims of the war in Darfur.

The first public signal of dissatisfaction with the Prosecutor was registered in July 2006 when the Court invited Antonio Cassese, the first president of the International Criminal Tribunal for the former Yugoslavia (ICTY), and Louise Arbour, the UN High Commissioner for Human Rights, to submit *amicus curiae* briefs, a kind of peer review. Both challenged Moreno Ocampo's performance. Addressing the Prosecutor like a teacher dressing down a particularly inept student, Cassese assailed every aspect of Moreno Ocampo's investigations but especially his failure to undertake even "targeted and brief interviews" in Darfur. Moreno Ocampo argued that Darfur was too dangerous for investigations and that victims and witnesses couldn't be protected from the wrath of the Sudan government. Cassese disagreed. He had led a UN Commission of Inquiry into Darfur in 2004 and had vigorously sought out and interviewed numerous witnesses in Darfur and Khartoum. Unlike Cassese, who mentioned Moreno Ocampo 36 times, Arbour made no personal reference to the Prosecutor. But she too told him how to do his job. She called for "an increased visible presence of the ICC in Sudan"

SOURCE: Julie Flint and Alex de Waal, "Case Closed: A Prosecutor without Borders," *World Affairs*, Spring 2009. Reprinted with permission of the Helen Dwight Reid Education Foundation

and made clear her belief that Moreno Ocampo was proceeding down the wrong track. Speaking with the authority of experience, she said, "It is possible to conduct serious investigations of human rights during an armed conflict in general, and Darfur in particular, without putting victims at unreasonable risk." Colleagues said Moreno Ocampo was enraged. He asserted that he was already "successfully carrying out an investigation" based entirely on evidence that could be gathered in safety outside Sudan. The Prosecutor dug in. From then on, senior staff said, it was "utter lunacy."

Although the Sudan government's minimal cooperation with the ICC ground to a halt in early 2007, court sources say that in 2006 an ICC delegation visiting Khartoum was invited to travel to Darfur. The invitation, like so many of the government's promises, may well have come to nothing. But Moreno Ocampo didn't call Khartoum's bluff. He didn't push at the door. The ICTY had made a point of opening branch offices in precisely the areas most hostile to it. Cassese's experience was that, with due care and courage, witnesses could be protected and evidence assembled. But Moreno Ocampo insisted that investigations inside Sudan were neither safe nor necessary. The OTP's original senior trial attorney for Darfur, Andrew Cayley, described the difference with the UN inquiry: "Cassese went personally to Kober prison and interviewed very sensitive witnesses. He demanded access with nothing more than a Security Council resolution. The OTP got no further than the Hilton Hotel." By the end of 2008, the Court had granted victim participation rights to just eleven Sudanese, as opposed to 171 Congolese and 57 Ugandans, and not a single case for witness protection on behalf of Darfurians had been presented to the judges.

The Prosecutor's next step was to issue a summons for two Sudanese whom he alleged were responsible for massacres. On February 27, 2007, he demanded that Ahmed Harun, minister of state for the interior and head of the "Darfur desk" that coordinated military and security operations in the region, and Ali Kushayb, a militia commander, present themselves in The Hague. Unlike in a domestic court, the ICC has a "Pre-Trial Chamber" of three judges who decide whether cases meet a relatively low threshold of reasonable grounds to conclude that a crime has been committed within the Court's jurisdiction. The Prosecutor has the option of public or sealed applications, with the latter offering the possibility of surprise arrests. A summons is the most modest step of all. The Pre-Trial Chamber considered the Prosecutor's request and, deciding that the men would never turn up of their own accord, issued arrest warrants.

Cassese damned the prosecutor's initiative with faint praise, saying "Better tiny steps than total inertia." Many in the OTP were dumbfounded by what several called Moreno Ocampo's "idiotic" insistence on summonses. The ICTY had shown how effective sealed warrants could be, and the ICC professionals believed that secrecy was their best, and possibly their only, chance of having Harun arrested—when he traveled abroad, as indeed he did in the very month the summons was issued. Was Moreno Ocampo still trying to win some cooperation from Khartoum? Colleagues find that hard to believe. Said one, "By the time Harun and Kushayb were named there had been several visits to Khartoum"—although not by Moreno Ocampo, who has yet to set foot in Sudan—"and it was abundantly clear that the Sudanese are masters at stonewalling, world-class prevaricators. It was obvious that the only way to get people delivered was a sealed warrant—unless you wanted to be seen to be doing something but not actually to be doing anything."

The role of ICC Prosecutor was always going to be extraordinarily difficult, under competing pressures from supporters and powerful detractors like the United States. Moreno Ocampo's greatest asset was an exemplary cadre of professional staff for whom working at the ICC was more than a career—it was a vocation. "I loved this job," an early recruit to the OTP told us. "It was my life." The Prosecutor had the opportunity to draw upon the accumulated expertise of existing international tribunals and some of the world's finest lawyers and investigators. This asset was rapidly squandered. Increasingly, Moreno Ocampo's staff found it difficult to agree with their own Prosecutor, whose penchant for publicity and extravagant claims rather than fine detail was the polar opposite of their own work ethic.

As the pressures on him mounted, Moreno Ocampo, in the opinion of many of his colleagues, began to "cut corners." They were incredulous when he announced publicly that he planned to intercept a plane on which Harun was scheduled to fly to Saudi Arabia for the Haj. If he really sought to arrest Harun, why advertise his own plan? The Prosecutor's harshest critics accused him of grandstanding: he knew, they said, that if the cases he was building ever came to court, and proved to be flawed, it wouldn't be on his watch. Some wondered if he was "making peace with the fact that he is never going to get these people arrested." Others suggested he was taking a maximalist position, very publicly, as the only way of showing the impact of the crimes committed.

As internal criticism grew louder, Moreno Ocampo listened less and took closer personal charge than ever. Many in the Investigations Division felt sidelined; in the Prosecutions Division, insufficiently consulted. A senior team member said the Prosecutor was "the most complicated and difficult" manager he had ever worked for, emotionally volatile and obsessed with micromanaging. Some tried to raise concerns, privately deploring the absence of "a culture in which objectivity and a critical review of the evidence with all its shades drives the institution." A key member of the OTP left, saying privately that he was fearful of having to defend an indefensible position a few years down the line. A second followed, saying the Prosecutor ran the OTP like a medieval kingdom. A third told us the OTP was run "like a police state," with a "culture of fear" that was "very real," and "sapping." He quit too.

Senior ICC staff who had worried over Moreno Ocampo's earlier caution were now puzzled by his zealous pursuit of the biggest culprits he could identify—and especially his determination to charge President Bashir with genocide, including for his policies toward the displaced camps in Darfur. Their concern was not so much that the Prosecutor was aiming too high, but the cavalier way in which he went about it. "The Prosecutor doesn't have the reflexes of a prosecutor, bringing to bear a sound judgment as to what is legally doable," one told us. Another said: "He cut corners in the Court's core business." Several felt he would have been better advised to confine his charges to the events of 2003–04, when, according to the Court's own crime base data, about 90 percent of the killings took place. . . .

The most strenuous public advocates of the Court also began to express their worries, albeit mainly in private. In September 2008, Human Rights Watch (HRW) wrote to the Executive Committee of the ICC to express serious concern over poor management practices in the OTP and about the effect this was having on the Court's investigations (and to criticize the prosecutor's "due process violations" in a matter relating to his own behavior, of which more later). HRW said the departure of senior staff in the OTP was having "a direct impact on the efficiency of investigations, and is particularly regrettable where due at least in part to the failure to develop a sufficiently supportive work environment." . . .

We have been told, by several sources, that Moreno Ocampo at first ruled out pursuing the Sudanese leadership. By the autumn of 2007, however, he had his sights on the president. In the words of one former colleague, "He jumped to the very top. He did not wish to have advice from attorneys." In addition, investigations into the Darfur case had diminished rather than expanded, and the Prosecutor was continuing to rely heavily on secondary material, including the 2005 Cassese Commission's sources—many of whom were unnamed and could therefore never be produced in a courtroom. . . .

In December 2007, Moreno Ocampo signaled his direction publicly in a briefing to the Security Council. Before going to New York, he had drafted a presentation outlining his theory that Bashir had designed a "two-stage" genocide—massacres in the villages in 2003–04, and then the "slow death" of the Fur, Masalit, and Zaghawa tribes in displaced camps. Colleagues had expressed concern, questioning the strength of his argument for genocide in the camps, and Moreno Ocampo reluctantly accepted a revised text. To their dismay, he repeated his original claims when he spoke in New York. . . .

There is much speculation, inside and outside the ICC, at how Moreno Ocampo arrives at his figures for death rates in Darfur. Unpublished UN monitoring figures for 2008 range from 60 to 350 violent fatalities a month, for an average of about 130. The activist group Genocide Intervention Network has a similar number, of around 150 a month. Moreno Ocampo has a very different figure. Speaking at a conference at Yale University on February 6, this year, the Prosecutor claimed that "as of today, 5,000 people are dying each month in Darfur," including through "slow death" by hunger and disease. The OTP itself possesses no specialist epidemiologists or demographers who might generate such figures, and no one working in Darfur proposes figures even remotely close to these. While some estimates for mortality during the peak of the crisis in 2004 generated figures this high, a specialist review of mortality data undertaken by the U.S. General Accountability Office wrote off high-end estimates as unreliable. In the last two years, relief agencies have warned of increasing malnutrition whenever the World Food Program cuts its rations or fighting erupts, but there is no evidence of a generalized famine on the scale that the Prosecutor insists is underway. Moreno Ocampo's arithmetic is simply fantastical.

Most of the controversy over the Bashir case has focused on the prudence of indicting a head of state in a fragile country prone to conflict. After a decade of attempts to coerce or overthrow the regime, the U.S. and European governments decided in 2001 to pursue the path of negotiation, leading in January 2005 to a peace agreement that brought a commitment to democratic elections and an end to twenty-one years of war between north and south. Slowly and painfully, with many setbacks and much resistance from the Sudan government, the key provisions of the "Comprehensive Peace Agreement" are now being implemented. There are serious problems still, especially over delineation of the north-south border, but a ceasefire has held most of the time, the northern army has withdrawn from almost all parts of the south, and a power-sharing government is functioning. Elections have been scheduled for this year and a referendum on self-determination for South Sudan for 2011. In Darfur, international efforts have focused on sustaining humanitarian access and deploying an international peacekeeping force, now approaching its mandated size of 26,000 men.

All this could be endangered by targeting Bashir directly. Many Sudanese fear that an arrest warrant could make things significantly worse, perhaps bringing about the very sorts of atrocities that the ICC is meant to deter. Moreno Ocampo disagrees. "For people in Darfur, nothing could be worse," he told *Foreign Policy* magazine. "We need negotiations, but if Bashir is indicted, he is not the person to negotiate with." Not even Darfur's rebel Justice and Equality Movement (JEM) has a position as militant as this—in Doha, Qatar, on February 17, JEM signed a "Declaration of Intent" with the government for a peaceful settlement of the conflict.

During the seven months that the ICC judges deliberated, Bashir made his position perfectly clear: "We are not looking for problems, but if they come to us we will teach them a lesson they won't forget." . . . Minutes after the arrest warrant was issued, Khartoum began expelling relief agencies, threatening at least 70 percent of humanitarian aid to 4.7 million people.

Less attention has been paid to the substance of the arrest warrant and the fact that the Pre-Trial Chamber threw out the genocide charges, Moreno Ocampo's principal reason for prosecuting despite the obvious risks. The judges wrote that "the Prosecution acknowledges that it (i) does not have any direct evidence in relation to Omar Al Bashir's alleged responsibility for the crime of genocide and (ii) its allegations concerning genocide are solely based on certain inferences that, according to the Prosecution, can be drawn from the facts of the case." In a remarkable humiliation for Moreno Ocampo, they proceeded (with one dissenting opinion) to dismiss those inferences. This will not have come as a surprise to the Prosecutor's most informed critic, his former senior trial attorney for Darfur. "Serious disagreement remains as to whether Al Bashir and the Sudanese government intended actually to destroy, in part, the Fur, Masalit and Zaghawa peoples of Darfur," Andrew Cayley wrote beforehand in a commentary on the genocide charges. "It is difficult to cry government-led genocide in one breath and then explain in the next why 2 million Darfuris have sought refuge around the principal army garrisons of their province. One million Darfuris live in Khartoum where they have never been bothered during the entire course of the war." Rony Brauman, a founder and former president of Médecins Sans Frontières—which has teams on the ground in Darfur—heaped scorn on the Prosecutor. "Can one seriously imagine Tutsis seeking refuge in areas controlled by the Rwandan army in 1994?" he asked. "Or Jews seeking refuge with the Wehrmacht in 1943?"

For Western nations committed to the ICC, and with interests in political stability and cooperation, Moreno Ocampo looks a lot less attractive than he once did. . . . Sudanese whose vocation is human rights find themselves torn: they want to see Moreno Ocampo pursue the highest ranking suspects and establish the principle that there can be no impunity for the most horrific crimes, but they remain fearful of a backlash in which ordinary Sudanese will once again find themselves in the firing line. They also fear that their hopes for a relaxation of Sudan's security laws and expectations for moderately free elections will be dashed when Bashir concludes that the Republican Palace is his safest, and perhaps only, safe house.

Moreno Ocampo is a man who diminishes with proximity. Six years after he became Prosecutor, the priceless human capital invested in his office is draining away. Lawyers and investigators who served in the OTP, and who count among the brightest and the best of their profession, say they believe the Court's reputation, and perhaps even its life, is at risk. Their desire to make a success of the court remains as strong as ever it was—but not under the current Prosecutor. "My time in the ICC was a mixture of a fascinating time and a terrible time," one of these exiles said shortly before Moreno Ocampo demanded Bashir's arrest. "The Prosecutor was erratic, so irrational sometimes that you felt despair. He uses his charisma in a negative way. Everyone in the OTP felt disrespected. But I still have a dream that one day—along with some other good people—I will be able to return."

CHAPTER SEVEN

Coping

How does one come to terms with genocide? Can it be done? This chapter attempts to bring into full view the human suffering that is an invariable consequence of genocide. It is concerned with the promise—and limits—of coping by way of self-examination. In the wake of the Holocaust, survivors turned like never before to art and autobiography in efforts to extract meaning from their extraordinary ordeals. This coping strategy continues into the present. Some of the most recent additions to the vast output of oral, visual, and written recollections, for example, are the drawings by children in Darfur. The selections brought together here give pride of place to those who suffered under the burden of having to live with the loss of life, identity, or self in the aftermath of genocide. It is mostly their voices that are being heard. A small selection of interpretative accounts frames and complements these moving first-person pieces.

Perhaps supreme among all efforts at giving voice to suffering is Paul Celan's haunting, modernist poem "Deathfugue," which is reproduced here in full. Autobiographical or quasi-autobiographical writings come from Jean Améry, Primo Levi, Saul Friedländer, and Charlotte Delbo, renowned writers all. Their theme is the suffering and survival of the Holocaust. Orhan Pamuk, the world-renowned author of *Snow*, writes of coping with genocide denial, recalling his recent brush with Turkey's criminal justice system for having acknowledged as historical fact the Armenian genocide. Writings by Rezak Hukanović and Roméo Dallaire feature less well-known examples of personal coping. Both were directly affected by the violence in the Balkans or Rwanda—one as a survivor, the other as a bystander.

Although the majority of selections in this chapter are first-hand accounts, a number of writings by scholars—including Theodor Adorno, Karl Jaspers, John Marcucci, and Linda Green—help readers discern what genocide can mean, in all senses of the word, to those whose lives have been wrecked by it.

Related is the review by David Denby, film critic at the *New Yorker*, of Claude Lanzmann's pathbreaking and much debated documentary depicting the Holocaust memories of both victims and perpetrators in *Shoah,* which raises complicated issues of remembering and forgetting. Another take on the problem of witnessing is provided by Lawrence Langer's seminal work, *Holocaust Testimonies.* Finally, there is coping by way of memorialization, with James Young guiding readers on a tour of Yad Vashem, perhaps the world's best-known site of institutionalized coping with the horrors of the Holocaust.

107 • Deathfugue (Paul Celan)

Perhaps the most haunting poem about genocide ever composed, "Deathfugue" was penned by Paul Celan, a Jewish Holocaust survivor from Romania whose parents were murdered in Ukraine. Inspired by accounts of concentration camp survivors who were returning to Romania late in 1944, the modernist poem (with its spliced and recombined sentence fragments as well as demanding imagery) was intended by Celan to be a literal depiction of Jewish suffering. In the eyes of some interpreters, the creativity of Celan's language and its metaphorical density constitute acts of defiance against the German idiom that he was unable to leave behind. John Felstiner's remarkable translation comes close to conveying the evocative language of the German original, notably the singsong rhythm that, in combination with the poem's fugue aspect, is its defining arrangement. As a poetic device, Felstiner subtly reintroduces the original language of some fragments, including Deutschland (Germany), "goldenes Haar" ("golden hair"), and "aschenes Haar" ("ashen hair"), and he retains the poem's final line, "der Tod ist ein Meister aus Deutschland" ("Death is a master from Germany"). The effect of this unexpected culmination in the German is one of apt disturbance.

Black milk of daybreak we drink it at evening
we drink it at midday and morning we drink it at night
we drink and we drink
we shovel a grave in the air there you won't lie too cramped
A man lives in the house he plays with his vipers he writes
he writes when it grows dark to Deutschland your golden hair Margareta
he writes it and steps out of doors and the stars are all sparkling
    he whistles his hounds to come close
he whistles his Jews into rows has them shovel a grave in the ground
he commands us play up for the dance

Black milk of daybreak we drink you at night
we drink you at morning and midday we drink you at evening
we drink and we drink
A man lives in the house he plays with his viper he writes
he writes when it grows dark to Deutschland your golden hair Margareta
your ashen hair Shulamith we shovel a grave in the air there you won't lie too
    cramped
He shouts jab this earth deeper you lot there you others sing up and play
he grabs for the rod in his belt he swings it his eyes are so blue
jab your spades deeper you lot there you others play on for the dancing

Black milk of daybreak we drink you at night
we drink you at midday and morning we drink you at evening
we drink and we drink
a man lives in the house your goldenes Haar Margareta

SOURCE: Paul Celan, "Deathfugue," in John Felstiner, *Paul Celan: Poet, Survivor, Jew* (New Haven, Conn.: Yale University Press, 1995), 31–32. Reprinted with permission of the editor and translator.

your aschenes Haar Shulamith he plays with his vipers
He shouts play death more sweetly Death is a master from Deutschland
he shouts scrape your strings darker you'll rise then as smoke to the sky
you'll have a grave then in the clouds there you won't lie too cramped

Black milk of daybreak we drink you at night
we drink you at midday Death is a master aus Deutschland
we drink you at evening and morning we drink and we drink
this Death is ein Meister aus Deutschland his eye it is blue
he shoots you with shot made of lead shoots you level and true
a man lives in the house your goldenes Haar Margarete
he looses his hounds on us grants us a grave in the air
he plays with his vipers and daydreams
   der Tod ist ein Meister aus Deutschland

dein goldenes Haar Margarete
dein aschenes Haar Shulamith

108 • Homines Ludentes (Jean Améry)

Born Hans Mayer, the Austrian writer Jean Améry, a member of the Belgian Resistance and an Auschwitz survivor, changed his name in the wake of World War II to dissociate himself from Germany, embracing the French language and culture instead. With the publication of Jenseits von Schuld und Sühne *(later translated into English as* At the Mind's Limits*) in 1966, Améry gained worldwide renown. Searching and thought-provoking, the book insists that the reality of Auschwitz— and that of the Holocaust—defies comprehension.*

When the big Auschwitz trial began in Frankfurt in 1964, I wrote the first essay on my experiences in the Third Reich, after twenty years of silence. At first, I did not consider a continuation; I merely wanted to become clear about a special problem: the situation of the intellectual in the concentration camp. But when this essay was completed, I felt that it was impossible to leave it at that. . . .

    I cannot say that during the time I was silent I had forgotten or "repressed" the twelve years of German fate, or of my own. For two decades I had been in search of the time that was impossible to lose, only it had been difficult for me to talk about it. Then, however, once a gloomy spell appeared to be broken by the writing of the essay on Auschwitz, suddenly everything demanded telling. That is how this book came about. At the same time, I discovered that while I had contemplated a good many questions, I had not articulated them with nearly enough clarity. Only in the process of writing did I recognize what it was that until then I had

SOURCE: Jean Améry, *At the Mind's Limits: Contemplations by a Survivor of Auschwitz and Its Realities*, translated by Sidney Rosenfeld and Stella P. Rosenfeld (Bloomington: Indiana University Press, 1980), xiii, 6, 7, 10, 11, 12, 19–20. Reprinted with permission of the publisher.

indistinctly caught sight of in half-conscious intellectual rumination and that hesitated at the threshold of verbal expression. . . .

In the beginning, at least, the intellectual still constantly searched for the possibility to give social expression to his thought. [But] in Auschwitz everything intellectual gradually took on a doubly new form: on the one hand, psychologically, it became something completely unreal, and on the other hand, to the extent that one defines it in social terms, a kind of forbidden luxury. . . . Not only was rational-analytic thinking in the camp, and particularly in Auschwitz, of no help, but it led straight into a tragic dialectic of self-destruction. . . . First of all, the intellectual did so easily acknowledge the unimaginable conditions as a given fact as did the nonintellectual. Long practice in questioning the phenomena of everyday reality prevented him from simply adjusting to the realities of the camp, because they stood in all-too-sharp contrast to everything that he had regarded until then as possible and humanly acceptable. As a free man he always associated only with people who were open to humane and reasonable argumentation, and he absolutely did not want to comprehend what truly was not at all complicated: namely, that in regard to him, the prisoner, the SS [*Schutzstaffel*, Defense Guard] was employing a logic of destruction that in itself operated just as consistently as the logic of life preservation did in the outside world. . . .

[For the unintellectual] the camp logic was merely the step-by-step intensification of economic logic, and one opposed this intensification with a useful mixture of resignation and the readiness to defend oneself. The intellectual, however, who after the collapse of his initial inner resistance had recognized that what may not be, very well could be, who experienced the logic of the SS as a reality that provided itself by the hour, now took a few fateful steps further in his thinking. Were not those who were preparing to destroy him in the right, owing to the undeniable fact that they were the stronger ones? Thus, absolute intellectual tolerance and the methodical doubting of the intellectual became factors of his autodestruction. . . . More than his unintellectual mates the intellectual in the camp was lamed by his historically and sociologically explicable deeper respect for power; in fact, the intellectual always and everywhere has been totally under the sway of power. He was, and is, accustomed to doubt it intellectually, to subject it to his critical analysis, and yet in the same intellectual process to capitulate to it. . . .

In the camp the intellect in its totality declared itself to be incompetent. As a tool for solving the tasks put to us it admitted defeat. However, and this is a very essential point, it could be used for its own *abolishment*, and that in itself was something. For it was not the case that the intellectual—if he had not already been destroyed physically—had now become unintellectual or incapable of thinking. On the contrary, only rarely did thinking grant itself a respite. But it nullified itself when at almost every step it ran into uncrossable borders. The axes of its traditional frames of reference then shattered. . . .

We did not become wiser in Auschwitz, if by wisdom one understands positive knowledge of the world. We perceived nothing there that we would not already have been able to perceive on the outside; not a bit of it brought us practical guidance. In the camp, too, we did not become "deeper," if that calamitous depth is at all a definable intellectual quantity. It goes without saying, I believe, that in Auschwitz we did not become better, more human, more humane, and more mature ethically. . . . We emerged from the camp, stripped, robbed, emptied out, disoriented—and it was a long time before we were able even to learn the ordinary language of freedom. Still today, incidentally, we speak it with discomfort and without real trust in its validity.

And yet, the time in the camp was not entirely without value for us (and when I say us, I mean the nonreligious and politically independent intellectuals). For we brought with us the certainty that remains ever unshakable, that for the greatest part the intellect is a *ludus* [game] and that we are nothing more—or, better said, before we entered the camp we were nothing more—than *homines ludentes* [men who play]. With that we lost a good deal of arrogance, of metaphysical conceit, but also quite a bit of our naïve joy in the intellect and what we falsely imagined was the sense of life. . . . Mostly, a few weeks in camp suffice to bring about . . . philosophical disillusionment, for which other, perhaps infinitely more gifted and penetrating minds must struggle a lifetime.

109 • The Question of German Guilt (Karl Jaspers)

A psychologist by training and a philosopher by vocation, Karl Jaspers, born in 1883, was removed from his post at the University of Heidelberg by the Nazis in 1939. On account of his moral fortitude during the "Third Reich," he became an important voice in post–World War II Germany. Through his postwar writings and radio broadcasts, Jaspers laid the foundations for the return of a civic culture. In The Question of German Guilt, *published in 1947 at the time of the Allies' Trial of the Major War Criminals at Nuremberg, Jaspers distinguishes four types of guilt — criminal, political, moral, metaphysical — and explores how guilty Germans are for the destruction of the European Jews.*

Almost the entire world indicts Germany and the Germans. . . . We Germans are indeed obliged without exception to understand clearly the question of our guilt [for World War II and the Holocaust], and to draw the conclusions. What obliges us is our human dignity. First, we cannot be indifferent to what the world thinks of us, for we know we are part of mankind—are human before we are German. More important, however: our own life, in distress and dependence, can have no dignity except by truthfulness toward ourselves. The guilt question is more than a question put to us by others, it is one we put to ourselves. . . .

Discussions of the guilt question often suffer from a confusion of concepts and points of view. To arrive at truth, we must differentiate. I shall begin by drafting a scheme of distinctions that will serve to clarify our present German situation. The distinctions are, of course, not absolutely valid. In the end, what we call guilt has one all-embracing source. But this can be clarified only by what is gained by means of the distinctions. . . . It is only after we have thought a thing through and visualized it from all sides, constantly surrounded, led and disturbed by feelings, that we arrive at a true feeling that in its time can be trusted to support our life.

We must distinguish between: (1) *Criminal guilt*: Crimes are acts capable of objective proof and violate unequivocal laws. Jurisdiction rests with the court, which in formal proceedings can be relied upon to find the facts and apply the law. (2) *Political guilt*: This, involving

SOURCE: Karl Jaspers, *The Question of German Guilt* (1947), translated by E. B. Ashton (New York: Fordham University Press, 2000), 21, 22–23, 24, 25, 26, 27, 30, 41, 67–68. Reprinted with permission of the publisher.

the deeds of statesmen and of the citizenry of a state, results in my having to bear the consequences of the deeds of the state whose power governs me [and] under whose order I live. Everybody is responsible for the way he is governed. . . . (3) *Moral guilt*: I, who cannot act otherwise than as an individual, am morally responsible for all my deeds, including the execution of political and military orders. It is never simply true that "orders are orders." . . . Jurisdiction rests with my conscience, and in communication with my friends and intimates who are lovingly concerned about my soul. (4) *Metaphysical guilt*: There exists a solidarity among men as human beings that make each co-responsible for every wrong and every injustice in the world, especially for crimes committed in his presence or with his knowledge. If I fail to do whatever I can to prevent them, I too am guilty. If I was present at the murder of others without risking my life to prevent it, I feel guilty in a way not adequately conceivable either legally, politically or morally. That I live after such a thing has happened weighs upon me as indelible guilt. . . .

This differentiation of concepts of guilt is to preserve us from the superficiality of talk about guilt that flattens everything out on a single plane, there to assess with all the crudeness and lack of discrimination of a bad judge. . . . All these distinctions become erroneous, however, if we fail to keep in mind the close connection between the things distinguished. Every concept of guilt demonstrates (or manifests) realities, the consequences of which appear in the spheres of the other concepts of guilt. . . .

The consequences of guilt affect real life, whether or not the person affected realizes it, and they affect my self-esteem if I perceive my guilt. (a) Crime meets with *punishment*. It requires that the judge acknowledge the guilty man's free determination of his will—not that the punished acknowledge the justice of his punishment. (b) There is *liability* for political guilt, consequently reparation is necessary and further loss or restriction of political power and political rights (on the part of the guilty). If the guilt is part of events decided by war, the consequences for the vanquished may include destruction, deportation, extermination. Or the victor can, if he will, bring the consequences into a form of right, and thus of moderation. (c) The outgrowth of moral guilt is insight, which involves *penance and renewal*. It is an inner development, then also taking effect in the world of reality. (d) The metaphysical guilt results in a *transformation of human self-consciousness before God*. . . . This self-transformation by inner activity may lead to a new source of active life, but one linked with an indelible sense of guilt in that humanity which grows modest before God and submerges all its doings in an atmosphere where arrogance becomes impossible. . . .

The guilt question received its universal impact from the charges brought against us Germans by the victors and the world [in the wake of World War II and the Holocaust]. . . . There can be no doubt that we Germans, every one of us, are guilty in some way. Hence there occur the consequences of guilt. (1) All Germans without exception share in the political liability. All must cooperate in making amends to be brought into legal form. All must jointly suffer the effects of the acts of the victors, of their decisions, of their disunity. We are unable here to exert any influences as a factor of power. Only by striving constantly for a sensible presentation of the facts, opportunities and dangers can we . . . collaborate on the premises of the decisions. In the proper form, and with reason, we may appeal to the victors. (2) Not every German— indeed only a very small minority of Germans—will be punished for crimes. Another minority has to atone for National-Socialist activities. All may defend themselves. They will be judged by the courts of the victors, or by German courts established by the victors. (3) Probably every German—though in greatly diverse forms—will have reasons morally to analyze himself. Here, however, he need not recognize any authority other than his own conscience. (4) And probably every German capable of understanding will transform his approach to the world and himself in the metaphysical experience of such a disaster. How that happens none can prescribe, and none anticipate. It is a matter of individual solitude. What comes out of it has to create the essential basis of what will in future be the German soul.

110 • The Meaning of Working through the Past
(Theodor W. Adorno)

Working through the past is an imperative frequently invoked in the aftermath of genocide. But what exactly does it entail? The acclaimed German sociologist and philosopher Theodor Adorno, cofounder of the Frankfurt School of critical theory, attempts an answer in this highly influential and widely debated 1959 essay. By tracing the history and engaging with the various connotations of the phrase "working through the past" (which in the German original is "Aufarbeitung der Vergangenheit"), Adorno opens a window onto the psychological state of a society replete with perpetrators, thereby shedding light on the politics of coping. The philosophical ruminations gained a broader audience when a radio version was aired in Germany in 1960. Aside from its general themes, the essay was a radical intervention in the conservative world of postwar Germany, for Adorno shone a bright light on the convenient "forgetting of National Socialism" that he diagnosed around him. By denouncing the "obstinate conviction of those who do not want to hear anything of" the Holocaust, he contributed to creating in West Germany the conditions that eventually gave rise to an official memory of the destruction of the European Jews.

The question "What does working through the past [Aufarbeitung der Vergangenheit] mean?" requires explication. It follows from a formulation, a modish slogan that has become highly suspect during the last years. In this usage "working through the past" does not mean seriously working upon the past, that is, through a lucid consciousness breaking its power to fascinate. On the contrary, its intention is to close the books on the past and, if possible, even remove it from memory. The attitude that everything should be forgotten and forgiven, which would be proper for those who suffered injustice, is practiced by those party supporters who committed the injustice. I wrote once in a scholarly dispute: in the house of the hangman one should not speak of the noose, otherwise one might seem to harbor resentment. However, the tendency toward unconscious and not-so-unconscious defensiveness against guilt is so absurdly associated with the thought of working through the past that there is sufficient reason to reflect upon a domain from which even now there emanates such a horror that one hesitates to call it by name.

SOURCE: Theodor W. Adorno, "The Meaning of Working through the Past" (1959), in Rolf Tiedemann, ed., *Can One Live after Auschwitz? A Philosophical Reader* (Stanford, Calif.: Stanford University Press, 2003), 3–4, 5–6. Reprinted with permission of the publisher.

One wants to break free of the past: rightly, because nothing at all can live in its shadow, and because there will be no end to the terror as long as guilt and violence are repaid with guilt and violence; wrongly, because the past that one would like to evade is still very much alive. National Socialism lives on, and even today we still do not know whether it is merely the ghost of what was so monstrous that it lingers on after its own death, or whether it has not yet died at all, whether the willingness to commit the unspeakable survives in people as well as in the conditions that enclose them. . . . Nobody disputes the fact that in Germany it is not merely among the so-called incorrigibles, if that term must be used, that the past has not been mastered. Again and again one hears of the so-called guilt-complex, often with the association that it was actually first created by the construction of a German collective guilt. Undoubtedly there is much that is neurotic in the relation to the past: defensive postures where one is not attacked, intense affects where they are hardly warranted by the situation, an absence of affect in the face of the gravest matters, not seldom simply a repression of what is known or half-known. . . . Despite all this, however, talk of a guilt complex has something untruthful to it.

Psychiatry, from which the concept is borrowed with all its attendant associations, maintains that the feeling of guilt is pathological, unsuited to reality, psychogenic, as the analysts call it. The word "complex" is used to give the impression that the guilt—which so many ward off, abreact, and distort through the silliest rationalizations—is actually no guilt at all but rather exists in them, in their psychological disposition: the terribly real past is trivialized into merely a figment of the imagination of those who are affected by it. Or is guilt itself perhaps merely a complex, and bearing the burden of the past pathological, whereas the healthy and realistic person is fully absorbed in the present and its practical goals? Such a view would draw the moral from the saying: "And it's as good as if it never happened," which comes from Goethe but, at a crucial passage in *Faust*, is uttered by the devil in order to reveal his innermost principle, the destruction of memory. The murdered are to be cheated out of the single remaining thing that our powerlessness can offer them: remembrance.

The obstinate conviction of those who do not want to hear anything of it does indeed coincide with a powerful historical tendency. . . . Empirical findings, for example, that the younger generation often does not know who Bismarck and Kaiser Wilhelm I were, have confirmed this suspicion of the loss of history. Thus the forgetting of National Socialism surely should be understood far more in terms of the general situation of society than in terms of psychopathology. Even the psychological mechanisms used to defend against painful and unpleasant memories serve highly realistic ends. . . . The effacement of memory is more the achievement of an all-too-alert consciousness than its weakness when confronted with the superior strength of unconscious processes. In the forgetting of what has scarcely transpired there resonates the fury of one who must first talk himself out of what everyone knows, before he can then talk others out of it as well.

Surely the impulses and modes of behavior involved here are not immediately rational insofar as they distort the facts they refer to. However, they are rational in the sense that they rely on societal tendencies and that anyone who so reacts knows he is in accord with the spirit of the times. Such a reaction immediately fits in well with the desire to get on with things.

111 • The Gray Zone (Primo Levi)

Primo Levi's notion of the "gray zone" is one of the most unsettling ideas coming out of the work of this Italian chemist and Auschwitz survivor. Levi developed his concept in The Drowned and the Saved, *his 1989 collection of analytical essays aimed at approximating "understanding" of the death camp experience. The zone Levi speaks of refers to the moral ground among inmates, the grayness to the uncertain moral boundaries of this zone. Thus the gray zone was inhabited by "prisoner-functionaries" who were ready to collaborate with the Nazi authorities in order to ensure their own survival. They ranged from Kapos (thought to be short for the German* Kameradschaftspolizei, *which loosely translates as "comrade police" and refers to prisoners who aided Nazi concentration camp personnel in the policing of their fellow inmates) who supervised and brutalized their fellow inmates to Sonderkommandos, or "special squads," whose task it was to prepare, work, and empty the gas chambers and crematoria.*

Have we—we who have returned—been able to understand and make others understand our experience? What we commonly mean by "understand" coincides with "simplify": without a profound simplification the world around us would be an infinite, undefined tangle that would defy our ability to orient ourselves and decide upon our actions. In short, we are compelled to reduce the knowable to a schema: with this purpose in view we have built for ourselves admirable tools in the course of evolution, tools which are the specific property of the human species—language and conceptual thought.

We also tend to simplify history, but the pattern within which events are ordered is not always identifiable in a single, unequivocal fashion, and therefore different historians may understand and construe history in ways that are incompatible with one another. Nevertheless, perhaps for reasons that go back to our origins as social animals, the need to divide the field into "we" and "they" is so strong that this pattern, this bipartisan—friend/enemy—prevails over all others. Popular history, and also the history taught in schools, is influenced by this Manichean tendency, which shuns half-tints and complexities: it is prone to reduce the river of human occurrences to conflicts, and the conflicts to duals—we and they, Athenians and Spartans, Romans and Carthaginians. . . .

The *desire* for simplification is justified, but the same does not always apply to simplification itself, which is a working hypothesis, useful as long as it is recognized as such and not mistaken for reality. The greater part of historical and natural phenomena are not simple, or not simple in the way that we would like. Now, the network of human relationships inside the Lagers [i.e., the Nazi concentration camps] was not simple: it could not be reduced to the two blocs of victims and persecutors. Anyone who today reads (or writes) the history of the Lager reveals the tendency, indeed the need, to separate evil from good, to be able to take sides, to emulate Christ's gesture on Judgment Day: here the righteous, over there the reprobates.

The young above all demand clarity, a sharp cut; their experience of the world being meager, they do not like ambiguity. In any case, their expectation reproduces exactly that of

SOURCE: Primo Levi, *The Drowned and the Saved*, translated by Raymond Rosenthal (New York: Vintage, 1989), 36–38, 39–40, 41, 42, 43–44. Reprinted with permission of the publisher.

the newcomers to the Lagers, whether young or not; all of them, with the exception of those who had already gone through analogous experience, expected to find a terrible but decipherable world, in conformity with that simple model which we atavistically carry within us— "we" inside and the enemy outside, separated by a sharply defined geographic frontier. Instead, the arrival in the Lager was indeed a shock because of the surprise it entailed. The world into which one was precipitated was terrible, yes, but also indecipherable: it did not conform to any model; the enemy was all around but also inside, the "we" lost its limits, the contenders were not two, one could not discern a single frontier but rather many confused, perhaps innumerable frontiers, which stretched between each of us.

One entered hoping at least for the solidarity of one's companions in misfortune, but the hoped for allies, except in special cases, were not there; there were instead a thousand sealed off monads, and between them a desperate covert and continuous struggle. . . . Rarely was a newcomer received, I won't say as a friend but at least as a companion-in-misfortune; in the majority of cases, those with seniority (and seniority was acquired in three or four months; the changeover was swift!) showed irritation or even hostility. The "newcomer" (*Zugang*: one should note that in German this is an abstract, administrative term, meaning "access," "entry") was envied because he still seemed to have on him the smell of home, and it was absurd envy, because in fact one suffered much more during the first days of imprisonment than later on, when habituation on one hand and experience on the other made it possible to construct oneself a shelter. He was derided and subjected to cruel pranks, as happens in all communities with "conscripts" and "rookies," as well as in the initiation ceremonies of primitive peoples: and there is no doubt that life in the Lager involved a regression, leading back precisely to primitive behavior. It is probable that the hostility toward the Zugang was in substance motivated like all other forms of intolerance, that is, it consisted in an unconscious attempt to consolidate the "we" at the expense of the "they," to create, in short, that solidarity among the oppressed whose absence was the source of additional suffering, even though not perceived openly. . . .

Now, one mustn't forget that the greater part of the memories, spoken or written, of those who came back begin with the collision with the concentrationary reality and, simultaneously, the unforeseen and uncomprehended aggression on the part of a new and strange enemy, the functionary-prisoner, who instead of taking you by the hand, reassuring you, teaching you the way, throws himself at you, screaming in a language you do not understand, and strikes you in the face. He wants to tame you, extinguish any spark of dignity that he has lost and you perhaps still preserve. . . . I remember now that the local Yiddish and Polish term to indicate privilege was *protekcja*, pronounced "proteksia," and is of obvious Italian and Latin origin. . . . The ascent of the privileged, not only in the Lager but in all human coexistence, is an anguishing but unfailing phenomenon: only in utopias is it absent. It is the duty of righteous men to make war on all undeserved privilege, but one must not forget that this is a war without end. Where power is exercised by few or only one against many, privilege is born and proliferates, even against the will of the power itself. On the other hand, it is normal for power to tolerate and encourage privilege.

Let us confine ourselves to the Lager, which (even in its Soviet version) can be considered an excellent "laboratory": the hybrid class of the prisoner-functionary constitutes its armature and at the same time its most disquieting feature. It is a gray zone poorly defined, where the two camps of masters and servants both diverge and converge. This gray zone possesses an incredibly complicated internal structure and contains within itself enough to confuse our need to judge. The gray zone of *protekcja* and collaboration springs from multiple roots. . . . In contrast to a certain hagiographic and rhetorical stylization, the harsher the oppression, the more widespread among the oppressed is the willingness, with all its infinite nuances and motivations, to collaborate: terror, ideological seduction, servile imitation of the victor, myopic desire for any power whatsoever, even though ridiculously circumscribed in space and time, cowardice, and, finally, lucid calculation aimed at eluding the imposed orders and order. All these motives, singly or combined, have come into play in the creation of this gray zone, whose components are bonded together by the wish to preserve and consolidate established privilege vis-à-vis those without privilege.

Before discussing separately the motives that impelled some prisoners to collaborate to some extent with the Lager authorities, however, it is necessary to declare the imprudence of issuing hasty moral judgment on such human cases. Certainly, the greatest responsibility lies with the system, the very structure of the totalitarian state; the concurrent guilt on the part of individual big and small collaborators (never likable, never transparent!) is always difficult to evaluate. It is a judgment that we would like to entrust only to those who found themselves in similar circumstances and had the opportunity to test for themselves what it means to act in a state of coercion.

112 • When Memory Comes (Saul Friedländer)

Saul Friedländer, a professor of history at the University of California, Los Angeles, survived the Holocaust in France, hidden away in a Catholic boarding school. Aside from major contributions to the history of the destruction of the European Jews, he is the author of a very personal account of remembrance and forgetting in the wake of genocide. When Memory Comes *was published in 1979 and widely praised. In it Friedländer tells of his unsettling encounters with his past while he was traveling in Germany in the 1960s and 1970s. On these occasions, he felt conflicting emotions. On the one hand, the country reminded him of danger, made him feel entrapped and desolate. On the other hand, it was impossible to block out pleasant feelings of familiarity: "the language, the streets, the songs, the waters of the Rhine." But these feelings gave way to strangeness as soon as he heard the protestations of ordinary Germans not to have known anything, not to have done anything. "Words, phrases, denials," as the survivor puts it.*

At my guardian's, recent events were one subject of our conversations. For instance, near our little city the Vichy militia—or was it Germans?—had flung some thirty Jews into a well and then crushed them to death beneath a pile of stones they threw in after them. Of these stories, those dealing with the camps themselves naturally impressed me more than the rest. The names of Belzec and Maidanek struck me particularly. I wanted to write.

SOURCE: Saul Friedlander, *When Memory Comes*, translated by Helen R. Lane (New York: Farrar, Straus and Giroux, 1979), 155–56, 143, 144–46. Reprinted with permission of the publisher.

On Saturday night after dinner, everyone left for the movies except me. I contemplated the oilcloth on the dinner table, still covered with crumbs and spots of grease, then stared at the damp spots on the wallpaper. I was trying to hypnotize myself somehow, to put myself in a different state so that the first words of a poem would burst forth from me. But nothing happened. The spots remained spots, and Belzec and Maidanek disappeared in a distant fog, despite the various things that I could call to mind. It was only much later, on thinking about these efforts, that I understood that what was missing was not literary talent, but rather a certain ability to identify.

The veil between events and me had not been rent. I had lived on the edges of the catastrophe; a distance—impassable, perhaps—separated me from those who had been directly caught up in the tide of events, and despite all my efforts, I remained, in my own eyes, not so much a victim as—a spectator. I was destined, therefore, to wander among several worlds, knowing them, understanding them— better, perhaps than many others—but nonetheless incapable of feeling an identification without any reticence, incapable of seeing, understanding and belonging in a single immediate, total movement. Hence—need I say?—my enormous difficulty in writing this book. . . .

Classes have begun again. Students are soaking up sunshine on the lawn in front of the seminar room; at the entrance to the library there is the usual busy traffic back and forth that marks the beginning of a school year. . . . Anyway, what are the values being transmitted here? . . . And what are the values that I myself can transmit? Can experience as personal, as contradictory as mine rouse an echo here, in even the most indirect way? I am not sure. But must I then limit myself to the neutral indifference of the technician, or alternatively pretend that I have roots, play at normality, and return to clear thoughts, those which help one to live and, perhaps, to die? Isn't the way out for me to attach myself to the necessary order, the inescapable simplification forced upon one by the passage of time and one's vision of history, to adopt the gaze of the historian?

In 1961, . . . I finally started back on the road to the university. Through the shifting prism of eyewitness accounts, stories, documents in archives, I tried to grasp the meaning of a period and reestablish the coherency of a past, my own. Through interviews as well. And so it was that at the end of 1962 I left for Aumühle, in northern Germany near the Danish frontier, to meet there the man who had commanded the German navy and after Hitler's suicide had become, for just a few days, the head of the Reich in ruins, ex–Grand Admiral Doenitz, sentenced to ten years' imprisonment by the Nuremberg Tribunal. . . . When I reached Mannheim the peaceful, unshadowed landscape that slipped by on both sides of the road suddenly began to look different to me. I would not call it anxiety or panic, but a strange feeling of desolation: this Autobahn was shutting me up in Germany forever; on every hand were Germans, nothing but Germans. I felt caught in a blind trap. In the ponderous cars going past me, the faces seemed suddenly bloated with a rancid, reddish grease; on the shoulder of the road the signs— in German!—represented so many cold injunctions, issued by an all-powerful, destructive, police-state bureaucracy.

Since then, I have often returned to Germany. More than once, the same sensation has come over me, though less intense and more complex. On the one hand—danger, a trap, desolation—but at the same time a feeling of familiarity, pleasant familiarity: the language, the streets, the songs, the waters of the Rhine that I had seen only once, at Kehl, the hillsides covered with grapevines, the old castles and the baroque churches—everything was thoroughly familiar to me. And so at the archives in Bonn, Koblenz, or Freiburg, I would read my records, those of the Ministry of Foreign Affairs of the Reich, those of the Ministry of Propaganda, and others; but when night came, how many times have I hesitated between the attractions of a *Weinstube* [wine bar] as familiar as everything else and the imperative need to pack my suitcases immediately, flee instantly, go back across the border at all costs . . . .

It was only at this time in my life, when I was around thirty, that I realized how much the past molded my vision of things, how much the essential appeared to me through a particular prism that could never be eliminated. But did it have to be eliminated? A great number of us go through life this way, insensible to a whole range of shades and tones, though, despite everything, the eye still manages to penetrate, in certain situations, far beyond the neutral, aseptic, normal meanings that reality presents. If our reactions may sometimes seem strange, let there be no mistake about it: behind the harmless surface of words and things, we know that at any and every moment abysses await us.

I have a precise memory of my conversation with Admiral Doenitz, but it is as though it has been transposed into fantasy. He received me at nightfall, sitting at a massive desk. Behind him, large windows overlooked a garden. The daylight was fading; no one turned on the lights in the room, and so we were talking in twilight. "I assure you that I knew nothing about the extermination of the Jews." Words, phrases, denials. I was tired all of a sudden, tired in advance. Did one only have to deny the past, deny it steadfastly, in order for that past to disappear forever? What was I doing here, in front of this enigmatic man, who was not going to give me so much as a glimpse of the world I was seeking to unveil? It was almost dark now and the narrow halo of light that illuminated the desk gave the figure, the room, the interview a vaguely fantastic quality: "Sir, can you give me your word of honor as a German grand admiral that you knew nothing?" The response came immediately, clipped words without a shadow of hesitation: "I give you my word of honor as a German grand admiral that I knew nothing."

A few months ago I saw Joachim Fest's film, *Hitler: A Career,* in a movie theater in Munich. The dazzling rise, the titanic energy, the Luciferian fall: it is all there. As for the extermination of the Jews, a few words in passing, no more. An inconsequential shadow on this grandiose tableau. For anyone who does not know the facts, the power and the glory still remain, followed by a veritable vengeance of the gods; or the long roll calls in the night, in front of the Feldherrnhalle, illuminated by thousands of torches, draped in flags bearing the swastika:

"Felix Alfahrth!"
"Present!"
"Andreas Bauriedl!"
"Present!"

For anyone who does not know the facts, the mystical communion with the brownshirt revolution and its martyrs still remains. Thus is evidence transformed over the years, thus do memories crumble away.

113 • Useless Knowledge (Charlotte Delbo)

Author of Auschwitz and After, *the French writer Charlotte Delbo ranks among the most important intellectuals to have turned their experiences as concentration camp survivors into art and commentary. Unlike the work of Eli Wiesel and Primo Levi, Delbo's autobiographical writings, published
in 1995, are not immediately accessible. For example, she reflects on her return from Auschwitz-
Birkenau by creating an assemblage of widely different text formats: poems, vignettes, fragments.
Her theme, here and elsewhere, is the impossibility of comprehending the genocide experience, which,
in turn, explains her adoption of a decidedly postmodern literary style.*

> O you who know
> did you know that hunger makes the eyes sparkle that thirst dims them
> O you who know
> did you know that you can see your mother dead
> and not shed a tear
> O you who know
> did you know that in the morning you wish for death
> and in the evening you fear it
> O you who know
> did you know that a day is longer than a year
> a minute longer than a lifetime
> O you who know
> did you know that legs are more vulnerable than eyes
> nerves harder than bones
> the heart firmer than steel
> Did you know that the stones of the road do not weep
> that there is one word only for dread
> one for anguish
> Did you know that suffering is limitless
> that horror cannot be circumscribed
> Did you know this
> You who know.

. . . You may say that one can take away everything from a human being except the faculty
of thinking and imagining. You have no idea. One can turn a human being into a skeleton
gurgling with diarrhea, without time or energy to think. Imagination is the first luxury of a
body receiving sufficient nourishment, enjoying a margin of free time, possessing the rudi-
ments from which dreams are fashioned. People did not dream in Auschwitz, they were in a
state of delirium. And yet, you might counter, each had a stock of memories? No, one couldn't
be sustained by one's past, draw on its resources. It had become unreal, unbelievable. Everything that had been our previous experience had unraveled. To speak was our only escape, our

SOURCE: Charlotte Delbo, *Auschwitz and After*, translated by Rosette C. Lamont (New Haven, Conn.: Yale
University Press, 1995), 168, 255, 268, 242, 258, 225. Reprinted with permission of the publisher.

mad raving. What did we speak of? Material, usable things. We had to omit anything that might awaken pain or regret. We never spoke of love. . . .

Each one had taken along his or her memories, the whole load of remembrance, the weight of the past. On arrival, we had to unload it. We went in naked. You might say one can take everything away from a human being except this one faculty: memory. Not so. First, human beings are stripped of what makes them human, then their memory leaves them. Memory peels off like tatters, tatters of burned skin. That a human being is able to survive having been stripped in this manner is what you'll never comprehend. And I cannot explain it to you. . . . The survivor must undertake to regain his memory, regain what he possessed before: his knowledge, his experience, his childhood memories, his manual dexterity and his intellectual faculties, sensitivity, the capacity to dream, imagine, laugh. If you are unable to gauge the effort this necessitates, in no way can I attempt to convey it. . . .

> Perhaps our expectations were enhanced
> by expectations
> of what we were awaiting.
> Every part of us stretched
> towards what we were waiting for
> our hands
> hard
> gentle
> sensitive
> impatient
> ready to grasp
> our hearts ready to give
> impatient
> avid
> inexhaustible
> our hands and hearts
> stretched towards what we were awaiting
> which was not awaiting us. . . .

As for myself, I felt at a loss at once, as soon as I came back to Paris. . . . I know the difference between before and after. Over there we had our entire past, all our memories, even memories from long ago passed on by our parents. We armed ourselves with this past for protection, erecting it between horror and us in order to stay whole, keep our true selves, our being. We kept on dipping into our past, our childhood, into whatever formed our personality, our character, tastes, ideas so we might recognize ourselves, preserve something of what we were, not letting this situation dent us, annihilate us. We tried to hang on to who we were. Each one of us recounted her life thousands and thousands of times, resurrecting her childhood, the time of freedom and happiness, just to make sure all this had existed, and that the teller was both subject and object. Our past was our lifeline and reassurance. But since I came back, everything I was before, all my memories from that earlier time, have dissolved, come undone. It is as though my past had been used up over there. Nothing remains of what was before. . . .

I know myself through and through
a knowledge
born from the depths of despair
You find out soon enough
you should not speak with death
for it is useless knowledge.
In a world
Where those who believe they are alive
are not
all knowledge becomes useless
for the one possessed of that other knowledge
it is far better to know nothing
if you wish to go on living.

114 ♦ Lanzmann's *Shoah* (David Denby)

David Denby, film critic at the New Yorker, *reviews one of the most ambitious and pioneering film projects ever realized: Claude Lanzmann's nine-and-a-half-hour documentary film* Shoah, *released in 1985. Yet* Shoah *is no ordinary documentary. It does not reconstruct and explain in any conventional sense of the word. Nor does it depict violence or death or remains. Instead Lanzmann, who edits* Les Temps Modernes, *the journal founded by Jean-Paul Sartre and Simone de Beauvoir, merely intersperses oral testimonies from perpetrators, survivors, and bystanders. Its loose and unusual structure notwithstanding, the extraordinary film, as Denby points out in this review, creates a contemplative atmosphere in which to consider the meaning of the Holocaust.*

Simon Srebnik, a Polish-born Jew, is one of exactly two survivors of Chelmno, the small improvised, little-known killing center in northwestern Poland where the Nazis began the systematic gassing of the Jews on December 7, 1941 (that's right, the same day). By the time the camp was closed, in January 1945, about 400,000 men, women, and children had been murdered there—in gas vans, with carbon monoxide. At the beginning of Claude Lanzmann's extraordinary nine-and-a-half-hour documentary, *Shoah*, we see Lanzmann and Srebnik walking across the beautiful meadow in Chelmno where bodies were once incinerated; and we hear the villagers of Chelmno say how much they liked Srebnik, who was only thirteen when he lived in the camp and who was a graceful and jaunty boy with a beautiful tenor voice.

Later in the film Lanzmann reunites Srebnik with some of the villagers. They all stand together on the steps of a large church—the same church, as it happens, in which Jews were locked up, sometimes for days and without food, before being put into the vans. And we see that the villagers, laughing and nodding their heads, remember Srebnik and really do like him; they are glad that he is still alive. But then Lanzmann asks them why they think the Jews were

SOURCE: David Denby, "Out of Darkness," *New York Magazine*, October 28, 1985, 130–33, reprinted in Stuart Liebman, ed., *Claude Lanzmann's Shoah: Key Essays* (Oxford: Oxford University Press, 2007), 73–75, 76. Reprinted with permission of the author and publisher.

exterminated, and even as the resurrected Srebnik stands among them, they say—can it be possible, so many years later, in *this* town—they say that the Jews were all rich, the Jews murdered Christ, the Jews. . . . Not one says the word "Nazis."

I admit that even after reading the rapturous early accounts of Lanzmann's film in the *New York Times* and in *Newsweek's* international edition, I was not eager to see it. Having absorbed my share of books and films on the Holocaust, I doubted I was capable of learning more, feeling more, understanding more. Numbness, I thought was beginning to set in, a prospective fatigue that was, in its way, one of the intended side effects of the enormous crime. But now I've seen *Shoah*, and it turns out to be far more original in technique, far stranger and more obsessive than the early accounts suggested. Lanzmann has redeemed the catastrophe from banality. He has also made one of the three or four greatest documentaries in the history of the cinema.

Shoah (the word means "annihilation" in Hebrew) ranks with Marcel Ophüls's *The Sorrow and the Pity* as a moral inquiry. Lanzmann, like Ophüls, is a gently persistent but finally implacable interviewer who manages to coax astounding revelations from his subjects. Whatever else it is, *Shoah* is a collection of remarkable speech (the text has been published by Pantheon). From the lips of old Nazis, unconscious self-accusations fall gaily and shamelessly into the air, catalogs of lies, swindles, willful delusion, and forgetting. The Jewish survivors Lanzmann chose, who were among those forced to assist in the work of the camps, and hence in the destruction of their own people, appear to be consciously avoiding rhetoric and emotion; they are somber and impressive, and two of them reach a pitch of bitter anguish—despair and the elation of survival inextricably mixed—that leaves one shattered. Mere witnesses to the disaster calmly fill in details, but a few climb to levels of incomparable eloquence or stupidity. One of the former, Jan Karski, an aristocratic Pole who tried, and failed, to arouse the outside world to what was going on, gives a long, declamatory account of his experiences that bears comparison with one of the racked, climatic speeches of a Shakespearean tragedy.

Like Ophüls, Lanzmann uses a circular rather than a table-of-contents or merely chronological way of organizing the material. Themes are introduced, developed, momentarily dropped, then varied, recapitulated, all in a widening spiral of reference and emotion. The film is beautifully paced, with a kind of musical feeling for repetition, meditation, crescendo, release. One adapts to the slow unfolding, the obsessive circling; Lanzmann, like all great film artists, changes one's sense of time. . . . *Shoah* is a film about history, and yet Lanzmann flying brazenly in the face of convention and common sense, uses not a single moment of archival footage in his 561-minute work. No, not one foot of newsreel; not a single still photo; no music, no narrator, no artifacts of the period; no radio speeches by Goebbels or Hitler, no diaries of SS officers. This is a movie about history as it is remembered as well as made—an account, then, of memory and forgetting, in which the fog and distortion of time and untruth matter as much as the recovered moment and the actual record.

As his survivors, executioners, and witnesses talk, Lanzmann moves his camera around the outskirts of the death camps as they look today. He approaches, gliding through the woods, and stops; approaches and stops again; and finally enters into their heart. The gigantic Auschwitz-Birkenau complex looks virtually the same as it did in 1945, when the Soviets liberated it. But the ruins of the other Polish camps that Lanzmann uses—Chelmno, Sobibor, and Treblinka—have been cleared away, the land covered with grass and trees (usually planted by the Nazis) and a variety of memorial monuments. At first one experiences feelings of be-trayal. Surely this is an anticlimax! One longs for a sulfurous photograph of the camp in opera-tion. But then, as the horrifying testimony—the stories of people herded, stripped, gassed, burned—continues over the idyllic images, Lanzmann's point becomes clear to us. The Nazis tried to make the earth swallow up their victims. For instance, the Sobibor stationmaster, who today is a traumatized man, describes an uncanny experience: In 1942, when the camp was being built (right next to the station), "there were orders shouted in German, there were screams, Jews were working at a run, there were shots." But finally the camp was finished, and as he was riding his bicycle home one night, the first transport—maybe 40 cars—rolled in. The next morning he returned. Silence. Absolute silence. All the Jews had vanished.

Today the clearing next to the station is again silent, as are the forests at Sobibor and the rivers where the ashes were dumped. Lanzmann's camera violates the stillness; he cannot make the ground crack, heave, and yield up its dead, but he can at least disturb the insensibil-ity of nature; he can end, by the mere act of remembering, the collusion of mass murder and "healing" time. As we watch these sequences, with their feral words and calm images, we have to re-create the Holocaust in our own heads; Lanzmann will not allow the familiar pictures, which have an almost pornographic appeal, to do the work for us. This is why this movie could bring about a change in consciousness even in people who have read and thought about these things many times before.

Lanzmann, 59, was a student leader in the French Resistance during the war and worked for years as a writer and editor at *Les Temps Modernes*, the intellectual quarterly founded by Sartre. His instincts are reportorial—and also topographical and archaeological. Again and again, he walks over the ground, pacing it off himself or with someone who was there: This is where the train stopped; this is where the ramp was; this is where the Polish peasants, whose fields abutted on the Treblinka station, stood and made signs of throats being cut for the Jews waiting in the cattle cars—according to the peasants, a courageous warning of what was to come. (Then why do they sound so jocular when recounting it?) . . .

The trains become a recurring image for Lanzmann. Again and again, he shows freight cars rumbling through the Polish countryside; the melancholy sound of those wheels, which normally has such lyrical, nostalgic associations for us, becomes a kind of musical motif of de-spair. The rhythm of *Shoah* envelops and mesmerizes. Reading about this movie isn't enough: You must see it.

115 • Holocaust Testimonies (Lawrence L. Langer)

In his 1991 book, Lawrence Langer constructs a foundational account about the nature and func-tion of survivor testimonies, with particular reference to videotaped Holocaust testimonies. Langer, a professor emeritus of English at Simmons College, reflects on the differences between written and oral testimonies and calls for new forms of interpretation when dealing with the latter. More specifically Langer asks us to "suspend our sense of the normal and to accept the complex immediacy of a voice

SOURCE: Lawrence Langer, *Holocaust Testimonies: The Ruins of Memory* (New Haven, Conn.: Yale University Press, 1991), ix–x, xi–xii, xiii, 2–3, 17, 19–20, 21. Reprinted with permission of the publisher.

reaching us simultaneously from the secure present and the devastating past." What is necessary—but almost impossible to achieve—says Langer, is for a listener to become attuned to the extraordinariness of the accounts, not to recoil in fear, confusion, shame, horror, skepticism, or disbelief, but to embrace the strangeness. What is required of audiences, then, are strategies for making the strange familiar.

About six years ago, when I first began looking at videotaped Holocaust testimonies, I was watching an interview with a Mr. and Mrs. B., who were on camera together. Each had been in several camps, including Auschwitz; both had lost virtually every member of their families. Their son and daughter are present in the interview too, and at the very end the camera draws back to reveal the entire family sitting together. The interviewer asks Mr. and Mrs. B. what they are left with, what their ordeal has done to them. Her children sitting next to her, Mrs. B. confesses: "We are left with loneliness. As long as we live, we are lonely." Mr. B., his children sitting next to him, looks down, an utterly forlorn expression on his face, shrugs his shoulders, and whispers barely audibly: "Nothing to say. Sad." Then he shakes his head and weeps quietly as his wife describes how deprived her children were because while growing up they lacked grandparents and relatives to give them the affection and small presents that other children received.

The interviewer then asks the daughter the same question: How does she feel about her parents' experience (which, in addition to Auschwitz, included the Lodz ghetto, as well as Dora-Nordhausen for Mr. B. and Bergen-Belsen for Mrs. B.)? The daughter seems to speak from a different world: "First of all, I think I'm left with a lot of strength, because you can't have parents like this who survived some very, very ugly experiences [a *mammoth* understatement, for anyone who has seen the interview] and managed to build a life afterwards and still have some hope. You can't grow up in a household like that without having many, many strengths, first of all. And second of all, something that I have as a child of survivors which second and third generation American people don't have is still some connection with the rich Jewish cultural heritage which is gone now. That is my connection." . . . While watching this sequence of moments on the initial tape, I remember thinking: "Wait a minute! Something's wrong here! Either someone's not listening, or someone's not telling the truth!" This was of course a naive response. But what I was reacting to was this: Despite the presence of their children, the parents speak of being lonely and sad. The daughter, if we listen carefully to the tenor of her words, . . . draws on a vocabulary of chronology and conjunction, while *they* use a lexicon of disruption, absence, and irreversible loss. It took me some time to realize that all of them were telling a version of the truth as they grasped it, that several currents flow at differing depths in Holocaust testimonies, and that our understanding of the event depends very much on the source and destination of the current we pursue. . . .

Moral formulas about learning from experience and growing through suffering rapidly disintegrate into meaningless fragments of rhetorical consolation as the testimony of these interviews proceeds. When I began to examine them, I was already suspicious of commentaries and memoirs that celebrated the resourceful human spirit in the face of the Holocaust disaster. As I continued to watch them, I felt that my suspicions were confirmed. A heritage of heroism encountered the awful facts of this particular catastrophe and found that the only honest judgment was to declare the confrontation "no combat." When former victims, entreating our

sympathetic understanding, insist that the situations in which they found themselves in ghettos and camps were "different," they are making a specific appeal to us to abandon traditional
assumptions about moral conduct and the "privileged" distinctions between right and wrong
that usually inspire such assumptions. The events they endured rudely dispel as misconcep-
tion the idea that choice is purely an internal matter, immune to circumstance and chance. . . .
From the point of view of the witness, the urge to tell meets resistance from the certainty that
one's audience will not understand. The anxiety of futility lurks beneath the surface of many
of these narratives, erupting occasionally and rousing us to an appraisal of our own stance that
we cannot afford to ignore. . . .

    Testimony is a form of remembering. The faculty of memory functions in the present to
recall a personal history vexed by traumas that thwart smooth-flowing chronicles. Simultaneously, however, straining against what we might call disruptive memory is an effort to reconstruct a semblance of continuity in a life that began as, and now resumes, a normal existence.
"Cotemporality" becomes the controlling principle of these testimonies, as witnesses struggle
with the impossible task of making their recollections of [for example] the [concentration or
death] camp experience coalesce with the rest of their lives. If one theme links their narratives
more than any other, it is the unintended, unexpected, but invariably unavoidable failure of
such efforts. . . .

    A written narrative is finished when we begin to read it, its opening, middle, and end al-
ready established between the covers of the book. This *appearance* of form is reassuring (even
though the experience of reading may prove an unsettling challenge). Oral testimony steers a
less certain course, like a fragile craft veering through turbulent waters unsure where a safe
harbor lies—or whether one exists at all! . . . When the witness in an oral [and videotaped]
testimony leans forward toward the camera . . . , apparently addressing the interviewer(s) but
also speaking to the potential audience of the future—asking: "Do you understand what I'm
trying to tell you?"—that witness confirms the vast imaginative space separating what he
or she had endured from our capacity to absorb it. Written memoirs, by the very strategies
available to their authors—style, chronology, analogy, imagery, dialogue, a sense of character,
a coherent moral vision—strive to narrow this space, easing us into their unfamiliar world
through familiar (and hence comforting?) literary devices. The impulse to *portray* (and thus
refine) reality when we write about it seems irresistible. Describing the SS man who greeted
her and her mother on the ramp at Auschwitz, Barbara T. writes: "his pale blue eyes dart from
side to side like a metronome," and . . . one has the uneasy feeling of the literary *transforming*
the real in a way that obscures even as it seeks to enlighten. . . .

    Until now, we have depended almost entirely on written narratives of the [concentration
and death] camp experience to gain insight into the nature of that atrocity. For the moment, I
shall suggest no more than that videotaped oral testimonies provide us with an unexplored
archive of "texts" that solicit from us original forms of interpretation. Reading a book that tries
to carry us "back there" is an order of experience entirely different from witnessing someone
like Barbara T. vanishing from contact with us even as she speaks, momentarily returning to
the world she is trying to evoke instead of recreating it for us in the present. Yet her presence
before us dramatically illustrates the merging of time senses (so often revealed by witnesses
in oral testimony) that *creates* meaning through the very manner of her narrative. A complex

kind of "reversible continuity" seems to establish itself in many of these testimonies, one foreign to the straight chronology that governs most written memoirs.

A further distinction may be necessary here. Normal oral discourse—the speech, the lecture, the political address—assumes that the audience is no mystery and that competent presentation and substantial content will rouse and hold an audience's interest. And that is generally true. But the first effect of many of these testimonies is just the opposite, no matter how vivid the presentation: they induce fear, confusion, shame, horror, skepticism, even disbelief. The more painful, dramatic, and overwhelming the narrative, the more tense, wary, and self-protective is the audience, the quicker the instinct to withdraw. Unlike the writer, the witness lacks inclination and strategies to establish and maintain a viable bond between the participants in this encounter.

To reverse the direction of that initial estrangement, a viewer [of videotaped oral testimonies] must find some entry into the realm of disrupted lives and become sensitized to the implications of such disruption. In other words, we should not come to the encounter unprepared—yet we do. We have little choice. It is virtually useless . . . to approach the experience from the reservoir of normal values, armed with questions like "Why didn't they resist?" . . . [Oral testimonies] impose on us a role not only of passive listener but also of active *hearer*. This requires us to suspend our sense of the normal and to accept the complex immediacy of a voice reaching us simultaneously from the secure present and the devastating past. That complexity, by forcing us to redefine our role as audience *throughout* the encounter, distinguishes these testimonies from regular oral discourse as well as from written texts.

116 • Yad Vashem (James E. Young)

Memorialization is one means of coping with genocide. James Young, a leading scholar of the practice and a professor of English and Judaic studies at the University of Massachusetts, Amherst, embarks on a walk through Yad Vashem, the Holocaust Martyrs' and Heroes' Remembrance Authority in Israel. Established in 1953, Yad Vashem serves as Israel's official memorial to the Jewish victims of Nazi genocide. Young's 1993 chapter serves as an expert guide, revealing the meaning of both the art and the architecture that are on display in Jerusalem on Mount Herzl.

Of all the memorial centers in Israel, only Yad Vashem Martyrs' and Heroes' Remembrance Authority bears the explicit imprimatur of the state. Conceived in the throes of the state's birth and building, Yad Vashem would be regarded from the outset as an integral part of Israel's civic infrastructure. It would both share and buttress the state's ideals and self-definition.

An eclectic amalgamation of outdoor monuments, exhibition halls, and massive archives, Yad Vashem enacts the state's double-sided memory of the Holocaust in dozens of media. Yad Vashem functions as a national shrine to both Israeli pride in heroism and shame in victimiza-

SOURCE: James E. Young, *The Texture of Memory: Holocaust Memorials and Meaning* (New Haven, Conn.: Yale University Press, 1993), 243–44, 245–46, 247, 250–52, 253, 254–55, 256, 257, 258, 260. Reprinted with permission of the publisher.

tion, a place where Holocaust history is remembered as culminating in the very time and space now occupied by the memorial complex itself. As if trying to keep pace with the state's own growth, Yad Vashem has continued to expand its reservoir of images, sculptures, and exhibitions: as the state and its official memory of the Holocaust evolve, so too will the shape of memory at Yad Vashem. In its roles as the national Memorial Authority, Yad Vashem is the final arbiter of both Holocaust memory in Israel and the very reasons for memory. . . .

In 1952, the minister of education and eminent Israeli historian Benzion Dinur submitted to the parliament a bill for the establishment of Yad Vashem. As always in the Knesset, debate was long and tangled, though the bill itself enjoyed an almost unheard-of consensus among Israel lawmakers. On 18 May 1953, spurred on by the imminent unveiling of a "memorial to the unknown Jewish martyr in Paris," the Knesset unanimously passed what was officially called the "Law of Remembrance of Shoah and Heroism—Yad Vashem" (Hok hazikaron hashoah vehagvurah—yad vashem), after which the entire assembly rose for a minute's silence in memory of the victims. On 19 August, one day after the Paris memorial's unveiling, the law passed its final reading and became the first remembrance law of the land.

In its immediate temporal context, in fact, the link between the Holocaust and the establishment of the state was palpable for legislators in ways lost to and occasionally denied by subsequent generations. This was partly the result of the fact that national independence followed liberation of the camps by three years, as well as of a sense that Israel's War of Independence was fought as an extension of the Jews' struggle for survival in Europe. In the words of Nachum Goldman, former President of the World Jewish Congress, "If the State came into being, it was not only by virtue of the blood spilt by those who fell in the battles for its existence, which is the highest price, but also, indirectly, because of the millions murdered in the Holocaust." In this view, the blood spilt for Israel's independence is seen to mingle with that spilt in Europe's slaughterhouses. If the state came about by virtue of the blood spilt in both places, it is little wonder that the murdered Jews of the Holocaust would be conferred posthumous Israeli citizenship, for in this scenario they, too, have given their lives for Israel. Conversely, once martyrs of the Holocaust are united with those who fought and died for the state, the War of Independence itself might be said to have begun not in 1947, but in 1939.

Even more significant to many of Israel's leaders at the time, however, was the overt political cause and effect between the Holocaust and the UN vote for Israeli statehood. For even in the practical side of its birth, the state of Israel was tied closely to other nations' perceptions and recent memory of the Holocaust. In order to persuade the UN commission appointed to study the partition of Palestine into Jewish and Arab states, Goldman reported, Abba Eban and David Horowitz spent much of their time recalling to the delegates the story of the Holocaust. In their retellings, they were able to establish a persuasive link between Holocaust and statelessness, between rehabilitation and national rebirth. As a consequence, the commission visited displaced persons camps in Germany on fact-finding missions to determine the depth of Zionist commitment among survivors—and came away stunned by what they saw and heard. . . . All of which was fresh in the minds of legislators as they sought to embody the link between Holocaust and statehood in what would become Israel's preeminent national shrine.

As defined by the Law of Remembrance of Shoah and Heroism, the memorial at Yad Vashem thus commemorates a reflexively Israeli understanding of the Holocaust, including "the six million members of the Jewish people who died a martyr's death at the hands of the

Nazis and their collaborators"; "the communities, synagogues, movements . . . and cultural institutions destroyed"; "the fortitude of Jews who gave their lives for their people"; "the heroism
of Jewish servicemen, and of underground fighters"; "the heroic stand of the besieged ghetto
population and the fighters who rose and kindled the flame of revolt to save the honor of their
people"; "the sublime, persistent struggle of the masses of the House of Israel, on the threshold of destruction, for their human dignity and Jewish culture"; "the unceasing efforts of the
besieged to reach Eretz Israel in spite of all obstacles, and the devotion and heroism of their
brothers who went forth to rescue and liberate the survivors"; and "the high-minded Gentiles
who risked their lives to save Jews." . . .

In bestowing posthumous citizenship on the victims, the state effectively created an
invisible but ever-present shadow population of martyrs. As the state's newest citizens, these
martyrs are understood in this context as having been murdered not only because they were
Jews, but because they were Israelis as well. The function of memory in this project is precisely
what it has always been for the Jewish nation; in addition to bringing home the "national
lessons" of the Holocaust, memory would work to bind present and past generations, to unify
a world outlook, to create a vicariously shared national experience. These are the implied
functions of every national memorial, of course, merely made visible in Israel's legitimation of
such memory. . . .

Today, the official route for visitors begins with the "Avenue of the Righteous Gentiles,"
a promenade lined with trees planted by non-Jews to honor their rescue of survivors during
the war. The end of the walk is crowned with a very small, fragile-looking rowboat used by
Danish fishermen to ferry some six hundred Jews out of Nazi-occupied Denmark on the eve
of their roundup. Just beyond the boat, the memory path leads up a short flight of steps, from
Gentile to Jewish heroism, into the Warsaw Ghetto Square, bordered by a reproduction of
[Nathan] Rapoport's Ghetto Monument. . . . From the Warsaw Ghetto Square, we enter glass
doors of the historical museum's open lobby, where we are confronted with a wall-sized monumental relief by Naftali Bezem, entitled *M'shoah l'tkumah* (From Shoah to Rebirth). . . . Somewhere between figuration and abstraction, these surreal pictographs trace Israel's conceptual
matrix of the Holocaust: Shoah, Revolt, Immigration, Rebirth. Thus introduced, the History
Museum itself is divided into three principal sections, their sequence echoing more literally
the symbolic narrative of the bas relief. . . .

As we enter the last room of the exhibition, the hall of names, we pass alongside the Baal
Shem Tov's words, gilded in gold lettering, a distillation of this memorial's raison d'être in
Israel: "Forgetting lengthens the period of exile! In remembrance lies the secret of deliver-
ance." With these words in mind, we walk outside into the blindingly bright light of Jerusalem,
the present moment. . . . From here, visitors ascend steps back up to the Hall of Remembrance
plaza, an open square overlooking the ghetto fighters' square below and the Jerusalem hills
behind, now ringed with shiny white new neighborhoods. The cool darkness of the Ohel
Yizkor (Memorial Tent), standing adjacent, invites us in. . . . The floor panels of the Ohel
Yizkor—literally, Tent of Remembrance—bear the names of twenty-two of the largest concentration camps and are arranged in rough geographical order. . . . In one corner, directly
beneath an open skylight, an eternal flame flickers amid a sharp-pronged sheath of bronze. . . .
Since this stone entombs the remains of victims, it might be regarded mire literally as a collective matzevah for unknown victims, a crypt. . . .

With its four-cornered ceiling rising to the small opening far above the eternal flame, and its walkway circling along the perimeter of names and tomb, the memorial tent objectifies emptiness and absence. The building and its form seem unyielding and permanent, stone-heavy and rock-hard to the touch. It is a space where one's eyes cannot readily fix on anything but the names on the floor, the flame and slab covering ashes. Our glance is first drawn downward by the flame, bringing us into the repose of prayer, and then it turns inward, as if to surround memory on the inside. Here we stand silently to meditate the order of events, or memory, created for us here. . . .

From [the Memorial Tent] visitors can walk around to the synagogue and plaza adjacent to the Hall of Remembrance, whence they can walk either to the art museum and Jewish soldiers' monument behind, or traverse a path alongside the Pillar of Heroism to the children's memorial. If we take the first way, we come to Bernie Fink's monument, Soldiers, Ghetto Fighters, and Partisans. In this installation, the artist has arranged six great oblong hexagonal granite blocks in two stacks of three, so that a window in the shape of a Jewish star is formed. The window is, in turn, bisected by the blade of a stainless steel sword. The six blocks are intended to recall the six million victims; the blade recalls the fighters; and the star represents the Jewish people. . . . Though its parts might commemorate the victims, in its wholeness, it projects itself as a victory monument. . . .

Behind us, in the very center of the complex, stands the tallest memorial at Yad Vashem. . . . Built not long after the Yom Kippur War, the tower seeks to unite past fighters of the ghetto with current Israeli soldiers. . . . Together with Rapoport's Ghetto Museum and Fink's monument to Jewish soldiers, this, the largest, most visible monument at Yad Vashem, thus reminds us of the distinction between martyrs' and heroes' monuments. Where the memory of the heroes is concretized in presence, in thrusting vertical figures, an uprising form, the martyrs are generally recalled by their absence: the Hall of Remembrance, the children's memorial. . . . In its realization, the children's memorial works at several levels, some highly evocative, others overly so. . . . From here, we continue into what seems at first to be a planetarium: the dancing light of five memorial candles is splintered into millions of sparks, like stars, reflected in the dark hall by five hundred angled mirrors on the walls and ceilings. . . . The architect seems to be reminding us that not only is memory illusory, but so are the monuments whose surfaces necessarily reflect our memory back to us. . . . A path descends from here to the kiosk, where books, postcards, and trinkets are sold. . . .

If Yad Vashem is indeed second only to the Western Wall in its sacredness as a shrine of Israel's civil religion, . . . then it also becomes more than just a civic shrine. . . . For . . . the new civil religion in Israel invites a certain confusion between traditional and civil religion. After substituting civil religious values like heroism, bravery, and courage for traditional values like faith and patience, the minister of the civil religion would have all forget that such substitutions were made. As a result, not only are traditional Jewish paradigms and holy sites reinvested with civil religious meaning, but civic sites and their meanings acquire a certain religious fervor. . . . If the objective of civil religion is to sanctify the society in which it functions . . . , then we cannot ignore the simultaneous sanctification of particular images of the Holocaust produced in sacred places like Yad Vashem. For such sanctification not only integrates, legitimizes, and mobilizes society, it also makes some interpretations of events holier than other interpretations. While this may well be the traditional prerogative of the state, critical visitors must also retain the right to remark the ways divine authority tends to accrue to a state's institutions. In all these ways, Yad Vashem continues to function as Israel's ever-legitimizing national shrine par excellence.

117 • Khmer Meanings of Pain (John Marcucci)

Although not concerned with coping per se, John Marcucci's 1994 essay delivers observations about the meaning of pain in Cambodia, which forces one to allow that suffering in the aftermath of genocide, both physical and psychological, may very well be experienced rather differently across time and space. By juxtaposing Khmer conceptions of pain, rooted as they are in Buddhism, and Judeo-Christian conceptions of pain, Marcucci draws attention to "pain as a cultural process," thus implicitly raising questions about possible—and impossible—ways of coping with social suffering in the wake of genocide. In order to truly understand the social construction of pain in Cambodia and elsewhere, Marcucci advocates participant observation, the anthropological method of data collection that centers on a researcher's complete immersion in the field. Immersion is achieved by partaking in and simultaneously observing the practices of the setting under investigation.

[The anthropologist] Clifford Geertz has claimed that human experiences are formulated into a "web of meaning" abstractly defined as culture. This chapter concerns the "web of meaning" the Khmer give to pain. The meanings of pain derive from sensate experiences recognized by complex cultural processes that contribute to and maintain ethnic identity.... I propose that the cultural concept of pain, particularly the sharing of pain, is a major element by which the Khmer distinguish their identity and provide meaning to their existence. Indeed, the range and complexity of the meanings of pain span cosmological, biological, and chemical reactions. This perspective on pain, so suited to the generalist perspective of anthropology, has received scant attention, for most study is directed to the medicalization of pain, especially alleviating, controlling, and managing its perception and expression....

For the Khmer, pain reveals experiences of suffering and healing, and their act of sharing the experiences of pain continually contributes to the process of meaning. Theravada Buddhism as practiced by the Khmer is a major belief system and it formulates the meaning of pain.... Pain as a sensate experience is accorded critical values and meanings in Khmer culture. Judeo-Christian Americans may believe that pain is either given or taken away by God, and other American conceptions emphasize biological and chemical causes of pain and symptom alleviation.... Khmer also acknowledge the natural scientific aspects of pain and its alleviation, but such knowledge of "nature" is not separated from their cosmological world view based on Buddhism. The natural and spiritual aspects of pain are mutually inclusive for the Khmer. Beyond Buddhism, another important part of Khmer cosmology is spiritism (or animism), a belief that magical spirits cause misfortune and affliction encourages people to take

SOURCE: John Marcucci, "Sharing the Pain: Critical Values and Behaviors in Khmer Culture," in May M. Ebihara, Carol A. Mortland, and Judy Ledgerwood, eds., *Cambodian Culture since 1975: Homeland and Exile* (Ithaca, N.Y.: Cornell University Press, 1994), 129, 130, 131–33, 134, 135, 140. Reprinted with permission of the publisher.

personal responsibility in coping with these problems. . . . In fact, it is the quotidian experiences of pain that provide individuals the ways for sharing pain through social interactions with others, particularly family members. Among the various means of socializing individuals to the group, Khmer medical practices offer a common, and often daily, means of providing a cultural context for the experience of pain.

The study of pain [especially in the context of genocide] requires a methodological approach that does not contrive the meaning and expression of pain, because meaning and behaviors vary and occur in different situations, and because the values assigned to beliefs about pain differ across cultures. . . . The approach to the study of pain as a cultural process is enhanced by the method of participant observation because the experience of pain remains within the "web of meaning" and is not removed from its social and cultural contexts. The following examples of the Khmer experience of pain are offered as a preliminary view that emphasizes the sharing of pain. . . .

I use the terms "affliction" and "infliction" to stress how closely related the experiences of pain can be, but differ regarding the meanings given within the context of the pain experience. Afflictions of suffering, in the sense I use it, describe conditions during which the endurance of pain becomes difficult and relief is usually sought. In contrast, inflictions of pain are sensations that are endured because of a perceived benefit or integration as a part of life. . . . Although French and other western pain medications, such as aspirin compounds, are known and used by the Khmer, the Khmer medical treatments of pinching, cupping, coining, and moxibustion are significant acts that contribute to the cultural processes of sharing the meaning of pain. "Pinching" involves literally squeezing the skin together until it becomes red. "Cupping" and "coining" obtain the same result by placing small cups over the skin or scraping the skin with a coin. "Moxibustion" involves putting a small amount of kapok (fibers from the ceiba tree) on the skin, . . . lighting it, then placing a small bottle over it. The vacuum created by the fire and the bottle creates a small reddish circle. . . . American providers of medical care to Khmer . . . have viewed these medical practices as forms of physical abuse, because the Khmer cultural conception of inflicting pain conflicts with American cultural values, which see pain only as suffering and as an experience that has only negative aspects and should be avoided. . . .

In numerous medical encounters, biomedical practitioners voiced their amazement about the absence of expressions of pain among the Khmer. Exemplifying these cultural differences is the case of a Khmer man with shrapnel wounds. Over a five-month period he sought medical treatment for his hand, which was becoming dysfunctional, as well as for sites on his abdomen and groin. During a series of examinations, physicians [erroneously] determined that his medical condition was not serious. They often remarked about the patient's lack of pain because he did not grimace or yell out when they pressed and prodded his wounds. . . . Khmer medical practices inflict pain, but the context of meaning accorded that sensation is the benefit of healing and the restoration of harmony. The infliction of pain as a part of treatment not only restores humoral balances to the body, . . . but also communicates to others the status of the individual's affliction of suffering. . . . Usually a person interacting with the afflicted person does not confront the meaning of the . . . affliction, . . . but rather responds in a caring and supportive manner. The offering of kindness and concern often helps the afflicted person discuss his or her troubles and conditions of pain. This social sharing of pain responds to one of the causes of pain, that is, social isolation or feeling the pain alone. . . .

The way the Khmer share their pain distinguishes values relating to suffering and healing. Critical behaviors in the social context of illness demonstrate how pain is endured as a part of healing. The Khmer believe that pain received during medical treatments is an infliction for healing, but this pain is only part of the experience. The restoration of health is dependent on treating the affliction—the perceived cause of pain. . . . Thus, an absence of behavior that expresses pain should not be misconstrued to mean that the Khmer are stoical or have a biological response to pain different from that of Americans. Nor should their expressions of pain be confused with somatization, a label often applied to patients of nonwestern cultures, which attributes emotional causes to physical distress. The Khmer teach us a particular cultural understanding of pain, suffering, and healing in their way of sharing beliefs and values.

118 • Fear as a Way of Life in Xe'caj (Linda Green)

Many observers believe the two-year cycle of collective violence perpetrated by Guatemala's army against the country's Mayan population in the early 1980s constitutes a case of genocide. At times referred to as the "silent Holocaust," the systematic scorched-earth campaign—under the cover of a counterinsurgency operation— led to the destruction of more than six hundred villages and their inhabitants. In a 1994 journal article, Linda Green, an anthropologist at the University of Arizona, chronicles the psychosocial consequences of the Guatemalan genocide, focusing in particular on the routinization of fear. The phrase captures the ways extraordinary emotions such as fear and terror are so omnipresent in a community or society that experiencing them is no longer perceived as unusual, but as entirely normal. The women in Green's case study suffer from chronic illnesses and diseases that largely stem from an inability to cope with "the new normal."

Fear is a response to danger, but in Guatemala, rather than being solely a subjective personal experience, it has also penetrated the social memory. And rather than an acute reaction it is a chronic condition. The effects of fear are pervasive and insidious in Guatemala. . . . The spectacle of torture and death and of massacres and disappearances in the recent past have become more deeply inscribed in individual bodies and the collective imagination through a constant sense of threat. In the altiplano fear has become a way of life. Fear, the arbiter of power—invisible, indeterminate, and silent. . . . Fear became the metanarrative of my research and experiences among the people of Xe'caj. Fear is the reality in which people live, the hidden state of (individual and social) emergency that is factored into the choices women and men make. Although this "state of emergency" in which Guatemalans have been living for over a decade may be the norm, it is an abnormal state of affairs indeed. . . .

Fear is elusive as a concept; yet you know it when it has you in its grips. Fear, like pain, is overwhelmingly present to the person experiencing it, but it may be barely perceptible to anyone else and almost defies objectification. Subjectively, the mundane experience of chronic fear wears down one's sensibility to it. The routinization of fear undermines one's confidence in interpreting the world. . . . While it is true that, with repetitiveness and familiarity, people

SOURCE: Linda Green, "Fear as a Way of Life," *Cultural Anthropology* 9, no. 2 (1994): 227, 228, 230, 231, 238, 233, 234, 246–47, 249. Reprinted with permission of the American Anthropological Association.

learn to accommodate themselves to terror and fear, low-intensity panic remains in the shadow of waking consciousness. One cannot live in a constant state of alertness, and so the chaos one feels becomes infused throughout the body. It surfaces frequently in dreams and chronic illness. In the mornings, sometimes my neighbors and friends would speak of their fears during the night, of being unable to sleep, or of being awakened by footsteps or voices, of nightmares of recurring death and violence. After six months of living in Xe'caj, I too started having my own nighttime hysteria, dreams of death, disappearances, and torture. Whisperings, innuendos, and rumors of death lists circulating would put everyone one edge. . . .

The terror and fear that pervaded daily life were not immediately perceptible to me. Military checkpoints, the army garrison, and civil patrols were clearly visible; yet daily life appeared "normal." The guerilla war, which reached an apex in the early 1980s, had ended at least in theory if not in practice. Although guerilla troops moved throughout the area, clashes between them and the army were limited. The war had reached a stalemate. While the army claimed victory, the guerillas refused to admit defeat. The battlefield was quiescent, yet political repression continued. Scorched-earth tactics, massacres, and large population displacements had halted, but they were replaced by selective repression and the militarization of daily life. . . . The use of camouflage cloth for clothing and small items sold at the market [in Xe'caj] is a subtle, insidious form of daily life's militarization. Wallets, key chains, belts, caps, and toy helicopters made in Taiwan are disconcerting in this context. As these seemingly mundane objects circulate, they normalize the extent to which civilian and military life have commingled in the altiplano. . . . The presence of soldiers and ex-soldiers in communities is illustrative of lived contradictions in the altiplano and provides another example of how the routinization of terror functions. . . .

The women have never recovered from their experiences of fear and repression; they continue to live in a chronic state of emotional, physical, and social trauma. . . . Certainly the ways in which the widows of Xe'caj experience their personal emotions of suffering may be construed as idiosyncratic and discrete. That these bodily expressions are also cultural renderings of collective social and political trauma, however, is a fact not lost on the women themselves. The invisible violence of fear and terror becomes visible in the sufferings and sicknesses of the body, mind, and spirit of the widows of Xe'caj. Their silenced voices speak poignantly through their bodies of their sadness, loneliness, and desolation, of chronic poverty and doubt. The women suffer from headaches, gastritis, ulcers, weakness, diarrhea, irritability, inability to sleep, weak blood—disorders usually clustered under the syndrome of posttraumatic stress—and of "folk" illnesses such as *nervios* (nerves), *susto* (fright), and *penas* (pain, sorrow, grief). Simply to categorize their sufferings, however, as either manifestations of clinical syndromes or culture-bound constructions of reality is to dehistoricize and dehumanize the lived experiences of the women. . . .

[In other words,] the sicknesses that the women of Xe'caj are experiencing are more than metaphors of their suffering; they are expressions of the rupture of the intricate and immediate connections between the body, mind, and spirit and are expressed in social relations between the individual, social, and body politic. . . . While I am not arguing that the ongoing chronic pains that the women experience are in themselves a form of social resistance, they do serve to connect the women to each other in their hardships and as such become a mechanism for social commentary and political consciousness. The women speak of their sufferings and illnesses in terms of the violence and oppressions that they suffer as Mayas. . . . Western medicine can in some instances alleviate their symptoms, but it cannot heal their problems.

119 • On Trial (Orhan Pamuk)

Novelist and Nobel laureate Orhan Pamuk tries to make sense of genocide denial in his native Turkey, where any mention of the large-scale atrocities committed by the Young Turks against Armenians in the early twentieth century is subject to punishment under Article 301 of the country's Criminal Code. In 2005 Pamuk was charged with insulting the Republic of Turkey under the provision on account of an interview in which he stated that one million Armenians and thirty thousand Kurds had been killed in the Ottoman Empire. The charges were eventually dropped. The following commentary from the New Yorker *stems from a time when this outcome was not yet known to the author.*

In Istanbul this Friday—in Şişli, the district where I have spent my whole life, in the courthouse directly opposite the three-story house where my grandmother lived alone for forty years—I will stand before a judge. My crime is to have "publicly denigrated Turkish identity." The prosecutor will ask that I be imprisoned for three years. I should perhaps find it worrying that the Turkish-Armenian journalist Hrant Dink was tried in the same court for the same offense, under Article 301 of the same statute, and was found guilty, but I remain optimistic. For, like my lawyer, I believe that the case against me is thin; I do not think I will end up in jail.

This makes it somewhat embarrassing to see my trial overdramatized. I am only too aware that most of the Istanbul friends from whom I have sought advice have at some point undergone much harsher interrogation and lost many years to court cases and prison sentences just because of a book, just because of something they had written. Living as I do in a country that honors its pashas, saints, and policemen at every opportunity but refuses to honor its writers until they have spent years in courts and in prisons, I cannot say I was surprised to be put on trial. I understand why friends smile and say that I am at last "a real Turkish writer." But when I uttered the words that landed me in trouble I was not seeking that kind of honor.

Last February, in an interview published in a Swiss newspaper, I said that "a million Armenians and thirty thousand Kurds had been killed in Turkey"; I went on to complain that it was taboo to discuss these matters in my country. Among the world's serious historians, it is common knowledge that a large number of Ottoman Armenians were deported, allegedly for siding against the Ottoman Empire during the First World War, and many of them were slaughtered along the way. Turkey's spokesmen, most of whom are diplomats, continue to maintain that the death toll was much lower, that the slaughter does not count as a genocide because it was not systematic, and that in the course of the war Armenians killed many Muslims, too. This past September, however, despite opposition from the state, three highly respected Istanbul universities joined forces to hold an academic conference of scholars open

SOURCE: Orhan Pamuk, "On Trial," *New Yorker,* December 19, 2005. Reprinted with the permission of Condé Nast Publications.

to views not tolerated by the official Turkish line. Since then, for the first time in ninety years, there has been public discussion of the subject—this despite the specter of Article 301.

If the state is prepared to go to such lengths to keep the Turkish people from knowing what happened to the Ottoman Armenians, that qualifies as a taboo. And my words caused a furor worthy of a taboo: various newspapers launched hate campaigns against me, with some right-wing (but not necessarily Islamist) columnists going as far as to say that I should be "silenced" for good; groups of nationalist extremists organized meetings and demonstrations to protest my treachery; there were public burnings of my books. Like Ka, the hero of my novel *Snow*, I discovered how it felt to have to leave one's beloved city for a time on account of one's political views. Because I did not want to add to the controversy, and did not want even to hear about it, I at first kept quiet, drenched in a strange sort of shame, hiding from the public, and even from my own words. Then a provincial governor ordered a burning of my books, and, following my return to Istanbul, the Şişli public prosecutor opened the case against me, and I found myself the object of international concern.

My detractors were not motivated just by personal animosity, nor were they expressing hostility to me alone; I already knew that my case was a matter worthy of discussion in both Turkey and the outside world. This was partly because I believed that what stained a country's "honor" was not the discussion of the black spots in its history but the impossibility of any discussion at all. But it was also because I believed that in today's Turkey the prohibition against discussing the Ottoman Armenians was a prohibition against freedom of expression, and that the two matters were inextricably linked. Comforted as I was by the interest in my predicament and by the generous gestures of support, there were also times when I felt uneasy about finding myself caught between my country and the rest of the world.

The hardest thing was to explain why a country officially committed to entry in the European Union would wish to imprison an author whose books were well known in Europe, and why it felt compelled to play out this drama (as Conrad might have said) "under Western eyes." This paradox cannot be explained away as simple ignorance, jealousy, or intolerance, and it is not the only paradox. What am I to make of a country that insists that the Turks, unlike their Western neighbors, are a compassionate people, incapable of genocide, while nationalist political groups are pelting me with death threats? What is the logic behind a state that complains that its enemies spread false reports about the Ottoman legacy all over the globe while it prosecutes and imprisons one writer after another, thus propagating the image of the Terrible Turk worldwide? When I think of the professor whom the state asked to give his ideas on Turkey's minorities, and who, having produced a report that failed to please, was prosecuted, or the news that between the time I began this essay and embarked on the sentence you are now reading five more writers and journalists were charged under Article 301, I imagine that Flaubert and Nerval, the two godfathers of Orientalism, would call these incidents *bizarreries*, and rightly so.

That said, the drama we see unfolding is not, I think, a grotesque and inscrutable drama peculiar to Turkey; rather, it is an expression of a new global phenomenon that we are only just coming to acknowledge and that we must now begin, however slowly, to address. In recent years, we have witnessed the astounding economic rise of India and China, and in both these countries we have also seen the rapid expansion of the middle class, though I do not think we shall truly understand the people who have been part of this transformation until we have seen their private lives reflected in novels. Whatever you call these new élites—the non-Western bourgeoisie or the enriched bureaucracy—they, like the Westernizing élites in my own country, feel compelled to follow two separate and seemingly incompatible lines of action in order to legitimatize their newly acquired wealth and power. First, they must justify the rapid rise in their fortunes by assuming the idiom and the attitudes of the West; having created a demand for such knowledge, they then take it upon themselves to tutor their countrymen. When the people berate them for ignoring tradition, they respond by brandishing a virulent and intolerant nationalism. The disputes that a Flaubert-like outside observer might call *bizarreries* may simply be the clashes between these political and economic programs and the cultural aspirations they engender. On the one hand, there is the rush to join the global economy; on the other, the angry nationalism that sees true democracy and freedom of thought as Western inventions.

V. S. Naipaul was one of the first writers to describe the private lives of the ruthless, murderous non-Western ruling élites of the post-colonial era. Last May, in Korea, when I met the great Japanese writer Kenzaburo Oe, I heard that he, too, had been attacked by nationalist extremists after stating that the ugly crimes committed by his country's armies during the invasions of Korea and China should be openly discussed in Tokyo. The intolerance shown by the Russian state toward the Chechens and other minorities and civil-rights groups, the attacks on freedom of expression by Hindu nationalists in India, and China's discreet ethnic cleansing of the Uighurs—all are nourished by the same contradictions.

As tomorrow's novelists prepare to narrate the private lives of the new élites, they are no doubt expecting the West to criticize the limits that their states place on freedom of expression. But these days the lies about the war in Iraq and the reports of secret CIA prisons have so damaged the West's credibility in Turkey and in other nations that it is more and more difficult for people like me to make the case for true Western democracy in my part of the world.

120 • The Tenth Circle of Hell (Rezak Hukanović)

Rezak Hukanović is a survivor of a Serb concentration camp that was erected in northern Bosnia and Herzegovina in 1992. The detention and execution of Muslims and Croats in this area took place in the context of the disintegration of the former Yugoslavia. The Serb quest for hegemony over the federation's constituent republics (Slovenia, Croatia, Bosnia, Kosovo, Montenegro, and Vojvodina) incited varieties of violence in the Balkans, from war to genocide. The municipality of Prijedor became infamous as the site of three concentration camps set up by Serbs: Omarska, Trnopolje, and Keraterm. With these camps (and many others like them), Serb forces sought to "ethnically cleanse" (a terrible euphemism) the region. Hukanović was a poet and journalist in Prijedor; in 1992 he became an inmate in the Omarska concentration camp, as he recalls in his memoir The Tenth Circle of Hell, *a disturbing account of the terror of detention.*

SOURCE: Rezak Hukanović, *The Tenth Circle of Hell: A Memoir of Life in the Death Camps of Bosnia*, translated by Colleen London and Midhat Ridjanović (New York: Abacus, 1998), 85–86, 88–91, 92, 93–94. Reprinted with permission of the publisher.

The Omarska camp wasn't surrounded by barbed wire, but it was as secure as a stone fortress. It was encircled by three rings of guards, with thirty guards in each ring. One ring was in the camp, the second some fifty yards beyond, and the third about one hundred yards from the first ring. The first and second group kept an eye on the camp itself, to make sure no prisoners tried to run away; the third protected the camp from any possible invaders.

Only two prisoners managed to get through all three rings and escape. The first was captured by residents of the nearby Serb village, Gradina, and brought back. He was killed immediately. The second got about six miles from Omarska, making it to the ruins of his village, Kozaruša; he hid out there in the rubble for a month or so. When he relaxed a bit, he set off for Prijedor. There he was shot in the leg and captured. Later he was brought back to the Omarska camp. No one knows what happened to him after that. Some say he died of infections, since his wounds were never treated. Such deaths, of course, were commonplace, especially from wounds inflicted by sharp, rusty objects. After a day or two of bleeding, the area around the wound would swell and turn purple. Then a scab would form as pus continued to run from the wound. One prisoner even took worms out of his own head wound, the kind that normally appear on corpses when they start to rot. . . .

Most of the victims who came through Omarska were from Kozarac; their homes had been hit the hardest. The residents of Kozarac were either killed on the spot or driven out in the long columns of pain flowing from the points of the daggers held by former neighbors. They were marched into the camps around Prijedor: Brezičani, Keraterm, Trnopolje, Omarska. Among the two thousand people from Kozarac crammed into Omarska were Kasim Grozdanić, a fifty-five-year-old shopkeeper, and his son Suad, nicknamed "Sudo" by his friends. They spent their days as prisoners in the hangar, the building across the runway from [another] dorm. . . . First they were placed in "Twenty-Six," the notorious dorm above the hangar, and then down below in the hangar's huge hall where more than one thousand prisoners spent their days.

The bare cement, covered with puddles of gasoline and dirty motor oil, was all they had to sleep on. The space they slept in was surrounded by a ring of barbed wire. There were smaller dorms upstairs, where between forty-five and fifty prisoners were kept. In the highest part of the hangar, about forty-five feet above the floor, pigeons nestled in between the asbestos room and the huge steel girders. At every flap of their wings, lice plummeted off their feathers onto the poor wretches below. The unbearable stench made everyone nauseous. There were no windows that opened anywhere, only tiny glass brick skylights at the peak of the roof. Occasionally the guards opened the big doors through which broken equipment had been ferried in and out in the old days.

Kasim and Sudo were right by the steps in the hangar that led to the small dorms, the former offices of the mine administrators. . . . Sudo was just twenty-four. The spark of manhood was in his eyes, since he had left youth behind. . . . His skin had begun to sag and wrinkle. His skinny legs stuck out, as if planted in the cement. Like so many others, he had contracted dysentery from the bad food and filthy conditions. Could there be any misery worse than this, rushing for the toilet every second, as your bleeding guts try to force themselves out? Often such a prisoner couldn't make it and lost control, the excrement running down the legs of his pants as it soiled the bodies huddled along the floor on the way to the toilet. There was always a guard in the hangar next to the toilet, ready to administer a beating. Sudo got so weak he couldn't even go and eat. . . .

"Take off all your clothes, everything," one of the guards shouted angrily. "We can't even go into the hangar because of your stink." Another guard held a thick rubber hose that blasted a stream of water onto the asphalt surface. Kasim felt unspeakable shame that his son had to see and endure such humiliation. The skinny bodies looked even more pathetic without the rags covering them. . . . Sudo twisted, turning his back to the water. Biting his lower lip from pain, he tried to protect himself with his hands as he avoided looking at his father. Kasim tried to use his own body to shield his son from the powerful impact of the water. Some men screamed as the water pounded their open wounds. . . . That night Sudo ran a fever and the pains in his stomach got worse. . . . Sudo's breathing became more difficult, then softer and shorter. Life slowly ebbed from his withered body. Little by little, the light of his twenty-four years extinguished itself. "Please, Dad . . . ," and his last words withered on his lips. A heavy, dead silence reigned throughout the hangar. Off in a corner, someone cursed God.

121 • Shake Hands with the Devil (Roméo Dallaire)

Roméo Dallaire was the force commander of the United Nations Assistance Mission for Rwanda. He received his commission in late 1993, a few short months before the onset of genocidal violence in the central African country. When the genocidal campaign got under way in earnest on April 6, 1994, Dallaire, with no mandate to stop the killing, found himself at the mercy of Rwanda's géno-cidaires because his calls for reinforcements went unheeded at the United Nations headquarters in New York. His self-proclaimed failure in Rwanda caused Dallaire to veer into depression. In his 2003 memoir, he describes his difficulties coping with the memories of genocide.

This book is long overdue, and I sincerely regret that I did not write it earlier. When I returned from Rwanda in September 1994, friends, colleagues and family members encouraged me to write about the mission while it was still fresh in my mind. Books were beginning to hit the shelves, claiming to tell the whole story of what happened in Rwanda. They did not. While well-researched and fairly accurate, none of them seemed to get the story right. I was able to assist many of the authors, but there always seemed to be something lacking in the final product. The sounds, smells, depredations, the scenes of inhuman acts were largely absent. Yet I could not step into the void and write the missing account; for years I was too sick, disgusted, horrified and fearful, and I made excuses for not taking up the task.

Camouflage was the order of the day and I became an expert. Week upon week, I accepted every invitation to speak on the subject; procrastination didn't help me escape but pulled me deeper into the maze of feelings and memories of the genocide. Then the formal processes began. The Belgian army decided to court-martial Colonel Luc Marchal, one of my closest colleagues in Rwanda. His country was looking for someone to blame for the loss

SOURCE: Roméo Dallaire, *Shake Hands with the Devil: The Failure of Humanity in Rwanda* (Toronto: Random House, 2003), xi–xii, xviii. Reprinted with permission of the publisher.

of ten Belgian soldiers, killed on duty within the first hours of the war. Luc's superiors were willing to sacrifice one of their own, a courageous soldier, in order to get to me. The Belgian government had decided I was either the real culprit or at least an accomplice in the death of its peacekeepers. A report from the Belgian senate reinforced the idea that I never should have permitted its soldiers to be put in a position where they had to defend themselves—despite our moral responsibility to the Rwandans and the mission. For a time, I became the convenient scapegoat for all that had gone wrong in Rwanda.

I used work as an anodyne for the blame that was coming my way and to assuage my own guilt about the failures of the mission. Whether I was restructuring the army, commanding 1 Canadian Division or Land Force Quebec Area, developing the quality of life program for the Canadian Forces or working to reform the officer corps, I accepted all tasks and worked hard and foolishly. So hard and so foolishly that in September 1998, four years after I had gotten home, my mind and my body decided to give up. The final straw was my trip back to Africa earlier that year to testify at the International Criminal Tribunal for Rwanda. The memories, the smells and the sense of evil returned with a vengeance. Within a year and a half, I was given a medical discharge from the army. I was suffering, like so many of the soldiers who had served with me in Rwanda, from an injury called post-traumatic stress disorder. With retirement came the time and the opportunity to think, speak and possibly even write. . . .

After one of my many presentations following my return from Rwanda, a Canadian Forces padre asked me how, after all I had seen and experienced, I could still believe in God. I answered that I know there is a God because in Rwanda I shook hands with the devil. I have seen him, I have smelled him and I have touched him. I know the devil exists, and therefore I know there is a God.

122 • Children's Drawings of Darfur (Carla Rose Shapiro)

An independent curator currently affiliated with the history department at the University of Toronto, Carla Rose Shapiro introduces a most interesting way of coping with genocide: drawings. What is more, she pays attention to the renderings of survivors whose experiences are only infrequently featured in accounts of large-scale social violence: children. Bringing to bear interpretive techniques from the arts, Shapiro offers a close reading of the style and substance of the stark, evocative sketches drawn by children who had been engulfed in the Darfur crisis that were showcased in the 2005 exhibition and catalogue The Smallest Witnesses: The Conflict in Darfur through Children's Eyes, *curated by Human Rights Watch.*

The Smallest Witnesses is a traveling exhibition produced by Human Rights Watch [HRW]. In The Smallest Witnesses, drawings of children are the primary medium of expression, giving voice to the youngest victims of the crisis in Darfur and standing as graphic testimony about

SOURCE: Carla Rose Shapiro, "Visual Advocates: Depicting Darfur," in Amanda F. Grzyb, ed., *The World and Darfur: International Response to Crimes against Humanity in Western Sudan* (Montreal: McGill-Queen's University Press, 2009), 226–27, 228–29, 231–32, 233, 234. Reprinted with permission of the publisher.

the atrocities these children have witnessed and experienced. The precious sketches that document these child-survivors' experiences are concrete evidence of their lives and struggles and an expression of their need to bear witness to the catastrophe that befell individuals, families, and entire communities. . . . These disturbing and vivid images of violence are one of the few extant visual records created by witnesses of the Darfurian genocide. There is a language that approximates the horrors of the genocide . . . that includes scenes of GOS- [government of Sudan] and Janjaweed-perpetrated attacks and the aftermath of the destruction.

On a research trip devoted to assessing the issue of sexual violence, Dr. Annie Sparrow, a pediatrician, and Olivier Bercault, a HRW lawyer, visited seven Darfurian refugee camps along Sudan's border with Chad and the border town of Tine. Sparrow and Bercault gave children paper and implements for drawing while their parents, teachers, or guardians were being interviewed. The children were not prompted to draw; the drawings happened spontaneously, without any instruction or guidance. Sparrow and Bercault also visited schools located in these refugee camps, where many children shared the drawings they had sketched in their notebooks. It is from all these sources that the drawings in *The Smallest Witnesses* are gleaned. The first version of the exhibition included twenty-seven original drawings—a representative sample of the hundreds of drawings collected by HRW researchers during their field research in Sudan and Chad. . . . The drawings are accompanied by captions, more extensive text and background information about the conflict in Darfur, an account of how the drawings were collected, interpretive material related to the content of the drawings, and excerpts of testimony providing context about the artists' renderings. Supporting the in situ exhibition materials is an exhibition catalogue, available in both hard-copy form and as a downloadable PDF document on the HRW website. It is interesting to note that the exhibition text does not refer to the ethnic cleansing and human rights crisis occurring in Darfur as genocide. . . .

Language is not a significant part of these children's artistic expressions; where language does appear on the "canvas," there are just a few words in Arabic. Perhaps this absence of language indicates that drawing, rather than words, was a more accessible vehicle of expression for the victims of this genocide. . . . Art is a non-threatening medium that is empowering to children because they are able to set their own representational and creative boundaries. This sense of safety in the art allows them to render and express their experiences, helping to make whole what has been shattered by trauma. The children who contributed their artwork were provided with an even greater sense of safety by knowing that pseudonyms would be used to preserve their anonymity. . . .

The drawings are valued less for the quality of their rendering than for the unique glimpses they offer of the perceptions of child survivors of the Darfurian genocide, and for the detailed and specific references they provide about the perpetrators of theses crimes and their means and methods of mass murder. A range of artistic and drafting skills are presented; many drawings are quite elementary—stick figures and rough outlines of objects—while others show a more sophisticated graphic quality. But the technical rendition does not take away from their power to convey essential truths. The drawings have a raw, unedited quality that conveys an organic genuineness. It is their very simplicity that makes their messages universal, and it is their candid quality that adds to their emotional resonance. In a universe filled with graphic images of violence, these drawings still have the power to shock, but with none of the sentimentality to which they were surely prone. While emotionally moving, they are never maudlin, nor do they appear to seek such forms of attention.

There is no mistaking that these drawings were made by the hands of children. From a distance we see features typical of all children's art—roughly hewn figures, skewed spatial relations, virtually absent perspective, colors that seep beyond bold and uneven lines. With few exceptions, the palette is muted, punctuated only by swaths of color denoting violence and fear—the blood from a corpse, the amber light of burning huts, aggressive tones beside victims being raped, and sometimes a bright green of a soldier's uniform. What is atypical for children's art are the subjects of these compositions, which quickly makes obvious that these "artists" are the victims of war. The images are painfully vivid and direct, affording little room for interpretation beyond the obvious gravity of the scenes of destruction being depicted.

The drawings include common representational motifs in art created by children who have experienced trauma. Children of war tend to draw airplanes as symbols of power, burning houses, projectiles, trajectories, and cadavers. Such things are common in the Darfur drawings: planes and helicopters raining down bombs upon village huts, machine-gun-clad Janjaweed militia, figures suggestive of mass fleeing, and other forms—fallen, outstretched, sometimes bloody—which suggest death. For the few compositions where the imagery is ambiguous or difficult to read, accompanying first-person accounts clarify the subject matter. What, at first glance, appears to be a picture of men dancing with women actually portrays Sudanese soldiers taking women away to be raped. In compositions that are purposefully more abstract, one senses that these less defined, more fluid lines are expressive of the chaos of the moment of Janjaweed violence—swirls in one drawing represent Janjaweed running after a screaming family, torn apart in this moment of terror.

The "visual vocabulary of war" evident in *The Smallest Witnesses* is expressed as five broad themes that predominate in these compositions: the bombing of villages, civilians fleeing for their lives, the rape of women and girls, corpses, and the actions of the Janjaweed. Several of the drawings picture scenes of villages being bombed by planes and helicopters and then burned to the ground. Musa, age fifteen, and his cousin Zania, eight, both show the aftermath of an Antonov aircraft bombing their village; Musa's mother, father, and brothers were all killed in the attack. The cousins depict the same scene with striking similarity—simple line drawings show a series of triangular huts; plane and Janjaweed attacks set the huts ablaze in shades of yellow, orange, and red. . . . Another genre of drawing depicts groups of civilians fleeing for their lives. The trauma of witnessing mass death, and subsequent exile and separation, are expressed through these drawings via a powerful simplicity of means. Taha, age thirteen, from North Darfur, drew such a landscape—planes showering bombs across a village, causing wide chaos, destruction, and death. The figures that appear are punctuated by broad strokes of red crayon, suggestive of those who did not make it. . . . [However,] it is the actions of the armed Janjaweed, on horses and camels, that, by far, dominate the mind's eye of *The Smallest Witnesses* artists.

The Janjaweed are most expressive of the children's subjectivity, for it is in the menacing figures, their automatic rifles spraying bullets at unarmed villagers, that the viewer most acutely senses the fear these children experienced. In the notebook belonging to Abd al-Rahman, age thirteen, from West Darfur, there are numerous stylized Janjaweed, one or two riders atop horses and camels, the grip of their guns and their postures signaling a "hunt" for their victims. The Janjaweed loom large in Abd al-Rahman's memory; by comparison, one victim [appears] as a minute presence on the very edge of the page. . . .

The significance of the images the children share goes beyond their value as personal expressions of trauma and compelling works of art; these drawings are an evidentiary visual record. The drawings corroborate eyewitness testimonial evidence and the documentation of the crimes committed by the GOS and Janjaweed as collected by HRW and other NGOs that have a presence in the region. The children's drawings display an uncanny familiarity with the military aircraft, artillery, and guns they have seen used (MiG-21S, Antonov aircraft, AK-47S, FAL rifles, and Kalashnikovs), and, rather than drawing generic armaments, some sketches include enough detail to identify the actual weapons, as determined by arms experts who have reviewed the artwork. It is also noteworthy that a series of these drawings has been submitted to the International Criminal Court (ICC) for consideration.

These drawings illustrate aspects of the crisis in Darfur that have evaded photographers and television crews. For example, these drawings portray Sudanese government officials and Arab militias attacking villagers together. The fact that the Sudanese soldiers are clearly distinguished from the militia fighters by their dress—the soldiers wear uniforms, the militiamen do not—further underscores the accuracy of the children's portrayals. . . .

From the exhibited works we are given few glimpses of the optimism present in the drawings of child survivors of other conflicts. The drawings in *The Smallest Witnesses* show, without reserve, the legacy of trauma held by children exposed to genocidal violence—depictions of loss: loss of childhood, loss of identity, and loss of family and community. The children's compositions are distilled into stark, acute, life-and-death struggles. There is no apparent place for escapism or decoration. Noticeably absent are birds, butterflies, hearts, and other life-affirming images found in drawings by children of other wars. The figurations of the Darfurian artists are literal—bombs, fire, and utter devastation. . . .

The drawings that comprise *The Smallest Witnesses* speak with poignant immediacy about the human cost of the Darfurian genocide. These compelling sketches function on multiple levels—as works of art, as historical documents, and as avenues of catharsis. While fear and political uncertainty do not permit the children to put their names to their artwork, each drawing gives a human and individual expression to the overwhelming tragedy of genocide. The drawings are also a collective and comprehensive condemnation of the crimes perpetrated by the GOS and the Janjaweed. If, in our contemporary familiarity with images of violence, we have become inured to tragedy, *The Smallest Witnesses* invites us to look at the human cost of genocide in a new way.

CHAPTER EIGHT

Compensation

Who should pay for genocide, and how? This chapter's emphasis is on the promise and limits of rectifying—in monetary and symbolic terms—the effects of genocide. In this chapter, compensation deals with apologies, restitution, and reparations. The suffering brought on by genocidal violence has both material and nonmaterial dimensions. In addition to death on a vast scale, genocidal campaigns destroy property, livelihoods, identities, and cultures. These losses place an enormous burden on survivors, on the relatives of those who perished, and on future generations not themselves directly affected by large-scale social violence. In an effort to ameliorate at least the most obvious forms of suffering, physical and otherwise, societies have experimented with different tools.

Apologies are one of the most frequently demanded responses in the aftermath of genocide. Potentially they are a way of compensating symbolically for the violation of the moral contract that at one time bound perpetrators and victims. Governments are reticent to issue apologies for genocidal pasts, lest they create a opening for the litigation of damages in a court of law. Restitution in times of large-scale violence revolves around the restoration of lost property to its rightful owner. Restitution in the context of the genocide in Srebrenica, for example, might involve the return of a house that was seized from a Muslim family by local Serbs in the course of the destruction. Or, to give an example from Rwanda, it might cover the return of goats or cattle to a farmer whose livestock was looted by marauding *génocidaires*. The purpose of restitution is to bring about (or at least approximate) the state of affairs that existed before the violation occurred. Reparations usually speak to both material and nonmaterial forms of suffering. Effective reparations seek to both recognize (not unlike apologies) and address (not unlike restitution) the harms that collective violence caused. However, because resource constraints (not to mention political opposition) are invariably a factor, payments of collective reparations, if they materialize at all, will usually not suffice to restore sustainable livelihoods to victims of genocide. It is for this reason that many reparations schemes are forward-looking, which is to say they are directed toward uprooting structural inequalities and the underlying causes of genocide rather than helping individuals make ends meet.

The first three selections are all concerned with the institution of the apology. After a general discussion of "dos" and "don'ts" by Aaron Lazare, the infamous—and by most accounts insincere—"Clinton apology" that the former U.S. president offered in Rwanda in 1998 for having failed to stop the 1994 genocide is featured. Then Haydie Gooder and Jane Jacobs explore with a critical eye the grassroots movement in Australia of making available so-called sorry books in which ordinary Australians repent for the sins committed in their name by a government still refusing to issue an official apology to the country's indigenous population.

The remainder of the chapter addresses—in both theory and practice—the multiple and thorny issues involved in providing restitution and reparations. In an influential contribution to the philosophical debate over both of these compensatory strategies, Jeremy Waldron raises important questions about the moral appropriateness of responding to historic injustice. His argument is based on examples of indigenous claims in his native New Zealand. William Bradford too is concerned with theoretical matters; against the background of the genocide of Native Americans, he juxtaposes three types of justice: justice as supersession, justice as compensation, and justice as restoration. By contrast, John Authers, Christian Tomuschat, and Gilbert Bitti and Gabriela González Rivas turn from theory to practice. Authers introduces readers to the convoluted history of the international negotiations over compensation for forced and slave laborers in Nazi concentration camps. Tomuschat turns from the Holocaust to international crimes in the Balkans and takes issue with the International Court of Justice's recent refusal to issue a reparations order in the case of *Bosnia and Herzegovina v. Serbia and Montenegro*. Bitti and González Rivas imagine the future of compensation; as practitioners at the International Criminal Court, they discuss the Court's reparations mechanism as well as the recently established Trust Fund for Victims. If we believe their verdict, the immediate future for compensation in the wake of genocide does not look bright.

Does a reckoning with genocide demand material compensation (restitution, reparations), or might symbolic compensation (apologies) suffice? This chapter is meant to help formulate answers to these questions.

123 • On Apology (Aaron Lazare)

An apology, when sincere, may serve to compensate for suffering and loss in the aftermath of genocide. In his 2004 book, Aaron Lazare, the former chancellor and dean of the University of Massachusetts Medical School, outlines the four requirements of an "effective" apology. First, it is essential to correctly identify to whom the apology is owed. Second, the wrongdoing that prompted the apology must be acknowledged in detail. Third, the apologizing party must recognize the extent of the suffering that victims have endured. Fourth, for an apology to be effective, it must communicate that the wrongdoing violated a moral contract between the wrongdoer and the wronged. Lazare goes on to illustrate these requirements with reference to an apology offered by the former president of Germany, Richard von Weizsäcker, for his country's extermination of the European Jews in the Holocaust.

The most essential part of an effective apology is acknowledging the offense. Clearly, without such foundation, the apology process cannot even begin. As self evident as that statement may seem, we should not assume that acknowledging an offense is a simple task. The reason that this part of the apology can be so challenging is that the acknowledgment may involve as many as four parts: (1) correctly identifying the party or parties to whom the apology is owed; (2) acknowledging the offending behavior in adequate detail; (3) recognizing the im-

SOURCE: Aaron Lazare, *On Apology* (Oxford: Oxford University Press, 2004), 75, 77, 80–81. Reprinted with permission of the publisher.

pact these behaviors had on the victim(s); and (4) confirming that the grievance was a violation of the social or moral contract between the parties. An effective apology requires that the
parties reach an agreement on all four parts, although it is common for one or more of the
parts to be implicit—that is, not verbally stated. . . .

Clarifying the details of the offense assumes particular importance in public apologies
because the parties offering the apology and/or parties receiving the apology may consist of
many, sometimes even millions of people. If the offense is not described in enough detail,
conflicting interpretations may result, often with destructive consequences. Because these
apologies are frequently codified in written form and then become part of the history of both
parties, the offending party must "get it right" the first time, with no ambiguity and no need
for later attempts to restate the original understanding. Lack of forthrightness at the outset
can prolong the acknowledgment stage, leading people to question the validity of the subsequent apology. . . .

[One] illustration of an effective acknowledgment is from Richard von Weizsacker, president of the Federal Republic of Germany. During a speech to the Bundestag [Germany's
lower house of Parliament] commemorating the fortieth anniversary of the end of the war in
Europe, von Weizsacker detailed the grievances inflicted on the victims of Germany during
World War II. . . . He began by emphasizing the importance of such honesty. "We need and
we have the strength to look the truth straight in the eye—without embellishment and without distortion," he said. Later, he repeated the point, "Remembering means recalling an occurrence honestly and undistortedly so that it becomes a part of our very being. This places
high demands on our truthfulness."

His description of the offending behaviors with its long list of victims is specific and un-
flinching. "Today we mourn all the dead of the war and the tyranny," he said. "In particular we
commemorate the six million Jews who were murdered in German concentration camps[;]
. . . all nations who suffered in the war, especially the countless citizens of the Soviet Union
and Poland who lost their lives[;] . . . the Sinti and Romany Gypsies, the homosexuals and the
mentally ill[;] . . . the people who had to die for their religious or political beliefs[;] . . . the
hostages who were executed. We recall the victims of the resistance movements in all countries
occupied by us. As Germans, we pay homage to the victims of German resistance—among
the public, the military, the churches, the workers and trade unions, and the Communists."

He also describes the impact offending behaviors had on the victims who survived.
"Alongside the endless army of the dead, mountains of human suffering arise," he observed,
"grief over the dead, suffering from injury or crippling or barbarous compulsory sterilization,
suffering during air raids, during flight and expulsion, suffering because of rape and pillage,
forced labor, injustice and torture, hunger and hardship, suffering because of fear of arrest and
death. . . . Today we sorrowfully recall all this human suffering. . . . There can be no reconciliation without remembrance."

The painful acknowledgment of Germany's multiple offenses is complete in every detail:
It enumerates the many victims of Nazi Germany (Jews, Gypsies, homosexuals, the mentally
ill, Poles, Soviets, among others), the reason for their victimization (religious and political
beliefs, among others) and the nature of their suffering (rape, pillage, forced labor, torture,
hunger, and death, among others). Von Weizsacker does not try to diminish the enormity of
the offense by offering rationalizations or excuses. He clearly identifies the responsible parties,

as he admonishes all Germans "to face the consequences with due responsibility." Remembering and acknowledging, he emphasizes, is the only path to reconciliation. It must, he declares, become "part of our very being."

124 • Remarks by the President of the United States at Kigali Airport, March 25, 1998 (William J. Clinton)

During his 1998 tour of Africa, U.S. President Bill Clinton insisted on a stopover in Rwanda in order to apologize to the victims of the 1994 genocide for America's inaction. His remarks are reprinted here in full. Aside from the widely held belief that the "Clinton apology" was insincere, it is perhaps best remembered for the location at which it was offered (Kigali airport), the time the president spent in the country (three and a half hours), and the fact that the engines of Air Force One were never shut off.

I have a great delegation of Americans with me, leaders of our government, leaders of our Congress, distinguished American citizens. We're all very grateful to be here. We thank the Diplomatic Corps for being here, and the members of the Rwandan government, and especially the citizens. I have come today to pay the respects of my nation to all who suffered and all who perished in the Rwandan genocide. (Applause.)

It is my hope that through this trip, in every corner of the world today and tomorrow, their story will be told; that four years ago in this beautiful, green, lovely land, a clear and conscious decision was made by those then in power that the peoples of this country would not live side by side in peace. During the 90 days that began on April 6 in 1994, Rwanda experienced the most intensive slaughter in this blood filled century we are about to leave. Families murdered in their home, people hunted down as they fled by soldiers and militia, through farmland and woods as if they were animals.

From Kibuye in the west to Kibungo in the east, people gathered seeking refuge in churches by the thousands, in hospitals, in schools. And when they were found, the old and the sick, women and children alike, they were killed—killed because their identity card said they were Tutsi or because they had a Tutsi parent, or because someone thought they looked like a Tutsi, or slain like thousands of Hutus because they protected Tutsis or would not countenance a policy that sought to wipe out people who just the day before, and for years before, had been their friends and neighbors. The government-led effort to exterminate Rwanda's Tutsi and moderate Hutus, as you know better than me, took at least a million lives. Scholars of these sorts of events say that the killers, armed mostly with machetes and clubs, nonetheless did their work five times as fast as the mechanized gas chambers used by the Nazis.

It is important that the world know that these killings were not spontaneous or accidental. It is important that the world hear what your President just said—they were most certainly not the result of ancient tribal struggles. Indeed, these people had lived together for centuries

SOURCE: "Remarks by the President to Genocide Survivors, Assistance Workers, and U.S. and Rwanda Government Officials," the White House, Office of the Press Secretary, March 25, 1998, http://clinton2.nara .gov/Africa/19980325-16872.html

before the events the President described began to unfold. These events grew from a policy aimed at the systematic destruction of a people. The ground for violence was carefully prepared, the airwaves poisoned with hate, casting the Tutsis as scapegoats for the problems of Rwanda, denying their humanity. All of this was done, clearly, to make it easy for otherwise reluctant people to participate in wholesale slaughter. Lists of victims, name by name, were actually drawn up in advance. Today the images of all that haunt us all: the dead choking the Kigara River, floating to Lake Victoria. In their fate we are reminded of the capacity in people everywhere—not just in Rwanda, and certainly not just in Africa—but the capacity for people everywhere to slip into pure evil. We cannot abolish that capacity, but we must never accept it. And we know it can be overcome.

The international community, together with nations in Africa, must bear its share of responsibility for this tragedy, as well. (Applause.) We did not act quickly enough after the killing began. We should not have allowed the refugee camps to become safe haven for the killers. (Applause.) We did not immediately call these crimes by their rightful name: genocide. (Applause.) We cannot change the past. But we can and must do everything in our power to help you build a future without fear, and full of hope. (Applause.) We owe to those who died and to those who survived who loved them, our every effort to increase our vigilance and strengthen our stand against those who would commit such atrocities in the future—here or elsewhere. (Applause.) Indeed, we owe to all the peoples of the world who are at risk— because each bloodletting hastens the next as the value of human life is degraded and violence becomes tolerated, the unimaginable becomes more conceivable—we owe to all the people in the world our best efforts to organize ourselves so that we can maximize the chances of preventing these events. And where they cannot be prevented, we can move more quickly to minimize the horror.

So let us challenge ourselves to build a world in which no branch of humanity, because of national, racial, ethnic or religious origin, is again threatened with destruction because of those characteristics, of which people should rightly be proud. Let us work together as a community of civilized nations to strengthen our ability to prevent and, if necessary, to stop genocide. To that end, I am directing my administration to improve, with the international community, our system for identifying and spotlighting nations in danger of genocidal violence, so that we can assure worldwide awareness of impending threats. It may seem strange to you here, especially the many of you who lost members of your family, but all over the world there were people like me sitting in offices, day after day after day, who did not fully appreciate the depth and the speed with which you were being engulfed by this unimaginable terror.

We have seen, too—and I want to say again—that genocide can occur anywhere. It is not an African phenomenon and must never be viewed as such. We have seen it in industrialized Europe; we have seen it in Asia. We must have global vigilance. And never again must we be shy in the face of the evidence. (Applause.) Secondly, we must as an international community have the ability to act when genocide threatens. We are working to create that capacity here in the Great Lakes region, where the memory is still fresh. This afternoon in Entebbe [Uganda] leaders from central and eastern Africa will meet with me to launch an effort to build a coalition to prevent genocide in this region. I thank the leaders who have stepped forward to make this commitment.

We hope the effort can be a model for all the world, because our sacred task is to work to banish this greatest crime against humanity. Events here show how urgent the work is. In the northwest part of your country, attacks by those responsible for the slaughter in 1994 continue today. We must work as partners with Rwanda to end this violence and allow your people to go on rebuilding your lives and your nation. Third, we must work now to remedy the consequences of genocide. The United States has provided assistance to Rwanda to settle the uprooted and restart its economy, but we must do more. I am pleased that America will become the first nation to contribute to the new Genocide Survivors Fund. (Applause.) We will contribute this year $2 million, continue our support in the years to come, and urge other nations to do the same, so that survivors and their communities can find the care they need and the help they must have. (Applause.)

Mr. President, to you, and to you, Mr. Vice President, you have shown great vision in your efforts to create a single nation in which all citizens can live freely and securely. As you pointed out, Rwanda was a single nation before the European powers met in Berlin to carve up Africa. America stands with you, and we will continue helping the people of Rwanda to rebuild their lives and society. (Applause.) You spoke passionately this morning in our private meeting about the need for grass-roots effort in this direction. We will deepen our support for those grass-roots efforts, for the development projects which are bridging divisions and clearing a path to a better future. We will join with you to strengthen democratic institutions, to broaden participation, to give all Rwandans a greater voice in their own governance. The challenges you face are great, but your commitment to lasting reconciliation and inclusion is firm. Fourth, to help ensure that those who survived in the generations to come never again suffer genocidal violence, nothing is more vital than establishing the rule of law. There can be no peace in Rwanda that lasts without a justice system that is recognized as such.

We applaud the efforts of the Rwandan government to strengthen civilian and military justice systems. I am pleased that our Great Lakes Justice Initiative will invest $30 million to help create throughout the region judicial systems that are impartial, credible, and effective. In Rwanda these funds will help to support courts, prosecutors, and police, military justice and cooperation at the local level. We will also continue to pursue justice through our strong backing for the International Criminal Tribunal for Rwanda. The United States is the largest contributor to this tribunal. We are frustrated, as you are, by the delays in the tribunal's work. As we know, we must do better. Now that administrative improvements have begun, however, the tribunal should expedite cases through group trials, and fulfill its historic mission. (Applause.)

We are prepared to help, among other things, with witness relocation, so that those who still fear can speak the truth in safety. And we will support the War Crimes Tribunal for as long as it is needed to do its work, until the truth is clear and justice is rendered. Fifth, we must make it clear to all those who would commit such acts in the future that they too must answer for their acts, and they will. In Rwanda, we must hold accountable all those who may abuse human rights, whether insurgents or soldiers. Internationally, as we meet here, talks are underway at the United Nations to establish a permanent international criminal court. Rwanda and the difficulties we have had with this special tribunal underscores the need for such a court. And the United States will work to see that it is created. (Applause.)

I know that in the face of all you have endured, optimism cannot come easily to any of you. Yet I have just spoken, as I said, with several Rwandans who survived the atrocities, and just listening to them gave me reason for hope. You see countless stories of courage around you every day as you go about your business here—men and women who survived and go on, children who recover the light in their eyes remind us that at the dawn of a new millennium there is only one crucial division among the peoples of the Earth. And believe me, after over five years of dealing with these problems I know it is not the division between Hutu and Tutsi, or Serb and Croatian and Muslim in Bosnia, or Arab and Jew, or Catholic and Protestant in Ireland, or black and white. It is really the line between those who embrace the common humanity we all share and those who reject it. (Applause.)

It is the line between those who find meaning in life through respect and cooperation and who, therefore, embrace peace, and those who can only find meaning in life if they have someone to look down on, someone to trample, someone to punish and, therefore, embrace war. (Applause.) It is the line between those who look to the future and those who cling to the past. It is the line between those who give up their resentment and those who believe they will absolutely die if they have to release one bit of grievance. It is the line between those who confront every day with a clenched fist and those who confront every day with an open hand. That is the only line that really counts when all is said and done. . . .

And so I say to you, though the road is hard and uncertain, and there are many difficulties ahead, and like every other person who wishes to help, I doubtless will not be able to do everything I would like to do, there are things we can do. And if we set about the business of doing them together, you can overcome the awful burden that you have endured. You can put a smile on the face of every child in this country, and you can make people once again believe that they should live as people were living who were singing to us and dancing for us today.

That's what we have to believe. That is what I came here to say. (Applause.) That is what I wish for you. (Applause.)

Thank you and God bless you. (Applause.)

125 • Australia's "Sorry Books"
(Haydie Gooder and Jane M. Jacobs)

In 1998, in response to the Australian government's inability or unwillingness (or both) to extend a sincere apology to the country's indigenous Australians for the suffering they were forced to endure during the colonization of the continent, ordinary Australians seized the moment. Responding to a groundswell of discontent, the advocacy organization Australians for Native Title unceremoniously opened informal "Sorry Books" all over the country. Functioning not unlike guest or condolence books, they generated more than half a million signatures and a great variety of apologies to the Aboriginal and Torres Strait Islander population. In a discerning article published in 2000, Haydie Gooder and

SOURCE: Haydie Gooder and Jane M. Jacobs, "'On the Border of the Unsayable': The Apology in Postcolonizing Australia," *Interventions* 2, no. 2 (2000): 229–30, 232, 235, 239, 240–41, 242, 245. Reprinted with permission of Taylor & Francis.

Jane Jacobs recount the origins and effects of this unusual grassroots movement in Australia. Contrary to many conventional, laudatory accounts, they argue that the Sorry Books may have ultimately been less about the suffering of the country's indigenous populations and more about the "desires of those settler Australians who sought absolutism for past sins."

In May 1997, some 1,800 indigenous and settler Australians met at the nation's first official Convention on Reconciliation. The audience waited expectantly as conservative Prime Minister John Howard made the speech that would formally open the Convention. They waited for much more than an official opening. That same month the findings of an Inquiry by the Human Rights and Equal Opportunity Commission into the Separation of Aboriginal and Torres Strait Islander Children from their Families had been released in a report entitled *Bringing Them Home*. The Inquiry investigated the painful consequences of the forced removal, in the name of assimilation, of "half-caste" Aboriginal and Torres Strait Islander children from their families and homes. The Inquiry into the "Stolen Generation" brought into public view a previously hidden part of the nation's history. In one of its many and wide-ranging recommendations, the Inquiry called for those involved in forced removals (governments, churches, police forces and welfare agencies) to apologize to indigenous Australians. It was the delivery of a formal apology from the nation for which delegates of this inaugural Reconciliation Convention waited.

The Prime Minister was far from oblivious to the expectations of his audience. His speech admitted past injustices to indigenous Australians, what he described as "the most blemished chapter in our history," an acknowledgment that was met with reserved applause. But the qualification that "Australians of this generation should not be required to accept guilt and blame for past actions and policies over which they had no control" received jeers from an increasingly dissatisfied audience. Among the admissions and the qualifications, the longed for apology was given:

> Personally, I feel deep sorrow for those of my fellow Australians who suffered injustices under the practices of past generations towards indigenous people. Equally, I am sorry for the hurt and trauma many people here today [strong applause] . . . Equally, I am sorry for the . . . hurt and trauma many here today may continue to feel as a consequence of these practices.

This apology was delivered nervously to an impatient and disgruntled audience. Some had already risen and turned their backs in a gesture of not listening. Although delivered by the central figure of national authority, the Australian Prime Minister, this apology seemed unable to do the work required of it. No doubt disappointed by the failure of his apology, and struggling to be heard above the jeering, back-turned audience, Prime Minister John Howard ended his speech in what could only be described as a state of mild hysteria. Departing from the safety of his script, with raised voice and clenched fist, he defended recent government policies that had significantly eroded the material and symbolic gains that had come with recognition of native title in the early 1990s. Instead of settling things down, this defensive apology activated in utterly unexpected ways all whom it implicated. An apology was given, but it was considered neither appropriate nor adequate. . . .

Yet the call for an apology, and the failure of the Federal Government to deliver a "proper" version of this apology, has also brought together large numbers of settler Australians in a collective expression of sympathy towards Aborigines and Torres Strait Islanders. This is a group we dub the "sorry people." In the absence of a proper national apology there has been a proliferation of "minor" apologies, an unprecedented outpouring of popular sympathy towards indigenous Australians from these "sorry people." It is with the mass performative of saying sorry in postcolonizing Australia that this essay is largely concerned.

One might imagine that "sorry people"—being non-indigenous, mainly white (and mostly from an Anglo-Celtic background), and largely middle class—are empowered enough by their placement in the structure of a settler nation to resist any destabilizing ill-effects that might come from a call for an apology. But it would appear that this group feels itself called upon to play a special part in the process of reconciliation. . . . These guilt-afflicted settler Australians feel the legitimacy of their national subjectivity to be compromised. They begin to experience a form of settler melancholia. The proliferation of apologies from settler "sorry people" is a symptom of this melancholia and testifies to the strange (and estranging) rewirings of circuits of power in postcolonizing settler contexts like Australia. . . . For the sympathetic settlers, who come to be touched by guilt, there is a sense that they have lost a properly constituted national selfhood. . . . Not only has there been a seemingly irreparable rupture in the settler sense of a place in the nation but, for some, the legitimacy of the very nation itself has been called into question. . . .

Within a year of the release of the *Bringing Them Home* report, a number of [Australian] state leaders had offered apologies on behalf of their [subnational] governments and their constituents. Similarly, police forces around the nation began to apologize for their role not only in the implementation of the laws and policies of forcible removal of children but also for their role in having enforced other unjust laws. Perhaps the most rapid response to the call for an apology came from those church groups that had played such a direct role in the removal and custody of children in the Stolen Generations. This flurry of official apology-giving amplified the absence of an [improved, more appropriate] official apology from the Prime Minister on behalf of the government of the day. . . .

The various formal apologies from governments and organizations have been accompanied by a proliferation of personal apologies from ordinary Australians. . . . The central site through which these ordinary apologies have been expressed are the "Sorry Books." The first Sorry Book (actually consisting of four volumes) was opened for signing on Australia Day 1998 at a media event at the Museum of Contemporary Art, Sydney. The book was initiated by Australians for Native Title, a voluntary political group concerned with supporting Aboriginal and Torres Strait efforts to have their native title recognized. . . . The idea of the Sorry Book captured the imagination of settler Australians and the practice of "opening" Sorry Books spread rapidly. It flowed through the network of largely non-indigenous political groups that had formed to support native title claims and the process of reconciliation. It was taken up by church and other community groups and encouraged by the Trade Union movement. It spread into schools and on to university campuses and was incorporated into the public face of state institutions like museums, libraries, parliaments and municipal offices. It was embraced by private enterprise with Sorry Books appearing in Body Shops, bookstores and shopping malls. A Sorry Book was even opened in London so that diasporic Australians could offer their apologies. By May 1998, just four months after the original Sorry Book was opened, it was estimated that over a thousand Sorry Books had been opened nationwide and over a million signatures and personal apologies collected.

From the outset a set of specifications for "proper" Sorry Books had circulated and many of the books conformed to these specifications. For example, most Sorry Books opened with this statement, taken from the original book:

> By signing my name in this book, I record my deep regret for the injustices suffered by Indigenous Australians as a result of European settlement and, in particular, I offer my personal apology for the hurt and harm caused by the forced removal of children from their families and for the effect of government policy on the human dignity and spirit of Indigenous Australians. I would also like to record my desire for Reconciliation and for a better future for all our peoples. I make a commitment to a united Australia, which respects this land of ours, values Aboriginal and Torres Strait Islander heritage and provides justice and equality for all.

In this statement we see many of the features of [a] proper apology: the admission of trespass, the implied acknowledgment of responsibility, an expression of regret, and a promise of a future in which injury will not recur. A website and brochures offered additional specifications about the paper quality and size (if possible A4 archive paper set in a ring binder) as well as the type of pen to be provided for signing (a water- and fade-proof, black pigment, ink pen). . . .

The Sorry Books came to play an important role in National Sorry Day, the first of which was held on 26 May 1998, the anniversary of the release of the findings of the *Bringing Them Home* report. . . . And while on this day many new Sorry Books were opened and signed, so others, filled over the past year, were delivered ceremoniously to Aboriginal and Torres Strait Islanders elders as a public performative of the giving of an apology. . . . It would seem that for many non-indigenous participants in the Sorry Events it was the *performative* of the apology that was centrally important. One had to be seen to be saying sorry. . . . The "on-record" apology is proof of a settler subject actively transforming him- or herself from "colonialist" into that fantasized subject of the postcolonial nation. Perhaps it is unsurprising that one newspaper inadvertently referred to Sorry Day as "a national day of atonement." Such a slip confirms that standing center stage of this event was not the sorrow of the Stolen Generations, but the desires of those settler Australians who sought absolutism for past sins. . . .

In apologizing, settler Australians ask indigenous Australians to see them more as they would like to see themselves: as settlers who properly belong, who have a kind of indigeneity. We might ask whether a situation such as this, where settler subjects are no longer seen as "settler," is actually a little *too* postcolonial? For at the heart of every apology is a set of truths which should not and cannot be forgotten. And at the heart of indigenous peoples' power in Australia, as elsewhere, is the claim that they were here first, that they belong. What might be the implications of "dispossessed" settlers acquiring their own indigenized sense of belonging? Does this mark the beginning of reconciled coexistence, or inaugurate a more penetrating stage of occupation? Indeed, when the settler nation fantasizes about coexistence, is it engaged in remembering or in forgetting?

126 · Superseding Historic Injustice (Jeremy Waldron)

Reparations and related forms of financial compensation for genocidal suffering are regularly subject to intense controversy. In a 1992 journal article, the legal philosopher Jeremy Waldron, who hails from New Zealand but teaches at the University of Oxford and at New York University, considers from a multitude of perspectives the precarious moral questions that arise when money enters the debate over transitional justice. In particular Waldron examines problems inherent in the use of counterfactual analysis for determining financial entitlements. He assesses the conditions under which entitlements to compensation for historic injustice, such as genocide, may be overtaken by circumstances and thus fade. Expressed more simply, he finds that entitlements that are derived from historic injustice often have a half-life: they last only so long. Based on a consideration of contending philosophical arguments, Waldron cautions that not all entitlements that were denied in the distant past survive as entitlements in the present.

The history of white settlers' dealings with the aboriginal peoples of Australia, New Zealand, and North American is largely a history of injustice. People, or whole peoples, were attacked, defrauded, and expropriated; their lands were stolen and their lives were ruined. What are we to do about these injustices? . . . What is it to correct an injustice? How can we reverse the past? If we are talking about an injustice that took place several generations ago, surely there is nothing we can do now to heal the lives of the actual victims, make them less miserable or to reduce their suffering. The only experiences we can affect are those of people living now and those who will live in the future. . . .

But then there is a sense in which we can affect the moral significance of past action. Even if we cannot alter the action itself we may be able to interfere with the normal course of its consequences. The present surely looks different now from the way the present would look like if a given injustice in the past had not occurred. Why not therefore change the present so that it looks more like the present that would have obtained in the absence of the injustice? Why not make it now as though the injustice had not happened, for all that its occurrence in the past is immutable and undeniable? This is the approach taken by [the philosopher] Robert Nozick in his account of the role played by a principle of rectification in a theory of historic entitlement. . . .

The trouble with this approach is the difficulty we have in saying what would have happened if some event (which did occur) had not taken place. To a certain extent we can appeal to causal laws or, more crudely, the normal course of events. We take a description of the actual world, with its history and natural laws intact, up until the problematic event of injustice (which we shall call event "E"). In the actual course of events, what followed E (events F, G, H) is simply what results from applying natural laws to E as an initial condition. For example, if E was your seizure of the only water hole in the desert just as I was about to slake my thirst, then F—the event that follows E—would be what happens normally when one person is deprived of water and another is not: you live and I die. So, in our counterfactual reasoning, we replace E with its closest just counterpart, $E+$ (say, we share the water hole), and we apply

SOURCE: Jeremy Waldron, "Superseding Historic Injustice," *Ethics* 103, no. 1 (1992): 4, 7–8, 9, 10, 12, 13–16, 24–25, 27–28. Reprinted with permission of the University of Chicago Press.

the laws of nature to that to see what would have happened next. Presumably what would have happened next is that we both slake our thirst and both survive. . . .

But what if some of the events in the sequel to E+ are exercises of human choice rather the inexorable working out of natural laws? Is it possible to say counterfactually how choices subsequent to E+ would have been made, so that we can determine what state of affairs (H+) would obtain now in a society of autonomous choosers, but for the problematic injustice? . . . The problem quickly becomes intractable particularly when the counterfactual sequence is imagined to extend over several generations, and where the range of choices available at a given stage depends on the choices that would have been taken at some earlier stage. This is not a mere academic difficulty. Suppose (counterfactually) that a certain peace of land had not been wrongfully appropriated from some Maori group in New Zealand in 1865. Then we must ask ourselves, What would the tribal owners of that land have done with it. . . ? To ask this question is to ask how people would have exercised their freedom if they had had a real choice. Would they have hung on to the land and passed it on to future generations of the tribe? Or would they have sold it—but this time for a fair price—to the first honest settler who came along? And, if the latter, what would he have done with it? Sold it again? Passed it on to his children? Lost it in a poker game?

Part of our difficulty in answering these questions is our uncertainty about what we are dong when we try to make guesses about the way in which free will would have been exercised. . . . I do not mean that the exercise of human choice is necessarily unpredictable. We make predictions all the time about how people will exercise their freedom. But it is not clear why our best prediction on such a matter should have moral authority in the sort of speculations we are considering. . . . A more general difficulty has to do with our application of rational choice in counterfactual reconstruction. People can and often do act freely to their own disadvantage, and usually when they do, they are held to the result. A man who actually loses his land in a reckless though involuntary wager and who accepts the justice of the outcome may be entitled to wonder why, in the attention we pay to aboriginal reparations, we insulate people from the possibility of similar vicissitudes. . . . The issue is particularly acute because the reparations that these counterfactuals support are likely to have a wide effect on holding across the board. . . . Ultimately, what is raised here is the question of whether it is possible to rectify particular injustices without undertaking a comprehensive redistribution that addresses all claims of justice that may be made. The counterfactual approach aims to bring the present state of affairs as close as possible to the state of affairs that would have obtained if some specifically identified injustice had not occurred. But why stop there? . . . Why not try to make things even better than they would have been if that particular unjust transaction, or any unjust transaction, had not taken place? . . .

The implications of this example are clear for the historic cases we are considering. Instead of regarding the expropriation of aboriginal lands as an isolated act of injustice that took place at a certain time now relegated firmly to the past, we may think if it as a persisting injustice. The injustice persists, and it is perpetuated by the legal system as long as the land that was expropriated is not returned to those from whom it was taken. On this model, the rectification of injustice is a much simpler matter than the approach we discussed in the previous section. We do not have to engage in any counterfactual speculation. We simply give the property back to the person or group from whom it was taken and thus put an end to what otherwise [would] be its continued expropriation. . . . What, if any, are the difficulties with this approach? It does not involve any of the problems of counterfactual reasoning that we identified earlier, but does it face any other problems? As I see it, the main problem is the following. Are we sure that the entitlement that was originally violated all those years ago is an entitlement that survives into the present? The approach we are considering depends on the claim that the right that was violated when white settlers first seized the land can be identified as a right that is still being violated today by settlers' successors in title. Their possession of the land today is said to be as wrongful vis-à-vis the present tribal owners as the original expropriation. Can this view be justified?

It is widely believed that some rights are capable of "fading" in their moral importance by virtue of the passage of time and by the sheer persistence of what was originally a wrongful infringement. In the law of property, we recognize doctrines of prescription and adverse possession. In criminal procedure and in torts, we think it important to have statutes of limitations. The familiarity of these doctrines no doubt contributes to the widespread belief that, after several generations have passed, certain wrongs are simply not worth correcting. . . . The view that a violated entitlement can "fade" with time may seem unfair. The injustice complained of is precisely that the rightful owner has been dispossessed. It seems harsh if the fact of her dispossession is used as a way of weakening her claim. It may also seem to involve some moral hazard by providing an incentive for wrongdoers to cling to their ill-gotten gains, in the hope that the entitlement they violated will fade away because of their adverse possession.

Still, the view that certain rights are prescribable has a number of things to be said in its favor. Some are simply pragmatic. Statutes of limitations are inspired as much by procedural difficulties about evidence and memory as by any doctrine about rights. It is hard to establish what happened if we are inquiring into the events that occurred decades or generations ago. There are nonprocedural pragmatic arguments also. For better or worse, people build up structures of expectation around the resources that are actually under their control. . . . Upsetting these expectations in the name of restitutive justice is bound to be costly and disruptive. There may be reasons of principle as well. One set of reasons has to do with changes in background social and economic circumstances. If the requirements of justice are sensitive to circumstances such as the size of the population or the incidence of scarcity, then there is no guarantee that those requirements (and the rights that they constitute) will remain constant in relation to a given resource or piece of land as the decades and generations go by. . . .

Consider the following example. On the savanna, a number of groups appropriate water holes, in conditions where it is known that there are enough water holes for each group. So long as these conditions obtain, it seems reasonable for the members of given group, P, to use the water hole they have appropriated without asking permission of other groups with whom they share the plains; and it may even seem reasonable to exclude members of other groups from the casual use of their water holes, saying to them, "You have your own water hole. Go off and use that, and leave ours alone." But suppose there is an ecological disaster, and all the water holes dry up except the one that the members of P are using. Then in these changed circumstances, notwithstanding the legitimacy of their original appropriation, it is no longer in order for P to exclude others from their water hole. . . . In the new circumstances, it may be incumbent on them to draw up a rationing scheme that allows for everyone in the territory to be satisfied from this one resource. . . .

Next, suppose as before that in circumstances of plenty various groups on the savanna are legitimately in possession of their respective water holes. One day, motivated purely by greed, members of group Q descend on the water hole possessed by group P and insist on sharing that with them. . . . That is an injustice. But then the circumstances change, and all the water holes of the territory dry up except the one that originally belonged to P. The members of Q are already sharing that water hole on the basis of their earlier incursion. But now that circumstances have changed, they are entitled to share that water hole; it no longer counts as an injustice. It is in fact what justice now requires. The initial injustice by Q against P has been superseded by circumstances. . . . I do not think this possibility—of the supersession of past injustice—can be denied, except at the cost of making one's theory of historical entitlement utterly impervious to variations in the circumstances in which holdings are acquired and withheld from others. If circumstances make a difference to what counts as a just acquisition, then they must make a difference also to what counts as an unjust incursion. And if they make a difference to that, then in principle we must concede that a change in circumstances can affect whether a particular continuation of adverse possession remains an injustice or not. . . .

Entitlements that fade with time, counterfactuals that are impossible to verify, injustices that are overtaken by circumstances—all this is a bit distant, I am afraid, from the simple conviction that, if something was wrongly taken, it must be right to give it back. The arguments I have made may seem to deflate a lot of the honest enthusiasm that surrounds aboriginal claims and the hope that now for the first time in centuries we may be ready to do justice to people and peoples whom we have perennially maltreated. The arguments also seem to compromise justice unnecessarily, as they shift from the straightforward logic of compensation to an arcane and calculative casuistry that tries to balance incommensurable claims. But societies are not simple circumstances, and it does not detract one bit from the importance of justice nor from the force of the duties it generates to insist that its requirements are complex and that they may be sensitive to differences in circumstance. . . .

It is true that in may cases the complexity of these issues does not diminish our ability to recognize acts of injustice—stark and awful—like direct expropriation and genocide. The fallacy lies in thinking that the directness of such perception and the outrage that attends it translate into simple and straightforward certainty about what is to be done once such injustices have occurred.

127 • Acknowledging and Rectifying the Genocide of American Indians (William C. Bradford)

William Bradford, formerly a professor at Indiana University School of Law, considers the promise —and limits—of a series of rectificatory schemes for coming to terms with the historic injustice perpetrated against American Indians. In a 2007 essay, he examines in turn approaches centering

SOURCE: William Bradford, "Acknowledging and Rectifying the Genocide of American Indians: 'Why Is It That They Carry Their Lives on Their Fingernails?'" in Claudia Card and Armen T. Marsoobian, eds., *Genocide's Aftermath: Responsibility and Repair* (Oxford: Blackwell, 2007), 240, 242–45, 246, 247. Reprinted with permission of the publisher.

on supersession, compensation, and restoration. Supersession as an approach to historic injustice is mindful of the contemporary injustice that could result from land restitution or redistribution. Its proponents are therefore wary of calls for rectifying the genocide of American Indians. Advocates of compensation accept more readily the need to rectify past injustice. However, their focus is purely remedial in the sense that they aim to restore or compensate without dwelling on the logic and meaning of the destruction of indigenous populations. Restoration is the most comprehensive of the three approaches to historic injustice because its focus is on making victimized communities whole again. This involves addressing not only material losses but also structural inequalities and the psychological consequences of suffering. While Bradford finds some merit in the pursuit of restorative justice, he ultimately concludes that none of the surveyed approaches is able to offer the full measure of relief that American Indians desire.

The United States murdered millions of Indians so as to depopulate their land and eliminate rival polities within a colonial state structured on it. The survivors and their descendants . . . have been under cultural assault to this day. This malign history has rendered Indians the most materially deprived and legally exposed group in the nation, and the scars of this genocide are manifested in an ongoing cycle of unemployment, infant mortality, suicide, homicide, substance abuse, homelessness, and poor health. . . . The next section will review existing theories of justice that suggest avenues toward the remediation of the genocide of the American Indians. Extant theories cluster around three distinct approaches: supersession, compensation, and restoration.

While the historical record establishes a factual predicate presumptively obligating the United States to remedy the genocide of Indians, proponents of the Justice as Supersession (JAS) theory reach a very different conclusion. . . . Although JAS theory recognizes that the historical record has an important place in a theory of justice, for JAS theorists the historical injustices must be weighed against the current injustice that would be inflicted upon innocent owners now in possession of erstwhile Indian lands if those lands were stripped away and restored to Indian ownership. . . . In other words, while injustice may have been inflicted in centuries past, injustice is perishable, and the accreting rights of non-Indians in Indian lands have incrementally extinguished any present claims for its restoration. . . .

Justice as Compensation (JAC) is similarly landcentric. JAC theorists ignore the process whereby Indian land was depopulated and contend quite simply that where land has been acquired unjustly through fraud or force, either it must, regardless of whether or not it has subsequently been lawfully transferred, be restored to its rightful owner or full compensation must be paid. . . . By accepting the duty to restore or compensate and thereby settling the normative question, JAC theorists are free to direct their energies to prudential issues, such as membership in the remedial class, the form that compensation is to assume, and the identities of the parties from whom restoration or compensation must issue. Nevertheless, many who would otherwise recognize the duty to afford redress to Indians for land expropriation point to relevant treaties and statutes, the Indian Claims Commission (ICC), and a host of federal Indian benefits programs as evidence that compensation has already been paid and claims settled. Even those JAC theorists who would accept that further measures of compensatory relief are still due Indian claimants insist that amounts be negotiated through the political process rather than be determined in accordance with some rational, objective standard. . . .

Justice as Restoration (JAR) aims at a more holistic approach. For proponents of JAR, in-kind compensation, even if theoretically equivalent in value to that which was taken, is insufficient to rectify the original injustice; restoration of the illicitly appropriated property itself is essential to "set unjust situations right." Even more significantly, JAR does not limit its remedial scope to the issue of land rights; rather, it extends to those "injustices that may in fact loom larger in the minds of the victims or their descendants—murder, torture, enslavement, discrimination and degradation." . . . JAR contends that theories which purport to remedy a genocidal history solely "through the language of property" forfeit transformative opportunities whereby to reconcile victims and wrongdoers. Accordingly, in conjunction with land restoration and apologies, JAR theorists call for rehabilitative measures designed to heal the injured psyches of individuals and groups. . . .

At its core, JAS [Justice as Supersession] theory is a not terribly subtle justification for genocide. While JAS theorists may highlight the pragmatic and utilitarian approach to preserving the interests of the non-Indian majority, stripped off its academic veneer JAS theory is little more than the medieval dogmas once enunciated by conquistadors as justification for their adventures in the Americas. . . . Simply put, JAS categorically rejects any moral or legal obligations from the genocide. . . . JAC [Justice as Compensation] theory, in contrast, rejects the premise that history is dead insofar as the obligation to render justice for past wrongs is concerned and that the passage of time can and has rendered good a thief's title. . . . However, JAC theory is far too quick to assume that cash and Indian land are commensurable. . . . Cash, however beneficial to its recipients, cannot restore to Indians the capacity to self-determination on their aboriginal landmass, nor can it bring dead ancestors back to life. Even if Indian tribes could be persuaded to surrender their claims for cash, the fair value would be so great as to threaten the national fisc and spark a racialized political firestorm.

Indian tribes currently control only fifty-two million acres, or 2.6 percent, of the U.S. continental landmass. The ICC, charged with assessing relative U.S. responsibility for expropriation of Indian lands, estimated that 35 percent of the two billion acres making up the United States—a total of 750 million acres—is legally Indian land. Assuming [for argument's sake] that the median value of an acre is $1,000, the fair market cost to compensate Indians would exceed $750 billion. Even assuming that nothing close to fair market value would be paid, and even if the award were reduced by the amounts paid through federal benefits programs or by the ICC, the enormity of any proposal that would offer even "payment on the cheap" would still have macroeconomic consequences. . . .

Of the three theories, only JAR embraces restoration of Indian land, and only JAR is theoretically amenable to consideration of the non-material injuries that occupy a central place in the Indian claim for redress for genocide. Furthermore, only JAR would hold the United States accountable under moral, as opposed to strictly legal, principles, and only JAR would even attempt to induce the United States to repudiate past acts of egregious injustice. . . . However, the most radical JAR theorists are oblivious to the broad externalities the application of their theory might spawn. . . . Thus, while much of JAR is germane, neither it nor the other theories surveyed afford the full measure of relief.

128 • Compensation for Forced and Slave Laborers
in Nazi Concentration Camps (John Authers)

Most compensations for genocidal suffering have been made in connection to the Holocaust. John Authers, a correspondent for the Financial Times, *details the drawn-out international negotiations over compensation for forced and slave laborers who toiled in Nazi concentration camps for the benefit of German companies. In a contributed essay to* The Handbook of Reparations *(2006), he describes the stages and stumbling blocks, legal and otherwise, that accompanied the contentious quest for reparatory justice and explains why the eventual settlement, signed in July 2000, satisfied none of the parties involved.*

In June 2001, fifty-six years after the end of the World War II, the *Bundestag*, Germany's parliament, voted to approve a law that would create a new foundation charged with giving DM10 billion (approx. US$5 billion at the exchange rates prevailing at the time) to former laborers forced to work for the Third Reich. In addition, the money would also be used to restitute beneficiaries of unpaid life insurance policies written on the lives of Holocaust victims, and owners of businesses that had been confiscated, or "Aryanized," by the Nazis. The German lawmakers believed that more than 2 million people still living might qualify for payments, which would be distributed via five national governments and two large international non-governmental organizations (NGOs). Half of the funds came from the German government, with the rest coming from German companies that had profited from using slave labor during World War II.

The law came into being only after lawsuits in the USA against many of Germany's largest and most powerful companies were initiated, and involved international negotiations among eight different governments. The first former laborers received their payments in June 2001. Payments continue at the time of this writing. By June 2005, after four years of the process, a total of 4.18 billion [euros] (approx. US$1.93 billion) had been paid to 1.62 million claimants. This accounted for 96 percent of the funds that had been earmarked for laborers. . . . "Slave laborers"—those, mostly Jewish, who had worked in concentration camps in conditions of extreme cruelty—received DM15,000 (about $7,500) each. "Forced laborers"—those, mostly Slavic, who had been forced to work for the Nazi effort, but in more humane conditions—received about DM5,000 each. . . .

The foundation that came into being in 2001 was the result of direct negotiations between the German government and international civil society organizations, with no overseeing body such as the UN or a court. Thus the amounts paid were contingent far more on the balance of negotiating strength than on any objective factors for assessing a fair amount to pay for the damage caused. Instead, the foundation was endowed with a fixed amount after much argument. This was divided among the claiming parties, again as the result of a negotiating process. These negotiations started in early 1999, at the behest of the governments of the USA and Germany. They lasted—amid great rancor—until the formal signing of the agreement in

SOURCE: John Authers, "Making Good Again: German Compensation for Forced and Slave Laborers," in Pablo de Greiff, ed., *The Handbook of Reparations* (Oxford: Oxford University Press, 2006), 420, 421, 432, 433, 434–35, 439. Reprinted with permission of the publisher.

July 2000. At this stage, Germany still required "legal peace"—the dismissal of the [class action] lawsuits [that had been filed in U.S. courts by lawyers requesting a total US$37 billion] against German companies. This took a year to achieve. . . .

The number of parties involved [in the international negotiations] ensured that finding a consensus would be difficult. Eight sovereign governments (Germany, the USA, Israel, Poland, the Czech Republic, Russia, Belarus, and Ukraine) had seats at the table. So did the Conference on Jewish Material Claims Against Germany (representing the interest of Jewish survivors), the German "Industry Initiative" (the organization set up by German industrial groups to represent them on the issue), and fifty-one different law firms, mostly from the USA. The talks were further complicated by the decision to include property restitution, as well as compensation for slave labor. This meant that once a size for the overall pie had been fixed, there were disputes among claimants over distribution. . . .

Once the DM$10 billion figure had been settled in December 1999, the issue of how to distribute the money remained. This led to a falling out between the Jewish organizations and the representatives of the Eastern Europeans over the distinctions that should be made between "slave laborers" and "forced laborers." Jewish campaigners, arguing that reparations should be to some extent proportional to the degree of suffering inflicted, accused Jewish lawyers who wanted to equate or minimize the difference in payments to the different kinds of laborers as "a disgrace to the memory of the Holocaust." There were also issues over dividing the money between those who had property claims against the German government and laborers. . . .

Slave and forced laborers each received a "rough justice" amount. . . . In another move to enable swift payments, the burden of proof was set very low. The Jewish survivors had mostly been covered by previous reparations efforts, and therefore could be traced swiftly. Definitions with arbitrary cut-off points made the justice rougher, but also allowed for ease of administration. No attempt was made to assess applicants' current needs. Prior compensation that the victims had received was also excluded from calculations—those already compensated separately by other German restitution schemes received no less than those who had received nothing. There was also no differentiation in terms of how long they had served as a laborer, a possibility that had been mooted at one point by the Jewish side in the negotiations. . . . The German foundation designed the process so as to keep very tight control of payments. . . . Money in proportion to the expected number of claimants was given to each government (and to the Conference on Jewish Material Claims Against Germany for the Jewish claimants, and the International Organization for Migration [IOM] for all non-Jewish claimants outside the Central and Eastern European countries). . . .

Virtually no party to the reparations process was satisfied with the outcome. The lengthy legal delays clearing the foundation meant that by some estimates as many as 10 percent of the eligible population alive at the time the reparations agreement was signed in principle in July 2000 died in the year which then elapsed before money started to be disbursed. The process also raised hopes and increased frustration for the remaining survivors. Many Jewish Holocaust survivors objected to the designation of the Conference on Jewish Material Claims Against Germany to receive their money, claiming that it was insufficiently accountable. On the German side, many complain—although generally not in public—that they are victims of moral blackmail, and that their Jewish interlocutors understated the importance of money already paid out to them in the reparations programs of the 1950s. However, by comparison with other attempts at restitution at about the same time (regarding stolen property in Austria and France, unpaid insurance policies across Europe, laundered stolen gold, and dormant Swiss bank accounts), the process was a relative success.

Many Jewish organizations put great weight on the German president's decision to accompany the payouts with a formal apology. This gave the gesture much more moral and symbolic value. There was a general acceptance on all sides that the crimes being compensated were so terrible that full justice was impossible. Thus even a token gesture commanded a wide degree of assent.

129 • The International Court of Justice's Refusal of a Reparation Order in *Bosnia and Herzegovina v. Serbia and Montenegro* (Christian Tomuschat)

The International Court of Justice's very influential decision in Bosnia and Herzegovina v. Serbia and Montenegro *also included a finding on the Bosnian quest for financial compensation. In short, the Court decided that the death of more than seven thousand Bosnian Muslim men and boys in Srebrenica did not warrant a reparation order for the benefit of the next of kin of the victims, even though Serbia was found to have failed to prevent and punish these international crimes. Christian Tomuschat, professor of international law emeritus at Humboldt University in Berlin and a former member of the International Law Commission, elucidates the judges' reasoning and questions their wisdom in this 2007 journal article.*

The judgment of the International Court of Justice (ICJ or the Court) of 26 February 2007 must have left the Muslim population of Bosnia and Herzegovina in a state of perplexity and bitterness. First of all, the finding that Serbia, at the relevant time the Federal Republic of Yugoslavia (FRY), did not commit genocide was contrary, in their eyes, to what they as the victims had witnessed as first-hand evidence. Second, the finding that Serbia violated its obligation to prevent genocide is not accompanied by any tangible consequential finding. The Court confines itself to stating that "a declaration of this kind is 'in itself appropriate satisfaction.'" No reasons are given for this rather cursory treatment of the request for reparation. Thus, the death of more than 7000 Bosnian Muslim men entails no substantial reparation for the benefit of the next of kin of the slaughtered victims. Serbia receives a blame which has a legal character but this boils down to no more than a gesture of moral reprobation—and that disposes of the matter. It is true that the perspective of the layman cannot be determinative. To establish legal responsibility in accordance with the applicable rules of international law is a complex juridical process which cannot be accomplished solely by looking at the relevant facts. These facts need to be assessed and evaluated by lawyers—but even lawyers will find it hard to follow the Court's convoluted line of reasoning. . . .

SOURCE: Christian Tomuschat, "Reparation in Cases of Genocide," *Journal of International Criminal Justice* 5, no. 4 (2007): 906–7, 908–9, 910–11. Reprinted with permission of Oxford University Press.

The Court set the course when it determined that Serbia was not directly responsible for the atrocities committed at Srebrenica, arguing that the murderous actions of the Bosnian Serbs could not be attributed to the FRY, a neighboring state which was intimately linked to the Republika Srpska but which had no effective control over the perpetrators, not even a decisive influence. However, logic would seem to require that the failure of the Serbian Government, specifically acknowledged by the Court, to halt the mass killing in and around Srebrenica should give rise to an obligation on the part of Serbia to compensate for the damage suffered by the victimized population and thereby also the state of Bosnia and Herzegovina.

The Court starts out from the well-known proposition enunciated in the *Factory at Chorzow* case of the Permanent Court of International Justice according to which "reparation must, so far as possible, wipe out all the consequences of the illegal act and re-establish the situation which would, in all probability, have existed if that act had not been committed." It is a matter of common knowledge that this proposition has also found its way into the Articles on State responsibility drafted by the International Law Commission (ILC) and "taken note of" by the UN General Assembly. The relevant requirements were met. By not taking any initiative to prevent the genocidal occurrences as they had to be envisaged on the basis of available indicia the Government of Serbia committed a breach of its obligations under Article I of the Genocide Convention. Obviously, *restitutio in integrum* could not be ordered by the Court. The dead could not be brought back to life. Under such circumstances, the ILC Articles suggest that compensation should be paid (Article 36). The Court explicitly refers to this subsidiary secondary rule as well. However, it seeks to demonstrate that the failure to abide by the duty of prevention incumbent on the FRY had no nexus relating it to the tragic outcome at the end of the causal chain. . . .

The Court acknowledges that as a remedy of last resort Bosnia and Herzegovina is entitled to reparation in the form of satisfaction. In an extremely short passage of its holdings, the Court concludes that a declaration to the effect that the Respondent has failed to abide by its duty of prevention is in itself appropriate satisfaction. As is well known, the ILC Articles on State Responsibility do not explicitly mention any form of satisfaction that would have a financial dimension. But Article 37(2) is not exhaustive as may be easily gleaned from its wording ("Satisfaction may consist . . .") as well as from the Commentary of the ILC. Moreover, there exist clear precedents in international practice which show that the full range of forms of satisfaction includes symbolic monetary damages as well. Thus in the *Rainbow Warrior* case, the Arbitral Tribunal stated unambiguously that

> an order for the payment of monetary compensation can be made in respect of the breach of international obligations involving, as here, serious moral and legal damage, even though there is no material damage.

No such order was made by the Tribunal, however, since New Zealand had not requested the award of monetary compensation. This is exactly the ground which the Court relies on in denying any financial reparation to the Applicant under the head of satisfaction. . . . Even a superficial reading of the submissions of the Applicant, however, shows that Bosnia and Herzegovina sought to obtain full reparation for any kind of the damage which had been inflicted upon it. Already in the application Bosnia and Herzegovina requested "reparation for damages to persons and property as well as to the Bosnian economy and environment . . . in a sum to be determined by the Court." . . . It would be hard to contend that the scope *ratione materiae* of these formulations is so narrow as not to include monetary compensation under the head of satisfaction. . . .

It is undeniable, on the other hand, that an international judge enjoys a large measure of discretion in awarding satisfaction. In trying to find support for its overly succinct manner of addressing the issue of satisfaction, the Court refers to the *Corfu Channel* case of 1949 where, indeed, the finding that Albania had breached its international obligations vis-à-vis the United Kingdom had been deemed to constitute the appropriate form of satisfaction. However, can the two cases really be put on the same level? Precedents should never be resorted to without a careful consideration of their factual context. When mines exploded in the Corfu Channel, British ships were damaged, and a number of British sailors were injured and died. But it was, conversely, Albania that requested satisfaction for the unlawful passage of ships through Albanian waters. Albania had not suffered any tangible, material damage. What was at stake was a violation of the sovereign rights over its coastal sea. Its claim for satisfaction had almost no legitimacy since the Court came to the conclusion that Albania was responsible for the explosions caused by the mines and for the damage and loss of human life that resulted therefrom.

Here, by contrast, more than 7000 men were murdered in cold blood. Therefore, can one really equate the *Corfu Channel* case with the *Srebrenica* case? No doubts should be permitted: the Court was not well-advised to refer to a case dating back almost six decades and dealing with a factual background that was fundamentally different from the circumstances of the instant case. To deal with the death of 7000 persons as if it were *un petit rien*, namely purely legal injury not requiring anything else than a toothless declaration of a breach, does not appear to do justice to the moral harm inflicted on the victims and their next of kin. We do not mix up the killing itself with the failure of the Belgrade authorities to discharge their responsibilities under Article I of the Genocide Convention. But the intimate relationship between the two phenomena is self-evident. There was at least a strong possibility that those 7000 lives could have been saved, and in any event the then FRY Government deliberately hazarded the consequences of its inertia. Therefore, in making a determination on the right form of satisfaction, the genocidal tragedy itself could not be left aside.

The Court could have found guidance in the case law of the European Court of Human Rights. The Strasbourg Court has indeed evolved a jurisprudence which in many instances deems a declaration of a violation to constitute sufficient reparation. But it deviates from this line whenever an applicant has suffered considerable emotional distress and anguish, in particular because of the loss of a close relative. . . . Another formulation to be encountered in the judgments of the Strasbourg Court focuses on "anguish and feelings of helplessness and frustration" experienced by the applicant as a consequence of a breach of its obligations by a state party [as articulated in *Xenides-Arestis v. Turkey*, December 7, 2006]. Clearly, in the human rights field the judges take into account the degree of pain and suffering endured by the victims. It is hard to understand why the international judge at The Hague dismisses any such considerations, without even addressing the issue. The praetorian statement . . . that a simple declaration indicating the occurrence of a breach constitutes appropriate satisfaction fails to comply with the duty of any judge to support his decision by explicit reasons. This is all the more deplorable since the proceedings in the case had been going on for 14 years. There was ample time to assess every facet of the relevant facts. Instead, the Court rushes through the issue of satisfaction as if it intended to avoid giving it due consideration.

130 • The Reparation Provisions in the Rome Statute of the International Criminal Court (Gilbert Bitti and Gabriela González Rivas)

In certain respects, the future of compensation for genocidal suffering looks more hopeful than its past. Gilbert Bitti and Gabriela González Rivas, formerly chief and legal officer of the Victims Participation and Reparations Unit at the International Criminal Court (ICC), discuss the Court's reparations mechanism as well as the recently established Trust Fund for Victims, which is independent of the ICC. In addition to explicating procedures, their 2006 essay raises serious questions about the ICC's readiness to mete out reparatory justice in response to genocide and other international crimes.

One of the great innovations of the International Criminal Court ("ICC" or the "Court") is the role extended to victims. A concerted effort to establish effective international law mechanisms for the protection of the rights of victims was made during the drafting of the Statute of the International Criminal Court (the "Rome Statute" or the "Statute"), the Rules of Procedure and Evidence (the "Rules"), and the Regulations of the Court (the "Regulations"). . . . The Rome Statute [among other things] allows victims to apply for reparations for the harm they have suffered as the result of the commission of a crime under the jurisdiction of the Court. The ICC has "the discretion to award individual or collective reparations, in the form of compensation, restitution, and rehabilitation."

Furthermore, in September 2002 the Assembly of States Parties of the ICC established a Trust Fund for Victims ("Trust Fund") for the benefit of victims of crimes within the jurisdiction of the Court, and the families of such victims, to complement the Court's reparations function. The Trust Fund is independent of the Court and plays a dual role. It may be asked by the Court to help implement reparations awards ordered against a convicted person. The Trust Fund is also able to utilize the contributions it receives to finance projects for the benefit of victims, and will, therefore, be in a position to help victims receive some form of reparations even when the convicted person does not have sufficient assets. . . .

[As far as the definition of "victim" is concerned,] Rule 85 provides as follows: "For the purpose of the Statute and the Rules of Procedure and Evidence: (a) 'Victims' means natural persons who have suffered harm as a result of the commission of any crime within the jurisdiction of the court; (b) Victims may include organizations or institutions that have sustained direct harm to any of their property which is dedicated to religion, education, art or science

SOURCE: Gilbert Bitti and Gabriela González Rivas, "The Reparation Provisions for Victims under the Rome Statute of the International Criminal Court," in International Bureau of the Permanent Court of Arbitration, ed., *Redressing Injustices through Mass Claims Processes: Innovative Responses to Unique Challenges* (Oxford: Oxford University Press, 2006), 299, 300, 306–7, 309, 312–13, 314, 317, 321, 322. Reprinted with permission of the publisher.

or charitable purposes, and to their historical monuments, hospital and other places and objects for humanitarian purposes." . . . The framework within which the Court may award reparations is set out in Article 75 ("Reparations to victims") of the Rome Statute. . . . The [reparations] procedure will usually be instigated at the request of victims. Rule 94 of the Rules ("Procedure upon request") requires the application to be made in writing (unless the person is unable, due to disability or illiteracy, to make a written application) and filed with the Registrar. The application may be made at any stage of the proceedings, even prior to the commencement of an investigation: the victim is under no obligation to link his or her application to a specific case before the Court. That task will be performed by the Court itself.

However, although request for reparations may be filed months or years before the arrest or conviction of the person responsible for the harm suffered, it is crucial to note that the reparations proceedings before the Court are intrinsically linked to the criminal proceedings before it; the Court cannot hear reparations proceedings in the absence of criminal proceedings against the person responsible for the harm suffered by the victims. For this reason, victims have a particular interest in closely following the progress of investigations and prosecutions and in intervening in those proceedings, to the extent permitted by Article 68, paragraph 3, of the Statute. If the investigation is not successful, the victims will lose the opportunity to have their requests for reparations dealt with by the Court, thus making it very important for victims to intervene in the selection of situations and cases to be investigated . . . by the Court. . . .

A request for reparations is required to contain the following particulars: (a) the identity and address of the claimant; (b) a description of the injury, loss or harm; (c) the location and date of the incident; (d) where restitution assets, property or other tangible items is sought, a description of them; (e) any claims for compensation; (f) any claims for rehabilitation and other forms of remedy; and (g) to the extent possible, any relevant supporting documentation, including names and addresses of witnesses. . . . When a request for reparations has been filed (or the victims have given a written undertaking that they will do so), the victims may request the pre-trial chamber, at any time after the issuance of a warrant of arrest or a summons to appear before the Court under Article 58, to seek the cooperation of States Parties to take measures for the identification, tracing and freezing of proceeds, property, and assets and instrumentalities of crimes. The pre-trial chamber may also, in accordance with Rule 99 of the Rules, do so on its own motion or at the request of the Prosecutor. . . . The trial chamber may hear witnesses and examine their evidence for the purposes of making a reparations order "at the same time as for the purposes of the trial." . . . The decision on reparations will usually be issued separately, after the decision on conviction. . . .

The Court may, where appropriate, "order that the award for reparations be made *through* the Trust Fund." The role to be played by the Trust Fund in the distribution of awards for reparations is set out in Rule 98 of the Rules. Individual awards for reparations shall be made directly against a convicted person and are not to be deposited with the Trust Fund unless, at the time of making the award, it is impossible or impracticable to make individual awards directly to each victim. The role of the Trust Fund is thus limited . . . to collective awards: indeed Rule 98, paragraph 3 clarifies that the Court may order that "an award for reparations against a convicted person be made through the Trust Fund where the number of victims and the scope, forms and modalities of reparations makes a collective award more appropriate." . . .

It may, arguably, be much more difficult for the Court to determine thousands of claims than to decide on several criminal cases for each situation. In its current setting, it is difficult to see how the Court will be able to manage [its] role [as arbiter of reparations], unless it receives substantial assistance either from within the Court (and therefore a substantial increase of its budget) or from outside the Court, through commissions or panels of experts which will act at the request of the Court and report to it. If such a system is not established, it is likely that the Court will only be in a position to award reparations on a collective basis, leaving the implementation of those awards to the Trust Fund either directly or through an international or national organization. Even with limited ambition, it is likely that the reparation functions of the Court will take time and effort, and require a substantive modification to the Court's structure, both in chambers and its Presidency. . . .

How will the entire system created by both the Court and the Trust Fund address the views, preoccupations, and needs of the victims of crimes within the jurisdiction of the Court? The consideration of this dilemma is only at a very early stage despite the fact that fundamental decisions concerning victims before the ICC were made seven years ago at the Rome Conference. It is now a question of implementation.

CHAPTER NINE

Cures

What, if anything, can be done about genocide? Can it be prevented? Can it be anticipated? What are appropriate responses once it has occurred? As recent developments in Darfur attest, the imperative of devising solutions to the problem of genocide is of continuing relevance for international peace and security. In recognition of this relevance, in 2012 the administration of U.S. President Barack Obama established the Atrocities Prevention Board (APB). Initially headed by Samantha Power, the journalist–turned professor–turned ambassador, the APB is tasked with creating a sounder organizational foundation for U.S. responses to mass atrocities and genocide. This chapter provides selections from the writings of a diverse group of scholars and practitioners as well as from public documents pertaining to the question of "cures" for genocide, broadly defined. The purpose is to acquaint readers with some of the knowledge necessary for evaluating policy responses such as the APB as well as institutional designs conceived by NGOs (e.g., the so-called responsibility to protect, or R2P), international organizations (e.g., the Office of the UN Special Adviser on Genocide), and governments (e.g. Vietnam's 1978 intervention in Cambodia).

The writings in this chapter illuminate long-standing and new advances in the ongoing quest to end genocide. They are suggestive of both progress and regress in efforts at uprooting the proverbial "problem from hell," a phrase famously coined by former U.S. Secretary of State Warren Christopher. Seven excerpts in this chapter directly speak to the question of military intervention. Two of the works address an insufficiently covered topic: the mechanics of military deployment. James Kitchens offers an important reassessment of the popular argument that the bombing of Auschwitz could have substantially altered—or even halted—the course of the Holocaust. Alan Kuperman provides a revisionist account of a comparable argument in the Rwandan case. Stephen Morris, Samantha Power, and Geoffrey Robinson approach the same topic from a vantage point where the demands of domestic politics and international affairs intersect. Morris examines a rarely mentioned, successful military intervention in times of genocide: Vietnam's invasion of Cambodia. Power delves into U.S. decision making regarding the 1994 genocide in Rwanda and elaborates why America stood by when that country's Tutsi population was targeted for total destruction. Robinson explains why genocide was stopped in East Timor.

The final two pieces on military intervention tackle the thorny relationship between law and morals. The first is the conclusion that the Independent International Commission on Kosovo reached in its assessment of the legality and legitimacy of the NATO intervention in the province of the former Yugoslavia: that the controversial military operation was "illegal but legitimate." The second is presented by the political theorist Michael Walzer. Deeply influenced by the Kosovo example, Walzer advances a pragmatic sketch of the conditions under which he believes military intervention to strangers is morally permissible, indeed morally required. The military intervention in Kosovo also opened the door for policy-oriented deliberations about the demands of a muscular humanitarianism that eventually led to the formulation of the idea of a "responsibility to protect." Two of the selections pertain to this development. The juxtaposition of the original formulation of R2P, as developed by Canada's International Commission on Intervention and State Sovereignty, with the watered-down concept of R2P as adopted at the 2005 United Nations World Summit in New York, gives a sense of the continuing resistance on the part of sovereign states to commit to the prevention of genocide.

However, the extensive focus on the question of military intervention, as important as it is, should not distract from other essential writings. Michael Barnett's sociological approach to decision making inside the UN Secretariat at the time of the Rwandan genocide brings into sharp relief the workings of international organizations, as does Dawit Toga's detailed empirical exploration of the many rounds of the Abuja talks, which the African Union oversaw in an attempt to help negotiate a peaceful settlement for the conflict in Darfur. Another international organization is at the heart of Karen Smith's analysis. She illuminates governmental attitudes in the European Union and in select European countries toward genocide prevention. Given the controversy that was sparked by the International Commission of Inquiry on Darfur (ICID), selections from the report are featured. The ICID is of immediate relevance for the question of cures because it represents one of the international community's most common responses to mass atrocities: the appointment of an international commission of inquiry. The ICID is also important to study because—controversially at the time—it bucked the trend to describe the collective violence in Sudan's Darfur region as genocide. Together with the highly critical op-ed by Andrew Natsios, the extract from its report makes for an illuminating discussion of the much-debated Darfur case. Rounding off the selection of pieces on the international community are the provisions from the UN Genocide Convention that ostensibly demand action in times of genocide, and William Schabas's pithy interpretation of these provisions. As he points out in no uncertain terms, the Convention—contrary to widespread belief—did not establish a "duty to prevent" genocide.

More recent policy responses to genocide have made use of quantitative methods. Exemplary of this trend is the scholarship of Barbara Harff and Matthew Krain. Both, although in slightly different ways, are working on the mathematical forecasting of genocide. Elizabeth Levy Paluck's and my contributions are concerned with pathways to interethnic cooperation in the aftermath of genocide. Whereas I reflect critically on superficial conceptions of reconciliation—a frequently prescribed strategy to prevent a renewal of violence—Paluck studies media interventions in the aftermath of conflict. She reports findings from a field experiment in postgenocide Rwanda, where an education entertainment radio soap opera appears to have led to some changes in behavior vis-à-vis former adversaries.

The diverse set of writings in this chapter—like those in the previous chapters—may instill in readers wariness of moral absolutes and reticence about easy prescriptions. This is the least we owe the subject of genocide, this darkest of human phenomena.

131 • The Bombing of Auschwitz Reexamined
(James H. Kitchens III)

In a 1994 journal article, the historian James Kitchens III reconsiders the contentious question of whether or not bombing the gas chambers and crematoria of Auschwitz would have been feasible or even desirable in the early 1940s. Taking issue with David Wyman's influential proposition from 1984, proffered in The Abandonment of the Jews, *that indifference—not inability—prevented the Allies from launching an air raid on the concentration camp complex in Poland, Kitchens argues that a series of far more benign factors, all influenced by military science, drove the American and British decisions to forgo the bombing of Auschwitz.*

One of the most curious—even bizarre—legacies of the Holocaust is the question of whether the Allies could, and should, have used their air power to destroy the gas chambers and crematoria at Auschwitz and the rail net feeding them. For a decade or so, it has been argued that the camp's location and layout were well known and that the installations and rails vital to its operations could have been easily and precisely neutralized from the air, had not insensitivity, indifference, and even antipathy prevented it. Critics, on the other hand, argue that aerial bombing of Auschwitz or its vital railroads was technically infeasible and militarily chimerical. . . .

The initial inspiration for bombing concentration camps or railroads to counter the Holocaust may be traced to early summer 1944 . . . [when] the Slovak Orthodox rabbi Dov Weissmandel, horrified by the incipient deportation of hundreds of thousands of Hungarian Jews to Auschwitz, begged the Allies to block the movement by bombing the Košice-Prešov rail line. . . . In late June 1994, the U.S. War Department rejected the Košice-Prešov rail bombing plea on the grounds that it was impractical and would require diversion of too many essential resources; in August, the British Air Ministry also refused aerial rescue operations, citing poor intelligence, hazards and high casualties, and dubious results. . . . Thus, no German concentration camps were deliberately attacked from the air before war's end, and no discernible efforts were made to single out deportation railroads for special attacks. . . .

Against this backdrop, in May 1978 David S. Wyman, professor of history at the University of Massachusetts, published a startling article entitled "Why Auschwitz Was Never Bombed" in the American Jewish Committee's magazine *Commentary*. The title told all: Wyman proposed to disclose how the camp could have been bombed but was not. . . . Despite spasmodic publicity in the early eighties, the bombing question really did not catch the public eye until late 1984, when Wyman incorporated a refined and annotated version of his *Commentary* article into a weighty monograph titled *The Abandonment of the Jews*. . . . As early as April 1944, Wyman postulated, the Allies had aerial photographs of the Auschwitz-Birkenau concentration camp, and additional evidence became available during May and June through the detailed report of two escapees, Rudolf Vrba and Alfred Wetzler. . . .

Adherents of camp bombing from Wyman onward have consistently maintained that Allied leadership possessed enough, and sufficiently exact, intelligence about . . . Auschwitz

SOURCE: James H. Kitchens III, "The Bombing of Auschwitz Re-examined," *Journal of Military History* 58, no. 2 (1994): 233–34, 235, 236, 237, 245–46, 247, 248, 249–50, 252, 253, 258, 259, 260, 261, 262, 263–64, 265. Reprinted with permission of the Society for Military History.

buildings [housing the gas chambers and crematoria] to mount the kind of attack necessary to destroy them. Two types of evidence for this are usually cited, photos derived from USAAF [U.S. Army Air Forces] reconnaissance over the I. G. Farben Monowitz complex ("Buna") near Auschwitz and the report of escapees Vrba and Wetzler. It is true that images of Birkenau appeared on aerial photographs as early as April 1944, but as [other scholars] have pointed out, the death camp appeared only accidentally and was wholly incidental to the interpreters' work. None of them was tasked to look for concentration camps; their prints and viewing equipment were primitive; none of them had the experience or interpretation guides to make the images speak intelligibly. . . . Under these circumstances, it is not surprising that Auschwitz's true nature passed unnoticed under the photo interpreters' stereoscopes. In the context of overall intelligence appreciation, it also should be noted that there was no historical precedent for genocidal installations like Auschwitz and that before the end of 1994, at least, the Allies lacked enough solid intelligence about the "Final Solution" to adequately comprehend its hideous import.

Bombing advocates maintain, however, that when combined with aerial photographs the Vrba-Wetzler report should have precipitated immediate and decisive action from Washington or London. . . . On the surface, the report appears to be a sickening revelation about what was going on in Auschwitz, and so it was. But in fact, as intelligence collateral for analyzing the camp as a precision bombing target the report had severe limitations. Neither escapee was a trained observer, and their page-and-a-half description of Birkenau's crematoria was almost exclusively concerned with the ghastly details of operation rather than militarily useful targeting data such as building structural design, materials, foundations, and the like necessary for the selection and placement of ordnance. Potential low-flying hazards such as high tension wires and radio transmission towers were nowhere mentioned, and chimneys and forested areas were only vaguely indicated. . . . The escapees' report did not even estimate the gas chambers and crematoria's outside dimensions, nor did it reliably locate them on the ground. . . . Finally, expert photo interpreters might, with enough time and effort, have correlated aerial photographs with the Vrba-Wetzler report, but the authors themselves remained in Slovakia, inaccessible for person-to-person debriefing or clarification of the information they had provided. In sum, the militarily useful intelligence available to the Allies about Auschwitz came late and was much shakier than Wyman suggests. . . .

Presuming adequate intelligence about Birkenau and Auschwitz I, their nature and location still presented insurmountable obstacles for precision bombing. One major problem was sheer range. The Auschwitz complex lay about 620 miles from Fifteenth Air Force heavy bomber bases around Foggia [in Italy] and approximately 525 miles from the Adriatic island airfield on Vis, operational after 2 May 1944. Thus, Auschwitz was barely within the theoretical range of B-25 medium bombers, P-38 fighter-bombers using an external drop tank, and D.H.98 Mosquito light bombers. Simple distance, however, was inseparably intertwined with factors of terrain, tactics, winds and weather, useful bomb load, air defenses, and crew performances. . . . To attack Auschwitz via direct route out of either southern Italy or Vis required crossing the Dalmatian Alps, ranging above five thousand feet. Flying heavily escorted in formation above the highest ridges, heavy bombers had no difficulty with the mountains, but a low-level attack by medium or light bombers or fighter-bombers would have been much more difficult. . . .

On arriving in the target area, attackers faced a dispersed, dauntingly complex objective consisting of five widely spaced buildings (four at Birkenau, one over a mile away at Auschwitz I) which had to be identified and attacked in concert with little loiter time and no release error. In making such attacks, weather also played a part. The atmosphere over mountainous Balkan terrain was likely to be more turbulent than over the sea or northwest European plain. Accurate precision bombing required perfect visibility, yet over southern Poland such weather was unusual and its prediction problematical. How, then, have bombing adherents proposed to attack the Auschwitz complex?

One proposal, high altitude raiding by four-engined heavy bombers, . . . can be immediately discounted. B-17s and B-24s . . . cruised at 180 to 190 mph and were designed to bomb from fifteen to thirty thousand feet. . . . Normal bomb patterns from the heavies extended hundreds of yards from the aiming point, and it was quite common for bombs to fall a mile or more away from the target. . . . It is true that Allies were occasionally able to carry out surgical stabs at well-known, high-priority targets, and bombing advocates have usually cited this kind of operation as optimal for raiding Auschwitz. Typically, it is suggested that twin-engined Lockheed P-38 fighter-bombers or De Hallivand D.H.98 Mosquitos could have bombed selected buildings with precision and surprise. . . .

Capable of carrying a ton of bombs at nearly three hundred mph close to the ground, the all-wood Mosquito was one of World War II's wonder planes. Highly versatile, it was built in over two dozen versions and performed well in many roles. . . . The similarity of the dramatic Mosquito operations [in other theaters of war] to the problem of attacking Auschwitz's gas chambers and crematoria, however, is vague at best, and in a close comparison, Auschwitz emerges as a well-nigh invulnerable target. . . . Few, if any, of the special Mosquito raids attacked more than one building, while there were *five* discrete objectives at Auschwitz. Mosquito fighter-bombers had no defensive armament and could not dogfight with interceptors; flying unescorted they relied solely on surprise and lightning speed for success. . . . Thus, flying over 620 miles in radio silence, crossing the Alps in some semblance of cohesion at low altitude, then sneaking through German air defenses with enough fuel to make a coordinated precision attack on five targets and return home beggars belief. . . . Furthermore, no Mosquito fighter-bombers were stationed in the Mediterranean in the summer of 1944, and none could be moved there. . . .

During 1944–45, 140 Wing [of Great Britain's Royal Air Force] typically employed from six to twenty aircraft against single-building targets on its most-demanding low-level strikes. . . . If one assumes a strike force of just eight aircraft to destroy each target at Auschwitz, a strike force of forty aircraft, or two full squadrons, would have been required. In 1944–45, this amounted to one-half of the very best Mosquito fighter-bombers crews in Britain. Had such a force been transferred to the Mediterranean Theater for a death camp raid, . . . other German military installations would have been sacrificed. . . . Such agonizing questions of asset allocation lay at the heart of military science, and Allied air leaders probably had them in mind when they responded negatively to pleas for an attack on Auschwitz-Birkenau in mid-1944. . . .

Although Wyman hesitates about trying to bomb railroads serving the extermination camps, other bombing adherents have advocated it. But as [one scholar] pointed out . . . , a successful line-cutting campaign requires day-in, day-out attacks over the entire system that serves a selected area—in this case, all of occupied Europe. Unless all routes are simultaneously interdicted and remain cut, alternative routes, repair gangs, and make-do will largely negate the effort. Thanks to their operations analysis sections, Allied air staffs knew this resources-results equation with great exactitude....

Two other vital observations about the bombing question cannot be overemphasized: attacking Auschwitz might have been illegal under international law, and it would certainly have been morally dubious. Under the Hague Convention of 1907 (Hague, IV), Article 25, "the attack or bombardment, by whatever means, of towns, villages, dwellings, or buildings, which are undefended is prohibited." The U.S. War Department's Basic Field Manuel FM 27-10, *Rules of Land Warfare*, issued in 1940, ... gave three examples of "defended places." Only by torturing the third example, "a place that is occupied by a combatant military force," could Auschwitz-Birkenau have qualified as a legitimate target for bombardment....

Yet, the underlying dilemma is as plain today as fifty years ago: Would it be moral to kill a minimum of several hundred internees in trying to save others—with no assurance of success—and if so, what tragic ratio would have been acceptable? Ultimately, this is a philosophical or theological dilemma, not a historical one, and it is not the historian's duty to resolve it. Arguments, however, that camp inhabitants would have died anyway, or that the symbolism of bombing would have justified it, or that some within Auschwitz might have welcomed death from the air appear specious. In general, Allied leaders were convinced that the innocent should be spared if possible and, weighing out the possibilities, acted accordingly....

Looking back from 1992, the bombing of Auschwitz emerges as a peculiar, and peculiarly difficult, historical conundrum. No bombing took place, and asking why decades later has as yet produced only conjecture. The Wyman thesis attributes the Allied avoidance of death camp bombing to callousness, insensitivity, and even antisemitic prejudice in high circles.... To date, however, the Wyman school has adduced only inferential and circumstantial evidence that Auschwitz remained inviolate because of indifference or outright antipathy for the plight of European Jews.... More—much more—than inference is required.

132 • The Prevention of Genocide (UN Genocide Convention)

Given the confusion that surrounds the provisions dealing with the prevention of genocide in the 1948 Genocide Convention, an examination of Articles I and VIII is in order. Although the famous international treaty came about, among other reasons, in response to the perception, held especially by a number of developing countries, that the crime of "peacetime genocide" had been neglected in the Allied proceedings against leading Nazis at the International Military Tribunal at Nuremberg, it is historically and legally inaccurate to suggest that the governments that were present at the creation of the Genocide Convention had the goal of imposing any binding obligation on member states to respond to genocidal violence. Contrary to conventional wisdom, neither of the aforementioned provisions imposes any kind of "duty to intervene" on state parties. Article VIII in particular gives states extremely wide latitude in designing a response to genocidal acts ("may call upon the competent organs" or "to take such action as they consider appropriate"). One of the most important facts

SOURCE: Convention on the Prevention and Punishment of the Crime of Genocide, adopted by Resolution 260(III)A of the United Nations General Assembly, December 9, 1948.

about the drafting history of the Genocide Convention is that nothing was further from the minds of the drafters than compelling state action in the event of genocide.

ARTICLE I

The Contracting Parties confirm that genocide, whether committed in time of peace or in time of war, is a crime under international law which they undertake to prevent and to punish.

ARTICLE VIII

Any Contracting Party may call upon the competent organs of the United Nations to take such action under the Charter of the United Nations as they consider appropriate for the prevention and suppression of acts of genocide or any of the other acts enumerated in article III.

133 • What Duty to Intervene? (William A. Schabas)

The 1948 Genocide Convention does not impose on contracting parties a "duty to intervene" in cases of genocide. In the latest edition of his 2000 book on genocide and international law, William Schabas, professor of international law at Middlesex University, explains why. As a principal reason he cites the lack of advocacy networks in international human rights in 1948. Not explicitly mentioned in this extract, but of equal importance during the drafting process, was the strength of the idea of sovereignty as a foundation of both international law and politics. Until very recently it was inconceivable that governments would even consider subscribing to a principle that would in any way circumscribe their absolute sovereign right to noninterference in their domestic affairs, a right that is enshrined in Article 2 of the UN Charter. In the late 1940s, the international human rights movement was still in its infancy. This meant that humanitarian concerns, though commonplace today, made virtually no difference to the calculations of states at the time. Quite the opposite: a number of authoritarian and totalitarian regimes were concerned during the making of the Genocide Convention that they could become the targets of human rights activists. Consequently these countries made sure that Articles I and VIII of the international treaty would not amount to more than mere expressions of goodwill.

Although the Genocide Convention's title speaks of both prevention and punishment of the crime of genocide, the essence of its provisions is directed to the second limb of that tandem. The concept of prevention is repeated in article I: "The Contracting Parties confirm that genocide, whether committed in time of peace or in time of war, is a crime under international law which they undertake to prevent and punish." Of course, punishment and prevention are intimately related. Criminal law's deterrent function supports the claim that prompt and appropriate punishment prevents future offenses. Moreover, some of the "other acts" of genocide imply a preventive dimension. Prosecution of conspiracy, of attempts and above all of

SOURCE: William A. Schabas, *Genocide in International Law: The Crime of Crimes*, 2nd edition (Cambridge: Cambridge University Press, 2009), 520–21, 533, 538, 579. Reprinted with permission of the publisher.

direct and public incitement are all aimed at future violations. . . . Finally, in article VIII of the Convention, the States parties are authorized to "call upon the competent organs of the United Nations to take such action under the Charter of the United Nations as they consider appropriate for the prevention and suppression of acts of genocide or any of the other acts enumerated in article 3." . . .

Some twenty years [after the adoption of the Genocide Convention in 1948], the General Assembly thought sufficiently highly of the role of article VIII to include the same text, *mutatis mutandis*, in the International Convention on the Suppression and Punishment of the Crime of Apartheid. Yet most commentators have tended to dismiss article VIII as relatively insignificant. Nehemiah Robinson [author of the first commentary on the 1948 Genocide Convention] observed that the "low value" the drafters gave to the provision is shown by the fact that it was originally deleted. . . . The laconic references to the prevention of genocide in articles I and VIII of the Convention are all that remain of considerably more extensive proposals aimed at attacking the origins of the crime. The further "upstream" that international law was prepared to go in preventing genocide, the more likely it was that it would trench upon "matters which are essentially within the domestic jurisdiction of any state," to borrow the language of article 2(7) of the Charter of the United Nations. The failure to adopt these more far-reaching provisions highlights the still relatively underdeveloped condition of international human rights law in 1948, when the Convention was adopted. While the drafters of the Convention were prepared to admit, albeit with great caution, international intervention when genocide had in fact been committed, they were loath to accept such activity when it was only threatened.

134 • Why Vietnam Invaded Cambodia (Stephen J. Morris)

When Vietnam invaded Cambodia on December 25, 1978, it effectively brought to an end the Cambodian genocide that had turned the neighboring country into a wasteland during the previous five years. The Vietnamese invasion is one of the few examples of a successful military intervention in response to genocidal violence. However, as Stephen Morris of Johns Hopkins University's Paul H. Nitze School of Advanced International Studies illustrates in his book, published in 1999, not all good things necessarily go together when the international community responds to genocide. In fact Morris shows that Vietnam's invasion was motivated less by humanitarian concerns than by geopolitical fears.

Vietnam invaded Cambodia because it saw the action as a means of simultaneously achieving two purposes: ending the military attacks begun by Khmers Rouges and satisfying a long-standing ambition to dominate its weaker neighbor. The first purpose, were it the only purpose, could have been achieved by actions short of full-scale invasion and occupation. An alternative response might have included an intensification of the counterattacks inside

SOURCE: Stephen J. Morris, *Why Vietnam Invaded Cambodia: Political Culture and the Causes of War* (Stanford, Calif.: Stanford University Press, 1999), 229–31, 232–34. Reprinted with permission of the publisher.

Cambodia's eastern provinces, which would have quickly destroyed Khmers Rouges offensive capabilities; the creation of a coordinated indigenous Cambodian armed resistance; and the temporary seizing of several eastern Cambodian provinces in conjunction with the pursuit of a sincere negotiation strategy to secure peace, involving China as an intermediary (which China had briefly tried of its own volition in 1977). That Vietnamese response would have avoided the several political and economic costs that Vietnam suffered for over a decade as a result of the negative international reaction to its invasion and occupation of Cambodia. On the other hand, without Khmers Rouges provocations, the Vietnamese would probably not have invaded, since they would have lacked a legitimizing public rationale. In other words, Khmers Rouges provocations provided a convenient pretext for a Vietnamese action that also had other less easily legitimizable purposes. But this does not tell us the whole story. For the behavior of the two local belligerents was affected by their relations with the two major communist powers, the Soviet Union and China.

It is customary for historians to distinguish between long-term, medium-term, and short-term or triggering causes. The long-term cause of Vietnam's invasion was Vietnamese imperial ambitions. Vietnamese political elites have aspired for centuries to dominate their weaker neighbors. This ambition was first displayed by the Vietnamese emperors, who modeled their courts on the political culture of the Chinese imperial court. . . . The imperial ambitions of the Vietnamese communists were realized in Laos, where Vietnamese forces installed a client regime in 1975. They were thwarted in Cambodia by a combination of the resilience of Cambodian nationalism, the desire of the external powers at Geneva in 1954 to guarantee Cambodian sovereignty, and the political skills and international prestige of Cambodia's first post-independence leader, Prince Norodom Sihanouk. The eventual ascension to power in 1975 of a communist movement [the Khmer Rouge] not under Vietnamese control seemed to ensure the security of Cambodia from Vietnamese domination. Yet this newly victorious communist movement soon began to act in such a provocatively aggressive way as to provide a pretext for the Vietnamese to justify their invasion and occupation of Cambodia. This was the immediate or triggering cause.

The Khmers Rouges, who emerged from an organizational embryo created by the Vietnamese communists, were not always hostile to their fellow revolutionaries. A genuine solidarity based upon Marxist-Leninist "proletarian internationalism" existed during the early years of the movement. The divergence of Vietnamese and Cambodian communist political interests during the 1960s and the clear manifestation of Vietnamese ambition to control the Cambodian revolution during the early 1970s, slowly turned the Khmers Rouges leaders against their former mentors. At some stage in this political metamorphosis the Khmers Rouges leaders became ideological disciples of Mao Zedong. . . . But the Khmers Rouges decision for military confrontation [with Vietnam] was irrational and counterproductive for a variety of reasons. . . . [Most important,] it was a decision taken without consulting Cambodia's external patron, the People's Republic of China. . . .

The intermediate causes of the [1978 Vietnamese] invasion and war were the attitudes and policies of the external powers in relation to each other and in relation to the two local Indochinese nations. To understand why the major communist powers became involved in the conflict, making full-scale war between Vietnam and Cambodia more likely, one has to consider the foreign policies of Cambodia, Vietnam, the Soviet Union, and China. As we have seen, the Khmers Rouges were ideological disciples of Mao Zedong. Because of this ideological affinity, the Khmers Rouges were natural allies of the Chinese communist regime until Mao's death in September 1976, and the arrest of his ultraleft allies, the Gang of Four, the following month. The shift by Mao's successor, Deng Xiaoping, toward more moderate domestic policies weakened Chinese authority in the minds of the Khmers Rouges. . . . This shift by the Khmers Rouges leaders from the original alliance with China based upon both an ideological inspiration and common political and military strategic mutual interests was not understood by the Vietnamese leaders. Hanoi continued to see the China-Cambodia relationship as one of master and servant, in which Khmers Rouges aggressiveness was merely the acting out of a script that had been written in Beijing. Cambodia was described as a Chinese dagger pointed at the heart of Vietnam. . . . The Vietnamese leaders' flawed vision of the China-Cambodia relationship prevented them from responding to apparently genuine mediation attempts by China in 1977. . . .

In 1978 when the Vietnamese leaders' anxiety over their pro-Soviet policy fused with their fear of a Chinese–Khmers Rouges conspiracy, their persecutory policy climaxed. Hundreds of thousands of ethnic Chinese residents of northern Vietnam were expelled to China. This policy had the serious consequence of intensifying Beijing's anger with Hanoi. . . . It also consolidated the previously ambivalent Beijing–Phnom Penh alliance. . . . Vietnamese actions in the context of the Sino-Soviet conflict provided a new security dimension to Chinese attitudes toward Cambodia. Vietnam's decision in the late 1960s to tilt toward the Soviet Union in its foreign policy line—in particular on many foreign policy issues that were irrelevant to Vietnamese national security but were matters of contention between the Soviet Union and China—angered Beijing. Given the massive assistance that Beijing had been providing the Hanoi leaders for over 20 years, Beijing came to regard Hanoi's pro-Moscow tilt as insulting in its ungratefulness. More ominously, Beijing came to perceive Hanoi as a mere servant of Soviet foreign policy. This was an exaggeration of the closeness of the Soviet-Vietnamese relationship at the time. But China's anger at the ostensible insult was genuine, as was its deep fear of Soviet military encirclement. Thus when the Vietnamese subsequently clashed with the Khmers Rouges . . . , China came to see the struggle for Cambodia as a struggle for or against Soviet "social imperialist" expansion. China redefined what was originally a local issue into an issue of great global significance.

Finally, one has to consider the role of the Soviet Union. Without the political, military, and economic support of the Soviet Union and its East European satellites, the Vietnamese communists would not have even contemplated challenging China's political preferences in Southeast Asia. Of course, the Soviet Union did not determine Vietnamese imperial ambition, but it made the realization of that ambition at least plausible. That Soviet policy in Indochina after 1970 was as much concerned with curbing Chinese influence as it was in undermining American power can be seen in the Soviets' Cambodia policy. Instead of supporting the communist FUNK [National United Front of Cambodia] insurgency's Beijing-based front government, nominally headed by Prince Sihanouk, the Soviets continued to recognize the pro-American, anticommunist government of Lon Nol until the last weeks of the 1970–1975 war. This Soviet policy had a clear albeit unintended consequence: it confirmed the Khmers Rouges' sense that the Soviet Union was their enemy and that the subsequent Soviet-Vietnamese alliance was a conspiracy aimed at Cambodia.

In reality, the Soviet-Vietnamese alliance, by the time it was formalized in 1978, was a conspiracy aimed at China. The Vietnamese communists, distrustful of even their most powerful sponsor, had failed to tell the Soviet Union of their plan to invade and occupy Cambodia until after the event. Nevertheless, subsequent Soviet willingness to assist the Vietnamese in establishing what amounted to a regional hegemony under Soviet auspices exacerbated China's concern for the threat to its own security. Soviet policy thereby produced more important unintended consequences in that it accelerated the process of Chinese-American rapprochement, and it resulted in the formation of a unified international coalition (led by China, the Association of Southeast Asian Nations [better known by its acronym, ASEAN], and the United States) opposed to Soviet foreign policy throughout the region. This in turn ensured China's ability to revitalize the Khmers Rouges from bases in Thailand, and thereby guaranteed that the Vietnamese invasion would result not in a swift military victory but instead in a protracted war.

135 • Bystanders to Genocide in Rwanda (Samantha Power)

In her 2001 article in the Atlantic Monthly, *journalist Samantha Power, who subsequently became a professor of practice at Harvard University's John F. Kennedy School of Government and a member of U.S. President Barack Obama's National Security Council, chronicles the evolution of U.S. decision making in response to the unfolding genocidal campaign in Rwanda in 1994. She argues that the administration of U.S. President Bill Clinton actively sought to dampen enthusiasm for action and to preserve the public's sense—and, more important, its own—that the adopted policy of nonintervention was not merely politically astute but also morally acceptable.*

In the course of a hundred days in 1994 the Hutu government of Rwanda and its extremist allies very nearly succeeded in exterminating the country's Tutsi minority. Using firearms, machetes, and a variety of garden implements, Hutu militiamen, soldiers, and ordinary citizens murdered some 800,000 Tutsi and politically moderate Hutu. It was the fastest, most efficient killing spree of the twentieth century. . . . Why did the United States not do more for the Rwandans at the time of the killings? Did the President [Bill Clinton] really not know about the genocide, as his marginalia suggested? Who were the people in his Administration who made the life-and-death decisions that dictated U.S. policy? Why did they decide (or decide not to decide) as they did? Were any voices inside or outside the U.S. government demanding that the United States do more? If so, why weren't they heeded? And most crucial, what could the United States have done to save lives? . . .

Each of the American actors dealing with Rwanda brought particular institutional interests and biases to his or her handling of the crisis. Secretary of State Warren Christopher knew little about Africa. At one meeting with his top advisers, several weeks after the plane crash [that killed the presidents of Rwanda and Burundi and, on April 6, set off the genocidal campaign], he pulled out an atlas off his shelf to help him locate the country. . . . Officials in the State Department's Africa Bureau were, of course, better informed. Prudence Bushnell, the deputy assistant secretary, was one of them. . . . Just two weeks before the plane crash the State Department had dispatched Bushnell and a colleague to Rwanda in an effort to contain the escalating violence and spur the stalled peace process.

Unfortunately, for all the concern of the Americans familiar with Rwanda, their diplomacy suffered from three weaknesses: First, ahead of the plane crash diplomats had repeatedly threatened to pull out UN peacekeepers in retaliation for the parties' failure to implement [the] Arusha [accords]. These threats were of course counterproductive, because the very Hutu who opposed power-sharing wanted nothing more than a UN withdrawal. . . . Second, before and during the massacres U.S. diplomacy revealed its natural bias toward states and toward negotiations. Because most official contact occurs between representatives of states, U.S. officials were predisposed to trust the assurances of Rwandan officials, several of whom were plotting genocide behind the scenes. . . . An examination of the cable traffic from the U.S. embassy in Kigali to Washington between the signing of the Arusha agreement and the downing of the presidential plane reveals that setbacks were perceived as "dangers to the peace process" more than as "dangers to Rwandans." . . . Even after the Hutu government began exterminating Tutsi, U.S. diplomats focused most of their efforts on "re-establishing a cease-fire" and "getting Arusha back on track." . . . The third problematic feature of U.S. diplomacy before and during the genocide was a tendency toward blindness bred by familiarity: the few people in Washington who were paying attention to Rwanda before [President Juvénal] Habyarimana's plane was shot down were those who had been tracking Rwanda for some time and had thus come to expect a certain level of ethnic violence from the region. . . . And because the U.S. government had done little when some 40,000 people had been killed in Hutu-Tutsi violence in [neighboring] Burundi in October of 1993, these officials also knew that Washington was prepared to tolerate substantial bloodshed. When the massacres began in April, some U.S. regional specialists initially suspected that Rwanda was undergoing "another flare-up" that would involve another "acceptable" (if tragic) round of ethnic murder. . . .

On April 9 and 10, in five different convoys, [U.S.] Ambassador [to Rwanda] [David] Rawson and 250 Americans were evacuated from Kigali and other points. . . . While the United States evacuated overland without an American military escort, the Europeans sent troops to Rwanda so that their personnel could exit by air. . . . In the three days during which some 4,000 foreigners were evacuated, about 20,000 Rwandans were killed. . . . Just when did Washington know of the sinister Hutu designs on Rwanda's Tutsi? . . . Whatever the inevitable imperfections of U.S. intelligence early on, the reports from Rwanda were severe enough to distinguish Hutu killers from ordinary combatants in civil war. . . . On April 26 an unattributed intelligence memo titled "responsibility for Massacres in Rwanda" reported that the ringleaders of the genocide, Colonel Théoneste Bagosora and his crisis committee, were determined to liquidate their opposition and exterminate the Tutsi populace. A May 9 Defense Intelligence Agency [DIA] report stated plainly that the Rwandan violence was not spontaneous but was directed by the government, with lists of victims prepared well in advance. The DIA observed that an "organized parallel effort of *genocide* [was] being implemented by the army to destroy the leadership of the Tutsi community." . . .

Even after the reality of genocide in Rwanda had become irrefutable, when bodies were shown choking the Kagera River on the nightly news, the brute fact of the slaughter failed to influence U.S. policy except in a negative way.... A discussion paper on Rwanda, prepared by an official in the Office of the Secretary of Defense and dated May 1, testifies to the nature of official thinking. Regarding issues that might be brought up at the next interagency working group, it stated, "1. *Genocide Investigation*: Language that calls for an international investigation of human rights abuses and possible violations of the genocide convention. Be Careful. Legal at State was worried about this yesterday—Genocide finding could commit [the U.S. government] to actually 'do something' [emphasis added]." At an interagency teleconference in late April, Susan Rice, a rising star on the NSC [National Security Council] who worked under Richard Clarke [who was orchestrating the U.S. response to the Rwandan genocide at the National Security Council and, in the wake of the terrorist attacks of September 11, 2011, in the United States became known as a "counterterrorism czar"], stunned a few of the officials present when she asked, "If we use the word 'genocide' and are seen as doing nothing, what will be the effect on the November [congressional] election?" ...

The genocide debate in U.S. government circles began the last week of April, but it was not until May 21, six weeks after the killing began, that Secretary [of State Warren] Christopher gave his diplomats permission to use the term "genocide"—sort of. The UN Human Rights Commission was about to meet in special session, and the U.S. Representative, Geraldine Ferraro, needed guidance on whether to join a resolution stating that genocide had occurred. The stubborn U.S. stand had become untenable internationally.... Notably Christopher confined permission to acknowledge full-fledged genocide to the upcoming session of the Human Rights Commission. Outside that venue State Department officials were authorized to state publicly only that *acts* of genocide had occurred. Christine Shelly, a State Department spokesperson, had long been charged with publicly articulating the U.S. position on whether events in Rwanda counted as genocide. For two months she had avoided the term, and as her June 10 exchange with the Reuters correspondent Alan Elsner reveals, her semantic dance continued.... *Elsner*: What's the difference between "acts of genocide" and "genocide"? *Shelley*: Clearly not all the killings that have taken place in Rwanda are killings to which you might apply that label.... *Elsner*: How many acts of genocide does it take to make genocide? *Shelley*: Alan, that's just not a question that I'm in a position to answer....

Once the Americans had been evacuated, Rwanda largely dropped off the radar of most senior Clinton Administration officials. In the situation room on the seventh floor of the State Department a map of Rwanda had been hurriedly pinned to the wall in the aftermath of the plane crash, and eight banks of phones had rung off the hook. Now, with U.S. citizens safely home, the State Department chaired a daily interagency meeting, often by teleconference, designed to coordinate mid-level diplomatic and humanitarian responses. Cabinet-level officials focused on crises elsewhere. [National Security Adviser] Anthony Lake recalls, "I was obsessed with Haiti and Bosnia during that period, so Rwanda was ... a 'sideshow,' but not even a sideshow—a no show." At the NSC the person who managed Rwanda policy was not Lake, the national security adviser, who happened to know Africa, but Richard Clarke, who oversaw peacekeeping policy, and for whom the news from Rwanda only confirmed a deep skepticism about the viability of UN deployments. Clarke believed that another failure [like the botched intervention in Somalia] could doom relations between [the U.S.] Congress and the United Nations. . . .

During the entire three months of the genocide, Clinton never assembled his top policy advisers to discuss the killings. Anthony Lake likewise never gathered the "principals"—the Cabinet-level members of the foreign-policy team. Rwanda was never thought to warrant its own top-level meeting. When the subject did come up, it did so along with, and subordinate to, discussions of Somalia, Haiti, and Bosnia. . . . [Relatedly,] the editorial boards of the major American newspapers discouraged U.S. intervention during the genocide. . . . What is most remarkable about the American response to the Rwandan genocide is not so much the absence of U.S. military action as that during the entire genocide the possibility of U.S. military intervention was never even debated. Indeed, the United States resisted intervention of any kind. . . . On April 15 Christopher sent one of the most forceful documents to be produced in the entire three months of the genocide to Madeleine Albright at the UN—a cable instructing her to demand a full UN withdrawal [from Rwanda]. The cable which was heavily influenced by Richard Clarke at the NSC . . . was unequivocal about the next steps. . . . Christopher wrote that there was "insufficient justification" to retain a UN presence. . . . The UN Security Council now made a decision that sealed the Tutsis' fate and signaled the militia that it would have free rein. The U.S. demand for a full UN withdrawal had been opposed by some African nations, and even by Madeleine Albright, so the United States lobbied instead for a dramatic drawdown in troop strength. On April 21, amid press reports of some 100,000 dead in Rwanda, the Security Council voted to slash UNAMIR's [UN Assistance Mission in Rwanda] forces [from an already reduced presence] to 270 men. . . .

The Administration employed several devices to keep down enthusiasm for action and to preserve the public's sense—and, more important, its own—that U.S. policy choices were not merely politically astute but also morally acceptable. First, Administration officials exaggerated the extremity of possible responses. Time and again U.S. leaders posed the choice as between staying out of Rwanda and "getting involved everywhere." In addition, they often presented the choice as one between doing nothing and sending in the Marines. . . . Second, Administration policymakers appealed to notions of the greater good. They did not simply frame U.S. policy as one contrived in order to advance the national interest or avoid U.S. casualties. Rather, they often argued against intervention from the standpoint of people committed to protecting human life. . . . Many internalized the belief that the UN had more to lose by sending reinforcements and failing than by allowing the killing to proceed. . . . A third feature of the response that helped to console U.S. officials at the time was the sheer flurry of Rwanda-related activity. U.S. officials with a special concern for Rwanda took their solace from mini-victories—working on behalf of specific individuals or groups (Monique Mujawamariya; the Rwandans gathered at the [H]otel [des Mille Collines]). Government officials involved in policy met constantly and remained "seized of the matter"; they neither appeared nor felt indifferent. Although little in the way of effective intervention emerged from mid-level meetings in Washington or New York, an abundance of memoranda and other documents did. Finally, the almost willful delusion that what was happening in Rwanda did not amount to genocide created a nurturing ethical framework for inaction. "War" was "tragic" but [unlike genocide] created no moral imperative.

136 • The Rwandan Genocide and the Limits
of Humanitarian Intervention (Alan Kuperman)

Contrary to Power, Alan Kuperman, an associate professor of public policy at the University of
Texas at Austin, is skeptical about the difference that a military intervention could have made in the
context of the Rwandan genocide of 1994. Focusing not on questions of political will or moral obliga-
tion but solely on military strategy, Kuperman's 2001 book examines the logistical challenges that
would have been involved in mounting a U.S. military operation in central Africa. To this end, he
compares and contrasts three typical modes of interventions: maximum, moderate, and minimal.
He concludes that, under the most realistic scenario, a U.S. military intervention could not have
prevented the genocide but might have saved an estimated 75,000 to 125,000 Tutsi from death—
about 15 to 25 percent of those who ultimately lost their lives.

If the United States had decided to launch an intervention immediately upon determining
that genocide was occurring in Rwanda, a key question would have been how fast an adequate
force could have been transported to the theater and begun operations there. . . . This chapter
analyzes the retrospective potential of three types of U.S. military intervention: maximum,
moderate, and minimal. None envisions full-blown nationwide policing or long-term nation
building by American troops. . . .

A maximum intervention would have required deployment of a force roughly the size
of a U.S. division—three brigades and supporting units, comprising about 15,000 troops. The
rules of engagement would have permitted deadly force to protect the lives of endangered
Rwandans. After entering and establishing a base of operations at Kigali airport, the force
would have focused on three primary goals: (1) halting armed combat and interposing between FAR [Forces Armées Rwandaises] and RPF [Rwandan Patriotic Front] forces on the
two main fronts of the civil war in Kigali and Ruhengeri; (2) establishing order in the capital;
and (3) fanning out to halt large-scale genocidal killing in the countryside. None of these
tasks would have been especially difficult or dangerous for properly configured and supported
U.S. troops once in Rwanda. However, transporting a force of appropriate size 10,000 miles
to a landlocked country with limited airfield capacity is not a trivial exercise, and would have
taken considerably longer than some retrospective appraisals have suggested. For example,
one unrealistic estimate is that of Iqbal Riza, deputy to the director of UN peacekeeping during the genocide and later chief of staff to UN Secretary-General Kofi Annan. Riza has asserted that—given the requisite will—sufficient troops and tanks to stop the genocide could
have been airlifted to Rwanda in two days. . . . His estimate is low by at least a factor of ten.

The first brigade to arrive would have been responsible for Kigali—coercing the FAR
and RPF to halt hostilities, interposing between them, and policing the capital. The second
brigade could have deployed one of its battalions north to halt the civil war in Ruhengeri,
another as a rapid-reaction force in case U.S. troops drew fire, and a third to begin stopping
large-scale genocide outside Kigali. The third brigade would have been devoted entirely to

SOURCE: Alan Kuperman, *The Limits of Humanitarian Intervention: Genocide in Rwanda* (Washington, D.C.:
    Brookings Institution Press, 2001), 52, 63, 64–65, 66, 67, 68, 70, 71, 73, 76, 77, 109. Reprinted with permis-
    sion of the publisher.

halting killing in the countryside. Military personnel requirements for such an effort would have been roughly 2,000 to halt war in Kigali, 1,000 to halt war in the north, 3,000 to police Kigali, 1,500 for a rapid-reaction force, and 6,000 to stop the genocide in the countryside, in addition to perhaps 1,500 support personnel for peace operations, making a total of about 15,000 troops. The 3,000 troops to police Kigali would have represented a ratio of at least ten per thousand of population in the capital. . . . The entire division-size task force would have been airlifted to the theater. Owing to constraints on the rate of airlift, . . . the time required to deploy the intervention force would have been a function of its weight. Estimates of the weight and other characteristics of a division-size task force built around one brigade each from the 101st, the 82nd, and a light division can be taken as the average of those divisions —26,550 tons, including 200 helicopters and 13,373 personnel. . . . At the maximum credible rate of 800 tons daily, such a task force would have required thirty-three days of airlift. . . . In Rwanda, the delay before deploying into the field would have been even longer because of the distance and difficulty of the airlift. Thus U.S. troops would not have begun stopping genocide in the countryside until about three weeks after the president's order, or May 11, 1994.

Optimists such as Human Rights Watch have suggested that genocide would have stopped spontaneously throughout Rwanda upon arrival of a Western intervention force in Kigali—or possibly even earlier upon the mere announcement of a deployment. . . . This is dubious. Genocide was in full swing throughout Rwanda by the time [U.S.] President [Bill] Clinton had enough information to reasonably issue an order on April 20, 1994. To stop the killing everywhere at once would have required the extremist ringleaders to issue clear and direct orders over the radio and through military channels to cease and desist. There is little reason to believe they would have done so spontaneously because they did not do so during Operation Turquoise [which the government of France apparently intended to protect internally displaced persons, refugees, and civilians in danger in Rwanda], even after their French allies urged them to halt the killing. . . . More likely, the announcement of Western intervention would have accelerated the killing as extremists tried to finish the job and eliminate witnesses while they had a chance. Such was the trend ahead of the RPA [Rwandan Patriotic Army] advance, as militias attempted to wipe out remaining Tutsi before the rebels arrived. . . .

The only plausible way for late-arriving interveners to have stopped the genocide without deploying to the countryside would have been to capture the ringleaders and force them to issue the appropriate orders. This mission would have been difficult because the extremist leaders retreated to Gitarama on April 13, ten days before American forces realistically could have arrived in Kigali. Even had the ringleaders been captured and so coerced, genocide might not have stopped immediately in the countryside, especially if the rebels had continued their offensive, which terrified the Hutu populace and motivated the Hutu militias to try to finish off the remaining Tutsi civilians, who were seen as natural allies of the advancing rebels. . . . Large-scale genocide could have been stopped during the fourth or fifth week after the deployment order, or sometime between May 15 and May 25. . . . According to [a] model of the genocide's progression, . . . such an intervention would have enabled about 275,000 Tutsi to survive the genocide, as compared with the 150,000 who actually did. . . .

A more modest intervention designed to reduce force requirements and the risk of casualties would have refrained from deploying U.S. troops to any area in Rwanda in which FAR and RPA troops were actively engaged in combat. In late April, this approach would have confined U.S. troops to a zone consisting of six prefectures in southern and western Rwanda that were still free of two-sided military combat but already consumed in genocide—Butare, Cyangugu, Gikongoro, Gisenyi, Gitarama, and Kibuye. . . . Three main objectives would have been set: (1) to deter and prevent entry of organized military forces into the zone; (2) to halt large-scale genocide there; and (3) to prepare for a hand-off to a UN force. By the time of the intervention, the zone would have included about 4 million residents. . . . Large-scale genocide in the zone probably could have been stopped within three weeks after the deployment order, or by May 11, 1994. The [aforementioned] model of the genocide's progression suggest that about 200,000 Tutsi within this zone could have been kept alive by such an intervention, about twice the 100,000 who actually did survive in this portion of Rwanda. . . . Moderate intervention thus could have spared about 100,000 Tutsi from death, or about 20 percent of the genocide's ultimate toll. Interestingly, moderate intervention would have saved almost as many lives as maximum intervention in Rwanda. . . .

To further reduce the risk of casualties, a minimal intervention would have attempted to mitigate the genocide without introducing U.S. ground troops into Rwanda. Instead it would have relied on air power from bases in neighboring countries. . . . Each of the [available] air power strategies would have had drawbacks. Coercion [by way of air strikes] might not have worked because of the difficulty of finding and targeting extremists and their military assets. Airborne policing would have been only a stopgap measure, dependent on cobbling together a follow-on ground force and unable to prevent smaller acts of genocide in the meantime. Facilitating safe passage [to neighboring countries] would have protected only those Rwandan Tutsi able to make their way to major exit routes, left many others to die, and created refugee crises in neighboring states. U.S. helicopters also would have been vulnerable to antiaircraft fire, and any resulting casualties could have undercut American public support for the mission. Nevertheless, each of the air power options also had the potential to save tens of thousands of Rwandan Tutsi from demise. . . . Based on the model of the genocide's progression, about 300,000 Rwandan Tutsi were still alive in late April 1994, of whom about 150,000 subsequently perished. If minimal intervention had been able to avert half these later killings, it could have spared about 75,000 Tutsi from death, or 15 percent of the genocide's ultimate toll. . . .

A realistic U.S. military intervention launched as soon as President Clinton could have determined that genocide was being attempted in Rwanda would not have averted the genocide. It could, however, have saved an estimated 75,000 to 125,000 Tutsi from death, about 15 to 25 percent of those who ultimately lost their lives, in addition to tens of thousands of Hutu. Rwanda represents a particularly tough case for intervention in some respects, including its rapid rate of killing and inaccessible location. However, it would have been relatively easy in other respects, such as the limited military strength of potential adversaries and the country's small size. By contrast, humanitarian intervention is much more challenging in a country with the population and territory of [Democratic Republic of] Congo, or the armed forces of the former Yugoslavia.

137 • Inside the UN in 1994 (Michael Barnett)

Author of Eyewitness to a Genocide, *published in 2002, the political scientist Michael Barnett examines decision making within the United Nations during the 1994 genocide in Rwanda. At the time, Barnett, a professor of international affairs and political science at George Washington University, was on sabbatical at the UN and thus uniquely poised to analyze the goings-on in the much-maligned international organization. He draws our attention to the organizational dynamics at New York headquarters, notably to what he calls the UN's bureaucratic culture. This culture, says Barnett, generated a calculated and staged performance that was designed to discourage military intervention.*

The story of Rwanda is quickly becoming received, predictably so, as a sorrowful parable about how humanity responds to crimes against humanity and genocide. To speak of Rwanda is to summon images of individuals and institutions who cared little or not at all, whose responsibilities were easily consumed by self-interests, and who medicated themselves with hollow expressions of concern. I aim to disturb this future of the Rwandan genocide. I want to replace the secure conclusion that unethical behavior begat indifference with the discomforting possibility that for many in New York the moral compass pointed away from and not toward Rwanda. To do so necessitates the reconstruction of the moral universe at the UN at this particular moment.

Anyone who has ever worked in an organization recognizes that its inhabitants use a discourse and reason through rules that are molded by a common identity. While this discourse and these rules are usually unintelligible to those who are outside the organization, for those inside the organization these rules and discourse can have such power that they mold their identities and ways of knowing and thinking about the world. The UN is no different in this regard. It too contains a discourse and formal and informal rules that shape what individuals care about and the practices they view as appropriate, desirable, and ethical in their own right. The centrality and distinctiveness of this moral universe have often been overlooked, and for a simple reason: the authors of many of the more popular accounts have allowed the genocide to govern their reading of the past. Historical hindsight (and a good dose of indignation) can induce even the most conscientious investigators to impose their own moral demands on the central decision makers, leading them to conclude that the very failure to act by logical necessity demonstrates an absence of ethical scruples.

Many inquiries have projected a false morality that derives from a false methodology. The methodological error is to impose one's own moral sensibilities, commitments, and categories on a radically different moment. When moral sensibilities are driven by knowledge of an outcome that was not known to those whose actions are considered, the consequence is a radically ahistorical reading of the past. . . . I do insist that in historical inquiry we should attempt to understand how the participants themselves looked forward upon objects or events that we now observe in the rearview mirror. I intend to develop what the historian

SOURCE: Michael Barnett, *Eyewitness to a Genocide: The United Nations and Rwanda* (Ithaca, N.Y.: Cornell University Press, 2002), 4–5, 7, 9–10, 47–48, 58, 59, 60, 103, 114, 118, 124, 128. Reprinted with permission of the publisher.

R. G. Collingwood called an "empathetic reconstruction." By reconstructing the moral universe in New York in 1993 and 1994, I hope to contribute to the understanding of the ethics of nonintervention. . . .

My decision to give prominence to the UN's culture crystallized after I reflected on my personal experiences [Barnett served as political officer at the U.S. Mission to the United Nations in 1994 while on sabbatical] and listened carefully to the accounts and testimonies of various participants. The UN was not a totalizing institution that transformed fairly independent-minded diplomats and international civil servants into bloodless bureaucrats, but it did profoundly influence how they looked at and acted upon the world. Government officials and UN staff came to know Rwanda as members of bureaucracies; the bureaucratic culture situated and defined their knowledge, informed their goals and desires, shaped what constituted appropriate and inappropriate behavior, distinguished acceptable from unacceptable consequences, and helped to determine right from wrong. Bureaucracy is not only a structure; it is also a process. Bureaucracies are orienting machines. They have the capacity to channel action and to transform individual into collective conscience. The existing stock of knowledge, the understanding of what constitutes proper means and ends, and the symbolic significance of events were organizationally situated. . . .

The UN is more than an instrument of member states. It is also the concrete expression of the hopes and ideals of the international community. UN staff often talk about the UN as if it were a church, suggesting that they are guardians of a religion whose tenets are transcendental. Even doubting states observe the High Holidays. New York, as headquarters is referred to by UN hands, developed peacekeeping rules that limited who would qualify for relief and assistance; developed a system of thought that helped them to maintain a faith in the values of the international community, even while acting in ways that potentially violated those values; and developed a sense of powerlessness that could lead them to deny their capacity for action. After sobering experiences in the field and a more realistic appraisal of the foundations of peacekeeping, New York developed a more precise and restricted set of rules to determine when peacekeeping was appropriate and how peacekeepers should operate in the field. Peacekeeping was appropriate when there was a "peace to keep"; peacekeepers should follow the principles of neutrality, impartiality, and consent. The reason for these rules was the recognition that the misapplication of peacekeeping was leading both to costly failures in the field and to fatal damage to the institution. But another consequence of these rules was the reduced likelihood that peacekeepers would be deployed during moments of mass suffering. Those at the UN, member states and staff alike, were overwhelmed by the sheer number of worthy cases. . . .

Roughly translated, the UN was interested in picking "winners," those places that had stability on the ground, and avoiding "losers," those places where stability was absent and humanitarian nightmares were present. . . . These rules represented an epoxy that bound together the desire to help with the desire to defend the organization and its ideals. Rwanda was born in these uncertain times. . . . The decision makers at UN headquarters were laboring under a superficial and at times incorrect reading of some of the basic features of Rwanda politics. However welcome and essential [nuanced, scholarly accounts of the pre-1994 period] are for generating a more complete understanding of the Rwandan genocide, they are, in some ways, irrelevant and even detrimental to the task of reconstructing the view from the UN. Such a reconstruction must include four essential features. First, policymakers can and should be easily forgiven if they did not possess an anthropologist's understanding of the culture or a historian's knowledge of the crooked path that made Rwanda what it was. . . .

Second, the constant juggling of operations meant that there was little time to master Rwandan history or synthesize the discrete pieces of information that were consumed sporadically over time. Few had the luxury to obtain a detailed understanding of a conflict that was of marginal importance, and most had to satisfy themselves with an undergraduate lecture's worth of knowledge. . . . Third, the scarcity of time produced a highly instrumental approach to information. . . . It means, in short, putting aside the very complexity that historians and anthropologists have reproduced dutifully in their postgenocidal studies. Knowledge that was relevant was knowledge that could be applied quickly to understand and address immediate concerns. . . . Bureaucratic knowledge, by necessity, flattens and shoehorns history into already established boxes and cubicles; information that is sought is information that conforms to already established modalities. . . . Fourth, the broad categories that were used to diagnose and remedy civil wars and ethnic conflict also produced a way of seeing and knowing Rwanda. . . . Bureaucratic categories and organizational boxes do more than simply separate relevant from irrelevant information. They also produce the social optics that policymakers and bureaucrats use to see the world. Before policymakers can act, they first must come to create a definition and understanding of the situation, and that understanding is mediated by how the institution is organized to think.

For instance, the very vocabulary of the "failed state" was omnipresent at this moment, and many states in turmoil were given that label. This meant that the very Rwanda that devel opment agencies found to be a model of efficiency only a few years before was constructed as a "failed state" by those in New York. This label would have important implications for how policymakers later came to describe the violence. . . . Attempting to re-create the view from New York means that we have to take seriously the fact that heavily overworked individuals were overseeing an operation of marginal importance, were highly economical and instrumental in the knowledge that they sought to understand Rwanda and ultimately create policy toward it, and were using the categories available from the organizational culture in which they were embedded to do so. It means appreciating how past interpretations are projected into the present circumstances, and considering how the stock of knowledge and recent events that are organizationally (and not simply individually) lived and experienced structure the present demands and responses. . . .

All eyes in New York assumed that they were seeing a civil war. The [Security C]ouncil was well aware of the obscenely high civilian death toll and the gruesome conditions on the ground. But because they predicted that sustained violence would be connected to a civil war, that is what they saw. . . . In retrospect it is possible to see the civil war and the coming genocide as running along in two semi-independent streams. At the time, however, the council could only see a civil war. . . . The claim that Rwanda was a civil war gave force to the argument that the UN's sole function under the circumstances was to try to negotiate a cease-fire. . . . Because the [UN] Secretariat was primed and predisposed to associate all violence with civil war, it was likely to overlook potentially contradictory information. Organizational and psychological theories suggest why it might have been insensitive to new information. The crisis environment and high uncertainty would have encouraged staff to rely on decisional shortcuts that were based on their personal experiences from recent events and broader organizational ways of knowing.... [The Secretariat's] handling of the information, however tragic and consequential, was understandable and excusable. These were awful but not indictable mistakes committed by decent individuals....

The Secretariat gave a calculated and staged performance that was designed to discourage intervention. Its preferences were born not from cynical, immoral, or purely instrumental reasons. It rank-ordered its responsibilities and calculated the risks associated with different types of action. There were peacekeepers to protect. Also to consider was an organization that might not survive another failure [like the ill-fated intervention in Somalia]. Protecting the organization from further harm or exploitation was, from the Secretariat's view, ethical, legitimate, and desirable.... To intervene in Rwanda in this post-Somalia moment and under these circumstances, therefore, risked not simply another failure but the exhaustion of a much hoped-for ideal. Although remaining indifferent to the killings might be a sin if judged in isolation, once balanced against the (higher) commitment to the international community's cathedral there emerged mitigating circumstances that made the council's actions part of a record of "self-defense" of the organization.

The reasons the council forwarded were connected to a moral compass that pointed away from Rwanda, not toward it, thus legitimating a stance that onlookers at the time and critics at later moments assumed was amoral and devoid of legitimation principles. But principles and reasons proved to be a spiritual guide and moral comfort to those at the UN, instilling confidence in the belief that their actions were necessary and proper. To let killings be at this moment was not a sign of their shallow commitment to the international community. Instead, it was evidence of it.

138 • "Illegal but Legitimate": The 1999 NATO Intervention in Kosovo (Independent International Commission on Kosovo)

The Independent International Commission was formed on the initiative of Göran Persson, Sweden's prime minister at the time, to inquire into the legality and legitimacy of the NATO intervention in the Yugoslav province of Kosovo. The publication in 2000 of the Kosovo Report by the Commission was of tremendous import for the future of humanitarian intervention, notably for the development of the concept of R2P, the responsibility to protect. The high-level, nongovernmental panel found, among other things, that the bombing campaign against Serbia was "illegal but legitimate." By calling into question the inviolability of sovereignty as a foundational principle of the international system, the Kosovo Report opened the door for deliberations about an "emerging doctrine of humanitarian intervention" in the face of severe human rights or humanitarian abuses.

From the early 1990s onwards, governments and international institutions were aware of the impending conflict in Kosovo. There were plenty of warnings, and moreover, the Kosovo con-

SOURCE: Independent International Commission on Kosovo, *Kosovo Report: Conflict, International Response, Lessons Learned* (Oxford: Oxford University Press, 2000), 1–2, 4, 163, 164, 166–68, 169, 172, 174, 175. Reprinted with permission of the publisher.

flict was part of the unfolding tragedy of the break-up of Yugoslavia. Yet prior to 1998, the international community failed to take sufficient preventive action. There were some diplomatic initiatives especially in 1992–3, but they were confused and not backed by sufficient high-level pressure. . . . The decision to exclude Kosovo from the Dayton negotiations, and the lack of results achieved by the strategy of non-violence, led many Kosovar Albanians to conclude that violence was the only way to attract international attention. It was during this period that the KLA [Kosovo Liberation Army] groups first made their appearance. Until late 1997 they were small resistance groups who pursued hit and run, low level guerilla warfare, hoping for international intervention. The Serbian response to the initial KLA attacks was, as expected, brutal and was also directed against civilians. The Serbian massacre of 58 people in Prekazi/Prekaze in February 1998 became a turning point. The internal war had escalated. . . . This armed conflict between the KLA and the FRY [Federal Republic of Yugoslavia, the Serbia-led rump state of the former Yugoslavia] lasted from February 1998 to June 1999 although it escalated after March 1999 when the NATO air campaign supervened. It can be characterized both as an armed insurgency and counterinsurgency, and as a war (against civilians) of ethnic cleansing. . . .

The Commission concludes that the NATO military intervention was illegal but legitimate. It was illegal because it did not receive prior approval from the United Nations Security Council [UNSC]. However, the Commission considers that the intervention was justified because all diplomatic avenues had been exhausted and because the intervention had the effect of liberating the majority population of Kosovo from a long period of oppression under Serbian rule. . . .

Any assessment of the legality of recourse to force in Kosovo and Serbia under NATO auspices should not lose sight of several elements of the surrounding circumstances. There was an impending and unfolding humanitarian catastrophe for the civilian Kosovar Albanian population. . . . [Slobodan] Milosevic [the president of the FRY at the time] was an adversary with a track record of manipulation and criminality, and one whom few trusted to implement international agreements. After the autumn of 1998, authorization for coercive action appeared politically impossible to secure under UN auspices, because of the expected Russian and Chinese vetoes. In addition to these prior conditions, the results of the NATO action have an important bearing. Although the intervention produced a temporary and severe worsening of the ordeal faced by the Kosovar Albanians, over time it averted their worst fears of ethnic cleansing, and had the emancipatory effect for them of dismantling the oppressive Serb police and paramilitary structure. . . . This complex of circumstances raises a central question— are the constraints imposed by international law on the non-defensive use of force adequate for the maintenance of international peace and security in the contemporary world? . . . If international law no longer provides acceptable guidelines in such a situation, what are the alternatives?

In responding to these challenges, the Commission considers the international law controversy provoked by the NATO campaign. It also puts forward an interpretation of the emerging doctrine of humanitarian intervention. This interpretation is situated in a gray zone of ambiguity between an extension of international law and a proposal for an international moral consensus. In essence, this gray zone goes beyond strict ideas of *legality* to incorporate more flexible views of *legitimacy*. . . .

International law as embodied textually in the UN Charter is on the surface clear with respect to the permissible scope for the use of force in international life. The threat or use of force by states is categorically prohibited by Article 2(4). The sole exception set forth in Article 51 is a right of self-defense, but only if exercised in response to a prior armed attack across an international frontier, and then only provisionally. A claim to act in self-defense must be promptly communicated to the UNSC, which is empowered to pass final judgment. The UNSC, in discharging its responsibility for international peace and security under Chapter VII [of the UN Charter] is empowered to authorize the use of force. This narrow interpretation of the legal framework governing the use of force was strongly endorsed by a commanding majority within the International Court of Justice [i.e., the UN's judicial organ] in the Nicaragua case decided in 1986. The only other relevant directive as to the use of force is contained in Article 53, which allows regional organizations to engage in enforcement actions provided that they do so on the basis of UNSC authorization. Although there is a subsidiary argument about implied authorization to use force once a conflict has been formally treated by the UNSC as a threat to international peace and security under Chapter VII of the UN Charter, it remains difficult to reconcile NATO's recourse to armed intervention on behalf of Kosovo with the general framework of legal rights and duties which determines the legality of the use of force.

It is, however, possible to argue that, running parallel to the Charter's limitations on the use of force, is Charter support for the international promotion and protection of human rights. In this vein it has been asserted that, given the unfolding humanitarian catastrophe precipitated by the Serb pattern of oppressive criminality toward the Albanian civilian population in Kosovo, the use of force by NATO was legitimate, as it was the only practicable means available to protect the Albanian Kosovars from further violent abuse. The main difficulty with such a line of argument is that Charter restrictions on the use of force represented a core commitment when the United Nations was established in 1945—a commitment which has reshaped general international law. In contrast, the Charter provisions relating to human rights were left deliberately vague, and were clearly not intended when written to provide a legal rationale for any kind of enforcement, much less a free-standing mandate for military intervention without UNSC approval. Human rights were given a subordinate and marginal role in the UN system in 1945, a role that was understood to be, at most, aspirational. . . . Any evidentiary claim based on human rights would face the additional legal obstacle posed by Article 2(7) which forbids intervention, even by the United Nations, in matters that fall essentially within the "domestic jurisdiction" of states. Even serious infractions of human rights were considered to be matters of domestic jurisdiction when the Charter was drafted, and were not thought to provide any grounds for an external use of force. . . .

However, the Commission recognizes that, in the more than fifty years of UN existence, the status of human rights has changed dramatically. . . . Such developments have led Secretary-General Kofi Annan and his two predecessors, Javier Perez de Cuellar and Boutros Boutros Ghali, to insist that the evolution of international human rights standards and support for their implementation has now reached the stage where norms of non-intervention, and the related deference to sovereign rights, no longer apply to the same extent in the face of severe human rights or humanitarian abuses. . . . This process of evolution could suggest that interventionary force to uphold human rights is less inconsistent with the spirit of the UN Charter and general international law than has been suggested by some. . . .

One way to analyze the international law status of the NATO campaign is to consider legality a matter of degree. This approach acknowledges the current fluidity of international law on humanitarian intervention, caught between strict Charter prohibitions of non-defensive uses of force and more permissive patterns of state practice with respect to humanitarian interventions. . . . The Chapter VII resolutions [by the UNSC] prior to March 1999 usefully support this analysis, as does the one-sided rejection of the Russian-sponsored resolution of censure after the intervention. . . . Rather than defining the Kosovo intervention as a precedent, most NATO supporters among international jurists presented the intervention as an unfortunate but necessary and reasonable exception. Nevertheless, NATO cannot hope to preclude states, and especially other regional organizations, from referring to its claims of intervention in Kosovo as a precedent. . . . The Kosovo "exception" now exists, for better or worse, as a contested precedent that must be assessed in relation to a wide range of international effects and undertakings. . . . Finally, eventual assessment of the "Kosovo principle" will also be strongly influenced by the ultimate outcome in Kosovo—whether the international action is seen as producing stable and humane governance, or the opposite.

139 ✦ How Genocide Was Stopped in East Timor (Geoffrey Robinson)

The UN response to the collective violence that seized East Timor in 1999 is one of the rare cases in which an international consensus in favor of military intervention was brokered quickly and action was swift. Geoffrey Robinson, professor of history at the University of California, Los Angeles, explains how this unusual outcome came about in his 2010 book, "If You Leave Us Here, We Will Die." According to Robinson, four factors merit particular attention: (1) the perception on the part of the UN Security Council that Indonesia (the occupying power of East Timor at the time) was disregarding the UN as an organization; (2) the perceived failure of the international community to respond to crimes in Rwanda and Srebrenica; (3) the perceived success of the NATO intervention in Kosovo earlier that year; and (4) the restraint shown by East Timor's resistance movements in answering the Indonesian onslaught.

Nineteen ninety-nine was a bad year in East Timor. Between January and late October, at least fifteen hundred civilians were killed among a total population of well under a million. Some of the victims were shot dead; others were decapitated, disemboweled, or hacked to death with machetes. Many were beaten or tortured, while women and girls were singled out for rape and other crimes of sexual violence. The vast majority of the victims were real or suspected supporters of East Timor's independence from Indonesia, including Catholic clergy,

SOURCE: Geoffrey Robinson, *"If You Leave Us Here, We Will Die": How Genocide Was Stopped in East Timor* (Princeton, N.J.: Princeton University Press, 2010), 1–3, 185, 202–4, 205. Reprinted with permission of the publisher.

local UN staff, and political activists. The perpetrators were overwhelmingly members of armed East Timorese militia groups and their Indonesian army patrons. The worst of the violence followed the announcement, on September 4, that 78.5 percent of the population had voted for independence in a UN-supervised referendum held just days earlier. Twenty-four years after invading and occupying the tiny former Portuguese colony, the Indonesian army and its local allies were not about to let it go without a fight. Over the next few weeks, the capital Dili along with many other towns and villages were burned to the ground. Warehouses, shops, and homes were looted, their contents loaded onto trucks and ships, and then taken to Indonesia. The systematic violence also fueled the displacement of the population on a massive scale. By the time it ended, at least four hundred thousand people had been forced to flee their homes, and an estimated 70 percent of the country's infrastructure had been burned or destroyed. . . . The swiftness with which the violence spread as well as its apparently orchestrated character led some observers to fear an impending genocide. That was not an idle fear. In the late 1970s, at least a hundred thousand East Timorese, and perhaps twice that number, had died as a direct consequence of the Indonesian invasion and occupation. Yet even as the possibility of a second genocide was being discussed, the tide suddenly turned.

In response to mounting public outrage, in mid-September the United States and other key governments finally took steps to rein in the Indonesia army and its militia proxies, cutting military ties to Indonesia and threatening to suspend economic aid. Under this unprecedented pressure, Indonesian authorities agreed to accept international assistance to restore order. Then, in another unusual move, the UN Security Council authorized the deployment of a multinational military force under Chapter VII of the UN Charter. That force landed about one week later, and within a week or two of its deployment, the worst of the violence had stopped and the distribution of humanitarian assistance had begun. . . . What finally brought about the surprising international military intervention of late September? . . .

There is no simple answer to that question. Indeed, a close examination of the events of late 1999 reveals their highly contingent quality and indicates how easily things have turned out differently. It reveals that among the most powerful states, notably the United States, resistance to intervention persisted for several days after the violence had begun to spiral out of control, and that the eventual decision to intervene was the consequence of an unusual conjuncture of events and conditions, including dramatic media coverage, the existence of a long-standing network of NGO and church organizations, and the surprisingly effective diplomacy of the UN Security Council and the secretary-general himself. . . . An additional factor was the openness toward the idea of international humanitarian intervention that existed, if only briefly, at the turn of the millennium. The principle that state sovereignty might legitimately be infringed by the international community in order to protect a people from gross human rights abuse or humanitarian catastrophe was being forcefully articulated, above all by [UN Secretary-General Kofi] Annan, and somewhat belatedly by [U.S. President Bill] Clinton. . . . The near consensus that the Kosovo campaign [that had been conducted just a few months earlier] had been a success made a similar response in East Timor far more likely than it would otherwise have been. . . .

Equally important was the sense that in East Timor, the principles and integrity of the United Nations were being openly attacked by Indonesia. In their statements on behalf of intervention, UN officials and member states referred repeatedly, often angrily, to the fact that

Indonesia had broken its promises to and solemn agreements with the United Nations—to maintain security and honor the result of the [referendum] ballot. . . . This sense that the post-ballot violence was a brazen attack on the United Nations itself was reinforced by the fact that local and international UN personnel were themselves the target of some of the violence. . . .

The notion that the United Nations itself was being attacked stimulated an unusual consensus among its member states and the Secretariat staff on the need for action. That consensus, in turn, paved the way for the swift and forceful diplomacy of the Security Council on the issue. Of particular importance was the Security Council's visit to Jakarta and Dili from September 8 through September 12 [1999], in the course of which international pressure on Indonesia mounted to unprecedented levels. Through their personal experience of the violence and of the mendacity of Indonesian officials, the Security Council delegation was effectively transformed into a powerful advocate for international action. Likewise, Annan's personal commitment and his energetic diplomacy at the height of the crisis were critical in bringing about a change within the United Nations and among key powers, including the United States.

Historical memory unquestionably played a part as well. From the start of the UN mission in East Timor, the 1994 genocide in Rwanda and the 1995 massacre in Srebrenica were on the minds of UN officials in Dili and New York, and they must have played a role in the deliberations of various states. The parallels were difficult to ignore, especially for those with some direct involvement in the earlier debacles. That group included Clinton, [U.S. Secretary of State Madeleine] Albright, Annan, and Annan's chef de cabinet, Iqbal Riza. Partly for the sake of the United Nations' reputation, but also for much more profound moral reasons, some of these people seemed determined that civilians would not be abandoned in East Timor. . . .

Finally, a case can be made that the intervention in East Timor was driven by decisions and actions of a handful of individuals, some of them powerful, and others scarcely known. [José Alexandre (Xanana)] Gusmão's [since 1981 the commander of both the political and military wings of the resistance, namely Fretilin (Frente Revolucionária de Timor Leste Independente) and Falintil (Forças Armada de Libertação de Timor-Leste), respectively] decision to adopt a policy of restraint in the face of the mounting violence, and the ability of the CNRT [Conselho Nacional de Resistência Timorense, a nonpartisan national coalition of political parties that was formed in 1998 and led abroad by Nobel Peace Prize laureate and East Timor's incumbent president, José Ramos-Horta] and Falintil leadership to make that decision stick, helped to ensure that the postballot violence was properly understood by international observers to be one-sided and wholly unjustifiable. Had the CNRT and Falintil opted instead to respond to the violence in kind, as they certainly would have done, the international consensus on the need for swift intervention on humanitarian grounds would quickly have evaporated. . . .

[On September 15, 1999], the Security Council passed resolution 1264 authorizing the establishment of a multinational force under Chapter VII of the UN Charter. That force had begun to deploy in East Timor within another week. Led by Australia, but comprised of units from several other states, including Malaysia, Thailand, the Philippines, and New Zealand, it immediately set to work rounding up militias, and in some cases killing them. Despite protests from some in Indonesia about its behavior, Interfet [the UN acronym for the International Force for East Timor] met little resistance from either militias or the TNI [Tentara Nasional Indonesia, the Indonesian military], and by late September, the violence had largely ended.

The pivotal role of the multinational force in halting the violence was highlighted by the fact that where Interfet troops were slow to deploy, serious violence continued. . . . Interfet also facilitated the timely delivery of humanitarian assistance to the many tens of thousands of people who had been displaced. In striking contrast to the almost total absence of international humanitarian assistance in the late 1970s, emergency relief began to be delivered within a few weeks of the onset of the humanitarian crisis. The speed and efficiency with which that assistance was delivered almost certainly averted a major humanitarian crisis.

In all of these ways, Interfet helped to prevent killing and death on a massive scale. At the same time, there were problems that it could not solve, and that no military intervention could reasonably have been expected to address. Nor, as it turned out, could they be solved by the UN Transitional Administration in East Timor (UNTAET) that governed the territory between October 1999 and May 2002, or by the fledgling government of Timor-Leste that followed it.

140 • The Argument about Humanitarian Intervention (Michael Walzer)

In a journal article published in 2010, the political philosopher Michael Walzer, professor emeritus at the Institute for Advanced Study in Princeton, challenges conventional wisdom about the theory and practice of humanitarian intervention. This article arguably constitutes the most important— and yet one of the least known—contributions ever made to the burgeoning literature on the topic. Walzer explains why he is not unduly concerned with unilateral interventions, even when they are undertaken by self-interested governments, including authoritarian ones. At the same time, he warns against inflated expectations about what international responses can reasonably accomplish. His is a case for minimalism when thinking about the ends of humanitarian intervention, which he conceives primarily in military terms. Walzer is particularly wary of invoking the language and substance of human rights in the context of humanitarian intervention. Instead he wants to minimize the use of force and its duration. To this end, says Walzer, in times of large-scale violence, we must focus on ending the killing—nothing more but nothing less.

In the old days, "humanitarian intervention" was a lawyer's doctrine, a way of justifying a very limited set of exceptions to the principles of national sovereignty and territorial integrity. It is a good doctrine, because exceptions are always necessary, principles are never absolute. But we need to rethink it today, as the exceptions become less and less exceptional. The "acts that shock the conscience of humankind"—and, according to the nineteenth-century law books, justify humanitarian intervention—are probably no more frequent these days than they were in the past, but they are more shocking, because we are more intimately engaged by them and with them. Cases multiply in the world and in the media: Somalia, Bosnia, Rwanda, East Timor, Liberia, Sierra Leone, and Kosovo in only the past decade. The last of these has dominated recent political debates, but it isn't the most illuminating case. I want to step back a bit,

SOURCE: Michael Walzer, "The Argument about Humanitarian Intervention," *Dissent* 41, no. 1 (2002): 29–37. Reprinted with permission of the University of Pennsylvania Press.

reach for a wider range of examples, and try to answer four questions about humanitarian intervention: First, what are its occasions? Second, who are its preferred agents? Third, how should the agents act to meet the occasions? And fourth, when is it time to end the intervention?

The occasions have to be extreme if they are to justify, perhaps even require, the use of force across an international boundary. Every violation of human rights isn't a justification. The common brutalities of authoritarian politics, the daily oppressiveness of traditional social practices—these are not occasions for intervention; they have to be dealt with locally, by the people who know the politics, who enact or resist the practices. The fact that these people can't easily or quickly reduce the incidence of brutality and oppression isn't a sufficient reason for foreigners to invade their country. Foreign politicians and soldiers are too likely to misread the situation, or to underestimate the force required to change it, or to stimulate a "patriotic" reaction in defense of the brutal politics and the oppressive practices. Social change is best achieved from within.

I want to insist on this point; I don't mean to describe a continuum that begins with common nastiness and ends with genocide, but rather a radical break, a chasm, with nastiness on one side and genocide on the other. We should not allow ourselves to approach genocide by degrees. Still, on this side of the chasm, we can mark out a continuum of brutality and oppression, and somewhere along this continuum an international response (short of military force) is necessary. Diplomatic pressure and economic sanctions, for example, are useful means of engagement with tyrannical regimes. . . . But these are still external acts; they are efforts to prompt *but not to preempt* an internal response. They still assume the value, and hold open the possibility, of domestic politics. . . . But when what is going on is the "ethnic cleansing" of a province or country or the systematic massacre of a religious or national community, it doesn't seem possible to wait for a local response. Now we are on the other side of the chasm. The stakes are too high, the suffering already too great. . . . This is the occasion for intervention.

We will need to argue, of course, about each case, but the list I've already provided seems a fairly obvious one. . . . We are best served, I think, by a stark and minimalist version of human rights here: it is life and liberty that are at stake. With regard to these two, the language of rights is readily available and sufficiently understood across the globe. . . . In practice, even with a minimalist understanding of human rights, even with a commitment to nothing more than decency, there are more occasions for intervention than there are actual interventions. . . . It is hypocritical, critics say to the "humanitarian" politicians or soldiers, to intervene in this case when you didn't intervene in that one—as if, having declined to challenge China in Tibet, say, the United Nations should have stayed out of East Timor for the sake of moral consistency. But consistency isn't an issue here. We can't meet all our occasions; we rightly calculate the risks in each one. We need to ask what the costs of intervention will be for the people being rescued, for the rescuers, and for everyone else. And then, we can only do what we can do.

The standard cases have a standard form: a government, an army, a police force, tyrannically controlled, attacks its own people or some subset of its own people, a vulnerable minority, say, territorially based or dispersed throughout the country. . . . The attack takes place within the country's borders; it doesn't require any boundary crossings; it is an exercise of sovereign power. There is no aggression, no invading army to resist and beat back. Instead, the rescuing forces are the invaders; they are the ones who, in the strict sense of international law, begin the war. But they come into a situation where the moral stakes are clear: the oppressors or, better, the state agents of oppression are readily identifiable; their victims are plain to see. Even in the list with which I started, however, there are some nonstandard cases—Sierra Leone is the clearest example—where the state apparatus isn't the villain, where what we might think of as the administration of brutality is decentralized, anarchic, almost random. It isn't the power of the oppressors that interventionists have to worry about, but the amorphousness of the oppression. I won't have much to say about cases like this. Intervention is clearly justifiable but, right now at least, it's radically unclear how it should be undertaken. Perhaps there is not much to do beyond what the Nigerians did in Sierra Leone: they reduced the number of killings, the scope of the barbarism.

"We can only do what we can do." Who is this "we"? The Kosovo debate focused on the United States, NATO, and the UN as agents of military intervention. These are indeed three political collectives capable of agency, but by no means the only three. The United States and NATO generate suspicion among the sorts of people who are called "idealists" because of their readiness to act unilaterally and their presumed imperial ambitions; the UN generates skepticism among the sorts of people who are called "realists" because of its political weakness and military ineffectiveness. The arguments here are overdetermined; I am not going to join them. We are more likely to understand the problem of agency if we start with other agents. The most successful interventions in the last thirty years have been acts of war by neighboring states: Vietnam in Cambodia, India in East Pakistan (now Bangladesh), Tanzania in Uganda. These are useful examples for testing our ideas about intervention because they don't involve extraneous issues such as the new (or old) world order; they don't require us to consult Lenin's, or anyone else's, theory of imperialism. In each of these cases, there were horrifying acts that should have been stopped and agents who succeeded, more or less, in stopping them. So let's use these cases to address the two questions most commonly posed by critics of the Kosovo war: Does it matter that the agents acted alone? Does it matter that their motives were not wholly (or even chiefly) altruistic?

In the history of humanitarian intervention, unilateralism is far more common than its opposite. One reason for this is obvious: the great reluctance of most states to cede the direction of their armed forces to an organization they don't control. But unilateralism may also follow from the need for an immediate response to "acts that shock." Imagine a case where the shock doesn't have anything to do with human evildoing: a fire in a neighbor's house in a new town where there is no fire department. It wouldn't make much sense to call a meeting of the block association, while the house is burning, and vote on whether or not to help (and it would make even less sense to give a veto on helping to the three richest families on the block). . . . In cases like these, anyone who can help should help. And that sounds like a plausible maxim for humanitarian intervention also: who can, should.

But now let's imagine a block association or an international organization that planned in advance for the fire, or the scream in the night, or the mass murder. Then there would be particular people or specially recruited military forces delegated to act in a crisis, and the definition of "crisis" could be determined—as best it can be—in advance, in exactly the kind of meeting that seems so implausible, so morally inappropriate, at the moment when immediate action is necessary. The person who rushes into a neighbor's house in my domestic example and the political or military commanders of the invading forces in the international cases would still have to act on their own understanding of the events unfolding in front of them and on their own interpretation of the responsibility they have been given. But now they act under specified constraints, and they can call on the help of those in whose name they are acting. This is the form that multilateral intervention is most likely to take, if the UN, say, were ever to authorize it in advance of a particular crisis. It seems preferable to the different unilateral alternatives, because it involves some kind of prior warning, an agreed-upon description of the occasions for intervention, and the prospect of overwhelming force.

But is it preferable in fact, right now, given the UN as it actually is? What makes police forces effective in domestic society, when they are effective, is their commitment to the entire body of citizens from which they are drawn and the (relative) trust of the citizens in that commitment. But the UN's General Assembly and Security Council, so far, give very little evidence of being so committed, and there can't be many people in the world today who would willingly entrust their lives to UN police. So if, in any of my examples, the UN's authorized agents or their domestic equivalents decide not to intervene, and the fire is still burning, the screams can still be heard, the murders go on—then unilateralist rights and obligations are instantly restored. Collective decisions to act may well exclude unilateral action, but collective decisions not to act don't have the same effect. In this sense, unilateralism is the dominant response when the common conscience is shocked. If there is no collective response, anyone can respond. If no one is acting, act.

In the Cambodia, East Pakistan, and Uganda cases, there were no prior arrangements and no authorized agents. Had the UN's Security Council or General Assembly been called into session, it would almost certainly have decided against intervention, probably by majority vote, in any case because of great-power opposition. So, anyone acting to shut down the Khmer Rouge killing fields or to stem the tide of Bengalese refugees or to stop Idi Amin's butchery would have to act unilaterally. Everything depended on the political decision of a single state. Do these singular agents have a right to act or do they have an obligation? I have been using both words, but they don't always go together: there can be rights where there are no obligations. In "good Samaritan" cases in domestic society, we commonly say that passersby are bound to respond (to the injured stranger by the side of the road, to the cry of a child drowning in the lake); they are not, however, bound to risk their lives. If the risks are clear, they have a right to respond; responding is certainly a good thing and possibly the right thing to do; still, they are not morally bound to do it. But military interventions across international boundaries always impose risks on the intervening forces. So perhaps there is no obligation here either; perhaps there is a right to intervene but also a right to refuse the risks, to maintain a kind of neutrality—even between murderers and their victims. Or perhaps humanitarian intervention is an example of what philosophers call an "imperfect" duty: someone should stop the awfulness, but it isn't possible to give that someone a proper name, to point a finger, say, at a particular country. The problem of imperfect duty yields best to multilateral solutions; we simply assign responsibility in advance through some commonly accepted decision procedure.

But perhaps, again, these descriptions are too weak: I am inclined to say that intervention is more than a right and more than an imperfect duty. After all, the survival of the intervening state is not at risk. And then why shouldn't the obligation simply fall on the most capable state, the nearest or the strongest, as in the maxim I have already suggested: Who can, should? Nonintervention in the face of mass murder or ethnic cleansing is not the same as neutrality in time of war. The moral urgencies are different; we are usually unsure of the consequences of a war, but we know very well the consequences of a massacre. Still, if we follow the logic of the argument so far, it will be necessary to recruit volunteers for humanitarian interventions; the "who" who can and should is only the state, not any particular man or woman; for individuals the duty remains imperfect. Deciding whether to volunteer, they may choose to apply the same test to themselves—who can, should—but the choice is theirs.

The dominance that I have ascribed to unilateralism might be questioned—commonly is questioned—because of a fear of the motives of single states acting alone. Won't they act in their own interests rather than in the interests of humanity? Yes, they probably will or, better, they will act in their own interests as well as in the interests of humanity; I don't think that it is particularly insightful, merely cynical, to suggest that those larger interests have no hold at all (surely the balance of interest and morality among interventionists is no different than it is among noninterventionists). In any case, how would humanity be better served by multi-lateral decision-making? Wouldn't each state involved in the decision process also act in its own interests? And then the outcome would be determined by bargaining among the interested parties—and humanity, obviously, would not be one of the parties. We might hope that particular interests would cancel each other out, leaving some kind of general interest (this is in fact Rousseau's account, or one of his accounts, of how citizens arrive at a "general will"). But it is equally possible that the bargain will reflect only a mix of particular interests, which may or may not be better for humanity than the interests of a single party. Anyway, political motivations are always mixed, whether the actors are one or many. A pure moral will doesn't exist in political life, and it shouldn't be necessary to pretend to that kind of purity. The leaders of states have a right, indeed, they have an obligation, to consider the interests of their own people, even when they are acting to help other people. We should assume, then, that the Indians acted in their national interest when they assisted the secession of East Pakistan, and that Tanzania acted in its own interests when it moved troops into Idi Amin's Uganda. But these interventions also served humanitarian purposes, and presumably were intended to do that too. The victims of massacre or "ethnic cleansing" disasters are very lucky if a neighboring state, or a coalition of states, has more than one reason to rescue them. It would be foolish to declare the multiplicity morally disabling. If the intervention is expanded beyond its necessary bounds because of some "ulterior" motive, then it should be criticized; within those bounds, mixed motives are a practical advantage.

When the agents act, how should they act? Humanitarian intervention involves the use of force, and it is crucial to its success that it be pursued forcefully; the aim is the defeat of the people, whoever they are, who are carrying out the massacres or the ethnic cleansing. If what is going on is awful enough to justify going in, then it is awful enough to justify the pursuit of military victory. But this simple proposition hasn't found ready acceptance in international society. Most clearly in the Bosnian case, repeated efforts were made to deal with the disaster without fighting against its perpetrators. Force was taken, indeed, to be a "last" resort, but in an ongoing political conflict "lastness" never arrives; there is always something to be done before doing whatever it is that comes last. So military observers were sent into Bosnia to report on what was happening; and then UN forces brought humanitarian relief to the victims, and then they provided some degree of military protection for relief workers, and then they sought (unsuccessfully) to create a few "safe zones" for the Bosnians. But if soldiers do nothing more than these things, they are hardly an impediment to further killing; they may even be said to provide a kind of background support for it. They guard roads, defend doctors and nurses, deliver medical supplies and food to a growing number of victims and refugees—and the number keeps growing. Sometimes it is helpful to interpose soldiers as "peacekeepers" between the killers and their victims. But though that may work for a time, it doesn't reduce the power of the killers, and so it is a formula for trouble later on. Peacekeeping is an honorable activity, but not if there is no peace. Sometimes, unhappily, it is better to make war.

In Cambodia, East Pakistan, and Uganda, the interventions were carried out on the ground; this was old-fashioned war-making. The Kosovo war provides an alternative model: a war fought from the air, with technologies designed to reduce (almost to zero!) the risk of casualties to the intervening army. I won't stop here to consider at any length the reasons for the alternative model, which have to do with the increasing inability of modern democracies to use the armies they recruit in ways that put soldiers at risk. There are no "lower orders," no invisible, expendable citizens in democratic states today. And in the absence of a clear threat to the community itself, there is little willingness even among political elites to sacrifice for the sake of global law and order or, more particularly, for the sake of Rwandans or Kosovars. But the inability and the unwillingness, whatever their sources, make for moral problems. A war fought entirely from the air, and from far away, probably can't be won without attacking civilian targets. These can be bridges and television stations, electric generators and water purification plants, rather than residential areas, but the attacks will endanger the lives of innocent men, women, and children nonetheless. The aim is to bring pressure to bear on a government acting barbarically toward a minority of its citizens by threatening to harm, or actually harming, the majority to which, presumably, the government is still committed. Obviously this isn't a strategy that would have worked against the Khmer Rouge in Cambodia, but it's probably not legitimate even where it might work—so long as there is the possibility of a more precise intervention against the forces actually engaged in the barbarous acts. The same rules apply here as in war generally: noncombatants are immune from direct attack and have to be protected as far as possible from "collateral damage"; soldiers have to accept risks to themselves in order to avoid imposing risks on the civilian population.

Any country considering military intervention would obviously embrace technologies that were said to be risk-free for its own soldiers, and the embrace would be entirely justified so long as the same technologies were also risk-free for civilians on the other side. This is precisely the claim made on behalf of "smart bombs": they can be delivered from great distances (safely), and they never miss. But the claim is, for the moment at least, greatly exaggerated. There is no technological fix currently available, and therefore no way of avoiding this simple truth: from the standpoint of justice, you cannot invade a foreign country, with all the consequences that has for other people, while insisting that your own soldiers can never be put at risk. Once the intervention has begun, it may become morally, even if it is not yet militarily, necessary to fight on the ground—in order to win more quickly and save many lives, for example, or to stop some particularly barbarous response to the intervention. That's the moral argument against no-risk interventions, but there is also a prudential argument. Interventions will rarely be successful unless there is a visible willingness to fight and to take casualties. In the Kosovo case, if a NATO army had been in sight, so to speak, before the bombing of Serbia began, it is unlikely that the bombing would have been necessary; nor would there ever have been the tide of desperate and embittered refugees. Postwar Kosovo would look very different;

the tasks of policing and reconstruction would be easier than they have been; the odds on success much better.

Imagine the intervening army fully engaged. How should it understand the victory that it is aiming at? When is it time to go home? Should the army aim only at stopping the killings, or at destroying the military or paramilitary forces carrying them out, or at replacing the regime that employs these forces, or at punishing the leaders of the regime? Is intervention only a war or also an occupation? These are hard questions, and I want to begin my own response by acknowledging that I have answered them differently at different times.

The answer that best fits the original legal doctrine of humanitarian intervention, and that I defended in *Just and Unjust Wars* (1977), is that the aim of the intervening army is simply to stop the killing. Its leaders prove that their motives are primarily humanitarian, that they are not driven by imperial ambition, by moving in as quickly as possible to defeat the killers and rescue their victims and then by leaving as quickly as possible. Sorting things out afterward, dealing with the consequences of the awfulness, deciding what to do with its agents—that is not properly the work of foreigners. The people who have always lived there, wherever "there" is, have to be given a chance to reconstruct their common life. The crisis that they have just been through should not become an occasion for foreign domination. The principles of political sovereignty and territorial integrity require the "in and quickly out" rule. But there are three sorts of occasions when this rule seems impossible to apply. The first is perhaps best exemplified by the Cambodian killing fields, which were so extensive as to leave, at the end, no institutional base, and perhaps no human base, for reconstruction. I don't say this to justify the Vietnamese establishment of a satellite regime, but rather to explain the need, years later, for the UN's effort to create, from the outside, a locally legitimate political system. The UN couldn't or wouldn't stop the killing when it was actually taking place, but had it done so, the "in and quickly out" test would not have provided a plausible measure of its success; it would have had to deal, somehow, with the aftermath of the killing.

The second occasion is exemplified by all those countries—Uganda, Rwanda, Kosovo, and others—where the extent and depth of the ethnic divisions make it likely that the killings will resume as soon as the intervening forces withdraw. If the original killers don't return to their work, then the revenge of their victims will prove equally deadly. Now "in and quickly out" is a kind of bad faith, a choice of legal virtue at the expense of political and moral effectiveness. If one accepts the risks of intervention in countries like these, one had better accept also the risks of occupation. The third occasion is the one I called nonstandard earlier on: where the state has simply disintegrated. It's not that its army or police have been defeated; they simply don't exist. The country is in the hand of paramilitary forces and warlords— gangs, really—who have been, let's say, temporarily subdued. What is necessary now is to create a state, and the creation will have to be virtually *ex nihilo*. And that is not work for the short term.

In 1995, in an article called "The Politics of Rescue," published in [*Dissent*], I argued that leftist critics of protectorates and trusteeships needed to rethink their position, for arrangements of this sort might sometimes be the best outcome of a humanitarian intervention. The historical record makes it clear enough that protectors and trustees, under the old League of Nations, for example, again and again failed to fulfill their obligations; nor have these arrangements been as temporary as they were supposed to be. Still, their purpose can sometimes be a legitimate one: to open a span of time and to authorize a kind of political work between the "in" and the "out" of a humanitarian intervention. This purpose doesn't cancel the requirement that the intervening forces get out. We need to think about better ways of making sure that the purpose is actually realized and the requirement finally met. Perhaps this is a place where multilateralism can play a more central role than it does, or has done, in the original interventions. For multilateral occupations are unlikely to serve the interests of any single state and so are unlikely to be sustained any longer than necessary. The greater danger is that they won't be sustained long enough: each participating state will look for an excuse to pull its own forces out. An independent UN force, not bound or hindered by the political decisions of individual states, might be the most reliable protector and trustee—if we could be sure that it would protect the right people, in a timely way. Whenever that assurance doesn't exist, unilateralism returns, again, as a justifiable option.

Either way, we still need an equivalent of the "in and out" rule, a way of recognizing when these longstanding interventions reach their endpoint. The appropriate rule is best expressed by a phrase that I have already used: "local legitimacy." The intervening forces should aim at finding or establishing a form of authority that fits or at least accommodates the local political culture, and a set of authorities, independent of themselves, who are capable of governing the country and who command sufficient popular support so that their government won't be massively coercive. Once such authorities are in place, the intervening forces should withdraw: "in and finally out." But this formula may be as quixotic as "in and quickly out." Perhaps foreign forces can't do the work that I've just described; they will only be dragged deeper and deeper into a conflict they will never be able to control, gradually becoming indistinguishable from the other parties. That prospect is surely a great disincentive to intervention; it will often override not only the benign intentions but even the imperial ambitions of potential interveners. In fact, most of the countries whose inhabitants (or some of them) desperately need to be rescued offer precious little political or economic reward to the states that attempt the rescue. One almost wishes that the impure motivations of such states had more plausible objects, the pursuit of which might hold them to their task. At the same time, however, it's important to insist that the task is limited: once the massacres and ethnic cleansing are really over and the people in command are committed to avoiding their return, the intervention is finished. The new regime doesn't have to be democratic or liberal or pluralist or (even) capitalist. It doesn't have to be anything, except non-murderous. When intervention is understood in this minimalist fashion, it may be a little easier to see it through.

As in the argument about occasions, minimalism in endings suggests that we should be careful in our use of human rights language. For if we pursue the legal logic of rights (at least as that logic is understood in the United States), it will be very difficult for the intervening forces to get out before they have brought the people who organized the massacres or the ethnic cleansing to trial and established a new regime committed to enforcing the full set of human rights. If those goals are actually within reach, then, of course, it is right to reach for them. But intervention is a political and military process, not a legal one, and it is subject to the compromises and tactical shifts that politics and war require. So we will often need to accept more minimal goals, in order to minimize the use of force and the time span over which it is used. I want to stress, however, that we need, and haven't yet come close to, a clear understanding of what "minimum" really means. The intervening forces have to be prepared to use the weapons they carry, and they have to be prepared to stay what may be a long course. The international community needs to find ways of supporting these forces—and also, since what they are doing is dangerous and won't always be done well, of supervising, regulating, and criticizing them. . . . Since there are in fact legitimate occasions for humanitarian intervention, since we know, roughly, what ought to be done, we have to argue about how to do it; we have to argue about agents, means, and endings. There are a lot of people around today who want to avoid these arguments and postpone indefinitely the kinds of action they might require. These people have all sorts of reasons, but none of them, it seems to me, are good or moral reasons.

141 • Why *Not* Genocide in Darfur?
(International Commission of Inquiry on Darfur)

In response to international concern over mounting violence and displacements in Darfur, Kofi Annan, secretary-general of the United Nations, in October 2004 appointed the International Commission of Inquiry on Darfur, a fact-finding panel headed by Antonio Cassese, the former president of the UN International Criminal Tribunal for the former Yugoslavia in The Hague. The Commission was tasked with reporting on the nature and salience of the atrocities in the western part of Sudan. It was to provide a preliminary assessment as to whether international crimes, notably genocide, had been committed. After visits to the field, the Commission controversially concluded in its 2005 report that although "Government forces and militias under their control had attacked civilians and destroyed and burned down villages in Darfur, contrary to the relevant principles and rules of international humanitarian law," it had not found evidence of genocide carried out at the behest of the Sudanese government.

The International Commission of Inquiry on Darfur (henceforth the Commission) was established pursuant to United Nations Security Council resolution 1564 (2004), adopted on 18 September 2004. The resolution, passed under Chapter VII of the United Nations Charter, requested the Secretary-General rapidly to set up the Commission. In October 2004, the Secretary-General appointed a five member body (Mr. Antonio Cassese, from Italy; Mr. Mohammed Fayek, from Egypt; Ms. Hina Jilani, from Pakistan; Mr. Dumisa Ntsebeza, from South Africa, and Ms. Theresa Striggner-Scott, from Ghana), and designated Mr. Cassese as its Chairman. . . . The Commission assembled in Geneva and began its work on 25 October 2004. The Secretary-General requested the Commission to report to him within three months, i.e., by 25 January 2005.

In § 1, resolution 1564 (2004) sets out the following tasks for the Commission: "to investigate reports of violations of international humanitarian law and human rights law in Darfur by all parties"; "to determine also whether or not acts of genocide have occurred"; and "to

SOURCE: International Commission of Inquiry on Darfur, *Report of the International Commission of Inquiry on Darfur to the United Nations Secretary-General Pursuant to Security Council Resolution 1564 of 18 September 2004*, January 25, 2005, http://www.un.org/News/dh/sudan/com_inq_darfur.pdf, paragraphs 1, 2, 20, 21, 22, 24, 75, 76, 630, 631, 632, 633, 634, 640, 641, 644, 645, 647, 649.

identify the perpetrators of such violations"; with a view to ensuring that those responsible are held accountable." . . . The Commission first visited Sudan from 8 to 20 November 2004. It met with a number of high level officials, including the First Vice-President, the Minister of Justice, the Minister for Foreign Affairs, the Minister of Interior, the Minister of Defense, the Minister of Federal Affairs, the Deputy Chief Justice, the Speaker of Parliament, the Deputy Head of the National Security and Intelligence Service, and members of the Rape Committees. It met with representatives of non-governmental organizations, political parties, and interested foreign government representatives in the Sudan. In addition, it held meetings with the United Nations Advance Mission in the Sudan (UNAMIS) and other United Nations representatives in the country. . . .

From 11 to 17 November 2004, the Commission visited Darfur. It divided itself into three teams, each focusing on one of the three states of Darfur. Each team met with the State Governor (*Wali*) and senior officials, visited camps of internally displaced persons, and spoke with witnesses and to the tribal leaders. In addition, the West Darfur team visited refugee camps in Chad and the South Darfur team visited the National Security Detention Center in Nyala. . . . The Commission's investigation team was led by a Chief Investigator and included four investigators, two female investigators specializing in gender violence, four forensic experts and two military analysts. Investigation team members interviewed witnesses and officials in Khartoum and accompanied the Commissioners on their field mission to the three Darfur States. . . . A second visit to Darfur took place between 9 and 16 January 2004. During this visit, the Commission focused on interviewing witnesses particularly in detention centers, and also met with some officials, members of civil society, and UN staff in Khartoum. . . .

The conflict in Darfur opposes the Government of Sudan to at least two organized groups of rebels, namely the Sudan Liberation Movement/Army (SLM/A) and the Justice and Equality Movement (JEM). . . . The first of two groups of insurgents took up arms against the central authorities in or around 2002. However, the scale of rebel attacks increased noticeably in February 2003. The rebels exercise de facto control over some areas of Darfur. The conflict therefore does not merely amount to a situation of internal disturbances and tensions, riots, or isolated and sporadic acts of violence. . . . All the parties to the conflict (the Government of Sudan, the SLA and the JEM) have recognized that this is an internal armed conflict. . . . The Commission concludes that the Government of Sudan and the Janjaweed are responsible for a number of violations of international human rights and humanitarian law. Some of these violations are very likely to amount to war crimes, and given the systematic and widespread pattern of many of the violations, they would also amount to crimes against humanity. . . .

In particular, the Commission finds that in many instances Government forces and militias under their control attacked civilians and destroyed and burned down villages in Darfur contrary to the relevant principles and rules of international humanitarian law. . . . The impact of the attacks on civilians shows that the use of military force was manifestly disproportionate to any threat posed by the rebels. In addition, it appears that such attacks were also intended to spread terror among civilians so as to compel them to flee the villages. From the viewpoint of international criminal law these violations of international humanitarian law no doubt constitute large-scale war crimes. . . . The Commission finds that large-scale destruction of villages in Darfur has been deliberately caused, by and large, by the Janjaweed during attacks, independently or in combination with Government forces. Even though in most of the incidents the Government may not have participated in the destruction, their complicity in the attacks during which the destruction was conducted and their presence at the scene of destruction are sufficient to make them jointly responsible for the destruction. There was no military necessity for the destruction and devastation caused. . . . The destruction of so many villages is clearly a violation of international human rights law and humanitarian law and amounts to a very serious war crime. . . .

It is undeniable that mass killing occurred in Darfur and that the killings were perpetrated by the Government forces and the Janjaweed in a climate of total impunity and even encouragement to commit serious crimes against a selected part of the civilian population. The large number of killings, the apparent pattern of killing and the participation of officials or authorities are among the factors that lead the Commission to the conclusion that killings were conducted in both a widespread and systematic manner. The mass killing of civilians in Darfur is therefore likely to amount to a crime against humanity. . . . It is apparent from the information collected and verified by the Commission that rape or other forms of sexual violence committed by the Janjaweed and Government soldiers in Darfur was widespread and systematic and may thus well amount to a *crime against humanity*. The awareness of the perpetrators that their violent acts were part of a systematic attack on civilians may well be inferred from, among other things, the fact that they were cognizant that they would enjoy impunity. The Commission finds that the crimes of sexual violence committed in Darfur may amount to rape as a crime against humanity, or sexual slavery as a crime against humanity. . . .

The Commission concluded that the Government of Sudan has not pursued a policy of genocide. Arguably, two elements of genocide might be deduced from the gross violations of human rights perpetrated by Government forces and militias under their control. These two elements are, first, the *actus reus* [physical element] consisting of killing, or causing serious bodily or mental harm, or deliberately inflicting conditions of life likely to bring about physical destruction; and, second, on the basis of a subjective standard, the existence of a protected group being targeted by the authors of criminal conduct. Recent developments have led members of African and Arab tribes to perceive themselves and others as two distinct ethnic groups. . . . The tribes in Darfur supporting rebels have increasingly come to be identified as "African" and those supporting the Government as "Arabs." However, the crucial element of genocidal intent appears to be missing, at least as far as the central Government authorities are concerned.

Generally speaking the policy of attacking, killing and forcibly displacing members of some tribes does not evince a specific intent to annihilate, in whole or in part, a group distinguished on racial, ethnic, national or religious grounds. Rather, it would seem that those who planned and organized the attacks on villages pursued the intent to drive the victims from their homes, primarily for purposes of counter-insurgency warfare. . . . The Commission does recognize that in some instances, individuals, including Government Officials, may commit acts with genocidal intent. Whether this was the case in Darfur, however, is a determination that only a competent court can make on a case-by-case basis. . . . The conclusion that no genocidal policy has been pursued and implemented in Darfur by the Government authorities, directly or through the militias under their control, should not be taken as in any way detracting from the gravity of the crimes perpetrated in that region. Depending upon the circumstances, such international offenses as crimes against humanity or large-scale war crimes may be no less serious and heinous than genocide. This is exactly what happened in Darfur, where massive atrocities were perpetrated on a very large scale, and have so far gone unpunished. . . .

The Commission has collected sufficient and consistent material (both testimonial and documentary) to point to numerous (51) suspects. Some of these persons are suspected of being responsible under more than one head of responsibility, and for more than one crime. . . . The Commission decided to withhold the names of these persons from the public domain. . . . The Commission instead will list the names in a sealed file that will be placed in the custody of the United Nations Secretary-General. The Commission recommends that this file be handed over to a competent Prosecutor (the Prosecutor of the International Criminal Court, according to the Commission's recommendations), who will use that material as he or she deems fit for his or her investigations. . . . With regard to the judicial accountability mechanism, the Commission strongly recommends that the Security Council should refer the situation in Darfur to the International Criminal Court, pursuant to Article 13(b) of the Statute of the Court. Many of the alleged crimes documented in Darfur have been widespread and systematic. They met all the thresholds of the Rome Statute of the International Criminal Court. The Sudanese justice system has demonstrated its inability and unwillingness to investigate and prosecute the perpetrators of these crimes. . . . The Security Council should, however, act not only against the perpetrators but also on behalf of victims. In this respect, the Commission also proposes the establishment [of] an International Compensation Commission, consisting of fifteen (15) members, ten (10) appointed by the United Nations Secretary General and five (5) by an independent Sudanese body.

142 • The African Union Mediation in Darfur (Dawit Toga)

Much has been written—not always helpfully—about the African Union's (AU) role in the unsuccessful settlement of the crisis in Darfur. Dawit Toga, a political analyst in the AU's Conflict Management Division, reconstructs in detail the long and winding road to mediation failure in this 2007 essay. As a close observer of and participant in the multistage process, he provides an indispensable guide to the various stages of the Abuja talks—the internationally mediated, inter-Sudanese peace negotiations between the government and rebel groups—and the multiple issues that scuttled this international effort at civil war settlement. Toga points in particular to the low incentives that the various parties to the negotiations had to come to any viable agreement and to the inexperience with which the rebel groups approached the various rounds of bargaining over the future of Darfur.

Under the mediation of the president of Chad, Idriss Déby, on September 3, 2003, in Abéché, Chad, the GoS [government of Sudan] and the SLM/A [Sudan Liberation Movement/Army] signed a ceasefire agreement. The agreement called for the cessation of hostilities for forty-five

SOURCE: Dawit Toga, "The African Union Mediation and the Abuja Peace Talks," in Alex de Waal, ed., *War in Darfur and the Search for Peace* (Cambridge, Mass.: Global Equity Initiative, 2007, 215, 216–17, 218, 219–20, 221–22, 223–24, 226, 227, 228, 229, 230–31, 232, 233, 234–35, 240–41, 242–43, 244. Reprinted with permission of the publisher.

days, the control of irregular groups, and the cantonment of SLM/A forces at locations to be agreed upon. In addition, the parties agreed to start comprehensive political talks to address the political and socioeconomic undercurrents of the conflict within fifteen days of the signing of the agreement. At their second meeting, on November 4, 2003, the parties agreed to extend the ceasefire for a month, committed themselves to facilitate humanitarian assistance, and agreed to meet in N'djamena [the capital of Chad] on December 16, 2003. However, this meeting never took place. Although the September ceasefire agreement contributed to the lessening of fighting between the GoS and the SLM/A, violence intensified against the civilian population. The Janjawiid continued to deliberately target the groups they viewed as providing the bulk of the support for the SLM/A and JEM [the Justice and Equality Movement, the other major insurgent group in the territory of Darfur].

On the part of the African union (AU), the containment of the conflict was viewed as essential. To that end, diplomatic missions were launched. Arresting the spread of [the] Darfur conflict was also considered essential, in part to insulate the ongoing Naivasha peace process concerning southern Sudan from its adverse effects. In early March 2004, senior AU officials held consultations with GoS officials in Khartoum to firm up the AU's role in the conflict. Sudanese authorities expressed their view that although they considered the Darfur issue to be an internal one, they had no objection to the AU's participation in the N'djamena talks. On March 26, 2004, once the green light was given by the GoS, AU Chairperson Alpha Konaré [the former president of Mali] dispatched a senior AU team to N'djamena. . . .

The initial round of the inter-Sudanese talks on Darfur started on March 31, 2004, in N'djamena, under the auspices of President Déby. The GoS, however, [ironically now] objecting to the presence of the international community, did not attend the official opening of the talks. The GoS also refused to have face-to-face negotiations with the SLM/A and JEM. As a result, the initial articulation and presentation of the positions of the parties were made through proxy negotiations. . . . On April 8, in the presence of Chairperson Konaré, as well as international observers and facilitators, the two parties signed a Humanitarian Ceasefire Agreement on the Darfur conflict and a protocol on the establishment of humanitarian assistance in Darfur. The parties agreed to: [1] Cease hostilities . . . ; [2] Establish a Joint Commission and a Ceasefire Commission, with the participation of the international community, including the African union; [3] Release all prisoners of war and all other persons detained because of the armed conflict in Darfur; [4] Facilitate the delivery of humanitarian assistance . . . ; [5] Create a team of military observers for the ceasefire, protected by an armed force jointly called the African Union Mission in Sudan (AMIS). . . .

In its meeting of May 25, 2004, the AU's Peace and Security Council requested that the AU Commission [for Peace and Security] take all necessary steps to ensure the effective monitoring of the Humanitarian Ceasefire Agreement of April 8. The council referred in particular to the deployment of an "observer mission" with the required civilian component and, if necessary, a protection force, to support the work of the Ceasefire Commission (CFC). To that end, the AU Commission [for Peace and Security] convened in Addis Ababa [on] May 27–28 in a meeting that brought together the GoS, the SLM/A, and JEM, as well as the Chadian mediation group and members of the international community. The meeting culminated with the signing, by the Sudanese parties, of an agreement on the modalities for the establishment of the CFC, and the deployment of observers in Darfur. The AU and its partners, namely the UN, the EU, and the U.S., witnessed the signing of the agreement.

As stipulated in the agreement, the CFC is made up of the AU, as chair; the international community, as deputy chair (the international community was represented by the EU, through France); the Chadian [m]ediation [group], the GoS, JEM, and the SLM/A. . . . The operational arm of the CFC is the African Union Monitoring Mission, composed of observers from the parties, the Chadian mediation [group], AU member states, and other representatives of the international community. . . . The CFC's headquarters is located in al Fashir [the capital of North Darfur]. . . . Initially, the AU Observer Mission was composed of twelve members of the CFC and 132 observers, sixty of which were from African Union member states, thirty-six from the Sudanese parties, eighteen from the Chadian mediation [group] and the rest from the international community (the EU and the U.S. had eighteen observers). The support staff, consisting of translators and interpreters, was made up of twenty-four people. Taking into account the volatile situation in some parts of Darfur, the agreement made provisions for a 270-person protection force for the Mission. . . .

When the Inter-Sudanese Peace Talks on the conflict in Darfur resumed in Addis Ababa on July 15, the senior leadership of JEM and the SLM/A refused to attend the talks, choosing instead to send junior representatives. The GoS sent a senior delegation. . . . In retrospect, it can be stated that although we were unable to agree on an agenda and on a concrete framework on how to proceed, the Addis Ababa meeting sensitized the mediators and allowed [them] to better understand the issues at stake. . . . As the international community's concern about the widening conflict in Darfur increased, so did their desire for action-oriented policies. Indeed, the crisis in Darfur was discussed on July 24 by the U.S. Congress, which adopted a resolution characterizing the human rights abuses in Darfur as "genocide." The resolution further called on the U.S. to lead an international effort to resolve the conflict and consider multilateral—or even unilateral—intervention, and to impose targeted sanctions on the government. The UN Security Council also tabled a draft resolution on Darfur, outlining specific timelines for actions to be taken by the government and raising the possibility of sanctions if they were not carried out. . . . The AU also accelerated the timetable for restarting the political dialogue. To that end, throughout July, high-level consultation by the then-chairperson of the AU, President Olusegan Obasanjo [the former president of Nigeria], and the chairperson of the AU Commission [on Peace and Security], with the parties and other stakeholders continued. . . .

The second round of the Inter-Sudanese Peace Talks on the conflict in Darfur (hereafter referred to as the "Abuja talks") formally opened in Abuja, Nigeria on August 23, 2004, by President Obasanjo and the AU chairperson. Both parties were represented by high-level delegations. The parties met in a closed session, under the chairmanship of President Obasanjo, and agreed the following day to a four-point agenda: humanitarian issues, security issues, political questions, and economic and social affairs. . . . On September 1, the parties concluded the discussion on humanitarian issues, agreeing on a protocol on the improvement of the humanitarian situation in Darfur. The protocol addressed the issues of free movement and access for humanitarian workers . . . and the assistance and protection of civilians. . . . The mediation [team] felt that although . . . remaining gaps in the respective positions of the parties on the security protocol would not allow for the signing of an agreement, it would still be possible for the parties to formally sign the Protocol on Humanitarian Issues. However, while the government [of Sudan] expressed its readiness to sign immediately, the [insurgent] movements [SLM/A and JEM] declined, but reaffirmed their commitment to the provisions of the protocol. The Abuja talks were formally adjourned on September 17.

The third round of the Inter-Sudanese Peace Talks on the conflict in Darfur convened in Abuja, from October 21 to November 10, 2004. The objective of this round was to continue deliberating on the remaining items on the agenda adopted during the second round. In the meantime, the UN Security Council had met twice on Darfur and passed resolutions 1556 and 1564. The first resolution demanded that the GoS take "substantial, irreversible and verifiable" actions to improve security for civilians in Darfur. This included taking immediate action on its commitment to disarm the Janjawiid, and to apprehend and bring to justice those who had committed human rights violations and other atrocities. . . . The second resolution established the International Commission of Inquiry into [sic] Darfur, to investigate the grievous human rights abuses perpetrated during the conflict. . . .

[Returning to the third round of the Abuja talks,] a plenary session to finalize the security protocol was held on November 2. The GoS delegation reiterated the two clarifications they sought from the mediation team during the separate consultations they held with the AU secretariat. These two issues related to the replacement of the term "Janjawiid" with "armed militias" as stipulated in the N'djamena Humanitarian Ceasefire Agreement, and to the provision calling for the parties to refrain from conducting hostile military flights in and over Darfur. . . . The GoS felt that the issue of military flights was non-negotiable, and the movements insisted on its inclusion. The movements insisted that, in light of the aerial bombings that had taken place in the course of the conflict, and their traumatizing effect on the civilian population, a no-fly zone should be imposed as part of the confidence-building measures and the efforts to facilitate the return of IDPs [internally displaced persons] and refugees. The mediators made it clear that these demands were unacceptable. . . . In a dramatic turn of events, on the evening of November 4 the SLM/A and JEM accepted the draft security protocol at the start of the plenary session, and expressed their readiness to sign it. . . . Subsequently, the movements hardened their positions. Indeed, in a separate consultation held with the AU mediators . . . , they argued that the humanitarian and security protocols should be signed before they started discussions on the draft DoP [Declaration of Principles, about the nature of the conflict and the future of governance in Sudan]. . . . Given the divergent positions of the parties on the DoP and the movements' attempt to delay the consideration of the DoP, the mediators felt it was necessary to end the third round of the Abuja talks that day.

The fourth round of the Inter-Sudanese Peace Talks on the conflict in Darfur was held in Abuja from December 11 to 21, 2004, and it turned out to be the least productive. It was essentially aimed at finalizing the draft of the DoP discussed during the third round. However, the talks were complicated from the outset as the GoS, more by design than coincidence, [had] launched a military operation on December 8, ostensibly to clear roadblocks mounted by the SLM/A. The two movements then decided to suspend their participation until the government stopped its offensive and withdrew its forces. . . . Therefore, despite the efforts of the AU leadership and the international community, the fourth round was adjourned with very little progress. . . .

Dr. Salim Ahmed Salim, former secretary-general of the OAU [Organization of African Unity], was appointed as the Chairperson's Special Envoy and Chief Mediator for the Abuja talks. The fifth round of the Inter-Sudanese Peace Talks resumed under his watch on June 10 and lasted until July 5, 2005. This round was devoted to finalizing the Declaration of Principles, which was initially discussed during the previous two rounds. This round of the talks had been delayed much longer than anticipated, partly due to the deteriorating security situation on the ground as well as the split within the SLM/A leadership. During several consultations during the interim, the SLM/A leadership had repeatedly requested more time, wanting to organize a general congress of the movement before designating new leadership and negotiators.

After extensive negotiations, the DoP was signed on July 5, 2005. . . . Key provisions in the DoP included: the establishment of a federal system of government with an effective de-volution of powers, and a clear distribution of responsibilities between the national and other levels of governance . . . ; the equitable distribution of national wealth, to ensure the effective-ness of the devolution of power in Darfur . . . and to ensure that due consideration will be given to the socioeconomic needs of Darfur; and finally, that power sharing and wealth shar-ing shall be addressed in accordance with . . . fair criteria to be agreed upon by the parties. . . . It should be noted that the adoption of the DoP during the fifth round of talks was extremely difficult due to the complexity of the issues being discussed. . . . Progress at this round was also marred by side issues such as the presence of Eritrea and the role of Chad as co-mediator, which prevented, for days, the beginning of the discussions on the agenda items.

The sixth round of the Inter-Sudanese Peace Talks on the conflict in Darfur opened in Abuja on September 15, 2005. . . . By October 10, after extensive consultations, the mediators finalized and provided to the two parties for their consideration a harmonized text that in-cluded the parties' respective positions on the criteria and guidelines for power sharing. . . . The unresolved issue of leadership in the ranks of the SLM/A remained the single obstacle hindering progress in the talks. The delegation led by Abdel Wahid Nur contained only a few of the SLM/A members affiliated with Minni Minawi [the leader of the largest SLA faction, whose real name is Suliman Arcua Minnawi], who rarely, if ever, attended any of these talks. . . . On October 20, the sixth round was adjourned. Prior to beginning the seventh and final round of the Abuja talks, Minawi informed the AU of his desire to unilaterally convene the movement's congress. The AU cautioned him of the need for an all-inclusive conference that would reflect the wide diversity of its membership. . . . Notwithstanding this advice, the con-ference was held in Haskanita, from October 29 to 31, 2005, and the movement elected a new "leadership" of the SLM. . . . The conference and the "elections" deepened the division within the SLM, creating serious implications for the peace process and other efforts to end the con-flict in Darfur. . . . For the AU, it became evident that the upcoming seventh round would be the critical phase of the Abuja talks and the consolidation of the movement's leadership would be absolutely critical to making progress and arriving at a lasting solution.

The seventh round of the Inter-Sudanese Peace Talks on the conflict in Darfur opened in Abuja, on November 29, 2005, and ended after more than five months of long, difficult, and frustrating negotiations, on May 5, 2006. The negotiations took place within three categories: power sharing, wealth sharing, and security arrangements. . . . In a series of incremental steps, the Abuja talks had shifted from being chaired by the Chadian government, to being co-chaired by the AU and the Chadians, to being chaired exclusively by the AU. This final shift occurred during the seventh round, by which time relations between Sudan and Chad had deteriorated to the point at which President Déby declared that his country was in a state of war with Sudan. During the early months of 2006, N'djamena hosted a series of meetings in which Chad provided political and military support to elements of the Darfur movements, while the GoS supported Chadian insurgents. . . .

On April 25, the chief mediator [for the AU] submitted to the parties a comprehensive set of proposals for a Darfur Peace Agreement, affirming that the draft DPA was the culmination of intensive deliberations and negotiations conducted by the AU mediation team, with the support of the facilitators and international partners, and that it represented a fair, comprehensive, and workable solution to the conflict in Darfur. . . . Before the deadline of April 30, the government of Sudan, while expressing reservations on some aspects of the document submitted by the chief mediator, formally informed the mediation team that it accepted the draft as a good basis for an agreement to end the conflict in Darfur. For their part, the movements continued to express concerns over some aspects of the document, which, according to them, did not fully address their original demands and aspirations in some of the fundamental areas. . . . The chairperson of the AU and the president of Nigeria appealed to the parties to continue with the negotiations until an agreement was reached. Consequently, the special envoy . . . extended the deadline for the Abuja talks by forty-eight hours. In the meantime, on May 2, U.S. Deputy Secretary of State [Robert] Zoellick [the current president of the World Bank], U.S. Assistant Secretary of State for African Affairs [Jendayi] Frazer, and UK Secretary of State for International Development Hilary Benn joined the mediation. . . . [They] consulted with the parties and proposed amendments to the draft DPA.

On the second day of [the extended negotiations], Minawi and his SLM group, after sustained engagement by the leaders and the international partners, confirmed their acceptance of the DPA as amended and expressed their readiness to sign it. For their part, Abdel Wahid and his SLM group, and Khalil Ibrahim Mohamed of JEM felt that the draft agreement did not address most of their fundamental areas of concern. They, therefore, announced that they were unable to sign the agreement unless substantial modifications were made to address those concerns. Following intensive consultations at the highest level, and despite the negative response from the leadership of SLM–Abdel Wahid and JEM, the DPA was signed at 5:55 p.m. on May 5, 2006, by Majzoub al Khalifa, on behalf of the GoS, and by SLM/A Chairperson Minawi. Immediately after the signing ceremony, fourteen members of [the recalcitrant] SLM–Abdel Wahid, led by Abdel Rahman Musa, who was until then chief negotiator of that group, handed in a letter that expressed their wish to join the peace process and to be included in the implementation mechanisms. . . .

Although the DPA was signed by the GoS and the SLM-Minawi, because two of the parties involved in the negotiations declined to sign it, President Obasanjo announced that efforts should continue to bring those two movements on board. Consequently, the AU announced that the agreement should remain open for signatures until the meeting of the Peace and Security Council on May 15. . . . While these ongoing negotiations succeeded in narrowing the areas of disagreement between the parties, no agreement was reached. The outstanding areas of difference were: [1] In security arrangements, the SLM–Abdel Wahid demanded that SLM/A forces be allowed a greater role in guaranteeing the security of returning IDPs and refugees, and monitoring the disarmament of the Janjawiid. In a letter to Abdel Wahid on

May 14, Majzoub al Khalifa [on behalf of the GoS] accepted these demands as consistent with the DPA. [2] Concerning wealth sharing, the SLM/A demanded a substantial increase in the GoS's initial payment into the Compensation Fund, from $30 million to $200 million. The GoS responded that it had put no ceiling on the amount of compensation to be paid, but did not specify any additional amount to be provided. [3] Regarding power sharing, the SLM/A demanded greater representation in the legislature and executive bodies of the Darfur state and local governments. The exact demands were not spelled out. The GoS replied that consideration could be given to greater representation when the SLM/A had assigned the DPA. Efforts to bring the SLM/A and JEM into the DPA continued into June but did not succeed, leaving the DPA with only the signatures of Majzoub al Khalifa and Minni Minawi. The supporters of Abdel Wahid and JEM condemned the DPA and vowed to oppose it.

The Inter-Sudanese Peace Talks on the conflict in Darfur suffered from a number of significant shortcomings that made the process frustrating and flawed. The most important of these shortcomings were internal to the conflict itself, and the structure and strategies of the belligerent parties. The peace negotiations were launched when the conflict between the SLM/A and JEM on the one side, and the GoS on the other, was itself less than six months old—at a time when both parties believed they could advance their positions on the battlefield. Therefore, each was a reluctant negotiator from the outset. Until the very end of the talks in May 2006, the parties tended to see the Abuja talks as a tactical forum, rather than the central stage on which a solution to Darfur's conflict would be found. . . .

The movements in particular suffered a chronic and systematic problem of cohesion and representation. This was unsurprising for the young insurgent groups, which had been precipitously thrust into the world's spotlight without having had the opportunity to establish political organization in the field, and which were led by relatively young and inexperienced political leaders. They were not only ill-prepared for negotiating with an experienced and skilled adversary, but also suffered problems of disunity that only increased with each passing month. However, the GoS was not innocent of inconstancy. It repeatedly reneged on its commitments and presented hard-line negotiating positions as its bottom line without indicating where flexibility was possible or necessary. Rarely did any of the parties work constructively with the mediation [team] in search of solutions. Under these circumstances, a negotiated settlement was always going to be very slow, and ultimate success was improbable.

143 • Genocide and the Europeans (Karen E. Smith)

Karen Smith, a political scientist at the London School of Economics, offers a useful account of European perspectives on genocide, focusing in particular on the ways countries such as France, Germany, and the United Kingdom responded to the Darfur crisis. In her 2010 book, Smith shows that most European governments as well as the European Union have been reticent to describe the large-scale atrocities in western Sudan as genocide.

SOURCE: Karen E. Smith, *Genocide and the Europeans* (Cambridge: Cambridge University Press, 2010), 222–23, 224, 225, 227, 228–29, 249, 253. Reprinted with permission of the publisher.

In stark contrast to the U.S. government's use of the term genocide in relation to Darfur, no European government has used the term consistently, and almost never since the UN commission's report [referring to the 2005 report of the UN's International Commission of Inquiry on Darfur, partially reproduced in this *Reader*] was published. Government ministers and officials often justified their non-use of the term by referring to the UN's classification of the conflict as not (yet, at least) a genocide; this even though the exact same governments in the case of Germany and the UK used the term genocide to describe Kosovo when few others had. As in previous cases, backbench and opposition MPs have used the term, as have activists, journalists and editors. There is, however, also more outright opposition to the use of the term from respected human rights organizations and experts . . . which means that in Europe there is less of a groundswell of public opinion pushing for governments "to do something about genocide in Darfur."

When the genocide debate was in full swing in the USA, in the summer of 2004, European governments were under some pressure to take a stance. In September 2004, the European Parliament passed a resolution on the Darfur region which—rather gingerly—urged the "Sudanese authorities to end impunity and to bring to justice immediately the planners and perpetrators of crimes against humanity, war crimes and human rights violations, which can be construed as tantamount to genocide." Nationals MPs began asking questions in parliaments about their governments' response to the conflict. In August, the EU High Representative for the Common Foreign and Security Policy, Javier Solana, sent his special representative on Sudan, Peter Feith, and a small team to Darfur for five days. They were there to investigate the possibilities for EU assistance to the African-Union mission, but on his return to Brussels, Feith told the media: "We are not in the situation of genocide there. . . . But it is clear there is widespread, silent and slow killing going on and village burning of a fairly large scale." In September the Council of the EU declared that it "would welcome steps by the UNSG [UN secretary-general] to establish as soon as possible an international commission of inquiry in order to immediately investigate all violations of human rights and humanitarian law in Darfur, and to determine whether acts of genocide have occurred."

The position that it was up to the UN to decide whether it was genocide or not remained the position of most EU member states. In early August, the Swedish Prime Minister Goran Persson declared that labeling the situation in Darfur a genocide was irrelevant and would make no difference to those being murdered. The Belgian Cooperation Minister dismissed the use of the term genocide as inappropriate and simplistic. The Dutch Foreign Minister, Bernard Bot, said that the EU had to wait for the UN report. . . . However, the Czech Foreign Minister, Cyril Svoboda, did suggest it was genocide, on 6 September. But once the UN commission of inquiry had decided it was not a case of genocide, then this became the official stance of European governments. When the UN commission issued its report, the EU welcomed it and condemned the crimes being committed in Darfur. A string of EU declarations —and of European Parliament resolutions—since then do not use the term genocide at all. Indeed, EU declarations tend not to even single out the government side for having been primarily responsible for atrocities (in contrast to the various UN reports . . .). . . .

As for the three countries [namely France, Germany, and the United Kingdom] on which this book focuses, the debate followed similar lines. . . . In general, the German government did not use the term before the UN commission's report was published—though there were members of the coalition parties (SPD [Social Democratic Party], Alliance 90/The Greens) who did, and even the odd slip by members of the government. Foreign Minister Joschka Fischer, who had been so outspoken regarding genocide in Kosovo, was much less keen on using the term in the case of Darfur. In September 2004, he called it "a humanitarian catastrophe with genocidal potential." . . .

The British debate was quite similar to the German one: the government generally avoided the use of the term, while backbench and opposition MPs did not. In April 2004, . . . MPs asked the government whether it considered that genocide had taken place in Darfur and what action would be taken as a result. The government's standard response was: "We and the UN agree that what is happening in Darfur cannot be described as genocide." This is a rather curious stance, given that the UN had not "agreed" that it was not genocide; the reports of the UN missions to the region that April do not make such a definitive finding (and were in any event not published until May). . . . The extent to which the UN commission of inquiry's "finding" regarding genocide brought the debate to a halt is evident in a report on Darfur by the House of Commons International Development Committee. The first witness to appear before the committee appeared in November 2004 and was quizzed on whether it was genocide or not. Witnesses who appeared later—and particularly after the UN report was published—were not. . . .

Likewise France also held off calling the situation in Darfur a genocide, preferring that the UN decided. Instead, terms such as "civil war" and "humanitarian disaster" were used. In mid-2004, the Secretary of State for Foreign Affairs, Renaud Muselier, said he "firmly believed" that it was a civil war, and that he agreed with Kofi Annan's comment that the situation was only "bordering on ethnic cleansing." Michele Alliot-Marie, the Defense Minister, declared [Darfur] a "humanitarian disaster" and argued that it could only be solved by political settlement. . . . And as in Germany and the UK, there were MPs who did use the term genocide, but government ministers usually did not.

European governments have generally been under less domestic pressure on Darfur than their American counterpart. There are pressure groups active on the issues . . . , and there have been rallies, concerts, protest marches and petitions aimed at pressing governments to take action to stop what is often (though not always) termed a "genocide" in Darfur. This activism undoubtedly has made it impossible for European governments to downplay Darfur. In the USA religious groups have been very mobilized on the issue and they have a particularly strong impact on political debate; in Europe, few religious groups have been active on the Darfur issue, with the exception of some Jewish organizations. But domestic pressure is of less salience in Europe than in the USA, and the issue was never going to appear at the top of policy-makers' agendas anyway, in an era of war in Afghanistan and Iraq, [nuclear] proliferation concerns in Iran and North Korea, and other similar serious crises. Furthermore, the unpopularity of the Iraq War arguably reduced the appeal of intervention, even for humanitarian reasons. . . .

The response by European governments to Darfur is similar to the Bosnia and Rwanda cases, in that the first impulse is to respond with humanitarian aid; coercive measures—even just sanctions on more than the four individuals targeted thus far—have been rejected as infeasible or undesirable (for a host of material and geopolitical reasons). The response to Darfur is also similar to Rwanda in the preference for "African solutions to African problems," which represents a step back from the cosmopolitan notion—proclaimed at the end of the Cold War—that human rights violations everywhere should be of concern to us all.... The spirit of a "responsibility to protect" is also not wholeheartedly embraced by European governments. Certainly there has been a backlash against the notion that in cases of gross violations of human rights (such as possible genocide) states should intervene without UN Security Council authorization. Support for the principle of the responsibility to protect reiterates that the responsibility is collective, of the international community as a whole. And we all know how difficult it is for the entire community to agree to act quickly, resolutely, decisively. European governments have not tried to assume a leadership role in building support for action under the principle of the responsibility to protect; arguably, in fact, their policies on Darfur demonstrate quite the opposite: responsibility is passed to other bodies such as the African Union.

Thus we are left with the unhappy conclusion that implementation of the social norm against genocide faces both countervailing economic and geopolitical interests on the one hand, and professed respect for multilateral practices and principles on the other. Further, the legal norm is not enough to enable action to prevent, much less stop, genocide. "Never again" is quite likely to be a hollow promise, for all the moral agonizing this produces.

144 • Obama, Adrift on Sudan (Andrew S. Natsios)

Cutting against the grain of much conventional wisdom about the Darfur crisis in this op-ed from 2009, Andrew Natsios, administrator of the U.S. Agency for International Development between 2001 and 2005 and subsequently special envoy for Sudan, calls into the question the wisdom of the administration of U.S. President Barack Obama in continuing to refer to the crisis in Darfur as "genocide." Natsios diagnoses a preponderance of campaign rhetoric, including "a dated view on Darfur," and a lack of unified leadership on Sudan in the higher echelons of the Obama administration. This intervention by a leading U.S. practitioner is relevant to any discussion about cures of genocide because it bemoans—correctly—the misleading narratives about the Darfur conflict that have informed decision making in the Obama administration. Natsios reminds readers that conflicts are not static but are constantly evolving. His message is that we are ignoring this complexity at our peril.

Thirty Sudanese political leaders will meet in Washington today with 170 observers from 32 countries and international organizations, as well as four African former prime ministers, to confront the issues that are slowly pushing Sudan over a cliff. The United States ought to be in a commanding position to mediate in these negotiations, as it did in the 2005 Comprehensive Peace Agreement that ended 22 years of civil war between Sudan's North and South. But disputes within the Obama administration are inhibiting U.S. efforts to stop Sudan's slide toward civil war at a time when unified American leadership is essential.

First, let's consider the situation. Some policymakers continue to call Darfur an ongoing "genocide," but in fact, the conflict has descended into anarchy. "Darfur today is a conflict of

SOURCE: Andrew S. Natsios, "Obama, Adrift on Sudan," *Washington Post*, June 23, 2009. Reprinted with permission of the author.

all against all," Rodolphe Adada, the joint African Union–United Nations special representative, told the UN Security Council in April. Between January 1, 2008, and March 31, 2009, he found some 2,000 fatalities from violence, one third of them civilian. The death of some 700 innocent civilians over a 15-month period, while morally repugnant, is not genocide. It is a low-level insurgency. More civilians died in southern Sudan during the past six months than in Darfur over the past 15 months. Despite such facts and extensive UN Security Office reports showing that genocide is not an accurate description, President Obama continues to use that weighted term.

Advocacy groups motivate their financial supporters and volunteers by associating today's low-level insurgency with the Sudanese government's massive atrocities of 2003 and 2004. This amounts to leading supporters through a time warp. Evidence shows that the deaths are less than half the 500,000 that [are] often cited, and that 96 percent of deaths took place during the first two years of the conflict. John Prendergast, co-founder of the Enough campaign to end crimes against humanity, said recently, "Most of these figures are wild estimates. They are simply crazily wild estimates." Well, such wild estimates are compromising American diplomacy.

The Obama administration should consider reducing sanctions on Sudan only in exchange for concrete Northern government concessions on critical issues. The North, of course, has a mixed history in carrying out its commitments, but its cooperation is key to securing peace. Yet U.S. use of the term "genocide" is reducing our diplomatic options. In the face of genocide, the United States could hardly act as a neutral mediator. No politician wants to explain why he or she remained complacent in the face of slaughter. What Sudan needs is a set of political deals to stitch the country back together before the state collapses. Advocacy groups that claim continuing genocide are under assault by respected scholars of Africa, such as Mahmood Mamdani and Alex de Waal, and they are retreating from their insistence during the Bush administration on military intervention in Darfur. But while many now claim to support a negotiated political settlement, they simultaneously undermine efforts to talk. In addition, the overuse use of a term such as genocide risks anesthetizing the American public and media; if the Sudanese government does one day unleash new atrocities on southern Sudan, no one will be listening.

The administration is focused more on a dated view of Darfur than on the risks of future atrocities that are likely to come from a new war between the North and South. Two events required under the 2005 peace agreement—national multiparty elections to be held in February 2010 and a referendum the following year on the secession of southern Sudan—will determine whether Sudan constructively addresses its internal political problems or descends into Somalia-like anarchy or Rwanda-scale atrocities. The risk of war rises exponentially without resolution of these issues: the status of oil-rich Abyei, preparation for the referendum on southern secession, and, after the referendum, the disposition of revenue from oil production (most of which is in southern Sudan, while the pipelines go through the North) between the North and South.

Using the term "genocide" feeds the International Criminal Court's indictment of President Omar Hassan al-Bashir—which has made meeting with him politically explosive. Some advocates insist that no American diplomat talk with him. How do you mediate a peace agreement if you can't speak to one side's leader? At this crucial moment, the long-suffering Sudanese people need unified American leadership behind a pragmatic policy of engagement. Instead, they have campaign rhetoric and diplomatic paralysis. We, and they, are headed toward disaster if we do not change course.

145 • What Role for Reconciliation? (Jens Meierhenrich)

In discussions, theoretical and otherwise, over the prevention of genocide, one idea has particular appeal: reconciliation. Often understood as the reestablishment of trust among former adversaries though an amalgam of truth, justice, forgiveness, and healing, the idea has acquired the status of a panacea and is being promoted the world over, notably in postgenocidal settings. However, at present we have little understanding of, let alone systematic data pertaining to, the phenomenon. I argue that reconciliation has been conceptualized and applied with insufficient rigor to balance moral ledgers. In response to this malaise, I propose a maximalist concept of reconciliation. On my argument, the achievement of reconciliation, properly understood, is extraordinarily demanding. It should not be applied to situations where former adversaries simply coexist but should be reserved for those rare occasions in which they genuinely and radically break with the violent past.

In the current international system, "there appears to be a global frenzy to balance moral ledgers. Talk of apology, forgiveness, and reconciliation is everywhere." Inasmuch as a burgeoning literature has reflected on the demands of justice in times of transition, no agreement exists on what is required for coming to terms with the past. This disagreement is partly due to the fact that reconciliation has been conceptualized—and operationalized—with insufficient rigor to balance moral ledgers, or to increase our understanding of them. In an attempt to penetrate the complexity of reconciliation, this article traces the genealogy of the term and takes issue with the proliferation of meanings in recent scholarship. It develops a conceptual analysis of reconciliation to reveal contending assumptions about its role in law and society. . . .

In everyday life, reconciliation means different things to different people, as exemplified by the entries in the Oxford English Dictionary (OED). The first available entry in the OED's Second Edition of 1989 defines *reconciliation* as the "action of reconciling persons, or the result of this; the fact of being reconciled," with the first usage found in 1386. Subsequent entries refer to the "reunion of a person to church" (1625) and "the purification, or restoration of sacred uses, of a church, etc., after desecration or pollution" (1533). The former of these meanings is characteristic of religious interpretations which portray reconciliation primarily as the solemn and public act of readmitting into church membership an excommunicated sinner. . . .

The verb *to reconcile* has seen a wider usage over the centuries. The collected meanings range from bringing a person "again into friendly relations *to* or *with* (oneself or another) after an estrangement" (1382, emphasis in the original) to bringing "back into concord, to reunite (persons or things) in harmony" (1429), and from efforts at restoring "to purity, to absolve

SOURCE: Jens Meierhenrich, "Varieties of Reconciliation," *Law & Social Inquiry* 33, no. 1 (2008): 196, 203–4, 206, 207, 208, 209, 210, 211, 212, 213, 214. Reprinted with permission of the American Bar Foundation.

or cleanse" (1430) to bringing "into a state of acquiescence (with) or submission *to* a thing" (1606, emphasis in the original). Also noteworthy are meanings revolving around the making "even or smooth" of impurities "so as to present a uniform surface" (1687).

While comprehensive, the conventional meanings of reconciliation are inadequate for furthering explanation and understanding in any systematic fashion. . . . The following is concerned with the formulation of a systematized concept. This involves the selection of shared and foundational attributes of reconciliation assembled from the broad constellations of meanings that have become associated with the idea through the universe of background concepts. . . .

With this in mind, I propose the following systematized concept of reconciliation: *reconciliation refers to the accommodation of former adversaries through mutually conciliatory means, requiring both forgiveness and mercy*, where *forgiveness* connotes the forswearing of resentment, "the resolute overcoming of the anger and hatred that are naturally directed toward a person who has done one an unjustified and non-excused moral injury," and *mercy* connotes the extension of an act of compassion to the undeserving person who has committed an unjustified and non-excused moral injury. . . .

Forgiveness is a constitutive element of reconciliation. . . . Yet my conceptualization of forgiveness departs from the existing literature. One study in this literature, for example, maintains that "reconciliation and forgiveness are *conceptually independent*, even if they often go together. . . . Arriving at an accommodation need not and perhaps should not involve the excusing of a wrong. It might, but need not, involve an apology or the offer of forgiveness." The author further remarks that "reconciliation might be psychologically possible where forgiveness is not." . . . Contra this conceptualization, I submit that the causal relationship between reconciliation and forgiveness runs in the *opposite direction*: forgiveness might be psychologically possible where reconciliation is not. This is so because forgiveness is epistemologically *less* demanding than reconciliation, which, in addition to forgiveness, requires the accommodation of former adversaries, thus demanding action (and credible commitments) from perpetrators *as well as* victims.

"To reconcile is an intersubjective process, an agreement to settle accounts that involves at least two subjects who are related in time." . . . It involves wrongdoers *as well as* those who have been wronged. It demands (in whatever form) the acceptance of responsibility from wrongdoers and (in whatever form) the allocation of forgiveness and mercy from those who have been wronged. Frequently, the dividing line between wrongdoers and those who have been wronged cannot be easily drawn, for all sides have committed wrongs. In these instances, *all* sides must (in whatever form) act for reconciliation to occur. In the case of forgiveness, by contrast, the action resides *solely* with those who have been wronged. . . .

Forgiveness is a necessary condition for reconciliation, but it is not a sufficient condition. Whereas forgiveness involves *unilateral action*, reconciliation necessitates *bilateral action*. The epistemologically demanding nature of reconciliation may even make necessary the mobilization of *multilateral action*. . . . It is for these reasons that reconciliation and forgiveness are *conceptually interdependent*. This narrow conceptualization represents a model of reconciliation that acknowledges the cost of reconciliation. It speaks to the fact that few creatures like us, in our private or public lives, are willing to forgive (let alone reconcile with) former adversaries, especially in times of transition. . . . We are not helped by "realistic" conceptions of rec-

NINE • Cures

onciliation that underestimate the cost of reconciliation, for data from Afghanistan to Colombia and from the former Yugoslavia to Rwanda amply demonstrate that the prospects for reconciliation continue to be slim in both municipal and international law and society. . . .

It is important to recognize the difference between forgiveness and mercy. Mercy is less personal than forgiveness. It has "a public behavioral dimension not necessarily present in forgiveness. I can forgive a person simply in my heart of hearts, but I cannot show mercy simply in my heart of hearts." . . . Jean Hampton . . . brings the distinction between forgiveness and mercy into even sharper relief:

> Whereas forgiveness is a change of heart towards a wrongdoer that arises out of our decision to see him as morally decent rather than bad, *mercy is the suspension or mitigation of a punishment that would otherwise be deserved as retribution, and which is granted out of pity and compassion for the wrongdoer.* What is "deserved" here refers to what is perceived as necessary to humble the wrongdoer and thereby vindicate the victim's value.

Mercy, according to this interpretation, involves treating a guilty party with the respect that it does *not* deserve. Or, put differently, "Mercy is a form of charity towards wrongdoers that justifies punishing them less severely than they deserve according to justice." Mercy, on this view, involves "the supererogatory tempering of deserved suffering." This understanding of mercy can be traced back to the ancient philosopher Seneca. . . . Yet this argument from just deserts, while important, is insufficient for our purposes. To make it relevant to a larger universe of cases, it must be complemented with insights about justice that have their origins in *other* philosophical traditions. . . . I propose that for reconciliation to exist in the sense defined above, merciful actions (which should be distinguished from merciful agents) must be motivated by *compassion*. This requirement does not make it inappropriate to impose . . . some hardship upon the potential beneficiary of mercy, but I maintain that this imposition must—ultimately—emanate from empathy. . . . By conceiving mercy in these terms, I attenuate the function of retribution in many existing conceptualizations of mercy. For mercy, properly understood, has *no* inherent connection with punishment—despite the fact that this connection frequently exists in practice.

The incorporation of forgiveness and mercy into the systematized concept makes reconciliation epistemologically demanding. This conceptual innovation is deliberate. If reconciliation is to retain its connotation of an ultimate achievement, we must rein in the conceptualization of reconciliation as a category of analysis and a category of practice. The formulation of realistic concepts of reconciliation that are more attainable in practice . . . is counterproductive, for if reconciliation is everywhere, it is nowhere. It is for this reason that the systematized concept of reconciliation developed in this article is narrow, or maximalist. The systematized concept calls for nothing less than an ethics of caring for the enemy. . . .

This underlines the *consensual* and *voluntary* nature of reconciliation as systematized herein. Absent either of these conditions, the accommodation of differences is coexistence at best. Reconciliation will be *consensual* if all affected parties choose to pursue accommodation. For reconciliation to be consensual it need not involve the settlement of underlying discordance. The necessity of consensus relates to the *process* of accommodation rather than its *substance*. Reconciliation will be *voluntary* if all of the affected parties choose to pursue accommodation out of their own volition. . . .

By making forgiveness and mercy an integral part of the systematized concept, my conceptualization draws attention to the mutually conciliatory means necessary for reconciliation, and the voluntary nature of the process. Absent the emphasis on forgiveness and mercy, the concept of reconciliation would be indistinguishable from the notion of coexistence. The concept of coexistence, however, must be distinguished from the concept of reconciliation. Defined as the toleration of former adversaries, coexistence is epistemologically *less* demanding than reconciliation. It requires no action other than a certain amount of restraint on the part of adversaries. . . .

Reconciliation, by contrast, demands more. It requires adversaries to share a present that is nonrepetitive: "To agree to a present that does not repeat requires both to create a 'sense of ending'—a radical break or rupture from existing relations—and to create a 'sense of beginning'—a departure into new relations of affinity marked not by cyclical violence but by trust and care." . . . Absent such a departure, we may encounter coexistence—but not reconciliation. "Reconciliation is thus a much more demanding and possibly unrealistic goal for postconflict peacebuilding, especially in the aftermath of genocide."

146 • Reducing Intergroup Prejudice and Conflict Using Media (Elizabeth Levy Paluck)

Psychologists have studied the determinants of intergroup prejudice and conflict for nearly a century. This notwithstanding, the discipline (like numerous others) has little understanding of what interventions reduce prejudice and intergroup conflict in the real world, especially in the context of largescale violence. In response to this lacuna, Elizabeth Levy Paluck, assistant professor of psychology and public affairs at Princeton University, set out to assess the effectiveness of one particular intervention in postconflict settings: radio. In the context of postgenocide Rwanda, Paluck explored whether an educational and entertainment radio soap opera designed by international donors to bring about healing in the depleted country was effective in reducing interethnic distrust. Based on a unique field experiment that combined quantitative and qualitative methods, she found that the radio program affected her respondents' behavior but not their beliefs. Paluck contends that the impact of listening to the radio in a group was more significant than the substance of the soap opera's message, which, according to this study, failed to substantially influence listeners' personal beliefs about intergroup prejudice and conflict.

Each year governments and organizations around the world pour millions of dollars into antiprejudice public service announcements, print and internet publications, and television and radio programs. . . . Education entertainment is a genre of media used globally for social change campaigns, including antiprejudice and conflict reduction campaigns. It weaves educational messages (e.g., about nonviolence or intergroup cooperation) into an entertaining radio or television show, typically a soap opera. Those interested in media campaigns against

SOURCE: Elizabeth Levy Paluck, "Reducing Intergroup Prejudice and Conflict Using Media: A Field Experiment in Rwanda," *Journal of Personality and Social Psychology* 96, no. 3 (2009): 575, 576, 577, 578, 581, 582, 583, 584. Reproduced with permission from the American Psychological Association.

prejudice find a bewildering array of theories at their disposal—theories of beliefs, norms, emotions, behaviors, and more. . . . Unfortunately, the existing evidence on media influence and prejudice reduction cannot adjudicate among these various theoretical perspectives. . . . In the entire literature, only 10 field experiments have been conducted on media's impact on prejudice—all involving television programs played in classroom settings for North American children. In response, this research departs from common practice. I test whether the media can reduce prejudice and conflict in a challenging real-world setting. In doing so, I take a grounded approach to theory building by measuring media impact on different components of prejudice and conflict. . . .

Musekeweya (moo-say-kay-way-ah), or *New Dawn*, is an education entertainment radio soap opera designed to address the mistrust, lack of communication and interaction, and trauma left by the genocide. The show's fictional story of two Rwandan communities parallels the history of cohabitation and conflict between Tutsis and Hutus, with each community representing one ethnic group (direct mention of ethnicity would be censored). Tensions arise from a land shortage, government favors granted to one community and not the other; intercommunity relations crumble, and the more prosperous community is attacked. The result is casualties, traumatization, and refugees—a situation paralleling, without directly referring to, the lead-up to and aftermath of the 1994 genocide. However, some characters band together across community lines, communicate with one another, and speak out against the powerful leaders who advocate violence.

The program's Rwandan scriptwriters weave into the storyline educational messages that are aimed at influencing listeners' beliefs about the roots and prevention of prejudice and violence and the symptoms of trauma and paths to healing. These messages teach that the roots of prejudice and violence are located in the frustration of basic psychological needs (e.g., for security, a positive identity, and belongingness) and that violence is the accumulation of a number of factors, including a lack of critical thinking, of open dissent, of active bystanders, and of meaningful intergroup connections. Messages about trauma emphasize that its symptoms can be understood, trauma is not "madness," and traumatized people can heal by talking with confidantes. The program's characters deliver these messages didactically to other characters—for example, a wise man who talks to community leaders about the sources of violence and a healer who teaches a traumatized character about her symptoms.

By portraying the characters as typical, realistic Rwandans, the show is also positioned to change perceptions of social norms—that is, to demonstrate to listeners what their peers do (descriptive norms) and should do (prescriptive norms) in situations that many real Rwandans face. The characters use popular proverbs and traditional songs and follow the routines of rural life (92% of Rwandans live in rural areas). Their key behaviors are revealed as they wrestle with problems known to all Rwandans, such as cross-group friendships, overbearing leaders, poverty, and memories of violence. For instance, scriptwriters portray positive behaviors through two Romeo-and-Juliet-like characters—a boy and a girl from different communities who pursue their love in the face of community disapproval. Instead of succumbing to a tragic end, the pair start a youth coalition for peace and cooperation, in defiance of the warmongering authorities.

I do not test the validity of the program's messages, but rather the two strategies of influence—one aimed at changing beliefs and the other at changing perceived social norms—

and the program's impact on its ultimate goal of changed behavior. The explicit goal of the radio program was to promote understanding of and belief in its messages, similar to a public education campaign. Thus, the first hypothesis is that the program will change listeners' beliefs with respect to program messages about prejudice, violence, and trauma. By portraying people and situations found in listeners' own lives, the reconciliation program should influence listeners' perceptions of descriptive norms regarding how Rwandans do behave and prescriptive norms regarding how Rwandans should behave in situations related to prejudice, conflict, and trauma. The third hypothesis is that behavior will change in the direction encouraged by the program—that people will be more willing to speak and even dissent about sensitive topics (e.g., community relationships and trauma) and to cooperate with one another, even across group lines. This behavioral change may be observed in conjunction with belief change, norm change, or neither of the two. Because neither empathy nor discussion was experimentally manipulated in the present study, documenting emotional and conversational reactions to the radio program can point to possible processes of change for future investigation. The literature reviewed above might predict that emotional and empathic reactions to radio characters and discussion will amplify media effects, although the predictions for discussion are less clear.

The study was designed to identify the causal impact of the radio program in the most naturalistic manner possible, within a stratified sample of the population, and along theoretically meaningful outcomes (beliefs, norms, and behaviors) and possible processes of change (emotion and discussion), using various measurement tools. Because Rwandans typically listen to the radio in groups, I used a group-randomized design in which communities were randomly assigned to the treatment (the reconciliation radio program) or control condition (a different radio soap opera about health). The communities were sampled from categories representing salient political, regional, and ethnic breakdowns of present-day Rwanda: eight general population communities from four different regions, two genocide-survivor communities and two Twa communities. . . .

I randomly assigned communities from each category to listen to the reconciliation or health program using a matched randomization procedure. Each community was first matched to the most similar community from the same category (general population, survivor, or Twa) according to a number of observable characteristics, such as gender ratio, quality of dwellings, and education level. Then, one community in each pair was randomly assigned to the reconciliation program and the other to the health program. This stratification of sites helped to balance and minimize observable differences between the communities ex ante.

Finally, I randomly selected 40 adults from official lists of all individuals living in each selected community, balancing for sex, age (half aged 18–30 years, half above 30 years), and family (no more than one person from an immediate family). Four Rwandan research assistants who represented Hutu and Tutsi ethnic backgrounds visited each community with me and located these individuals to explain the study. Our purpose—"to understand Rwandans' opinions about radio programs produced by the organization"—was defined broadly to avoid creating particular expectations. . . .

Over the course of 1 year, the same Rwandan research assistants visited each community to play that month's four 20-min episodes on a portable stereo for the group. Although research assistants were aware of the program differences, they were blind to specific research hypotheses. Participants gathered in their respective community spaces as they do for non-research occasions to listen to the radio. Control groups listened to an education entertainment radio soap opera that aims to change beliefs, norms, and behaviors about reproductive health and AIDS: *Urunana* (*Hand in Hand*; hereafter "health program"). Thus, program content was the only difference between the two conditions—the listening protocol and outcome measurements were the same. . . . At the end of 1 year, a team of 15 Rwandan researchers accompanied the regular research assistants and myself to each community for 3 days. We conducted individual interviews, focus groups, and behavioral observation with all 40 participants. . . .

Nine statements measured participants' beliefs with respect to the program's educational messages, and six statements measured perceptions of descriptive ("that is the way things are") and prescriptive ("that is the way things should be") norms portrayed in the program. . . . Questions about the health program tested the discriminant validity of the intervention, specifically whether the pattern of treatment effects reversed in favor of the control group on questions about health. Researchers measured participants' empathy for other Rwandans with four statements probing whether participants "imagine the thoughts or feelings of" Rwandan prisoners, genocide survivors, poor people, and political leaders. Participants organized into single-sex groups of 10 discussed four topics: intermarriage, violence prevention, trauma, and trust. As with the individual interviews, the goal was to assess personal beliefs and perceptions of social norms. Researchers also repeated questions from the individual interviews in the focus group to test whether individuals would voice the same opinions in front of their peers as they did privately. . . .

According to the monthly field notes, participants' emotional reactions to both soap operas were visible, audible, and frequent. In every listening session, researchers documented various emotional reactions, for example, crying out in pain when a character from the prosperous community was beaten, laughing and clapping during a reunion of the star-crossed lovers, and calling out in encouragement to the girl when the relationship was foiled again— "*ihangane sha*" ("hold on dear"). Such reactions seem to reflect what psychologists would label sympathy (feeling sorry for a character) and empathy (feeling an emotion parallel to the character's). In the individual interviews, reconciliation listeners expressed more empathy for real-life Rwandan prisoners, genocide survivors, poor people, and political leaders. An additive index of these empathic responses indicated a moderate and significant effect of the reconciliation program. . . . This effect holds when responses of genocide survivors are taken out of the analysis (on the grounds that their empathy for other survivors would be especially acute, but this was not the case). . . .

The reconciliation radio program did not change listeners' personal beliefs but did substantially influence listeners' perceptions of social norms. Normative perceptions were not empty abstractions but were realized by actual measured behavior, such as active negotiation, open expression about sensitive topics, and cooperation. This modulated pattern of effects, which was mirrored in the comparison radio condition, increases confidence that the results are not artifacts of experimental demand. Of more importance, this pattern carries a provocative implication for theoretical models of prejudice reduction: namely, that to change prejudiced behavior it may be more fruitful to target social norms than personal beliefs. . . .

That listeners' perceptions of social norms and their behavior changed without a corresponding change in their personal beliefs supports a classic and recently reinvigorated literature emphasizing the key role of social norms in the production of prejudice and conflict. Indeed, in some instances, reconciliation listeners endorsed norms in opposition to their stated beliefs—for example, they rejected proscriptions for intergroup marriage even though they believed that marriage between groups often causes tension. These results also support the pessimistic view that beliefs are difficult to change and that media do not effectively tell people what to think but instead communicate social norms, or what other people think. In contrast, these findings go against psychology's current inclination to examine prejudice via cognition rather than via social influence. . . .

Combining my descriptive data with previous theory and research, one could infer that emotional and group processes were critical to the present findings. For one, the impact of the radio intervention is inseparable from the impact of listening to the program in a group. Alone, people become aware of ideas communicated in radio programs, but in groups they also become aware of other people's awareness of those ideas. When group members react positively, their endorsement creates another vector of social influence on each listener, perhaps even encouraging group members to convince themselves of the idea. . . . Likewise, the dramatic narrative form of the radio program may have provoked emotional and imaginative processes critical to the changes observed. . . . Listeners' emotional empathic reactions to the soap opera characters may have transferred onto the real-life counterparts of the groups the characters represented (measured by the increased empathy for real-life Rwandans—prisoners, genocide survivors, the poor, and leaders). This explanation is consistent with claims made by the extended contact hypothesis that feelings from a vicarious relationship can generalize to the larger social group represented in that relationship. . . . The power of narrative media, including humor and drama, may also lie in its ability to allow people to think through difficult issues or to experience intergroup contact in a vicarious and less threatening way. More research is needed to examine this proposition, although some has started by demonstrating the power of narratives to stimulate empathy.

147 • Quantitative Risk Assessment (Barbara Harff)

Whereas the vast majority of genocide scholarship to date has been founded on qualitative methods, a select number of statistical studies do exist. Barbara Harff's work on the assessment of risks of genocide and political murder since 1955 is a case in point. An outgrowth of her collaboration with Ted Robert Gurr on the CIA's recently renamed State Failure Task Force, her modeling exercise led to the identification of six causal factors—political upheaval, prior genocide, ideological orientation of the ruling elite, regime type, ethnic character of the ruling elite, and trade openness—that jointly differentiate, with 74 percent accuracy, the thirty-five serious civil conflicts since 1955 that led to episodes of genocide and politicide from the ninety-one others that did not have genocidal consequences. These data, claims Harff, who is a professor at the U.S. Naval Academy, provide the basis for a global "watch list" that could identify countries in which the conditions for genocidal violence are present.

SOURCE: Barbara Harff, "No Lessons Learned from the Holocaust? Assessing Risks of Genocide and Political Mass Murder Since 1955," *American Political Science Review* 97, no. 1 (2003): 57, 58, 59, 61, 65, 66–67, 70, 72. Reprinted with permission of Cambridge University Press.

The Clinton Administration, in the aftermath of Rwanda, sponsored the use of social science analysis to explain genocides and ethnic conflict, with an eye to developing early warning systems to detect humanitarian disasters in the making. The study reported here was supported in part by two successive administrations and builds on years of prior research by those involved in the comparative study of genocide and similar phenomena. . . . This article expands on previous theoretical and empirical work by testing the effects of prior conflict, elite characteristics, regime type, and international context on the likelihood of geno-/politicide. The optimum model identifies six preconditions of genocide and politicide (political mass murder) that make it possible, using case-control procedure and logistic regression, to postdict accurately 74% of episodes that began between 1955 and the late 1990s. . . .

The following definition . . . is used to identify the universe of cases for comparative analysis. Genocides and politicides are *the promotion, execution, and/or implied consent of sustained policies by governing elites or their agents—or in the case of civil war, either of the contenting authorities—that are intended to destroy, in whole or part, a communal, political, or politicized ethnic group.* In genocides the victimized groups are defined by their perpetrators primarily in terms of their communal characteristics. In politicides, in contrast, groups are defined primarily in terms of their political opposition to the regime and dominant groups. . . . The general definition and operational rules guided the compilation and successive revisions of a list of genocides and politicides since World War II. This list is widely accepted by researchers, several of whom have used it for comparative research, sometimes adding or deleting a few cases.

The 37 cases cited in this analysis include all those that began after 1955. Several considerations led to the 1955 starting point. Most episodes in the late 1940s and early 1950s were continuations of prior conflicts, e.g., four cases in the USSR that followed through on Stalin's wartime campaigns against disloyal national peoples and potential dissidents. As a consequence of decolonization, many new, conflict-prone states entered the international system beginning in the 1950s, and as a practical matter, reliable data for most independent variables were sparse or nonexistent before then. . . . The 37 cases are deliberate and sustained efforts by authorities aimed at destroying a collectivity in whole or in part. The theoretical objective is to identify general conditions under which governments, and rival authorities in internal wars, choose such a strategy. . . . The approach taken here focuses on factors that affect the decision calculus of authorities in conflict situations, in particular, the circumstances that lead to decisions to eliminate rather than accommodate rival groups. . . .

The empirical work reported here was undertaken in the context of the State Failure project [funded by the Clinton administration], which uses a case-control research design common in epidemiological research but rare in empirical social science. The basic procedure is to match problem cases—people (or countries) affected by a disorder—to a set of controls that do not have the disorder. The State Failure project's researchers selected a set of controls by matching each problem case, in the year it began, with three countries that did not experience failures that year or in the preceding or ensuing several years. In effect, cases are selected on the dependent variable: Those experiencing failure are matched with otherwise similar cases that did not experience failure. Logistic regression is then used to analyze data on conditions in "problem" countries shortly before the onset of state failure with conditions in the controls. The results are expressed as regression coefficients and as odds ratios that approximate the relative risks associated with each factor. . . .

The task here is to distinguish countries where state failures led to genocides from those where they did not. The case-control method was adapted to the estimation of a structural model of geno-/politicide in this manner. First, the universe of analysis consists of all countries already in state failure. The dependent variable represents the conditional probability that a genocide or politicide will begin one year later in a country already experiencing failure. This avoids the problem of comparing the risks of genocide in Rwanda and Sudan with, say, the negligible risks in France and Canada. Instead, the objective is to examine countries experiencing episodes of internal wars and regime collapse and determine why geno-/politicide occurred during such events in Rwanda and Sudan but not, say, in Liberia or Nigeria. Second, the model is estimated using as cases all geno-/politicides since 1955, including multiple episodes that occurred in the same country. . . .

The general procedure was to estimate a best-fit model that included a limited set of [six] theoretically important variables [i.e., political upheaval, prior genocide, ideological orientation of the ruling elite, regime type, ethnic character of the ruling elite, and trade openness], then to seek to improve it by testing the effects of adding other variables and alternative indicators. The six-variable model . . . is the culmination of a long process of model estimation and indicator validation. All six variables have significant effects at the .10 probability level; three have significant effects at the .5 level. . . . Consistent with the theoretical argument, the greater the magnitude of previous internal wars and regime crises, summed over the preceding 15 years, the more likely that a new state failure will lead to geno-/politicide. . . . Arguments about the recurrence of geno-/politicide are also supported. The risks of new episodes were more than three times greater when state failures occurred in countries that had prior geno-/politicides. The effects of magnitude of political upheaval were weaker than those of prior genocide—it appears that habituation to genocide adds more to the risks of future genocide than the magnitude of internal war and adverse regime change per se. . . .

Theoretical arguments about the importance of elite ideologies and regime type are supported. Countries in which the ruling elite adhered to an exclusionary ideology were two and a half times as likely to have state failures leading to geno-/politicide as those with no such ideology. Failures in states with autocratic regimes were three and a half times more likely to lead to geno-/politicides than failures in democratic regimes. . . . Numerous indicators of ethnic and religious cleavages were evaluated but only one was significant in the final model. The risks of geno-/politicide were two and a half times more likely in countries where the political elite was based mainly or entirely on an ethnic minority. . . . Countries with low trade openness had two and a half times greater odds of having state failures culminate in geno-/politicide. High trade openness (and the underlying economic and political conditions it taps) not only minimizes the risks of state failure in general, but reduces substantially the odds that failures, if they do occur, will lead to geno-/politicides. . . .

Note that, since the analyses include all cases of state failure and all instances of geno-/politicide, issues of sampling error do not arise. The probability of genocide for a country in failure with no risk factors is .028. If the country is an autocracy but has no other risk factors, the probability is increased by .090. If the country has a minority elite but no other risk factors, the probability is increased by .069. The incremental effects of each risk factor are relatively small; their cumulative effect is large. Analysis of various combinations of risk factors shows that, if all risk factors are present in a failed state, the conditional probability of geno-/

politicide is .90, with a 95% confidence interval of .66 to .98. The only such country with all six factors in 2001 is Iraq. . . . A hypothetical country with the following combination of four risk factors—a high magnitude of past upheaval, a minority elite, low trade openness, and autocracy—has a conditional geno-/politicide probability of .52 (confidence interval, .27 to .77). Sierra Leone is a contemporary example. If such a failed state also had a past genocide, the probability increases to .79 (confidence interval, .43 to .95). Contemporary Rwanda and Burundi fit this pattern, i.e., they are challenged by rebels (are in failure) and have all risk factors except an exclusionary ideology. . . .

The structural model tested here identifies six causal factors that jointly differentiate with 74% accuracy the 35 [two of the 37 cases were not sufficiently separated in time and thus were eventually excluded from the analysis] serious civil conflicts since 1955 that led to episodes of genocide and politicide from 91 others that did not have genocidal consequences. . . . Some theoretical arguments about the causes of genocide are called into question by the results. First, indicators of ethnic and religious cleavages had ambiguous effects in the final model. Active discrimination against ethnic minorities is a significant causal factor leading to ethnic war, consistent with theories of ethnic conflict, but once ethnic and other civil wars have begun, discrimination does not help explain which of them are likely to lead to geno-/politicide. Second, levels of economic development, indexed here by infant mortality, make no difference in the likelihood of geno-/politicide once internal wars and adverse regime changes have begun. . . . It was also found, contrary to expectations, that economic interdependence is more important than international political linkages. The reason, I suggest, is that the international will to act is more important than political linkages in preventing escalation to geno-/politicide. . . .

The model [sketched here] provides a framework for assessing and comparing the vulnerability of countries with state failure to genocide and politicide. When the model is applied to current information, it provides the basis for a global "watch list" that identifies countries in which the conditions for a future episode are present. . . . The risk assessments generated using this approach not only signal possible genocides, but flag the actual and potential victims of human rights abuses in conflict-ridden countries everywhere. Timely and plausible assessments of the situations should make it easier to convince policymakers of the need to engage proactively in high-risk situations. Anticipatory responses should save more lives at less cost than belated responses after killings have begun.

148 • The Prediction of Genocide Onset (Matthew Krain)

Like Harff, Matthew Krain, a professor of political science at the College of Wooster, is devoted to the quantitative study of genocide, with a particular focus on genocide onset. In this 1997 article on the subject, Krain asks how important different configurations of political opportunity structure (e.g., position in the international system, war, regime type, regime change, types and number of societal

SOURCE: Matthew Krain, "State-Sponsored Mass Murder: The Onset and Severity of Genocides and Politicides," *Journal of Conflict Resolution* 41, no. 3 (1997): 333, 335, 336, 337, 338, 339, 340, 344, 346, 350, 355, 356. Reprinted with permission of Sage Publishers, Inc.

divisions) are for predicting a country's propensity for genocide. Based on a statistical analysis, he finds that civil wars are the most consistent predictors of genocide or politicide onset (as well as severity), although other openings in the political opportunity structure (such as wars and decolonization) do occasionally have important effects as well.

Recently, much work in the literature on political violence has focused on theories of political opportunity structure. An assumption of these theories is that "political violence is a function of the political opportunities and constraints of the immediate political environment." Elites do their best to keep opportunities for challenging the status quo at a minimum. However, openings in the political opportunity structure often lead to challenges to the elites because they signal the vulnerability of the state. . . . The connection between openings in the political opportunity structure and genocides or politicides appears to be an important one.

My assertion is that the mere status of a state—be it economic (i.e., place in the world economy), political (i.e., regime type, power concentration), or social (i.e., ethnic composition) —does not help us understand why genocides or politicides occur at particular points during a given regime and not at other points. For instance, why were Tutsi and Tutsi-sympathizing Hutu slaughtered in Rwanda in 1994 and not a decade before? Why were Bengalis killed in 1971 instead of a few years later? The answers lie in the events that open the political opportunity structure. The presence of such openings should increase the probability of the onset of state-sponsored mass murder and the level of its severity. . . . Major structural changes such as [external] wars, civil wars, extraconstitutional changes, or decolonization create "windows of political opportunity" during which elites may and must more freely act to consolidate power and eliminate the opposition. . . . Thus I construct the following hypotheses . . . :

Hypothesis 1: If a state is engaged in an external war, the probability of the onset of genocide or politicide and the degree of its severity will be greater than that for a state not engaged in an external war.

Hypothesis 2: If a state is engaged in a civil war, the probability of the onset of genocide or politicide and the degree of its severity will be greater than that for a state not engaged in a civil war.

Hypothesis 3: If a state experiences an extraconstitutional change, the probability of the onset of genocide or politicide and the degree of its severity will be greater than that for a state that does not experience an extraconstitutional change.

Hypothesis 4: If a state has a recent history of decolonization, the probability of the onset of genocide or politicide and the degree of its severity will be greater than that for a state without a recent history of decolonization. . . .

Hypothesis 5: States that centralize political power in a small number of institutions are more likely to be associated with the onset and high degree of severity of genocides and politicides than states that decentralize political power. . . .

Hypothesis 6: As the level of ethnic homogeneity in an aggressor state increases, the probability of the onset of genocide or politicide and the degree of its severity should increase. . . .

Hypothesis 7: States that are more marginalized within the world economy are more likely to be associated with the onset and increased severity of a genocide or politicide than states that are less marginalized within the world economy. . . .

Separate tests will determine what affects the onset and severity of state-sponsored mass murder. The time frame used in this study, 1948 to 1982, was the broadest possible range within the constraints of available data.... I rely on [Barbara] Harff and [Ted Robert] Gurr's data set, which presents a list of genocides and politicides from 1945 to 1987.... Onset of genocide or politicide is coded as a dichotomous variable—1 if the year of onset corresponds to any country year within the time window, 0 in all cases where there is an absence of geno-cide or politicide. Between 1948 and 1982, the period of examination in this study, there were 35 instances of the initiation of a genocide or politicide.... Severity was measured as the "number of victims." The number of victims is reported in many cases in ranges of estimates. In such cases, I employ the mean of these estimated bounds....

Using the [eight independent] variables above [war, civil war, extraconstitutional changes, decolonization, ethnic fractionalization, marginalization, power concentration, and duration], I ran two types of models: logit models examining the onset of genocide and politicide and negative binomial event-count models examining severity. An ordinary least squares (OLS) regression is inappropriate when onset is the dependent variable because the relationship between the independent variables and the dependent variable is nonlinear.... The results of the logit analysis on factors affecting the onset of state-sponsored mass murder are [as fol-lows]. Neither marginalization nor ethnic fractionalization are significant in any of the mod-els.... Civil war involvement appears to be the best predictor of genocide or politicide.... In addition, although not strongly significant or having strong effects on its own, decolonization, in combination with civil war, has a large effect (up to an almost 20% increase in the prob-ability) on the onset of state-sponsored mass murder.... [Turning to the negative binomial analysis,] power concentration, decolonization, ethnic fractionalization, and marginalization have no significant effect on severity, all else held constant. War, civil war, and extraconstitu-tional changes appear to have the only significant effects on severity....

To summarize my results, civil wars are the most consistent predictors of genocide or politicide onset although other openings in the political opportunity structure (wars, decolo-nization) do occasionally have important effects. Most notably, these variables have the great-est effect on the probability of onset when combined with at least one of the other political opportunity structure variables. This is intuitive because a combination of any two of these variables should create a wider (or longer) window of opportunity. Genocide and politicide are extreme policies that may require larger than normal openings in the political opportunity structure.... In addition, political opportunity structure variables also best account for the degree of severity of a given genocide or politicide. Although other variables such as ethnic fractionalization and power concentration may occasionally have some impact, it is marginal compared with the effect of "big opportunity" variables on severity.

Openings in the political opportunity structure are important in understanding what affects the onset and the degree of the severity of genocides and politicides. This study has shown that from 1948 to 1982, these relationships have been more important for predicting the occurrence and severity of genocides and politicides than more static, environmental components of opportunity such as levels of power concentration.... In that vein, this study presents evidence that state-sponsored mass murder should be studied in the context of the more general framework of conflict and political violence.... Concepts and findings from the vast literature on political violence may help us to better understand other conflict phenomena such as genocides, politicides, and war and civil war consequences.

149 • R2P: Responsibility to Protect, International Commission on Intervention and State Sovereignty

The responsibility to protect (R2P) quickly became a buzzword in the international community when it was first introduced. It was the brainchild of a Canadian group of experts called the International Commission on Intervention and State Sovereignty. Convened by the government of Canada in September 2000, the independent Commission deliberated and consulted for twelve months before issuing its recommendations. What follows is an excerpt from the Commission's hugely influential report, The Responsibility to Protect, *in which it urged the international community to henceforth "embrace the 'responsibility to protect' as a basis for collective action against genocide, ethnic cleansing and crimes against humanity."*

If intervention for human protection purposes is to be accepted, including the possibility of military action, it remains imperative that the international community develop consistent, credible and enforceable standards to guide state and intergovernmental practice. The experience and aftermath of Somalia, Rwanda, Srebrenica, and Kosovo, as well as interventions and non-interventions in a number of other places, have provided a clear indication that the tools, devices and thinking of international relations need now to be comprehensively reassessed, in order to meet the foreseeable needs of the 21st century.

Any new approach to intervention on human protection grounds needs to meet at least four basic principles: to establish clear rules, procedures and criteria for determining whether, when and how to intervene; to establish the legitimacy of military intervention when necessary and after all other approaches have failed; to ensure that military intervention, when it occurs, is carried out only for the purposes proposed, is effective, and is undertaken with proper concern to minimize the human costs and institutional damage that will result; and to help eliminate, where possible, the causes of conflict while enhancing the prospects for durable and sustainable peace. . . .

It is important that language—and the concepts which lie behind particular choices of words—do not become a barrier to dealing with the real issues involved. Just as the Commission found that the expression "humanitarian intervention" did not help to carry the debate forward, so too do we believe that the language of past debates arguing for or against a "right to intervene" by one state on the territory of another state is outdated and unhelpful. We prefer to talk not of a "right to intervene" but of a "responsibility to protect." . . . We seek to make a principled, as well as a practical and political, case for conceptualizing the intervention issue in terms of a responsibility to protect. The building blocks for the argument are, first, the

SOURCE: International Commission on Intervention and State Sovereignty, *The Responsibility to Protect: Report of the International Commission on Intervention and State Sovereignty* (Ottawa: International Development Research Centre, 2001), 11, 12, 13, 17–18, 49, 50. Reprinted with permission of the publisher.

principles inherent in the concept of sovereignty; and secondly, the impact of emerging principles of human rights and human security, and changing state and intergovernmental practice. . . .

On the one hand, in granting membership of the UN, the international community welcomes the signatory state as a responsible member of the community of nations. On the other hand, the state itself, in signing the Charter, accepts the responsibilities of membership flowing from that signature. There is no transfer or dilution of state sovereignty. But there is a necessary re-characterization involved: from *sovereignty as control* to *sovereignty as responsibility* in both internal functions and external duties. Thinking of sovereignty as responsibility, in a way that is being increasingly recognized in state practice, has a threefold significance. First, it implies that the state authorities are responsible for the functions of protecting the safety and lives of citizens and promotion of their welfare. Secondly, it suggest that the national political authorities are responsible to the citizens internally and to the international community through the UN. And thirdly, it means that the agents of state are responsible for their actions; that is to say, they are accountable for their acts of commission and omission. The case for thinking of sovereignty in these terms is strengthened by the ever-increasing impact of international human rights norms, and the increasing impact in international discourse of the concept of human security. . . .

The proposed change in terminology is also a change in perspective, reversing the perceptions inherent in the traditional language, and adding some additional ones: First, the responsibility to protect implies an evaluation of the issues from the point of view of those seeking or needing support, rather than those who may be considering intervention. Our preferred terminology refocuses the international searchlight back where it should always be: on the duty to protect communities from mass killing, women from systematic rape and children from starvation. Secondly, the responsibility to protect acknowledges that the primary responsibility in this regard rests with the state concerned, and that it is only if the state is unable or unwilling to fulfill this responsibility, or is itself the perpetrator, that it becomes the responsibility of the international community to act in its place. In many cases, the state will seek to acquit its responsibility in full and active partnership with representatives of the international community. Thus the "responsibility to protect" is more of a linking concept that bridges the divide between intervention and sovereignty, [whereas] the language of the "right or duty to intervene" is intrinsically more confrontational. Thirdly, the responsibility to protect means not just the "responsibility to react," but the "responsibility to prevent" and the "responsibility to rebuild" as well. It directs our attention to the costs and results of action versus no action, and provides conceptual, normative, and operational linkages between assistance, intervention and reconstruction. . . .

Because the prohibitions and presumptions against intervention are so explicitly spelled out in the [UN] Charter, and since no "humanitarian exception" to these prohibitions is explicitly provided for, the [UN] Security Council becomes of paramount importance. . . . There are many reasons for being dissatisfied with the role that the Security Council has played so far. But all that said, the Commission is in absolutely no doubt that there is no better or more appropriate body than the Security Council to deal with military intervention issues for human protection purposes. It is the Security Council which should be making the hard decisions in the hard cases about overriding state sovereignty. And it is the Security Council which should be making the often even harder decisions to mobilize effective resources, including military resources, to rescue populations at risk when there is no serious opposition on sovereignty grounds. That was the overwhelming consensus we found in all our consultations around the world. . . . The task is not to find alternatives to the Security Council as a source of authority, but to make the Security Council work much better than it has. . . .

Article 42 [of the UN Charter] authorizes the Security Council, in the event that non-military measures prove "inadequate" to decide upon military measures (as may be necessary) "to maintain or restore international peace and security." Although these powers were interpreted narrowly during the Cold War, since then the Security Council has taken a very expansive view as to what constitutes "international peace and security" for this purpose, and in practice an authorization by the Security Council has almost invariably been universally accepted as conferring international legitimacy on an action. . . . It is arguable that what the Security Council has really been doing in these cases is giving credence to what we described . . . as the emerging guiding principle of the "responsibility to protect," a principle grounded in a miscellany of legal foundations (human rights treaty provisions, the Genocide Convention, Geneva Conventions, International Criminal Court statute and the like), growing state practice—and the Security Council's own practice. If such a reliance continues in the future, it may eventually be that a new rule of customary international law to this effect comes to be recognized, but as we have already acknowledged it would be quite premature to make any claim about the existence now of such a rule.

150 • Responsibility to Protect Populations from Genocide, War Crimes, Ethnic Cleansing, and Crimes against Humanity (United Nations General Assembly)

Due to the success of the work of the International Commission on Intervention and State Sovereignty (ICISS)—notably the reception of its report, The Responsibility to Protect—*things moved quickly in the international realm. On September 20, 2005, the member states of the United Nations embraced the notion of the "responsibility to protect" as a (nonbinding) international norm in paragraphs 138–39 of the Outcome Document of the United Nations World Summit in New York. However, a comparison of this, the UN's rendering of R2P, with the more demanding version advanced by Canada's ICISS illustrates all too well the difference between theory and practice in devising cures for genocide, for the UN document is a substantially hollowed-out version of the ICISS proposal.*

138. Each individual State has the responsibility to protect its populations from genocide, war crimes, ethnic cleansing and crimes against humanity. This responsibility entails the prevention of such crimes, including their incitement, through appropriate and necessary means. We accept that responsibility and will act in accordance with it. The international community

SOURCE: UN General Assembly, 60th Session. *Draft Resolution Referred to the High-Level Plenary Meeting of the General Assembly by the General Assembly at Its Fifty-ninth Session* (A/60/L.1), September 20, 2005, paragraphs 138–40.

should, as appropriate, encourage and help States to exercise this responsibility and support the United Nations in establishing an early warning capability.

139. The international community, through the United Nations, also has the responsibility to use appropriate diplomatic, humanitarian and other peaceful means, in accordance with Chapters VI and VIII of the Charter of the United Nations, to help protect populations from genocide, war crimes, ethnic cleansing and crimes against humanity. In this context, we are prepared to take collective action, in a timely and decisive manner, through the Security Council, in accordance with the Charter, including Chapter VII, on a case-by-case basis and in cooperation with relevant regional organizations as appropriate should peaceful means be inadequate and national authorities are manifestly failing to protect their populations from genocide, war crimes, ethnic cleansing and crimes against humanity. We stress the need for the General Assembly to continue consideration of the responsibility to protect populations from genocide, war crimes, ethnic cleansing and crimes against humanity and its implications, bearing in mind the principles of the Charter and international law. We also intend to commit ourselves, as necessary and appropriate, to helping States build capacity to protect their populations from genocide, war crimes, ethnic cleansing and crimes against humanity and to assisting those which are under stress before crises and conflicts break out.

140. We fully support the mission of the Special Adviser of the Secretary-General on the Prevention of Genocide.

ONLINE RESOURCES

Avalon Project, Yale Law School

avalon.law.yale.edu/

A searchable collection of legal and other documents related to the Trial of the Major War Criminals at the International Military Tribunal at Nuremberg as well as the successor trials held under Control Council Law No. 10.

Center for Advanced Holocaust Studies, United States Holocaust Memorial Museum

www.ushmm.org/research/center

Portal to a searchable catalogue of both published and unpublished materials currently available in the USHMM archives as well as separate catalogues for Holocaust testimonies, photographs, and films.

Coalition for the International Criminal Court

www.iccnow.org

Access to the latest news regarding the ICC as well as relevant research materials collated by a leading international advocacy organization.

Documentation Center of Cambodia

www.dccam.org

Website highlights the work of this long-standing and highly regarded research institution in Phnom Penh, which has been documenting and analyzing the genocide in Cambodia for many years.

Extraordinary Chambers in the Courts of Cambodia

www.eccc.gov.kh/en

Official website containing relevant documents, legal instruments, up-to-date case information, and internal rules and regulations of the Extraordinary Chambers in the Courts of Cambodia.

Fortunoff Video Archive for Holocaust Testimonies, Yale University

www.library.yale.edu/testimonies

A collection of testimonies by individuals with firsthand experience of Nazi persecutions, including those who were in hiding, survived, stood by, resisted, or liberated. The website provides access to research guides, information about the archives, and excerpts from the interviews.

Genocide Studies Program, Yale University

www.yale.edu/gsp

Select scholarly publications, maps, and satellite images as well as databases, notably on Cambodia, Guatemala, the former Yugoslavia, Rwanda, and East Timor.

International Coalition for the Responsibility to Protect

www.responsibilitytoprotect.org

Website of a coalition of nongovernmental organizations aimed at strengthening available capacities for preventing and halting genocide, crimes against humanity, and war crimes. Offers an extensive document archive and up-to-date information about international crises and international responses thereto.

International Committee of the Red Cross

www.icrc.org

A portal to essential documents about and research on international humanitarian law, hosted by one of the first international organizations ever created.

International Criminal Court

www.icc-cpi.int

Official website containing relevant documents, legal instruments, judgments, and up-to-date case information for the International Criminal Court.

International Criminal Tribunal for Rwanda

www.ictr.org

Official website containing relevant documents, including judicial decisions, judgments, and legal instruments, and up-to-date case information for the International Criminal Tribunal for Rwanda.

International Criminal Tribunal for the former Yugoslavia

www.icty.org

Official website containing relevant documents, including judicial decisions, judgments, and legal instruments, and up-to-date case information for the International Criminal Tribunal for the former Yugoslavia.

International Crisis Group

www.crisisgroup.org

Website of an international advocacy organization that provides access to thematic as well as country-specific analyses in the area of international peace and security, with particular reference to political instability and mass violence.

International Justice Tribune

www.internationaljustice.nl

Online archive of the now defunct magazine, featuring reporting from and analysis of goings-on in the ad hoc international criminal tribunals as well as the International Criminal Court and domestic proceedings.

Minorities at Risk Project

www.cidcm.umd.edu/mar/

Website of a long-standing research project that compiles widely used quantitative data on conflicts of politically active ethnic groups to facilitate comparative analysis.

Office of the Special Adviser on the Prevention of Genocide, United Nations

www.un.org/preventgenocide/adviser

Official website containing key documents and statements by the adviser and related publications.

Online Encyclopedia of Mass Violence

www.massviolence.org

Searchable database of case studies, review articles, theoretical papers, and chronologies of large-scale social violence.

Oxford Bibliographies Online: Genocide

www.oxfordbibliographies.com, DOI: 10.1093/OBO/9780199743292-0074

Available by subscription, this online resource offers annotated links to a subset of readings included in this *Reader*.

Political Instability Task Force

globalpolicy.gmu.edu/political-instability-task-force-home

Website of a research consortium originally created at the behest of the U.S. government. The website provides access to several major cross-national data projects and resources related to the prediction of state fragility and its associated risks.

Relief Web, United Nations

www.reliefweb.int/rw/dbc.nsf/doc100?OpenForm

Searchable database for timely, reliable, and relevant humanitarian information and analysis. Organized by both information type, such as maps, analysis, news and professional resources, as well as country and emergency type.

Report of the Commission for Historical Clarification in Guatemala

http://shr.aaas.org/guatemala/ceh/report/english/toc.html

Provides online access to Commission's entire report, which found that agents of state had committed acts of genocide against Mayan people in Guatemala.

Sorry Books, Australian Institute of Aboriginal and Torres Strait Islander Studies

http://www.aiatsis.gov.au/collections/exhibitions/sorrybooks/introduction.html

An initiative by the group Australians for Native Title, the Sorry Books collect individual "apologies," in the form of simple signatures or personal messages, regarding the "Lost Generation" of Aborigine children.

Through a Glass Darkly: Genocide Memorials in Rwanda, 1994–present

www.genocidememorials.org

Interactive website featuring several thousand photographs, geographic data, and empirical vignettes of some of Rwanda's lesser known sites of memory.

War Crimes Studies Center, University of California, Berkeley

http://socrates.Berkeley.edu/~warcrime

Online portal to monitoring and thematic reports on trials relating to Sierra Leone, East Timor, Indonesia, Cambodia, and World War II.

Yad Vashem

www.yadvashem.org

Website of Israel's Holocaust museum provides access to its library collection as well as to its archives, which feature survivor testimonies, names of victims, and photographs.

INDEX

Romanov Dynasty (Russia),
112–13
Rome Statute. *See under* International Criminal Court
Roosevelt, Theodore, 83
The Roots of Evil (Staub), 155–57
Rosenberg, Alfred, 124
Rosenfeld, Sidney, 363
Roth, Walter, 194
Rousseau-Portalis Doctrine,
58–59
Rubenstein, Richard L., 133–34
Rummel, R.J., 56, 76–78
Rummel, Rudolph, 6
Russell, Lord John, 190
Russia. *See also* Soviet Union
Armenian population in,
116–17
Chechens in, 391
Holocaust restitution and, 415
imperial disintegration in,
112–13
Mongols in, 27
pogroms in, 19, 113
United Nations and, 443, 445
World War I and, 115
Rwabugiri (king of Rwanda),
148–49
Rwabukumba, Séraphin, 311
Rwanda
agriculture in, 145–46, 148
"ancient hatreds" explanation
regarding, 265
Arusha Accords and, 50, 147,
333, 433
autobiographical accounts
from, 361
Burundi and, 43, 241, 311
civil war in, 50–51, 103, 149,
167, 436, 441
Clinton apology in, 401–4
colonial legacies in, 147–48
comparisons to the Holocaust
and, 102
constitution in, 333
Democratic Republic of Congo
and, 278
dogs in, 267–68
educational media initiatives in,
473–77
environmental stressors in,
144–47
ethnic identity dynamics in,
50–51
flow and blockage symbolism
in, 243–45
foreign aid to, 308
gacaca jurisdictions in, 345–48

génocidaires' profiles in, 239–42
genocide in, 19, 49–51, 93, 97,
102–3, 144, 146–47, 149–50,
160, 162–63, 166, 172,
211–12, 235, 239–45,
253–54, 265–68, 286–87,
310–11, 333, 344, 393–94,
398, 401–3, 422–23, 432–42,
454, 467–68
Hutu in, 50–51, 102–3,
147–49, 235, 239–45,
265–67, 286, 307–9, 317,
333, 336–37, 343, 345–47,
401, 432–33, 437–38, 475
identity formation in, 147–149,
333–34
media coverage of, 253–54,
265–66
militias *(Interahamwe)* in, 241,
244, 287, 344
population growth and density
in, 145
post-genocide government in,
277, 307–9, 311–12
post-genocide trials and,
316–17, 332–35, 342–48
racialization of difference in,
147–49
radio soap operas in, 474–76
rape as a weapon of war in,
336–37
refugees from, 244, 265,
286–88, 311, 343–44
restorative *versus* retributive
justice in, 345–47
symbolic forms of killing in,
242–45
Tutsi in, 50–51, 97, 102–3,
147–49, 212, 235, 241245,
265–66, 286, 307–9, 317,
333, 336–37, 343, 345–47,
401–2, 422, 432–433,
436–38, 475
United Nations and, 265–66,
268, 287, 309, 311, 393, 403,
433–35, 439–42, 447
United States and, 103, 308,
401–4, 422, 432–38
International Criminal Tribunal
for, 403
Zaire and, 43, 286–87, 310–12
Rwandan Patriotic Front (RPF)
invasion of Rwanda (1990) by,
149, 167
post-genocide government of,
277, 287, 307–9, 311–12, 346
Rwandan ivil War and, 50, 103,
149, 347, 436–37

Rwandan genocide and, 244,
267, 310, 343
"Rwanda's Failing Experiment in
Restorative Justice" (Waldorf), 345–48
"Rwanda: Ten Years On"
(Reyntjens), 307–9
Rymond-Richmond, Wenona,
277, 288–92

Saint Bartholomew Massacre, 25,
28–29
Şakir, Behaeddin, 118
Şakir, Nazim, 118
Salim, Salim Ahmed, 463
Samaritan's Purse, 268, 272
Sambanis, Nicholas, 14, 49
San Miguel, Jerónimo de, 182–83
al-Saraj, Mubarak Muhammad,
250
Sarkar, Tanika, 246
Sartre, Jean-Paul, 6, 94
Saudi Arabia, 141, 269
"Save Darfur" campaign, 8–9, 98,
100, 102–3
Scales, Len, 29
Scanlon, John, 141
Schabas, William, 56, 65–67, 423,
428–29
Scheffer, David, 57, 88–91
Scheper-Hughes, Nancy, 56,
94–96
Scherman, Dave, 258
Schlieffen Plan, 198
Scipio Aemilianus, 25, 172
Scipio Africanus, 24, 172–73
Scipio Nasica, 172
Scully, Gerald, 105, 160–63
"The Secret Young-Turk Ittihadist
Conference and the Decision for the World War I
Genocide of the Armenians"
(Dadrian), 116–18
Seeley, Robert, 108
Seibel, Wolfgang, 171–72,
223–26
Selo, Borovo, 212
Selye, Hans, 298
Semanza case (ICTR), 335–37
Semelin, Jacques, 9, 16, 211–12
Seminole Indians, 178
Sendashonga, Seth, 308
Serbia. *See also* Serbs
Bosnia and Herzegovina wars
and, 47–49, 316
Chetnik nationalist movement
in, 212
Dayton Agreements and, 340